Praise for *The Creation of the Media*

"Daring and dazzling. No other work has integrated the history of communications so thoroughly, and no other work is likely to do so any time soon. Paul Starr's book is deeply informed by a rich comparative knowledge of the development of the media in other parts of the world. Underlying this complex but fascinating story is his commitment to understanding and preserving a liberal democratic society. *The Creation of the Media* is a major intellectual achievement, an indispensable work."

—Michael Schudson, Professor of Communication at the University of California, San Diego and author of *Discovering the News*

"A creative, illuminating history." —David Greenberg, *Newsday*

"*The Creation of the Media* provides the grand synthesis of the history of journalism and communications that has been needed for a long time. Starr writes with verve and authority."

—David Nasaw, Distinguished Professor of History, Graduate Center, City University of New York, and author of *The Chief*

"As the state has withdrawn from the fray, control over every form of mass communication has become more centralized. *The Creation of the*

Media can be read as an argument that this represents an alarming departure from a great American tradition. Once we understand the media in Starr's terms, we have to start caring about what those lobbyists who stand in the corridor outside the Senate Commerce Committee hearing room actually do."

—Nicholas Lemann, *The New Yorker*

"Paul Starr's masterful study makes plain how deep are the roots of the media's splendors and miseries alike. It's easy to gesture airily at 'structures' but Starr fills in the blanks with his thorough account, emphasizing differences between America's communications system and others'. Anyone who thinks entrepreneurs make media all by themselves, indifferent to government policy and culture, will find *The Creation of the Media* especially illuminating."

—Todd Gitlin, Professor of Journalism and Sociology at Columbia University and author of *Letters to a Young Activist*

"*The Creation of the Media* is a book no journalist—and probably no citizen—should be without."

—David Propson, *New York Sun*

"The *Creation of the Media* is first and foremost a sweeping narrative history of American media from the Revolution to World War II. And it is the best such history ever written. . . . This is truly a case where the whole adds up to much more than the sum of its parts."

—David Paul Nord, *The Book*

THE CREATION OF THE MEDIA

Political Origins of Modern Communications

PAUL STARR

A Member of the Perseus Books Group
New York

To Daniel Bell

Hardcover edition first published in 2004 by Basic Books,
A Member of the Perseus Books Group.
Paperback edition first published in 2005 by Basic Books.

Designed by Trish Wilkinson
Set in 11-point New Caledonia by the Perseus Books Group

The Library of Congress has cataloged the hardcover as follows:
Starr, Paul, 1949–
The creation of the media : political origins of modern communications / Paul Starr.
p. cm.
Includes bibliographical references and index.
ISBN 0-465-08193-2 (hardcover)
1. Mass media—United States—History. 2. Mass media—Political aspects—United States—History. 3. United States—Politics and government. I. Title.
P92.U5S646 2004
302.23'0973—dc22 200302915

ISBN 0-465-08194-0 (paperback)

05 06 07 / 10 9 8 7 6 5 4 3 2 1

ALSO BY PAUL STARR

The Discarded Army: Veterans After Vietnam

The Social Transformation of American Medicine

The Logic of Health-Care Reform

Contents

Preface and Acknowledgments

THIS BOOK has taken a long time to write, and that is a good thing—at least it seems so in retrospect. Begun nearly a decade ago, the work on this project has allowed me to step back from the contemporary preoccupations that first led me to think about the communications media and the information revolution. The feverish speculation of the past decade did not take place only on the stock market; there was plenty of it in the world of ideas. In writing this book, I took the slow road, plunging into the past rather than levitating into the future. During the boom, history may have appeared irrelevant to those who believed the Internet "changed everything." But now that familiar patterns have reasserted themselves, perhaps the long view will get a hearing.

The term "media" in this book's title may be taken in two senses: first, as the various modern channels of communication created from the early seventeenth to the mid-twentieth centuries (the press, postal and telecommunications networks, the movies, and broadcasting); second, as a set of powerful institutions ("the media") that, to the despair of grammarians, people generally speak of as singular rather than plural. That structure, I argue, came into existence only toward the end of this history.

Some readers may be surprised that the author of *The Social Transformation of American Medicine* would write *The Creation of the Media*. But the two books have much in common as studies of the sources of power in the modern world, the structuring of ascendant industries, and the disappointment—or at least ambiguous realization—of democratic ideals. Both books are at least as much about America as they are about either medicine or media. I did not set out to write parallel accounts, and in many ways they are different. There is also far too much historical contingency in each narrative for me to suggest that the developments in either one have followed an inexorable course. Powerful tendencies have been built into the institutions, but the lesson of the past, it seems to me, is that we can still make new choices about them—and politics has been, and continues to be, the primary means of making those choices.

It would have been impossible for me to undertake a project of this scale without the support of family, friends, and colleagues. I owe great thanks to Princeton University, to its Center for Arts and Cultural Policy Studies, and to my colleagues and students in sociology and American studies. I also owe a particular debt to those who have given me the benefit of their knowledge and critical reactions during the work on this project, including Paul Dimaggio, Hendrik Hartog, Richard R. John, Stephen Holmes, and Eszter Hargittai. Research assistants over the years—Jonathan Steinberg, Chuck Auletta, and Lauren Cusick—have helped out on specific factual issues. I also want to thank my agent, Bill Leigh, and Jo Ann Miller and others at Basic Books.

The unpredictable factor in any author's work is the course of life itself. Although personal tragedy interrupted my work on this book, heaven has smiled again—and I thank my wife Ann for her love, support, and, not least of all, knowledge of literature and history.

Paul Starr
Princeton, New Jersey

Introduction

The Political Origins of Modern Communications

DURING the past several decades, the "information revolution" has served as a defining conception of our time. Yet, as remarkable as the recent wave of innovation has been, it is only the latest phase of a centuries-long process that has been punctuated by a series of upheavals in communications and information at least as revolutionary as our own. Out of these upheavals have come the modern media—not just the various means of communication, but the array of powerful institutions that everyday references to "the media" imply. Technology and economics cannot alone explain the system of communications we have inherited or the one we are creating. The communications media have so direct a bearing on the exercise of power that their development is impossible to understand without taking politics fully into account, not simply in the use of the media, but in the making of constitutive choices about them.

By *constitutive* choices I mean those that create the material and institutional framework of fields of human activity. My premise here is that the constraints in the architecture of technical systems and social institutions are rarely so clear and overpowering as to compel a single design. At times of decision—*constitutive moments,* if you will—ideas and culture come into play, as do constellations of power, preexisting institutional legacies, and models from other countries. Although the people directly involved in the decisions may not be aware of their long-term implications, institutions and systems once established often either resist change or invite it in a particular direction. Constitutive choices emerge in a cumulative, branching pattern: Early choices bias later ones and may lead institutions along a distinctive path of development, affecting a society's role and position in the world.

From the seventeenth to the mid-twentieth centuries, the constitutive choices about the modern media—chiefly the press, postal and telecommunications networks, cinema, and broadcasting—took place in the context of larger political and economic transformations. As the most powerful nation-states in the world emerged in Europe and North America, the architects of those states took a direct hand in shaping communications for both instrumental and symbolic purposes. Political movements, particularly beginning in the eighteenth century, also began to set limits on state power, including the right to discuss public questions freely. This liberal constitutionalist tendency was more hospitable than earlier absolutist regimes to the flourishing of communications on a wider and more commercial basis. Other factors, such as the international position of a state, its stability and coherence, and the balance of forces at critical moments of decision, also affected national paths of development. As the market for print media and other cultural goods expanded, early institutional differences—notably among continental European countries, Great Britain, and the United States—led to widening divergences in the communications industries and popular media.

It is a particular argument of this book that the United States has followed a distinctive developmental path in communications ever since the American Revolution. The origins of that path lie in the country's founding as a liberal republic and its response to the peculiar challenges of building a nation on a continental scale. The consequences, albeit unintended, have been to endow the United States with a source of economic, political, and even military advantage and to make the American media a formidable power in themselves. America's leading role in the contemporary information revolution may seem simply to reflect its position as the world's dominant economy and most powerful state. But in the early nineteenth century, when the United States was neither a world power nor a primary center of scientific discovery, it was already a leader in communications—in postal service and newspaper publishing, then in development of the telegraph and telephone, later in the movies, broadcasting, and the whole repertoire of mass communications. This pattern of early leadership and persistent advantage in communications stems fundamentally from constitutive, political decisions that led the United States from its founding on a course sharply diverging from the patterns in Britain, elsewhere in Europe, and even in Canada.

The American path is not reducible to a simple opposition to government and preference for free markets. While restraining state authority in some respects, American law and policy have also actively used government to promote communications. The constitutional provisions for the press and the Post Office illustrate the apparent polarities of a limited and interventionist state: Although the Bill of Rights denied the federal government any authority to regulate the press, the Constitution made the Post Office the one nationalized industry, and the new government soon set about building a comprehensive postal network. Rather than conflicting with one another, however, the two policies were complementary: The Post Office was used to subsidize the press, and both contributed to the extension of communication—in particular, the distribution of political news—beyond earlier boundaries. These policies, like many later ones, were born of supremely political objectives, though they also had important economic consequences. The government's role in the early development of the Internet is only the latest example of policies that have not only restrained the power of the state but also made positive use of it to promote communications—and ended up, albeit without any deliberate plan in this and other instances, generating new economic and social possibilities.

Unintended consequences are usually invoked to explain cases of good intentions gone wrong, but this is a more positive story from the standpoint of economic growth. America's leading role in the information economy is at least partly a case of unexpected payoffs. In a country where politics is richly despised, a legacy of politically based competitive advantage lies at the foundation of new wealth. At the same time, the continuing transformation of communications has created new hierarchies of private power and put at risk some of the political aspirations that originally helped to set the process in motion. The American framework of communications has been a remarkable engine of wealth and power creation, so much so that its influence now extends over not merely a continent, but the world. Yet that very achievement raises uneasy questions about the media's structure, role, and relation to popular self-government.

Revolutions as Constitutive Moments

The rise of modern communications is usually told as a narrative of revolution, from the printing revolution in early modern Europe to the electronics and computer revolutions of the twentieth century. In the usual understanding of the term, a "communications revolution" is a radical change in both communications and society resulting from the introduction of a new medium. The putative social changes stemming from a new technology, however, may be slow in coming, hard to isolate from other contemporary developments, and related less to a medium's intrinsic properties than to constitutive choices about its design and development. Revolutionary shifts in communication may also come from other sources besides technology. The alternative followed here is to conceive of communications revolutions as radical changes in the framework of communication, whether precipitated by technology, politics, cultural shifts, or other causes.[1]

Constitutive choices are choices about how things are built and how they work—their design and rules of operation. In the case at hand, these are choices about the material and institutional framework of communications and information (for example, the basic structure of networks and legal principles regulating the press). Insofar as such choices emerge from slowly crystallizing cultural practices or gradual economic and political change, there may be no clear moments of decision. But at times constitutive choices come in bursts set off by social and political crises, technological innovation, or other triggering events, and at these pivotal moments the choices may be encoded in law, etched into technologies, or otherwise embedded in the structure of institutions.

A variety of mechanisms—call them mechanisms of *entrenchment*—make it difficult to revoke such decisions. Written constitutions are typically intended to be difficult to change; entrenchment is purposeful. Laws and regulations are often tenacious because bureaucracies and private organizations are built up on the basis of their provisions and develop an interest in their perpetuation. When the telegraph first emerged, the decision about whether to run it as a state or private enterprise was relatively open; change became far less likely after the rise of Western Union in the United States and government telegraph bureaucracies in Europe. What is true of organizations is also true of technologies themselves. Once technological development moves in a particular direction, strong inertial forces favor continuing down that path. Initial choices in design also develop into more elaborate systems as individuals and firms pursue complementary innovations. Things that work satisfactorily come to be thought of as right: Laws, methods, and systems that appear to be successful become the basis of standards, often gradually appearing to be natural and inevitable, as if they could be no other way. Invention is often the mother of necessity. Network technologies and institutions based upon them develop particularly strong inertial tendencies because of the interconnections and interdependencies they create. As a result, instead of following a single, universal route of progress from tradition to modernity, social and economic development may take a distinctive direction from an early point—in the current phrase, social and economic systems may be "path-dependent," unable to "shake off the effects of past events."[2]

Constitutive choices about communications, in the approach I take in this book, fall into three broad areas: *first,* the general legal and normative rules concerning such issues as free expression, access to information, privacy, and intellectual property; *second,* the specific design of communications media, structure of networks, and organization of industries; and *third,* institutions related to the creation of intangible and human capital—that is, education, research, and innovation. All three of these, especially the first, are relevant to the development of the "public sphere"—the sphere, that is, of public discussion, public knowledge, and public opinion.[3]

The great political revolutions of the modern world, including the American, the French, and both Russian revolutions (1917 and 1991), all raised the most fundamental questions about communications and knowledge, as they did about politics: Who will have the right to speak and to publish? Who will be subject to surveillance? What access will ordinary people have to information and debate about public issues? What incentives will they have to invest in creating and disseminating knowledge? In each case, revolutionary changes in politics brought about revolutionary changes in communications. Some old-regime structures survived into the new era, but for communications, as for other areas of social life, the ideological beliefs of the revolutionaries mattered a great deal, particularly in constitutive decisions about the public sphere. The restriction or protection of free speech, popular assembly, and private association are only the most obvious examples. Through a variety of decisions about their own practices—the writing down and publishing of constitutions, publication of laws, opening up of legislative sessions, disclosure of votes, public accounting of taxes and expenditures, dissemination of economic and social data—modern states have also determined the transparency of their operations and the ability of the press and the public to monitor and criticize them.

As a new technology emerges, so do new choices about the purposes and organization that will guide its development—whether, for example, they will primarily be military or civilian, governmental or private, or non-profit or commercial. At issue may be the technology's architecture—the complex of standards that define the workings of a technological system or a major segment of it—as well as the methods for settling architectural disputes, such as by national or local regulation or international agreement, through private standard-setting organizations, or by competition among private firms for architectural dominance in the market. Different architectures often embody different values. They may make governmental control easy, or they may make it difficult. They may facilitate external monitoring, or they may protect anonymity and privacy. They may enable greater diversity and decentralization in the sources of expression, or they may favor greater uniformity. In the case of computational technologies, the underlying code may be open to scrutiny and revision, or it may be proprietary and closed. A new technology may have particular consequences because of its architecture, not because that is the only way it could be. Architectural choices are often politics by other means, under the cover of technical necessity.[4]

The advent of a new technology may also create an occasion for a larger restructuring of rules and relationships. At moments of change, a typical question is how, if at all, the state will translate the rules and policies for an old medium into rules and policies for a new one. Will it adopt, with minor revisions, the same legal and regulatory framework and mode of organization, or fundamentally transform them? The development of the telegraph, for example, posed a choice as to whether legal principles previously applied to print and postal communication would apply to telegraphic messages; after the motion pictures developed, the question became whether the legal framework governing the press would apply to the cinema. And, more recently, the rise of the digital media has upset older legal models and posed new questions about whether existing laws and norms should apply to such forms of communication as e-mail.[5]

Wars, economic shocks, and other events may also provoke a generative crisis—one that shakes up older institutions and creates the opening for new choices about previously settled rules and practices. World War I was a generative crisis for communications in many of the countries drawn into the conflict. International pressures of other kinds may also precipitate internal upheavals. The more a society is tied into the world economy, the more likely constitutive moments will arise from changes in international communication regimes—that is, the norms and policies institutionalized in various kinds of international agreements, such as those governing copyright, telecommunications, and the broadcast spectrum.

As an episodic process, constitutive development reflects the particular conjuncture of forces and ideas at the moment when a political upheaval takes place, a new technology is introduced, or some other event reopens settled institutional patterns. But not all constitutive decisions work out equally well. Institutions created under unusual conditions may not survive; later developments may undo them or create pressure to conform to standard national patterns. International competition, conflict, and coordination also provide an imperfect "discipline" on the range of decisions sustainable in the long run. These are some of the mechanisms that create wider uniformities despite variable influences in particular societies. But, in the exceptional case, a constitutive "mutation"—a new institutional form, technological system, or social practice born of a particular historical conjuncture—may also set a new pattern in a society and even in the world.

Communications and Power

It is one thing to explain why an open public sphere and independent media originate in a particular country. It is another thing to explain why they persist and spread. Social institutions, including forms of government, are the result not only of forces that create them in the first place, but of forces that affect their survival. To be sure, some corrupt governments and other self-aggrandizing institutions may become entrenched despite poor performance and the unhappiness of the people who suffer under them. And, alas, even the highest virtues may not guarantee that institutions endure. But their survival and diffusion may have a lot to do with their relationship to power.

For centuries, the idea of free and open public communication about matters of political importance did not appeal to the great and powerful.

Francis Bacon's equation, "Knowledge is power," may be read not simply as an endorsement of knowledge but also as a warning about its perils. For fear of the power others might acquire against them, ruling elites have often kept knowledge secret, limited public discussion, and controlled religion, education, and science so as to prevent their subjects from acquiring sensitive information and dangerous ideas. Yet in the modern world, notwithstanding that interest, the sphere of public information has grown, independent channels of civil society have increased, and scientific and educational institutions have gained greater autonomy. While hard-won political struggles have been immediately responsible for these developments, a more systematic reason may explain their diffusion and consolidation.

Attempts by states to restrict communication and monopolize knowledge suffer from an internal difficulty. Inasmuch as they impair the widespread social capacity to create wealth, restrictions on knowledge and communication undercut the long-term ability of a state to sustain its power internationally and meet a variety of internal demands. As a result, informational and communicative capacities present a dilemma to those who hold power. More highly developed and widely distributed capacities may promise more control over the forces of nature, economic growth, greater military strength, and other advantages. But by enabling people to communicate and organize independently, such expanded capacities may also destabilize and undermine the existing order from within. How states respond to that knowledge-power dilemma holds great consequences. Different responses imply different constitutive choices about communications, and because early choices lead down different developmental paths, the legacy of old responses may affect a society long after it attempts to shed them.

Consider the strategic options and potential aftereffects of a regime that limits communicative capacities in the hope of minimizing internal social and political risks. In the extreme case—a "closed society"—a state afraid of popular participation or subversion may try to seal itself off from the wider world, refuse to invest in literacy and education, and ban independent ownership of the means of communication. Or, without entirely closing itself off, a state may selectively invest in education, communications networks, or other resources while jailing dissidents and demanding ideological conformity from journalists, researchers, and others in exchange for privileges—the typical strategy of an authoritarian state hoping to modernize. Control may be particularly effective if, instead of exercising direct supervision, a state can rely for enforcement primarily on partnerships with strategic elites, such as a printing guild or the directors of a broadcasting authority, in whom the state vests a communications monopoly. Control and centralization have a long historical connection. From ancient empires that kept scribes close at hand to the absolutist states of early modern Europe that centralized printing in their capitals, regimes seeking to censor communication have often tried to confine it geographically. And even when the regimes change, the imprint on the structure of communications may not disappear. Centralization tends to be highly persistent: France and Russia still display the highly centralized pattern of communications that state policy originally pursued centuries ago.

The development of telecommunications in the Soviet Union provides a twentieth-century example of the influence of state interests in control on decisions about technological systems. After taking power in 1917, the new Soviet rulers could have invested in telephone networks, as other nations were doing at that time, but chose instead to emphasize another emerging communication technology—loudspeakers. Down to its collapse in 1991, the Soviet Union and the countries under its control had markedly fewer telephones than the countries of Western Europe and North America, even allowing for differences in income. The Soviet regime did, however, invest in broadcasting, which it made into a loudspeaker of another kind; the Soviets favored vertical communications technologies that allowed the state to communicate with the people but neglected technologies for horizontal communications that would allow people to communicate with each other. This preference reflected the regime's general effort to repress the spontaneous organization of civil society. The telephone network built by the Soviets also routed long-distance calls through Moscow, a choice that had no economic logic but made it easier for the state to maintain surveillance. Reconstructing telecommunications became a major economic imperative after the Soviet system fell.[6]

If the costs of closed or restrictive regimes consisted only of the direct expenditures for surveillance and policing, a mere change of regime might remove them immediately. But deeper malformations—such as neglect of education and communications outside of the metropolitan "core," distorted allocations of investment in technology, and lack of popular trust in the privacy of communications—are likely to have long-lasting effects. The immediate costs to growth are clearest in the case of the closed society that loses access to trade and international scientific exchange. Authoritarian modernization may be more ambiguous in its results because such regimes may succeed in importing technologies and developing technical education, military research, and other informational capacities. But here, too, if the sparse record of authoritarian regimes in technological innovation is any indication, the costs over the long term are substantial. Insofar as these costs become apparent through military defeat, relative economic decline, or other ways, they may induce political change, including efforts to loosen old controls and mimic institutional structures thought to be more successful.

The opening up of restrictive systems of control may proceed either de facto or through law. In the case of a de facto opening, a society may have no strong central state authority, the governing elites may be too divided for the state to act consistently, or the state may lack the means to stop or screen communication from abroad. Examples of such states run from the Netherlands in the seventeenth century to Iran today. A de facto opening may serve as an initial stage before rights to independent communication and association are legally established, but the importance of such a phase is not just transitional. The de facto opening may do the work of "creative destruction," eroding legacies of control or averting their development in the first place.

Opening the public sphere under the protection of law requires more than the state's pledged absence from society. Constitutional and judicial protections of rights to free expression, access to information, privacy, and patent and copyright are as much of a "service" provided by states as welfare benefits or military defense.[7] Some work on state-building, however, focuses solely on administrative, military, and fiscal capacities and suggests that the formation of modern states primarily involves increases in the scale and scope of state activity.[8] But the rise of constitutional government also involves institutionalized limitations on state power and the creation of an independent judiciary. These aspects of state-building are particularly important for knowledge and communications, not only because of such legal guarantees as rights to free speech and intellectual property, but also because of constitutive decisions that limit discretionary political control of activities conducted under state authority. For example, instead of establishing universities and broadcasting networks as organs of the national government, a state may disburse funds to private and public organizations outside of the national government. Such provisions limit executive power, but they do not imply that the state is "weak," since they may increase public trust and thereby promote cooperation and support. The attempt to build in checks and balances may also prevent the state from adopting measures that in the long run would be destructive of its own authority. Just as better brakes on a train or car enable it to travel safely at higher speeds, so may constitutional limitations increase the power potentially available to a state in its hour of crisis.

Constitutive decisions about intellectual property, scientific research, and other issues affecting technological innovation have particular bearing on economic development. There is hardly a better example of constitutive choice than the definition of property rights; even the most basic question of what can be held as property is a matter of political decision. The idea of property rights in the radio spectrum would have mystified our ancestors, while the idea of property rights in people, that is, slavery, is abhorrent to us. Political decisions determine the particular rights that a form of property conveys; in the case of copyright and patents, for example, decisions in the eighteenth century set a limited duration for those rights. The development of intellectual property rights allowed authors and inventors to appropriate at least some of the economic value of their work. And this right of appropriation, not just the right to publish, has helped to enlarge the public sphere by creating incentives to produce and disseminate knowledge and new technology. The medieval guilds used secrecy to appropriate the gains from innovation, thereby keeping discoveries out of wider circulation and inhibiting further advance. The ingenuity of patent and copyright is that in exchange for a temporary monopoly, they encourage inventors and authors to disclose new knowledge, and when the rights finally expire, the property itself tumbles into the public domain. To large corporations, the prospective time limit is an incentive to develop not just isolated innovations but a continuous capacity for innovation so as to stay ahead of competitors. Insofar as antitrust and other policies prevent corporations from achieving gains through predatory tactics, they may encourage them to invest instead in patentable innovation.[9]

But intellectual property also suffers from inadequacies as a basis for innovation and even has its dark side. Patent and copyright convey a monopoly, albeit a temporary one. If patents are construed so broadly that they cover potential alternative inventions, they may suppress further innovation, at least for a time. Similarly, copyright can be so extended in scope and time as to inhibit both criticism and further development of ideas. Insofar as copyright and patent owners shape the law, they may succeed in bending it to their private advantage alone. Like the development of communications monopolies, such efforts illustrate the potential for private interests created under a liberal state to conflict with the wider interests it claims to advance. In addition, scientific research and other forms of inquiry, particularly those aimed at basic principles rather than applications, have such diffuse and long-term social benefits that individual intellectual property rights cannot fully capture returns on investment. Governmental and nonprofit support for education and research can fill the gap between social returns and individual rewards that would be left under a pure market-based regime. As the level of investment required for successful innovation increases, particularly at higher levels of development, an early bias against state support of science and technology can become a barrier to growth.

The demands of long-term economic growth ultimately required, therefore, not simply constitutional limitations on the state, but its active support in developing knowledge and communicative capacities. Restrictive-information regimes had to evolve into more open ones without, however, moving so far toward laissez-faire as to impair the state's ability to meet various developmental and external challenges. No single set of policies was necessarily optimal. But a state that provided positive support to communication, education, and creation of new knowledge and technology, while restricting its own powers of surveillance, censorship, and control, had the potential for developing comparative advantage in communications. Although many states today have adopted institutions and policies that more or less fit this description, the United States had a singular advantage in starting down that path at the point the nation was founded in the late eighteenth century.

The Path of American Development

Four waves of institution-building in American history hold special importance for communications. The American Revolution, the writing of the Constitution, and the development of such institutions as the Post Office, the common school, copyright law, and the popular press in the early republic left a legacy of foundational decisions that were especially important in shaping the legal and normative framework of the public sphere. New constitutive choices came with the rise of technological networks, beginning with the decision to privatize the telegraph in the 1840s and culminating in the system of regulatory and antitrust policy imposed on telecommunications beginning around 1907. Yet another wave came with the rise of the early mass media—first the mass press, then the motion pictures—when the dynamic tensions created by immigration and industrialization led to both wider diversity and tighter moral regulation, until repression crested just after World War I and a new legal framework for freedom of expression began to take shape in the 1920s. And, finally, though beyond the scope of this volume, the expansion of public investment in science, technology, and higher education during World War II and the early Cold War and the ensuing revolutions in computers, electronics, and telecommunications set off the most recent wave of institutional design and transformation.

As the United States developed internally, so the relationship of American communications to the external world changed. The young republic, like the earlier colonies, belonged to the dependent periphery of an Atlantic communications network centered in London. While standing apart from Europe and developing its own institutions, the United States by 1850 became more of an originator of communications technologies; by this period, it was already a leader in certain aspects of communications without being a center. It had graduated, in effect, from the dependent periphery to the independent semi-periphery in the world economy, while Britain remained the dominant power in communications, in part through its control, during the late nineteenth and early twentieth centuries, of the global submarine cable network. In the decades after World War I, as the United States gained economic and military power, it increasingly became the dominant global center in communications, communications technology, and entertainment for export, and by the late twentieth century, what had been the American exception in communications—private telecommunications and commercial broadcasting, for example—increasingly became the rule. In short, though the differences have by no means been completely eliminated, the divergence in communications that opened up between the United States and Europe in the eighteenth century has increasingly been settled on American terms.

Communications in America did not unfold in a uniform and linear way. Less open in its public life and lagging in every dimension of education and communications, the South both before and after the Civil War departed from the prevailing patterns elsewhere in the United States. During the antebellum era, the planter class limited public debate in the press and not only denied literacy to blacks but opposed public education for poor whites as well. Some of the changes that the Revolution set in motion elsewhere in the United States were therefore delayed in the South. Long after slavery, blacks throughout the nation were denied full participation in public discussion, rights of free expression, and access to education, and other resources. Women, though an increasingly important part of the reading public and other markets for cultural goods during the nineteenth century, also suffered various forms of political and educational exclusion. In the society at large, after a long expansion of the public sphere from the Revolution through the mid–nineteenth century, a more repressive tendency set in from the Civil War through World War I and its immediate aftermath. Both of those wars generated pressures for stronger state control of communications than was typical at other times. All these deviations from the society's ideal standards led to political struggles, and these struggles changed the practical working of communications, though the changes were often presented and understood as reaffirmations of founding principles.

No single idea, interest, or condition explains the distinctive path taken by communications in America. But the challenge of building a continental republic helps to account for much that was distinctive about the early direction of national policy and private investment. Of fundamental importance to the long-term development of communications were the responses to the initial demands of state- and nation-building through choices about the postal system and press. Relative to Europe—in particular to Britain and France, which will serve as our principal points of comparative reference—communications in America tended to exhibit a series of related characteristics: greater openness and transparency in the public sphere; higher levels of commercialization; greater decentralization; more rapid extension and ubiquitous penetration of communication networks; and greater receptivity to new products and technologies but relatively little support, until the twentieth century, for the more abstract sciences or theoretical innovation.

Why did American communications diverge from European patterns? The idea that the United States "was created differently, developed differently, and thus has to be *understood* differently"—and that it differs from other counties in ways both good and bad—has long been a theme of foreign visitors, social theorists, and historians alike.[10] Some of the same factors cited in such accounts influenced the distinctive course taken by communications in America. The absence of certain legacies of feudalism and absolutism, such as monopolistic printing guilds and centralized state censorship, had an early effect on American development. Even before the Revolution's affirmation of rights to freedom of the press, a de facto opening had created an embryonic public sphere during the late colonial period. The geopolitical position of the new nation was also a factor: Removed from foreign threats, the United States was under less pressure to develop a centralized state with a standing army, and for just this reason, it experienced less pressure to impose a military or security-minded framework on new communications technologies such as the telegraph. By the time the United States became more embroiled in international conflict, it had already established institutional patterns in communications that reflected its earlier situation. Moreover, from an early point, because of the country's rapid expansion west, Americans approached technical and organizational challenges in communications from a continental perspective—building postal, telegraph, and telephone networks on a far more extensive scale than any single nation in Europe. The sheer scale of these networks—and the enormous domestic market they helped to create—then had a pervasive effect on the productivity and competitive advantage of nearly all the communications industries, particularly telecommunications, motion pictures, and broadcasting.

At the nation's founding, however, Americans were concerned with building not just a continental nation but a republican one, and their choices about communications reflected distinctive ideological preoccupations, particularly about the role of the state. After the failure of the Articles of Confederation, the framers of the Constitution approached the problem of state-building with creative reluctance. No nation better illustrates the proposition that liberal state-building involves the building-in of limitations. Some theorists and historians have argued that the early American republic had no "state" at all, while others have contended that it did indeed have a state—as the South certainly discovered when trying to secede from it—but that there was no "sense of the state" because the federal government had limited administrative capacities until the end of the nineteenth century.[11] Communications does not fit this chronology. From the start, the Post Office was the one major exception to limited federal administrative capacities. But because its role was facilitative rather than extractive or controlling, it did not convey the image of a state standing over and apart from the people, even though it was the most visible federal presence in everyday life.

Precisely because of the interest in strengthening republican institutions, early American policy included strong positive commitments to information and communications, not merely the "negative liberty" of individual rights to free expression. While the Europeans taxed publications, the United States subsidized the growth of independent newspapers through cheap postal rates. Legal guarantees of postal privacy also exemplified a distinctive stance toward popular communication, simultaneously advancing it and protecting it from political control. The spread of popular education in the early republic similarly reflected a belief in what Americans themselves referred to as "the diffusion of knowledge," though again, in using the power of government, they minimized the risk of top-down control, in this case through locally financed and controlled schools. In still other policies, the American republic exemplified a new cognitive relationship between a people and its government through such commitments to transparency as public legislative sessions and concisely written and widely published state and federal constitutions. The public sphere did not simply emerge from material changes; it was created through politics—in the American case, through a revolution.

In some respects, however, the choices that shaped American communications were in tension with each other. Persistent internal conflicts have arisen from the relationship between democracy and capitalism in communications. While Americans preferred to see control of education and communications widely diffused, the constitutional tradition provided the means of combating excessive concentrations of power only in the state, not in the marketplace. In the mid–nineteenth century, when Western Union gained control of the telegraph industry and the Associated Press held a monopoly over wire-service news, Americans confronted a new form of centralized power for which they at first had no institutional response. As the problem of monopoly later intensified, antitrust policy and communications regulation became the settings in which these tensions were played out.

Capitalism is no newcomer to communications in America. From the beginning, even in the colonial era, printing and publishing were commercial in outlook, and advertising achieved earlier and wider acceptance in America than in Europe. American entrepreneurs also pioneered production for the mass market through innovations in cheap print and cheap public entertainment. While this was all evidence to critics of American vulgarity, it reflected the powerful confluence of democracy and capitalism in eroding certain forms of restricted communication. As a general rule, democratic interests tend to favor greater transparency, openness, intelligibility, and cheap access to information. In search of profits from wider markets, publishers and other entrepreneurs also often favor more accessible work that can be sold in greater volumes at lower prices (though their preferred strategies depend on the incentives created by intellectual property laws). During the nineteenth century, the joint expansion of the public sphere and commercial enterprise dramatically cut the cost of information and cultural goods. But because cheap culture was often disturbing to guardians of taste and morals, it met condemnation as indecent and subversive and triggered demands for new controls on expression or more wholesome alternatives. While the regulatory and repressive reactions sometimes gained sway, particularly in the late nineteenth and early twentieth centuries, the predominant American pattern was the brash pursuit of markets and publics in competition that was more open and unrestrained than was typically the pattern in Europe.

Another source of internal tension arose from what might be called the American culture of information, particularly if we think of information not as covering knowledge in all its forms but in a more specific, contrasting sense. "Information" often refers specifically to data relevant to decisions, while "knowledge" signifies more abstract concepts and judgments. As knowledge provides a basis of understanding, so information affords a basis of action. "Information" carries the connotation of being more precise, yet also more fragmentary, than knowledge.[12] From early in its history, American culture was oriented more to facts than to theory, more to practicality than to literary refinement—more, in short, to information than to knowledge. While the pattern originated in England, it was accentuated in America. "Those in democracies who study sciences are always afraid of getting lost in utopias," Alexis de Tocqueville observed in *Democracy in America.* "They mistrust systems and like to stick very close to the facts. . . . In America the purely practical side of science is cultivated admirably. . . . But hardly anyone in the United States devotes himself to the essentially theoretical and abstract side of human knowledge."[13] Though the point is sometimes contested, historians have frequently commented on this aversion to abstraction in nineteenth-century American science. The emphasis on the gathering of statistical data in both governmental and private decision-making practices is a reflection of the same cultural tendency.

A comparison of the historical development of Anglo-American and French journalism illustrates how this tendency found expression in communications. Nineteenth- and early twentieth-century American newspapers gave primacy to reporting the news, while French newspapers gave primacy to literary essays. American newspapers pioneered financial and sports reporting (filled with numbers, of course) and had far more foreign correspondents than did newspapers in France. American journalists invented the interview, and when the French finally imported it, they imported the word itself from English and recognized the technique as an American novelty. The highest aspiration of French newspaper writers was to achieve a reputation as a poet; newspaper writing commanded little prestige.[14] American journalists cared about "color" as well as facts, but the highest-prestige newspapers had an informational rather than a storytelling orientation.[15] The cultural framework of the public sphere was radically different in the two countries. Journalistic authority belonged to information in America and to literary distinction in France.

But the culture of information, like the reliance on the marketplace, had its limits. As technological innovation became increasingly dependent on advances in abstract scientific knowledge, America's lack of interest in theory could have become an obstacle to growth. The United States was not without resources for advancing science, thanks to private universities and foundations that had sought to emulate the German system of higher education and made substantial investments in scientific research. But America did not play the kind of leadership role in the advanced sciences that it played in other areas; the government devoted few resources to science and technology, except in agriculture. It took World War II to jolt America out of its older patterns. The coincident Atlantic migration of physicists and other scientists and intellectuals contributed to the institutional transformation, and then the Cold War helped to sustain the new pattern. Public investment in science and technology—channeled through institutions that continued, however, to be decentralized and competitive—proved instrumental in the emergence of computer science, advanced telecommunications, and other developments that led directly to the contemporary phase of the information revolution.

No single country is responsible for the making of modern communications, but the United States has played a singular role for the past two centuries in such developments as the constitutional protection of rights to free expression, the opening up of government to public scrutiny, the development of a comprehensive postal system, the rise of the popular press, the spread of literacy and primary education, the development and diffusion of the telephone, the invention of broadcasting, the development of satellite communications, the rise of the Internet, e-mail, and other recent changes too numerous to mention. The global influence of the American media and the American model now puts an even heavier responsibility on the United States than in the past. History is no basis for a complacent triumphalism about American technology and institutions, especially if the original grounds of policy are forgotten. Freedom is at stake now in choices about communications as it was at the founding of the republic. The question is no longer whether a post-industrial, information society is coming; it has come. But what kind of society it proves to be will ultimately be a political choice. If only because the future will hinge on decisions yet to be made, the political origins of modern communications ought to command our attention.

PART ONE

The Opening of the Public Sphere 1600–1860

CHAPTER ONE

Early Modern Origins

COMMUNICATIONS in Europe and America during the seventeenth and eighteenth centuries underwent a radical transformation, but not because of any revolution in communications technology. A printer from the 1500s magically catapulted into a print shop of the late 1700s would have found hand-operated, wooden presses little altered from his own time.[1] Viewed from the standpoint of social practices, politics, and institutions, however, the change in communications was enormous. Europe and its American colonies saw the introduction of regular, publicly available postal service; the first newspapers, scientific journals, and other periodicals appeared and, along with them, journalism emerged in its earliest forms. Commercial expansion, religious conflict, and the rise of more powerful nation-states altered the economic and political context of communications. While states generally sought to control information, they were not entirely successful; internal conflicts and the structure of the international system permitted more autonomous forms of communication even before free expression received legal protection. The market for print expanded, and the law of intellectual property began to take its modern shape. Most important, out of these developments a new sphere of public information, public debate, and public opinion emerged.

What was this new public sphere? Part of the difficulty in defining it lies in the ambiguity of the word "public." In one sense, public is to private as open is to closed, as when we speak of making something public. In another sense, public is to private as the whole is to the part, as when we speak of the public health or public interest, meaning the health or interest of the whole of the people as opposed to that of a class or individual.[2] The term "public sphere" combines both senses when conceived (as it will be here) as the sphere of openly accessible information and communication about matters of general social concern.[3]

Before 1600, the sheer underdevelopment of communications networks impeded flows of information and the development of a public sphere. To be sure, news and other information circulated by word of mouth, via privately carried letters and scribal publications, through ballads relating current events, and in occasional pamphlets and other printed works, but the absence of postal service and periodicals such as newspapers presented severe limitations. Regular means of exchange and publication provide not only a stream of fresh information but also the opportunity to respond to events as they unfold, to engage in the back-and-forth of debate, and to sustain relationships and affiliations. Publications weave invisible threads of connection among their readers. Once a newspaper circulates, for example, no one ever truly reads it alone. Readers know that others are also seeing it at roughly the same time, and they read it differently as a result, conscious that the information is now out in the open, spread before a public that may talk about the news and act on it.[4] Without a regular flow of communication, it is difficult to develop this sense of a public that extends beyond the limits of a local, face-to-face community.

Not only did European societies before 1600 lack the necessary communication networks for a public sphere; there were also normative and political barriers to its formation. Under the prevailing principles of political communication, ordinary people were not properly concerned with government; according to an English royal proclamation drafted by Francis Bacon in 1620, matters of state were "not themes or subjects fit for vulgar persons or common meetings." The privilege of discussing politics belonged exclusively to the few who could speak in government councils, and these discussions were supposed to be confidential. In England it was a crime to divulge parliamentary proceedings. The norms of discussion and decision-making in Parliament itself were also consensual rather than adversarial; open disagreements and organized political alignments were avoided. The development of the public sphere required the breakdown of "norms of secrecy and privilege" and the open acknowledgment and acceptance of political differences.[5]

In short, if a public sphere was to emerge—and no inexorable force of progress dictated that it would—two conditions had to be met: the creation of a new network infrastructure and the collapse of old norms, if not the fashioning of new ones. The rise of capitalism, with attendant increases in the circulation of commodities and information, contributed particularly to overcoming the infrastructural barriers. Markets themselves are information networks, and expanding commerce opened up new channels of communication. As printing and bookselling developed, information itself increasingly became a commodity. "One fact must not be lost sight of: the printer and the bookseller worked above all and from the beginning for profit," write Lucien Febvre and Henri-Jean Martin of the early history of the book in the fifteenth and sixteenth centuries.[6] Continually searching for new markets, printers and booksellers extended distribution networks and enlarged the reading public. In a variety of ways, state policy also created the bases of the public sphere. States reduced the infrastructural barriers to communications by developing roads and postal systems. Traditionally patrons of the arts, states in the seventeenth and eighteenth centuries also became patrons of the sciences and sponsors of learned academies and publications as they sought to centralize power in its symbolic as well as material forms.[7]

But neither the rise of capitalism nor state-building guaranteed a change in norms of secrecy about governmental proceedings or the development of openly accessible channels of public discussion. Ruling elites not only exercised direct control of print through censorship and surveillance but also sought to shape the organization of the book trade and the press to ensure that the dominant interests in publishing were aligned with those of the state. In the early phases of development (until 1695 in England and 1789 in France), states pursued this objective by granting privileges and monopolies to a limited number of favored printers and booksellers, who then shared the state's interest in suppressing illegal publications. Later, high taxes and other costs imposed on publishers by the state helped to limit the popular press. Since state policies both fostered and inhibited the public sphere, the role of the state does not lend itself to a simple generalization. If states had always been coherent, systematic, and effective, they might have created a sphere only of official ideology. But because their domination was far from single-minded and complete, something else was possible.

The Diffusion and Control of Print

The advent of printing around 1450 is the paradigmatic example of change in information technology, yet it was equally a change in economic organization. The production of manuscripts had been chiefly a monastic function, though commercial stationers in the later stages of the manuscript era began to produce and sell hand-copied books in quantities of up to several hundreds.[8] Had monasteries remained dominant in the era of the movable-type press, they would not have had the same incentives as commercial printers to expand the uses of print, and the technology might not have had the effects so widely attributed to it. But from the time of Gutenberg, printing was organized commercially, and as the technology spread, so did a capitalist framework in the book trade.

Publishing was associated with capitalism in part because the industry itself was a prime instance of capitalist development. It took considerable capital to finance not only the equipment in a shop but also the paper and other costs of production while awaiting sales, which were often slow in coming. The dependence on capital drew printing to cities where finance was available and created pressures to adapt the physical and cultural form of the book to wider markets. The earliest printed books, like the manuscripts that served as their models, were large, cumbersome folios written in Latin primarily for the clergy, the universities, and high officials. Printers and others acting as publishers had incentives, however, to find new texts they could sell, to bring them out in more portable sizes (the printed book was the original laptop), and to simplify typefaces and other elements to improve readability. Thus, the early book trade became divided between weighty volumes for the learned and "small-size literary or polemical works for a larger public."[9] Print could reach a wider public than manuscripts had because of lower costs; by 1470, according to one estimate, the same text cost between 50 percent and 80 percent less in print than in manuscript.[10] Nonetheless, in early modern Europe, the market for print comprised only a small fraction of the population because of the limits of both literacy and income, as well as high distribution costs due to the primitive condition of transport and communication.

Religious ideas and conflict contributed to the spread of print culture in the sixteenth and seventeenth centuries. Beginning in 1517 in Germany, the Protestant Reformation unleashed a tremendous surge in printing for two separate reasons. First, it set in motion a process that would later be repeated many times: the antagonistic expansion of a medium. Protestant leaders regarded the printing press as a means of propagating the truth and created their own presses to disseminate their beliefs; theirs was the first transformative movement in history spread, to a large extent, through the vehicle of print. With the Counter-Reformation beginning around 1570,

Catholics also turned to the press; in the antagonistic expansion of a medium, even the reluctant side in a conflict has no other choice but to adopt more powerful means of persuasion. Second, by calling on the faithful to read the Bible, Protestantism elevated the importance of literacy. The effort to incorporate reading into everyday lay religious practice was halting at first, but in the seventeenth century it gathered force with Pietism in Germany and Puritanism in England.[11] The positive association of Protestantism and economic development probably also contributed to the more rapid growth of literacy rates and the book trade in Protestant areas.[12]

Both the economic and the religious forces in the growth of printing helped to shape the international map of print. The geographically dispersed demand for books led to the early development of an international book trade; in the sixteenth century, fairs at Lyons and Frankfurt became important venues for the traffic in print. From its infancy, publishing was cosmopolitan, and a division of labor developed between the center and periphery of the trade. The early centers of publishing in Germany, Italy, and Holland dominated the production of texts in Latin that were originally the chief articles of international exchange, while publishers in the periphery specialized in the vernacular. England, which fell on the periphery of the European economy when William Caxton introduced printing in 1476, exemplified the pattern. Since continental printers could supply tomes in Latin more cheaply, the first printers in England concentrated on legal and literary texts in English.[13]

Religious conflict added another dimension to center-periphery relationships. As states and established churches sought to restrict heretical publications, they drove dissenters to other countries. The flight of the Huguenots from France in the late seventeenth century contributed to Holland's role as a center of Protestant publishing; similarly, English dissenters went across the channel to Holland to have their work printed. Extraterritorial publishers, moreover, found a market for the books and journals they produced all over Europe. Amsterdam became a center of Jewish publishing also because of an influx of refugees. As the lingua franca of the "republic of letters" changed from Latin to French in the seventeenth century, the Netherlands became a center of French-language publishing beyond the reach of the French state.[14] The development of such extraterritorial and transnational publishing complicated the efforts of states to control the printed word. It meant that rulers faced two distinct tasks: controlling domestic printers and regulating the influx of print across their borders.

Although some governments had originally sought to attract printers in the late 1400s, the policing of print became a focus of state interest in the sixteenth and seventeenth centuries. Control eventually extended across the entire sequence of activities, from the initial production or importation of texts through their distribution, and involved both religious and secular authorities. In 1543, the Catholic Church banned all books except those that had its approval, and in 1559 it issued its first Index of Forbidden Books. The long-run trend, however, in Protestant and Catholic countries alike, was toward centralized control in the hands of the state. Through several steps culminating in a proclamation in 1538, Henry VIII established a licensing system for all books in English. During the sixteenth century, the English government also prosecuted those responsible for troublesome publications on such grounds as treason, heresy, and "false news" concerning the magnates of the realm *(Scandalum Magnatum)*, though licensing proved the most efficient means of control. In a series of measures in France between 1535 and 1551, the king banned all books except those approved by censors and prohibited the importation of books from Protestant countries. Absolutism regarded censorship as a royal prerogative and open political debate as unthinkable, although the practice of censorship was often less systematic than the theory and law suggested.[15]

A key feature of policy in both England and France was the alignment of the dominant groups in the trade with the aims of the state. The control of any industry is likely to be more effective when enforcement becomes endogenous—that is, when those who run the industry have strong incentives to make state policy their own. This was the effect of state-granted monopolies and privileges in printing. In England, the Company of Stationers received a charter from the crown in 1557 that conferred on its members the exclusive right to own a press. Since the members of the company had to be freemen of London, this provision effectively kept printing centralized in the capital, an arrangement preferred by the government because it facilitated censorship. A series of other measures up through 1586 also had the purpose of limiting access to the press to a small number of people whom the government considered reliable. The charter vested the company with powers of search and seizure in pursuit of unlicensed books, and further state decrees strengthened its role in enforcing censorship.[16] In effect, the Stationers helped to carry out state censorship in exchange for monopoly privileges; indeed, repressive measures by the state sometimes originated in pressures from the Stationers to extinguish competitors. Although individual printers might gain by producing unlicensed work, the company as a whole had an economic interest in suppressing competition that matched the crown's political interest in suppressing unlicensed print.

In 1559 the Stationers adopted a rule requiring members to register a work ("copy") with the company in order to enjoy an exclusive right to print it; this rule gave the company's members the sole ability to make the written word their own property. The Stationers thereby turned the regulatory authority entrusted to them into a system of property rights. These rights were understood to be perpetual, not lapsing, like later copyright, after some fixed period. From early in the 1500s, the crown had also awarded a series of monopolies to various London printers over specific classes of books. These "patents" covered such categories as legal texts, Bibles, almanacs, and grammars and became lucrative sources of income to the leading printers while also, like the Stationers' charter, promoting the centralization of publishing in London and thereby facilitating censorship. The patents gradually came under the control of the dominant members of the Stationers' Company, and in 1603 many of the existing patents were merged together and incorporated as the English Stock; all shares were held by members of the Stationers, most of them by the company's inner circle. The creation of the English Stock strengthened oligarchic control of the industry.[17]

Likewise, in France an absolutist state sought to make censorship endogenous to the book trade. Louis XIV's ministers adopted policies favoring a small group of printers in Paris, ruining smaller printers in the capital and destroying the centers of provincial publishing; the state followed the same policy toward the paper industry, concentrating production so as to monitor the flow of supplies to printers more effectively. The architects of centralized state power in France thereby imprinted a centralized structure on French publishing. Like the Stationers' Company, the Paris Book Guild accumulated monopolies over the most profitable classes of legal, religious, educational, and literary works and could therefore be counted on to help police the realm of print against illegal intruders. By virtue of the texts it monopolized, the guild's economic interests were closely tied to France's official culture. As in England, those with dissident ideas did not merely confront state censorship; they faced an entire literary and cultural system that spanned the state, the dominant cultural institutions, and the publishing industry.[18]

Despite the entrenched power of this system, it did not fully succeed in limiting access to information and proscribed ideas. The system drove critics and dissenters to develop clandestine or extraterritorial capacities for publishing and disseminating their work. It led authors to use what Annabel Patterson calls "functional ambiguity" to pass the censors in licensed publications.[19] And it helped to sustain a manuscript culture long into the age of the printing press. Precisely because print was regulated, many writers felt they had more freedom in manuscript and often deliberately chose to circulate their work in that form. Manuscript literature also continued to circulate because of the "stigma of print," the disdain for publicity and commercialism that lingered among poets and other writers into the seventeenth century.[20] One aspect of this persistent scribal culture was manuscript news, which characteristically took the form of handwritten newsletters.

Yet while potential targets of censorship used these evasive techniques, they did so at a cost. Clandestine publishing carried risks of discovery and punishment, and the necessary precautions limited dissemination. Indirect and ambiguous language limited accessibility to readers in a different way. And manuscript literature, by its nature, was more expensive than print and therefore less accessible to the public. States in the sixteenth and seventeenth centuries may not have had the capacity or the determination to enforce censorship systematically, but the risks and burdens they imposed by episodic enforcement were sufficient to hamper the development of a public sphere. Indeed, while they might fail to block the circulation of individual forbidden books or pamphlets, states proved to have more control over a new institution of peculiar importance to the public sphere—newspapers.

Networks and News

The development of newsletters, as the term itself suggests, was closely related to the growth of postal service. The late medieval world had seen the emergence of private mercantile networks that were channels for postal communication. In the late fifteenth and sixteenth centuries, several private postal networks were created, and one of these, run by the Thurn and Taxis family initially under the sponsorship of the Hapsburg emperor, expanded until it linked together much of Europe, at its peak employing 20,000 couriers. Although parts of the Thurn and Taxis network lasted for centuries—in the Low Countries until 1794, and in parts of Germany until 1866—the more enduring postal services developed directly under state authority. The French postal system dates from the late 1400s, the English from 1516, though in both cases these initial services were established only for official use and had limited reach. Nonetheless, by the early 1600s the French and English authorities realized that by opening the post to the public, while maintaining it as a monopoly, they could pay for its cost and, not incidentally, keep their opponents under surveillance. Gradually, both France and England began putting postal communication on a modern basis—that is, with service on regular schedules, open to the public at large, and linked to networks in other countries. In the 1620s, the English post connected with the Thurn and Taxis network on the continent.[21]

Postal networks supported the creation of news networks. By 1600, there were correspondents exchanging economic and political intelligence across Europe, though direct access to such information was limited primarily to merchants, bankers, diplomats, and nobles. Commodity price currents (listing the prices of commodities trading on local markets) and exchange rate currents (giving rates for buying and selling foreign bills of exchange) were being published in major commercial centers by the late 1500s, beginning in Italy; surviving copies of the commodity price currents date from the 1580s, but some evidence suggests that these forerunners of financial news publications began forty years earlier.[22] A handwritten periodical referred to as a *gazzette* circulated in Venice around 1550; surviving copies suggest that by 1556, one such newssheet was appearing weekly, but it is unclear whether it was publicly available.[23] People living in a capital often included news in private letters to their kin or patrons in the provinces. Out of this practice evolved commercial newsletters, or *nouvelles à la main,* distributed through the mails and passed from hand to hand all over Europe. In London by the late 1500s, commercial newswriters were providing an "aristocratic news service," sometimes to as many as a hundred or more clients. Typically addressed to a gentleman in the country, scribal newsletters reported events in chronological order, usually in a sentence or two. Though in some ways antecedents of newspapers, the newsletters did not carry essays and arguments to sway their readers' opinions, nor did they purport to speak for the public.[24] Pamphlets and books served as the primary means of carrying on political and religious argument. The sixteenth century also saw the appearance of printed newsbooks and broadsides reporting single events of major importance. In Cologne in 1594, a volume of mainly military news, *Mercurius Gallobelgicus*, began appearing on a semi-annual basis, earning it the designation of the first news periodical, but a semi-annual volume in Latin plainly belongs to a different species from the newspaper. With these qualified exceptions, if news was printed before 1600, it wasn't periodical; and if it was periodical, it wasn't printed.[25]

The first publicly available reports of sundry recent events printed regularly on at least a weekly basis—in other words, the first newspapers, by at least one definition—appeared in Europe around the turn of the seventeenth century. Strasbourg and Wolfenbüttel may have had the first printed newspapers in 1609; within the next decade, there were weeklies in Basel, Frankfurt, Vienna, Hamburg, Berlin, Amsterdam, and Antwerp.[26] The first newspaper to appear in London came from Amsterdam in 1620; printed in English, it carried foreign news that had been translated from Dutch corantos. By 1622, English publishers began regularly issuing corantos under licenses from the crown that permitted them only to carry foreign news.[27] When two papers appeared in Paris in 1631, the king conferred a monopoly on the one published by Théophraste Renaudot, a physician, social reformer, and court favorite, who had created an information-exchange bureau in Paris. Authorized to publish both domestic and foreign news, Renaudot's *Gazette* became the official organ of the state.[28]

The appearance of newspapers in the same period in so much of Europe suggests how closely interconnected its economic and communication networks had become. The advent of newspapers, like the book trade, was related to the rise of capitalism, but there was a critical economic difference between books and newspapers. While books made publishers thirsty for capital because of slow returns on investment, newspapers were typically cheaper to print and sold by subscription payable in advance. Newspapers did not need infusions of capital so much as a continually refreshed supply of their distinctive raw material: news. The growth of trade and markets helped to make that supply possible. Expanding markets increased the appetite for information about the wider world—the predominance of foreign news in early papers is a telling sign of reader interests—while simultaneously creating channels for the flow of news and new possibilities for disseminating it. "The newspaper depends upon its own special lines of communication, inward and outward, bringing information to it and taking the printed copies to the readers," writes Anthony Smith. "These lines of supply were laid down over many generations, but seemed to 'jell' suddenly and simultaneously over a vast terrain at the beginning of the seventeenth century."[29] The spread of newspapers from one country to another was itself a network phenomenon: Much of the content of individual papers consisted of news items taken from other papers, thanks to the emerging international postal network. As newspapers put information into public circulation, they made it easier for printers elsewhere to duplicate their enterprise. Or, if we think of the newspapers themselves as forming a communications network, the more "nodes" transmitting information, the more any individual paper could offer at little extra cost to itself.

As with other forms of print, the state played a shaping role in the development of newspapers. Newspapers could be especially dangerous to authority because of the immediacy and potential political sensitivity of news; they also seemed an affront and a vulgarity to some guardians of custom and social prerogative who upheld the traditional norms of privilege in political communication. What business did newspaper readers have knowing about things that did not concern them? Writing about the traditional norms of secrecy and privilege in England, David Zaret points to an "inverse relationship" between access and substantive discourse: "Access was greatest for purely symbolic displays of sovereign authority, least so for modes of communication that featured substantive discussions and debates."[30] When newspapers first appeared, they were heavily censored, if not shut down entirely; those that were permitted to develop were primarily court gazettes, founded to monopolize the news and to report and celebrate the ceremonial life of the court. In other words, they extended the display of authority rather than the substantive discussion of politics. Political news was generally from abroad; domestic news consisted primarily of lurid, strange, or miraculous reports. The model for the newspaper was a chronicle of historical and providential events, not a vehicle for public discussion. By the end of the century, however, journals with at least some independence of the state were beginning to assume an accepted, albeit restricted role in political communication. This new role emerged in two principal forms—one, a national press; the other, transnational.

England's Opening

It was in England that the most significant change in the role of a national press took place during the seventeenth century. After the initial debut of newspapers in the 1620s, Charles I banned them entirely for six years beginning in 1632, and in 1637 the Star Chamber introduced a rigorous system of licensing for the press as a whole. But with the coming of the English Revolution, the entire structure of control temporarily collapsed. In 1641, the Star Chamber was abolished, licensing and censorship ceased, the Stationers' monopoly broke down, and the number of printers soared. The ensuing years of armed conflict saw another instance of the antagonistic expansion of the press as both Parliament and the king sponsored competing publications. In the struggle for public opinion, the traditional norms of secrecy that had long governed political communication broke down, and new practices emerged. For example, from the beginning of the Long Parliament in 1641, speeches in the House of Commons found their way into print, and parliamentary leaders began to authorize publication of what had previously been confidential proceedings. Although Parliament passed new legislation to regulate printing in 1643, it failed to reestablish control. In addition to a flood of broadsides, pamphlets, declarations, and petitions, the 1640s saw the appearance of newsbooks that unlike the earlier corantos reported domestic political news and sought to sway opinion. Competing newsbooks offered royalist and parliamentary as well as independent versions of battles and other events. This was also the era when censorship began to be attacked in principle, with John Milton's essay *Areopagitica* (1644) against licensing of the press and the more radical libertarian ideas of the Leveller John Lilburne. But the revolutionary efflorescence of the public sphere was short-lived. In 1649, the Commonwealth reimposed licensing and censorship of print (the Puritan revolutionaries had closed all theaters in 1642), and in the mid-1650s Oliver Cromwell's Protectorate stiffened press controls and closed down public discussion. The revolutionary decades, however, had irreversibly transformed Parliament from a council into a legislature—that is, from a body operating on a confidential and consensual basis, charged with doing the king's business, into a genuine source of authoritative decision-making, powerful in its own right. It would not be long before that power again became the focus of adversarial politics and public debate.[31]

When the Stuarts were restored to the throne in 1660, they brought with them a determination to keep information and political discussion under strict control. Nearly the entire pre-1641 information regime was rebuilt, now, however, through legislation rather than as the sole prerogative of the king. In 1662, Parliament gave authority for licensing publications to the secretary of state and limited the number of master printers to twenty, nearly all in London. Under this Licensing Act, all copy entered into the Stationers' Register had to be licensed, and all licensed publications had to be entered into the register to prove ownership; the Stationers' copyright system thereby gained the force of law. The Licensing Act also conferred a monopoly of news on the state. Sir Roger L'Estrange, appointed as licenser in 1663, disclosed the regime's attitude toward public discussion when in 1663 he wrote that "a Public Mercury should never have My vote; because I think it makes the Multitude too Familiar with the Actions, and Counsels of their Superiours; too Pragmaticall and Censorious, and gives them, not only an Itch, but a kind of Colourable Right, and License, to be Meddling with the Government."[32] This objection, however, apparently did not apply to a tightly controlled court gazette. That year L'Estrange bought the only newsbook to survive the Interregnum, *The Kingdom's Intelligencer*, and in 1665 the government created an official publication along the same model as the *Gazette de France*. For most of the next three decades, the *London Gazette* was England's only newspaper; the words "Printed By Authority" ran under its logo, announcing its special relationship to the state.

The system of licensed printing monopolies, however, was approaching its end. From 1679 to 1682, during a political crisis, the Licensing Act lapsed, unleashing a spate of short-lived metropolitan newspapers. Then, with the overthrow of the Stuarts in the revolution of 1688, the monarchy definitively lost the authority to impose licensing by royal prerogative. For a while, licensing continued under parliamentary authority. But with divisions in Parliament, consensus about what ought to be censored broke down, and a growing body of opinion objected to the Stationers' monopoly on economic grounds and looked to competition as a way of bringing down prices. After licensing lapsed in 1695, it was never renewed, though bills were repeatedly introduced during the next decade to restore the system.

The end of licensing of the press was undoubtedly a landmark in the history of free speech, even though it was not the result of a deliberate, liberally minded decision to end state control of the printed word. The government at first expected to use the law of treason to punish subversive publications, but when Parliament effectively barred that option by making treason convictions more difficult in 1696, the government turned to the law of seditious libel as a functional substitute.[33] The abandonment of licensing ended requirements for prepublication clearance, but not the risk of being punished for criticism of the government. Eighteenth-century English legal authorities held that liberty of the press meant only freedom from advance censorship, not from penalties applied after publication. Moreover, while the government allowed two theaters to reopen in London during the Restoration, it maintained tight control over what continued to be regarded as an especially dangerous means of expression. And Parliament, the theater of the state, still did not accept public scrutiny of its own deliberations; newspapers remained barred from reporting parliamentary debates until the late 1700s.[34]

Nonetheless, after 1695 England unquestionably saw an increase in the circulation of political news and the vitality of public discussion in the press. The explanation for this shift lies in complementary structural changes in publishing and politics. The lapse of the Licensing Act precipitated rapid growth in both metropolitan and provincial printing, and as the number of printers increased, so did competition and variety. Pamphlets continued to be the principal vehicles for political writing well into the eighteenth century. But immediately after the end of licensing, London newspapers became more numerous and more frequent: The first triweeklies appeared in 1695, the first daily in 1702, and by 1712 about twenty newspapers were publishing in London every week. The first provincial papers proliferated just after the turn of the century.[35] The lapse of licensing also ended the Stationers' monopoly of literary property, setting off a protracted battle that Parliament partially resolved in 1710 when it adopted a copyright act that, for the first time, imposed time limits on literary property.[36] An immediate political consequence of the new structure of publishing was that it helped critics of the government gain access to print. The end of monopoly undermined the endogenous control of the industry; the state could no longer count on a corporate body like the Stationers to serve as its agent in censorship.

Changes in the structure of politics created a functional role for an opposition press. The late seventeenth century, even before 1688, saw a shift in the nature of parliamentary selection. In the early 1600s, qualified electors in counties and boroughs had given their assent, usually by acclamation, to men chosen for the House of Commons chiefly on the basis of social precedence, without any public opposition. When contests erupted, they were typically personal and seen as a threat to peace and good order. By 1678, in contrast, electoral contests were common, rivals actively sought office, and standard rules emerged for polling voters. These were still contests within the social elite, but they were representative of a shift from consensual to adversarial politics that created new occasions for public debate. In 1694, at nearly the same time that it failed to renew the licensing system, Parliament adopted a bill requiring elections every three years; during the next two decades, there were ten general elections, and for the first time, intense electoral competition between two parties, Whigs and Tories, which alternated in power. Political competition helped to generate interest in political news and argument, but perhaps even more important was the effect of the parties on each other, as antagonism once again contributed to the growth of the press. At first only the party out of power sought to mobilize public opinion through the press, but under Robert Harley (earl of Oxford), Tory governments in the early 1700s began to operate a concerted propaganda effort both in power and out. As of 1702, there was only one government newspaper, the *London Gazette*; by 1713, when Harley's machine was at its peak, the ministry was supporting five London newspapers, each serving a somewhat different audience. In addition, it underwrote a considerable volume of pamphlets. Modern politicians can only be envious of the talent Harley recruited: His two leading writers were Daniel Defoe and Jonathan Swift, and it was Swift who served as chief of propaganda, supervising the party hacks and printers. Repeatedly rejecting calls for the restoration of licensing and censorship, Harley opted instead for a strategy of permanent propaganda and selective prosecution of the government's opponents in the press.[37]

To control criticism, the English government after 1700 turned to a basis of criminal prosecution rarely used while licensing had been in effect. Benefiting from a change in judicial interpretation, the government began to frame its charges against dissenters as violations of the common law of seditious libel. A century earlier, judges had conceived of seditious libel as defamation of individual magistrates, but the term had gradually taken on an extended meaning that included libel of the state, and in a case in 1704 Chief Justice John Holt stripped seditious libel entirely of its older sense of individual defamation and ruled that words bringing the government into disrepute were criminal: "If men should not be called to account for possessing the people with an ill opinion of the Government," the chief justice declared, "no Government can subsist; for it is very necessary for every Government, that the people should have a good opinion of it." In pursuing such cases, the state could secure general warrants for searches of homes and offices (that is, without specifying the object of a search), and it could bring charges without an indictment by grand jury. Not even proof of a statement's truth could be offered in defense; under a Star Chamber precedent from 1606, the truth of a libel aggravated the crime. Although defendants were entitled to jury trials, juries were permitted to rule only on whether the accused had made the statement; judges decided whether it was libelous. Thus, after the end of prepublication censorship, the state had not only legal authority, but also expedient legal principles, to silence critics.[38]

During the eighteenth century, the volume of prosecutions for seditious libel varied depending on political circumstances; the government was sometimes unable to get convictions but nonetheless brought charges to intimidate authors and printers into silence or flight abroad, to jail low-ranking employees of newspapers, and to impose higher costs on newspaper owners. The government targeted not only genuine radicals outside the two dominant parties but also journalists associated with the parliamentary opposition. Under the Tories, for example, the Whig editor of the *Flying Post* took flight himself and went into exile after being convicted of seditious libel in 1713.[39]

Besides relying on propaganda and prosecutions, Harley's government in 1712 also introduced a third policy that was destined to evolve into a primary method of controlling the press. This was the stamp tax. The occasion was yet another effort to restore licensing, in this instance a proposed bill that would have required printers to register every press with the government and to list on every publication the names and addresses of the author, printer, and publisher. Instead of this measure, however, the government decided to extend a tax that had been imposed the previous year on calendars and almanacs. Known as a stamp tax because stamps were required on printed items to show the tax had been paid, the duty amounted to a halfpenny per half sheet (one penny per full sheet) for every copy, plus one shilling per advertisement. Since the typical paper at the time was printed on a half sheet and sold for a penny, the burden on most newspapers (not counting the duty on advertisements) was equivalent to a 50 percent sales tax. While the prospective revenue was part of the motivation, at least some members of the government anticipated that the tax would stifle opposition newspapers.[40] Yet, in this initial form, it failed to do so. Although four newspapers immediately ceased publication, the press was able to recover, in part because the Whigs stepped up subsidies to their publications. Printers, moreover, soon found a loophole in the law that allowed them to pay only two shillings for an entire edition run off on one and a half sheets (six pages). In 1725, however, Parliament tightened both the law and its enforcement, and in 1757, 1776, 1789, and 1797, it continued to push up rates until the retail price of a single copy of a newspaper hit 6*d*, nearly a day's pay for a typical wage-earner. Political motives were clearly at work. During the Parliamentary debate on a stamp tax increase in 1776, Lord North said the demand for newspapers arose from a foolish curiosity and that newspapers, therefore, were a luxury that could stand higher taxation.[41] The government did not suppress newspapers outright, but higher prices kept in check their numbers and circulation, which otherwise would have risen more substantially. The stamp tax made it impossible to operate a popular press that was at once cheap and legal. The printers and hawkers of cheap papers that tried to escape unstamped in the search for a more popular audience suffered the legal consequences, including periodic arrest. Like the earlier licensing laws, the stamp tax shaped the structure of the industry so as to minimize the chances of a popular opposition press emerging that could threaten the government. It also had a more subtle effect in shaping the conception of the public as consisting only of the upper strata of society.

While the stamp tax provided an indirect means of influencing the press, the British government also continued the more direct, old-fashioned method of simply paying writers and owners of newspapers for their support. This kind of intervention reached a peak under Harley's Whig successor, Robert Walpole, who maintained an elaborate network of informants in the press while using bribery and prosecutions to limit the strength of opposition publications. In 1722, troubled by the *London Journal*, the government simply bought it. The English press in the eighteenth century did include oppositional elements, but they were severely constrained and manipulated.[42] After a brief period during the 1730s when control of the theaters broke down, Walpole obtained legislation for a full-scale licensing system for theatrical performances.[43]

The development of postal communication from the Restoration through the eighteenth century reflected the same shift in England's information regime: The means of public communication were expanded, but society was kept in check. In the mid-1600s, regular horse posts were established on the six major roads that radiated out of London into the provinces. Under the Turnpike Act of 1660, the roads themselves began to be improved, and postal service was then extended beyond the Six Roads across England. A wave of turnpike construction a century later upgraded the routes from the major centers in the provinces to London and to each other, and by 1760 the Post Office offered regular service among the provincial centers as well as to and from London. Private competition was not welcome; in 1680, a London merchant named William Dockwra started a penny post in London only to have it taken over by the Post Office two years later. The Treasury had the dominant hand in postal policy. In 1711—and again in 1765, 1784, and several more times at the turn of the century—postal rates were raised to levels that, like the stamp taxes, reduced the volume of popular communication.

Our image of the post office as a routine bureaucracy does not capture its importance in the era before telegraphy. By the eighteenth century, writes Kenneth Ellis, the British Post Office was "the centre of imperial communications, controlling a large fleet of packets; a propaganda and intelligence organ, serving as the government's mouthpiece, eyes, and ears; and an important source of patronage, employing hundreds of officials, postmasters, and sailors."[44] Officials, peers, and members of Parliament enjoyed the privilege of franking mail, which they used in enormous volumes for their private benefit. Several officials used their privilege to operate a profitable newspaper distribution business. The government franked its own publications as well as pamphlets and newspapers that supported its policies. By the 1760s, the volume of metropolitan newspapers being sent for free by the government to the provinces equaled the total circulation of the provincial press.[45] In the second half of the eighteenth century, the Post Office also began to carry the opposition press, including papers franked by opposition members of Parliament, but postal clerks scrutinized publications to weed out those that exceeded the limits of allowable dissent.

The same concern for keeping society in check also constrained the development of education and literacy. In the seventeenth century, England experienced an "educational revolution" as schools became more widely available through efforts largely independent of the state. But the spread of schooling fell far short of becoming universal; the adult male literacy rate in England, measured by signatures, stalled at around 60 percent through the eighteenth century. Nor was there any felt urgency to reduce illiteracy; much of the English elite believed that educating the great mass of the population would only unfit them for the drudgery they needed to perform, mislead them about their expectations in life, and thereby increase discontent.[46]

Partly as a result of the limits of literacy, the "public" of this period still comprised only a small minority of the population. Estimates of newspaper readership for the eighteenth century are highly speculative. Although there are some figures for circulation, more than one person typically read a copy, but no one knows whether the average ratio of readers to copies was three, five, ten, twenty, or more. For estimates of the *total* weekly newspaper audience, however, the correct multiplier is likely to be at the lower rather than at the upper end of that range, because many of the same people who read one paper read others. (In other words, total newspaper circulations cannot be added up and multiplied by ten or twenty because of overlap among their readers.) In 1704, according to an internal Treasury report, there were nine newspapers, all in London, with a total weekly circulation of 43,800 copies—about one copy for every 133 people in England and Wales. By 1750, when dailies were more common and provincial weeklies had spread, the total number of newspaper stamps issued indicates one copy per week for every 45 people.[47] These numbers suggest a sharply restricted readership. In the 1790s, Edmund Burke estimated the political reading public at 400,000, about 5 percent of the population.[48]

Many people no doubt listened as newspapers were read aloud in taverns and other public places or heard about the news secondhand. But the limits of newspaper sales prevented those who ran the papers from acquiring the power and autonomy that their successors would be able to achieve on the basis of larger circulations and greater revenue from both readers and advertisers. A larger market would later permit newspapers to employ more substantial staffs, to gather information directly instead of relying on authorities, and to exert a stronger influence of their own. They were not yet in that position in the eighteenth century.

France and the Transnational Public

The appearance of a semiautonomous national press in England after 1695 stands in some contrast to the development of the press in France. Down to the revolution, the French state continued to exercise direct supervision over the realm of print through prepublication censorship and an extensive system of book police. Approval for publication could come in the form of a *privilège,* which conferred an exclusive right to publish, or a tacit permission, which the regime granted to works that it was willing to allow without formal approval. Censorship wasn't completely effective, but that doesn't mean it was inconsequential. The state committed substantial resources to enforcement. By 1750, there were 130 censors; over the entire period from 1659 to 1789, 17 percent of the prisoners in the Bastille were sent there for offenses related to the book trade.[49]

Royal privileges structured the entire domain of print, reserving various areas of publishing to specific printers; there was no legal way to start a new periodical without obtaining a privilege. According to a comparative study, French periodicals were not only less numerous than those in Britain and North America but also less varied. By 1750, there were fewer than 50 French-language periodicals, but nearly a hundred in Britain and North America. Literacy was lower in France, standing at about 40 percent among adult men. But the French population in 1750 was so much greater—about 21 million, compared to about 8 million in Britain and the American colonies—that the literate public was probably about two-thirds larger in France. The explanation for the more limited number of French publications may lie, therefore, not in the number of readers but in the effect of the two regimes on the market. English publishers had more freedom to create new publications and sought wider markets by making the content of periodicals more varied and practical. French periodical publishers, in contrast, sought monopoly privileges and cultivated a more limited, aristocratic readership.[50]

It is easy, however, to overstate the differences between Britain and France. Not only did the British government check any threat from public communication through the use of prosecutions, taxes, and favors. Britain also retained many of the characteristics of an old-regime society: The monarchy and the church remained dominant institutions, and deferential relations to superiors permeated social life.[51] In France by mid-century, and increasingly after 1750, the influence of the Enlightenment was widely felt among the elite. Censorship was no longer as strict as it had been, and publishers found it easier to contrive a rationale for new publications.[52] The divisions within the French state itself, particularly between royal authorities and the *parlements,* created space for public discussion. What the French read, moreover, did not correspond exactly to what was printed in France.

As a result of the regulation of domestic publishing, extraterritorial printers had come to assume a major role in the French public sphere. Many of the great works of eighteenth-century French literature were published not in France, but in the Netherlands or Switzerland, and circulated through semiclandestine networks. The underground traffic, as Robert Darnton has described it, mixed Voltaire and Rousseau with pornography in a class of forbidden books all promiscuously labeled "philosophical."[53] Extraterritorial newspapers faced more constraints, however, because they depended upon the postal system to reach French readers from their publishing base in the semi-independent principalities and neighboring countries around the periphery of France. In addition, their correspondents inside France could obtain information and send reports to their editors only if they had the forbearance and cooperation of the state. But rather than try to bar these newspapers entirely—which would likely have failed—French officials developed a modus vivendi with them. Ministers used the extraterritorial press to plant stories that would have greater credibility precisely because they did not come from censored domestic publications. Paradoxically, the officials had to accept the extraterritorial newspapers' uncensored reports (including criticism of the state by the parlements) in order for the papers to have credibility as a channel for ministerial leaks. In return for their ability to circulate in France, the newspapers did not explicitly attack French authority.[54]

But the French-language extraterritorial press had a larger importance. Although there were several hundred newspapers in Europe by the mid-1700s, most of them were censored, official gazettes. Many elite readers across the continent subscribed to a French-language extraterritorial newspaper to obtain news not only about other countries but also about their own. The most important center for such publications was the Dutch Republic, which had long been a leader in producing books for export. The Dutch did not protect freedom of the press as a matter of principle; in fact, the number of books banned in the United Provinces increased during the eighteenth century.[55] But the Netherlands lacked a strong central government capable of enforcing any control; power resided in the cities, and thus printers could move from one location to another to evade censorship. The authorities were also much less concerned about publications exported abroad than about those read at home. As a result, an independent press was able to develop that reported news of diplomacy, wars, and other major political events to an elite readership across Europe.

By the mid-eighteenth century, the foremost of these newspapers was the *Gazette de Leyde,* which had appeared continuously since 1677. According to Jeremy Popkin, the Leiden paper presented a picture of the world that differed from the one in the court gazettes: The central actors in its pages were ministers rather than monarchs, and the news included the domestic political conflicts that the court gazettes were unable to report. Written in sober language, and unwilling to publish contributions by interested parties, the paper relied on its own network of paid, albeit mostly part-time, newswriters in perhaps eight to ten cities, including Paris, London, Hamburg, Vienna, and St. Petersburg. The Leiden gazette's circulation provided the revenue to support this network. A profitable enterprise, it apparently refused any payments by governments or other groups, and it carried relatively little advertising. While generally sympathetic to constitutional government and civic republicanism, the paper sought to give an impartial chronicle of events; it was, Popkin says, the "newspaper of record" of its time, as well known to its elite public as the *New York Times* is today.[56]

Histories of the press and the public sphere that have concentrated on publications within the major European states have neglected the significance of this phenomenon. But as the Leiden paper and its competitors show, a transnational market for news had already emerged by the eighteenth century, and on the basis of that market, editors and entrepreneurs were able to create a commercially sustainable, transnational journalism. By exporting papers to many countries (and often selling virtually none at home), the transnational papers gained a degree of autonomy from state control that newspapers produced and sold within a single country could not readily achieve. The European state system, Popkin suggests, was too fragmented to permit joint action to suppress the news, and states instead began to use the transnational press to publicize their views of events. "By at least the mid–seventeenth century," he writes, "the European state system had come to accommodate publications that served no other purpose than to collect the news and arguments put forward by the major powers so that those interested could weigh all sides to a dispute."[57] The public that could participate in this sphere of discussion was limited; it cost far more to subscribe to an extraterritorial newspaper such as the *Gazette de Leyde* than to a domestic paper, although both were available in select coffeehouses and reading rooms. The transnational press, however, anticipated the critical public role that high-level, independent, commercial journalism could play as a mediator and shaper of elite opinion.

The De Facto Public Sphere

These developments, both national and transnational, created a different model of political communication from the one that had traditionally dominated political thought. Internal political divisions and conflicts among states broke down the normative obstacles to open discussion, allowing new practices to take shape. Although states still sought to control public information and debate in seventeenth- and eighteenth-century Europe, a public sphere began to emerge de facto. The new possibilities of public communication were already on view during the English Revolution and in the Netherlands before John Locke and others formulated the theory of representative government in the late seventeenth century.[58] The Dutch Republic was a model for the English; England, for the French. De facto freedoms created a basis in experience for theoretical reflection and revolutionary legal principles that would in time give affirmative protection to popular communication.

The de facto emergence of a public sphere ran counter to the trend toward more centralized state power. With the development of central bureaucracies, professional armies, and new systems of finance in the early modern period, Europe saw the rise of the most powerful states in the world, capable of extracting and mobilizing far more resources than ever before from their own and other peoples. Improved informational capacities were part of that transformation. States had obvious interests in transportation and communication networks and the development of scientific and technical knowledge. As James Scott has shown, states sought not only to gather more intelligence, but also to change society in a variety of ways to make it more "legible." For example, they required people to adopt surnames so as to be more easily identified for purposes of taxation and conscription, and they demanded that linguistic minorities adopt the national language.[59] State-building interests, however, cannot explain the decline in the norms of political secrecy. Rulers did not simply acquire new means of monitoring society; the public also began to acquire new means of monitoring their rulers. Society did not just become more legible to the state; the state became more legible to the public.[60] The public sphere benefited in some ways from state-building, but it did not derive solely from it.[61]

Both in Britain and on the continent, the beginnings of independent journalism depended on complementary changes in politics and markets. Starting in the 1690s, divisions between Whigs and Tories in England had opened up the space for a more competitive press that included opposition newspapers. So, too, the fragmentation of power in both the Netherlands and the European state system as a whole opened up the space for a competitive, semiautonomous transnational press. In both cases, a market for news emerged that provided an alternative to the state as a basis of financial support, but the market was limited primarily to an elite public. British policy helped to ensure that result through the stamp tax; France did the same by preventing an independent press from developing inside its borders. The public sphere did not develop entirely from the top down; there were episodes of popular political contention, such as the English Revolution, when new forms of communication developed outside the ruling elite. But, given hostile state policy, independent popular media were not yet sustainable.

The public sphere of early modern Europe should not be mistaken for a democratic ideal, as if reason reached its highest and most cultivated form amid the heady aromas of eighteenth-century London coffeehouses and the perfumes of Paris salons, only to slide down a path to degradation in later centuries. While the early modern public sphere represented a shift away from political secrecy, it was still socially exclusive, subject to the mundane influences of money and status, and routinely manipulated by those in power. Public opinion may have emerged as a new force in politics, but the public sphere that European states allowed to develop in the early modern period sharply limited the opinion that could be heard. Except in some highly restricted ways, the public sphere did not yet provide society with a means of self-government.

CHAPTER TWO

New Foundations

THROUGH the mid–eighteenth century, Britain's colonies in North America experienced changes in communications similar to those that were unfolding in Europe. The dynamic varied from one region to another, but an embryonic public sphere generally emerged once communications networks developed if and when there were significant political cleavages and competition among printers. Purely local factors, however, cannot explain the larger transformation of the late eighteenth century.

The American colonies, like the English provinces, Wales, Scotland, Ireland, and the British West Indies, occupied a peripheral position in an Atlantic communications system centered in London. Most of what the colonists in America knew about the world went through an English filter, as it was from London that they primarily received books, ideas, and news. The institutional models for postal service, schools and colleges, civic associations, and newspapers and other kinds of publishing, including the governing legal doctrines, also came primarily from England. Through the mid-1700s, the British North Atlantic was becoming more integrated. Shipping increased in frequency, speed, and dependability; postal communication was established on a more regular and reliable basis; the flow of consumer goods from England rose; and the volume of information communicated in books and periodicals grew. These developments put the colonists in closer touch with London's metropolitan culture, allowing them to become, in some respects, more English than they had been before.[1] But the political conflict that culminated in the Revolution led Americans in a contrary direction, to reject membership in the empire as well as key elements of British law, ideology, and practice and to define their new nation in opposition to them. It was out of this revolutionary transformation of the British legacy that the distinctive American framework of communications emerged.

The Revolutionary era—the period extending from the pre-Revolutionary crisis beginning roughly around 1765 through the writing of the Constitution and the Bill of Rights—was as much the foundational period for communications as it was for government in the United States. Not only did the de facto public sphere of the late colonial era gain constitutional affirmation. The developments in this period also set in motion a political process that in the early republic elaborated and extended the new American pattern and established the design of such important institutions as the Post Office and the common school.

By the early 1800s, European visitors to the United States were struck by the abundance of communications circulating among ordinary Americans. Newspapers were more common in America than anywhere else; even small towns and villages often had their own printers and newspapers. Literacy was exceptionally high; the development of common schools in the northern states had made the white population the most literate and best educated in the world. Americans, as Alexis de Tocqueville famously observed, created civic associations for every conceivable cause; prominent among these were academies, libraries, lyceums, and other institutions to spread knowledge. The American postal system was also exceptionally comprehensive, extending even to remote villages on the frontier. While traveling by mail coach in Kentucky and Tennessee in December 1830, Tocqueville marveled at the "astonishing circulation of letters and newspapers among these savage woods." A few months later, in frontier Michigan, he came across a crude cabin off the main roads: "You think that you have finally reached the home of the American peasant. Mistake." The cabin's owner was literate, even willing to advise him on what it would take to make France prosperous. The backwoodsman, Tocqueville wrote, "talks the language of a town; he is aware of the past, curious about the future, and ready to argue about the present." Contrary to expectations, he was "a very civilized man prepared for a time to face life in the forest, plunging into the wildernesses of the New World with his Bible, ax, and newspapers."[2]

The web of communications that Tocqueville observed was not a predictable legacy of European settlement, much less a product of the environment. Just across the Great Lakes in what was still British North America, postal service was limited, newspapers were scarce, schools were few, and literacy was less extensive. This contrast between Americans and Canadians stemmed partly from their varying cultural and colonial heritages, but the political transformation of American society in the previous half-century had accentuated those early differences. The Americans had carried out a revolution, while the Canadians had not.[3] And after becoming independent, the Americans had decided not just to allow communication and education to develop, but to promote them in a deliberate effort to create a new society and a more powerful nation.

Colonial Legacies

Although the development of communications in seventeenth- and eighteenth-century colonial America paralleled the changes taking place in Britain, the conditions were substantially different. The colonies were not just peripheral to metropolitan Britain; they were also subordinate and inferior to it in a self-conscious cultural as well as political sense.[4] Distance did have its advantages. The printing monopoly of the Stationers' Company before 1695 never extended to America, and penalties for criticism of colonial authorities eased after the initial period of settlement in the first half of the seventeenth century. But long after settlement, the colonies lacked the institutional and financial means to support the level of book publishing and other forms of cultural expression possible in the cosmopolitan centers of Europe. Nonetheless, by the mid–eighteenth century, the growth of printing, postal service, and particularly newspapers created the basis for a public sphere that was to emerge in fully politicized form during the struggle with Britain.

Variations in colonial rule offer particularly vivid examples of the political shaping of communications. A state that attempts to suppress independent centers of communication at home has all the more reason to do so when ruling at a distance. As the French monarchy censored and policed publishing within its borders, so it sought to control print communication in its colonies. Printing presses were simply banned in Quebec, so books had to be imported, and there were no newspapers. French rule produced more widespread illiteracy in New France than in France itself. Education was left to the Catholic Church, which even at the end of French control in 1763 maintained schools or teachers in fewer than 20 of 123 parishes and districts. Overall, the literacy rate as late as 1750–1765 was about 25 percent, only 11 percent in rural areas.[5]

The British colonies in America were not subject to comparable policies. Colonial governments had authority to regulate communication, but they varied in the regime they imposed on it. Seventeenth-century Massachusetts, beginning with the Pilgrim settlement at Plymouth in 1620 and the founding of the Massachusetts Bay Colony in 1630, developed as a radically different society from the Chesapeake and the Middle Colonies, and this contrast was nowhere more evident than in printing and education.[6] Animated by religious ideas, the Puritan settlers of Massachusetts aimed to create a model Christian commonwealth in the wilderness. Though expecting to rely on agriculture for sustenance, they included a relatively large number of educated men and made churches and schools central institutions in their communities. In 1636, they founded the first college in the colonies (Harvard), and in 1639 they established their own printing press, the first in British America. (The Spanish had established a press in Mexico a century earlier.) Tightly knit villages and towns organized around nuclear families carried out critical social functions. In 1647, after earlier requiring each family to teach its children how to read, the colony required communities to provide for organized instruction in reading and writing if they had more than fifty families and to establish a Latin grammar school if the number of families exceeded one hundred.

Economically, seventeenth-century Massachusetts was relatively egalitarian; land was widely distributed, and differences in wealth were modest. Politically as well, participation was exceptionally widespread among adult men. Although the original charter lodged all power in a General Court representing only the shareholders in the Massachusetts Bay Company, the franchise was quickly widened to include all male church members. A majority of men qualified as "freemen" and could vote in province elections, except for a period of crown intervention in the 1680s, and nearly all men were eligible to vote in town affairs.[7] The political order was based on ideas of voluntary consent expressed in the extraordinary document that was the first to be issued in print in the English colonies of North America—the freeman's oath:

> I am being (by God's providence) an Inhabitant, and Freeman, within the jurisdiction of this Commonwealth, do freely acknowledge my self to be subject to the government thereof, and therefore do here swear, by the

> great and dreadful name of the Everliving God, that I will be true & faithful to the same, and will accordingly yield assistance and support thereunto, with my person & estate, as in equity I am bound. . . . Moreover, I do solemnly bind my self, in the sight of God, that when I shall be called, to give my voice touching any such matter of this state, (in which freemen are to deal) I will give my vote and suffrage as I shall judge in mine own conscience may best conduce & tend to the public weal of the body, without respect of persons, or favor of any man, so help me God in the Lord Jesus Christ.[8]

Devised by the colony's governor, John Winthrop, and printed on the eve of the English Revolution, this was a seditious declaration; unlike the freeman's oaths administered by English guilds to newly admitted members, it included no acknowledgment of the crown's authority. While the exact meaning of freemanship in Massachusetts changed during the seventeenth century, it generally conveyed rights of participation in the province's affairs in exchange for the assumption of certain public obligations. At times, a majority of men took the oath; many others declined to do so to avoid the obligations it entailed. As a voluntary contract, explicitly invoking "mine own conscience" as a guide to judgment about the public weal, the freeman's oath expressed the core elements of a political philosophy that was radical for its time. It was almost certainly chosen for its symbolic importance to be the first English document printed in America.[9]

Yet the participatory basis of Puritan rule did not signify either popular control or a receptiveness to alternative views. While enjoying a wide franchise, the Massachusetts colonists were deferential to their leaders. All political officials were subject to election, with terms of only one year, and some did lose their positions; yet, overall, the Puritan elite maintained control not just of formal authority but also of public discussion. Indeed, the Bay Colony was in some ways like a one-party dictatorship led by intellectuals who served as both its ministers and its magistrates.[10] Although not all differences of opinion were suppressed, dissenters were frequently banished from the colony (this was famously the origin of the settlements in Rhode Island and Connecticut); similar processes of exclusion and separation kept the peace in individual towns. Especially before the 1640s, criticism of officials or the government in New England (as in the southern colonies) frequently met with severe penalties, including "bodily correction" through such means as whipping or cutting the ears and public humiliation in the pillory or the stocks, as well as exile.[11] Puritan ideology gained its power, moreover, from its role as an internal discipline, a point the Puritans themselves well understood: "When Laws may be read in men's lives," stated the Massachusetts statutes, "they appear more beautiful than in the fairest Print, and promise a longer duration, than engraven in Marble."[12] Just to make sure, the authorities controlled and censored the press, seized manuscripts, and suppressed imported works, such as Quaker publications. They also vigorously prosecuted a wide range of crimes of the tongue besides sedition. Under a law originally enacted in 1641, men had "full freedome" to voice "any advise, vote, verdict, or sentence in any Court, Counsell, or Civill Assembly" if they did so "orderly and inofensively," yet magistrates meted out severe punishment for a variety of forms of disapproved speech, from blasphemy (a capital offense) to mere swearing.[13]

Puritanism today calls to mind these restrictions on expression and conduct rather than the expansive effects of early literacy, education, and printing. But while Puritan control of public life would decline, the Puritan impetus to the development of communications and education (including higher education) gave Massachusetts "early mover" advantages. As of 1700, Boston had emerged as the center of printing and the book trade in the colonies, and although the town's early printers produced relatively little of intellectual distinction, they laid the institutional basis for the later development of New England publishing.[14] Literacy rose to near-universal levels among men in colonial New England because its early settlers made the support of schools a community obligation. Compliance was initially limited, particularly in new settlements, but by the late colonial era literacy extended far down the social hierarchy and out into the countryside.[15] Overall, male literacy in New England rose from 60 percent in 1660 to 70 percent by 1710, then to 85 percent by 1760.[16] Female literacy, which probably ranged from 30 to 40 percent in the early 1700s, rose to about 60 percent by the 1760s—and these figures, based on signature rates, probably understate the proportion of women who could read. Reading, writing, and arithmetic were taught as a sequence, and many girls were taught only to read; the manual skill that women were thought to need was not writing, but knitting and sewing.[17] In the rest of the American colonies, education remained a private and voluntary responsibility as in England, and illiteracy was far more widespread. In Virginia, literacy among white men rose from 46 percent in the 1640s to 62 percent by about 1710, and then remained unchanged for the rest of the colonial period. As a result of limited education for women and the denial of literacy to slaves, three out of four people in colonial Virginia were "largely or entirely confined within the oral medium."[18]

The social order and information regime of the Chesapeake in the seventeenth century offer a stark contrast to Massachusetts. Virginia was founded in 1607 not on religious ideals but as a commercial enterprise, and after early schemes for enrichment failed, it became oriented toward raising a single export crop, tobacco. As a result of early disasters, the colony was placed under royal control in 1624. Whereas whole families migrated from England to Massachusetts, the immigrants to the Chesapeake region were disproportionately single men. Community institutions were weak, social and economic inequalities were extreme even before slavery became dominant, and political power was highly concentrated in the planter class. "I thank God, there are no free-schools, nor printing; and I hope we shall not have these [for a] hundred years," the royal governor of Virginia, William Berkeley, wrote to London in 1671, "for learning has brought disobedience, and heresy, and sects into the world, and printing has divulged them, and libels against the best government. God keep us from both!"[19]

As a result of deliberate policy, Virginia continued without any press through the first three decades of the eighteenth century. In the 1680s, a printer tried to establish a shop but was forced to leave before issuing a single work; he then moved to Maryland, where he was jailed for printing the proceedings of the assembly, told never to publish anything concerned with politics again, and thereafter primarily confined himself to printing blank legal forms. Unlike Massachusetts, the Chesapeake had no booksellers. While books and other sources of knowledge were distributed in a hierarchical pattern throughout colonial America, the shape of the hierarchies was not the same. In New England, book ownership ran from the large collections of Harvard Library and prominent ministers down to the Bibles, almanacs, and sermons of many ordinary readers. In the Chesapeake, large collections belonged to the wealthiest planters, and books were scarce outside the elite. So restricted was the sphere of print during the seventeenth century that, except for two London imprints, the laws of Virginia and Maryland were generally available only in manuscript form—and the manuscripts varied, in some cases missing entire statutes. In their official business, the Chesapeake colonies operated almost entirely in a pre-Gutenberg, scribal culture.[20]

The Middle Colonies in the seventeenth century followed a pattern in print communication that was surprisingly closer to the Chesapeake's regime than to New England's. Pennsylvania was founded on principles of religious toleration, and the governing Quakers had long experience in England with clandestine publishing. William Penn himself brought along a printer's apprentice named William Bradford in 1682 when he visited the lands granted to him. Nonetheless, as ruling authorities in Pennsylvania, the Quakers initially suffocated publishing. After Bradford settled in Philadelphia in 1685, his first publication, an almanac, offended Quaker leaders, who told him "not to print any thing but what shall have Lycense from ye Councill."[21] In 1692, he was jailed during another conflict with Quaker authorities, and, after his release, left for New York, where he took a salary as the government printer and avoided any work that could get him into trouble. Twenty years later, his son Andrew established himself in Philadelphia in a position parallel to his father's in New York. As monopoly printers, the two Bradfords produced nothing that would offend their official patrons and little of popular interest.[22]

Neither readers nor authors in the colonies, however, had to rely on local printers; they imported books from London and sent manuscripts across the Atlantic to be published. Distance did not prevent even the earliest immigrants from maintaining contact with the world they had left behind. At first, in the absence of regular postal service, the colonists depended on ships' captains, seamen, and travelers to provide an informal courier service for letters to and from family and old associates. Isolated from the turmoil in seventeenth-century England, the colonists also hungered for news of public events brought to them by passengers as well as letters and publications in arriving ships. In the 1640s, copies of civil war newsbooks circulated in New England; in 1685, the issue of the *London Gazette* reporting the death of Charles II was reprinted in Boston. Massachusetts took the first step to put transatlantic communication on a more organized basis in 1639 when the General Court designated the house of Richard Fairbank as the site for all letters that "are brought from beyond the seas, or are to be sent thither." The colony appointed a postmaster in 1677 and created a General Letter Office in Boston in 1693, the year that regular postal service connecting Philadelphia, New York, and Boston began. A year earlier, the crown had granted a twenty-one-year monopoly on American postal service to an Englishman, Thomas Neale, who had never even been to America. But because of slow progress and Neale's death, the crown repurchased the patent in 1707, and a few years later Parliament placed the colonial system under the control of the British Post Office.

As in Europe, newspapers developed in tandem with postal service, although the relationship between the two was not evident in the first, abortive attempt to create a colonial news periodical. In 1690, a Boston printer and coffeehouse proprietor named Benjamin Harris—a refugee from London, where he had been jailed for unlicensed publishing—brought out a single edition of a four-page paper, *Publick Occurrences, Both Forreign and Domestick,* intending to publish it monthly, or "if any Glut of Occurrences happen, oftener." The paper furnished original reports and commentary primarily about local events, such as a fire in Boston, smallpox cases, and the fall harvest, as well as the war with Indian tribes then in progress. It was in that context that Harris denounced military cooperation with the Iroquois, who were allies of the British. Within days, the governing council banned the paper on the grounds that it was unlicensed.[23]

When a newspaper was established successfully more than a decade later, it had a fundamentally different character. In 1702, John Campbell took over as postmaster after the death of his father, who had held the position since 1693. At first Campbell continued the practice of sending an occasional handwritten newsletter to the governor of Connecticut and perhaps others; then, in 1704, he began weekly publication of the *Boston News-Letter,* the first regularly published paper in the colonies. Although the shift from manuscript to print suggests a larger market, even the published version, according to Campbell himself, never sold more than 300 copies. Unlike Harris, Campbell condensed most of the items in his pages from the London papers, steering clear of sensitive news close to home. He conceived of his role as that of a functionary, not a journalist, treating the newspaper as an extension of his work as postmaster. For every edition he secured the governor's advance approval; the paper was not an official publication, but it bore the same words as the *London Gazette,* "Published by Authority."[24] Bland and unimaginative, this was the initial model for newspapers in the colonies. The Bradfords established papers along the same lines: Andrew Bradford's *American Weekly Mercury* in Philadelphia in 1719 and William Bradford's *New-York Gazette* in 1725. Like the court gazettes in Europe, these papers posed no challenge to authority; they primarily chronicled events across the Atlantic but provided little information about developments at home, much less any critical discussion of politics. Monopoly newspapers had little incentive to do otherwise; in each case, the publisher was either a postmaster or a government printer and therefore dependent on the authorities for his livelihood.

The emergence of public debate in the press came with the shift from monopoly to competition in printing and newspapers and with the more general growth and increasing diversity of colonial societies. Some of the original, sharp contrasts among the colonies softened in the eighteenth century. Founded on religious principles, New England became more commercial, a change reflected in the shift of printing from Cambridge, where the press had been an instrument of Puritan authority, to Boston, where printing was more of a business. Meanwhile, the Chesapeake and the Middle Colonies were developing stronger community and cultural institutions, although they continued to lag behind New England in literacy and education. The American colonies experienced tremendous growth in every dimension: The population multiplied from high rates of internal growth as well as migration; settlements expanded geographically; and per capita income doubled from 1650 to 1770, making the colonies among the most prosperous areas in the world.[25] The political development of the colonies matched these trends. Increasingly strong colonial assemblies gained ground in legislation and policy-making, including taxation. Although the assemblies were originally neither open to the public nor democratic in a modern sense, debates about policy increasingly spilled into print in both pamphlets and newspapers. The Massachusetts Assembly took a historic step when in 1715 it began publishing its debates and votes. By 1730, colonial governors' instructions no longer included even nominal authority to license the press.[26] Haltingly, from a press that was entirely controlled by authority, there developed a more open public sphere.

Already, during the seventeenth century, there had been a decline throughout the colonies in the severity of punishment for criticism of both individual officials and government. In 1625, the Virginia General Court convicted Richard Barnes of "base and detracting speeches concerning the governor" and, before banishing him from the colony, ordered both his arms broken, his body beaten, and his tongue "bored through with an awl." While particularly gruesome, these penalties reflected the harsh practices of the time. A study of 1,244 seditious-speech prosecutions in the seventeenth-century colonies, drawn from records of courts, councils, and assemblies, provides the most exhaustive analysis of actual enforcement of censorship. Among punished cases of seditious speech in the 1620s, more than 50 percent involved "bodily correction"; the proportion fell to just under a third in the 1630s and then under one-tenth for the rest of the century. Humiliation punishments and banishment for seditious speech declined in a similar pattern.[27] The 1640s, the decade when Parliament overthrew and executed a king, proved a watershed in the colonies; afterward, colonial government never recovered its extreme harshness. Instead of trying to punish all "base and detracting" speech, officials increasingly targeted prosecutions at speech that they viewed as posing a danger to government.[28] This shift scarcely signaled the triumph of free expression; nonetheless, it meant a reduction in the risks associated with critical discussion of public issues, even though the laws against seditious speech remained unchanged. Suits for defamation or slander, a principal business of courts during the 1600s, also declined toward the century's end.[29]

The transformation of newspapers in eighteenth-century colonial America came in two stages. The first, beginning around 1720, saw the advent of competition and the emergence of public debate in the press; the second, beginning in 1765, involved the active, partisan engagement of newspapers in political conflict. Throughout the century, the absence of regulatory obstacles to newspapers contributed to their growth. No guild regulations limited entry into printing, and the Stamp Tax of 1712 did not apply to the colonies (although stamp duties were briefly in force in New York and Massachusetts during the French and Indian War). Boston had two newspapers by 1719, three by 1721, four a decade later, and five by 1735, when the population was still just 15,000. The city's second newspaper, like its first, was established by a postmaster who sided with authority, but the third paper, the *New-England Courant,* represented a departure in both content and style. Founded by the young printer James Franklin and a circle of writers critical of the Puritan leadership, the *Courant* introduced controversy to the colonial press. The triggering issue was Cotton Mather's proposal in June 1721 to use inoculation to fight smallpox, an idea that the *Courant*'s writers relentlessly mocked. But while contesting authority in Boston, the *Courant* represented an Anglicizing influence in its literary style, which its writers, including James Franklin's apprentice, his sixteen-year-old brother Benjamin, copied from London's exemplar of polite letters, *The Spectator.*[30] In September 1723, the younger Franklin fled Boston and his brother's abuse, and the *Courant* folded two years later. Nonetheless, by the next decade Boston's papers were providing a forum for debate about public issues.

Newspaper controversy came to Pennsylvania and New York in the same period with the arrival of second printers. Competitors to the Bradfords' monopoly started newspapers that provided the opposition with a voice and thereby compelled the Bradford papers to adapt to a more contentious public sphere. In Philadelphia, the shift began with an eccentric printer, Samuel Keiner, who in December 1728 started *The Pennsylvania Gazette, or the Universal Instructor,* in which he intended, among other things, to reprint the contents of a recently published encyclopedia, beginning in his first issue with a long disquisition on the letter *a.* The paper mysteriously languished for lack of readers, and the following September—sadly, before Keiner was able to reach entries beginning with *b*—he sold the paper to his journeyman. This was none other than the now-transplanted Benjamin Franklin, who reoriented Keiner's paper to news, added to it his own sprightly prose, and shortened its title to *The Pennsylvania Gazette*: "As a typical second newspaper," writes James N. Green, "it was livelier, more local, and better written than the *Mercury.*"[31] It also had a different political orientation. Pennsylvania was deeply divided between the interests allied with descendants of the Penn family, who believed that authority belonged with the colony's proprietors, and an opposing faction that viewed authority as residing in the elected assembly. The latter were known as the "popular" party, even though a restrictive franchise limited voting to a narrow group. Both Bradford and Franklin operated their printing businesses chiefly with an eye to making money. But while Bradford supported the proprietary party, Franklin became the champion of the popular party and an ally of one of its leaders and Bradford's enemies, the lawyer Andrew Hamilton. Control of a newspaper was critical to Franklin's influence. To the proprietary party, he was, as Thomas Penn put it, "a dangerous man," but "as he is a sort of tribune of the people, he must be treated with regard."[32]

The advent of newspaper contention in New York also involved political conflict and competing printers. In 1732, a new royal governor, William Cosby, removed the colony's chief justice, Lewis Morris, who had refused to go along with Cosby's claim to half the salary of the official who had temporarily served as governor before his arrival. Intending to expose Cosby's abuse of power, the faction allied with Morris the next year engaged a little-known printer, John Peter Zenger, to bring out a paper. Although the politicians behind the *New-York Weekly Journal* wrote the articles attacking Cosby, it was Zenger who was indicted for seditious libel and spent eight months in jail awaiting trial. To defend him, the Morrisites called on the Pennsylvanian Andrew Hamilton, who quickly conceded at the trial that Zenger had printed the newspaper. But Hamilton insisted, contrary to English law, that there was no libel because the charges were true. The jury's acquittal of Zenger, in defiance of the court's instructions, marked a critical step in the development of the press, not so much for its effect on the law as for its political significance. The case had no force as a legal precedent; even if it had, the standard that Hamilton had asked the jury to uphold offered no protection to the press for opinions that could not be proved. Nonetheless, heralded throughout the colonies, the Zenger verdict vindicated the idea that the press could serve as a guardian of popular liberty by scrutinizing government.[33] Moreover, while royal officials still had authority to suppress seditious libel, they virtually gave up trying to do so after the Zenger trial. Between 1735 and the American Revolution, the risk of being tried for seditious libel by British colonial authorities effectively disappeared.[34]

The development of political controversy in the press in Boston, Philadelphia, and New York followed a similar pattern to the emergence of the public sphere in Europe in the eighteenth century. Fragmentation among political elites and competition in the market together contributed to breaking up the monopoly of court gazettes and opening up public political debate. Yet the American pattern diverged in some respects. While Zenger's paper owed its existence to a political faction, colonial newspapers were typically established and owned by their printers, who were not subordinate, as their counterparts were in Britain, to a powerful class of booksellers. The independent printer-publisher engaged in the newspaper business was an American phenomenon. Book-making dominated the European trade; newspapers, the American one. On both sides of the Atlantic, printers were artisans who worked with their hands running the presses, but in America they also took on nearly every other role in producing newspapers, including editor, writer, business manager, and—because they put their own capital at risk—publisher. These roles affected their social status. Except for Franklin, colonial printers did not rise to positions of political power and great wealth; indeed, they often struggled to make a living, but many won respect and influence, served as officials in their local communities, and achieved a measure of economic security.[35]

Colonial printers, however, did not free themselves from dependence on government. Government printing contracts and advertising revenue from official notices were often critical to their success. Franklin's business received an enormous boost when he became public printer for Pennsylvania; he also served in that capacity at various times for Delaware, New Jersey, and Maryland. The post office was another source of entanglement between government and the press. By the end of the colonial period, it was rare for a printer to serve as a postmaster, but earlier the two roles were prominently commingled. In Boston, not just Campbell but his five successors as postmaster ran a newspaper. Franklin, who was appointed Philadelphia's postmaster in place of William Bradford in 1737, personified the printer-postmaster connection. The dual role put printers at the hub of the local information network in a community and gave them an edge over their competitors in distributing papers to subscribers; three years after becoming postmaster, Franklin denied Bradford use of the mails to distribute his *Mercury*. Yet as a royal functionary, the printer-postmaster himself was at risk of losing his privileged position if he vexed the authorities.[36] Neither printers nor authors enjoyed any legal guarantees of free expression. Ironically, after Zenger it was not royal authorities but colonial assemblies that posed the primary threat to freedom of the press. Charging breach of privilege, they repeatedly threw printers in prison, fined them, and forced them to humble themselves and pledge to be more respectful and compliant.[37]

In the face of both economic and political pressures, most printers sought to remain studiously neutral. Later on, during the Revolution and in the early republic, the majority of newspapers would take on a partisan identity. Through most of the colonial era, however, there was no system of partisan politics to support partisan journalism. And with only a limited local demand for their services, printers typically maximized their potential clients and advertisers by not taking sides in local controversies.[38] Printers sometimes claimed that their neutrality assured liberty of the press, by which they meant the liberty of contending parties to use the press to air their opinions. In other words, a free press was one that was open to all points of view (a common carrier), not one that exclusively expressed a viewpoint of its own. Printers, Benjamin Franklin wrote in 1731, believed that "when Men differ in Opinion, both Sides ought equally to have the Advantage of being heard by the Publick. . . . Being thus continually employ'd in serving all Parties, Printers naturally acquire a vast Unconcernedness as to the right or wrong Opinions contain'd in what they print; regarding it only as a Matter of their daily labour." More commonly, however, printers avoided offending the powerful by keeping divisive issues entirely out of their newspapers, stifling debate rather than promoting it.[39]

Cultural subservience to metropolitan Britain also limited the capacity of American printers to articulate a distinctive viewpoint. Through the mid–eighteenth century, newspapers largely conveyed news from overseas received via Britain. From 1723 to 1765, according to calculations by Charles Clark, the *Pennsylvania Gazette* dedicated 48.9 percent of its news space to continental Europe, 18.4 percent to the British Isles, and 10.8 percent to the West Indies and Latin America, compared to only 4.8 percent to Pennsylvania and 16.4 percent to the rest of British North America. Of the space given to news, 58 percent was devoted to diplomatic and military affairs, 9 percent to royalty and the nobility. The practical needs of merchants and others for information about foreign markets and British policy cannot be the entire explanation for the overwhelming dominance of foreign reports. As Clark argues, the news also served as a means of ritually affirming the colonists' participation in the imperial system; the news from London reflected not just a metropolitan view, but the perspective of the British elite. While the wealthy and powerful were treated with respect, lesser people "found their way into the news as the unnamed subject of an anecdote intended to evoke sympathy, scorn, amazement, or, more frequently, amusement."[40]

A variety of aspects of colonial communication continued to reflect the hierarchies of British culture and society. Much of the regulation of speech in the colonies aimed at ensuring deference and suppressing insubordination among slaves, indentured servants, and women. According to the prevailing norms of everyday communication, common folk kept their eyes down and caps off when talking with gentlemen, who may have numbered one out of ten white men in the North and one out of twenty-five in the South.[41] Attitudes and policies toward education reflected the same kinds of assumptions about inequality. Except perhaps in New England, the colonists had not broken from the educational views of the English elite epitomized by Bernard Mandeville's comment that "should a Horse know as much as a Man, I should not like to be his Rider."[42]

Yet elements of British culture were also resources for colonial opposition. As the writers in the *Courant* deployed the irreverent wit of *The Spectator* against authority, so many in the colonies called on the republican ideas associated with the "country" tradition in British politics. This tradition had its origins in the radical political thought of the mid–seventeenth century but was known to the colonists best through its early eighteenth-century exponents, who attacked the "court" party dominating the English government as a corrupt and overweening power that was undermining ancient liberties and the proper balance of the British constitution. None of these critics was more important to the colonists' thought than the Radical Whigs John Trenchard and Thomas Gordon, the authors of a series of articles known as *Cato's Letters,* published serially in the *London Journal* and then as a book beginning in 1720.[43] It was here that the colonists found a powerful defense of a free press as a "bulwark of liberty." Soon after the essays appeared in Britain, colonial newspapers were quoting and reprinting them. In July 1722, for example, while James Franklin was imprisoned for criticizing the governor of Massachusetts for failing to control pirates, his younger brother took over the paper and quoted from Trenchard and Gordon: "In those wretched Countries where a Man cannot call his Tongue his own, he can scarce call any Thing else his own. Whoever would overthrow the Liberty of a Nation, must begin by subduing the Freeness of Speech; a *Thing* terrible to Publick Traytors."[44] Dissenting thought that had been marginal to British politics would become central to politics in America; the *Boston Gazette* would reprint Trenchard and Gordon's essay on free speech seven times between 1755 and 1780. In the 1760s, the colonists also took an increasing interest in the natural-rights liberalism of John Locke, and as the conflict with Britain developed, colonists employed both republican and liberal ideas in justifying their positions. In 1767, Samuel Adams wrote to an Englishman, "We talk the language we have always heard you speak."[45] In fact, Adams and other defenders of colonial liberty had listened selectively. And although they borrowed their language, they were about to do something with it that had not yet been accomplished on the other side of the Atlantic.

The Revolution and the Public Sphere

A common view holds that the American Revolution was not a genuine revolution but only a political revolt, a mere war of independence that failed to make deep changes in society. "Although the American War of Independence is often cited as a revolution that established democracy, it was in fact merely a defense of existing democratic institutions against

Britain's attempt to circumvent them to increase its revenues from the colonies," a leading sociological analyst of revolutions writes.[46] Originally, in the 1790s and early 1800s, it was conservative critics of the French Revolution who sought to distinguish it from the American Revolution on the grounds that the Americans merely sought to restore preexisting rights. By the twentieth century, many analysts on the left also took the view that the American Revolution failed to qualify as a social revolution because it did not overthrow a ruling class. While some historians have argued that there was no revolution because the colonies were already democratic, others have denied there was a revolution because the new republic left blacks, women, and unpropertied white men disenfranchised and, therefore, wasn't democratic at all.[47]

An alternative view has insisted ever since the Revolutionary War itself that it was a true revolution in the structure of government and basis of society. To say that the American Revolution was "merely" political rather than social presupposes that politics and society can be separated and that politics is of secondary importance. But colonial society under English rule was, as Gordon Wood argues, a "web" of political relationships—a chain of domination and dependency that extended from the king through the aristocracy and gentry down to the meanest servant. In overthrowing monarchy, the revolutionaries transformed this system of rank and subordination. Servitude among the white population virtually disappeared. The rights of siblings to share in inheritance became more equal. Critics began to attack slavery—and while failing in the South, they succeeded after Independence in ending slavery in the North.[48] The limitations of the Revolution from a later standpoint should not obscure the changes it brought about. It was only during the Revolutionary era that the term "democracy" came into widespread use and acquired its positive connotations.[49] While the individual colonies had representative assemblies, their laws could be, and sometimes were, disallowed by the crown; all but two colonies had royal governors, and only in Massachusetts and Virginia were the legislatures clearly dominant. Many of those who enjoyed lucrative colonial offices owed them to the crown and came from loyal and privileged families.[50] The Revolution dispossessed much of this elite; indeed, the loyalists who fled to Canada and elsewhere—many of whom had their property confiscated—were five times as large a group, relative to population, as the émigrés who fled the French Revolution.[51]

But changes in class structure ought not to be the sole criterion distinguishing a social revolution. If we ask whether the American Revolution was revolutionary, surely part of the answer lies in the effects on the structure of the public sphere. The Revolution brought new assumptions about institutions that had pervasive effects on American society. While the colonies enjoyed de facto liberties, they had no guarantees of those rights from royal authorities or colonial legislatures; the very idea of constitutional protections did not exist. The "British constitution," universally admired by colonial leaders for its balance among royalty, nobility, and commons, was only a conceptual model of government, not a legal constraint on it. There was no distinction in Britain between what was legal and what was constitutional, and thus no possibility of any law being found unconstitutional. The American Revolution created a republic on a national scale, and it established the idea of a formal, written constitution that was antecedent to government and spelled out its structure and limits. While sovereignty in Britain after 1689 was thought to reside in Parliament, the U.S. Constitution would vest sovereignty in the people. The premise of this constitutional order was that the people and their liberties came first, government second; or, as James Madison put it, while power had granted liberty in Europe, liberty granted power in America.[52]

These new political foundations, as well as the changes in social relations that flowed from the Revolution, had profound effects on communication. Colonial elections had chosen only local leaders, but elections in the new nation, as well as the revolutionary and constitutional struggles in its formation, confronted voters with more distant and abstract issues. As participants in a wider theater of political decisions, citizens of the Revolutionary era and early republic had new reasons to be interested in events and ideas more removed from their immediate surroundings. Republican ideology held up a new standard of good conduct: The responsible citizen was informed and kept up with the times.[53] Self-government, in other words, generated greater demand for information, particularly for news and newspapers. And those who sought office (and later the parties that organized politics) had reason to promote newspapers that could influence public opinion. The Revolution did not level all political inequalities; rule by local notables would persist long past the Revolution in many parts of the country. But by legitimating the idea that ordinary people could govern themselves, the Revolution dignified their right to speak up—literally, without self-consciously bending and averting their eyes while addressing people of higher status. The doctrine of popular sovereignty implied a wide range of free expression. Even apart from the Bill of

Rights, the Revolution disinhibited political speech and transformed Americans' sense of their rights; from the beginning of the republic, its citizens "lambasted their leaders, excoriated public policies, and acted as if their governments were their servants."[54]

The Revolution generated particularly strong popular beliefs in a free press because the events that led up to the war helped to identify the press with the patriotic cause. A critical formative experience was Britain's attempt to impose a key element of its communication regime on the colonies. In March 1765, faced with a looming debt from its war with France, Parliament imposed a stamp tax on the colonies, effective the following November. The colonists famously opposed the measure on the grounds that it was taxation without representation, but the specific nature of the tax also mattered. As if designed to inflame the most articulate, the stamp tax fell on printers, lawyers, merchants, and even college students, among others. Printers faced heavy duties on pamphlets, almanacs, legal forms, and newspapers. They would owe British authorities a halfpenny on each copy of a newspaper printed on "half a sheet," a penny if printed on larger sheets, and two shillings on every advertisement (roughly a 50 percent levy on gross advertising revenue). Writing from London to his partner in Philadelphia, Franklin estimated that the Stamp Act would cut both newspaper subscriptions and advertising in half. The sheer magnitude of the taxes betrayed an indifference to the fate of the press, if not a deliberate effort to limit its circulation. The most repressive provision doubled taxes on publications in foreign languages, which might have killed off Philadelphia's German-language papers.[55]

Far from stifling the press, however, the Stamp Act politicized it. At first, many colonists reacted with anger and "silent consternation," as one later recalled, but were unsure how to proceed, for lack of any tradition of opposition to British policy. Despite their financial self-interest, printers were among those to respond slowly and seemed resigned at first to pay the tax; even as popular resistance developed, some printers continued to adhere to their customary neutrality. But others put their newspapers at the service of the resistance by reporting protests, championing the cause, and perhaps most important, providing a forum for discussion and helping to turn what could have been mere disorder into a more coherent opposition movement. On August 14, 1765, a group of patriots in Boston burned an effigy of the prospective stamp distributor, who asked the next day to be relieved of the post. Twelve days later in Boston, in an uprising with different origins, a mob looted the houses of customs officials and the lieutenant governor. These two riots drew sharply different responses from newspapers that took a leading role in the opposition. The first riot, aimed specifically at intimidating the stamp distributor, became a model for actions in other cities and drew praise, while the second was condemned, in the words of the *Boston Gazette,* as "utterly inconsistent with the first Principles of Government, and subversive of the glorious cause."[56] The radicals at this point were far from revolutionaries, and the press served as an instrument for both propelling and braking their movement.

The Stamp Act crisis led to the first intercolonial cooperation against the British as well as the first newspaper campaign against them. The two were related. Newspapers copied items from one another and thereby exposed their readers to news and opinion from other colonies. When opponents of the Stamp Act organized themselves as the Sons of Liberty in the fall of 1765 and began coordinating their resistance, they created correspondence circuits with their own riders to communicate with one another but were generally more interested in publicizing their activities than in concealing them. Newspapers, in Pauline Maier's words, "remained the prime vehicle of uniting the population" as the strategy of resistance evolved from the intimidation of stamp distributors to the nonimportation agreements that eventually proved to be the key to getting Parliament to repeal the tax.[57] The role of newspapers in the Stamp Act resistance exemplified the seeming paradox that while the press contributed to Anglicization by transmitting British culture and opinion, it also contributed to Americanization by fostering a sense of the colonists' common situation. In both cases, it reduced colonial insularity. From 1763 to 1765, there was a sharp increase in the frequency of newspaper references to the colonists as "Americans."[58] Postal policy had also been a factor in this process of integration. In 1753, Franklin had been appointed deputy postmaster general for North America, a position he initially shared with William Hunter, a Virginia printer. They not only put postal service on a more frequent and reliable basis but also began allowing newspapers in the colonies to exchange copies for free.[59] Together, the postal network and newspaper exchanges created the infrastructure for a proto-national public sphere.

As printers during the Stamp Act crisis began to identify their interests with resistance to the British, so patriot leaders came to identify their cause with the printing press. In a series of newspaper articles that formulated a potent myth of America's founding, John Adams framed the Stamp Act as a violation of the colonists' deepest traditions. The earliest settlers, he wrote, had come to America in search of liberty and believed that "knowledge diffused generally thro' the whole body of the people" could preserve their descendants from tyranny. Accordingly, they established colleges and grammar schools. "But none of the means of information are more sacred, or have been cherished with more tenderness and care by the settlers of America, than the Press. Care has been taken, that the art of printing should be encouraged, and that it should be easy and cheap and safe for any person to communicate his thoughts to the public." All this was now threatened by the design of the British "to strip us in great measure of the means of knowledge, by loading the Press, the Colleges, and even an Almanack and a News-Paper, with restraints and duties."[60]

The opponents of British rule had other occasions to affirm their support for the press as the crisis with Britain intensified over the next decade. In 1768, asked by the Royal Council to take action against the *Boston Gazette* because of its attacks on the royal governor, the Massachusetts House instead resolved, using language from Trenchard and Gordon: "The Liberty of the Press is a great Bulwark of the Liberty of the People: It is, therefore, the incumbent Duty of those who are constituted the Guardians of the People's Rights to defend and maintain it."[61] As they came to depend on the printers, the patriot cause and revolutionary struggle elevated freedom of the press to the status of a fundamental and emblematic right.[62]

The Revolution enlarged the public, and that enlarged public transformed politics. Earlier political writers, including colonial pamphleteers, had typically assumed a limited audience of gentlemen and made extensive use of classical allusions and complex ironies, but the mobilization of popular opinion for a revolution required more accessible prose. At the beginning of 1776, a pamphlet appeared that forthrightly made the case for an independent republic. *Common Sense* would go through twenty-five editions, selling an estimated 150,000 copies and reaching an audience several times that large in a single year. It was "the greatest sale that any performance ever had since the use of letters," according to its author, Thomas Paine, and he may have been right if that is understood as short-term penetration of a society, not to mention long-term impact on it. Like his later books, *The Rights of Man* (1791) and *The Age of Reason*

(1794–1796), *Common Sense* was revolutionary in its style as well as its content. The traditional assumption was that writing for a popular audience meant abandoning refinement for vulgarity, but Paine's style was neither vulgar nor refined. Relying on simple metaphors and referring to no other literature except the Bible, he showed it was possible to discuss complex problems of government in language that was lucid and exciting. Intending to enable even the barely literate to read his work, he once wrote, "I shall therefore avoid every literary ornament and put it in language as plain as the alphabet."[63]

The approach of the Revolution made it impossible for printers to maintain their old strategy of editorial neutrality. Although some delayed a choice as long as possible, newspapers broke about two to one in favor of the Revolution.[64] By the outbreak of fighting in 1775, while there were no dailies in the colonies, the four-page weekly newspaper was a potent force; the number of papers, which had risen to fourteen by mid-century, reached thirty-seven in 1775. In Boston, the circulation of the two leading revolutionary papers jumped during the pre-Revolutionary crisis—to 2,000 for the *Boston Gazette* and to 3,500 for the *Massachusetts Spy*, according to their printers—but these were exceptional; the average circulation in New England was probably around 600 at the time.[65] On the eve of the Revolution, total circulation per capita was still lower than in England, but how much lower is unclear. Comparative estimates for 1775 put colonial newspapers per capita at between 28 percent and 91 percent of English levels, depending on the source of data and the exact measure.[66] The Revolution itself did not bring further growth in the newspaper press; during the war years, when paper and other supplies were scarce, the number of newspapers remained unchanged, though growth resumed afterward. Yet numbers may be beside the point; the pre-Revolutionary crisis had already transformed the uses of the press, as is apparent from the pattern of distribution of the Declaration of Independence. The official printing consisted only of a hundred copies, which members of the Continental Congress sent to printers in their home states. Although we think of the Declaration as a written document with its famous signatures, Americans at the time generally read it printed in their local newspapers or heard it proclaimed in public places.

The French Revolution, sometimes seen as the moment of birth of the modern public sphere, provides a useful reference point in understanding the American transformation. The "revolution in print" in France was, if anything, more abrupt and electrifying than the one in America. After having been stifled by censorship and monopoly under the Old Regime, the press suddenly mushroomed, especially in Paris. During the year after the summoning of the Estates General in July 1788, more than 10 million pamphlets were printed; 140 new periodicals were started in 1789, and although many were short-lived, by the end of that year there were dozens of newspapers of varying political viewpoints.[67] While the Old Regime allowed just thirty-six printers in Paris before 1789, soon hundreds of print shops appeared, and the old Parisian printers who produced books for the church, the schools, and other institutions of the Old Regime collapsed and went bankrupt.

In one sense, French publishing moved in an American direction from 1789 to 1793. Just as newspapers dominated books in the American printing trade, so in France there was a shift from books to newspapers, pamphlets, sheet music, and other kinds of ephemeral literature—more "democratic" literary forms written "for (and often by) people with little money to spend and little leisure time to read."[68] On the other hand, the revolutionary press in France, unlike America, was concentrated in the capital in close proximity to the events of the Revolution, and newspapers reported daily events with a breathless immediacy that marked a turn toward a new and more modern sense of journalistic time. At the height of the French Revolution, newspaper circulation reached 300,000 copies per day, a far greater level than in America. But while the growth of the French press was greater and more sudden than in America, the surge was short-lived. As the French Revolution turned more repressive, many newspapers were suppressed, and journalists lost their lives in staggering numbers: The Terror in 1793–1794 cost the lives of one-sixth of the journalists active in Paris just three to four years earlier.[69]

In America, freedom of the press survived the Revolution, and so did the journalists. The loyalist printer James Rivington was hung in effigy, but that was as close as he or other loyalist printers came to the gallows. Patriot mobs threatened them harm and shut down loyalist presses, undoubtedly an abrogation of free speech.[70] But newspapers continued to print criticism of public officials even in the midst of the fighting. Writing as "Leonidas" in the *Pennsylvania Packet,* for example, Benjamin Rush accused Revolutionary leaders of embezzling public funds, and he suffered no penalty for it, even though one member of the Continental Congress demanded that the *Packet*'s printer be brought before the bar of Congress. "When liberty of the Press shall be restrained," another delegate argued, "take my word for it, the liberties of the people shall be at an end." Other incidents also suggest that the revolutionaries accepted criticism in the press but drew the line at what they regarded as the loyalists' treason.[71]

In later years, it seemed self-evident to the Revolutionary generation that a free press had played a vital role in the struggle, even as they came to disagree about what freedom of the press ought to mean. In a letter to John Adams in 1789 about the free-press clause of the Massachusetts Constitution, William Cushing, the commonwealth's chief justice, wrote: "Without this liberty of the press could we have supported our liberties against british administration? or could our revolution have taken place? Pretty certainly it could not, at the time it did."[72] The vital role that the press played was not merely as a vehicle of "propaganda," as some interpretations have it. The term "propaganda" suggests a one-way process in which those who initiate communication shape others' attitudes and knowledge, but communication did not simply flow from top to bottom, from elites to masses, from center to periphery. From the earliest phases of the Revolutionary conflict, the press had served as a means by which the colonists had debated their common interests, developed a national identity, and created capacities for cooperative action. In an 1803 book reflecting on the previous century, a writer named Samuel Miller noted that instead of merely stating facts, newspapers had assumed a more important function: "They have become the vehicles of discussion in which the principles of government, the interests of nations, the spirit and tendency of public measures, and the public and private characters of individuals are all arraigned, tried, and decided. Instead, therefore, of being considered now, as they once were, of small moment in society, they have become immense moral and political engines, closely connected with the welfare of the state, and deeply involving both its peace and prosperity."[73]

Like the English and French revolutions, the American Revolution generated an eruption of public debate in print; the difference was the outcome. The pre-Revolutionary crisis in America established the press as the central venue of public discussion independent of government, and the conflict and its immediate aftermath consolidated the status and rights of the press and the priority of open debate as a means of conducting politics in the new republic. None of the European dynastic states had previously experienced a comparable transformation, and notwithstanding the French Revolution, neither France nor the other principal nations of Europe would see such changes on a sustainable basis until well into the nineteenth century. It was the American Revolution that turned this page in human history.

Constitutional Choices

There may be no better evidence of the new structure of the public sphere in the new nation than the Constitution itself and the debate that accompanied its adoption. During the Revolutionary era, beginning in the states, Americans invented the practice of calling constitutional conventions and writing constitutions. Not only were these constitutions written, but perhaps more to the point, they were also printed and published, and widespread publication was central to their legitimacy. After Pennsylvania's state constitution was approved, Paine later wrote in *The Rights of Man,* "Scarcely a family was without it. Every member of the Government had a copy; and nothing was more common when any debate arose on the principle of a bill, or on the extent of any species of authority, than for the members to take the printed Constitution out of their pocket, and read the chapter with which such matter in debate was connected." Printed constitutions gave Americans a foundation not only for government but also for judging what government did. Widely distributed, intensively read, and continually invoked, a constitution could become, in Paine's phrase, a "political Bible."[74]

The federal Constitutional Convention of 1787 was conducted in secret, and in this regard, the process looked backward to an earlier era of restricted elite communication. But to belabor the secrecy in Philadelphia is to miss the more telling fact. The document that the framers produced ran only 5,000 words and was written in plain English, and in this sense it was a model of transparency. Indeed, it may have seemed more intelligible to the ordinary reader at the time than it does now, when no one can approach it unaware of more than two centuries of disputed constitutional interpretation. On the day the convention adjourned, September 17, 1787, the Constitution was already set in type; by early October, newspapers throughout the original thirteen states had reprinted it, typically on two or three pages. From the calling of the convention, the press had devoted intensive coverage to constitutional issues, and once the Constitution was published, much of the debate about it occurred in the public space that newspapers provided. A nation peacefully debating adoption of its organic law had no historical precedent—this, too, was revolutionary. The articles now known as *The Federalist*, by James Madison, Alexander Hamilton, and John Jay under the collective pseudonym "Publius," have proved to be the most enduring contributions, but at the time they were rarely reprinted outside of New York, and other essays by federalists* were better known.[75]

Opposition to the Constitution came from diverse sources loosely grouped together under the name "anti-federalist," though the crux of their case was that the proposed plan called for too powerful a national government that was not federal enough. The opponents ranged from such elite figures as Elbridge Gerry of Massachusetts and George Mason, Richard Henry Lee, and Patrick Henry of Virginia to many others of a "middling sort" as well as more radical, plebeian voices. The anti-federalists saw in the Constitution dark possibilities for recreating the kind of remote, imperious, extravagant, and aristocratic government that they had earlier experienced under the British; they objected particularly to the consolidation of tax and judicial powers in the government, the insufficient provisions for popular representation, and the absence of a bill of rights. But they formulated no alternative, failed to organize effectively ("They had no plan whatever," Madison observed), and lacked newspapers of their own to spread their views. One-fourth of the nation's papers gave no space to the anti-federalists, and the median number of anti-federalist pieces published by other papers was only four, amid a flood of essays and letters in favor of the Constitution. Federalist domination of the debate seemed to the anti-federalists to validate the threat to the public sphere that they saw in the Constitution's failure to guarantee freedom of the press. But though their views may have been underrepresented in print, the anti-federalists' participation in the debate may have helped to reconcile them to the result: The political outcome of ratification was not only that the Constitution was adopted, but also that the opponents did not contest its legitimacy afterward—indeed, they quickly disappeared as a distinct force and became part of a loyal opposition

*I leave "federalist" lowercase when referring to supporters of the Constitution, but capitalize "Federalist" when referring to the political party that took shape in the 1790s after the new government was established. Some original federalists, such as Madison, did not become Federalists.

seeking to modify the new government rather than overturn it. During the ratification debate, a subtle change was already shifting politics in a more popular direction. The ratifying conventions were open to the press and had a more democratic tenor than the Constitutional Convention; all sides, even men who in Philadelphia had questioned popular rule, now cast themselves as the people's champions. The federalist gentry would continue to dominate politics in most parts of the country for the next decade, but the Revolution had set in motion a process that, step by step, would undermine the old rhetoric and customs of political exclusion.[76]

The general affinity between the Revolution and the printing press did not guarantee that the government issuing from the Revolution would foster free communications. The suppression of the loyalist press could have been an omen of things to come. From the outset, however, the ideal of a free press received legal affirmation. As a preface to its constitution of 1776—the most democratic of the ten that were written that year and the next—Pennsylvania adopted a Declaration of Rights stating: "That the people have a right to freedom of speech, and of writing, and publishing their sentiments, therefore, the freedom of the press ought not to be restrained." The Pennsylvania Constitution itself added: "The printing presses shall be free to any person who undertakes to examine the proceedings of the legislature, or any part of the government." These are the first constitutional protections of free speech adopted anywhere.

It was uncertain, however, whether the new principles established by the Revolution overturned earlier restrictive understandings of freedom of the press. English legal doctrine, as we have seen, held that liberty of the press signified only the absence of prior censorship; known to Americans through William Blackstone's *Commentaries on the Laws of England* (1765–1769), this view was often identified with Blackstone's name. Under the common law of seditious libel, the British government could still punish anyone who spoke or wrote words that tended to encourage disrespect for authority or breach of the peace. During and after the American Revolution, the states had accepted the common law as their own without explicitly making an exception for seditious libel. Even Zenger's defense had not challenged the principle that words were punishable as crime if their truth could not be established and they had the "bad tendency" of encouraging disrespect and disorder. Because there were so few cases after Zenger, seditious libel law had received little further legal, philosophical, or public attention at the time of the Revolution.

At the Constitutional Convention, the prevailing view was that a bill of rights was unnecessary because the new government would have only those powers the Constitution expressly gave it. Madison, among others, defended this position. But after the convention, it quickly became apparent that the framers had underestimated public support for explicit guarantees of personal liberty, and the state ratifying conventions often called specifically for amendments guaranteeing free speech. The Virginia ratifying convention resolved: "That the people have a right to freedom of speech, and of writing and publishing their sentiments; that the freedom of the press is one of the greatest bulwarks of liberty and ought not to be violated." Ratification may have succeeded in Virginia and several other states only because supporters promised they would immediately seek amendments including guarantees of rights. The same demand became an issue in the elections for the first Congress. Hoping to avoid a second constitutional convention that would weaken the new federal government, the federalists accepted a bill of rights as a necessary concession to public opinion. Thus the immediate origin of the constitutional guarantees of freedom of speech and of the press, among other rights, lay in the demands of popular consent and public discussion during the elections for the ratifying conventions and the first Congress.[77]

Won over to the cause by Thomas Jefferson and elected to the first Congress in a closely contested race, Madison became responsible for drafting the amendments to the Constitution in the House of Representatives. The political alignments now shifted. Because it would remove the chief popular complaint against the new government, the prospective Bill of Rights gained support among federalists while losing support among anti-federalists. The amendments, an anti-federalist in Congress wrote to Patrick Henry, "shall affect personal liberty alone, leaving the great points of the Jud[iciar]y and direct taxation etc. to stand as they are" and were therefore "good for nothing, and I believe as many others do, that they will do more harm than benefit." Madison's persistence became crucial as congressional attention focused on other urgent matters in establishing the new government. His proposed draft of what became the First Amendment echoed the resolution of the Virginia ratifying convention: "The people shall not be deprived or abridged of their right to speak, to write, or to publish their sentiments; and the freedom of the press, as one of the great bulwarks of liberty, shall be inviolable." In the House, the amendment appears to have passed without controversy; there is no record of the exact vote or of any opposition.[78]

In the Senate, which conducted its deliberations in secret at the time, there is also no record of any debate, only of actions taken. An amendment proposed in the Senate would have protected freedom of speech in "as ample a manner" as the common law had provided "at any time." But the senators rejected this change, which because of its reference to the common law would likely have authorized the government to impose criminal penalties for seditious libel.[79] The Senate, however, initially changed the amendment to read, "That Congress shall make no law, abridging the freedom of speech, or of the press, or the right of the people peaceably to assemble and consult for their common good, and to petition the government for a redress of grievances." With no record of the discussion, it is impossible to know whether the new phrasing in the active voice ("Congress shall make no law . . . ") was merely a clarification or a substantive change and, if the latter, whether it was intended to make the injunction more imperative or more narrow than Madison's construction ("The people shall not be deprived . . . "), which could be construed as applying to power in any form. In fact, Madison proposed another amendment in the Bill of Rights that would have explicitly barred the states from infringing freedom of speech and other rights; in the House debate, he called this "the most valuable amendment on the whole list," for "if there was any reason to restrain the government of the United States from infringing upon these essential rights, it was equally necessary they should be secured against the state governments."[80] The House passed this amendment, but the Senate did not; restraint on the power of the states would be left to their own constitutions.

The Senate combined the free-speech provisions with those relating to religion and, as a result, the final amendment emerging from negotiations read: "Congress shall make no law respecting an establishment of religion, or prohibiting the free exercise thereof, or abridging the freedom of speech, or of the press, or the right of the people peaceably to assemble, and to petition the government for a redress of grievances." Each of these provisions had a distinct history up to that time; only later did they come to be understood jointly as protecting "freedom of expression." The apparent priority of free expression in the Bill of Rights is mere historical accident. It was only because the states never ratified the first two amendments adopted by Congress that what we know as the First Amendment came first.

The historical background of the press clause in the amendment suggests that the Founders were concerned not just with individual rights but also with the institutional role of the press. In its "Address to the Inhabitants of Quebec," the Continental Congress in 1774 had declared that besides advancing "truth, science, morality, and arts in general," freedom of the press promotes discussion "whereby oppressive officers are shamed or intimidated, into more honourable and just modes of conducting affairs."[81] The first Pennsylvania state constitution also referred to the role of the press in scrutinizing government, and Madison's draft of the First Amendment, like so many eighteenth-century declarations, spoke of the press as one of the "great bulwarks of liberty." These statements ascribe to the press a vital political role in enabling the people to exercise their supervision over the government. The spare, final version of the First Amendment, however, omits any language to this effect, leaving it ambiguous as to whether the amendment refers only to an individual right to publish or to the distinctive rights of the press as a political institution. The latter might include, for example, rights of access to information about the government that could enable the press, as the Continental Congress put it, to "shame" public officials into "more honourable and just" conduct.[82]

Perhaps the single most important question about the First Amendment was whether it was intended to provide broader guarantees of free speech than had existed under British rule, particularly in regard to the common law of seditious libel.[83] On this question, however, the intentions of the framers are impossible to establish. The single most relevant but inconclusive fact is that the Senate explicitly rejected language that would have made the common law the framework of free-speech protection. Like the first Congress, the state legislatures that ratified the Bill of Rights left too sketchy a record of their deliberations to determine any shared intent. Later recollections of key participants about their earlier understandings are also contradictory. Most legal and philosophical discussion of free speech in America may have gone no further than the claim of truth as a defense made during the Zenger trial. But, in practice, Americans had gone far beyond Zenger, and popular views rejecting criminal liability for criticism of the government limited "when and how officials could apply legal restraints to political discussion."[84]

The final draft of the First Amendment did not qualify free-speech rights in any way, though qualifications were discussed at the time. Even Jefferson privately recommended to Madison language permitting punishment of "false facts affecting injuriously the life, liberty, property, or reputation of others or affecting the peace of the confederacy with foreign nations."[85] The provisions of many state constitutions explicitly indicated that while people enjoyed a right of free speech, they could be held responsible for its "abuse." Perhaps the members of the first Congress who voted for what we know as the First Amendment hesitated to include any qualifying language because they aimed to quiet public anxiety about the new government's powers. Perhaps they were willing to vote for an unqualified protection of free speech only because it limited the federal government and not the states; in the early republic, the First Amendment was one of various provisions dividing power in the federal system.[86] For whatever reason, the First Amendment stands as a guarantee, with no explicit exceptions, that "Congress shall make no law . . . abridging the freedom of speech, or of the press."

Why Rights Mattered

By itself, the mere wording of the First Amendment did not guarantee freedom of speech, broad or narrow in construction. Few words have been susceptible to more varied interpretations. The real meaning of the amendment was determined through political conflict, and this conflict was not long in coming. Some have claimed that for the nation's first century, the Bill of Rights "seemed hardly to matter" because the Supreme Court did not cite its provisions in striking down any law.[87] But this is to overlook the central role of the Bill of Rights in politics, particularly in the political contest that soon enveloped and transformed the new government.

In the 1790s, as Jefferson, Madison, and their followers broke off to form an opposition Democratic-Republican (or Republican) Party, an opposition press emerged that sharply criticized the Federalist administration, including President Washington. The vast majority of papers at the time were Federalist in their sympathies or politically neutral; as a practical matter, it was difficult to sustain a Republican newspaper because the merchants who were the chief advertisers strongly supported the administration. As secretary of state, Jefferson helped to underwrite the earliest of the Republican papers, the *National Gazette,* by providing a sinecure to its editor, Phillip Freneau, but the paper, established in late 1791, lasted only two years. During the mid-1790s, a small number of independently published urban papers upheld the Republican viewpoint. None of these nettled the Federalists more than the leading organ of radical Republicanism, the Philadelphia *Aurora,* edited by Benjamin Franklin Bache, grandson of Benjamin Franklin. Bache even accused Washington of having bungled military strategy during the Revolution, and he charged Washington's successor, John Adams, with arrogance and corruption.[88] During Washington's presidency, Hamilton repeatedly urged prosecutions for seditious libel, but the administration took no action. Finally, in the late 1790s, when the United States faced the threat of war with France, the Federalists struck back against their critics in what would prove to be a defining battle over freedom of speech.

Centered in New England, the Federalists had become the party of conservative nationalism, unabashedly in favor of rule by the rich and the wise. The press, said one of their leaders, Fisher Ames, "has inspired ignorance with presumption, so that those who cannot be governed by reason are no longer to be awed by authority."[89] As the French Revolution became a European war, the Federalists feared the spread of Jacobinism and sympathized with the British. During Washington's second term, the United States negotiated an agreement with Britain, the Jay Treaty, ratified in 1795, to which the French Directory retaliated by seizing American ships and refusing to receive an American representative. The crisis seemed headed toward war after Adams became president in 1797; there was even feverish talk of a French invasion of the United States as France was triumphant on the European continent. In this context, the Federalists, who had long tarred Jefferson and his party as the "French faction," regarded opposition to their leadership as disloyalty to the government. A direct assault on the Republican press, weak as it was, would eliminate this threat from within and assure the Federalists continued control of public opinion.

Their first target in the press was Bache of the *Aurora,* who was arrested for seditious libel in June 1798. This was the first legal move by the federal government to claim jurisdiction in cases of allegedly seditious speech. A justice of the Supreme Court, however, had already expressed his personal opinion that the government could not punish seditious libel without express statutory authority. To overcome this objection, the Federalists were advancing a bill through Congress that would be known as the Sedition Act and make it a crime to "write, print, utter or publish . . . any false, scandalous and malicious writing or writings" against the government, the Congress, or the President, "with intent to defame."[90] (A companion measure, the Alien Act, gave the president unlimited power to control foreign-born troublemakers who had not become citizens.) Federalists who even before the Bill of Rights had denied that the Constitution gave the federal government any authority to regulate the press now claimed exactly that power. To secure support from more moderate Federalists in the House, the sedition bill had to be modified in a more liberal direction. The final legislation, which barely passed in the House by a vote of 44 to 41, required proof of malice, allowed truth as a defense, and permitted juries to rule on the law as well as the facts. In these respects, the Sedition Act was more libertarian than the common law as state courts continued to interpret it. The partisan character of the Sedition Act, however, was evident from two features. It was limited to Adams's term of office, and it did not make it a crime to defame the vice president, Thomas Jefferson, leader of the opposition.

If it had been a crime to defame Jefferson, Federalist editors would have landed in jail. Instead, Republicans were convicted and imprisoned. Bache died in the yellow fever epidemic of 1798 before his case went to trial. The first victim of the Sedition Act was Matthew Lyon, a member of Congress and former printer from Vermont, who had come to America as an indentured servant and risen to political success partly by means of the newspaper he published. Detested by the Federalists as a coarse upstart, Lyon—who had written that under President Adams "every consideration of the public welfare was swallowed up in a continual grasp for power, in an unbounded thirst for ridiculous pomp, foolish adulation, and selfish avarice"—was convicted and sentenced to four months in prison. There were eventually fifteen indictments and ten convictions under the Sedition Act as well as several additional common-law prosecutions and convictions in the states. Initially, the Federalist campaign succeeded in silencing much of the Republican press, including the leading urban papers from which others reprinted articles.[91]

This turn toward repression of press freedom in the 1790s was a transatlantic development in the aftermath of the French Revolution. In France itself, a series of measures beginning as early as 1793 had already greatly restricted the latitude of the press. In September 1797, the regime banned many newspapers, subjected the rest to police control, and introduced a stamp tax that drastically reduced print runs.[92] In Britain, fear of the revolutionary forces being unleashed led to intensified prosecutions of seditious libel and new repressive measures. The government made inciting hatred of the government a high misdemeanor, suspended habeas corpus, created a system of registration for the press, and adopted a Law Against Seditious Meetings. These measures, which enjoyed popular support in Britain, were a direct influence on the Federalists.

In the United States, however, the repressive strategy backfired. Republican editors imprisoned by the Federalists under the Sedition Act became popular heroes; Lyon was reelected to Congress while he was still in jail. Even more important, the Federalists' attack galvanized supporters of the Republican cause to establish new organs in greater numbers than had existed before. The initial strategy adopted by Jefferson and Madison to combat repression was a failure; they hoped to get the states to declare the Sedition Act invalid, but only Kentucky and Virginia adopted such measures, in 1799, and the entire effort raised anxieties about the potential for a breakdown of national government. Nonetheless, a changing international situation and the gathering force of the Republican movement turned events in Jefferson's favor. By the fall of 1798, the crisis with France had already begun to abate and English victories ended worries about a French invasion of America. As Adams sought a peaceful settlement with France, the more extreme Federalists denounced him in terms that should have earned them their own indictments for seditious libel. By the election campaign of 1800, the country had eighty-five Republican papers, up from fifty-one in the spring of 1798. Moreover, unlike much of the traditional press, including many Federalist papers that professed a high-minded impartiality, the new partisan papers created by Republican printers and editors openly declared their political sympathies and were organized to contest political power.[93]

When Jefferson and the Republicans upset the Federalists in 1800, the United States passed a milestone with the first peaceful transfer of power from one party to another. It also passed another milestone. For the first time, a party demonstrated how a national network of newspapers could influence public opinion and help win the presidency and control of the government. This was a new model of political insurgency. The Federalists themselves, though ultimately unsuccessful in regaining power, gave the Republicans the ultimate compliment by attempting to imitate their strategic use of the press: "Fas est et ab hoste doceri" (It is proper to be taught by one's enemy), the Federalist Fisher Ames later wrote.[94] After the election, Jefferson pardoned all who were still in prison for violating the Sedition Act, declared the law a "nullity," and allowed it to lapse.

Judicial actions during the battle over the Sedition Act are no measure of the political significance of the First Amendment. The role of the courts in constitutional disputes was not yet established, and with Federalist judges controlling the bench, the Republicans did not appeal the constitutionality of the Sedition Act to the courts. They did appeal to the public, however, on the grounds that the First Amendment had expressly denied the federal government the power to regulate the press. It was through public opinion, state legislatures, and eventually national elections that they sought to uphold their rights. The conflict over the meaning of the First Amendment was not only an argument about federal power; after all, Republicans also favored corresponding protections for free speech in state constitutions. Freedom of speech, Madison argued during the 1790s even before the Sedition Act, was essential to the very idea of popular sovereignty. It is in the nature of republican government, he had said in 1794, "that the censorial power is in the people over the Government, and not in the Government over the people."[95]

Still, there were contradictions. In his first inaugural address, Jefferson famously declared: "If there be any among us who would wish to dissolve this Union or to change its republican form, let them stand undisturbed as monuments of the safety with which error of opinion may be tolerated where reason is left free to combat it." Privately, however, he encouraged "a few prosecutions" of Federalist editors by state governments controlled by his own party, and there were several such cases.[96] Far from disappearing, the law of seditious libel became firmly established in nineteenth-century state courts. In New York in 1804, Alexander Hamilton, defending a Federalist editor named Harry Croswell, proposed that liberty of the press was "the right to publish, with impunity, truth, with good motives, for justifiable ends though reflecting [adversely] on government, magistracy, or individuals."[97] This highly restrictive definition—offering no protection to opinion published for motives disapproved by a court—was incorporated into a statute in New York the following year and influenced other states. At the federal level, though cases were rare, judicial doctrine also followed Blackstone more than Madison throughout the nineteenth century. Except in one minor case, the Supreme Court did not uphold a single claim based on the First Amendment until after World War I.[98]

Yet we tend to read too much into judicial rulings because of the subsequent role of judges in expanding civil liberties during the twentieth century. The traditional basis of a free press lay not in courts, but in politics and in the fragmented and decentralized structure of American institutions. Americans had accepted a journalism that was often scurrilous in its criticism of government and politicians. Controlling the press from the federal level was difficult, while it was relatively easy to start new publications, as Republican printers and editors showed in 1800. After Madison succeeded Jefferson, he made no effort to control dissent, not even during the War of 1812, when the New England papers were rife with seditious sentiment. During the Mexican War, President James Polk made no effort to control any paper other than the one that spoke for his own party.[99] The record of American government on freedom of speech during the antebellum era was far from pristine. Not only were slaves denied free speech; beginning in the mid-1830s, the South also suppressed any dissent about slavery in the press, and similar efforts to silence abolitionists, including mob violence, took place in the North.[100] These, however, were exceptions to the relatively open system of communications America enjoyed in the period before the Civil War.

The contrast in institutional outcomes with France is once again instructive. The French press not only lost its freedom during the Revolution; Napoleon also returned it to the centralized, monopolistic organization that the monarchy had maintained. By 1810, Napoleon permitted only four newspapers in Paris and only one in each provincial *département*—all of which were subjected to censorship by local prefects. Why the French lost their liberty in the Revolution is one of the great problems of modern history. It was not only because of the threat posed by royalist and foreign opposition that the Revolution turned to repression; the revolutionary leaders made choices that reflected their assumptions and beliefs about government. Assuming that the people had one true interest, and afraid of disagreement as a source of weakness, they left little room for public differences of opinion. The French revolutionaries' response to the American Constitution exemplified their frame of mind; they thought the bicameral legislature and elaborate checks and balances were an irrational residue of English tradition: Why not repose the full power of the state in a single assembly?[101] They couldn't see the rationale for structural constraints that would make a government think twice.

After the American Revolution, the men who had led it were also concerned about the threats to the survival of the republic. Like their French counterparts, they worried about consolidating their revolution and keeping the republic together, and this concern influenced their thinking about communications, knowledge, education, and even language. But their ideas were different, so the choices they made and the institutions they shaped were different—as Tocqueville discovered almost a half century later when he traveled to America and found stagecoaches dropping off newspapers in the wilderness.

CHAPTER THREE

America's First Information Revolution

THE CONSTITUTIVE choices about communications after the American Revolution involved more than the rights to free expression codified in the First Amendment and state constitutions. The early republic also faced basic decisions about postal service, the press, schools, and other institutions that affected the capacities for knowledge and communication. What would Americans know about their country and the world? How could a nation spread over so vast a territory maintain itself and its republican form of government? What knowledge should be public and what private?

The institutions that Americans created in the first decades after Independence reflected a new understanding of the political imperatives for information and communication. Old ideas about who should know what no longer made sense: Popular sovereignty implied a change in the cognitive relationship between the state and the people. Traditionally, the state obtained knowledge about its individual subjects but disclosed little about itself, except what served the interests of those in power. But if the people were to be sovereign, they had to have the means of understanding their government, keeping up to date about distant events, and communicating with each other. Since the seventeenth century, the development of communications, particularly of newspapers and postal services, had begun to provide Europeans and Americans with regular information about the public world. But at the time of the American Revolution, the actual public embraced far from a majority of people, the scope of such information was limited, and its cost was high. By the 1830s, the public had expanded, the scope of knowledge was broader, and the cost had fallen. These changes did not happen solely through the invisible hand of the market. Once again, political decisions played a critical role.

The Creation of the News Network

Washington Irving's "Rip Van Winkle," published in 1820, tells the story of a man suddenly thrust into the new political society that had emerged after the American Revolution. After awakening from a sleep that began before the Revolution and lasted twenty years, Rip walks into his old village. "The very character of the people seemed changed. There was a busy, bustling, disputatious tone about it, instead of the accustomed phlegm and drowsy tranquility." Rip finds the very language incomprehensible: "A lean, bilious-looking fellow, with his pockets full of hand-bills, was haranguing vehemently about rights of citizens—elections—members of congress—liberty—Bunker's Hill—heroes of seventy-six—and other words, which were a perfect Babylonian jargon to the bewildered Van Winkle." He had arrived in the midst of an election. "The orator bustled up to him, and, drawing him partly aside, inquired 'on which side he voted?' Rip stared in vacant stupidity."[1]

In the early republic, American journalism took on some of the air of Rip Van Winkle's village: There was a bilious, disputatious, partisan tone about it. National as well as local politics often took the form of quarrels over personal reputation that spilled into print, governed by a shared understanding—the historian Joanne Freeman calls it a "grammar of political combat"—that included rules for the choice of weapons, from gossip to paper war to the ultimate step, an "interview" with pistols on the field of honor. While the printed word had its lofty functions, it also had its more blunt and brutal uses. "For god's sake, my dear Sir," Jefferson wrote Madison in 1793, urging him to criticize Hamilton in print, "take up your pen, select the most striking heresies, and cut him to peices [*sic*] in the face of the public."[2] Hamilton himself was not shy about using words as weapons and ultimately lost his life in a duel after a reference to some of his aspersions on Aaron Burr found their way into a newspaper. Editors, too, flung charges at each other, sued one other, and dueled not just with words but with real bullets. "Scurrility, assaults, corruption, blatancy were commonplace," the historian Frank Luther Mott writes of the press from 1800 to 1830, which he disapprovingly calls "the dark ages of partisan journalism."[3] The intensified conflict in print, at once personal and partisan, stood in contrast to the more classical, public style of eighteenth-century debate, so often conducted behind a veil of pseudonyms. Still, in scores of communities Americans developed little newspapers to relay important political news to their readers, to support their friends and attack their enemies, and to argue for their view of the world. The democratization of the American press—often identified with the "penny press" of the 1830s—was already in progress.

After the end of the Revolution, printing presses multiplied rapidly "not only in seaports," the printer Isaiah Thomas later recalled, "but in all the principal inland towns and villages."[4] While pamphlets, sermons, sheet music, and books came from these presses, the printer's single most important business was typically a newspaper. Mostly small weeklies, often published by a single printer and an apprentice, the papers required an investment of only a few hundred dollars and depended on income from both subscriptions and advertising. Some began when a group of people from a newspaperless community committed themselves to buying a minimum number of subscriptions and invested in the enterprise or gave the printer credit. Others started at the invitation of a political sponsor. Although often described as "partisan," the papers of this era were not all the same. Some editors still adhered to the old ideal of a neutral, open press, and many others were partisan only in the sense of identifying with a party's viewpoint, though the party exercised no control over them. The description of journalism in the early republic as "partisan" has created a misunderstanding that most newspapers from the beginning were creatures of political parties. But America's first parties, the Federalists and Democratic Republicans, had so little organization that it is misleading to suggest newspapers were generally subordinate to them. Rather, newspapers were the organizational base on which a more modern party politics began to take shape. The agitation leading up to and during the War of 1812, like the election of 1800, led to a surge in political journalism. But it was only with the advent of America's "second party system," beginning in the election campaign of 1828, that parties assumed a major role in creating and guiding newspapers, and partisan newspapers became the focal point of sustained party activity.[5]

In the early republic, though aided by governmental subsidies, newspapers had to survive on a commercial basis. In 1784, the first issue of the first daily in the United States, the *Pennsylvania Packet and Daily Advertiser,* gave more than 60 percent of its space to advertising; after 1800, advertising generally filled more than half the column inches in newspapers and in some papers frequently reached four-fifths or even nine-tenths the space. The names of daily papers reflected their commercial orientation: The word "advertiser" appeared in the title of 5 of 8 dailies published in 1790 and 20 of 24 dailies in 1800, though the proportion then subsided, down to 21 of 42 in 1820.[6]

Between 1790 and 1835, while the population grew from 3.9 million to 15 million, the number of newspapers in the United States climbed eleven-fold, from 106 to 1,258.[7] For every 100 households, there were 18–19 newspaper subscriptions in the 1780s; by the 1820s, there were just over 50. That does not prove that more than 50 percent of households received a paper, since some families received more than one, but it does show a remarkably broad distribution of newspapers in an era when, according to some historians, newspaper readership was supposedly restricted to a political and economic elite. William Gilmore's study of villages and farms in Vermont and New Hampshire along the Upper Connecticut River Valley—on "the far fringes of American life," as he says—shows the remarkable transformation in reading habits in the early republic. By the 1820s, he estimates, three-fourths of families included at least one adult who engaged in life-long reading, and that reading had become more varied, secular, and particularly focused on a "new activity"—keeping up with the times through newspapers.[8]

Nowhere in Europe was there anything like this profusion of newspapers and newspaper reading. In 1775, newspaper circulation per capita had been greater in England than in America. In 1835, after travels in America, the English writer Richard Cobden pointed out that despite a larger population, the British Isles had only 369 newspapers, of which only 17 were daily, while the United States, according to an almanac for 1834, had 1,265 newspapers, of which 90 were daily. Cobden calculated that per capita newspaper circulation was six times higher in the United States than in the British Isles.[9] Based on historical statistics now available, he seems to have overestimated the American edge, but the per capita circulation in the United States in 1835 was probably two to three times greater than in Great Britain.[10] No reliable general data on European newspaper circulation are available; it is striking, nonetheless, that one British writer who attempted to compile such data in 1880 estimated that, as of 1840, total weekly circulation in the United States, with a population of 17 million, had surpassed that of all of Europe, with 233 million inhabitants.[11]

Travelers often find causes for what they admire abroad in conditions they want to emulate at home. To Cobden, one of Britain's leading apostles of free trade, the explanation for America's abundance of papers was, naturally enough, the absence of stamp duties and taxes on paper, type, or ink. To Tocqueville, who was preoccupied with the centralization of power in France, the explanation for America's abundance of newspapers was its decentralized structure of government, which, he thought, created demand for news of local affairs.[12] If Tocqueville were correct, American newspapers should primarily have carried news about local politics. But, as in the colonial era, the papers continued to publish a preponderance of national and world news and little news about their local communities. According to a study of papers in rural New York, the country printer did not believe that "his readers would pay for information which they could secure by word of mouth from their neighbors."[13]

Yet Tocqueville was right to think that democratic government in America promoted an abundance of newspapers. Political participation gave more Americans reason to make themselves informed about the nation, and when competing parties developed in the 1820s, they created newspapers to build support and strengthen their connections to voters. Government itself intervened in the market for news in two ways to support the press. General subsidies available to all newspapers, without respect to party, reduced the cost of obtaining and publishing news from a distance. And selective subsidies available to some newspapers from their patrons in public office helped to support partisan news chains linking together papers with similar political orientations.

The postal system exemplifies the distinctiveness of American policy as a positive force in communications. Just before the Revolution, the colonial Post Office had 67 offices, or about 4.5 per 100,000 inhabitants. These offices were located only in the major towns along the eastern seaboard and served primarily as a medium for commercial correspondence. As in other respects, the English had left a legacy, but a limited one. By 1831, the federal government had built a comprehensive network reaching towns and villages deep in the interior and employing more than

8,700 postmasters, or just over three-fourths of the entire federal civilian workforce. This network far exceeded the postal systems of any other country. As of 1828, according to estimates by the historian Richard R. John, the number of post offices per 100,000 inhabitants had grown to 74 in the United States, compared to 17 in Great Britain and 4 in France.[14] In fact, the per capita volume of mail was about the same in the United States as in France, but the American postal network was more comprehensive.[15] The French authorized a new post office only where it could generate $200 in revenue, a principle that would have closed 90 percent of the post offices in the United States.[16]

A radical new conception of postal communication emerged in the earliest years of the republic. In an "Address to the People of the United States" in 1787 in support of the new Constitution, the physician and Revolutionary leader Benjamin Rush argued that "knowledge of every kind" had to be circulated "through every part of the United States" in order to adapt the "principles, morals, and manners of our citizens to our republican form of government." The new government, Rush thought, could achieve these ends by extending postal service throughout the country and distributing newspapers for free.[17] Five years later, this vision of the postal service as a medium of civic communication and nation-building was embodied in the legislation that became the new system's charter, the Post Office Act of 1792. The law, as John points out, had three key elements: It made Congress itself responsible for designating postal routes, gave newspapers special discount rates and privileges, and categorically barred government officials from violating the privacy of letters.

By assuming direct control of postal routes, Congress opened a direct political channel for local demands that would spur the development of a broader network. The clamor from localities for new post offices and post roads was incessant, but Congress was not merely acceding to local interests; it wanted to tie the western territories to the union, and postal service helped to achieve that purpose. From 1792 to 1828, Congress established 2,476 new postal routes, abandoning the principle that every route had to be self-supporting. In 1825, it authorized the postmaster general to designate a post road to the courthouse of any new county seat. As the Post Office did not run a deficit in this period, the federal government was, in effect, using surpluses from the older states to subsidize service into newer ones; almost half of every dollar in revenue from the mid-Atlantic states went to support routes in the South and West.[18] The expansion of the postal system meant extending mail delivery not just to the states beyond the Alleghenies, but to the less populated parts of eastern states. By 1820, for example, there were 443 post offices spread through the state of Massachusetts (which then included Maine).[19]

In contrast, British North America as of the 1830s had a far more limited postal system. From Quebec east to New Brunswick, there were more than 100,000 people but only seven post offices. While the Canadian Post Office returned a surplus annually to the British Treasury, it was unable to respond to continual pleas for service from new settlements. Rates were high, and the volume of postal communication was low. In 1846, an assembly petitioned the queen for more adequate postal service so Canadians might be on an equal footing with the citizens of the United States. A historian of the Post Office in British North America, a former civil servant himself, concedes that rates were "exorbitant" but adds that "after all, the post office was but little used by the mass of the people" and "loyal people bear many things of that kind easily."[20]

In the United States, the subsidies to newspapers adopted in 1792 were critical to the emergence of the first national news network. Under the Articles of Confederation in 1785, the postmaster general had insisted that the Post Office had no obligation to carry newspapers, and after adoption of the Constitution it was unclear what policy the new government would take. In the debate leading up to the 1792 legislation, some congressmen suggested that the Post Office carry newspapers selectively to avoid being deluged. But others insisted on admitting all newspapers because, if the government could refuse to carry some papers, it could manipulate the press and public opinion—and this view in favor of unrestricted distribution prevailed. In another debate, Washington, like Rush, favored free postal service for newspapers, while Madison argued for a small charge to be collected by the postmaster from the recipient because it would encourage reliable delivery—and Madison's view prevailed. The rates established in 1792 called for a charge of 1 cent for newspapers sent up to 100 miles and 1.5 cents if sent further, which represented substantial savings to a publisher who had been paying private carriers.[21]

This postal subsidy would have been less important if most papers were distributed solely within the cities and villages where they were published, but even small-town papers had many subscribers who lived at a distance. A study of the subscription books of two small-town Ohio papers in the 1820s, the *Ashtabula Sentinel* and the *Mansfield Gazette*, finds that a majority of subscribers to both papers lived out of town; indeed, 47 percent of the *Sentinel*'s subscribers and 34 percent of the *Gazette*'s lived more than 20 miles away.[22] Not all of these copies necessarily went by U.S. mail. But by expanding the area from which a newspaper could draw subscribers, the Post Office made possible a larger subscription base and thus enabled more newspapers to develop. In the late 1830s, the Post Office was delivering about one-fourth of all newspapers, although the proportion was declining.[23] In addition, postmasters collected and remitted subscription fees.

Even newspapers that distributed most of their copies without use of the mails benefited from another postal subsidy. The 1792 law codified the right of newspapers to exchange copies for free with one another, and by the 1840s the average newspaper received an astounding 4,300 exchange copies a year.[24] Editors relied on other papers for the nonlocal news that filled most of their columns. In effect, the federal government was encouraging local papers to become outlets for a national news network that the government itself did not control. To obtain news from this network, editors paid only the marginal cost of producing extra copies of their own papers for exchange.

As a result of low-cost distribution and free exchange, the postal service carried a prodigious volume of newspapers—indeed, by 1830, 2 million more newspapers than letters. In 1832, newspapers made up 95 percent of the weight of postal communication and only 15 percent of the revenue.[25] Federal officials and members of Congress also used the franking privilege to send out rivers of public documents, which were also a source of items for local editors. Because the postal system overall was generally self-supporting, the cost of the press subsidy and franked government publications was borne by ordinary correspondence, which was primarily commercial in origin.

The Post Office in Canada, in contrast, had no regular provisions for carrying newspapers. Newspaper publishers had to negotiate distribution with the deputy postmaster general, Thomas Stayner, who by 1830 had quadrupled the price from its level in 1790. Under British law, Stayner was allowed to pocket all the charges to newspapers as a perquisite of his office; a colonial assembly discovered that his profits nearly equaled the total amount paid in compensation to all 137 postmasters in Upper Canada.[26] Newspaper publishers complained bitterly about the high charges and objected to the lack of free exchange with other Canadian papers. Newspapers developed much more slowly in Canada than in the United States during the first half of the nineteenth century, and postal policy was probably a factor.[27]

By 1835 in Britain, the Post Office gave free transport to all newspapers that paid the stamp tax, but the tax had been raised to 3.5*d* per copy in 1797 and to 4*d* in 1815, effectively restricting newspapers to people with higher incomes. After the Napoleonic Wars, a wave of unrest in Britain saw the emergence of radical publications that evaded the stamp duties. In 1819, Parliament adopted the Six Acts, which included provisions to apply the newspaper duty to more publications and a new statute requiring all publishers to deposit a large amount of "caution money" (£300 if they lived in London) as a bond in the event of any future conviction for seditious or blasphemous libel. The particular reason for demanding caution money—a requirement adopted by France the next year—was to discourage the ownership of newspapers except by the wealthy. The Six Acts succeeded in severely restricting radical publications during the 1820s and, together with the stamp taxes, so held back the development of newspapers that there was no growth in per capita circulation of legal newspapers in Britain between 1815 and 1835, although unstamped papers emerged again in the 1830s. While state policy sought to make political news expensive, it exempted religious and moral tracts from taxation, giving them an advantage in shaping public opinion. The tax on advertising had a drastic effect on newspaper revenue: During the late 1820s, New York's dailies alone published more advertising than all the newspapers in Great Britain. In 1836, the government reduced the stamp taxes, but newspaper prices fell only from 7*d* to 5*d*, still too high for regular purchase by working-class readers, though enough for a 70 percent increase in circulation in the next six years. Taxes continued to hold back circulation growth, however, until the final tax was lifted in 1855.[28]

Thus, different political decisions in America and Europe were a key source, though not the only cause, of America's early edge in newspapers and newspaper reading. In Britain and other European countries with stamp duties and requirements for caution money, the state taxed newspapers; in the United States, the state subsidized them. European policy restricted the circulation of newspapers by raising their cost; American policy increased their circulation by reducing their cost. In one case, taxes on advertising limited the ability of newspapers to become commercially self-sufficient and independent of the state; in the other, tax-free advertising enabled newspapers to grow with the expansion of commerce. The United States admitted newspapers into the mails at any post office, whereas other countries generally allowed newspapers only to be sent from the capital.

While the federal government provided postal subsidies to all papers, public officials also dispensed selective benefits to the press through government printing contracts, fees for legal notices, salaries for official posts, and other means. Out of their own funds, wealthy political leaders sometimes provided start-up capital for newspapers. The first notable examples of such political patronage came during Washington's first term, when Hamilton, secretary of the treasury, and Jefferson, secretary of state, each helped to establish and subsidize the publication of a newspaper in the capital. Not only did cheap postage enable these papers to circulate nationally; free exchange allowed editors elsewhere to receive them at no cost, thereby helping to sustain two national networks of loosely affiliated Federalist and Republican papers. From Jefferson's administration to 1820, federal patronage of the press was of relatively minor importance, but the groundwork was laid. In 1789, Congress had authorized the secretary of state to pay newspapers in each state for publishing the laws enacted each year. And in 1819, dissatisfied with the quality of printing of its own journals and reports, Congress abandoned the practice of awarding contracts to the low bidder and voted that each house would separately elect a printer for the next session. These decisions created the two major sources of federal patronage of the press. In one case, the secretary of state dispensed modest sums of money to large numbers of papers throughout the country; in the other, the houses of Congress directed substantial sums to one or two newspapers in Washington, D.C. The profits on congressional printing were considerable; during the first five years after 1819, the beneficiary of congressional patronage, the *National Intelligencer*, enjoyed profits of 55 percent, according to a subsequent congressional investigation. Printing contracts from other executive departments for such items as forms and directives also included hidden subsidies, though of lesser magnitude. Separate executive and legislative patronage developed at the state level as well.[29]

All of this took on new significance when political parties assumed a more structured form in the 1820s. The presidential election of 1824, though not fought on a party basis, foreshadowed the development: Three of the five candidates (Secretary of State John Quincy Adams, Secretary of War John Calhoun, and Secretary of the Treasury William Crawford) were able to use their positions to support a newspaper in Washington advocating their candidacy, while two others (Senator Andrew Jackson and Speaker of the House Henry Clay) were not. Jackson, after losing the contest despite winning the popular vote, decided that a newspaper in the capital was vital to prevailing at the next election, and in 1826 his supporters established the *United States Telegraph* in Washington under the editorship of Duff Green. During the election campaign, they also created several dozen new papers around the country, while the Jacksonians in Congress accused Clay, now secretary of state, of using his patronage to reward newspapers supporting the administration. This was the first time that patronage became a political issue. But after Jackson won, he provided an even greater windfall to the journalists of his own party in the form of appointments (fifty-nine journalists received positions), and Green became printer to both houses of Congress. At first, the *Telegraph* served as the president's journalistic organ—until Green lost Jackson's confidence by getting too close to Calhoun. Jackson then brought in an editor more to his liking, Francis Preston Blair, whose *Globe* took over the *Telegraph*'s role and began receiving executive and later congressional printing contracts. Congressional patronage of the press, as well as the institution of a quasi-official presidential newspaper, lasted until 1860, when Congress established the Government Printing Office.[30]

If the American government had had a more unified structure, political patronage could easily have produced a more uniform press. The fragmentation of authority, however, limited the impact of patronage. This was an indirect effect of the system of checks and balances. At the federal level, the houses of Congress and the executive branch were often under the control of opposing parties or factions; additional power centers lay in the states. Since power was divided, so was patronage. Moreover, most newspapers even in the early 1800s relied principally on advertising and subscriptions. Selective government subsidies did not prevent an opposition press from developing, new parties from forming, or opposing parties from winning office. During the period between 1828 and 1860, there were frequent changes of party control; the presidency changed party hands six times, and instead of a fixed governmental press, eleven different papers served as presidential organs.[31] While patronage was a central element in government-press relations in the antebellum era (particularly in

Washington, D.C., and in the state capitals), it was less important in determining the overall character of the press than the nonselective, general promotion of newspapers through postal and tax policies.

Partisan interests were also at work in the postal network. Members of Congress who obtained new post offices for their districts gained credit with constituents, and parties that won the presidency—most notoriously Jackson's Democrats—used the Post Office for patronage appointments. But the postal system, like the Constitution, did not require men to be angels to achieve its original purposes. For all its flaws, the Post Office did knit together the republic and contribute to the diffusion of knowledge, as Rush and Madison had hoped it would. Previous political thinkers had not imagined that a large republic could survive partly because they had not foreseen how improved communication could maintain a vital connection between representatives and their constituents. They had not understood how new institutions (even without new technologies) could create publics larger than face-to-face communities. Nor had they anticipated the new rules of knowledge that a republic might establish—the new commitments about what the government would make public and what people could keep private.

Privacy and Public Knowledge

The rise of constitutional democracy did not shift social life in either a public or private direction. It did both. Constitutional limitations on state power changed the rules of information disclosure. On the one hand, constitutionalism required that more of government, including law itself, be public; on the other, it sought to protect individuals against arbitrary intrusion into their private lives. While originating in Britain, these commitments to publicity and privacy were still far from their modern form before the American Revolution.

Although the revolutionaries did not speak of a "right to privacy," one of their complaints against British rule was intrusion into their dwellings and use of general warrants for search and seizure of their possessions. The general warrant had a long historical association in Britain with the attempt to control communication, from the enforcement of censorship before 1695 through the prosecutions of seditious libel. Most provisions in the Bill of Rights restated rights that the English had enjoyed under the common law, but one element that grew specifically out of the Revolutionary era was the Fourth Amendment: "The right of the people to be secure in their persons, houses, papers, and effects, against unreasonable searches and seizures, shall not be violated, and no Warrants shall issue, but upon probable cause, supported by Oath or affirmation, and particularly describing the place to be searched, and the persons or things to be seized." The reference to "papers" underlines the historical connection of the Fourth Amendment to freedom of expression.[32]

At the time the United States established its postal system, state surveillance of letters was routine in Europe. Even in Britain, where the law nominally barred opening private letters except by warrant, the Post Office regularly intercepted mail of potential interest to the government. "By custom," writes Kenneth Ellis, "mail was opened freely on suspicion, or in search of designated letters, or on informal orders from Under Secretaries of State, a method possibly preferred by ministers wishing to read the correspondence of opposition leaders." The Post Office was a primary center of the government's intelligence operations, with its own espionage agents and deciphering branch. Its "secrets office" monitored foreign diplomats, domestic dissenters, and even the government's own ministers, keeping the king and the government's inner circle apprised of intrigues and disaffection.[33]

The colonial mail was no exception to the pattern of state surveillance; letters with potentially valuable intelligence were intercepted in transit. In the early colonial era, moreover, travelers often deposited letters they had carried in bags that hung in taverns, where mail might be looked over and read by people to whom it wasn't addressed. Only informal norms discouraged prying eyes. Envelopes did not come into use until the mid–nineteenth century, and although letters were often sealed with wax, the seals were liable to break, or be broken.[34] Privacy began to receive some official attention in the late colonial era. After Franklin and Hunter took charge of the Post Office in 1753, they developed such protections as requiring postmasters "not to suffer the Letters to lie open in any Place, to which Persons, coming to your House, may have Access." They had postmasters and riders take an oath not to detain letters except "by an express Warrant in Writing under the Hand of one of the principal Secretaries of State for that purpose."[35] The colonists, however, had little confidence in the security of the mail and often used pseudonyms and ciphers for delicate correspondence, and after Franklin's dismissal in 1774 Americans were quick to establish their own mail system even before the Declaration of Independence.

In the young republic, the Post Office became the most visible everyday presence of the federal government, but unlike traditional postal systems, it did not serve as a system of surveillance to extend state power. The 1792 act committed the government to the privacy of letters, which is not to say that the postal system entirely succeeded in protecting confidentiality. Prominent figures often complained that their letters were opened in transit and divulged; if passing along sensitive gossip in a letter, they "usually took precautions, using nicknames, pseudonyms, initials, or ciphers to conceal the subject of their accusations."[36] But, except perhaps for the crisis of 1798–1800, the violations appear to have been local and to have diminished in the early nineteenth century. There is no evidence of any organized "secrets office" in the Post Office before the Civil War.

By the 1830s, Americans took pride in the sanctity of the mails as evidence of the comparative advantage of American institutions. The wording of postal legislation in 1825 did not appear to allow even for carrying out a judge's warrant to open a letter; the only letters the Post Office had authority to open were those that landed in the "dead letter" office after postmasters were unable to deliver them. It was not until 1877 that the Supreme Court declared, in an obiter dictum, that the Fourth Amendment's provisions against search and seizure barred the government from violating the privacy of sealed letters.[37] During the nineteenth century, there were some notable exceptions: southern states' interception of antislavery pamphlets and newspapers in the antebellum period and Union interception of letters suspected of providing information about troop movements during the Civil War. Ironically, the 1877 Supreme Court ruling that letters were protected by the Fourth Amendment came in a decision that authorized the Post Office to exclude publications and other mail the government deemed morally repugnant. This was the beginning of an era when the government did, in fact, use its control of the postal system to impose a set of moral strictures on communication.

But, as with the violations of the First Amendment, these instances should not obscure the more general pattern during the antebellum era. Americans seem to have been unafraid of any government surveillance of the mail, and the confidence was largely justified. As government promoted communication by creating the postal system, so it also promoted communication by restricting its own power over the mail.

Like the Post Office, the census illustrates both the active role of government in the spread of knowledge and the changes that America brought about in an old institution.[38] Censuses, like postal service, have an ancient lineage, but in ancient Greece and Rome and even in early modern societies the census was an instrument of state control, not of public knowledge. Censuses originated as a method of registration and surveillance of persons and property, often for conscription and tax assessment; statistical information was not the object. The term "census" comes from Latin, and in Rome it referred to "a register of adult male citizens and their property for purposes of taxation, the distribution of military obligations and the determination of political status."[39] The Roman censor was also charged with the control of manners; hence the etymological association between "census" and "censorship." As late as the sixteenth century, Jean Bodin in a classic work on statecraft described a census as "nothing else but a valuation of every mans [*sic*] goods," useful not only for levying taxes, but also for determining the number and age of men available for war and public works, the needs of cities in the event of a siege, the resolution of civil disputes, and "the discovery of every mans estate and faculty, and whereby he gets his living, therby to expell all drones out of a commonweale."[40]

Statistical information and reasoning in politics have modern origins, but those origins also reflect interests of state. In its original use, "statistics" referred to information about states, regardless of whether the information was numerical. In seventeenth-century England, William Petty and others pioneered a quantitative approach to public policy known as "political arithmetic" that sought to make rational calculation a tool of statecraft. Petty's study *Political Arithmetic* compared the military and economic resources of England, France, and Holland and sought to demonstrate the superiority of English power.[41] Similarly, the earliest quantitative work on national income, by Gregory King in 1696, sought to estimate potential revenue, and early studies of mortality rates were prompted in part by the interest in calculating the cost of government annuities.[42] Political arithmetic, according to one of its practitioners, aimed to "help any ruler to understand fully that strength which he is to guide and direct." It was only in the second half of the eighteenth century that English dissenters transformed political arithmetic into an instrument for controlling government and its power over society.[43] This alternative view of statistical knowledge influenced the new institutional practices Americans adopted.

As the Constitution had authorized a governmental post office, so it also specifically required a government census, and in 1790 the United States became the first nation to inaugurate a periodic census, publish the statistical findings, and use them in the organization of government. The primary impetus for the decennial census was the decision to apportion the House of Representatives and Electoral College on the basis of population. Political representation gave Americans a positive reason for complying with the census. The Founders anticipated the federal government would also use census information to apportion tax obligations among the states. In the *Federalist* number 54, Madison argued that by making both political representation and taxes dependent on the count, the Constitution had given the states two symmetrical interests so well balanced as not to encourage either an overstatement or an understatement of their true population.[44]

In the early years of the republic, Congress was divided over whether to extend government statistical inquiries beyond the bare requirement of an enumeration. Supporters of broadened inquiry thought such information would be valuable in helping legislators serve their constituents; they conceived of society as consisting of diverse groups and of politics as a sphere of interests. The opponents viewed the object of government as the pursuit of an undifferentiated common good; for them, empirical investigation was irrelevant.[45] The gradual expansion of the census reflected the victory of the pluralist understanding. By mid-century, the census was evolving into a more comprehensive enterprise. Nineteenth-century congressional debates suggest that support for federal provision of statistics was based primarily on political purposes, such as the need of legislators themselves for information even on matters where proposed social or economic legislation was ultimately rejected. Support for the census also arose because it was seen as producing evidence of national achievement and the success of the American experiment in democracy.[46]

But as more questions were added to the census, it began to represent more of an intrusion into private life. Concerned more about accuracy than about privacy, the enumerators during early censuses posted two copies of their lists in public places, giving the names of each head of household and the number of persons in each home, so local citizens could check for mistakes. This practice does not appear to have caused any controversy. As early as 1810 and 1820, however, economic questions provoked some resistance, judging from incomplete returns, and the addition of more delicate personal questions—in 1830 the census asked about physical defects and in 1840 about insanity—stirred uneasiness. By the 1840 census the government began to pledge that those involved in the enterprise would keep information confidential.[47] As in the case of the postal system, the record was not perfect—for example, General William Sherman obtained census returns to guide his march through Georgia in 1864—but the premises of state information-gathering had changed.

In its treatment of information about individuals and populations, the American census inverted the ancient pattern. In the classical census, the state obtained information about persons and kept secret information about its people. The American census tried to assure anonymity to persons and publicity to facts about population. Behind this inversion of what was secret and what was public lay a more profound change. The traditional census assumed a coercive relationship between a state and its subjects; the American census presumed—and through a balancing of interests, sought to create—a cooperative relationship between the state and its citizens. As the United States barred officials from using the postal system for surveillance, so it separated the census from surveillance.

The Post Office and the census had to make credible commitments of privacy for the same reason that deliberative assemblies in America were forced to yield to demands for publicity. They had to secure the cooperation and trust of citizens who were presumed competent. In its first years, the U.S. Senate tried to follow the old practice of closing its doors to the public and the press, but secrecy raised suspicion. "Secrecy in your representatives," Philip Freneau, editor of the short-lived Jeffersonian paper, the *National Gazette,* warned his readers, "is a worm which will prey and fatten upon the vitals of your liberty."[48] Secret sessions also meant that senators' brilliant performances in the chamber did not receive coverage in their home-state papers, a disadvantage in building support for a second term.[49] When the Senate voted to make its sessions public after four years, it was acceding not just to the demands of the press but to the new rules of knowledge in a democracy.

The Democratization of Competence

Education was another element in the enlargement of both the public sphere and individual communicative competence. The beliefs of the

Founders about education paralleled their ideas about the postal system and the press; all three means would promote "the diffusion of knowledge" and the principles of liberty on which the survival of the republic depended. Education assumed particular importance in light of the growing popularity of Lockean theories of psychology and child-rearing. If external influences, especially early in life, determined thought and behavior, education could wield enormous power by impressing upon the young not just the beliefs but also the moral character appropriate to a republic. Schools and colleges would be necessary to achieve these aims, and America would somehow have to develop a system for organizing such institutions.[50]

In the early republic, however, Americans did not agree upon the ways and means of accomplishing these ends. Unlike the postal system or the census, education was not understood as a federal responsibility—the U.S. Constitution did not refer to it at all—and no single piece of national legislation encapsulated the liberal republican vision. Early state constitutions often gave education broad endorsement but left vague the method of organizing and paying for it. Among the Founders, Jefferson and Rush were the most explicit about how their states ought to organize schools to achieve republican purposes, but they failed to win sufficient support to carry out their plans. One influential historical account points to these failures as evidence that the Revolution had little impact on education.[51] For example, Jefferson's proposed three-tier system for Virginia, consisting of free elementary schools, twenty regional academies, and aid for the ten most promising needy students at the College of William and Mary, was defeated three times by state legislators who would not vote for the necessary taxes.[52]

In the North, however, partly because of the educational legacy of the colonial era, support for schooling fared better. Besides requiring local communities to establish schools, New England colonial governments had also set aside land to generate income to cover school costs when founding new townships. These precedents were imitated and extended in the northern states after Independence. As early as 1789, Massachusetts renewed requirements for local communities to maintain schools. In 1795, New York State voted significant funds for local schools, and that same year Connecticut sold its land in the Western Reserve for $1.2 million, created a permanent school fund, and started using the interest to pay teachers' salaries. Schools took a variety of forms—the boundary between "public" and "private" was not yet clearly delineated. But increasingly in the villages and rural areas where most Americans lived, communities supported an elementary school open to all the children in a district. This emerging system of "common schools" represented a break from the traditional hierarchy of upper-tier Latin grammar schools and lower-tier "dame" schools.

Although statistics are sketchy, the evidence suggests that school enrollments rose significantly during the half century after the Revolution. Between 1800 and 1825 in New York State, school enrollment of children under age twenty climbed from 37 percent to 60 percent. For the nation as a whole by 1830, the enrollment of the white school-age population was probably about 35 percent—higher than for any other country at that time. Even including blacks, the proportion receiving some schooling in the United States in 1830 was greater than in Britain or France and probably second only to Prussia.[53]

This early expansion of schools occurred primarily through local efforts, but the federal government played an earlier and more significant role in stimulating the development of common schools than is usually appreciated. The origins of federal support go back to the Ordinance of 1785, which divided land in the Northwest Territory into townships of 36 square miles and reserved 1 square mile for support of "public schools." (This was the "old Northwest," which later became Ohio, Indiana, Illinois, Michigan, Wisconsin, and part of Minnesota.) Ultimately, the federal government gave the states land grants totaling 77.6 million acres for public schools—more than three times as much as the 22.7 million acres it later gave the states in the more famous provisions for land-grant colleges, hospitals, and other public institutions. At first, federal land grants were given only with the general requirement that they be applied to schools, and some of the states squandered their endowments. But during the nineteenth century, federal stipulations about the use of land grants became more specific. Federal land grants, note David Tyack and his colleagues, "primed the pump of state school finance and led to greater state regulation of common schools."[54]

Perhaps the single most important aspect of the transformation of education that followed the Revolution was the increased enrollment of women. Female illiteracy declined rapidly in the late eighteenth century. In New England, as of 1760, about 40 percent of women were unable to sign their names; for women born between 1766 and 1795, however, the rate of signature illiteracy was cut to under 20 percent. Even so, the rate for all women remained higher than the rate among men (which was about 10 percent for those who died around 1790). By the 1850 census, the gap in literacy between adult men and women had been closed; these data suggest that girls were learning how to read and write at rates equal to those of boys by 1830 and perhaps as early as the Revolutionary era.[55]

Although not all women who learned to write learned in school, the rise in female literacy developed along with broader support for women's education. In the mid-1700s in New England, it had already become common for girls to attend the lower schools, and in the era of the Revolution they probably began gaining admission to the upper-tier schools from which they had long been excluded. In the 1790s and early 1800s, many new schools for girls were also established.[56] This change was consistent with the republican ideas of the Revolution, although those ideas fell far short of assuring equality to women. In a widely reprinted essay of 1787, Rush argued that women should receive an education so they could instruct their sons in the principles of liberty and serve as "stewards and guardians of their husbands' property."[57] This conception of "republican motherhood" favored education for women not to equip them for the same occupations as men, much less for public life, but to enable them to perform their responsibilities in the domestic sphere more effectively. Another early advocate of education for women, Judith Sargent Murray, also argued that education would enable a woman to be independent if she remained unmarried or became a widow. The chief rival view held that education was ill-becoming a woman, reducing her charms and attractiveness in marriage, but this opinion seems to have diminished after the Revolution. By 1800, a consensus had emerged about the desirability of literacy and education for women; from a modern standpoint, it was a limited conception of female education—but a revolution nonetheless.[58]

This transformation had a double effect because it increased not only the communicative competence of women but also their ability to educate their children. In New England, the chief responsibility for education within the family began to pass from the father to the mother in the colonial era.[59] In the nineteenth century, even with the growth of schooling many Americans continued to learn to read at home, and accounts of family life suggest that reading to children at an early age became a more widespread practice. (The invention of the kerosene lamp in 1830 may also have facilitated reading in the evening.) The same era also saw an explosion of books and magazines of advice to mothers about managing the household and raising their children. Thus it is too simple a generalization to say, as some sociologists have, that the family was displaced by the school. Because of the rising literacy of mothers, the educational capacity of the family in the nineteenth century may have *increased*—which was, more or less, what Rush had envisioned.

The educational concerns of the Founders were expressed in the substance as well as the extent of education. Noah Webster, today identified with the dictionary that he first published in 1828, played a key role in articulating the educational and linguistic implications of American political ideas. In the 1780s, Webster was a young schoolmaster and lawyer, an early proponent of a stronger national government, and one of the ardent publicists for the Constitution during the battle for ratification. He saw reform of language as pursuit of the Revolution by other means. "Let us seize the present moment," he declared in a series of lectures published in 1789, "and establish a *national language,* as well as a national government."[60] Although Webster, like other Federalists, would become increasingly conservative, there was a radical foundation to his theory of language that he never repudiated. He believed that just as the people were sovereign over their government, so they were sovereign over language and could revise the rules of grammar and spelling—and it was his role to codify and disseminate these new rules. In 1783, he had published the first edition of what became known as the "blue-back speller," which would eventually sell an estimated 60 million to 100 million copies. The term "speller" suggests it taught children how to spell, but it was actually the text most often used to teach Americans how to read—and, because reading was taught through oral recitation, how to speak correctly. Webster hoped to minimize the growth of dialects, which in Britain were associated with regional and class distinctions; by enabling Americans to write and speak alike, his schoolbooks could, he thought, contribute to national harmony and power.[61] And this was no mere vain ambition: In the early national period, Webster's speller and his many other schoolbooks probably provided more uniformity of curriculum than any state, much less the federal government, imposed in America's schools.

The prevailing vision of popular education in the early republic emphasized the priority of "useful knowledge." This utilitarianism did not exclude religious and moral instruction, which was thought to be highly useful, but it militated against some kinds of instruction deemed luxuries that were believed likely to encourage indulgence and degeneracy. Women did not need to learn French, according to Rush, because there were more than enough "useful books" in English (and perhaps more than enough dangerous books in French). But the emphasis on practicality also had a positive side in making certain skills more accessible than they ever had been in the past. One of the most striking examples was instruction in arithmetic. Before 1800, arithmetic was widely understood as a commercial skill that most children did not need to learn, and texts in the subject were so thoroughly dedicated to commercial applications that the fundamental principles were ill understood and ill taught. The same mathematical operation would be presented as one rule for money, another rule for weights and measures. Because of the tangle of rules that needed to be memorized, arithmetic was believed to be extremely difficult to learn—and as then conceived, it was. Beginning in the 1820s, instruction in arithmetic underwent a transformation as the concepts were simplified and made more broadly accessible. Before the nineteenth century, numeracy was an esoteric skill; the use of statistics was an arcane mystery. But with the diffusion and simplification of arithmetic, Americans became not only more literate but also more numerate.[62]

These developments in the accessibility and scope of education contradict the view—propagated by Horace Mann and other educational reformers of the 1830s and later adopted by many historians—that the half century after the Revolution was an era of educational decline. But to correct that perception is not to minimize what the reformers who led the common-school movement set out to do. By the 1830s, as the historian Carl Kaestle puts it, America had schools but not school systems; the common-school movement sought to make education more public and more systematic. States had previously provided aid to many educational institutions that, in our terms, were privately run. Gradually, the idea took shape not only that schools should be primarily financed through public funds, but that this money should go exclusively to publicly controlled schools and that these schools should be free, nonsectarian, and open to all children. The common-school reformers also campaigned for state boards and superintendents that would set minimum standards, but it is misleading to think of these as "bureaucracies" in the modern sense because their functions at first were more hortatory than regulatory. As late as 1890, the median number of employees of state departments of education was two, counting the superintendent. Local communities decided how much money to spend, what teachers to hire, and what curriculum and texts to use. The school was a general resource for the community, often providing the only space for public meetings, exhibits, and lectures attended by adults.[63]

As the postal system created wider access to communication, so, too, the rise of the common schools expanded access to knowledge for adults and children alike. What the federal government in 1792 did for postal communication, the common-school movement did for schools: It established the institutional principles for carrying out the republican creed. The nineteenth century would see further growth in schooling (higher enrollments, longer sessions, more years in school, and so on), but that growth largely took place within the framework of public education established in the 1830s and 1840s. This framework was shaped mainly under state and local government, but as the federal government "primed the pump" of educational finance, so it played a crucial role in consolidating the common-school vision as national policy. The Constitution required that Congress admit new states to the union only if they had a republican form of government, and by the late nineteenth century, Congress interpreted this provision to mean that new states must have free, nonsectarian public schools. So while the older state constitutions had only vague language about education, the western states typically had specific provisions for public schools to meet federal requirements and to measure up to the standards that by then were being set in the East and Midwest.[64]

By 1850, the growth of education in the United States had already produced a more literate population than the European average. The school enrollment rate in America, according to census data, was now up to 56.2 percent for whites, 47.2 percent overall.[65] Illiteracy among those twenty years of age or older, as measured in the census (that is, according to responses by heads of families), was 10.7 percent among white Americans, 22.6 percent among the whole population.[66] In contrast, about half of the European adult population could neither read nor write, according to Carlo Cipolla's summary estimate from studies of literacy in specific countries; including Russia, the European illiteracy rate in 1850 was roughly 60 percent.[67] The only country with a lower illiteracy rate than the United States was Sweden (at 10 percent); Prussia and Scotland both stood at about 20 percent. England and Wales were still at 30–33 percent, France at 40–45 percent, Italy and Spain 75 percent or higher. Again, Canada provides a particularly instructive contrast. In 1850, it remained under British rule—the part of British North America that had no revolution. As postal service and newspapers developed more slowly in Canada up to the 1850s, so did schooling. In Quebec as of 1838–1839, 73 percent of adults—88 percent of rural francophones and 40 percent of rural anglophones—were illiterate. Just south and east of Quebec, New England had long achieved nearly universal literacy, but "French-Canadian illiteracy seems to have been more on a level with that prevailing in Italy, Spain and the Balkans."[68] Illiteracy was falling sharply in English Canada in the middle decades of the nineteenth century but as of 1850 remained above the levels in the northern United States.

Within the United States, literacy rates varied directly with the spread of common schools. Growing numbers of district schools cut the average physical distance between school and home, a key determinant of whether children enrolled and actually attended. Parental literacy was also a factor in the literacy of children.[69] Thus there is little doubt that the growth of schooling was responsible for the rise in literacy—directly, by educating those who attended schools, and indirectly by educating mothers and encouraging the habits of life-long reading.

Some historians question, however, whether the growth in literacy had the benign effects that nineteenth-century editorialists and reformers associated with it.[70] No doubt the messianic advocates of literacy exaggerated its benefits, particularly in moral improvement. But the advantages of literacy were no myth. While some individuals may have prospered without becoming literate, the acute observer will not have missed the fact that in the modern world there are no prosperous and powerful countries with mass illiteracy. The long-term economic payoff of literacy and education is well established.[71] Nor is it imaginary to suppose that literacy gives people greater access to the knowledge required for full citizenship.

Marxist historians have maintained, however, that the growth of mass public schooling in the 1830s and 1840s served the particular interests of industrial capitalism. In the revisionist interpretation, schools did not teach valuable cognitive skills so much as the compliant behavior required by factories.[72] Curiously, some right-wing critics of public schools also make the same argument that schools followed the dictates of factory organization.[73] The difficulties with this explanation, however, are overwhelming. The rise of popular education in America preceded industrial capitalism. School enrollment rates were higher in rural than in urban areas. Variations in school expenditures in the early 1800s show no relationship to industrialization.[74] Schools were not imposed on Americans from above; in one community after another, Americans voluntarily created schools that they controlled, and they voted to tax themselves to pay for education. Moreover, industrial capitalism did not functionally require universal primary schooling; most children who attended school did not go into the factories, and the factories employed many immigrants who had never gone to school. Other capitalist countries didn't develop common schools. While factory owners did support schools, so did working-class groups at the time. If self-interest alone governed, capitalists might have preferred a traditional two-tier educational system instead of the new system of common schools. The common-school system that emerged actually corresponded closely to the program of working-class reformers in the early nineteenth century.[75]

American education certainly left much to be desired. Nineteenth-century observers often commented that although American education was more practical and more broadly disseminated than education in Europe, it lacked depth and richness. Throughout the nineteenth century, the United States did not have universities or library collections that were the equal of those in Europe, and American science and scholarship were less distinguished. America excelled in applying education to practical tasks. As early as the 1820s, for example, Americans began to develop means for instructing farmers in scientific agriculture. What distinguished American education in the half century after the Revolution was not the advance of the arts, sciences, and scholarship, but the diffusion of competence to ordinary people.

An American Revolution in Communications

Here, then, were some of the innovations that made up the first American revolution in information and communications: The United States established free speech as a constitutional principle, and the Constitution itself was written and published so that ordinary citizens could read it. Instead of taxing newspapers, the government subsidized them. It created a comprehensive postal network and assured postal privacy. It introduced a periodic census, published the aggregate results, and assured individuals anonymity. Primarily through local efforts, it extended primary schooling earlier to more of its population, including women.

The South conspicuously deviated from this pattern in critical respects. Unlike the states in the North and the Midwest, all but one of the states in the South rejected common schools before the Civil War. The southern states prohibited slaves from learning to read, and they rejected tax support for schools for all white children. Legislative votes in Virginia and Georgia show that the regions least dependent on slavery were the most inclined to support common schools; in the one state that established a common school system before the Civil War, North Carolina, a relatively low proportion of the white population owned slaves.[76] According to the 1850 census, illiteracy among native whites twenty years of age and older was 20.3 percent in the South, compared to 3 percent in the mid-Atlantic states and 0.42 percent in New England.[77] As of the same year, newspaper circulation per capita in the South was only one-fifth the level in New England and the mid-Atlantic states.[78] Libraries, lyceums, and other informational institutions were also much less developed. The South had an extensive postal network, but it imposed censorship on the mails. In July 1835, pro-slavery men invaded the Post Office in Charleston, South Carolina, to confiscate and burn a mass mailing by northern abolitionists; thereafter, in actions condoned by federal officials despite federal law, local postmasters effectively barred antislavery literature from reaching the South.[79]

The mid-1830s saw a decisive shift in the South away from the earlier liberal republicanism of the Founders. The South of Jefferson had become the South of Calhoun, and southerners—including southern editors—sacrificed free expression in the hope of averting black insurrection. Southern states enacted statutes prescribing severe penalties for anyone denying the legitimacy of slavery; the occasional dissenting voice was stilled by prosecution or mob violence, typically with the approval of southern authorities and newspapers. At the same time, abolitionists in the North were facing intense hostility. These events came to a head in 1837 when a mob in Alton, Illinois, killed an abolitionist publisher and destroyed his press. The incident strengthened the abolitionist argument that the "slave power" threatened the liberty of whites as well as blacks: As slavery had led the South to deny rights of free speech, so it was now threatening the rights of every American. The defense of the slave system led, by a certain logic, to a general hostility to the easy circulation of ideas. In an 1859 denunciation of cheap postage, popular newspapers, and other "modern improvements," the pro-slavery author George Fitzhugh wrote that the southern states ought to "tax heavily" all "foreign" books and periodicals.[80]

The restricted information regime in the South may appear to fit the view that the rise of industrial capitalism accounted for the pattern that prevailed in the North. But southern repression had much to do with slavery and little to do with agrarianism. The spread of literacy, schools, and newspapers in the North took place before industrialization, and as William Gilmore's study of rural New England shows, these developments penetrated far into the countryside. Industrial capitalism is even less plausible as an explanation for the development of postal service. Industrial "Second Wave" economies, according to Alvin Toffler, "required the tight coordination of work done at many locations. . . . The post office provided the first wide open channel for industrial-era communications."[81] But firms that coordinated work at many locations didn't develop until long after the Post Office created a national network. The Post Office, moreover, subsidized newspapers, not industrial communication—indeed, it charged higher rates to merchants to support the press and transferred money from the more industrial Northeast to the South and West. The advocates of narrowly economic explanations seem to regard the civic and political interests cited in debates over education and postal policy as a mere charade, as if no one could find such concerns compelling.

The timing of change also does not point to technological innovation as the driving cause of America's first information revolution. The advance of the postal system, the spread of newspapers, the creation of the modern census, and the rise of common schools—none of these depended on technology. All occurred before railroads and the electric telegraph. The various elements in this transformation, however, did reinforce one another. As more people became literate, the demand for books and periodicals increased, and as printed information became more prevalent, individuals had a growing incentive to become literate. Literacy increased the market for newspapers; newspapers campaigned for greater literacy and more schooling. Growing demand for books and periodicals encouraged investment in new printing technology to supply that demand more efficiently, and new technology helped cut the cost, increasing demand. But what set in motion these self-reinforcing processes?

There is considerable force to an explanation that emphasizes the early influence of both religious belief and the general process of commercialization. In the preindustrial era in Europe and America, Protestantism was a powerful force for literacy, and in the early nineteenth century there continued to be a relationship between schooling and evangelical Protestantism, though it was probably of diminishing explanatory importance.[82]

Similarly, although industrialization was not the original stimulus, capitalism undoubtedly played a role in driving the transformation. From the 1600s in Europe, and from the 1700s in America, the growth of long-distance trade had provided an impetus to the development of newspapers. The continuing growth of commercial relationships, even before industrialization, gave individuals more incentive to master skills in communication. In a world that increasingly relied on written contracts, for example, illiteracy was a source of dependency; illiterates had to rely on others to read and write for them. The law of contracts included some special protections for illiterates, but it could not possibly immunize them from the consequences of their own communicative disability.[83] The interests favoring literacy that arise out of capitalism are not simply those of capitalists; all those who buy and sell goods, services, and property—in other words, the vast majority of adults—have a rational interest in gaining the knowledge and skills relevant in a market economy.

Protestantism and the market economy, however, cannot explain why the United States moved ahead more quickly in communications than did the Protestant, commercial countries of Europe. Both the timing of change and international comparisons point to the decisive importance of politics. The transformation of postal service, news, education, and the census followed in the wake of the American Revolution. Between 1760 and 1810, Gordon Wood writes, Americans were transformed from "monarchical, hierarchy-ridden subjects on the margin of civilization" into "the most liberal, the most democratic, the most commercially minded, and the most modern people in the world. . . . It was the Revolution that was crucial to this transformation."[84] To say that these developments had political origins is not to say that the cause was the "state," if by that is meant the state as an aggrandizing, controlling force. Some of the key changes, such as the postal system, the census, and public education, critically involved law and policy and doubtless helped to make the United States more powerful. But the federal government promoted communications in part by desisting from the use of power: It conducted no surveillance of mail, refrained from using the census to maintain information about individuals, and helped to finance and stimulate development of the common schools at the local level, but did not control what the schools taught. The government promoted communications by making credible commitments not to control their content.

The politically driven transformation of the Revolutionary era was followed by an economic one. As of 1750, the northern and southern colonies had about the same level of wealth per capita, and at that point New France may have been no poorer. By 1840, however, the North had surged dramatically ahead as income per capita rose to a level about 50 percent greater than in either the South or Canada.[85] The extent of education in the North, as well as other aspects of its information regime, while not the entire explanation for the divergence in growth, may have been a source of regional advantage.

In the second half of the nineteenth century, many European countries and Canada would begin to catch up with the American movement toward broader communications and education. The taxes and other restraints on the press would be reduced in Great Britain and elsewhere. As of 1850, the Prussians and Scandinavians already had relatively advanced educational systems; Britain, France, and southern European countries would follow. The expansion of schooling in Europe, however, typically involved more centralized action. The share of education expenditures raised at the national level and the control by national governments were much greater than in the United States. Other forms of communication, such as book publishing and newspapers, were also more concentrated in a few metropolises, such as London and Paris. The United States had started down a distinctive path of development in communications that would influence its institutions long after its early head start in the half century after the Revolution.

CHAPTER FOUR

Capitalism and Democracy in Print

"IN THE FOUR corners of the globe, who reads an American book?" the editor of the *Edinburgh Review,* Sidney Smith, asked dismissively in 1820, insisting that although Americans were unparalleled in "self-adulation," they had done "absolutely nothing" since their independence for the sciences, arts, literature, or political economy. Even Europeans in the early 1800s who admired America's self-government, prosperity, and common schools were unimpressed by American literature and culture. "If the national mind of America be judged by its legislation, it is of a very high order," wrote the English journalist Harriet Martineau in 1837. "If the American nation be judged by its literature, it may be pronounced to have no mind at all." American writers were scarcely kinder to their culture, often scolding their fellow citizens for slavish dependence on imported books, ideas, and standards of taste. But the day would soon come, some prophesied, when America would have its own literature—"when the sluggard intellect of this continent," Ralph Waldo Emerson predicted, "will look from under its iron lids and fill the postponed expectation of the world."[1]

In fact, things were about to change, though not simply because of an awakening of genius. Growing literacy, schooling, and a burgeoning economy and civil society were generating larger markets for reading matter. And with those markets came both the rise of indigenous literary publishing and the transformation of print into a form of mass entertainment and information. America followed a different path from Europe in the development of both high culture and a popular press. During the sixteenth and seventeenth centuries in Europe, royal courts were the centers of high culture, and writers looked to royal and aristocratic patrons for material support and prestige. A patron might bestow gifts, finance publications, provide employment, or place a writer in an important or at least remunerative position. By the early 1700s, the growing market for print enabled writers to turn to a different source of patronage—the reading public—and by 1800, the market was large enough to enable the most popular authors to make a living solely from their writing. Nonetheless, the cultural vestiges of absolutism and aristocracy persisted. In France, Britain, and other countries during the nineteenth century, culture and communication continued to be concentrated in the capital, and there remained a strong distaste for commercialism.

In America, in contrast, no royal court or aristocratic patrons ever supported writers and publishers, and no single center dominated cultural life. And while English aristocratic ideals had lingering influence, literature in America was, if not born in the marketplace, at least raised there from infancy. America's high literacy rate and its rapidly growing population, fed by new waves of immigration, led to markets for print that were not just larger than those in European countries but also increasingly diverse. Thanks to the extension of schooling, the reading public even in the first half of the nineteenth century included growing numbers of women, young readers, working-class as well as middle-class adults, and new immigrants as well as some free blacks. The development of roads, canals, and railroads extended markets for books and periodicals geographically. From the chiefly local orientation of printers in the colonial era and early national period, there developed a national market for print. This socially and spatially enlarged market invited new strategies for publishing—new books for new readers and larger volumes of production at lower prices, in part through investment in new printing technology. Technological advances in related industries, notably papermaking, helped push down prices further.

The rise of publishing as a popular information and entertainment industry took place on both sides of the Atlantic in the nineteenth century, but under different conditions. The American constitutional and legal framework of printing and publishing led to an industry that was commercially freewheeling. Religious, civil, and political activity was also intensely competitive, and this pluralist competition found expression in print as well. From a relatively early period, price-cutting, technological innovation, and relentless popularization and pursuit of the mass market became the hallmarks of American publishing. Capitalism and pluralist democracy together stimulated this restless process. But there was also a strain of high-minded moralism in American culture and politics that would become an increasingly important regulatory influence on print and public entertainment, especially after the Civil War. New forms of cultural expression frequently met condemnation as vulgar, indecent, and dangerous from critics and guardians of public virtue, who demanded restraint and created their own, presumably more wholesome and virtuous, alternatives. The development of publishing reflected the collaboration and clash of these forces.

Publishing and the Limits of Copyright

The Constitution and Bill of Rights, besides providing for the Post Office and freedom of the press, explicitly sought to promote the development of information and communications in another way. As one of its last touches, in September 1787, the Constitutional Convention approved without dissent a provision in Article 1, Section 8, that became the basis of the U.S. copyright and patent system: "The Congress shall have Power . . . to promote the Progress of Science and useful Arts, by securing for limited Times to Authors and Inventors the exclusive Right to their respective Writings and Discoveries." Three years later, the first Congress approved copyright legislation.

Like the framework of English copyright from which it derived, the American system had two consequences of symmetrical importance. It created private rights to published work (though the original act mentioned only "maps, charts, and books") and at the same time provided for a legal public domain consisting of works on which copyright had lapsed or to which it had never applied. As a matter of constitutional principle, authors would receive "exclusive rights" to their work, but the short terms and narrow scope originally given copyright assured that the public would benefit from competition in publishing, low prices, and consequently wider diffusion of knowledge. The balance between these two interests has shifted over time, but federal law at first fostered a competitive market and broad public domain far more than it protected the interests of authors. For a century after it was adopted, copyright was exclusively available to U.S. citizens. While seemingly a benefit to American authors, this limitation undermined their competitive position, since publishers did not have to pay for rights to reprint books by foreigners. And although publishers lobbied for this limitation on copyright, it exposed them to the risk that a rival would reprint the same book at a lower price.

Risk is inherent in the book trade because each new book is a singular product, its market uncertain; hence the distinct role of publishers, who put capital at risk on books and arrange for their manufacture and distribution. Publishers have historically come from a variety of occupations in the trade, not just printing but also retail or wholesale book selling, papermaking, and binding. Financiers, patrons, and organizations of different kinds have also performed the role of publisher. In Britain and France, the monopolistic guilds that long limited entry into the trade reduced the publisher's risks of competition as well as the state's risks of subversion. In America, the doors to publishing were wide open—a good thing for free expression, but a source of heightened risk to the entrepreneurs of the printed word.

Despite the early growth of newspapers, book publishing had a slow start in colonial America. Short of capital and mindful of the difficulty of finding a market for substantial books, colonial printers concentrated on small projects, such as pamphlets, primers, catechisms, and chapbooks, requiring only modest amounts of paper and type. They kept their financial exposure to a minimum, even to the point of expecting authors to supply the paper, and generally stuck to the safe and well tested in their limited ventures in book publishing at their own risk. An ideal book, from a printer's standpoint, was a short "steady seller," such as a religious text in standard use. Almanacs, another steady seller, had the virtue of requiring local information that British sources could not supply.[2] Even Benjamin Franklin, whose great publishing success was his almanac, risked his own capital on only a small number of original books. Imports from Britain dominated the book trade, and colonial printers generally combined their printing business with bookshops where they sold their own and other publications. After Franklin retired from printing, his partner, David Hall, shied away from publishing books at his own risk and turned primarily to bookselling, for which he relied largely on imports. The printer James Rivington, who had been a London bookseller, was so closely tied to British publishing that he could obtain books soon after they were available in London and thus did "business in America almost as if there were not an ocean between him and England."[3] American printers complained that the British dumped books on the American market that they could not sell at home; in fact, the American colonies accounted for half of British book exports, and the traffic was increasing up to the time of the American Revolution. "Had it not been for American independence," Hugh Amory has argued, "London might ultimately have dominated the American [book] trade as thoroughly as it would Australia's where, even as late as 1953, 80 percent of the books sold were imports."[4]

The establishment of American copyright law in 1790 on the model Britain had adopted in 1710 might suggest that book publishing followed similar paths of development in the two countries. But the preexisting institutional framework of print and politics in Britain differed from the framework that emerged in America. Originating in a guild (the Stationers' Company), the British publishing industry continued to be dominated by a small oligarchy even after the lapse of government licensing of the press in 1695. Under the licensing system, London booksellers had enjoyed a legal monopoly on publishing, but after the law lapsed, they were able to work together to keep control of the trade. Since London remained not just the political capital but also the financial and cultural center of the empire, the centrifugal forces in publishing were overwhelming. While provincial printers proliferated in the early 1700s, they mainly did job printing and put out local newspapers, posing no competitive threat as book publishers; indeed, the new provincial shops that emerged to sell local papers extended the distribution network for books from London.[5] For the London booksellers, the chief problem caused by the lapse of licensing in 1695 was that it ended the Stationers' old system for regulating the ownership of "copy," which had become a significant form of wealth. Members of the trade invested in successful books, bought and sold shares in them, and bequeathed copy to their heirs. Between 1695 and 1703, they continued to try to persuade Parliament to revive the licensing system, but they finally shifted strategy and began pressing for recognition of copyright apart from censorship. In an influential pamphlet published in 1704, Daniel Defoe conveniently provided them with the altruistic rationale that the rights of authors needed protection. The pirating of "other Mens Copies," Defoe wrote, was "every jot as unjust as lying with their Wives, and breaking up their Houses."[6]

The bill that the booksellers sponsored would have established a perpetual property right in literary works, but that was not, in the end, what Parliament gave them. The Statute of Anne, passed in 1710 and generally regarded as the earliest legislative basis of copyright in its modern form, provided a mere fourteen years' protection for new publications (in line with the law of patents for mechanical inventions), renewable for another fourteen years if the author was still living. The statute extended the stationers' copyrights on works already in print for a single term of twenty-one years. But unlike the old system, the new one enabled authors and others besides booksellers to hold copyrights. As penalties for infringement, it called for fines and the destruction of unauthorized copies.[7] Yet the statute did not settle the issue. Interpreting the time limits only to apply to the penalties under the act, the booksellers continued to claim perpetual copyright under the common law. In the first legal tests, English courts upheld that claim, although publishers in Scotland and Ireland began issuing cheap reprints of the classics and challenging the London booksellers in provincial English markets. When one of the Scottish publishers, Alexander Donaldson, opened a shop in London offering books at 30 to 50 percent of customary prices, the booksellers sued, with every expectation of confirming their legal monopoly. But in an unexpected rebuff, the House of Lords ruled on appeal in favor of the Scottish reprint publisher that copyright was limited in term. This case, *Donaldson v. Becket* (1774), proved to be the definitive turning point in modern copyright law. It not only established that copyright was time-limited; it also led to the understanding that the copyright created by statute comprised all the property rights in a publication, instead of merely supplementing those established in common law.[8]

According to one interpretation of these developments, the new framework of copyright reflected a more general tendency toward Lockean ideas of "possessive individualism" and Romantic ideas about individual authorship.[9] English law did for the first time recognize authors (among others) as owners of literary property, but an interpretation emphasizing this aspect alone misses the symmetrical nature of a change that also set limits on literary property, created a public domain, and liquidated much of the capital that booksellers had invested in old copyrights. As it happens, John Locke himself played an important role in the debate about literary property, but his concern was the interests of readers, who he believed paid excessive prices for books because of the Stationers' monopoly. In a memorandum to Parliament in 1693, Locke argued it was "unreasonable and injurious to learning" for anyone to have exclusive rights to print classic texts; the "liberty, to any one, of printing them, is certainly the way to have them the cheaper and the better." Regarding "those who purchase copies from authors that now live and write," he proposed "to limit their property to a certain number of years after the death of the author, or the first printing of the book, as, suppose, fifty or seventy years."[10] It is a caricature not just of Locke, but also of classical liberalism generally, to suppose that property rights dominated all other considerations. In this instance, as in others, there was equal, if not greater, concern for limiting monopoly power and increasing public access to knowledge. The same was later true of changes in literary property during the French Revolution.[11]

The British book trade after *Donaldson* did, in fact, change in the direction sought by opponents of perpetual copyright. With older works now in the public domain, rival publishers began to reprint popular classics in new and less expensive editions. The end of perpetual rights shook the foundations of publishing because it made success dependent on the discovery of new books that would enjoy copyright protection at least for a limited term. These were not necessarily the same kinds of works as in the past. Whereas the old copyright regime made steady sellers highly desirable, the new regime favored books that would have large sales in a short period—novels, for example. The change also created a demand for new means of publicity and marketing. Innovation in publishing became necessary for survival; only a few of the old booksellers, such as Longmans, successfully made the transition to publishing in the new way. By the end of the eighteenth century, the book trade was being reshaped into a modern publishing industry as "publishers injected risk capital into new books, wholesalers distributed them, and at the end of the chain the retail booksellers laid them before the public."[12] Nonetheless, some old patterns persisted. Despite the introduction of remaindering in the 1790s by an interloper, James Lackington, who built London's biggest bookstore, the general practice was to publish new books in low volumes and at high prices. The trade was still able to restrain price-cutting. In the late eighteenth and early nineteenth centuries, it was not in Britain but in the United States that antimonopolistic sentiment and public policy decisively shaped the structure of publishing.

The impetus for copyright in America came from individual authors in the years just before the Constitutional Convention. Through private enactments, colonial legislatures had granted some patents for mechanical inventions, but they had no tradition of granting copyright, except for one isolated enactment in Massachusetts in the 1670s.[13] Yet almost as soon as the Revolution was over, authors descended on state legislatures in search of copyright protection. In 1782, with a manuscript of his grammar textbook in hand, the twenty-four-year-old Noah Webster began visiting state capitals in the hope of obtaining legal protection for his work. His cultural nationalism was evident in the petition he submitted to his home state, Connecticut: "America must be as independent in *literature* as she is in *Politics*, as famous for *arts* as for *arms*; and it is not impossible but a person of my youth may have some influence in exciting a spirit of literary industry."[14] Connecticut had already granted a songwriter copyright for a collection of psalmody, and in January 1783 it became the first state to pass general copyright legislation.[15]

That same month, in a letter to Elias Boudinot, president of the Confederation Congress, the poet Joel Barlow wrote, "As we have few Gentlemen of fortune sufficient to enable them to spend a whole life in study, or enduce others to do it by their patronage, it is more necessary, in this country than in any other, that the rights of authors be secured by law."[16] Under the Articles of Confederation, the Congress did not have authority to adopt a copyright law, but in May 1783 it encouraged the states to enact such legislation, and in the next several years, twelve of the original thirteen states did so, though the exact provisions varied. Since many participants in the Constitutional Convention in 1787 had served in the state legislatures that enacted these laws, the state experience directly influenced the decision to give the new Congress the authority the old one had lacked. Just as the Constitution sought to promote interstate commerce, so it sought to reduce the obstacles that authors and inventors confronted in obtaining legal protection separately from each of the states.[17]

Nonetheless, the constitutional provision "to promote the Progress of Science and useful Arts, by securing for limited Times to Authors and Inventors the exclusive Right to their respective Writings and Discoveries" suggests a shift in emphasis from the state laws of the 1780s. Two principal justifications of copyright appear in the petitions and laws of that period. One of these conceives of copyright as a natural right of the author; as Barlow put it in his 1783 letter, "There is certainly no kind of property, in the nature of things, so much his own, as the works which a person originates from his own creative imagination." The second rationale for copyright conceives of it as an incentive to produce a public benefit; Barlow made this argument as well, cautioning that America should not expect authors to publish "any works of considerable magnitude" until they had protection against piracy.[18] Although both views of copyright were in the air, the state laws emphasized the natural rights of authors, while the Constitution's emphasis on promoting the "Progress of Science and useful Arts," together with its express injunction that rights be for "limited Times," framed copyright as an incentive. While other provisions of the Constitution granting powers to Congress are silent as to purpose, the copyright and patent clause says explicitly that its object is a public benefit. This, at least, was to become the dominant legal view in the early republic.[19]

Following British precedent, the Copyright Act of 1790 limited the term of protection to just fourteen years, renewable for another fourteen if the author was living. The authors or proprietors of "maps, charts, and books" could have "the sole right and liberty" to such works, whether or not previously published, as long as they were U.S. citizens and met several procedural requirements involving deposit of copies with the government and public notice of copyright. Nineteenth-century courts interpreted the scope of copyright narrowly and the procedural requirements strictly. Since the Constitution authorized copyright only to promote "science and useful arts," judges denied protection to publications such as news reports; "a work of so fluctuating and fugitive a form as that of a newspaper," wrote Justice Smith Thompson in an 1829 opinion, could not qualify as science, nor apparently as a useful art.[20] Courts also denied copyright to advertising, market quotations, and other commercial information on the same grounds.

In a pivotal case in 1834, *Wheaton v. Peters*—the American counterpart to *Donaldson v. Beckett*—the Supreme Court held that common-law copyright applied only to unpublished work; once a book was published, it entered the public domain unless the author or proprietor established title by adhering exactly to the statutory procedures for copyright. Even a minor error in registration or public notice rendered a copyright void.[21] In a late nineteenth-century case, for example, the Court threw out the copyright on an entire book published in serial form because the copyright on a single installment had been defective. In *Wheaton* and other cases, the courts were skeptical of claims of copyright infringement by derivative works, such as abridgments. According to an 1853 decision, a translation of a work did not infringe on the copyright of the original and an author had no property right in a book's fictional characters.[22] In 1831,

Congress extended the initial term of copyright to twenty-eight years and broadened the scope to cover musical compositions; by 1870, it had expanded copyright to include translations and dramatizations. By and large, however, nineteenth-century copyright law took a restrictive view of intellectual property rights and gave priority to free expression, competition, and the public domain.[23]

The legal framework of copyright limited its early use; from 1790 to 1800, only 556 works were copyrighted out of an estimated 13,000 that were published.[24] Initially, even American authors made little use of copyright, except to protect schoolbooks and other texts that were frequently reprinted and thus commercially valuable. Literary publishing and copyright were barely acquainted with one another at this stage. As late as 1820, British reprints still accounted for 70 percent of all titles published. Thus, the great majority of books, as well as all newspapers, were in the public domain. The predominance of British reprints partly reflected the continuing appeal of older classics as well as the persistent sense of American cultural inferiority. Reprints of new books successfully published in Britain may have also seemed less risky to publishers than untested manuscripts by native authors. That rights to foreign books were free added to the weight of these considerations. At the same time, tariffs, varying from 8 percent to 15 percent between 1816 and 1860, helped to prevent imported books from competing with domestic reprints of British works, which, along with schoolbooks, were the biggest sources of profit for American publishers.[25]

Assisted by these copyright and trade policies, as well as by the expansion of schooling, indigenous publishing began to take off in the decades after Independence. The colonial printer-publisher had been more printer than publisher, but several leading members of the trade now turned to publishing in earnest, assuming the risks of publication and coordinating production and distribution. Mathew Carey of Philadelphia is generally acknowledged to have been the first to make publishing his principal business. To extend his geographic reach, Carey had more than fifty agents by 1790 distributing books up and down the eastern seaboard; he also began to invest in advertising and developed the largest wholesale operation for supplying his own and other publishers' books to local dealers. Cooperative agreements among publishers in different regions were critical in the early development of the industry. By exchanging books with each other, publishers could simultaneously diversify the stock in their retail bookstores and reduce the risk in any individual title. They also sometimes divided ownership of a book into shares; the primary publisher thereby limited potential losses, while the secondary publishers assured themselves a supply of the title. The reduction of risk lay behind other publishing practices as well. Publishers sought to transfer risk to authors through shared-risk contracts, which called for authors to put up part or all of the money to pay for their own publications. This was a shift "backward" in the supply chain. In the case of some costly books, they also sometimes transferred risk "forward" to consumers by selling advance subscriptions, which signaled demand for the book as well as reducing the publishers' exposure. Though the failure of some projects tainted the reputation of subscription books, they nonetheless became a significant part of the business.[26]

The absence of copyright on foreign reprints created the peculiar risk that after investing in an American edition, a publisher might find much of the market taken by a competitor. To avert that possibility, publishers tried to maintain an informal norm known as "courtesy of the trade," which meant leaving the market for a foreign book to the first publisher to issue it in America. But in the United States, unlike Britain, publishers did not form a self-regulating community, and trade courtesy broke down. The race to reprint new books by popular British authors was often so fierce that American publishers would pay British sources for advance sheets, which on reaching America would be rushed from the docks to the composing rooms and reprinted overnight for immediate delivery to bookstores. Although a few publishers did pay foreign authors for sheets or even for rights, market pressures limited what foreign writers could expect.[27] American editions, as a rough rule, sold at a quarter of the British price and in much larger quantities.[28] Price competition was built into the American market from the beginning, and as the reading public expanded to unprecedented size in nineteenth-century America, publishing at high volumes and low prices made more sense than ever.

The Revolution of Cheap Print

The first half of the nineteenth century saw dramatic changes in the economics of the printed word in both the United States and Europe, though the changes generally happened earlier and on a wider basis in America.

In the 1830s and 1840s, sharp reductions in prices for newspapers and books in America highlighted the advent of an era of cheap print. Now there were daily newspapers that instead of 6 cents per copy sold for a penny or two. Now there were novels that instead of an earlier price of $2 sold for 25 cents or less, when the same books in Britain cost the equivalent of more than $7. So steep were the declines in the price of print over so short a period that they amounted to an information price revolution, the first of several such episodes of declining prices that have profoundly affected information and culture during the past two centuries.[29] Two mid-nineteenth-century American cultural innovations, the "penny press" and the "dime novel," were actually named for their low price (as was the later English "penny dreadful"). These were criticized for being cheap in both senses of that word: low in price and low in taste. But low price did not necessarily mean lowbrow. Increasingly, book publishers issued even the most esteemed works in cheap as well as expensive editions to reach as wide a public as possible. The information price revolution also affected religious and political publishing as reading became a basis of mass persuasion for the first time in history.

Cheap print was not entirely unprecedented. In seventeenth- and eighteenth-century England and France, cheap collections of stories, ballads, and other miscellany had circulated among the lower classes. But since only a minority of the poor could read, most listened while a few read aloud; thus cheap print reached not so much a reading as a listening public.[30] The expansion of cheap print in the nineteenth century in America and Europe was on a much larger scale, and it took place during a great increase in popular literacy. Together these amounted to a cultural watershed. Traditionally, even in literate homes, books and other publications had been relatively rare and treasured objects; reading meant returning to a few texts, especially religious works. In the late eighteenth and early nineteenth centuries, Britain, France, and (somewhat later) Germany witnessed a "reading revolution," a shift, in Rolf Engelsing's terms, from "intensive" to "extensive" reading, exemplified by the rise of the novel.[31] The trajectory was not quite the same in America, where the shift, at least during the eighteenth century, was less to a literature of sensibility than to journalism and practical instruction. But with the explosion of print, reading became more varied, and readers scanned newspapers, magazines, and cheap books that they soon passed on or discarded. Intensive reading of religious and other works did not disappear, but reading became an increasingly common form of diversion as well as devotion. In addition, printed ephemera proliferated through the emerging urban landscape, as advertisers and political campaigns plastered walls with bills and broadsides, and groups of all kinds carried placards and banners in parades and other public events.[32] The changes in reading accompanying the rise of throwaway print are nicely captured in an autobiography of an American publisher reflecting in 1856 on his youth in Connecticut in the 1790s:

> Books and newspapers—which are now diffused even among the country towns, so as to be in the hands of all, young and old—were then scarce, and were read respectfully, and as if they were grave matters, demanding thought and attention. They were not toys and pastimes, taken up every day, and by everybody, in the short intervals of labor, and then hastily dismissed, like waste paper. The aged sat down when they read, and drew forth their spectacles, and put them deliberately and reverently upon the nose. . . . Even the young approached a book with reverence, and a newspaper with awe. How the world has changed![33]

The usual explanation for the rise of cheap print emphasizes new technology. Unquestionably, the full development of cheap print could not have happened without technological change. Print, however, had already become cheaper in America before technological advances played a significant role; new technology arrived once the process was under way, not at the beginning. This was no accident: The continuing expansion of print created an incentive for technological innovation. To conceive of technology as the causal force is to understate the prior importance of politics, culture, and markets in creating the conditions that allowed investments in new technology to pay off.

Cheap print was public policy in America. While European governments taxed newspapers and other publications, the United States let them go tax-free and even subsidized them, to a degree, through the postal system. The Stamp Act crisis during the Revolutionary era left behind a distinct bias against any special taxes on the press. In 1785, Massachusetts enacted a stamp tax on newspapers that was quickly repealed in the face of protests and ridicule; in its place, the state enacted a tax on advertising but repealed that as well in 1788 after newspaper advertising and profits dropped. The adoption of both of these taxes preceded adoption of the Constitution and Bill of Rights. In 1936, when the U.S. Supreme

Court ruled that a Louisiana tax on newspapers with more than 20,000 circulation violated the First Amendment, the Court declared that to its knowledge no state during the nation's previous 150 years had ever imposed a similar tax singling out the press.[34] The absence of any taxes on American newspapers in the early 1830s explains why entrepreneurs could dare to sell them for a penny each. At that time, British newspapers cost 7 pence, of which half consisted of taxes: "Paper and Print 3½ *d*. Taxes on Knowledge 3½ *d*," as the masthead of one London newspaper put it.[35] American opposition to higher prices for publications was also a source of opposition to measures extending copyright protection to foreign authors. Henry Clay introduced such legislation in 1837 but drew little support, and when Secretary of State Edward Everett negotiated a copyright convention with Britain in 1853, the Senate never even voted on it.[36]

The rise of cheap books and other forms of cheap print in the United States also reflected distinctive patterns of nineteenth-century American consumer markets. As the economic historian Nathan Rosenberg remarks, citing the cases of cutlery, guns, boots, and clothing, "Americans readily accepted products which had been deliberately designed for low cost, mass production methods" at a time when handmade goods persisted in Britain.[37] Books fit this pattern. Americans had not been primarily responsible for introducing new manufacturing technology to the production of books. On the contrary, most of the key advances in printing and papermaking before 1850 had traveled west across the Atlantic rather than the reverse. But the industrialization of book production proceeded more rapidly in the United States, where the market by the middle decades of the century was not only larger than in Britain but also apparently more sensitive to price than to quality, perhaps because elite readers constituted a smaller proportion of book buyers.[38]

The technological innovations affecting print in the early 1800s came not in the form of a single invention, but rather in a wave of related advances. Technological change often comes in clusters because of interdependencies in the various parts and processes that go into a product; an improvement in one component focuses attention on an impediment in production somewhere else, generating a succession of changes. The advances that cut the costs of producing print fell into three primary areas: papermaking, printing, and stereotyping. As of 1800, paper continued to be made by hand from rags in a process that, except for some improvements in reducing rags to pulp, had hardly changed since the fifteenth century. Consequently, the high cost of paper, as well as limits on its supply from shortages of rags, threatened to impede publishing as the demand for print rose. Half of the problem found a solution in a papermaking machine devised by a French inventor in 1798 and rendered commercially viable in 1807 by two London stationers named Fourdrinier. It was not until 1827, however, that the Fourdrinier machines arrived in America; other advances in papermaking in the same period helped to cut the cost of paper, though they yielded output of too low a quality to be used in making the finer grades. From 1828 to 1831, thanks to these innovations, paper fell in price 25 percent, from 16 to 12 cents a pound. The antebellum era also saw the first steps to find substitutes for rags, beginning with straw and soda wood pulp, which produced a further 30 percent drop in paper prices in the second half of the 1850s (and with wood-pulping technology introduced after the Civil War, even greater declines in the late nineteenth century). As these steps drove down paper prices, they removed a key constraint on print as a mass medium.[39]

The transformation of printing itself started with a shift in labor relations that preceded new technology. Printers in the late eighteenth century increasingly employed wage labor rather than apprentices and divided work between compositors and lower-paid pressmen. Part of the commercial payoff of new technology also lay in the expanded use of low-wage (often female) workers.[40] Beginning around 1800, modified hand-driven presses, some for the first time made of iron rather than wood, marginally improved productivity, but the more significant innovations came later, with the substitution of power-driven for hand presses and of presses working on the principle of the cylinder rather than the plane. In 1822, Daniel Treadwell of Boston introduced what proved to be a transitional model, a bed-and-platen press literally using horsepower, but horses shortly gave way to steam. The varying imperatives of book and newspaper printing then led to different technological patterns. A steam-powered bed-and-platen press devised by Isaac Adams in 1830 became standard in book manufacture, while steam-powered cylinder presses, first put into operation by the London *Times* in 1814, had their primary application in large-circulation newspapers. The relatively small print runs of individual American newspapers may account for their later adoption of the cylinder press, which began to be produced in the United States in the 1830s and then underwent further improvements. The impact of this whole series of developments on productive capacity was enormous. Per hour, the hand press allowed roughly 250 impressions; the Adams steam press of 1830, 500 to 1,000 impressions; a double cylinder Napier press of the same period, 3,000 impressions; and the Hoe Type Revolving Machine of 1846, the first rotary press, 12,000 impressions.[41] Like the advances in papermaking, the new presses cut costs and enabled both book and newspaper publishing to scale up to larger runs on faster timetables.

Stereotyping, which came to America around 1811 from England, solved other problems. Traditionally, to be able to reprint a book, a printer needed either to keep the type standing (a substantial capital cost) or to reset it (a substantial cost in labor). With stereotyping, the set type was used to make lead molds from which metal plates were cast, freeing the type for other uses (and releasing capital for other investments). Since stereotypes made it cheaper to reprint a book when the demand arose, the technology helped to modulate print runs, cut inventory costs, and reduce the risk of being stuck with unsold copies. By investing in plates, the owner could also run multiple presses without having to make correspondingly large investments in type or causing wear to the type itself. The plates themselves could be rented or sold as part of joint publishing or other arrangements. Thus, the technology was a source of flexibility as well as economies of scale.[42]

As these new production technologies were emerging, other developments helped to reduce obstacles that publishers faced in long-distance distribution. The construction of canals and railroads and improvement of postal service not only reduced the cost but also increased the year-round reliability of distributing many products nationally, including books and other publications. A national market was in the making, enabling entrepreneurs to derive profit from technologies that would not have been rational investments for them if they had been confined to local sales. And it was not only commercial publishers who took advantage of these new conditions. So did spreading networks of voluntary associations. Indeed, as David Paul Nord has pointed out, the first to adopt new printing technologies to reach a mass public were Evangelical Christian publicists, who saw the possibility of producing and disseminating Bibles and religious tracts so cheaply that they could afford to give them away for free to every household. The movement to establish Bible and tract societies had begun under Jefferson, whom the Evangelicals loathed as an infidel—once again, political and religious conflict instigated a search for more effective communications. By 1814, there were more than 100 local Bible societies, two years later the American Bible Society was established, and in the 1820s it was joined by the American Tract Society in a movement that had close ties with counterparts in England. Basing their publishing operations in New York City, which had become the center for stereotyping, both American organizations invested heavily in stereotypes and Treadwell presses to turn out Bibles and religious tracts in unprecedented quantities. The Evangelicals, Nord writes, first "proposed to deliver the same printed message to *everyone* in America," and by the 1820s, they were able to do it using techniques of distribution as well as production that were later adopted by abolitionists and other reformers.[43]

In commercial book publishing, cost-cutting technologies had particular value in the high-volume business in popular British reprints. The firm that most effectively exploited this opportunity in the late 1820s and 1830s was J. and J. Harper, later Harper & Brothers, the leading American publishing house of the era. Established as a printing firm in New York City in 1817, Harper began to turn itself into a publisher around 1825, depending almost entirely on British reprints. Among book publishers, Harper was the first to make stereotyping routine for books it expected to reprint; it installed a Treadwell horse-powered press by 1828 and a steam-powered press five years later, giving it the capacity to turn out a million volumes a year. The technology helped the Harper brothers underprice their rivals. For example, when a battle erupted with another publisher over the novels of the popular British writer Maria Edgeworth, Harper was able to issue her complete works in ten volumes at 75 cents each, while its American competitor charged $19.50 for the set and the British publisher the equivalent of $67. Cheap publishing was developing in England around the same time; the publisher John Murray started his *Family Library* in April 1829 with books selling at 5 shillings (or about $1.20).[44] Imitating the idea, Harper established its own *Family Library*, which in fifteen years grew to 187 titles sold in cloth for 45 cents each. The risk in purchasing costly capital equipment is being stuck with unused capacity during periods when sales are slow. By selling low-priced books in series, Harper tried to assure itself a large and steady market to match its capacity for high-volume production.[45]

Cheap reprints of religious literature and British fiction were just the beginning. Soon there followed another innovation in cheap print, also initially centered in New York, that would represent a major landmark in the emergence of print as a popular medium. This was the advent of the penny press.

New Publics, New Markets

Political as well as economic changes contributed to the growth of the newspaper-reading public in the 1820s and 1830s. State governments moved to extend the franchise to all adult white men, eliminating the economic barriers that previously kept many of them from voting. New York State eliminated property qualifications in 1821 and taxpaying requirements in 1826—reforms that tripled the size of the electorate for the state senate and doubled it for the assembly as well as for Congress.[46] Endowed for the first time with full political rights, many workers had new reasons to pay attention to the news, and political parties had new reasons to pay attention to them.

The parties themselves, which had slumbered during the "era of good feeling" after the collapse of the Federalists, were undergoing a revival and transformation. In the aftermath of Andrew Jackson's defeat in the 1824 presidential election, his supporters built a nationwide Democratic party organization that reached down to the local level and included a network of newspapers to communicate with the electorate. While Jacksonian Democrats were the leading edge of this expansion of the partisan press, the more fundamental cause lay in a structural change in political competition. During the 1830s, the Whigs, and in some areas the Anti-Masons, also built party organizations and started or co-opted newspapers. With the advent of this "second party system," voting participation climbed dramatically, from 27 percent in 1824 to 56 percent in 1828 and 78 percent in 1840.[47]

Though much criticized by later historians, the partisan press (and the patronage that supported it) may well have been critical to party efforts to raise voter turnout; given the postal subsidy to the press, newspapers were the most efficacious means for parties to communicate with their supporters in a predominantly rural society. While party committees hibernated between elections, newspapers provided a continuing organizational base for party activity. Their editors played a central role in politics, defining their party's position on issues, publicizing its candidates, and imposing discipline on wayward political figures.[48] During the same period, urban artisans began to organize labor unions and to establish workingmen's publications, and many other groups pursuing such causes as temperance and abolition created their own periodicals as the first step toward organization. "Only a newspaper can put the same thought at the same time before a thousand readers," Tocqueville wrote after his 1830 visit to America. The absence of traditional ties among Americans, Tocqueville thought, made newspapers all the more necessary for voluntary cooperation. "Newspapers make associations, and associations make newspapers."[49] Ten years earlier, this pattern would not have been as striking; Tocqueville's visit came at a moment when the mutually reinforcing rise of the press and growth of political participation were in full swing.

Reductions in the cost of paper and print in this era no doubt contributed to the proliferation of political and reform-oriented papers, most of them weeklies with fewer than a thousand subscribers. But the economies of scale in cheap print also opened up possibilities for journalism of a different kind. Several publishing entrepreneurs had the same idea in the early 1830s: At a penny a copy, they could sell a newspaper to a wider market, including working-class readers, generating increased profits from advertising and affording wide influence over public opinion. The first penny paper to succeed was the *Sun*, launched in New York City in September 1833 by the twenty-two-year-old printer Benjamin H. Day, who had connections to local labor groups and was looking to expand his business. "The object of this paper," he announced, emphasizing its commercial ambitions, "is to lay before the public, at a price within the means of every one, all the news of the day, and at the same time offer an advantageous medium for advertisements." The city then had eleven daily papers with a total circulation of 26,500. Two years later, having upgraded from a hand press to a steam press, the *Sun* alone had a circulation approaching 20,000, making it the largest in the nation and inviting a series of penny competitors. The most important of these (and the only other New York penny paper to survive the decade) was the *Herald*, established in 1835 by one of the most inventive promoters of the era, the journalist James Gordon Bennett, and destined to become, during the middle decades of the nineteenth century, the largest-circulation newspaper in the world. Penny newspapers also sprang up during the same decade in Boston, Philadelphia, Baltimore, Cincinnati, and other cities.[50]

The basic formula of the penny press was to obtain a higher circulation and therefore more advertising on the basis not only of a low price, but also of a livelier product and a broadened view of the readership. Cutting the price to a penny or two was a dramatic move at a time when the established dailies cost 6 cents a copy and annual subscriptions were $8 to $10. (Subscription rates of $2 or even $1.50 for the weekly papers that dotted the country were less of a deterrent to popular readership.) A physical change reflected the new uses and wider market of the penny press. Instead of the oversized sheets used by New York's established dailies, which measured 3 feet high by 2 feet wide (4 feet wide when opened up), the penny papers were 12 inches by 18 inches or even smaller. A reader of the large-format papers would be most comfortable spreading them out at a desk or table, whereas a penny paper could be read on the go. With this new format came new modes of distribution. Previously, American newspapers were available only by subscription or by purchase at a newspaper office, and editors had long complained of the difficulty of collecting subscription debts. Day, in contrast, sold the *Sun* for 67 cents per 100 copies to newsboys, who hawked them on the streets, and to carriers, who delivered them to subscribers; he thereby transferred the day-to-day risks to his distributors and acquired a sales force with incentives for maximizing circulation that matched his own interests.[51] He also put advertising on a cash basis, insisting on payment in advance, and adjusted rates as his circulation grew.

Depending entirely on revenue from readers and advertisers, the publishers of penny papers proclaimed their independence of any political party and represented themselves as the unfettered champions of the public in reporting the news. No data are available to determine the demographic composition of their readership, but contemporary testimony suggests the two principal New York penny papers of the 1830s, the *Sun* and the *Herald*, found readers among artisans and other workers, while the *Herald* also drew businessmen (one of Bennett's innovations was coverage of the stock market).[52] They did not show the same interest, however, in broadening their audience across racial lines; indeed, it was the *Sun*'s refusal to publish a letter from a black writer named Willis Hodges, protesting the paper's campaign to retain property qualifications for black voters alone, that led Hodges to establish one of America's first black newspapers.[53]

The successful penny papers changed the scope and style of newspaper coverage to appeal to the new readers they sought among white working men. According to an analysis of five large-format metropolitan dailies for

1831–1832, politics accounted for just over half and business just under one-quarter of editorial content.[54] Shipping news was a staple; crime was recorded, but not reported as a story. The penny papers, while not abandoning politics and business, were written to be entertaining and included news about a wider scope of social life. Imitating an innovation in the London press that had been the basis of two books reprinted in America, Day had a reporter visit the police court and write up the news about crime, often treating petty cases in a facetious or whimsical fashion. Ordinary people figured in human-interest items. The papers did not shy from conflict; Bennett, in particular, built circulation with vituperative attacks on the institutions and people he disliked, especially his competitors. And while the penny papers expanded the scope of news, they also expanded journalism beyond news, publishing outright hoaxes, such as a notorious series in the *Sun* in 1835 about a British astronomer's supposed discovery of strange forms of life on the moon.[55]

No episode better reveals the manifold changes in the practice of journalism brought about by the penny press than the murder in April 1836 of a prostitute known as Helen Jewett and the ensuing trial of her former client and lover, a dry-goods clerk related to an influential merchant and politician. Crime literature had already emerged as a staple of popular fascination. In the 1700s, short pamphlets with ministers' execution sermons had given accounts of murders; by the early 1800s, journalists and lawyers were writing pamphlets eighteen to twenty-four pages long narrating crimes in bloody detail; and by the 1830s, pamphlets chronicled murders involving sexual relationships. The penny papers "leaped on the Jewett case," Patricia Cline Cohen writes in a book about the murder, "framing their storytelling in the conventions borrowed from the popular pamphlet literature on fatal crimes" and developing "an aesthetic of erotic murder."[56] Immediately after the killing, Bennett reported a visit he had made to the brothel where the crime had taken place, described the corpse to his readers ("The perfect figure, the exquisite limbs, the fine face, the full arms, the beautiful bust, all, all surpassed in every respect the Venus de Medici . . . "), and published an interview with the woman who kept the house.[57] Admiring biographers and historians regard Bennett's reporting as exemplary of a new model of journalism as active fact-gathering. Yet his descriptions of the corpse and crime scene seem drawn as much from his imagination as from observation, and the interview may have been fictitious (as was a supposed letter of confession by an anonymous writer that the *Herald* published a few days later).[58] The penny press may well mark an early stage in the rise of reporting, but it also marks the advent of journalism as form of entertainment in which fidelity to facts was subordinate to the interest in a compelling story.

The penny papers are often described as America's first popular, commercial newspapers, independent of political parties and truly devoted to "news" in the modern sense, but this view needs qualification. Popularization and commercialization were long-term developments that had been under way for decades when the penny press emerged. Weekly papers throughout the country already constituted a popular press, and these papers certainly published news, albeit of a particular kind. Some major dailies had begun employing reporters to cover Washington in the 1820s. Advertising was also extensive before the penny press; the earlier papers were already devoting the majority of their column space to advertising—far more than was typical in Britain at the time—though their relatively small circulations limited what they could charge.[59] The penny papers advanced these trends in new ways because they produced and packaged news of more diverse kinds to appeal to a larger urban audience. As a specifically urban phenomenon, the penny press anticipated later developments, but that is also what made it unrepresentative of the times. Since the development of penny papers came at a time when relatively few Americans lived in urban settings (in 1830 just 4 percent of the population lived in cities with more than 25,000 inhabitants[60]), they were not typical of the journalism that most Americans read in Jacksonian America. Nonpartisan penny papers did not replace the earlier partisan press; at the time the penny press appeared, partisan papers were increasing in number. A U.S. Census report of 1850 estimated that 80 percent of newspapers were partisan, and the great majority of newspapers continued to identify with a party into the second half of the nineteenth century.[61] Despite their declarations of independence, the penny papers themselves were also scarcely free of partisanship. When he founded the *New York Tribune* as a penny paper in April 1841, Horace Greeley later recalled, he had been "incited" by "several Whig friends, who deemed a cheap daily, addressed more especially to the laboring class, eminently needed in our city, where the only two cheap journals then and still existing—*The Sun* and *The Herald*—were in decided, though unavowed, and therefore more effective, sympathy and affiliation with the Democratic party."[62]

Nonetheless, the penny papers were an editorial and entrepreneurial innovation of singular importance. In their quest for circulation, they became the first papers in the United States to publish extensive coverage of local news and to turn news itself into entertainment. In their orientation to circulation-building and advertising—because they sold their readers to advertisers as much as they sold copies to readers—the penny papers anticipated the modern structure of media enterprise. Even if politically "incited," successful newspaper publishers such as Greeley were economically stronger than their predecessors had been and could more easily stand on their own and exercise independent political influence.

Larger circulations and new technology transformed newspapers as enterprises. Bennett was able to found the *Herald* in 1835 with only $500 and at first served as the entire editorial and business staff, running the newspaper out of a basement office. By 1840, the start-up cost for a daily in New York City ranged between $5,000 and $10,000 and by 1850 amounted to as much as $100,000.[63] Rising capital requirements for metropolitan dailies reflected the change from a craft to a bureaucratic mode of production as urban newspapers became corporate enterprises with a more extensive division of labor. The role of editor had emerged separate from that of printer at the beginning of the 1800s (indeed, the word "editor," meaning "one who conducts a newspaper or periodical publication," dates from that time); the role of the reporter came into its own with the penny press in the 1830s. Thanks to increased economies of scale from new printing technology, the penny newspapers could generate far more income from their high circulations than earlier papers could generate from their limited readership. As a result, they were able to support a greater original news-gathering capacity than any previous private organization of any kind—as would become apparent during the Civil War, when the *Herald* alone was able to send sixty-three reporters to cover the conflict.[64]

Two aspects of the penny papers—their focus on local news and independent news-gathering—were representative of general trends in American journalism. According to a study of sixty-seven daily and nondaily newspapers published between 1820 and 1860, news became more localized in two senses. First, an increasing proportion of news stories concerned events in a paper's hometown or state, while relatively fewer stories reported events taking place abroad or in Washington, D.C. Second, local editors and reporters, who wrote only 25 percent of news articles in their own papers during the years 1820 to 1832, increased their share of the total to 45 percent by 1847 to 1860, while the proportion clipped from other newspapers (or, in the later period, received by telegraph) fell from 54 percent to 38 percent.[65] During the middle decades of the nineteenth century, newspapers added sections entirely devoted to local news, and "city editor" often became the second most important position.[66] In other ways, however, remarkably little changed. The survey of sixty-seven papers found no significant shift during the antebellum period in the general subjects of stories (there was no reduction in attention to politics) or in the level of readability.[67]

Yet the sensationalism of the penny press was part of a more general cultural tendency in the early nineteenth century that profoundly affected publishing in America. Even before the penny papers, a popular pamphlet literature had emerged that included the chronicles of deadly crimes as well as moral tracts with lurid stories of human depravity. The early nineteenth century, according to David S. Reynolds, saw a shift in the literature of moral reform. The conventional literature emphasized "hopeful themes or characters" such as "the blissful home, the nurturing parent, the angelic child, the idyllic village environment, and self-improvement through hard work and moral discipline," while a growing literature of a more ambiguous character explored "dark forces of the human psyche" and "the grisly, sometimes perverse results of vice, such as shattered homes, sadomasochistic violence, eroticism, nightmare visions, and the disillusioning collapse of romantic ideals." Ostensibly condemning vice, these writings were filled with salacious and violent details that sometimes raised doubts about their true intent. In the early 1830s, for example, an antiprostitution reformer and Presbyterian minister named John R. McDowall published an Evangelical weekly about sexual depravity, *McDowall's Journal,* which briefly enjoyed a national circulation in the tens of thousands before a grand jury declared that it promoted "lewdness." McDowall himself was then suspended and defrocked by his own church for doing "scandalous things, too bad to name" (apparently having sex with one of the prostitutes he was supposed to be reforming).[68] Reform and sensationalism mixed together in another way in the pages of George Wilkes's *National Police Gazette,* a popular national weekly begun in 1845. The paper provided a steady diet of crime news along with politically charged denunciations of abuses by the police and the courts and entertaining biographies of criminals, reproduced in pamphlet form as *Lives of the Felons.*[69]

From 1820 to 1860, published fiction also increasingly satisfied similar interests in the sensational, the morbid, the criminal, and the erotic.[70] A vital interplay developed between the popular press in its various forms and more serious works of the imagination. The decades from 1830 to 1860 that saw the eruption of the popular press also saw the beginnings of a genuine indigenous literary tradition in America with the publication of the major works of Nathaniel Hawthorne, Herman Melville, Emerson, Edgar Allan Poe, and Walt Whitman. Rather than being alienated from the dominant popular culture, as some critics have pictured them, the writers of the "American renaissance" were deeply influenced, Reynolds argues, by the "new rhetorical strategies of popular texts." The new forms of popular expression not only supplied raw material recast by the major writers, but also opened up cultural possibilities for probing the darker and more ambiguous aspects of life. The major writers of the era did not simply reproduce the sensationalism of the cheap press; avid readers of the crime narratives and other popular journalism of the day, they transformed the sensibility of their time into enduring literature.[71]

Although it had advanced further in the United States than in Britain in the 1820s, the revolution of cheap print hit book publishing in America with even greater force at the end of the 1830s. The success of the penny papers provided a model for a new format for cheap fiction, so-called "story papers," produced in a newspaper format to obtain cheap postal rates for national distribution. These were generally eight pages in length, cost 5 or 6 cents apiece, and included a half dozen or so serialized stories as well as other miscellany. The first, *Brother Jonathan* ("Cheapest Reading in the World"), appeared in New York in 1839, and when its founding editors fell out with their publisher, they created a second, *New World.* Yet another format for cheap fiction, the dime novel, originated as fifty-page "novelettes" sold as extras to the readers of *New World* before becoming an industry in their own right.[72]

The competition posed by these cheap formats helped to keep prices for books low. During their brief career, the story papers forced Harper to cut its prices on cheap editions of popular English writers to 25 cents and even less. Although the story papers succumbed after the Post Office in 1843 denied them the right to mail at low newspaper rates, the dime novels and other cheap publications remained popular for decades. As a result, the standard price for books in cloth during the 1850s was 50 cents, with small volumes costing half as much.[73] Some literary works were published in a variety of editions for different classes of readers. The traditional view had associated high culture with an exclusive public and expensively produced books; writers with high aspirations occasionally brought out their own work at great personal cost in fine editions. But now a writer such as Henry Wadsworth Longfellow, a crossover poet with a popular as well as elite public, issued his own books (he owned the plates as well as the rights) not only in morocco-bound editions but also clad in brown paper at a cheap price accessible to the general public.[74] In effect, the lure of the popular market broke down the traditional hierarchy of taste that had been expressed in the physical form of the book.

The expansion of the popular market for newspapers and books created new means of commercial support for both the public sphere and imaginative literature, expanding and diversifying them. Although Anglo-Protestant writers dominated the landscape, by 1850 the market was helping to underwrite a growing body of published work in English by members of various minority cultures—Jewish and Irish immigrants and African and Native Americans—whose autobiographies and novels paid close attention to the distinctive consequences of social identity.[75] In eighteenth- and nineteenth-century Europe, the growth of cultural markets enabled authors and artists to escape dependency on royal and aristocratic patronage. So, too, in nineteenth-century America the growth of a popular market enabled the penny papers (and subsequently other newspapers) to escape dependency on party patronage and to represent themselves as an impartial source of news. Explaining the rise of the penny press, Michael Schudson calls it a phenomenon of a democratic market society.[76]

One might say the same of publishing generally in that era. By the 1840s, publishers were beginning to take on the role of patron that no court or aristocracy had ever filled in America. Because they could reach a national market, publishers could connect writers to enough readers for the former to derive significant earnings from their work. Instead of the early emphasis on journalism and practical instruction, publishing also began to provide a channel for imaginative literature. To be sure, many of the major early nineteenth-century authors still read today never enjoyed a comfortable livelihood from their writing. Nonetheless, American writers were accounting for about half of fiction titles by 1850 despite their disadvantages in competing with copyright-free foreign reprints, and not all of the American work was ephemeral. "Suddenly," writes the critic Larzer Ziff of this era, "there were American books of the first rank, not by prevailing provincial standards but by the standards of world literature."[77] A new public had taken shape, and with it had come more highly capitalized commercial publishing enterprises that were capable of taking risks on original books. Explaining the relative dearth of literary achievement in the antebellum South, Thomas Nelson Page writes, "There was genius enough to have founded a literature, but there were no publishers generally, and there was never any public."[78] The North had both, which put its writers in a stronger position to found the national literature—and they did.

Center and Periphery in Antebellum America

From the Revolution to the Civil War, America followed a distinctively decentralized path in communications. As a predominantly rural republic with a federal system of government, the United States generally resisted policies that would have concentrated communicative capacities institutionally or geographically. In early nineteenth-century Britain and France, in contrast, the center dominated the periphery in two senses. Urban centers enjoyed a sharp advantage over rural areas in such means of communication as printing and mail delivery, and in each country the metropolis at the seat of government entirely dominated the publishing of newspapers and books and other aspects of cultural life. These patterns bore the thumbprints of power. Until 1695 in Britain and 1789 in France, both states concentrated printers in proximity to power the better to control them; before and after those dates, they also built up cultural institutions in or near the capital and focused postal development in political and commercial centers. Even when the formal monopolies on print broke down, the gravitational power of the center did not. Writers and artists continued to flock to the metropolis in search of patronage and bureaucratic positions. London's booksellers and newspapers continued to dominate the press as a whole, and the French Revolution, far from dispersing communicative capacities, concentrated them even more in Paris. By the end of the eighteenth century, Tocqueville wrote in *The Old Regime and the French Revolution,* "Paris had absorbed the intellectual life of the whole country at the expense of the provinces," and Napoleon only furthered the process.[79]

In the United States, however, the nation's capital did not draw culture and communication into a political orbit. Things might have turned out differently if the Founders had located the capital permanently in New

York City or Philadelphia and if they or their successors had established authoritative cultural institutions in the capital. The same committee at the Constitutional Convention that recommended the provisions for copyright also deliberated on a proposal to create a national university but decided that the power to create one was already implied in the general authority over the capital district granted to Congress. George Washington proposed a national university in his first inaugural address, reserved land for it in 1796, and in his will designated shares of stock to be used in support of such an institution. Congress, however, failed to approve the proposal, and the provision in Washington's will never resulted in an endowment. Jefferson also favored the idea, and probably the best chance for it came at the beginning of his second term, when the treasury was running a surplus and he was at the peak of his influence. But in 1806, Congress declined once again to act, this time on a bill drafted by Joel Barlow, who thought the cause was "opposition of the schools and colleges already established, and the indifference of the great majority of Congressmen to anything but the material development of the country." During the early republic, objections to a national university focused on its cost and constitutionality but may also have stemmed, as a 1902 congressional committee speculated, from a feeling that the proposal was a form of "class legislation in the interest of the few and best conditioned."[80] The early presidents, including Jefferson, believed in developing an educated republican elite, but the Congress was more wary.

Two related proposals, however, did win congressional approval. After James Smithson, an Englishman who had never set foot in America, left a large bequest to the federal government for "an institution for the increase and diffusion of knowledge among men," Congress voted, not without controversy and delay, to accept the funds. But the new Smithsonian Institution, at last established in 1846, seventeen years after Smithson's death, was to have no students and offer no degrees, nor was it given any authority over other institutions of learning and culture.[81] And in 1862, when Congress finally adopted legislation introduced by Congressman Justin Morrill to provide federal resources for higher education, it granted land to the states to establish colleges, principally for teaching "agriculture and mechanic arts," instead of a single national university dedicated to training a republican elite. The land-grant college system followed the same pattern as earlier federal provisions for primary education and postal communication; the form that Congress gave to the distribution of federal resources ended up strengthening the periphery more than the center.

Although Washington, D.C., was never a factor in book publishing, between 1828 and 1860 there were the makings of a nationally dominant, government-subsidized newspaper press in the capital. The system was based on the power of politicians to control the flow of two critical resources: money and information. This was the period when presidents and congressional majorities routinely used printing contracts and other means to subsidize friendly newspapers. The single biggest beneficiary was typically the president's quasi-official newspaper. Before 1840, the houses of Congress also gave Washington papers exclusive access to reporters' galleries and thereby privileged those papers in transmitting news of congressional deliberations to the public—this at a time when the publication of political news was the core function of newspapers. In the heyday of the Washington press corps during the 1820s and 1830s, local papers around the country were on the receiving end of political news chains originating in the capital.

Several congressional decisions and long-term structural changes, however, contributed to the breakdown of the privileged-press system. In 1840, responding to rising complaints from newspapers around the country, Congress admitted out-of-town journalists to its reporters' galleries, eliminating the monopoly previously held by the Washington press. In 1846, after battles over the choice of congressional printers had become increasingly bitter, Congress began awarding contracts to the low bidder, but six years later it restored the old system. The costs of congressional printing had now soared out of control, raising concerns across party lines. The real break came in 1860, when after repeated scandals and investigations, the fractured Democrats as well as rising Republicans voted overwhelmingly to establish a Government Printing Office with its own printing plant and employees—a measure that succeeded in sharply reducing costs. Around the same time, President James Buchanan withdrew support from the newspaper created to support his administration because of its sympathy for secession, and on assuming office Lincoln did not attempt to build up a newspaper of his own in Washington. By this time, the rise of powerful dailies around the country reduced the political advantage to be gained from a party organ in Washington. In addition, the increasing revenue and newsgathering resources of such metropolitan dailies as the *New York Herald* reduced the reliance of the press on political handouts of both information and money. These developments ended the possibility that subsidized newspapers in Washington would dominate news throughout America.[82]

Postal policies adopted by Congress also had an important decentralizing effect on the press. From the first postal legislation in 1792, free exchange—the policy allowing editors to exchange copies with each other at no postal charge—had subsidized the little weeklies by providing a steady flow of free copy to them. Local papers also enjoyed some protection from competition by big-city rivals because of the extra half-cent a copy postage on newspapers sent interstate more than 100 miles. During the mid-nineteenth century, however, some newspapers, notably the *New York Tribune,* succeeded in developing weekly "country" editions that threatened the circulation of small-town papers. But in 1851, Congress voted to allow all weeklies to be mailed free to subscribers within their immediate county.[83] Since members of Congress depended on the support of local newspapers, it is no surprise that they attended to their interests. Here, constitutional structure (specifically, the mode of representation in the House) tended to reinforce local control of communications.

By mid-century, Congress was also opening up cheap postal service for other uses. While newspapers had enjoyed cheap access to the system, the Post Office had kept rates high for private letters, treated magazines less favorably than newspapers, and excluded books altogether. Since 1816, the cost of sending a letter on a single sheet had ranged from 6¼ to 25 cents, depending on distance; the postage on a single letter sent more than 300 miles could cost a day's wages for a laborer. Because letter writers were unwilling to pay in advance, the recipients often bore the cost, and many letters (and much postage) went uncollected. Then, in two acts in 1845 and 1851, Congress reduced the rates and reformed the system, following the example of reforms first introduced in Britain.[84] Instead of charging for letters by the sheet, the Post Office would charge by weight. As of 1851, with some exceptions, Congress cut the postage for letters sent anywhere in the United States to a flat rate of 3 cents (prepaid) per half ounce, a level that would remain more or less unchanged for a hundred years. The same era saw the introduction of postage stamps, which became mandatory in 1855. The discrimination against magazines had eased somewhat in 1825, which was partly the reason for growth in magazines in the second quarter of the nineteenth century (though they remained far less widely read than newspapers). In the 1851 legislation, Congress authorized the Post Office to deliver books, and the next year it gave books discount rates. The increased postal distribution of books and magazines was especially important to people in small towns and rural areas, who had no convenient retail access.[85]

In the early republic, book as well as newspaper publishing was widely dispersed in America, most strikingly in New England, where even villages in rural areas had printers who turned out their own editions. Between 1790 and 1829, for example, Alexander Pope's popular *Essay on Man* appeared in seventy-seven editions in New England, published by printers in thirty-five different towns. In Massachusetts on the eve of the Revolution in 1775, newspapers were published in only two other places besides Boston; by 1820, the state had twenty-three towns publishing a total of fifty-three papers.[86] The spread of common schools, printing facilities, newspapers, and post offices helped to develop capacities and opportunities in rural areas that in Europe were generally limited to cities. America was remarkable not only for its high overall levels of literacy and education, but also for the comparatively high literacy and school enrollment rates of its rural inhabitants outside of the South. The production of culture in America was not strictly a metropolitan phenomenon. While aspiring French writers were inexorably drawn to Paris, often ending up in the lower circles of its literary life, Americans who sought success in print were sometimes able to achieve it from villages on the rural periphery. The absence of any metropolitan monopoly on publishing made possible what one historian has called America's "village enlightenment."[87]

In book publishing, nonetheless, the metropolitan industry soon dwarfed the little world of village printers. Three publishing centers had emerged by the early nineteenth century: Boston, the early leader in the colonial period; Philadelphia, which had surpassed Boston around 1790; and New York City, which became preeminent roughly from 1820. Although government policy did not directly determine the locus of publishing centers, it had an indirect effect via the copyright system. Since publishers' profits depended on rapid reprints of copyright-free foreign books, they had strong incentives to locate in seaports with deep harbors, where they could have quick access to arriving ships and ready connections to the interior. The profits from the reprint business helped to provide the metropolitan firms with the capital to dominate other kinds of publishing. While the three leading publishing centers accounted for about half of fiction titles by American authors from 1800 to 1810, they produced more than 90 percent of native fiction by the end of the 1840s.[88]

The three publishing centers took on distinctly different roles. Despite the preeminence of New England writers in the antebellum period,

Boston remained more of a regional center in publishing, and Philadelphia tended to dominate publishing for the South. New York catapulted ahead of its rivals as a result of its advantages as a center of finance, its superior links to the west via canals and later railroads, and its early lead in stereotyping and industrial-scale publishing. During the antebellum decades, the city saw the emergence of such publishing houses as Putnam, Appleton, E.P. Dutton, and Scribner's. Along with Harper, these firms would make up the single most powerful center in the industry, though during the nineteenth century the city never established the hegemony over publishing that London and Paris enjoyed in their countries. Moreover, as the literary historian William Charvat argues, publishing centers in nineteenth-century America did not have the same functional significance that such centers had in Europe, where they often brought together authors as well as publishers in stable literary circles. In America, writers were relatively dispersed and literary circles tended to be short-lived.[89]

In antebellum America, the principal dynamic forces affecting communications pulled in different directions: Democracy tended to be the decentralizing force; capitalism and technology, the centralizing forces. In Britain and France, in contrast, the state had already been a powerful force for centralization before 1800, and technological change and the growing scale of enterprise in the nineteenth century reinforced that pattern. Constitutional structure and political forces in the United States held back the centralizing tendencies of capitalism in communications that the state accentuated in Europe.

The Civil War might well have changed this pattern, and to some extent it did. The war and its aftermath produced a stronger central government for three separate reasons. The war effort itself led to an increase in the fiscal and administrative capacities of the federal government and precipitated a suspension of rights, including, in some instances, freedom of the press. The South had been the principal source of support for states' rights, and its defeat weakened devolutionary pressures. And after the war, the enactment of the Thirteenth, Fourteenth, and Fifteenth Amendments created rights under the federal Constitution that were enforceable against the states and would later be interpreted to mean that the original Bill of Rights applied to the states as well. This was a revolutionary change in America's constitutional system, and it set in motion a long-term process toward a more powerful national government.

A comparison with Canada is instructive here. Both nations were originally divided between two societies: Quebec had been incorporated into

British North America as a distinct society with its own language and established church, and the slave South had developed as a distinct society within the United States. But whereas Quebec remained—indeed, still remains—an effective devolutionary force in Canada's political development, the American South after the Civil War did not. This difference set the stage for later struggles: When movements for minority rights emerged in both countries, they demanded more provincial autonomy in Canada and greater authority for the national government in the United States.[90]

In communications, specifically, the Civil War confirmed and prolonged the dependent position of the South. From the colonial to the antebellum era, the South had lagged in every dimension of communicative capacity—literacy rates, publishing centers, newspaper circulation, and transportation and communications networks. As the North moved ahead during and after the Civil War, the regional inequalities in communications development only increased. For example, newspaper circulation per capita had been 3.7 times higher in the North than in the South in 1860; by 1870, circulation per capita in the North was 5.5 times greater than in the South, and even ten years later it was 5.1 times greater.[91] The war itself had boosted central control of the press. During the war, Lincoln shut down several opposition papers, notably in border states, and his secretary of war, Edwin Stanton, sought to manage the news from the front.[92] Even when the war was over, the federal government continued to try to shape the press and the public sphere far more intrusively than it had during the antebellum era. No effort, however, was made to revive the prewar system of congressional patronage and a quasi-official presidential newspaper. The final vestiges of federal patronage, State Department payments to newspapers for publication of federal laws, were eliminated in 1875.[93]

Although publishing was concentrated in the Northeast, new publishing centers emerged in Chicago, St. Louis, and other cities in the West. According to 1878 postal data on the volume of mailed publications, New York stood first with just under a third of the total (32.1 percent); then came Chicago (7.9 percent), Boston (6.6 percent), Philadelphia (5.4 percent), St. Louis (4.3 percent), and Cincinnati (4.1 percent).[94] No single house dominated book publishing: As late as 1914, the largest publisher, Harper, accounted for only 2 percent of the industry's sales. In the late nineteenth and early twentieth centuries, newspapers, magazines, higher education, and other cultural institutions continued to be highly decentralized in the United States compared to the typical pattern in countries descended from absolutist states. The difference in the early paths of development left long-lasting effects. Power mapped itself onto communications. The greater diffusion and fragmentation of power in America produced a wider dispersion of communicative capacities.

The Consequences of Political Choice

Some may be tempted to say that publishing in America before the Civil War reflected the workings of a free market. But while America certainly had a freer press and a freer market than existed in many other countries, publishing scarcely developed in isolation from political decisions. America's constitutional structure, intellectual property law, protective tariffs and other tax policies, public investment in common schools, government printing and other means of patronage, and postal rates and regulations all had shaping effects.

In certain respects, the development of newspaper and book publishing after the Civil War extended trends that had begun in antebellum America. The transformation of newspapers into large-scale enterprises shifted power and influence in the press. As printers had given way to editors as the dominant figures in journalism in the early 1800s, so editors gave way to publishers. The growth of commercial advertising gradually reduced and then virtually eliminated the role of political patronage in the economics of daily newspapers. The shift to advertising did not simply liberate the press to serve the public; it created new commercial incentives and pressures. In response to demands from advertisers, many nineteenth-century papers inserted paid "reading notices" into their regular news columns and published "puffs" for products (including laudatory book reviews for publishers). Some editors resisted these crude forms of influence, but there was an inexorable trend away from the early republican conception of the newspaper. Instead of viewing their readers as citizens and their function as engaging their readers in politics, newspaper publishers tended to see their readers as consumers and the provision of news as a means of support for the advertising that was the foundation of their business.[95] Still, the growing revenues and profits of newspapers provided an economic basis for press autonomy and power that the early printers and editors never enjoyed.

Great Britain and France, unlike the United States, continued to constrain the economic development and autonomy of the press well into the nineteenth century. Until the 1850s, governments in Britain used covert bribes as well as stamp taxes to keep newspapers in line and prevent them from becoming agents of popular discontent; under this regime, the *Times* of London, the voice of the governing elite, held a commanding position in both circulation and influence. Even afterward, at least until the 1880s, the daily press remained largely in the grip of an orthodox conception of journalism that called for an impersonal, highly deferential account of Parliament and public life. Restrained in their typography as well as their content, British newspapers of the mid-1800s made little compromise with the popular reader, using small, generic headlines ("Latest Intelligence") and packing in text as tightly as possible, with no illustrations or subheadings for visual relief and ease of comprehension. Growing advertising revenue, however, did enable British dailies to support independent news-gathering by their own correspondents; the *Times,* in particular, had the most formidable team of international correspondents of any paper in the world. French newspapers were far slower to acquire formal autonomy and the independent sources of income to sustain it. Until 1877, they were subject to highly repressive legal restrictions, and even after formal controls ended, the major dailies remained dependent upon political patronage, while advertising represented a small share of their income. As a result, the French press continued throughout the nineteenth century to speak in partisan terms, to cultivate a more literary style, and to put relatively little emphasis on news gathering. Information in French papers, according to a comparative study by Jean Chalaby, was less extensive, less recent, less frequent, and less grounded in reporting than information in British and American papers. For example, during the second half of the nineteenth century, French newspapers had hardly any international correspondents while the major American as well as British newspapers were sending reporters to cover wars around the world and had permanent foreign correspondents in major capitals.[96]

It was in the Anglo-American world and primarily in the United States, as Chalaby argues, that the shift occurred toward the distinctive modes of inquiry and discourse of modern journalism (or as Chalaby calls it, a "journalism of information"). In America, beginning with political coverage in the 1820s, reporting not only became the primary job of the journalist but increasingly took on a brash character, trespassing previously understood boundaries of newsworthiness. In the mid-1800s, American newspapers began to convey the gist of the news in large headlines, still single-column in width but often arrayed in multiple decks, depending on the importance of a story. The news interview was perhaps the most striking American innovation. Before 1860, though journalists talked with sources when reporting events, their articles did not quote from those conversations or even refer to them. When the words of the powerful appeared in print, they were typically in the form of a prepared speech or essay, not on-the-spot responses to a reporter's questions. In the 1860s, interviewing began to take shape both as a set of practices and as a distinct journalistic genre, and it soon became firmly institutionalized in America despite the view of many politicians and businessmen that it was an impertinence. Two decades later, when the first interviews appeared in Britain and (to a lesser extent) France, the innovation was explicitly recognized as American.[97] Cultural and institutional differences were probably both at work here. America's more egalitarian, less deferential culture fostered the invention of a mode of journalistic inquiry that subjected important people to questioning by mere reporters. At the same time, the highly competitive American market encouraged newspapers not just to record but to create news (as they did in interviews) and to use interviews as a way of publicizing and currying favor with powerful subjects. In short, American journalism became more of an independent and innovative source of information just as it became more of a means of advertising and publicity.

A parallel process affected book publishers. Renewed growth in cheap, popular reading in the late 1800s led critics to complain about the commercialization of literature, while at the same time, by virtue of their greater capital, the major publishing houses also became more capable of assuming risk for literary projects. The two decades after 1870 saw an explosion of cheap books, mostly foreign novels, similar to the wave of the 1840s. Public policy continued to play a role through the continued absence of copyright protection for foreign authors as well as the establishment of cheap rates for mailing books, just 2 cents a pound (cut to 1 cent in 1885). And once again, falling paper prices and new printing technologies, combined with new methods of marketing, intensified the process. At the lower end of the market, "fiction factories" churned out dime novels, while cheap editions of more serious books were so widely available that no work on a list of the fifty best books in the world, chosen in 1887 by students at the University of California, cost more than 30 cents.[98]

Just as the story papers of the 1840s led the major publishers to seek relief through a change in postal policies, so the flood of cheap reprints in the 1870s and 1880s helped publishers to discover a need to revise the copyright law. By the late nineteenth century, the denial of copyright to foreigners no longer had the same economic significance that it had had in the early republic. Foreign reprints had been a highly profitable business in the early nineteenth century, and as long as Americans were primarily importers of culture, their interest in cheap books provided a widely accepted justification for denying copyright to foreign authors. This denial may have hurt American writers and perpetuated cultural dependence on Britain, but it had an immediate economic rationale, or so many publishers claimed, and the Congress agreed. As books by American authors began to sell abroad, however, the balance of interests began to shift. Growing support by American publishers and authors for international copyright was an early sign of the shifting position of the United States in global cultural exchange. During the last decades of the nineteenth century, Britain was inundated by a tidal wave of popular American fiction, much of which generated no income to American authors and publishers for lack of secure international copyright protection. Meanwhile, in Europe during the 1870s and 1880s, a movement in favor of international copyright, led by such notables as Victor Hugo, culminated in the adoption of the Berne convention of 1887, which committed countries signing the agreement to give foreign authors the same treatment they provided to their own citizens.

These developments finally helped to bring about a change in American law almost exactly a century after the first Copyright Act of 1790. Instead of adopting the Berne convention, however, Congress in 1891 passed the Platt-Simmonds Act, which provided for reciprocal agreements with other countries to secure rights for American authors abroad and provide rights for foreign authors in the United States. Protectionism, however, had not disappeared; unlike the Berne convention, the act required that copyrighted books by foreign authors be manufactured in the United States. By eliminating the price advantage that foreign fiction had enjoyed while free of copyright, the legislation may have promoted a shift in publishing toward American novelists, though this was already happening beforehand. Some evidence also suggests a narrowing of differences in the content of books by foreign and domestic authors published in the United States.[99] Although cheap foreign reprints declined, the dime novels and other cheap books continued to be a fixture of the mass market.

In the early republic, advocates of policies favoring newspapers and cheap print as well as education and the postal service had argued that all of these would aid the "diffusion of useful knowledge." The institutions they created did not remedy the deepest injustices of their society, endow their posterity with wisdom, or avert civil war, but to a considerable extent they achieved their intended civic and commercial objectives. American newspapers carried news that helped their readers to act as competent citizens and enabled them to organize for public purposes. The channel that the press provided for communication between parties and the electorate raised levels of voting participation. Cheap print put information into broader circulation further down the social hierarchy than ever before. Cheap publications for farmers and mechanics, for example, diffused practical knowledge that contributed to the rapid diffusion of new technologies in nineteenth-century America. Even consumer advertising may have had economic benefits by permitting the more rapid introduction of new products in America than in Europe. In these and other ways, the politically driven path of development in American communications paid off economically.

But as tidal movements have their countercurrents, so in the late nineteenth century cheap print became the focal point of moral anxieties. Especially when first introduced, new forms of popular culture often seem to many people to be dangerous and vulgar. This was the initial elite response to the penny press and the dime novel. In the early years of the penny press, the six-penny papers attacked Bennett's *New York Herald* in a "moral war." Sensational fiction set off the same kind of disapproving response from both rival publishers and guardians of public taste. In the antebellum years, these efforts had little success—the *Herald* prospered and cheap fiction continued to be distributed. But after the Civil War, amid rising anxieties among older-stock elites, America entered a more repressive era in communications as in politics generally. Crusades for reform became crusades for restriction, employing the power of the state aggressively, though in the end with little success, to ward off tidal changes in American culture. New technologies also created new occasions for public decisions about communications and new opportunities for monopolizing as well as diffusing knowledge. These developments threatened to take American communications along a much different path from the one it had started on.

PART TWO

The Rise of Technological Networks 1840–1930

CHAPTER FIVE

The First Wire

THE ADVENT of the electric telegraph in the 1840s was as much a political as a technological milestone. The telegraph inaugurated a new phase in the history of communications, the rise of modern technological networks, and precipitated divergent national decisions about the role of the state that outlasted the telegraph itself. The new networks promised faster connections of people and places, of markets, armies, and governments—a change that was already in progress because of improvements in transportation. Steam power had only recently begun to accelerate movement on the oceans, rivers, and rails when the "lightning" of the telegraph decoupled communication from transportation altogether. But many obstacles stood in the way of stretching the new iron cords across continents. Different jurisdictions and systems had conflicting policies and standards that needed to be reconciled, and the new networks required large capital investments as well as innovations in engineering and management. As in other formative periods, new technologies posed new choices: Would state security, commercial, or other interests guide the development of the new networks? What form of organization would they take? What sources would provide the capital and assume the risks? And by what means would the networks be integrated so communication could flow uninterrupted over long distances and across borders?

European nations and the United States responded differently to these constitutive choices. In Europe, the domestic telegraph, and later the telephone, came under the control of the state and were often assimilated into the organization of the postal system. In the United States, in contrast, both the telegraph and the telephone were established as private enterprise and went through a phase of intense competition before evolving into monopolies and becoming subject to government regulation. (International submarine cable lines, primarily British, were also chiefly run as private businesses.) The differences between Europe and America involved more than ownership. American law and policy, as well as other conditions, were more favorable to telecommunications development and led to more rapid, early deployment of the technologies. Indeed, Americans played more of a pioneering role in developing both the telegraph and the telephone than one might reasonably have expected from the country's overall level of industrial and scientific development in the mid-nineteenth century.

Different patterns, however, emerged in the telegraph and telephone networks. The telegraph in America became a service primarily for business; the first national monopoly, it also served as the basis for an unprecedented private monopoly in the national distribution of news. Ironically, the telegraph in private hands proved to be a far more powerful means of centralized control of information than the federally operated Post Office had been in the pre-telegraphic era. The telephone, in contrast, served households as well as businesses, and telephone service became far more widely diffused in the United States—particularly outside of metropolitan areas—than in any country in Europe. Whereas the telegraph departed from the social patterns originally established with the Post Office, the telephone returned toward them.

Since the telegraph was the first electrical communications network—indeed, the first electrical technology of any kind to find practical application—it stands at the head of a long line of innovations, and many historians tend to see in it the shape of things to come. One popular history, for example, calls it the "Victorian Internet."[1] There is a danger, however, of reading the subsequent history of telecommunications into the beginnings; we may exaggerate what was of secondary importance in the past because it is of primary importance in the present. The novelty and tangibility of inventions also make them more easily understood as history's prime movers. At the time the telegraph and telephone were introduced, contemporary observers attributed to them vast social and economic effects, and historians have tended to do the same, often suggesting that the modern communications revolution begins with the telegraph.[2]

But as the previous chapters have shown, the telegraph arrived in a world already revolutionized, and its development continued a process that other forces had set in motion. Even in the dimension that the telegraph most directly affected—the speed of communication over long distances—the advances in postal service and transportation during the preceding decades had already resulted in considerable change. For example, the time it took for news to travel between Charleston, South Carolina, and New York City fell from 20.2 days in 1794 to 5.5 days in 1841; by that time, the news lag between Washington and Boston had fallen from 18 days in 1790 to only 2.8 days.[3] Taking a more skeptical view of the early social impact of the telegraph and telephone, several recent studies have underlined the limits of the initial uses of the technologies and cautioned against an overemphasis on new inventions at the expense of less dramatic changes, such as improvements in postal service, that affected a far larger volume of communication.[4] This more cautious view of early effects, however, should not obscure the profound long-run consequences of early choices about the telegraph and telephone. The new technologies created divergent possibilities. They could expand social connections, increasing the possibilities of association, exchange, and diffusion of information, but they also created new means of controlling communication that the state or private monopolists might use for their own purposes. Since the technologies themselves did not determine which possibilities would be realized, it is tricky to talk about their effects. The effects depended on the path of development they followed, and that path depended critically on political decisions.

A Path for the Telegraph

It may seem self-evident why Europeans adopted public enterprise and Americans private enterprise in telecommunications: Weren't the Europeans statists, while Americans were devoted to laissez-faire? Don't general differences in ideology or "policy paradigms" explain the specific differences in communications? Although the continental European development of the telegraph and telephone fits this straightforward account, neither America's original decision for private development in 1845–1846 nor Britain's later turn from private to state enterprise in 1870 has so easy an explanation.

Contrary to the mythology of laissez-faire, nineteenth-century Americans did not leave economic development entirely to private initiative. Government played a central role not just in the postal system but also in the two major transportation networks under construction in the decades preceding the telegraph. Between 1817 and 1824, the state of New York built the Erie Canal, a project so immensely successful that it led to a burst of government-financed canal construction. Beginning around 1830, states and cities also underwrote the development of railroads, such as the Baltimore & Ohio; most of this was originally in the form of mixed public-private investment rather than state enterprise. Altogether, public sources provided about 70 percent of the financing for canals as well as 25–30 percent of investment in railroads from 1815 to 1861, a period when Britain relied on private capital to build most of its canals and all of its railroads. Three principal reasons have usually been cited for the greater reliance on government in the United States. First, private capital was more scarce. Second, instead of connecting populated areas, many of the projects were "developmental": They connected a settled area with one that was expected to develop and, as a result, could not be expected to generate an immediate enough return to satisfy investors. And, third, states and cities competed with one another by investing in transportation projects that would improve their prospects for development.[5]

If this pattern had carried over to the telegraph, the United States would have been more likely than Britain to develop it under state auspices. As the leading historian of "internal improvements" in antebellum America writes, Americans did not consider the general strictures against governmental involvement in business activity to apply to communications.[6] To be sure, the investment in canals and railroads came from state and local government, not Washington, and the federal government as of the 1840s had relatively limited administrative capacities compared with Britain. But the Post Office was the one field in which the U.S. government did possess those capacities, and the extension of its activities to embrace the telegraph seemed a logical step to many at the time. The generally limited structural capacity of the federal government did not dictate the outcome. The causes that led America to private deployment of the telegraph were, in the first instance, conjunctural—that is, they arose from the conjunction of political forces at a critical, constitutive phase in the development of the new medium.[7]

The origins of the telegraph in Europe lay with concerns of state. The concept of the telegraph, indeed the word itself, which means "distant writer," came from a signaling system developed in revolutionary France and adopted primarily for military purposes. Conceived by Claude Chappe and first put into operation between Paris and Lille in 1794, the optical semaphore telegraph enabled operators stationed on a line of towers to send and relay messages by varying the positions of a large rotating bar with rotating arms. While the Chappe telegraph had obvious drawbacks—it was costly, limited in the information it could carry, and unusable at night or in bad weather—it did have strategic value. Napoleon used it to extend and maintain his empire, and the British erected their own visual telegraph to speed communication between London and England's southern coast. But in 1816, when the war in Europe was over, the British secretary of the Admiralty rejected a proposal for a new kind of telegraph based on electricity. "Telegraphs of any kind are now wholly unnecessary," he wrote, adding that none but the one in use would be supported. Made available for limited commercial use, optical telegraphs continued to develop, and by 1830 European governments operated about a thousand towers. When a private company set up a line between Paris and Rouen in 1834, the French government closed it down; three years later, France officially made the telegraph a state monopoly.[8]

In the United States, the federal government took no action on the optical telegraph, though proponents urged Jefferson as early as 1807 and Madison at the time of the War of 1812 to build one. The concept became widely enough known, however, for the word "telegraph" to be adopted in the names of dozens of newspapers, including the *United States Telegraph,* the leading Jacksonian organ from 1826 to 1831. Several small commercial optical telegraph lines, such as one from Martha's Vineyard to Boston, provided early notice of arriving ships. But these were not so profitable as to be widely imitated, and there appeared to be no prospect of governmental backing until 1837, when a petition urging development of an optical telegraph from New York to New Orleans led the House of Representatives to ask the secretary of the treasury to conduct an inquiry into "the propriety of establishing a system of telegraphs for the United States."[9] It was as a result of this inquiry that federal officials first witnessed a working prototype of a new alternative—an electromagnetic telegraph.

Ever since the late 1700s, scientists had been trying to use electricity to transmit intelligence, but fundamental limitations in knowledge stood in their way. Breakthroughs in two areas of science finally put the goal within reach. In electrochemistry, Alessandro Volta's invention of the battery in 1800 made it possible to supply a steady electrical current. And in electromagnetism, the key developments came in rapid succession after 1820, when Hans Christian Ørsted discovered that passing a current through a wire deflected the needle of a compass. Four years later, William Sturgeon invented the electromagnet by passing a current through a coil wound around a piece of iron, and by 1831 Joseph Henry had shown how to overcome the diminution of the current that otherwise limited electromagnetic effects to a short distance.

Bolstered by new knowledge, scientists began working on many different competing ideas for electric telegraphs. The principal designs in Europe were "needle" telegraphs in which an electric current conveyed information by giving direction to a needle pointing to letters and numbers on a dial. In 1837, the distinguished British scientist Charles Wheatstone, in uneasy collaboration with William Fothergill Cooke, obtained a British patent for the needle telegraph that would dominate early development of the medium in that country. Meanwhile, in America, beginning in 1832, Samuel F.B. Morse invented a telegraph on an entirely different model, using an electromagnet to move an armature, which recorded the message in dots and dashes. Morse first publicly demonstrated his telegraph in 1837, brought it to Washington the following February, and succeeded in getting the Commerce Committee of the House of Representatives to approve a bill to finance an experimental line. The measure, however, failed to gain approval from Congress as a whole. Traveling to Europe, he found it impossible to overcome the political obstacles there as well. The British government denied him a patent on a technicality, almost certainly because of influence exercised on behalf of Wheatstone and Cooke, and the French awarded Morse a patent but took no action to develop an electric telegraph. Meanwhile, Wheatstone and Cooke received private financing, and a German inventor obtained patronage from the king of Bavaria to build a line.[10]

The British were the first to deploy a regularly functioning electric telegraph over a substantial distance. In 1838, Cooke entered into a contract with the Great Western Railway to build a telegraph line of 13.5 miles, which opened the following July. The contract reflected a complementary relationship between the two emerging industries. While the railroads gave the telegraph a valuable right-of-way, the telegraph enabled railroads to coordinate trains and avoid collisions. By 1845, Cooke and Wheatstone were involved in deploying 550 miles of telegraph along railways, and when the Electric Telegraph Company was incorporated in

1846 to buy out their patents and develop the telegraph, its board of directors featured leading capitalists from the railroad industry. For the next twenty-four years, the development of the telegraph in Britain was left entirely to private capital.[11]

On the continent, where development generally began later than in Britain, the state took control of the electric telegraph as it had its optical predecessor. "Telegraphy should be a political instrument, and not a commercial instrument," the French minister of the interior stated in 1847. The locus of authority in the government reflected that understanding; the Interior Department, which controlled the national police, administered the French state telegraph until 1878.[12] As of the early 1850s, no one in France could send a telegraph without government permission. Even after European governments opened up the telegraph to more general public use, they still retained powers of surveillance; until 1865, they generally banned the private use of ciphers or codes so that all telegrams would be open to government scrutiny. In these respects, they repeated the early history of postal systems as mechanisms of state security. On the European continent, according to one historian, private entrepreneurs "simply failed to present their appearance. . . . The general public showed no desire to share in the use of this time-saving contrivance. . . . The public administrative and military authorities alone displayed any active interest in the improvement of existing means of communication."[13] The absence of private entrepreneurs may have stemmed, however, from the high political risk—the likelihood of nationalization—even if a private telegraph had been temporarily allowed.

Another factor that slowed the takeoff of the telegraph in Europe was political fragmentation. The value of telegraph communication depended on the savings in time, and as a general rule, time savings were greater the further the distance of a transmission. Long-distance telegraph networks in Europe, however, required negotiations among independent states. With Germany still divided, for example, twelve governments had to agree to build a single telegraph line from Berlin to the Belgian border. A telegraphic congress in 1850 led to the formation of an Austro-German Telegraphic Union and the standardization of continental telegraphy on the Morse system, but the fragmentation of authority continued to impede development.[14]

The United States benefited from the absence of these political and historical burdens. The nation covered a large and expanding territory, and the considerable distance of its commercial centers from one another made the telegraph especially valuable. Never having developed an optical telegraph for military purposes, Americans also did not approach the electric telegraph with the kind of legacy paradigm that weighed upon its development in Europe. The United States, however, was generally not in the forefront of scientific developments; all the fundamental advances leading up to the telegraph, except those of Joseph Henry, came from Europe. And the American who pioneered development of the telegraph labored for years without significant governmental or private patronage.

Morse's development of the electromagnetic telegraph is a study in the difficulties that confronted large-scale technological innovation in mid-nineteenth-century America. A painter by profession, educated at Yale but without personal wealth, Morse initially financed his research out of his own pocket, using space available to him at the University of the City of New York (now New York University [NYU]), where he was appointed professor in the fine arts in 1835. Then, when faced with both technical and political obstacles, he obtained help from others using the one material asset that was available to him: shares in the ownership of the eventual patent. On his own, as an amateur scientist and inventor, Morse was able to build a prototype in 1835 that operated successfully over a 40-foot line in his studio, but he lacked the scientific knowledge to scale it up to long distances and the mechanical skill to build more than a crude mechanism. In published work and classroom demonstrations at Princeton unknown to Morse, Joseph Henry had already solved the distance barrier and even foreseen the potential application to a telegraph, but Henry confined his own interests to scientific research and teaching.[15]

At this point, between 1835 and 1838, two people provided Morse with critical resources. Leonard Gale, a scientist at NYU who was familiar with Henry's discoveries, worked with Morse to extend the range of the telegraph to 10 miles (Morse himself contributed a key component, the relay, which extended it even further). And Albert Vail, a recent graduate and son of the proprietor of one of the most advanced iron works in America, brought his family's resources and personal ingenuity to the task of refining Morse's instruments. Both received a share in the future patent, which Morse did not obtain until 1840, though he filed a *caveat* (preliminary notice) with the Patent Office in 1837. And when Morse went to Washington in 1838 to seek the support of the Congress, he made a deal with the chairman of the House Commerce Committee, Representative Francis

O.J. Smith, who was impressed by the invention. In March, Morse signed an agreement giving Smith one-quarter of the American patent rights (and five-sixteenths of foreign rights) in return for his services. The next month, Smith's committee approved the bill and sent it to the floor of the House, without Smith publicly acknowledging his financial interest.[16] (The word "bribery" is strangely absent from the historical accounts of these events.)

After Congress failed to act in 1838, Morse continued to look to the federal government for help. In his 1838 approach to Congress, Morse had expressed a worry that if controlled by a "company of speculators," the telegraph could be "the means of enriching the corporation at the expense of the bankruptcy of thousands," but that "in the hands of Government alone" it could also do "vast mischief to the republic." As a solution to this dilemma, he proposed that the federal government own the rights to the telegraph, reserve a telegraph line for its own official use, and license private lines to promote "a general competition."[17] A year later, with the United States in the grips of an economic depression, Morse wrote to Vail that while the British and Germans were going ahead, "Whether ours is to be adopted depends on the Government or on a company, and the times are unfavorable for the formation of a company."[18]

In national politics at this time, the Whigs were the principal supporters of federal programs fostering "internal improvements." Morse's moment of political opportunity finally arrived when party control of the Congress and presidency switched hands after the Whig victory in the 1840 election. Still, considerable skepticism and ignorance surrounded the notion of an electric telegraph, even though the British had already deployed their version and Morse had a letter of endorsement from Joseph Henry as well as an earlier positive evaluation by Philadelphia's Franklin Institute. By this time, Smith was out of Congress and no help to Morse. Nonetheless, in 1842, by a margin of just six votes, 89 to 83, with 70 members not voting, the House passed a bill appropriating $30,000 for a test of Morse's telegraph. The Senate approved the measure only shortly before adjournment in March 1843, and President John Tyler signed it into law. Most of the support in Congress for Morse's telegraph—as for other developmental programs during the antebellum era—predictably came from representatives of northern states, where support for federally sponsored developmental measures was strongest.[19]

As a result of this legislation, the federal government financed and owned the first telegraph line in the United States—the first telegraph anywhere available for public use. In approving the funds, Congress was supplying the seed investment, or, as we might say today, the venture capital, and Morse himself took charge of the project, which involved building a line of 40 miles between Washington and Baltimore. At this point, many of the basic engineering problems, such as whether to put the telegraph lines above or below ground and how to insulate the wires, remained unsolved. The project, therefore, did for the telegraph what the Erie Canal had done for canal building and the Baltimore & Ohio had done for railroad construction: It served as a publicly financed engineering laboratory. Indeed, the project nearly failed when Morse and his colleagues used up $23,000 in laying underground wires that were so poorly insulated that the line didn't work; fortunately, they were able to correct their mistake and rebuild the line above ground rapidly enough to finish on time.

Since the federal government was sponsoring the new medium, the political class was naturally the chief audience for the first demonstrations of the telegraph. On May 1, 1844, with the line extending only as far as Annapolis Junction, Vail transmitted a message to Washington that the Whig Convention in Baltimore had nominated Henry Clay for president and Theodore Frelinghuysen for vice president. Since Clay's nomination had been a foregone conclusion, the vice presidential choice was the first genuine news ever carried by wire in America and, arriving before a train from Baltimore, the first public proof that the telegraph worked. On May 25, when service from Baltimore officially began, Morse telegraphed his famous message, "What hath God wrought?" And four days later, when the Democratic convention, also in Baltimore, nominated James Polk for president and Silas Wright for vice president, the telegraph transmitted not only the news from the convention, but also the response from Senator Wright in Washington declining the nomination. The role the telegraph played in these national political events assured maximum press exposure around the country, though it didn't necessarily gain Morse the political support he wanted. Ironically, the national platform adopted by the Democrats that year included a categorical rejection of the power "to commence or carry on a general system of internal improvements."[20]

Technically a success, the Baltimore-Washington line nonetheless appeared to be a practical failure. During the first year, it ran at only 15 percent of capacity; even while the service was free, few messages were sent, and when the government began to charge, the revenue did not cover expenses. At first, the telegraph was primarily a novelty (as a stunt, the operators played chess a city apart); the commercial practices that would eventually lead to greater use of the telegraph had not yet developed. Besides, the Baltimore-Washington line didn't save that much time in sending messages since it connected two nearby cities already linked by rail. Nonetheless, there was much influential support for the government to develop the technology nationally. Morse himself, in an appeal to Congress in December 1844, offered to sell all the rights to the government for an unnamed lump sum. Concerned that if the telegraph were left in the hands of "private individuals," they would be able to "monopolize intelligence," Clay wrote to Vail shortly before the 1844 presidential election that he thought "such an engine ought to be exclusively under the control of government." Similarly, a group of merchants in Baltimore saw government operation as preferable because a private owner could use the telegraph to manipulate markets at their expense. James Gordon Bennett spoke for the dominant view among the nation's editors when he wrote in the *New York Herald* that "government must be impelled to take hold" of the telegraph and develop it as part of the Post Office. Postmaster General Cave Johnson—to whom authority over the Baltimore-Washington line had been transferred—also argued in his annual report at the end of 1845 that the government should buy the rights from Morse, even though he doubted that the telegraph could ever generate enough revenue to pay for itself: "The use of an instrument so powerful for good or evil cannot with safety to the people be left in the hands of private individuals uncontrolled by law."[21] Nonetheless, Congress declined to purchase the rights from Morse or to develop the telegraph further and the next year instructed the postmaster general to lease or sell the Washington-Baltimore line.

Why did the federal government leave the deployment of the telegraph to private capital? The decision reflected the political configuration of the time, particularly as it affected the prevailing view of the proper relationship between government and business enterprise. The outcome of the 1844 election, though it may not have been the decisive factor, hurt the chances for federal acceptance of Morse's offer to sell rights to the telegraph. While the Whig candidate Clay favored federal control, the Democrats who won the election opposed federal financing of developmental projects. As president, Polk sought to enlarge the nation without enlarging the state; he championed the continental expansion of the United States but blocked major developmental legislation, effectively taking internal improvements off the national agenda.[22] There was a strong sectional aspect to the opposition to developmental legislation before the Civil War. As the conflict between slave and free states became central to national politics, southern opposition to measures that would strengthen the industrial North became a key obstacle to any such legislation. Once the South seceded, a series of developmental policies cleared Congress in the early 1860s. Federal purchase of the telegraph arose, however, during the preceding era, when southern votes held back such policies.[23]

The decision about the telegraph also came at a time when throughout the country, including the North, there was "an abrupt turning away from the policy of state action for internal improvements."[24] During the early 1840s, as a result of a deep depression, the failure of many of the canal and railroad development projects brought about a fiscal crisis in the states. Pennsylvania, Maryland, Indiana, Illinois, and Michigan temporarily defaulted on interest payments, and many states began to adopt constitutional and statutory restrictions on their entanglements with business enterprise. Although this "revulsion" against internal improvements did not, in fact, end state participation in railroads and other projects, it represented an important watershed. The states turned against these projects for one principal reason: "They lost money."[25] And that seemed to be the case with the telegraph; even the postmaster general, who favored purchase of the rights, was unsure it could ever pay its way.

Conversely, the 1840s also saw a turn by entrepreneurs toward reliance on private capital for projects that they expected to be profitable. The early railroad promoters looked to government for patronage; even in soliciting private funds, they originally framed the project as a matter of public benefit rather than profit. Later promoters, however, envisioned railroads as profit-making enterprises from the start.[26] The decision about the telegraph arose at a transitional moment. Morse's early pursuit of government patronage and the subsequent privatization of the telegraph followed the same path that railroad finance traveled.

Some might argue that European states conceptualized the telegraph as a military instrument because of the imperatives that war imposed upon them. The idea that war is the mother of the state is a staple of comparative history.[27] Yet the Mexican War, which began while the U.S. government was still deciding whether to buy out Morse, did not alter the decision to leave the telegraph in private hands. Nor, for that matter, did the Civil War alter the decision to privatize the American telegraph.

These wars, however, did not institutionalize either a large-scale military establishment or a military framework for technological development.

A federally owned and operated telegraph was probably more likely at the founding moment of the telegraph network, 1844 to 1846, than at any later time. Since Morse himself, as well as many commercial groups and newspapers, supported making the telegraph a permanent part of the Post Office, there would have been no private interest to override. The decision might have gone the other way if it had come up earlier, if the Whigs had won the 1844 election, or if the demonstration line, instead of stopping in Baltimore, had gone as far as New York City and generated a greater immediate return. And if the telegraph had become a service of the Post Office, it might have been used for patronage and generated other political interests that would have made it difficult to privatize later. (Some people at the time opposed a federal takeover precisely because of the potential for patronage.) For better or worse, once the twig was bent, the tree started to grow in a particular direction—private interests accumulated, ideological defenses developed, and what was once an open question became a hardened institutional reality.

Monopoly on the Wires

The new network industries of the nineteenth century—canals, railroads, and telegraph, which came in the industrial revolution's first wave, and gas and electrical supply, urban transit systems, and the telephone, which came in the second—had common economic characteristics that, sooner or later, prompted calls for government intervention. Capital costs typically represented a high proportion of total expenses. There were strong, if not always imperative, pressures toward integrated operation of the networks. And, as a result, whether or not they started that way, the industries tended toward consolidation, often amid the widespread belief that they were "natural monopolies."[28] State intervention could come at the initial deployment of the network. But if the industry started off entirely in private hands, the state might also intervene at a secondary point when market failures emerged and the industry developed into a monopoly or price-fixing cartel. During the 1840s, Britain and the United States were the only countries to leave the telegraph to private capital. In a relatively short period, however, many of the typical problems of competition in a network industry began to emerge, and by the mid-1860s both Britain and America had growing movements to nationalize the telegraph. But there the two countries' paths in telecommunications diverged, as the British government took over the domestic telegraph and made it a part of its postal system and the United States did not.

From the mid-1840s to 1870, while still in private hands, the British telegraph industry developed differently from its American counterpart. From an early date it had more of an international orientation. The first international submarine cable, between Dover and Calais, opened to the public in November 1851 and was soon followed by cables to Ireland and to Holland; later, submarine cables would extend to British colonies all over the world. International traffic became an important source of telegraph revenue in Britain as it did elsewhere in Europe, especially in such strategically positioned countries as Belgium.[29] The orientation of the American telegraph industry was almost entirely domestic, although as a result of the Mexican War and the extension of American territory to include Texas, California, and Oregon, the United States now reached across the continent and provided telegraph entrepreneurs with a vast frontier of development. Domestically, the British industry took the form of a relatively stable cartel that eventually involved two major companies and three smaller ones, each established to work different telegraph patents. The American industry, in contrast, first splintered into a large number of firms—more than fifty different companies, as of 1851—and then underwent consolidation, ultimately leaving a single corporation, Western Union, in control.

The greater ability of Britain's telegraph companies to achieve a modus vivendi and operate as a price-fixing cartel helped to trigger the series of events that led to the industry's undoing. In July 1865, opting for slower sales growth and higher profitability, the companies agreed to impose higher prices, triggering a wave of criticism. What especially mattered was the source of outrage: leading commercial interests and the press. In a view soon endorsed by the Association of Chambers of Commerce, the Edinburgh Chamber called for nationalization.[30] The leading newspapers, which had long-standing grievances with the service by the telegraph companies, turned sharply against them. Criticism had been growing during the previous decade even in quarters where one might least suspect it. In 1861, John Lewis Ricardo—the founding chairman of the Electric Telegraph Company, a nephew of the great economist David

Ricardo, and a leading free-trade advocate in his own right—sent a confidential memorandum to the chancellor of the Exchequer, William Gladstone, urging that the Post Office take over the telegraph.[31] While the memo did not immediately have any effect, it reflected the rise of an influential view that competition in telegraph services was inefficient. When opposition exploded in 1865, it tended to focus on the same litany of complaints concerning high rates, low reliability, and the inconvenient location of telegraph offices. Critics cited data (for 1859) showing that Americans used three times the number of telegrams per capita at less than half the cost per telegram, and they compared telegraph service in Britain unfavorably with that available through state telegraphs on the continent, particularly in Belgium and Switzerland.[32]

But the discontent with the telegraph industry in Britain might have resulted in other policies besides nationalization had it not been for the legacy of postal reform in Victorian Britain. In 1840, responding to a pamphlet by the reformer Rowland Hill and pressure from independent radical members of Parliament who held crucial swing votes, the government adopted policies that drastically simplified postal operations. Hill had argued that instead of charging varying rates according to distance, the Post Office could cut rates to a penny, payable in advance, for a letter sent anywhere in the United Kingdom. While revenue per letter would fall, volume would increase and the Post Office would achieve substantial savings because postmen would no longer spend time trying, often fruitlessly, to collect postage from recipients. As an aside in the second edition of his famous pamphlet, Hill suggested that payment of the postage could be validated through adhesive labels on the envelope. We know these as postage stamps.[33]

Although Hill's economic forecasts proved inaccurate, the penny post worked more or less as he had suggested. The volume of letters surged, and by 1853 unit costs in the Post Office were one-third their level in 1839; despite a temporary setback in revenues, the agency continued to operate in the black. The reforms were immensely popular because they transformed an institution that previously served as a means of taxation into a public service.[34] The penny post not only elevated the prestige of the Post Office; it also endowed a new generation of civil servants in the department with a fund of self-confidence. Moreover, it gave them a paradigm of successful reform, which might be summarized as follows: If you have a complex, high-cost, low-volume service, make it more efficient by reducing and simplifying prices, increasing volume, and cutting unit costs. Everyone will be better off.

When discontent increased with private telegraph service, a wide variety of groups could point to the Post Office as an exemplar of efficiency and competence. "No one ever charges the Post Office with lavish expenditure and inefficient performance of duties," the economist W.S. Jevons wrote in 1867. And when the Post Office turned to an energetic civil servant, Frank Ives Scudamore, to report on the telegraph, he naturally saw in the high prices, low volume, and poor service of the telegraph industry "precisely what we had in the postal system of the United Kingdom, before the year 1840." Claiming that the state telegraphs on the continent showed better results, Scudamore proposed that the government buy out the telegraph companies at a fair price, open new offices, cut rates to a uniformly low level, and make up the difference from higher traffic. The nationalized telegraph, he predicted, would still run a profit.[35]

Scudamore's report crystallized an emerging consensus in favor of nationalization. In the ensuing debate, the telegraph industry found itself almost entirely isolated. As *The Economist* commented, the industry was universally abhorred and the "Post Office is admitted to do its work very much better and more cheaply than any company." Although the British government had never before taken over a profitable industry, the support for nationalizing the telegraph did not signal an ideological upheaval. The postal reforms of 1840 were widely understood as entirely consistent with the free-trade legislation of the same period. The high rates previously charged by the Post Office had been a tax; by reducing this tax, the penny post lifted a burden from commerce. By extension, a postal takeover of the telegraph to simplify and reduce rates would also lift a burden from commerce and be consistent with liberal principles of free trade. The nationalization of the telegraph did not divide the major British political parties. Benjamin Disraeli's Conservative government initiated it during 1868, and Gladstone's Liberal government completed it in 1870. At first, advocates of a role for the Post Office aimed only to run a competing telegraph; in the end, fearing that the Post Office could not compete in telegraphy if private firms continued to dominate the most lucrative routes, Gladstone's government decided to buy up all the domestic telegraph lines. The chief issue was the terms, which in the end were exceedingly generous to the companies; the government paid twenty times profits, even though the industry had been engaged in price-fixing. So anxious was the government to complete nationalization expeditiously that it made other extraordinary concessions: cheap rates to the press and indefinite, free service to the railway companies, which had owned some of the telegraph lines.[36] Excluded from nationalization, the international submarine telegraph lines received a boost from the enormous amount of capital released by the government's purchase of the domestic business.

The telegraph in the United States followed a different trajectory, beginning with a far more rapid start-up than in Britain and elsewhere in Europe. Despite the fact that Cooke and Wheatstone began building telegraph lines in 1838 and Morse started only in 1844—and despite Britain's generally higher level of industrial development—by 1850 there were 12,000 miles of telegraph line in the United States compared to 2,215 miles in Britain. By 1853, the U.S. total had reached 23,000 miles. The volume of telegraph traffic relative to population was also higher during this early phase in the United States than in Britain and other European countries, except for small states such as Belgium that could subsidize domestic telegraph rates with the revenue from cross-border traffic.[37]

The astonishingly steep takeoff of the telegraph in America doubtless reflected the geopolitical differences mentioned earlier. The telegraph industry was unencumbered by the political fragmentation that impeded networks in Europe and by the security concerns that initially led European states other than Britain to frame the telegraph as a political rather than commercial device. Three other factors help to explain the telegraph's accelerated takeoff in America: first, the positive legacies of American communications in the pre-telegraphic era; second, the inability of the Morse interests to maintain internal cohesion and suppress competition during the industry's early development; and third, consistently pro-development government policy, directly favorable to the telegraph and indirectly favorable through its effects on railroads.

If private entrepreneurs "simply failed to present their appearance" when the telegraph was introduced in continental Europe, where did the entrepreneurs come from in the United States? By the 1840s, the political development of American communications had created a distinctive organizational legacy in two institutions, the postal system and the popular press, and it was from these that the first telegraph enterprises chiefly drew their top leadership. In May 1845, Morse and his colleagues established the Magnetic Telegraph Company, with half of the stock reserved for the patent owners. Three major figures emerged in the development that followed: Amos Kendall, who became president of the Magnetic and served as the agent for three-fourths of the patent owners; F.O.J. Smith, the congressman who held the remaining one-quarter of the patent rights; and Henry O'Rielly, who received a contract from the company to build a telegraph line to the west. Soon to become the leading protagonists in the contest for dominance of the industry, all three had experience with the press and politics and two with the Post Office. Kendall had been editor of a newspaper in Kentucky, became a leading figure in Jackson's kitchen cabinet, and served as postmaster general from 1835 to 1840 in the aftermath of the Post Office scandals in Jackson's administration. Smith had owned newspapers in Maine. O'Rielly had edited a newspaper in Rochester, New York, had served as a postmaster, and spoke like a true Jacksonian for rising western commercial interests.[38]

The press also became an important source of start-up capital and early demand for the telegraph. In Britain, which did not have a large, competitive popular press at the time, the start-up financing came from the railways, but American railroad leaders did not at first discern the value of the telegraph. Instead, the press stepped in when the Morse interests had trouble raising capital at the start. The largest investor in the Magnetic was William Swain, the owner of the Philadelphia *Public Ledger*, the city's leading penny paper. After Smith failed to raise money in Boston for a telegraph line linking that city and New York, he was able to get money from New York newspaper publishers, including Horace Greeley and James Gordon Bennett.[39] To newspaper men, the telegraph presented both a threat and an opportunity: a threat because the telegraph might provide more timely news directly to the public and displace newspapers, but an opportunity if telegraph dispatches could be used to stir excitement and sell more papers. The prompt response of leaders of the popular press reflected their immediate appreciation of the potential use of the telegraph and their interest in ensuring that it would be more a partner than a rival.

Kendall's original vision was to create an interlocking group of companies across the country that the Morse patent interests would control through their share of stock. New York would be at the hub of the network, with trunk lines to the major cities throughout the country. But the plan broke down for several reasons. Instead of building lines in different regions and working together, Kendall's group, Smith, and O'Rielly soon entered into litigation over O'Rielly's contract and began invading each other's territories. Kendall also failed to grasp the need for alliances with railroads in controlling rights-of-way. In addition, other inventors besides Morse were able to obtain patents on telegraph instruments, and new companies using this equipment erected lines along the same routes where Morse companies were already operating. Between 1847 and 1852, there was an explosion of entrepreneurial activity as companies raced to complete connections between commercial centers throughout the country. New lines sprang up along the main corridors in the Northeast, and three rivals built lines south to New Orleans. The steep ramping up of the telegraph industry, from 2,000 miles of line in 1848 to 23,000 four years later, occurred during this fiercely competitive phase. But many lines were so poorly built that they functioned only erratically. Just as Americans built railroads at a lower cost per mile and lower quality than the British, so they sacrificed standards of construction to achieve the greatest extension of competitive networks in the shortest time possible.[40]

The steep takeoff between 1848 and 1852, as well as the continued growth in the next decade, also reflected supportive law and public policy. At the inception of development, one state legislature after another granted charters to telegraph companies ceding to them rights-of-way on public roads and canals at no charge. All the states required was priority in sending messages to respond to public emergencies and to apprehend fugitives; a number of states also made it a misdemeanor to disclose a telegram to someone other than the person to whom it was addressed. State subsidies to accelerate telegraph development were of minor importance. The single biggest direct subsidy before the end of the Civil War would come from the federal government in 1860, when Congress passed the Pacific Telegraph Act guaranteeing $40,000 a year for ten years and free use of unoccupied public land to support a transcontinental telegraph. But perhaps even more important was the indirect benefit to the telegraph from governmental support of the railroads, not just at the state level, but through federal grants of land from the public domain that ultimately totaled 210,000 square miles (one-twelfth of the continental United States).[41] By the mid-1850s, railroad managers began to appreciate the value of telegraph lines alongside their tracks in dispatching trains and coordinating other operations. While the British generally built two sets of tracks for trains going in opposite directions, American railroads were able to use the telegraph to build single-track lines (with periodic turnoffs to allow for passing). Single-tracking yielded an immense savings of capital; one estimate indicates that the savings in 1890 in track alone were equal to two and a half years' steel production in the United States, and other related economies more than doubled the benefit of what is perhaps the single largest unambiguous instance of the economic payoff of the telegraph.[42]

Nineteenth-century American law generally provided a highly favorable environment for development of capitalist enterprise, and the telegraph was no exception. Like other entrepreneurs, those who pioneered the telegraph had no difficulty in creating corporations with limited liability (this was still not the case in Britain at the time of the formation of the first telegraph company in 1846). A key liability issue also later arose regarding damages from errors in telegrams—a mistaken message could, for example, lead to enormous financial losses on the stock market—but an influential state supreme court decision in 1867 (later upheld by the U.S. Supreme Court) ruled that telegraph companies could not be held responsible for such consequences.[43] Although the companies were not completely immunized, this ruling fit a general pattern in which the courts tended to shelter industry from liability.[44]

The patent system also functioned as an economic development policy. Recent research has shown that during the nineteenth century, the system led a "broad cross section of the population" to invest in inventive work as expanding markets increased the returns to invention.[45] The patent system aimed to reward inventors but not to create such broad rights as to stifle new inventions, and it succeeded in striking that balance in the case of the telegraph. The mere potential of a patent had enabled Morse to obtain crucial resources for developing his invention, and later he was able to get the normal fourteen-year term of his principal patent extended an additional seven years. But in the critical decision in which it upheld his patent, the Supreme Court rejected the broadest of his claims, which would have severely hindered competing inventions.[46]

As of the early 1850s, however, the telegraph industry was so fragmented that competition on many routes prevented any firm from making a profit. In addition, the lack of integration between contiguous lines often led to long-distance messages being lost or garbled as they were written down and transferred from one line to the next. Low profits and poor service—typical of the competitive phase of network industries—produced both internal and external pressures for unified operation.

The trend toward consolidation began slowly at first, aided by a court decision finding the Bain telegraph—one of the rivals to Morse's instrument—guilty of infringing his patent and by the financial collapse of

O'Rielly's telegraph empire. In 1853, Kendall tried to temper competitive forces through a voluntary association of the Morse companies, which at that point dominated the industry. But this approach proved less successful than the strategy of absolute conquest adopted by a group of Rochester businessmen led by Hiram Sibley, who controlled the New York and Mississippi Valley Printing Telegraph Company, a relatively small line until it merged in 1856 with the Erie and Michigan and was renamed Western Union. Taking advantage of the financial distress in the industry, Sibley's group bought up companies at a fraction of the original value (in one case buying stock literally for 2 cents on the dollar) and combined them into prosperous monopolies. In a crucial step, Western Union negotiated exclusive agreements with railroads to run telegraph lines along their rights-of-way. Its drive to dominance met a strong adversary after 1855, however, when a new company called the American Telegraph Corporation consolidated control of major eastern telegraph companies, including many of the original Morse lines. In 1857, six leading telegraph companies of the time adopted a set of agreements for interconnection and avoidance of competition that were supposed to leave each one sovereign in its territory.[47]

Two developments destabilized this entente and lifted Western Union to dominance over its rivals. In 1861, Sibley took up the incentives offered by Congress and completed the transcontinental telegraph, which immediately proved a huge financial coup. Beginning a few years earlier, some of the same investors who controlled American Telegraph were involved in the primarily British effort to lay a submarine cable across the Atlantic. But because the first attempt failed in 1856, a second line worked only briefly in 1857, and yet a third cable was lost at sea in 1865, American Telegraph did not receive the boost in traffic its investors had hoped for. The Civil War also had drastically different effects on the two companies. The principal trunk lines of American Telegraph ran north-south, whereas those of Western Union ran east-west and were mostly located in secure areas of the North. Once the war broke out, American's lines were cut and its revenues plunged, while Western Union prospered from a surge of wartime demand. Its complete triumph came soon after the war ended. In 1866, it combined with a third firm, United States Telegraph, and later the same year took over American Telegraph and gained a nearly complete monopoly throughout the country.

The formation of a single national network for telegraph through-traffic (small firms continued to own feeder lines) advanced one of the functions frequently attributed to the technology: the development of a single national market. As early as 1845, F.O.J. Smith wrote that the telegraph would bring "State street, in Boston, Wall street, in New York, Chestnut street, in Philadelphia, and the market of New Orleans, all into juxtaposition—*all into one street,* as it were!"[48] The rise of national commodity exchanges and futures trading did follow closely on the growth of the telegraph network, and intercity differences in prices for commodities shrank dramatically. Such developments, however, did not mean the telegraph "annihilated" all distances equally. The telegraph provided the leading cities with the strongest connections. In the early stages of development, the telegraph chiefly connected these centers, and even after the network became more extensive, the "higher-order" metropolitan stations continued to enjoy priority over lower-order stations.[49] This tendency to confer greater influence on the core than on the periphery was nowhere more evident than in the changing flow of news.

During the same decades that the telegraph industry was consolidating, another monopoly was taking shape in the related business of telegraph news. Between 1846 and 1848, New York City was at the center of an emerging telegraph network with connections north to Boston, west to Buffalo, and south to Washington and beyond. During that period—the exact date remains a matter of historical controversy—a half-dozen major New York newspapers entered into a number of working agreements to share the expense of telegraph reports as well as news gathered from ships arriving in New York's harbor. The rise of the penny press in the 1830s had already created a growing demand for timely news as well as the ability to pay for it, and such papers as the *Sun* and the *Herald* had been spending considerable sums to rush reports from Washington and elsewhere, first via pony expresses and then by express trains. Joint action by the largest and richest New York papers not only enabled them to avoid costly duplication in transmissions but also gave them an advantage over papers that they excluded. It was one of these excluded papers, bitter over being forced to bear telegraph costs alone, that first referred to the allied group as the "associated press" of the city. At first an informal designation, it became the name of the most powerful news service in the country.[50]

By the early 1850s, the New York Associated Press (NYAP) was providing two columns of news to major dailies throughout the United States. The key to its dominance was its command of European news, relayed by telegraph from the seaports in eastern Canada where it was first received;

the New York papers' combined financial resources were critical in maintaining control of this route in the face of repeated challenges (particularly from F.O.J. Smith, who controlled the major New England telegraph line). The NYAP obtained national news not through reporters of its own but via a network of agents around the country who rewrote items from local papers and transmitted them to New York, where they were consolidated into a single report along with the foreign news and then sent by telegraph to client newspapers. No competing news agency could offer a comparable product; as other regional press associations were formed, they initially were dependent on New York. In 1856, the NYAP contracted exclusively with American Telegraph in the East and Western Union in the West. That same year, it required client newspapers to make it their exclusive source of wire news, except for specials about party conventions and other political developments. With the triumph of Western Union over its competitors, there developed the first "bilateral monopoly" in the United States—a monopoly telegraph in close partnership with a monopoly news service.[51]

Much of the historical writing about the rise to dominance of Western Union treats it as inevitable on the premise that the telegraph was a natural monopoly and therefore more efficient under a single organization. This interpretation echoes the contemporary reaction of Morse himself, who wrote to Kendall after Western Union's victory that their telegraph interests were "now very much as you and I wished them to be at the outset, not cut up in O'Rielly fashion into irresponsible parts, but making one great whole like the Post Office system. . . . Its unity is in reality a public advantage if properly and uprightly managed."[52] After 1866, however, there were frequent challenges to Western Union from new telegraph companies; repeatedly, Western Union bought up these rivals, typically at an enormous premium, to protect its control of the market, until it eventually reached a modus vivendi with one surviving competitor. It is impossible to know for certain whether, under different policies, competition might have been maintained through the late nineteenth century at lower average costs. What we do know is that no legal barrier blocked the Western Union juggernaut. When the company achieved a national monopoly in 1866, it was the first national monopoly of any kind to emerge out of a previously competitive industry; no federal antitrust law existed, none would be passed until the Sherman Antitrust Act in 1890, and there was no effective antitrust enforcement until after 1900.

Still, Western Union's monopoly immediately stirred opposition, and in 1866 Congress passed legislation that attempted both to generate new competition in telegraph services and to establish a framework for nationalizing the industry. The Telegraph Act of 1866 permitted any company that accepted the terms of the act in writing to build telegraph lines along post roads, and it set a five-year period after which Congress might buy out telegraph companies for a price to be set through arbitration. Neither of these provisions, however, produced the results that reformers hoped for. Thanks to court decisions that undermined the intent of the act, the first provision did not yield new competition, and after five years Congress took no action to buy out Western Union. The act did, however, authorize the postmaster general to set rates of payment for telegraph services used by the federal government, and these rates may have led to some general price restraint.[53]

The decade after the Civil War, when Republicans in Congress were still pressing for an expanded role for the national government, was probably the period of peak opportunity to bring the telegraph back into the Post Office as it briefly had been at the beginning. The support for a postal telegraph included prominent Republicans, including President Ulysses S. Grant. Between 1866 and the end of the century, some seventy bills were introduced to put the Post Office in the telegraph business. Reformers had various ideas: The Post Office might build its own telegraph lines to provide a competitive service; it might offer telegraph service through contracts with private firms (as it contracted with railroads to carry letters); or it might purchase the existing companies. Farmers' groups, labor unions, and numerous local chambers of commerce supported postal telegraphy in one or another form. Seventeen congressional committees reported favorably on such proposals. In 1888, a petition circulated by the Knights of Labor for a postal telegraph drew signatures by more than a million people. But nothing was done.[54]

Comparison with Britain helps to put the failure of the postal telegraph movement in perspective. In the British case, a number of different factors aligned to produce nationalization. First, powerful interest-group opposition to the telegraph cartel emerged from commercial organizations and the press. Second, the success of postal reform had created a widely understood paradigm for solving the kind of problem that telegraph services appeared to present. Third, within the state itself—that is, inside the postal bureaucracy—there was a strong impetus to take over the telegraph. And, finally, both Liberals and Conservatives became convinced that rather than conflicting with their economic principles, nationalization of the telegraph was another species of free-trade legislation. This kind of configuration never developed in the United States. Though it provoked some interest-group opposition, Western Union never faced a rebellion from its primary business clients; though farmer and labor groups opposed the monopoly, their membership made relatively little use of the telegraph, and the issue was not a high priority for them. Although the Post Office provided a paradigm for reorganizing the telegraph as a public service, it had mixed significance. In view of the record of patronage in the department, members of the minority party (usually the Democrats in this period) may have worried that a postal takeover of the telegraph would enable the majority to entrench itself further. The persistent support for a postal telegraph from postmasters general suggests some internal bureaucratic pressure for expansion, but that relatively weak force was unable to shape the national debate.

One reason was the peculiar wiring of the public sphere in late-nineteenth-century America that tied the most powerful newspapers to the interests of Western Union. According to the agreement between the AP and Western Union, AP's member newspapers were bound not to encourage any alternative telegraph. Originally, in the mid-1840s, most editors had favored a takeover by the Post Office. After the Civil War, all major newspapers, with only one or two exceptions, opposed a postal takeover.[55] Unlike the British telegraph companies, Western Union had the press on its side and, in no small measure because of that means of attenuating hostile public opinion, was able to avoid the fate of its British counterparts.

Wiring the News

By the 1860s, the telegraph had become a firmly established medium for a critical, even if limited, type of communication. Too expensive for individual use except by the most affluent, it found its primary customers in finance and business, the state, and the press. It carried high-value, time-sensitive commercial and governmental communication as well as dispatches about breaking news of extralocal interest. During the Civil War, for example, where the Union armies advanced, telegraph lines followed, enabling President Lincoln—who spent long hours in the telegraph office at the War Department—to stay in direct communication with his generals as no other president previously was able to do in wartime.[56] By virtue of its role in disseminating news, the telegraph became the first national medium of mass communication. By virtue of its role in disseminating commercial information, it played a central role in the development of a national economy, and after the successful laying of a transatlantic cable in 1866, telegraph circuits began to link international markets more closely. As a result of technical improvements, service was now far more reliable than in the telegraph's earliest years. But how much information of what kind, between what places, with what degree of freedom, under what rules concerning privacy—all such matters depended not on the technology itself, but on the institutions and policies governing its development and use. This was conspicuous in the state telegraphs of Europe, but it was equally true of the private monopoly that came to dominate the telegraph in America. On the basis of the history of print, one might suppose that the free exchange of information and a flourishing public sphere would have been safer with the telegraph in the private sector. But a comparative analysis of the telegraph and the press in late nineteenth-century Britain and America suggests things were more complicated.

State control of the telegraph did not entail the same policies everywhere. Unlike the original security-minded takeovers in continental Europe, nationalization in Britain in 1870 brought to the telegraph a public-service ethos. The mandate of the Post Office was to improve service and reduce rates, and under Scudamore's leadership it immediately embarked on an expansion plan to make telegraph offices and hours more convenient to the public. Under a simplified set of tariffs, the average cost of a telegram dropped from 1*s* 7*d* to 1*s* 1*d*, and the volume of telegrams doubled in two years. Scudamore, however, had underestimated the costs of expansion and overestimated revenues; the economies of scale in postal operations that made the penny post a success were not available in the telegraph, and demand did not continue to grow as fast as he expected. Initially, receipts covered operating expenses but not the interest on the initial purchase or the costs of upgrading and enlarging the network. Scudamore himself was forced to resign when it was discovered that to finance expansion he had diverted funds from postal savings deposits. As a result of further rate reductions, wage concessions, and the rising cost of subsidies to the press and the railroads, the nationalized telegraph would later run an operating deficit. Nonetheless, it enjoyed great popularity. "Cheap telegrams," the *Daily News* commented in 1876, "have become a necessity of modern existence; and be they irksome or not, profits or no profits, the public must have them."[57]

Perhaps the most striking impact of the nationalized telegraph was on the press, which had reason to be enthusiastic about it. Before nationalization, the three major telegraph companies established a single Intelligence Unit to supply telegraph news, allowing no other wire service, except for the bureau for foreign news established by the German immigrant Julius Reuter after his arrival in London in 1851. The prevailing view among editors was that the telegraph industry's Intelligence Unit was not worthy of the name; they complained about errors and delays, the irrelevance of much of the material they were sent, and their inability to get the news they wanted. In 1865, a group of provincial newspaper proprietors, led by the owner of the *Manchester Guardian*, met to form their own cooperative wire service, but they were unable to overcome the opposition of the telegraph cartel. Three years later, they met again, established the Press Association, and threw their support to nationalization. During the parliamentary debate, seeking to allay any concerns about a government takeover, the postmaster general promised his department would provide the press with arrangements "more satisfactory than those in force"—and it did. A year after nationalization, the number of words transmitted daily in press messages more than tripled, and the number of provincial papers receiving telegraph news jumped from 144 to 365.[58]

Rather than ushering in censorship, nationalization opened wire service to competition. While the Press Association became the leading service, others were founded as well. The Central Press reflected a Conservative viewpoint; the later National Press Agency a Liberal one. By 1900, London alone had some twenty news services. Instead of centralizing control of information, nationalization in this case broke it up. The last of the stamp taxes—or as their liberal critics called them, the "taxes on knowledge"—had been eliminated in 1855, and the cheap telegraph rates for the press introduced in 1870 extended that policy. That same year, Parliament passed a landmark Elementary Education Act, which finally made universal primary education a responsibility of the state. Just as Britain had earlier inhibited a popular press, so these new policies helped to foster it. Cheap telegraph news was particularly associated with the rise of halfpenny evening papers read primarily by the working class, and it proved to be a major boon to the provincial press.[59]

During the late nineteenth century, however, states more often deliberately sought to concentrate wire service in a single company that loyally reflected official views. Successive governments in France had a close relationship with a news bureau founded by Charles Havas in 1835; similarly, the Prussian government used patronage to control the telegraph news bureau founded by Bernhard Wolff in Berlin in 1849 (Wolff, like Reuter, had worked for Havas before starting his own enterprise). In 1865, when Havas tried to buy out Wolff, Bismarck's personal banker Gerson Bleichröder arranged for new financing to keep the wire service in Prussian hands. Four years later, Bismarck's government entered into a secret contract with the new parent company, Continental Telegraph, giving the Wolff Bureau various privileges, including priority in telegraph transmission, which made it a virtual monopoly. In return, the state gained wide authority over the company's activities and personnel; Wolff "asks the government about every doubtful telegram and unconditionally follows the government's instructions," an official noted seven years later. In Britain, though the state did not directly control Reuters, the foreign news service was so reliably in line with official opinion that it was given exclusive access to internal government information, such as telegrams from India, and gained an aura as the semiofficial imperial news agency. Unlike France and Germany, Britain developed a divided market, with the Press Association and other bureaus supplying domestic telegraph news, while Reuters dominated the foreign wire (competing, in some respects, with the *Times* of London, which had its own foreign correspondents).[60]

In 1869, the three major state-sponsored wire services—Havas, Wolff, and Reuters—joined together to form an international cartel, agreeing to exchange news with each other and dividing up the international news business into regional spheres of interest where each company had exclusive rights. At this point, no American company belonged to the cartel, and Reuters was acknowledged as having the exclusive right to sell foreign news to the American market (AP became a member of the cartel only in 1893).[61] The development of the transatlantic cables, therefore, did not simply speed the arrival of European news but channeled it through a semiofficial British filter on its way to the American public. International cable news cut the time lag, but given the circuit such news traveled, it also helped to reestablish an older pattern of informational dependency on metropolitan Britain dating from the colonial era.

Within the United States, Western Union continued to dominate the telegraph industry after its triumph in 1866 but faced two constraints that limited its ability to exploit its market power. First, the postal telegraph movement created a political environment that was, to some extent, a functional substitute for government regulation. Britain's nationalization of the telegraph was widely discussed in America. Worried that the U.S. government might follow suit, Western Union's leaders at various times extended service or held rates in check to keep public opposition within manageable levels.[62] (Concern about the postal telegraph movement also led the company to provide members of Congress with free telegraph service—in effect, making the private telegraph a post office for officeholders.) Public opinion was critical in confining Western Union to its core business. In 1866 and again in 1881, the company was on the verge of trying to muscle the Associated Press aside and take over the wire-service business itself when it drew back, apparently out of concern that it could lose the battle over nationalization by alienating the most influential newspapers in the country. Western Union did, however, move into the distribution of commercial news and in 1871 acquired majority control of Gold and Stock, a pioneering financial information company that developed the stock ticker.[63]

The second constraint on Western Union was that its monopoly was not fully secure, at least not until the 1880s. The behavior of a dominant firm in an industry depends not only on whether there is competition but also on whether the market is contestable—that is, whether some other firm, perhaps one in an adjacent industry, can credibly threaten to enter the market, even on a "hit-and-run" basis.[64] The telegraph market was highly contestable by new firms if they were able to challenge it from a base in the railroad industry, and no one proved more a master of that strategy than the financier and railroad magnate Jay Gould. In 1874, when he took over the Union Pacific Railroad, Gould also took control of a subsidiary, the small Atlantic & Pacific (A&P) Telegraph, which operated telegraph lines on the Union Pacific and Central Pacific rights-of-way. During the next two years, while strengthening A&P's management and technology, Gould added telegraph lines along the Pennsylvania Railroad, the Baltimore & Ohio, and various other roads, until Western Union—its earnings and stock price battered—agreed in 1877 to buy him out at a huge premium.

So profitable was this hit-and-run entry that a few years later Gould tried it a second time, aided by an amendment passed by Congress in 1879 that gave him a legal weapon to break Western Union's exclusive hold on railroad rights-of-way. By 1880, Gould himself controlled 8,168 miles of railroad, more than any other individual or corporation in America. From this formidable position, he built up a new challenger, American Union Telegraph, until it, too, pummeled Western Union's earnings. This time, Gould bought into Western Union as its stock fell and then, as its largest shareholder, negotiated not only the purchase of American Union but also the surrender of Western Union itself to his control.[65] It was a staggering financial coup, but its brilliance was not what impressed the press and the public. In his day, Gould was the most reviled man in America, widely regarded as a financial schemer without moral principles. His takeover of Western Union set off alarms that he would now be in a position to monitor private telegraph traffic to manipulate the stock market. And it triggered concern that through his power over the Associated Press he would control "what has been the free press of America," as the anti-Gould *New York Times* lamented in February 1881.[66]

While Gould's takeover stimulated political opposition, Western Union under his leadership proved stronger than any challenger. "Your Company has attained such magnitude and strength, that it is no longer necessary to buy off any opposition," the president, Norvin Green, declared the following September, adding that competition was a "popular demand" and it might be "good policy . . . to indulge competing lines."[67] Under Gould's direction, however, Western Union did not prove so indifferent to competition, as it later bought out new rivals, including American Rapid in 1885 and the Baltimore & Ohio Telegraph in 1887. But thereafter it indulged its surviving, inferior competitor, a private company called, curiously enough, Postal Telegraph.

Just as American law facilitated the takeoff of the telegraph industry, so it provided a critical underpinning for Western Union to develop into an integrated national monopoly. In a key decision, *Pensacola Telegraph Company v. Western Union Telegraph Company* (1877), the Supreme Court struck down a Florida statute favoring an in-state telegraph company as a violation of the interstate commerce clause; the Court required states to treat corporations the same regardless of where companies were based. The telegraph and railroads are often identified as causes of the growth of a unified national market in the United States, and no doubt they contributed to it. But America's large national market did not emerge purely from the raw facts of geography, population, and technology. Although the Constitution laid the basis for a national market, it was not a self-fulfilling prophecy. The outcome of the Civil War prevented the market from being divided, and through *Pensacola* and other decisions delimiting the authority of the states and federal government the Supreme Court in the following decades protected the market from more subtle tendencies toward fragmentation.[68] It was this legal environment that permitted Western Union to create a national telegraph system and to have the effects on economic development so often attributed to the technology alone.

What difference did it make that Britain nationalized the telegraph and the United States left it in private hands? While both telegraph systems were monopolies, Western Union and the British Post Office had markedly different policies and conceptions of their role. As of 1868—that is, after Western Union gained its monopoly but before nationalization gave British consumers more ready access to the telegraph—telegraph use per capita was slightly greater in Britain, though almost exactly in line with Britain's relatively higher per capita income. By 1880, however, telegraph use was 34 percent higher in Britain than in the United States, even though the gap in income had closed. Per 100 people, there were 85 telegrams sent annually in Britain compared to 63 in America (but only 45 in France and 38 in Germany).[69] Without apology, Western Union almost exclusively continued to serve a business market; in 1887, according to its president, business messages accounted for 87 percent of traffic, the press for 8 percent, and personal messages for only 5 percent. Personal messages were more important in Europe, representing two-thirds of British and other European traffic, according to one estimate.[70] Some evidence does suggest that Western Union had higher levels of productivity than the British Post Office. Any attempt to compare the overall efficiency of the two systems, however, is complicated by differences in objectives. The British Post Office established new telegraph offices, extended hours, and kept rates cheap for newspapers despite clear evidence of unprofitability, just as the American postal system had long subsidized the press and maintained many post offices that could not be justified on grounds of efficiency. In both cases, commitments to public access were deemed more important than efficient operation.[71]

Nowhere is the contrast in outcomes of telegraph development clearer than in the case of the press. While the British Post Office provided the same low rates to all newspapers and opened wire service to competition, Western Union gave preferential rates to the members of the AP and refused to carry any other wire service. Britain's postal telegraph helped equalize power between the provincial and metropolitan press, whereas Western Union helped stronger papers dominate weaker ones. Like Western Union, the New York Associated Press did not enjoy a completely secure dominion. As cities rose in the West, the Western Associated Press (WAP)—the association representing newspapers between Pittsburgh and St. Louis, the Great Lakes and the Ohio River Valley—gained in strength and grew restive under New York's control. In 1866–1867, a battle broke out for control of telegraph news. After one of Western Union's aborted moves to enter the business, the NYAP and the WAP settled their dispute, formed a joint executive board, and maintained an only slightly altered regime.

Though turmoil continued within the organization, the basic structure of the AP remained in place for decades. In return for their exclusive use of Western Union, the members of the AP agreed to do nothing, in the words of an 1867 WAP circular to its membership, "to encourage or support any opposition or competing Telegraph Company." Member newspapers also agreed to use the AP exclusively for wire service; if a newspaper publicly criticized the AP, it risked losing its membership. In return for staying within these limits, an AP newspaper could blackball prospective rivals: No new members could join without the unanimous consent of the current AP members in the same city or area.[72] Not only, therefore, did AP itself enjoy a monopoly position; its member newspapers could also protect themselves against local competition. As a result, an AP franchise in a city became extremely valuable; an 1884 Census report put the value of a franchise in New York at $250,000.[73] Rising publishers such as Joseph Pulitzer made their fortunes by acquiring AP franchises; Pulitzer was willing to pay Jay Gould's price for the money-losing New York *World* because, as one of Pulitzer's biographers writes, "The *World* had that invaluable asset, an Associated Press franchise, itself worth a huge sum." Conversely, journalists who were unable to acquire a franchise, such as the radical Henry George, editor of the *San Francisco Herald,* found their enterprises severely handicapped.[74]

The value of AP franchises also reflected the expanded volume of news the agency was supplying. Clients of the WAP, who had received about 750,000 words a year in AP reports in 1866, were receiving more than 7 million words by 1882; small-town midwestern papers were now using the AP for as much as 80 to 100 percent of their news copy. The economies of scale and scope in providing such a service enabled AP to provide more comprehensive reports without a proportionate increase in costs. And by leasing private lines during the night from Western Union, it was able not only to cut costs but also to increase the size and frequency of reports at will.[75]

When the British nationalized the telegraph, they grafted it onto the postal network, and the telegraph became another way of posting a message. In the United States, three private networks—rail, wire, and news—were overlaid along the same routes. By the turn of the century, three-quarters of all telegraph lines were strung along railroad rights-of-way, railroad depots doubled as telegraph stations, and in the less populated areas of the country telegraph operators doubled as AP reporters. Western Union had exclusive contracts with the railroads; AP had exclusive contracts with Western Union; and individual newspapers had exclusive contracts with AP. These linkages made it difficult for rival news services to break in.

If this system of interlocking networks had any structural vulnerability, it lay in individual papers' interest in excluding local rivals from the AP, thereby creating a potential clientele for competing wire services. During the decades after the Civil War, AP membership stayed at about one-third of the nation's dailies (355 out of 971 in 1880). Beginning in 1869, a series of competing services developed to serve excluded papers but remained in a marginal position for lack of a telegraph network comparable to Western Union's. In 1884, the leader of the strongest of these competitors, the United Press (UP)—unrelated to the twentieth-century United Press—said at a Senate hearing, "I cannot see any future for an opposition press association unless there is an opposition telegraph company."[76] But UP enjoyed one legal advantage; as of this era, there continued to be no copyright protection for news reports, and UP took news from the early editions of AP papers to distribute to its members. (The Supreme Court did not uphold a copyright in news dispatches until a 1918 case involving the AP.[77]) In a secret agreement consummated in 1885, the two wire services began colluding with each other. AP agreed to supply news to UP (and UP to AP), UP pledged not to offer wire service at a lower price, and the top leadership of the AP received stock in UP. In 1892, the exposure of this collusion led to the collapse of the old AP and its reconstitution under new leadership, without, however, fundamental change in the exclusive arrangements with member newspapers. As the AP recovered its dominant position, UP declined and then went bankrupt in 1897.

A semblance of competition in wire service developed only after the turn of the century, when E.W. Scripps, the owner of a chain of newspapers, built up a news service that developed into a new, and longer-lasting, United Press. But it was not until 1945—fifty-five years after the passage of the Sherman Antitrust Act—that the Supreme Court ruled that the AP's exclusive arrangements with newspapers were an illegal restraint of trade.[78]

As a monopoly wire service during the second half of the nineteenth century, the AP represented an extraordinary concentration of influence. In a sense, it was the first institution in America capable of "broadcasting" national news. Two examples of the use of the AP illustrate its significance. In February 1862, undeterred by any concerns about the First Amendment, the secretary of war imposed military censorship on the telegraph. Favoring the AP with exclusives, the administration allowed no other news dispatches to be sent from Washington, and as testimony at 1862 congressional hearings established, the AP distributed, withheld, or tailored its reports as the administration wished. Censors, the head of the AP's Washington bureau wrote in his memoirs, "had to be very circumspect, for they feared arrest and imprisonment if they should, by inadvertence, suffer an obnoxious sentence to be telegraphed." The AP was not in a position to monopolize all war news—it had far fewer reporters on the front lines than a single paper, the *New York Herald*—but the government could use it as a means of manipulating the picture of the war reaching the vast majority of citizens in the North.[79]

The AP's monopoly continued to give it a strategic place in political communication after the Civil War. During the presidential election of 1876, the general agent of the AP was William Henry Smith, a former Republican politician who remained in frequent contact with other leaders in his party, particularly his close friend, Ohio governor Rutherford B. Hayes. Early in the 1876 campaign, Smith began using AP dispatches to tout Hayes for the Republican nomination and then played a pivotal role in eliminating the frontrunner, James G. Blaine, when supporters of a third candidate passed on information implicating Blaine in dubious stock transactions. After helping to clear the way for Hayes to win the Republican nomination, Smith had a central role in securing the general election. Hayes lost the popular vote to New York Governor Samuel Tilden, but the electoral-college vote hinged on the disputed outcome in South Carolina, Florida, and Louisiana (plus one disputed elector from Oregon). During the ensuing investigation by a special Electoral Commission created by Congress, Western Union secretly disclosed to Smith telegrams that Democrats were sending to and from the South, enabling Smith to anticipate their moves and send instructions to Hayes's representatives. The AP also obtained and disseminated legal opinions in support of the Republicans, failed to report Democratic protests when the commission gave Hayes the election on a party-line vote, and amplified the voices of Democrats who called for restraint among their supporters. The AP supported Hayes so faithfully that Democrats called it the "Hayesociated Press."[80]

While Western Union was turning over Democratic telegrams to the AP's general agent, the company publicly maintained an official policy guaranteeing that "all messages whatsoever" were kept "strictly private and confidential." The government itself had violated the privacy of telegrams during the Civil War. When fighting began, the War Department seized the copies that Western Union offices kept of all telegrams from the previous twelve months. During the impeachment of President Andrew Johnson, the Congress also authorized a wholesale seizure of telegrams, to which Western Union did not object, and in two additional investigations before the 1876 election, congressional committees obtained large numbers of telegrams as a result of dragnet searches. But when Congress subpoenaed the telegrams that had circulated during the battle over the election, Western Union initially refused to comply; the company finally acceded in January 1877 and turned over nearly 30,000 telegrams to a Senate committee chaired by a Republican. The telegrams, which the Democrats were never able to review, were kept for two months, returned to Western Union, and destroyed, although extracts from some messages implicating the Democratic candidate Tilden in a scandal—the so-called "cipher telegrams"—found their way into print.[81]

The issue of telegraphic privacy took a new turn after Jay Gould's takeover of Western Union in 1881, when there were widespread suspicions, albeit never proved, that he was monitoring messages to score gains on the stock market. Many states passed legislation imposing penalties on individual telegraph employees if they violated the confidentiality of messages, but these laws were never a basis for prosecuting Western Union itself, nor did they limit the power of Congress or the executive branch. In 1877, the Supreme Court ruled that the Fourth Amendment protected the privacy of letters carried by the Post Office, and a leading constitutional authority at the time argued that the decision ought to apply to telegrams.[82] But the Fourth Amendment provides a right against the government, not against a private company, and the Supreme Court did not extend its ruling to the telegraph. A series of state and federal decisions did, however, begin to require the government when conducting searches to specify telegrams by subject and date, instead of allowing wholesale seizures. Ironically, if the Post Office had taken over the telegraph, the stronger constitutional protection of postal privacy might have carried over to the new medium.

In regard to the critical issues of monopoly, free expression, and individual privacy, the advent of the telegraph posed new problems for which nineteenth-century American thought and institutions were unprepared. Americans had typically conceived of monopoly as originating in political favor and legal privilege. They did not have established legal principles and policies for dealing with monopolies such as Western Union that emerged in the market, and by the time that framework emerged during the Progressive era, the diffusion of the telephone was already eroding the telegraph's monopoly position. Similarly, Americans had generally believed that the way to preserve freedom of the press was to protect the press from the federal government; their ideas and experience had not prepared them to deal with a private monopolist and a new medium of communication. As newspapers and other businesses came to depend on the telegraph, state and federal law at first offered them only limited protection against discrimination by Western Union. In 1894, the Supreme Court declared that telegraph companies were "bound to serve all customers alike, without discrimination," but the Court refused to categorize the companies as "common carriers," like railroads. It was only in 1910, in amendments to the Interstate Commerce Act, that Congress defined telegraph and telephone companies unambiguously as common carriers, required to accept messages from any customer willing and able to pay.[83] American concerns about individual privacy, reflected in the Fourth Amendment's guarantees against unreasonable search and seizure, had also focused on infringements by government, not by a private corporation. Nineteenth-century law did not extend to the telegraph either the protection of individual privacy or the commitment to popular access to service that postal policy had provided.

In short, while Americans developed the telegraph early and fast, they did so without translating into a new technological context the underlying principles embodied in the First and Fourth Amendments and the postal system. The popular movements that upheld these principles did not have the political power in the late nineteenth century to overcome the institutional interests that early decisions about the telegraph had allowed to develop.

In sheer volume, the Post Office continued to carry far more messages than the telegraph. Thanks to railway mail, it was also able to move those messages more quickly than in the past, breaking down barriers of distance and tying markets and other institutions more closely together. The telegraph was not solely, or even primarily, responsible for the trend toward greater social integration in the second half of the nineteenth century. But in reshaping the American public sphere from its earlier, more decentralized structure, the telegraph triggered a radical, even revolutionary change. The American decision to develop the telegraph privately, while the Europeans put it under the aegis of the state, also proved to be a guiding precedent in the later development of both the telephone and broadcasting. One developmental path led to another. But in the United States, the telegraph influenced later networks in a negative sense as well: Western Union's almost exclusive focus on the business market left a void in popular communication that a more accessible and cheaper medium might fill. The telephone soon answered this description.

CHAPTER SIX

New Connections

Telephone, Cable, and Wireless

DURING the last quarter of the nineteenth century, the realities of a world wired for the telegraph confronted developers of new networks with a political challenge. When the telephone emerged in the mid-1870s, the telegraph was already an integral, working part of larger economic and political systems, and the interests, policies, and understandings built up over the previous three decades gave telegraph development an inertial force. When yet another network technology, the wireless telegraph, developed at the turn of the century, it, too, confronted inertial commitments to its wired predecessor. The new networks depended, therefore, not just on "demand" in the conventional economic sense, but also on whether the state and other dominant institutions would allow that demand to be fully expressed. In many countries, hostile or ambivalent policy toward the telephone slowed its early development. Yet states also faced strategic challenges and rivalries abroad that encouraged them to support new systems of communication despite entrenched resistance. This larger theater of international politics became critical in the rise of "wireless," as radio was originally called.

The telephone had its birth in America in 1876, coincidentally the year the United States celebrated its centennial, but it was not the accident of its national origin that by the turn of the century led to far wider diffusion and development of the technology in the United States than anywhere else. National differences in wealth, institutions, and policy affected the relative advance of new communications media. By 1900, the United States had the world's highest per capita income, and affluence enabled more Americans to afford telephones and other consumer goods. In addition, European state telegraph authorities circumscribed development of the telephone within more narrow limits than did American institutions. A familiar geographic pattern emerged: Just as schooling, newspapers, and other communicative resources had spread into small towns and rural areas earlier in the United States than in Europe, so, too, did the telephone. So wide a dispersion would never have happened except for legal and political decisions and habits of association that enabled many Americans unserved by the original telephone monopoly to join together and take control of the technology into their own hands.

Wireless followed a different trajectory, more closely linked to active state sponsorship. Unlike the telephone in its early stages, the wireless telegraph held military as well as commercial value because of its applications in marine signaling and transoceanic communication. Just as Britain had dominated the international submarine cable industry throughout the nineteenth century, so a British company quickly emerged as the dominant early force in wireless. But at the end of World War I, coming into its own as a world power, the United States was unwilling to accept a dependent position in global communications, and at a moment when America had a slight technological edge, federal officials and private corporations worked together to expel British interests from the nascent American radio industry and place it entirely under American control. Previously, while law and policy influenced communications, the impetus for development had not originated in a self-conscious effort to build up American strategic resources relative to the rest of the world. Radio opened a new phase.

A Path for the Telephone

In both Europe and America, the telephone could not simply follow the path of the telegraph because of one inescapable fact: The telegraph had come first. By the 1870s, a web of telegraph wires linked the cities and towns of North America and Europe, while undersea cables crossed the ocean between them, making up a vast, interconnected network pulsating with the urgent business of the time. The historical priority of the telegraph, however, had more of a dampening effect on growth of the telephone in the Old World than in the New. In Europe, the legal and bureaucratic interests in the telegraph "captured" the telephone, while in the United States the telephone escaped—not once, but twice.

In the rise of any new medium, a key factor is its relationship to the dominant technology of the day. Since organizations with a large stake in an existing technology are likely to try to preserve their investment—in today's idiom, they are reluctant to "cannibalize" their current business—any policies or legal decisions that give them influence over the new medium may retard its introduction. Part of the explanation for early differences in telephone development is that European policies often subordinated the telephone to the telegraph, whereas the telephone in America developed independently. After 1879, the American rights to the new invention went not to Western Union but to a new set of organizations, the Bell telephone companies, established initially by one of Western Union's leading public critics. This was the telephone's first escape. Yet, even in America, the cultural legacy of the telegraph as a medium of business communication hung over the telephone's early development and limited the managerial vision of its potential popular use. Moreover, from 1880 to 1893, the period when the Bell interests enjoyed a patent monopoly, they exploited that position by imposing high prices and concentrating their capital on developing the most profitable urban markets.

As the telephone eluded Western Union's control, however, so it also for a time escaped the limitations that the Bell system imposed upon it. From 1894 until 1907 (and continuing in lesser degree for another decade), the market broke open with a surge of independent commercial and nonprofit cooperative telephone enterprises. This opening, more than any other development, propelled the popular takeoff of the telephone in America, expanding its geographical range and allowing consumers to push its evolution in directions the Bell System had not planned. And while the telephone industry shifted back toward a monopoly around the time of World War I, it did so under new forms of regulatory and antitrust policy that encouraged Bell to maintain its position through technological leadership rather than simply reverting to its earlier strategy of exploiting the richest markets.

As an invention, the telephone originated in an effort to improve and extend the telegraph, not to replace it. During the 1860s and 1870s, telegraph inventors and promoters pursued several different avenues for profitable innovation, including a variety of devices for local telegraph services. As early as 1851, two inventors in Boston had devised and installed the first fire-alarm telegraph, and by the mid-1870s nearly eighty other cities had done the same. Beginning in 1871, "district telegraph" companies began installing signal boxes in homes and offices, enabling customers to press a key or turn a dial to signal a central district office for fire or police help or a messenger. Around 1870, the demand for private telegraph wires (connecting, for example, a home and a business) also began to increase as a result of the introduction of small "printing telegraphs," which permitted people who did not know Morse code to send messages by keying in letters. Because of their expense, such systems did not have a large market, nor did their development loom as a competitive threat to Western Union.[1]

William Orton, Western Union's president in this period, saw its business as lying primarily in two highly profitable areas where customers were relatively insensitive to price: long-distance commercial messages and financial information. It was in connection with the latter interest that Western Union had acquired control of the market-quotation company Gold and Stock, along with the services of the young Thomas Edison, whom Gold and Stock had on retainer developing improved stock tickers and related inventions. Orton was especially alert to technological innovations that could move more than one message at a time over a wire. By increasing the telegraph's information-carrying capacity, Western Union could reduce the capital it required for its network and prevent its rivals from gaining a technological edge. In 1868, Joseph B. Stearns received his first patent on a duplex telegraph, which allowed for two messages moving in opposite directions; three years later, Orton began financing Stearns's work, and he later acquired rights to his invention. Then, he put Edison to work on other duplex designs so no other company could gain access to the technology, and he acquired control of Edison's quadruplex, which could send two messages in both directions simultaneously—"the solution of all difficulties in the future of telegraphic science," Orton called it in 1874.[2]

Soon, however, several inventors were racing to devise a "harmonic" telegraph that could carry multiple messages at different tones or frequencies, and it was in the course of this search for a next-generation telegraph that the telephone emerged. One of the aspiring inventors, Elisha Gray, was the cofounder of an electrical equipment maker, Gray & Barton, later to be renamed Western Electric. Already the holder of numerous patents, Gray had the advantage of superior knowledge of electrical technology. The other leading aspirant, Alexander Graham Bell, still in his twenties, was a teacher of the deaf whose advantage lay in his understanding of acoustics. While the harmonic telegraph eluded them both, Bell directed his energies into the invention of the telephone, a device that Gray at first considered to be without commercial value when Bell displayed it at the Centennial Exhibition in Philadelphia in June 1876.[3]

Turning the telephone from a novelty into a network meant putting an infant up against a giant. In America, as in Europe, the telegraph seemed to meet the demand for instant communication, and it had certain advantages, such as producing a written record, while the telephone at its debut was cumbersome, unreliable, and limited in range. Some uncertainty also initially surrounded the exact function telephones would serve.[4] Bell himself did not have the capital or financial acumen to build a business, but his work as a teacher of the deaf had brought him into the household of Gardiner Greene Hubbard, a Boston Brahmin lawyer and entrepreneur, who by happy coincidence was the national nemesis of Western Union. Testifying opposite Orton in congressional hearings, Hubbard had argued for years that the telegraph monopoly neglected the interests of the public and that the federal government ought to charter a private company to offer a cheaper and more accessible telegraph service based in post offices. While acknowledging that Western Union was "unrivaled" as a telegraph for business, it was, Hubbard would write several years later, showing a weakness for puns, "a signal failure" as a "telegraph for the people." On learning of Bell's inventive work, he at once saw the commercial potential of a harmonic telegraph, though in time he also awoke to the possibilities of the telephone. As one of Bell's two earliest backers, later his father-in-law, and trustee of his business interests, Hubbard became the driving force in the earliest days of Bell Telephone, founded in July 1877.[5]

Despite its animus toward Hubbard, Western Union might have made a deal to gain control of the telephone at two points during its early development. The first opportunity came during the fall of 1876, when Hubbard seems to have approached Orton to discuss a sale of the rights. According to a widely repeated but possibly apocryphal story, he asked $100,000 for an outright purchase, which Orton declined to make, perhaps because he had earlier inspected Bell's harmonic telegraph and decided it was inferior to Gray's, distrusted Hubbard, and had already hired

Edison on a monthly retainer to do research on the "speaking telegraph." At that point, Bell's device worked only over short distances, and Orton may have initially seen it as the basis of yet another local telegraph service that did not fit into Western Union's business strategy.[6]

While Hubbard and others began organizing Bell Telephone during 1877, Orton scarcely ignored the potential of the technology. Late that year, combining Gray's patents with Edison's important new contributions and other patent claims, Western Union organized a new firm, American Speaking Telephone, which in early 1878 entered the telephone business in defiance of Bell's claims of patent infringement. Even after it began competing against Bell, Western Union still sought to negotiate a consolidation, but its effort to overwhelm or absorb Bell was short-lived. The following year, its own legal counsel advised that the company was going to lose the patent infringement suit Bell had brought, though Western Union had patents of its own that Bell needed. Meanwhile, in what was probably the decisive factor in the outcome, Gould's American Union Telegraph was mounting a frontal assault on Western Union and making overtures to Bell to form an alliance. (A primary expected value of the telephone, as a local network, was that it would feed messages to the telegraph for long-distance communication.) So, conserving its strength for its battle against Gould, Western Union folded its cards in November 1879 and ceded Bell the entire telephone business, including Gray's and Edison's telephone patents. For its part, Bell agreed to purchase the assets of American Speaking Telephone at cost, pay a 20 percent royalty on the sale or lease of its telephones during the life of the original patents, and channel to Western Union, insofar as it could, all the telegraph orders of its telephone subscribers.[7] Immediately, Bell's shares doubled in value to nearly $1,000, whereas the decisions about the telephone that Western Union made ultimately sealed its doom—but that was all they did. Unlike the mistakes that telegraph authorities in other countries made about the telephone, Western Union's blunders did not obstruct telephone development.

From 1880 to 1894, though it continued to fight off patent challenges and minor incursions, Bell had the industry to itself, and the growth of the medium during this period reflected both the incentives it faced and the strategy it adopted. A critical change had already taken place before 1880. At the outset, through local agents, Bell had leased phones to customers, who had their own lines built connecting two points; then, in 1878, beginning in New Haven, Connecticut, the first telephone exchange was introduced, enabling customers to connect with each other through a central switchboard. Instead of simply leasing phones, therefore, the telephone business now also involved the more complex and costly tasks of financing, building, and operating networks, and Bell's local agents evolved into operating companies with territorial monopolies. From 1880 to 1884, the number of subscribers tripled, but during the next decade growth slowed to an annual rate of 6 percent as the directors of the company chose to harvest dividends rather than invest in rapid expansion.[8]

But, however managed, the early telephone business confronted several underlying economic realities that made high growth rates costly to sustain. On the one hand, it was cheaper to build telephone networks where the installations were closer together; in other words, there were economies of *density*. On the other hand, the more telephones in a network, the higher was the average cost per phone because of more complex switching and concomitant capital investments. In other words, taking the telephone as the unit of measurement, increasing *scale* was associated with rising costs.[9] To be sure, telephone networks became more valuable to each individual phone user as more users were added. But because costs as well as benefits rose with network size, a telephone company could easily find itself in financial straits as its network grew if it failed to keep rates higher than its rising average expenses. At this stage of the industry, therefore, a monopoly telephone company might rationally choose to focus on limited markets that had a high density of customers who were relatively insensitive to price. That may explain why Bell was oriented almost entirely to an urban business market during this period and why, by sticking to that market, it generated a very high return on investment.[10] Only after its patent monopoly ended would it become clear to Bell's leadership that its early focus on the urban business market exposed the company to attack from the communities it had neglected.

During this phase, following the model of the telegraph industry, Bell also began to develop long-distance service. In 1884, it built a line between New York and Boston and the following year created a subsidiary, American Telephone and Telegraph (AT&T), to build long-distance lines throughout the country. By 1894, these lines connected cities in the Northeast and Midwest, though the quality of long-distance calling remained very poor. In the same period, Bell also pressed its smaller operating companies to merge into larger ones; New England Telephone and Telegraph, founded in 1883, consolidated eight smaller companies and became the most highly developed of these early regional enterprises. While New England Telephone and other Bell licensees could build toll lines linking their own exchanges, Bell reserved to AT&T the development of long lines connecting the operating companies with each other. During the early 1880s, in another deal with Western Union, Bell bought control of the electrical equipment manufacturer Western Electric, which it merged with other firms and made the exclusive supplier of telephones to Bell operating companies. The operating companies were bound to the national system, therefore, not only by contract but also through their dependence on its long-distance and manufacturing arms. The entire federation of companies made up the Bell System (control of which was transferred, for legal reasons, to AT&T in 1899). As of 1894, the system had 240,000 telephones, or one for every 225 Americans.[11]

Although telephone service spread only at a moderate pace in America during this period, adoption of the telephone proceeded even more slowly in the major European countries. Unlike the telegraph, the telephone was a Yankee import, and it was greeted with much uncertainty and ambivalence. In both Britain and France, the governments initially turned responsibility for the telephone over to the private sector while establishing policies that stifled investment. Concerned about potential loss of revenue, telegraph authorities in both countries immediately sought to confine the telephone in two ways: by setting geographical limits on telephone connections and by setting dates in the future when the state might take possession of the networks. In Britain, the institutional impediments were actually in evidence even before the telephone's invention: While he was working on the harmonic telegraph in 1874, Alexander Graham Bell wrote to the British Post Office, hoping to sell his invention, only to receive an imperious and discouraging response.[12] In the late 1870s, after Bell and Edison both obtained telephone patents, rival companies were established, but the British Post Office acquired licensing authority over telephone service as a result of a court ruling in 1880 establishing that the new device came within the government's telegraph monopoly. The telephone licenses were for specific districts, typically limited to a distance of 3 to 5 miles from an exchange, and the companies were not allowed to build trunk lines, lest they take business away from the telegraph. The government took a 10 percent royalty on telephone revenues, and it not only limited a license to thirty-one years but at specific intervals could also purchase a company's assets. A liberalized policy in 1884 allowed private trunk lines, but the government nationalized them eight years later. The telephone companies also ran into trouble at the municipal level, where they faced opposition getting access to rights-of-way. "The telephone," the Association of Municipal Corporations declared, "is a system for the benefit of capitalists and the more well to do people and not for the public at large."[13]

The high level of postal and telegraph services in Britain may have blunted popular demand for the telephone and been at least partially responsible for the government's lack of interest in its development. No competitive dynamic pushing telephone expansion emerged from the market. To avoid head-to-head rivalry after the expiration of their original telephone patents, the firms in the industry merged into a single National Telephone Company (NTC) in 1889. In the following decade, the government experimented with public-sector competition; it authorized municipalities to establish their own exchanges, though few did, and for a period the Post Office itself competed with the NTC in London. In 1905, however, after lurching through a series of policies, the government decided to purchase the NTC. But whereas the postal takeover of the telegraph in 1870 came with a mandate to cut prices and expand service, the nationalization of the telephone—completed in 1912—brought no comparable effort. The telephone, unlike postal or telegraph service, would have to pay its own way, and the government would not stoop to market it. A widespread view held that the telephone was a luxury good that the taxpayers had no reason to promote; as a London *Times* editorial in 1902 put it, the telephone was "not an affair of the million" but "a convenience for the well to do and a trade appliance for people who can well afford to pay for it."[14]

French policy was even more unfavorable to the telephone. Unwilling to spend public funds on the medium, the French government, beginning in 1879, granted local concessions for telephone service lasting only five years. The idea was to let the private sector assume the risk of a new business, giving the state time to see if it was worth taking over. Private capital could lose money on the telephone, but if the medium proved profitable, the government would step in: a policy nicely designed to depress investment. In 1885, the government itself began building long-distance lines but limited construction so as not to cause too rapid a depreciation of its investment in the telegraph. Four years later, it nationalized the local telephone carriers as well, not so much because of a positive commitment to improve telephone service as because of a defensive concern about the erosion of the state's telegraph monopoly. "Private ownership failed in France, as it did in virtually all of the European countries," one analyst comments, "because government actions inflated the riskiness of investment: concessions were granted for short periods of time with no certainty of renewal, restrictions were imposed on construction of long-distance facilities, and there was a serious threat of nationalization."[15] The telephone also continued to languish in France after the government took over because it refused to invest in facilities; municipalities could put up the funds to build telephone lines, which the government would then take over without any return of the capital. In the classic French pattern, communication capacities were concentrated in the capital; as of 1902, 44 percent of the telephones in France were in Paris alone, which already had its famous system of pneumatic tubes for local messages.[16]

Differences in government policy materially affected how quickly the telephone spread. By 1895, while the United States had one telephone for every 208 people, Britain had one for every 350 and France one for every 1,216. Germany—with one phone for every 397 people—had the widest diffusion among the continental Great Powers; unlike France, it had nationalized the telephone at the start and adequately financed capital expansion. (The difficulties of public ownership in Germany would become apparent after World War I, however, when the German telephone system was unable to keep up with hyperinflation because its rates required legislative approval, and the resulting financial pressures prevented it from maintaining investment at earlier levels.) As of 1895, telephones were most widespread in three of the smaller European countries: Luxembourg (one telephone per 160 population), Switzerland (one per 129), and Sweden (one per 115).[17] But while growth in European countries continued to be slow, it was about to take off in America.

The Technology of Civil Society

Telephone development in the United States surged after Bell's patent monopoly came to an end in 1894. By 1902, more than a thousand new independent telephone companies had emerged, primarily occupying territory unserved by the Bell System. Although some of the independents began in cities, they were especially strong in small towns, and they were concentrated in the North Central states. After opening an exchange in one town, independent companies often moved on to build exchanges among its neighbors and then began linking them together with short-haul lines. From small beginnings, some independents grew into significant regional companies and through alliances with other independents were able to provide toll service, though not over distances as long as those covered by the Bell System.[18]

A second, separate wave of independent development began around 1900, when rural areas witnessed an explosion of telephone development, often in the form of cooperatives started by small groups of farmers. From its inception, Bell had shown no interest in developing telephones in rural areas, and though the independent telephone companies were more likely to serve rural needs, they were also ambivalent about a market that they viewed as likely to be unprofitable and vexatious. Rural telephony became a genuine grassroots movement. Governed by elected boards, the rural co-ops made telephone service available at a cost they were determined to keep to a minimum. Sometimes using fence wire for transmission, they typically provided service on party lines and expected their members to install poles and wires and maintain them. A "central" or switchboard might be located in a farmhouse or village store. Though usually grouped with the independent telephone companies, the farmers' lines were a third force and did not necessarily side with the independents in the battle with Bell.[19]

While the independent telephone companies at first filled in the gaps Bell had left, the two networks increasingly overlapped by the turn of the century. In 1904, among communities with more than 5,000 people, 60 percent had dual service—that is, two competing telephone systems that did not interconnect with each other. The independents moved from the periphery to the center. From their base in smaller communities, they extended their networks into larger ones until nearly all major cities, with some notable exceptions, had dual service. Conversely, the Bell companies moved from the center outward, opening 3,500 new exchanges in communities with less than 10,000 population between 1894 and 1907. The Bell-independent rivalry at the turn of the century led to the same breakneck extension of networks that had characterized the early telegraph industry around 1850; when noninterconnecting networks compete with each other, the scope of connections they offer any individual user becomes a source of competitive advantage.[20]

As this dynamic unfolded, prices for telephone service fell sharply. Independent phone companies generally offered lower rates than Bell, and though Bell cut its rates everywhere, they were lower where it faced a rival. Overall, from 1895 to 1909, the revenue that Bell received per phone dropped by 55 percent. Since expenses per phone dropped by 45 percent, Bell claimed that the cause of lower rates was primarily improved efficiency, not competition.[21] Competition created pressure on Bell, however, not only to become more efficient, but also to adapt equipment, services, and rate plans to meet demands for low-cost service. In 1906, for example, Bell introduced a less expensive phone set for rural use, and it expanded party lines in order to make service available on a cheaper basis.[22]

The result of this process was an enormous expansion of telephone service. Instead of increasing at 6 percent a year as it had from 1885 to 1894, the annual compound growth rate surged to around 30 percent from 1895 to 1907. In 1894, there had been 285,000 telephones, nearly all of them in the Bell System; by 1904, there were 3.36 million, nearly half of them in independent systems. By 1907, the total reached 6.1 million; by January 1911, 7.6 million, which represented 67 percent of all telephones in the world. Per 100 population in 1911, there were 8.1 phones in the United States compared to 1.4 in Britain, 0.6 in France, and 1.6 in Germany. Even the relatively wealthy, small European countries that had earlier surpassed America now lagged behind; Luxembourg stood at 1.3, Switzerland at 2.1, and Sweden—the highest in Europe—at 3.4. (Sweden also had rural telephone cooperatives.) The density of telephones in the United States was eleven times greater than in Europe as a whole.[23]

American telephones, moreover, had a different social and geographical distribution. In Europe, telephones were heavily concentrated in urban areas, as they had been in the United States until the end of Bell's patent monopoly.[24] Telephone service, the British chancellor of the Exchequer declared in 1901, "is not desired by the rural mind"; more than one-third of all telephones in Britain were in London alone as late as 1913.[25] But in America, the growth of independent telephone companies and rural cooperatives enlarged the network. The rural share of American telephones rose from near zero in 1894 to 5.3 percent in 1902, 24 percent in 1907, and 38 percent in 1912. By the latter date, 30 percent of farms had a telephone, which was close to the rate of 35 percent for all American households.[26] The physical isolation of many farms seems to have made the telephone an especially desirable home improvement. Moreover, rural telephones served not just social but also business purposes; farmers could order supplies, obtain price information, and even use the telephone to listen to weather reports telegraphed by a federal agency to local telephone companies. "The rural telephone lines are now the best and most economical means of distributing weather information," the U.S. Department of Agriculture noted in 1905.[27]

The role of cooperative institutions underscores a key point about the expansion of telephone service at the turn of the century. While competition was crucial to the process, the development was a phenomenon not just of the marketplace but also of civil society. The midwestern areas of the country that saw the greatest development of rural telephone service were areas where agricultural cooperatives thrived. Instead of waiting for either the government or a corporation to provide telephone service to them, millions of ordinary people created their own telephone networks. Rather than having their needs defined for them, they defined those needs for themselves.[28] Whether the telephone led to more or less sociability is unclear, but it clearly benefited from habits of association already established. Even the rise of the commercial independents reflected a wide distribution of self-organizing capacities at the local level. One of the costs of nationalization in many other countries is that it left no room for the autonomous development of the telephone on the periphery of power.

The origin of this process, the expiration of the original Bell patents in 1893–1894, was not simply an inevitable legal event. During the monopoly era, Bell obtained 900 new telephone-related patents, primarily buying them from inventors who had no other market. The courts, however, thwarted Bell's efforts to use these new patents to perpetuate its control of the market. Bell had already enjoyed, one of its own attorneys acknowledged in internal correspondence in 1891, "a monopoly more profitable and more controlling—and more generally hated—than any ever given by any patent."[29] Its high prices and lack of interest in serving much of the country had created widespread resentment. The courts were, in effect, registering that political reality when they chose to interpret Bell's later patents so narrowly that the independent telephone companies and cooperatives could circumvent them with only minor technical modifications.[30] In short, Americans were able to "reinvent" the telephone because the courts loosened the grip that patents might have given Bell.

The opening of the telephone industry to non-Bell organizations also provided an avenue for technological innovations that Bell had rejected. It was the independent telephone companies, not the Bell System, that first adopted automatic dialing. In the traditional telephone exchange, an operator answered when someone picked up a phone, took the request for a call, and plugged one line into another. Bell's leaders conceived of the operator as providing a form of personal service analogous to a servant or secretary; after 1880, nearly all operators were women who spoke English without an ethnic accent. Bell's initial resistance to automatic dialing partly reflected its doubts about the reliability and flexibility of the technology, but in time even its own internal studies showed that automatic dialing would bring significant savings. Nonetheless, while the independent companies competed on price, Bell held to its vision of personal service until around the time of World War I, when it had difficulty recruiting enough operators who met its social criteria, ran into increased labor militancy, and finally recognized that consumers actually preferred the privacy of dialing the phone themselves.[31]

Although wide-open competition at the turn of the century set in motion the expanded adoption and use of telephones, the competitive market had its problems. In communities with two systems, many people with telephones could not connect with each other because they had service from competing companies. Some of the independent telephone companies were also poorly organized and financed, underestimated their costs, and went bankrupt. The rural telephone cooperatives, dedicated to keeping their fees low, suffered from chronic shortages of capital and were typically unwilling to extend service into new areas; little cooperatives proliferated, but they had to haggle with each of their neighbors over connections. The resulting inefficiencies in coordination prevented the cooperatives from developing into a larger-scale means of providing service. Even the independent telephone companies were incapable of providing high-quality long-distance service for want of the coordination that AT&T provided the Bell network. And there was an ugly underside to competition: Accounts of the era describe illicit schemes, including sabotage and bribery by both sides, designed to undermine the opposition.[32]

The rivalry between Bell and the independents had a political as well as an economic character. Adopting a populist rhetoric, with names such as Citizens or Home Telephone, the independents emphasized their local roots and portrayed Bell as a distant, eastern-dominated monopoly. In the debate about dual service, Bell claimed that two systems were wasteful, forcing some subscribers, mainly businesses, to pay for duplicate service, while the independents insisted that competition had reduced prices and opened up telephone service to more people than when Bell had a monopoly. During the first phase of the competitive era, from 1894 to 1907, Bell attacked competitors relentlessly. In addition to expanding its facilities and slashing prices, it pursued litigation against the independent telephone companies for infringing patents still in effect, refused to allow Western Electric to sell them equipment, and in nearly all cases denied them interconnection with its local exchanges or long-distance network. At the local level, Bell and the independents often fought over the award of municipal franchises. The municipalities had an early role in regulating the industry because of their control over rights-of-way, and they often used their power to extract such concessions as guaranteed low rates or the provision of free telephones to the local government. In many communities, the independents were able to win franchises because of public hostility toward Bell, while Bell was able to use its political influence and financial clout to prevent its rivals from gaining a foothold in New York, Boston, and Chicago. The failure of independent telephone systems to penetrate these centers was a serious handicap particularly in gaining business customers in other cities as well as in surrounding areas. At the turn of the century, however, long-distance telephone calling was still so minor a part of the business that the independents' limited access to long lines did not arrest their growth.[33]

Dual-service competition and battles over municipal franchises would prove to be only a transitional phase in the development of telephony. In later years, after Bell regained its dominance, many critics would attribute its success to its predatory behavior, while others would point to its efficiencies as an integrated system, particularly its superiority in long-distance. Both claims have a factual basis: Bell's actions were predatory, and it did enjoy efficiency advantages.[34] But neither was sufficient to prevent Bell from losing half the telephone market to the independents a decade after its patent monopoly ended. And neither of these explanations adequately captures the forces that shaped telephone systems in the early twentieth century, when developments within the industry intersected with a larger political change.

Hello, Regulation

Unlike the battles of the 1870s and 1880s over Western Union, the struggle over Bell's practices in the early 1900s took place at a time when public antagonism toward corporate power and the "trusts" had become a political force of real influence. The antitrust and regulatory policies toward business adopted in the United States during the Progressive era (1900–1918) may seem mild compared to state ownership, but they were actually far more elaborate than the regulation of business in Germany, Britain, and France at the time. None of the fifty largest British companies, for example, faced government-initiated lawsuits at the appellate level, while eleven of the fifty largest American corporations did. Although Theodore Roosevelt's trust-busting zeal is exaggerated in popular folklore, his administration (1901–1909) brought forty-four antitrust suits, while that of his successor, William Howard Taft (1909–1913), brought ninety. Among these were the prosecutions that resulted in the dissolution of two of the greatest trusts, Standard Oil and American Tobacco. The same era saw the federal government create the Antitrust Division in the Department of Justice and other administrative machinery to make effective regulation possible. In 1887, Congress had passed the Interstate Commerce Act to regulate the railroads and bar rate discrimination, but the agency established under the law, the Interstate Commerce Commission (ICC), had neither the power to set rates nor the necessary administrative capacity until Congress strengthened its authority in 1906. At the time, many states were establishing independent commissions to regulate public utilities, and these commissions, like the ICC, were developing the machinery and principles for rate setting. The central thrust of American regulation of business, however, continued to come in litigation and court decisions rather than through administrative rulings, and the chief focus of the law was competition. Antitrust enforcement was flexible, but the very discretion it left to prosecutors and judges augmented their power.[35]

This new political context—the Progressive conjuncture—shaped the outcome of conflicts over the telephone. If such giants as Standard Oil could be dissolved, AT&T had to worry about its possible exposure under antitrust law to an attack orchestrated by its rivals in business and its critics in the public arena. The growing possibility that rate setting, like antitrust, might extend to the telephone industry was also abhorrent to Bell, at least as its traditional leadership understood the company's interests. But just as its legal and political risks were increasing, so too was the financial strain on the Bell System from its efforts to respond to the independents by expanding facilities and cutting prices. The company's profits fell, its debt soared, and it was forced repeatedly to make new stock offerings, diluting the share owned by the board of directors. As these problems deepened, the Boston investors that had dominated Bell lost control of the company in 1907 to the Morgan banking interests, which brought in new management that drastically changed Bell's posture toward government as well as its relations with the independent telephone companies.[36] The shift at AT&T that then took place corresponded to a wider movement among the public-utility industries to trade their autonomy in setting prices for long-term market stability.

AT&T's new president, Theodore N. Vail, had begun his executive career as superintendent of railway mail in the Post Office. Recruited by Hubbard in 1878, he had served as Bell's original general manager, eventually leaving the company in 1887. On his return as president in 1907, Vail combined the old aspiration to create a telephone system analogous to the Post Office with the new imperative to restore the company's control of the market. Vail summed up his policy with the slogan, "One system, one policy, universal service." Telephone service, he wrote, "should be universal, interdependent and intercommunicating, affording opportunity for any subscriber of any exchange to communicate with any other subscriber of any other exchange." Though vague on the exact implications ("some sort of connection should be within the reach of all"), he suggested a "broadened" ideal of "a system as universal and as extensive as the highway system of the country which extends from every man's door to every other man's door."[37]

In the short run, however, universal service meant creating an integrated telephone network throughout the country, and in pursuit of that end, Vail had both a political and a business strategy. Instead of rejecting any role for government, he was willing to accept regulatory control, as long as it was by an independent commission that recognized the rights of investors and management to a fair return. Instead of holding Bell aloof from public opinion, Vail undertook what is widely regarded as the first major public relations campaign designed to improve a corporation's image. And instead of trying to suppress all independents, Vail began to accommodate some and acquire others, trying to absorb the opposition into a more broadly conceived system.

Five years earlier, Bell had begun to allow its operating companies to "sublicense" independent exchanges—that is, to connect with noncompeting independent systems if the latter would agree to several conditions, including purchase of equipment that met Bell's technical standards. Under Vail, Bell increasingly offered independents in communities where Bell did not operate the chance to interconnect with its network and to buy equipment from Western Electric. It also acquired competing companies wherever possible, though in some cases where a rival dominated the market, Bell conceded the territory if the independent company would connect with its network rather than with other independents. The purpose of this divide-and-acquire strategy was to limit the scope of the independent telephone system, and it worked. Between 1907 and 1912, the share of telephones operated by the independents dropped from 51 percent to 45 percent, and even more impressive, the proportion of all phones run by independents not connecting to Bell dropped to a mere 17 percent. By 1913, the share of cities with dual service fell from its peak of 60 percent to 37 percent.[38]

This shift away from dual-service competition reflected growing public support for a unified, regulated telephone system. Dual service had long been a nuisance from the standpoint of businesses that needed to have duplicate subscriptions, and after 1910 telephone competition seems to have lost support in public opinion. Increasingly, city councils and state agencies came out in favor of a unified telephone service. Even the opposition of the independent companies was weakening; in 1911, the association representing the independent telephone companies endorsed government regulation. The more independent companies connected to Bell's network, the greater was the support among the independents for the same policies that Bell favored. Before 1907, only eight states regulated telephones to any extent, and these were mostly southern states that used regulation to promote the industry rather than to control it. By 1914, however, regulation had spread to thirty states, and by 1920 to forty-two. In 1910, Congress gave the ICC authority to regulate interstate telephone traffic, though this was only a minuscule portion of the business. In the following years, the commission gave little attention to telephone rates and had little effect on the industry. As a practical matter, therefore, public supervision of the telephone industry fell to the states, where regulation was increasingly regarded as a substitute for competition. In several states during 1911 and 1912, public service commissions began to orchestrate the consolidation of the industry and the end of dual service.[39]

This turn was accompanied, however, by some ambivalence in public policy-making. While some state commissions were encouraging competing telephone companies to merge, other public officials believed such consolidations violated the antitrust laws. AT&T had also raised new antitrust concerns when it purchased a controlling interest in Western Union in 1909 and Vail became president of both companies. In 1912, the U.S. attorney in Portland brought an antitrust case against AT&T in connection with the acquisition of a small Oregon telephone company, and the following year, in an agreement with President Woodrow Wilson's attorney general, AT&T settled the case by making several concessions. It would divest itself of its holdings in Western Union, stop acquiring competing independents, and, under certain limited conditions, open its long-distance lines to independent exchanges. While the antitrust suit was still pending in 1913, state ownership had received the backing of Wilson's new postmaster general, who declared that the Post Office "should have control over all means of the communication of intelligence" and that it was investigating a takeover of the telegraph and telephone industries.[40] Satisfying the Wilson administration in the antitrust case helped to avert that threat. The antitrust settlement, particularly the telegraph-telephone divorce, drew a generally positive response in the press and had important long-term effects, but it did not preserve direct telephone competition. In 1921, Congress passed the Willis-Graham Act, allowing the purchase of competing telephone companies if the ICC approved, which over the next thirteen years it did in 271 of 274 proposed AT&T acquisitions.[41]

Like other constitutive moments in communications, the Progressive era left a distinctive imprint on institutions. In this case, the general shift toward government regulation under the banner of Progressive reform gave force and direction to specific dissatisfactions with the telephone market. Beginning in 1893, competition in telephone service had won popular approval by shaking the old Bell monopoly out of its complacency and forcing it to cut its rates and serve communities it had ignored. Competition, however, generated its own complaints: The division of a community into two nonintercommunicating networks diminished the value of any given telephone and increased the costs to subscribers who paid for duplicate subscriptions. Consumers stood to benefit from unified service if they could avoid becoming subject to an exploitative monopolist. In theory, there were several ways of achieving that objective. One option, mandatory interconnection of companies in the same territory, would have required too much duplication of physical assets to be efficient and too much administrative integration to allow for genuine competition. Another option was public ownership, but it failed to gain traction despite prominent support. Although three Canadian provinces took over telephone service in whole or in part, not one state did so in the

United States. The federal government actually did nationalize telephone service during World War I, but its administration was unpopular. Instead of reducing rates—as reformers expected would happen under public ownership—the government raised them, and it still ran a deficit. After a disillusioning one-year experiment, the industry was quickly returned to private control.[42]

A third possibility was to accept a monopoly telephone carrier in every area and use government regulation to limit the power of the monopolist to exploit its position. Under this approach, independent companies would survive in some local enclaves, while AT&T would run most local and regional systems, own the sole long-distance network, and serve as the network manager. Between 1906 and 1920, public policy gravitated toward this option. From Bell's standpoint, regulation by state commissions with long-term appointments (insulating their members from political pressure) was far preferable to the alternative policies: Dual-service competition and municipal regulation exposed the Bell System to ruinous instability, while dissolution under the antitrust laws and public ownership threatened its very existence. State courts already treated telephone companies as common carriers, subjecting them to such requirements as nondiscrimination among subscribers. As it turned out, state regulatory commissions did not add greatly to the companies' burdens, except for imposing higher technical standards, which worked in favor of Bell and against the independents. Regulatory restrictions on price competition also helped Bell to consolidate its position. Only in later decades would regulatory laws provide a platform for expanded public-service obligations under a more redistributive ideal of "universal service" than Vail had originally imagined.[43]

By 1920, the Bell System's share of the industry had risen to 66 percent; by 1932, to 81 percent. While public policy helped it to gain this dominant position, AT&T also owed its triumph to the organizational structure that it had created before regulation. The centralized direction that AT&T gave the Bell System enabled it to provide long-distance service that the independents could not match, and this edge became more valuable with advances in long-distance technology and the growth of the national economy. During the battle between the two systems, the Bell operating companies were tightly bound to AT&T, while the independents were only loosely affiliated with each other, allowing the Bell System to acquire individual independent companies or get them to connect to its network. In the process, Bell not only weakened the independent system but also aligned the interests of the surviving independents with its own. Once they held their own territories within a regulated system of local monopolies, independent telephone companies also shared an interest in rate-setting principles that protected their profits. Instead of fighting the independents, AT&T could increasingly count on local independent allies to represent its interests at the state level far more persuasively than it could itself. Peace within the industry was critical to the control of policy.[44]

As might be expected, there was one silent interest that lost out in this resolution of earlier tensions: people who did not yet have telephone service. As competition declined, the rate of increase in telephones had slowed down, back to about 6 percent a year between 1907 and 1917.[45] Nonetheless, the burst of growth during the competitive era had lifted telephone diffusion in the United States so far ahead of other countries that the American lead remained considerable. As of 1929, the American share of the world's telephones had dropped from 67 percent (in 1911) to 59 percent, which was to be expected as other areas developed. Per 100 population, the United States had 16.3 telephones, compared to 3.8 in Britain, 2.3 in France, 4.6 in Germany, and 1.7 for Europe as a whole.[46] The American pattern remained distinctive not just in overall density but in the dispersion of phone service beyond metropolitan areas. For a brief time, telephones were actually more common on farms than in cities—in 1920, the proportion of farm households with telephones hit 39 percent, compared to 35 percent for the rest of the country—but this was an anomaly. Rural telephony declined during the 1920s and continued falling sharply during the early 1930s as a result of the Great Depression and because the advent of radio and the spread of the automobile answered some of the same needs for information and sociability.[47]

Seen in continental terms, America's telephone system was far ahead of Europe's. By the mid-1920s, Americans had a long-distance network that enabled them to call virtually every other part of the country, while in Europe long-distance connections across borders and even across regions within countries were extremely limited. In 1927, while Bell was reporting an average delay of 1.5 minutes in placing long-distance calls, it took, on average, more than an hour to put through a call from Paris to Berlin.[48] As political fragmentation in Europe had slowed the takeoff of the telegraph during the mid–nineteenth century, so it obstructed the advance of the telephone in the twentieth. But as the poor interregional connections within countries indicated, this was not the only factor. Most European countries merged the telephone into the same government departments that administered postal and telegraph systems. Aside from the postage stamp, however, new inventions had not figured prominently in the annals of postal service, and the telegraph had become technologically mature in a relatively short time. State agencies are capable of sponsoring technological innovation (the military is a principal example), but previous experience had not oriented postal and telegraph authorities in that direction. From their standpoint, moreover, the telegraph already provided an efficient and profitable system of rapid long-distance communication. They saw no need to make the investments in scientific research and political cooperation required for a long-distance continental telephone network.[49]

In the United States, however, by divorcing the two wired networks, federal antitrust policy denied the telephone industry the option of relying on the telegraph for long-distance connections and instead gave it a powerful incentive to develop a long-distance system of its own. In this larger sense, telecommunications did not become a monopoly in the early twentieth century. A continental telephone network, moreover, turned out to be far more technologically demanding than a continental telegraph network had been. As a result, even though no such effect was planned, public policy in America—and not simply the size of the American market or the geographic distances in the country—inclined AT&T toward a much greater commitment to scientific research than either Western Union or any of the European telecommunications authorities had made. A recent analysis of the history of global communications notes that with only a few exceptions, "all of the fundamental technical problems of telephony were addressed and solved in America," and all were "put into practical form and entered service" first in the United States.[50] This one-sided American dominance of telephone technology was not characteristic of the other long-distance communications networks to develop in this era. The explanation for this pattern lies in geopolitics and public policy.

Wires, Waves, and Lines of Innovation

Two major private telecommunications industries emerged from the nineteenth century: the British submarine cable industry, operating, like its parent state, on a global scale, and the American telephone industry, operating, like its parent state, on a continental one. In each case, the political and economic context of the industry shaped business strategy and the focus of technological innovation: Long-distance submarine cable connections posed one set of problems, long-distance land lines another. When radio first developed at the turn of the century, Britain maintained the dominant position it had in cable. By 1914, however, the technological interests arising in long-distance telephony and wireless converged on the same innovations, America took the lead in radio technology, and the stage was set for a critical battle over control of the new medium.

Britain's dominance of international submarine cables during the nineteenth century stemmed fundamentally from its position as both the leading commercial power and the largest empire. These twin roles gave it both the incentive and the capacity to solve the technical as well as the financial problems in developing a global cable network. Geography served as an initial stimulus. As an island nation, Britain had a ready market for telegraph connections to the continent, and the efforts by British companies in the 1850s to meet that demand impelled them to search for improved means of insulating submarine cables from the corrosive effects of salt water. The best insulator identified was gutta-percha, a natural plastic from trees in Malaysia and Indonesia. Through its colonial possessions, particularly Singapore, Britain was able to control the trade in gutta-percha and assume a dominant position in the manufacture of submarine cables. As the industry developed, the British also constructed the largest cable-laying ships, including, in 1865, the *Great Eastern,* the first ship capable of carrying enough cable to span the Atlantic.[51]

Political developments in Britain in the 1860s accelerated the growth of international cable connections. When the first attempts to lay a transatlantic cable in the 1850s met with disaster, Parliament created a commission of inquiry, led by William Thomson (later Lord Kelvin), whose 1861 report was a milestone in electrical engineering; Thomson himself also made key scientific contributions to improving cable transmission. The successful deployment of a transatlantic cable in 1866 then fortified confidence in the entire industry. During the next several years, the parliamentary debate about nationalizing the domestic telegraph publicized the high profits in telegraphy, and when the government bought out the domestic companies at spectacularly high prices, it released £8 million for reinvestment, much of which went into submarine cables. By that point, the chief interest lay in connecting Britain with its empire. Overland telegraphs through Russia and Turkey linked Britain to India in 1865, but because they provided abysmal service and no security, two private British companies built new lines to India by 1870, including one that relied primarily on submarine cables through the Mediterranean, the Red Sea, and the Indian Ocean.[52]

The global cable network had manifest value for the empire. It enabled Britain to coordinate and direct its military forces more effectively and to exert greater control over its distant colonies and subject peoples. Like other technological advantages enjoyed by the dominant colonial powers in the second half of the nineteenth century—superior weapons, faster transportation, better means of controlling disease—the telegraph reduced the cost of imperialism and thereby contributed to its geographic extension.[53] Nonetheless, the government did not take the undersea cables directly into its own hands, preferring to leave them to private ownership and operation while subsidizing specific connections the state required. At the height of the subsidies, from 1893 to 1899, Britain devoted £170,000 annually to secret financing of cables, including a line down the east coast of Africa. Led by John Pender's Eastern group, which benefited from the government's close cooperation even more than from subsidies, British interests owned two-thirds of world cable mileage, a share that actually understates the extent of their control. While other countries owned feeder cables, British firms owned the main trunk lines to Asia, Africa, and the Americas and held exclusive cable landing rights at strategic locations; telegraph traffic around the world could hardly flow except through British lines and relay stations. Britain also monopolized the manufacture of cables, dominated cable deployment and repair (as of 1896, twenty-four out of the world's thirty cable ships were British), and developed the highest cable engineering skills. Though the Atlantic cables long operated as a price-fixing cartel, continued investments in improved technology increased the speed and capacity of cable lines and eventually brought down costs and prices. The architecture of the network as much as its ownership assured imperial control: Because the nodal points were under British authority, the government could monitor a large share of global telegraph communication, if it chose to do so.[54]

While Britain's network expanded through state subsidies, it was sustained over the long term by commercial traffic. The other European powers could not match this combined state and private support: France had a large empire but lacked a comparable position in global trade, while the

Germans had neither the colonial empire nor the global trading system. Both started building their cable networks later than Britain and lagged far behind in both mileage and secure control over their lines; France had to abandon some of its cables, and the Germans had failed to catch up before 1914. During the nineteenth century and even into the beginning of the twentieth, the United States was a junior partner to Britain in development of the Atlantic cables. A nominally American company, Commercial Pacific, built the major cable from the West Coast of the United States to Asia but was secretly controlled by Pender's Eastern. Even after American interests took control of the transatlantic cables in 1911, all American lines to Europe went through Britain, enabling the British government to monitor American traffic.[55]

As the leading sea power, Britain was the logical country in the waning years of the nineteenth century to develop a new communication technology that had marine signaling as its most promising early application. Radio was originally radiotelegraphy, the transmission of Morse code through the air. Because of its high expense, low reliability, and lack of privacy and security, early radio did not pose a threat to wired telegraph systems; rather, it promised to extend the telegraph to places unreachable by wire. Two physicists, James Clerk Maxwell and Heinrich Hertz, laid the scientific basis for radio: Maxwell, through his theoretical work in the 1860s on electromagnetic waves; Hertz, through experiments in the 1880s in which he produced radio waves with an electric spark and detected them with a "coherer" of iron filings. Further developments in the late 1880s and early 1890s improved the apparatus for producing and detecting signals. But no one had yet put these discoveries together into a usable—and profitable—technology until the arrival in Britain of Guglielmo Marconi in 1896.

Just twenty-two years old at the time, Marconi had studied physics at Livorno and Bologna and conducted experiments in the propagation and detection of electromagnetic signals on his father's estate. The support for his work came from his Scotch-Irish mother, born into the wealthy Jameson clan of whiskey distillers. Failing to win support from the Italian postal authority, Marconi moved with his mother to London, where he could take advantage of her family's money and social connections. Within a year, Marconi successfully demonstrated his system to influential officials and submitted his first patent for wireless telegraphy, and in 1897 he and his backers founded the Wireless Telegraph and Signal Company (later renamed Marconi's Wireless Telegraph). His technology, however, suffered from serious problems at this point. Spark transmitters scattered waves all over the electromagnetic spectrum, and his original receivers were unable to separate different signals; as result, he could transmit only one message in an area at a time, scarcely the basis of a commercially viable system. But in 1900—in work anticipated by the British physicist Oliver Lodge—Marconi patented a tuning dial to distinguish signals at different frequencies. This was the key step in scaling wireless up to commercial levels of traffic. In 1901 and 1902, defying the scientific establishment of his day, he also succeeded in communicating by wireless across the Atlantic, a triumph that added enormously to his international fame, though the transatlantic service he established was slow to yield a profit.[56]

In turning wireless into a business, Marconi faced political obstacles, both domestic and international, that proved no less challenging than the technical ones. As the British Post Office had looked askance on the telephone when it was new, so it now also refused to purchase Marconi's wireless or to allow Marconi to offer a competing telegraph service within Britain. He was more successful with the British War Office, which tested his system during the Boer War, and with the Royal Navy, which in 1900 placed a major order and three years later made Marconi its sole wireless supplier. The patronage of the navy opened the way to commercial business in ship-to-shore communication, including an important contract with Lloyd's for wireless stations on the ships it insured. In Britain and other countries, the Marconi Company built its own shore stations, leased stations for ships, and trained and supplied telegraph operators—in short, created an entirely self-contained system. When competitors emerged, Marconi refused to allow its operators to communicate with any station using another firm's equipment. This policy of nonintercommunication was similar to Bell's early refusal to connect with independent telephone companies, and it aroused the same antagonism—except that in Marconi's case, the issue had international implications.[57]

While Marconi had the support of maritime interests in Britain and Italy, his policy met protests in other countries on the grounds that the refusal of the largest wireless company to intercommunicate endangered the lives of those at sea. In Marconi's view, since other companies did not pay for maintenance of his marine network, they ought not to be able to use it; as others saw his policy, he was trying to create a monopoly not just over a business, but over the use of the electromagnetic spectrum. And although the Marconi Company may not have regarded itself as a political instrument, other countries viewed its attempt to control radio as an effort to extend British hegemony from the oceans into the ether. No nation objected to that possibility more than Germany. Hoping to use wireless to overcome its inferior position in cables, the German government cultivated its own wireless industry, arranging in 1903 for two small firms to merge into a larger radio company that became known as Telefunken. That same summer, Germany invited other countries to send delegates to Berlin to the first International Wireless Conference, which produced resolutions, over British and Italian objections, calling for all wireless stations regardless of equipment to communicate with each other. A second Berlin conference in 1906 adopted that principle in a treaty and also took up a German proposal to divide the radio spectrum between governmental and commercial uses, with the government, that is, the military, getting the most valuable wavelengths. In the end, after securing concessions on spectrum allocation, even Britain decided to sign the 1906 treaty, though Parliament ratified it only by a single vote. The Marconi Company, however, continued to follow its policy of nonintercommunication toward Telefunken until the two companies struck a deal several years later.[58]

During this early contest over wireless, the United States was divided in its sympathies. The American press hailed Marconi as a hero-inventor, but federal officials, particularly in the U.S. Navy, were hostile to the Marconi Company (and its American subsidiary) because of its nonintercommunication policy, British ownership, and practice of only leasing rather than selling equipment. The Navy at this time was undergoing a dramatic expansion as a result of America's imperial ambitions in the Caribbean and Pacific and the growing belief that sea power was the key to opening markets abroad and assuring future prosperity. Sea power had no greater champion than the president, Theodore Roosevelt, and the Navy's budget, which had doubled between 1896 and 1900, doubled again by 1905, until it represented one-fifth of federal spending. In early purchases of radio equipment, the Navy shunned Marconi, and at the international wireless conferences the military-dominated American delegations opposed Marconi's nonintercommunication policy. But the Navy itself was ambivalent and ineffective in its early attempt to develop wireless and, despite its nationalism, did little to nurture an American industry. Although it tested different instruments, it was slow to adopt any, and it lacked trained engineers and operators capable of running the equipment it ordered, most of it from Germany. Determined to get the lowest prices, it simply disregarded private patent rights: After one American inventor quoted a price the Navy deemed too high, the department had other suppliers copy his design. Meanwhile, naval officers resisted the use of wireless at sea because it threatened their autonomy.[59]

Nonetheless, an Interdepartmental Board of Wireless Telegraphy appointed in 1904 by Roosevelt recommended giving the Navy the lead role in wireless, including management of federal wireless operations and construction of a network of coastal stations. Although Congress never approved the board's report, it later became the basis of Navy claims to authority in making federal radio policy. Included in the report was a recommendation that the Navy offer free shore wireless service to all ships where no commercial station was available. Since at that point few such stations existed, the proposal would have effectively established military control over the primary business that wireless companies were developing. But Congress failed to support these ambitions, marine wireless emerged instead as a private enterprise, and—despite the Navy's determined efforts—the industry fell almost entirely under the control of American Marconi in 1911 when it won a patent infringement suit against its archrival, United Wireless, and absorbed its assets.[60] Marconi also continued to build up its transatlantic radiotelegraph service by constructing high-power, longwave transmitting stations on both sides of the ocean. Then, in 1912, the *Titanic* sank, and the press hailed Marconi operators as heroes for the role they played in the rescue of survivors.

The *Titanic* tragedy was the trigger for the most important early federal regulation of radio. Despite the Navy's support for the 1906 international wireless agreement, many Americans were dubious of the need for government control of the ether, and Congress had initially failed to ratify the convention. In 1910, after wireless proved the savior in a collision of ships at sea, Congress did take a first step toward regulation, requiring that any oceangoing steamer with fifty or more people aboard carry radio equipment, but it left unaddressed the growing problem of interference on the airwaves from competing military, commercial, and amateur radio operators. As soon as the *Titanic* went down, radio regulation moved up on the public agenda. Press reports noted that if one of two nearby ships had had its wireless working and its operator on duty (instead of its engines off and its operator asleep), it could have saved all the lives that were lost; the press also condemned amateur radio operators for the interference they caused and for transmitting falsely reassuring messages that the *Titanic* was being towed to port. Four months later, after first requiring all ships to have two wireless operators and an auxiliary power supply, Congress passed the landmark Radio Act of 1912. Among its provisions were requirements that all radio operators be licensed and that all ships have wireless stations; most important, it allocated bands of spectrum to different types of use, exiling amateurs to the less desirable shortwaves. By restricting interference by amateurs, the legislation indirectly benefited the company that dominated the private wireless business and that the Navy regarded with deep suspicion—Marconi.[61]

But despite its virtual monopoly of the industry, Marconi's position was weaker than it appeared because the company had failed to anticipate a shift in radio technology. While the spark system produced an intermittent signal scattered over a large band of frequencies, a new approach sought to produce a continuous wave at a single frequency. Continuous-wave radio was more efficient than a spark apparatus in channeling electrical energy into signals and, unlike spark, could transmit voices and music as well as dots and dashes. The pioneering figure in continuous wave was the electrical engineer Reginald Fessenden, a professor at what is now the University of Pittsburgh, who together with Ernst Alexanderson of General Electric (GE) developed the high-frequency alternator, one of three devices invented in the early 1900s to produce continuous-wave transmissions. As early as 1900, Fessenden transmitted voices over distances of up to a mile. A second device, the Poulsen arc, was invented by Valdemar Poulsen of Denmark but developed primarily in America by Cyril Elwell of Federal Telegraph (a private company, despite the name) under contracts from the Navy. Both the alternator and the Poulsen arc played brief, transitional roles in the shift to continuous-wave radio, and it was their development during World War I, under Navy patronage, that gave America a technological lead in radio by the war's end.[62]

But the device that held long-run importance was the third entry in the race for continuous wave, the triode vacuum tube. In 1907, searching for a better means of detecting radio signals, the American inventor Lee de Forest inserted a third element into a vacuum-tube diode invented by a British electrical engineer associated with Marconi, Ambrose Fleming. Although de Forest's triode, or "audion," as he called it, subsequently proved to be a fundamental advance, he was unable to develop it into a commercial product. The organization that did was AT&T, which saw in the new technology both threat and opportunity. As the work on continuous wave progressed during the first decade of the twentieth century, there began to be speculation in the press about the potential for a new wireless telephone system that might make the existing wired network obsolete. That, from Bell's standpoint, was the threat. The same technology, however, also held promise as a solution to the problems of transcontinental telephone service. That was the opportunity. It was at this point, the development of the vacuum tube and its application to long-distance telephony as well as radio, where the two lines of innovation in wires and waves came together.

Beginning in the 1880s, Bell focused its technological interests on improving its long-distance service in the conviction that it would not only be highly profitable, but also help maintain future control of the industry. "We need not fear the opposition in a single place," one of AT&T's lawyers wrote its president in 1901, "provided we control the means of communication with the other places."[63] The basic technical obstacle faced by AT&T was that signals grew weaker with distance. During the monopoly era, Bell addressed this problem through a variety of measures, including a better transmitter, stronger batteries to power the system, and improved wires to increase the efficiency of transmission. In 1899–1900, the nearly simultaneous discovery of the "loading coil" by a Bell engineer and a Columbia University physicist provided a means of doubling the range of long-distance calling to about 1,700 miles. While that advance extended lines from New York as far as Denver, it still left AT&T short of the capacity to provide transcontinental service.[64] To connect Americans coast to coast, it needed some kind of amplifier—what its engineers called a "repeater"—but all the known possibilities caused too much distortion.

This challenge provided the immediate impetus for AT&T to step up its commitment to research and development. Although it had employed some scientists and engineers since the 1880s, Bell's research had focused only on incremental technological improvements, and even this effort initially suffered when Vail took over in 1907 and made substantial cuts in spending. After a few years, however, budgets for research and development began to grow, and in 1911 Vail approved the establishment of a research laboratory at Western Electric, initially known as the Research Branch, to work on studies of fundamental principles, chiefly in the hope of a breakthrough on the repeater problem. This was the beginning of what later became Bell Laboratories.[65]

Political and legal developments at the time were pushing AT&T and other corporations toward a greater emphasis on research. Antitrust law played a critical role because it foreclosed some older strategies for growth. It limited mergers (after a key Supreme Court decision in 1904), and it prevented corporations from using an array of traditional tactics for driving their competitors out of business (especially after the passage of the Clayton Act and establishment of the Federal Trade Commission in 1914). Bell's 1913 antitrust settlement restricted its future acquisitions as well as its tactics and thus forced it to explore alternative means of raising its profitability, such as reducing its costs or developing new products and services. Research could furnish the knowledge to do these things. As some technology-based companies were showing—the German chemical and dye industries were important models—industrial research could generate new products and patents that enabled large corporations to control their markets by perfectly legal means. Several changes in patent law also encouraged companies to make such investments. A 1908 Supreme Court decision upholding the validity of patents on goods not in production gave corporations an incentive to accumulate a portfolio of patents for use as a defense against competition or in trades or cross-licensing agreements with other companies.[66]

From 1894 to 1914, competition in the telephone industry stimulated innovation in automatic dialing and lower-cost services. But if that intensely competitive market had continued, its low margins and high uncertainties would have made it difficult for any firm to make substantial investments in basic research. In a purely competitive market, AT&T would have been too concerned with its short-term survival to invest in new knowledge potentially convertible into profitable innovations only many years later. Regulation, in contrast, provided a stable environment for recovering long-term investments, and rate-setting agencies typically recognized research as a legitimate capital cost. As a result, AT&T could allocate research costs to its operating companies, which could pass them on to consumers. At the same time, public regulation also led Bell to worry about public opinion, and research was good public relations. Still concerned about sentiment in favor of public ownership, Bell continually sought to justify its performance on the grounds that it provided the highest-quality system in the world. A record of technological innovation could also bolster a defense against a future antitrust prosecution.[67]

As a result, government regulation of the telephone industry does not appear to have retarded technological change. On the contrary, the combined effect of antitrust policy (in foreclosing certain monopolistic strategies) and regulatory policy (in assuring long-term market stability) was to turn AT&T toward research and innovation as crucial bases of corporate growth. Perhaps the single most important step in that direction came in 1913, the same year that AT&T faced federal antitrust prosecution. Concluding that Lee de Forest's audion might hold the solution to the repeater problem—the key proved to be exhausting the gas in the audion and turning it into a high-vacuum tube—the company acquired rights to the device. In January 1915, after further work, AT&T met a self-imposed deadline for inaugurating transcontinental telephone service when it connected the aging Alexander Graham Bell in New York to his old assistant Thomas Watson, who was standing by in San Francisco. Like the start of transcontinental telegraph service, the event signaled the closing of a communications frontier. But unlike the earlier link, the new one also symbolized the emergence of a close, ongoing relationship between the communications industry and scientific research. Later in 1915, AT&T sent voice communication through the air for the first time between America and Europe.[68]

Ownership of rights to the vacuum tube now positioned AT&T to dominate wireless telephony; at the same time, GE and Federal Telegraph were also developing continuous-wave technologies ahead of Marconi. A new radio industry was in the making. The previous summer, however, war had broken out in Europe, and the international rivalries in long-distance communications technology assumed a new significance.

Communications and Strategic Advantage

World War I marked a turning point in the political understanding of communications. It brought to the surface the latent strategic implications of the changes in networks and the rise of the mass press throughout the industrial world during the preceding quarter-century. Control of communications circuits became critical to the conflict, and code-making and code-breaking for the first time took on the highest importance as arts of war. Mass propaganda, while hardly new, developed into a far more substantial enterprise, aimed at mobilizing a state's own citizens, demoralizing the enemy, and swaying the public in neutral countries. The war also drove the belligerents to invest in new communications technology, and much of this effort focused on radio. The conflict saw the development of air-to-ground communication, first used in dirigibles and planes to spot enemy forces, and it led to pioneering work in radio direction-finding to locate U-boats and other ships. As the use of radio spread from the naval to air branches and finally to the army, it opened up the potential for mobile command-and-control—and for new forms of warfare—that wired telegraph and telephone systems had not supported.[69]

To many military and political leaders, the political implications of these developments seemed clear: States needed, at a minimum, to prevent their vital communications circuits from falling under foreign control and, better yet, to assure themselves a technological edge over their rivals. In Europe, the war only confirmed earlier tendencies to state intervention. But in the United States, where strategic interests had played virtually no part in shaping communications, World War I brought more of a change—though in the end, after coming close to nationalization, America continued to shy away from state ownership.

The war underscored the strategic value of communications partly because the new networks of the time were highly vulnerable to an enemy that understood how to attack them. While cable and radio provided warring states with more rapid, long-distance communication, the available circuits were limited and poorly protected. The Allied Powers were able to achieve an unqualified victory in the battle for communications intelligence because they started out with stronger systems and quickly took advantage of German vulnerabilities. Britain's prewar dominance of submarine cable technology was a crucial asset. No sooner had Germany invaded Belgium on August 4, 1914, triggering Britain's entry into the war, than the British moved to cut the five undersea cables that linked Germany to the world overseas. Within a few weeks, the Allies also silenced most of the high-powered German wireless stations around the world that were capable of long-range communication. Germany, however, did not have a similar capacity to shut down the British, French, and Russian networks. Britain's cables were far more extensive than Germany's, and the British were able to repair them quickly whenever they were damaged. Allied circuits actually increased because the cables seized from Germany were diverted to Allied use.[70]

Nonetheless, like the Royal Navy's blockade of the German fleet, this communication blockade had limited impact on the fighting early in the war because the Central Powers were self-sufficient in critical resources. But the cutoff did have important political consequences. While the British were able to censor cable traffic and control the flow of European news, the Germans had only restricted access to the public in neutral countries, notably the United States before its entry into the war in April 1917. The disparity gave the British a considerable advantage in shaping American sympathies. According to a study of *New York Times* coverage, only 4 percent of front-page stories came from Germany during the first year of the war, while 70 percent came from the Allied side, primarily from London. Before America's entry, Germany did retain the ability to transmit its view of the war from a high-powered radio station near Berlin to one of two German-built stations in the United States, but American policy banning all but neutral communication limited the use of this link. Germany lacked secure channels of its own for military and diplomatic messages and needed to originate cables from such officially neutral countries as Sweden, exposing them to British interception. In 1917, in one of the war's greatest intelligence coups, the British decoded a telegram from German Foreign Secretary Arthur Zimmermann to the president of Mexico offering the return of Texas, Arizona, and New Mexico if Mexico would enter the war on Germany's side. Disclosure of the Zimmermann telegram in March 1917 helped to bring the United States into the war against Germany the next month.[71]

Britain's control of the channels of information was not, however, an unqualified blessing in the view of many American officials. Americans suspected that the British government was reading telegraph traffic between the United States and other countries and turning over commercially relevant information to British firms. Such concerns inspired a series of American moves in the immediate aftermath of the war. At the Paris Peace Conference, President Wilson unsuccessfully sought to prevent Britain from taking permanent possession of cables seized from Germany; he also proposed discussing a new international regime for cable communication, but to no effect. At home, meanwhile, officials in his administration were trying to free American radio from British interests, and these efforts proved more consequential, though not exactly as they were intended.

During the war, Wilson's secretary of the navy, Josephus Daniels, nearly succeeded in nationalizing the entire radio industry. By 1912, the Navy had begun to make the necessary changes in organization and leadership to assure the integration of wireless into naval operations. Daniels, who became secretary in 1913, believed the Navy had a mission to develop wireless, indeed, that government generally ought to own and manage the means of communication in the nation's best interests. During the more than two years of American neutrality after the war broke out in Europe, the Navy built the world's most advanced radio network through contracts with Federal Telegraph and GE for the most powerful continuous-wave transmitters yet constructed. These resources soon proved critical for communication with American forces overseas. Once the United States declared war, the Navy also took operational control of American Marconi as well as the two high-powered stations the Germans had built on the East Coast. Then, without congressional authorization, the Navy bought Federal Telegraph's wireless operations on the West Coast as well as its patents and, in another unauthorized acquisition, purchased Marconi's shore and ship network, giving it a monopoly of marine radio (229 coastal stations and 3,776 ship stations) by the end of 1918.[72]

But Daniels, who faced threats of impeachment for the Marconi purchase, was unable to persuade Congress to make nationalization permanent. While the Navy's management of radio had not been controversial during the war, wartime state ownership of the railroads and the telephone industry had brought higher rates and widespread public dissatisfaction. After the war, as Progressivism receded, the country was in no mood to adopt public ownership. Furthermore, Republican victories in the 1918 congressional elections effectively ruled out nationalization of radio.[73] Just as neither the Mexican War nor the Civil War altered the private path of the telegraph, so World War I did not alter the path of radio or the telephone in America. Indeed, the brief experience with nationalization seems to have put the issue to rest. During the nineteenth century, such major figures as Clay and Grant had supported federal ownership of the telegraph; the efforts by Wilson's postmaster general and navy secretary effectively ended the effort to nationalize communications in America.

With state ownership excluded, the question after the war became whether the nationalists in the Navy could find a politically feasible way to prevent American Marconi from acquiring continuous-wave technology and reestablishing its earlier primacy. The issue came to a head while Daniels was away in Europe during the spring of 1919, when key Navy officials asked GE as a matter of patriotism—supposedly at the request of President Wilson himself—to refuse to sell Marconi high-frequency generators. Instead, they proposed that GE create a new radio company under American ownership that would have a monopoly under a federal charter. But, despite the support of the assistant secretary of the navy,

Franklin D. Roosevelt, the officials who approached GE were in no position to offer the government's imprimatur. Neither Congress nor Secretary Daniels, once he got wind of the proposal, was willing to authorize a radio monopoly, and no charter ever materialized. The intervention by the Navy's leading radio officials nonetheless had a decisive impact. American Marconi's top executives became convinced that they had to free themselves of British ownership, and GE decided to enter the radio industry by purchasing British Marconi's controlling interest in the company. When it concluded the purchase, GE turned the old American Marconi into the operating core of the new company it created, the Radio Corporation of America (RCA). Soon after starting operation in December 1919, RCA took over the Navy's wireless stations, and the impetus for nationalization dissipated.[74]

Another obstacle, however, had to be overcome. During the war, to facilitate production of radio equipment by private companies, the Navy had removed all patent restrictions, assumed any liability for patent infringement, and set uniform standards for vacuum tubes and other components. New companies, including Westinghouse and Western Electric, entered the field, and instead of producing radios one at a time, as had been the rule before the war, manufacturers mass-produced thousands of sets with standardized parts. Standardized production, with its lower costs and simplification of procedures, was a key step toward the transformation of radio into a means of mass communication. After the war, however, the fragmentation of patent ownership loomed as an impediment to the growth of the industry. Although RCA at its inception received rights to GE's radio patents as well as those belonging to American Marconi, it lacked rights to essential patents owned by AT&T and Westinghouse. The legal status of the vacuum tube was particularly vexed. In 1915, British Marconi, which owned the patent on the Fleming diode, sued de Forest for infringement, while de Forest countersued Marconi for violating his patent on the triode. The next year, a court held that each was guilty of infringing the other's patent, making it impossible for either Marconi or AT&T (which had acquired most of de Forest's rights) to proceed alone.[75]

To avoid paralysis, GE invited AT&T and Westinghouse to join in an agreement that eventually involved cross-licensing 1,200 radio-related patents. If it had stopped there, the agreement would have left the companies free to compete with each other in radio and telecommunications, but instead it called for a territorial division of the emerging businesses. According to the initial terms, GE would manufacture 60 percent and

Westinghouse 40 percent of radio sets, RCA would be responsible for sales and distribution as well as for radiotelegraph services, and AT&T would have exclusive rights to telephone service (whether wired or wireless) and to interconnection of wired and wireless systems. Although the agreement incidentally mentioned sales of radio sets to "amateurs," it still conceived of radio as point-to-point communication. None of the parties yet anticipated the rise of broadcasting.[76]

In one respect, the creation of RCA followed the pattern already established in telecommunications. Despite the powerful tendency toward military socialism, American policy held back from state ownership: Nationalism prevailed without nationalization. Antistatism set limits to statist impulses. The suspicion of concentrated power blocked not only a federal takeover of radio, but also a federally chartered private monopoly. The intervention of Navy representatives, however, precipitated the formation of what soon came to be called the "radio trust." Geopolitical concerns that had never previously entered into the structure of American communications led to a new concentration of corporate power. This conjunction of military and domestic communications was a new development that anticipated a more extensive institutional convergence in the development of electronics, communications, and computers during World War II and the Cold War.

World War I, then, serves as a convenient marking point to divide the political development of American communications. From the early republic, America took a distinctive path in communications, beginning with the postal system, newspapers, and primary education, continuing with the growth of popular print, and reaching a further stage with the rise of technological networks, particularly the telephone. Though there are exceptions and limitations (communication no less than other aspects of American society was circumscribed by race and gender), the pattern had three general characteristics. First, the development of these media occurred earlier and more rapidly in the United States than in other countries. Second, the systems tended to be more geographically extensive and popularly accessible than in Europe; in particular, instead of being concentrated in metropolitan centers, they were more widely distributed in rural areas and small towns than was the pattern in European societies. And, third, despite America's lag in many areas of science, there was an exceptionally high level of technological innovation in communications.

These characteristics resulted from particular policies favorable to communications and from general features of the American constitutional and legal system. Republican government generated both ideological commitments and political interests in communications. At the nation's beginnings, for example, concerns about the survival of the republic influenced the decision to build a comprehensive postal network, and support for public education and other policies reflected a widespread belief that the diffusion of knowledge would generally strengthen republican institutions and add to the nation's wealth and power. At the same time, limits on state power (as in the guarantees of free speech and postal privacy) encouraged popular initiative in the public sphere and trust in the channels of communication. As the legal environment was generally favorable to economic development, so it was favorable to communications development. An unimpeded national market, created by the Constitution and elaborated through judicial decisions, was particularly important as a stimulus to continent-wide telegraph and telephone networks, particularly when compared with the effects of political fragmentation in Europe.

Able to develop into integrated national systems, the telegraph and telephone helped to tie the national market more closely together. This was one of the ways in which communications development fed into economic growth. The expansion of America's national market, Alfred Chandler argues, provided the basis for the emergence of high-volume, management-run, modern business enterprise, which became a critical source of competitive advantage for the United States relative to countries such as Britain and France where smaller-scale, family-run business was more entrenched. Chandler's history portrays the process as technology-driven, but this is only part of the story: Through its constitutional interpretations, the Supreme Court cleared away barriers that might have fragmented the national market despite technological change.[77] With that qualification, the Chandler hypothesis points to one of the ways in which America's distinctive path in communications may have conferred economic advantage. Continent-wide networks made it possible to achieve the efficiencies of high-volume enterprise.

Although the Chandler argument focuses on manufacturing, the benefits of American communications development may have also accrued to agriculture and other industries located in rural areas. From the expansion of the postal system, schooling, and newspapers in the early republic to the Post Office's introduction of rural free delivery in the 1890s and the rise of rural telephone systems at the turn of the century, rural America received earlier and more extensive access to communications than such areas elsewhere in the world. A series of federal programs—the Morrill Land Grant College Act of 1862, the agricultural experiment stations created under the Hatch Act of 1887, and the cooperative extension service established in 1914—are widely credited with generating "unprecedented payoffs in agricultural productivity."[78] The extension service was specifically concerned with assuring the diffusion of new scientific knowledge to farmers. But it was only a small part of the wider support given to communication in rural areas that facilitated the rapid take-up of new knowledge, cut farmers' information costs, and improved their productivity in other ways.

As the case of the telephone illustrates, America built a widely distributed national communications system through a kind of creative resistance to centralized power. At the turn of the century, law and policy antagonistic to prolonged monopoly opened up telecommunications to the forces of civil society and the market, enabling unserved communities to acquire telephone service. Even after the return to monopoly, the American suspicion of concentrated power, in the form of antitrust policy, contributed to the emphasis on research by limiting other strategies for growth. By forcing the divestiture of Western Union in 1913, antitrust policy also forced AT&T to build a national, long-distance network of its own, which required fundamental technical advances. The large installed base of telephones resulting from the early burst in popular adoption then supported high levels of investment in technological innovation under a rate-setting system that recognized research as a legitimate cost. When Bell Telephone Laboratories opened in 1925, it had more than 2,000 employees on its technical staff and a budget of $12 million to work on advances in electronics, radio, applied mathematics, and many other areas of science related to communications. During the next fifty years, the 18,000 patents its scientists received averaged out to about one per working day. When AT&T held up Bell Laboratories as a national resource, this was not just public relations. National policy was behind it, and when war came in 1917 and again in 1941, Bell Laboratories and Western Electric quickly converted to military research and production.[79] America's leadership in telecommunications, developed originally for civil purposes, thereby became a source of state power and strategic advantage.

But the long absence of military concerns from communications policy may have helped to create the lead in telecommunications in the first place. In early nineteenth-century continental Europe, the original military conception of the telegraph impeded its commercial development.

Security-minded telecommunications policies tended to militate against easily accessible, widely distributed networks, distorting both allocational priorities and architectural choices, to the disadvantage of long-term growth. A mere tool of civil society and local commerce, the telephone originally had little appeal to the military, in particular, and to the state, in general. States that were strong relative to civil society did not invest heavily in telephone service. That was the case in the major European states compared to America in the late nineteenth and early twentieth centuries. Similarly, the far greater domination of the state over civil society in the Soviet world helps to explain its lag relative to the West in the development of the telephone during the twentieth century.[80] As World War I illustrated, wartime state support could generate technological innovation in communications. But it is one thing to have individual spin-offs from military projects, and quite another to have a framework for communications shaped by state-security concerns.

As it turned out, the nationalist effort to build up American radio after World War I was not a brilliant success. The vision that inspired the Navy, GE, AT&T, and other participants in the birth of RCA in 1919 proved wrong in almost every respect. With the rise of broadcasting in the next two years, radio became an entirely different medium from what the partners in the radio trust had imagined. They soon found their agreement was obsolete and had to be rewritten; far from monopolizing the field, RCA at first had difficulty keeping up with new competitors that grabbed most of the business in making radio sets. The high-frequency alternators that the Navy did not want GE to sell to Marconi quickly became obsolete, and few of them were built. Despite the Navy's efforts, the British regained their dominant position in global communications during the 1920s, thanks to a new shortwave beam antenna system developed by Marconi. In short, nothing worked out the way the Navy or the private corporations planned. The world was about to shift under their feet, and even some of the most powerful organizations in America could not make it stand still.

PART THREE

The Making of the Modern Media 1865–1941

CHAPTER SEVEN

Great Transformations

The Early Mass Media and the Diversity Dynamic

DEEP CHANGES in society are often as important for the reactions they provoke as for the direct effects they produce. In both Europe and the United States during the nineteenth century, the growth of markets and industry sparked countermovements of protest, reform, and public regulation, all attempting to control the unsettling effects of economic upheaval. It was this double movement, Karl Polanyi argued, that characterized the "great transformation" of the nineteenth century.[1] America's great transformation, however, followed a different pattern from Europe's because of an additional dynamic overlaid upon industrialization and set in motion by a radical increase in ethnic diversity that affected nearly every aspect of American society, including communications.

During the early decades of the nineteenth century, immigration to the United States had been relatively limited; the foreign-born hit a low of 8 percent of the nation's population in 1830, rising only slowly in the decades before the Civil War. After 1870, the numbers of immigrants surged, and instead of originating in Germany and the British Isles, they came predominantly from southern and eastern Europe. Just at the moment that cities were exploding in size, the new immigrants settled in urban areas and formed an increasingly important part of cultural life as well as of the electorate. By the turn of the century, African Americans from the rural South were also migrating to northern and midwestern cities, a journey that brought them into closer relation with urban culture and into conflict with northern whites, both foreign-and native-born. Like the "great transformation" affecting all industrial societies, the increase in ethnic heterogeneity beginning in the 1870s had a double character. Immigrants and blacks brought new vitality to American culture, particularly the popular culture that became central to the emerging mass media. But the influx of new people with different cultural traditions also elicited reactive movements of protest, reform, and regulation that were concerned not just with overtly nativist and racist causes such as immigration restriction but also with culture and moral behavior.

This was the social and political context of a crucial phase in the constitutive development of modern communications. The half century before the outbreak of World War I in 1914 saw the establishment of the "mass media" as central social institutions in both Europe and North America.[2] Though the metropolitan penny papers in the antebellum United States had anticipated this development, only a small minority of Americans had lived in large cities before the Civil War. In Britain, France, and other European countries, restrictive state policies such as high taxes on the press, as well as low literacy rates, had held back the expansion of cheap popular newspapers in the early 1800s. It was in the second half of the nineteenth century, particularly after 1870, that the mass-circulation, metropolitan press became a dominant presence in the public sphere on both sides of the Atlantic. The same era also witnessed the growth of urban cultural institutions and new forms of popular entertainment, culminating at the turn of the century in the rise of the movies. But while American and European media shared many of the same tendencies, they traveled along different paths of development because of variations in social conditions and key political and legal decisions.

As of 1870, the communications media followed a more classically liberal and democratic pattern in America than in Europe. State intervention was more limited in the United States, which had a stronger tradition of an independent press and was now virtually alone in leaving the telegraph in private hands. Although democratizing forces in European societies were closing the earlier gaps in electoral participation and access to education, there was a critical difference in the sequence of development. In the United States, just as political democracy had preceded industrialization, so, too, had greater cultural democratization preceded the rise of the mass media. Much of early nineteenth-century American culture—theater, music, books, and newspapers—had a public that crossed class lines, and cultural entrepreneurs tended to adapt to popular demands for accessibility. In contrast, their European counterparts of the time often benefited from state patronage, catered to a more elite public, and used more elevated and restricted forms of expression that would not have been readily intelligible or appealing to working-class audiences. Like class distinctions, differences between high and popular culture that were blurred in America were more marked in Europe.

These early transatlantic contrasts became much attenuated during the late 1800s. In Europe, the spread of education and literacy, the mass press, and popular entertainment pushed cultural practices in a more democratic direction, which critics often identified as American, a characterization usually not intended as praise. Meanwhile, in the United States after the Civil War, culture and communications became in certain respects markedly less liberal and democratic than they had been earlier: The state imposed greater moral regulation on the press, and sharper distinctions emerged between "high" and "low" spheres of culture and entertainment as some Americans sought consciously to imitate European high culture. These repressive and hierarchical tendencies bred their own reaction in the form of modernist, progressive, and bohemian rebellion, especially after 1900. But throughout this period, up to the 1920s, the dominant American institutions, public and private alike, reflected relatively restrictive moral and cultural norms; the courts, in particular, were almost uniformly unsympathetic to claims of free speech by radical political as well as cultural dissidents, even as American society accommodated a wider range than ever of ethno-religious expression. In short, the United States simultaneously moved toward greater cultural restriction, hierarchy, and diversity as the early mass media were taking shape. Then, during and immediately after World War I, the restrictive impulse peaked in an outburst of repression and provoked so strong a backlash that the old legal and cultural framework of communications was shattered, and a new one emerged.

The Rise of Moral Censorship

Studies of state intervention in the nineteenth century usually emphasize such measures as factory legislation, public health, and social insurance, but there was also an increase in moral regulation, particularly relating to sex, popular culture, and the protection of children. In the United States, these concerns intersected after the Civil War in a growing public preoccupation with obscenity—or as we now call it, "pornography," a term that had not yet acquired its modern meaning.[3] Like other movements of moral reform, the campaign had a coercive side, aimed at suppressing vice, and a meliorist or didactic side, aimed at propagating alternatives thought to be more wholesome, pure, and uplifting.[4]

Obscenity had long been illegal, though there had been little effort to eradicate it. Beginning with Vermont in 1821, twenty-one states and four territories had adopted statutes banning obscenity before or during the Civil War, while courts elsewhere had held it punishable under the common law.[5] But the stringency of enforcement and volume of cases appear to have been limited, and the federal government had been involved in only one minor respect (a ban on the import of "indecent and obscene prints, lithographs, engravings and transparencies" in an 1842 tariff law). The years after the Civil War saw antiobscenity efforts turn into a public crusade and gain the authority of federal as well as stricter state law. For the first time, Americans created private organizations specifically aimed at suppressing obscene publications and other indecent items, undertook extensive prosecutions of people in the trade, and sent them to prison in significant numbers. In a key turn, Congress broke with earlier policy and authorized use of the Post Office as an instrument of censorship and moral regulation.

The United States was far from unique in trying to suppress obscenity; by the end of the nineteenth century, an international "social purity" crusade was attacking obscenity along with other forms of vice in a variety of countries where the rise of cheap print included a growing business in smut. Here, it seems, was a typical instance of a regulatory reaction to an expanding market that threatened the sense of order, but it was not merely a quantitative change in obscene items that drew a political response. A considerable amount of steamy and sensational literature circulated in America in the 1830s and 1840s without exciting congressional attention, aggressive local law enforcement, or organized demands for censorship. In the United States, as in Europe, the advent of moral regulation depended on the formation of a political force with the commitment and capacity to mobilize moral sentiment and to translate it into law and policy. That force emerged in the United States only after the Civil War.

Although some cultural critics associate the moral censorship of the late 1800s with the Puritanism of colonial New England, the more immediate model came from Great Britain. It was the British who established the cultural forms, organizational prototypes, and legal principles that moral reformers adopted in the United States. Victorian morality, as the term "Victorian" suggests, had British origins, though its influence eventually stretched across the ocean. The shift toward greater prudery in Britain actually started long before Victoria's accession to the throne in 1837. Beginning in the 1780s, two developments affecting the British elite were critical in arousing institutional efforts to curb sexual representations and expressions: an Evangelical religious revival, which identified obscenity as one of several sources of moral decay, and the alarm set off by the French Revolution that sexual immorality and political rebellion went hand in hand. In 1787, at the instigation of the Evangelical political leader William Wilberforce, George III issued a "Proclamation for the Encouragement of Piety and Virtue, and for the Preventing and Punishing of Vice, Profaneness and Immorality," which included strictures against obscene works. A Proclamation Society with leadership from high circles in the aristocracy and church then attempted to carry out the policy, but in 1802 a new group, the Society for the Suppression of Vice, replaced the first, bringing to the campaign a somewhat broader membership, greater energy, and more emphasis on policing. The vice society initiated prosecutions against dealers in obscene as well as blasphemous publications, sought to enforce observance of the Sabbath by discouraging any public entertainment on Sunday, and attacked a variety of forms of bawdy and disorderly public behavior. These efforts, undertaken against the backdrop of Britain's struggle with France, reflected a moral conservatism common in wartime as well as the specific conviction among the elite that undisciplined sexuality and radical politics were intertwined French influences threatening to overturn both church and state. While the vice society attacked obscenity, blasphemy, and disorderliness through coercive measures, religious tract societies and other groups cultivated moral and religious conformity through cheap publications and other didactic methods.[6]

In short, elite-sponsored campaigns aimed at changing moral and cultural life played a significant part in the beginnings of Victorianism, contributing to a general trend toward greater sexual reticence and delicacy of expression. The same period saw the first expurgated editions of English classics, such as *The Family Shakespeare,* first published in 1807 before being reissued in expanded form in 1818 by Thomas Bowdler. A century later, Bowdlerization would be seen as a clumsy corruption of literature, but the Victorians regarded it as evidence of their moral and cultural refinement, so superior to the coarseness and crudity of earlier times.[7] The same belief that repression represented moral progress inspired stronger official measures to suppress obscenity.

As of the early nineteenth century, British legal regulation of obscenity rested not on statute, but on common-law rulings that held, going back to 1728, that any work tending to corrupt morals, thereby threatening breach of the peace, represented an "obscene libel." Until the formation of the Society for the Suppression of Vice, however, prosecutions for obscenity were rare. By employing agents to seek out vendors of obscene items, the vice society provided a private, semiofficial means of law enforcement at a time when many in the elite were reluctant to expand the state itself. The organization was not a "pressure group" in the modern sense: Rather than exerting pressure upward on Parliament and the crown, it primarily applied pressure downward on the working classes. The group's practice of targeting the vices of the poor while ignoring those of the rich led to persistent accusations of hypocrisy, a charge its defenders handily rebutted on the grounds that it was mere kindness to reform the poor because they could least of all afford depravity. The rich kept their vices private, argued one Evangelical publication. "The vices of the poor, on the contrary, walk abroad, insult us in the marketplace, and elbow us in the streets." The vice society's primary concern with public order was evident in a legislative change that it secured in 1824: an amendment to the Vagrancy Act providing for summary conviction for public displays of lewdness and obscenity.[8] The operative hypothesis seems to have been something like today's "broken window" theory of crime control: If affronts to public order (such as a broken window on a street) do not meet an immediate response, they will lead to a self-reinforcing spiral of criminal activity.[9]

Gradually, however, a change took place in the underlying Victorian concern about smut and, accordingly, in the focus of censorship. By the mid–nineteenth century, instead of worrying that obscenity and blasphemy would invite rebellion and disorder among the lower classes, moral reformers became increasingly concerned that obscenity, in particular, would lead to private sensual indulgence, even—perhaps especially—among the better off. As a result, according to M.J.D. Roberts, the vice society shifted its efforts from "the regulation of working-class sexuality" toward "the 'protection' of that increasingly segregated and morally problematic section of the population—middle and upper-class youths and unmarried males."[10] This new focus, which went along with a growing Victorian panic about masturbation, may help to account for changes in the law. During the first half of the nineteenth century, though the vice society attacked obscene displays and prosecuted some purveyors of obscene materials, its efforts were intermittent, the legal means at its disposal were limited, and the trade continued to flourish, particularly in London's Holywell Street. By the 1850s, the failure to extirpate obscenity became a matter for legislation and more thoroughgoing enforcement. In 1857, prodded by Lord Campbell, Parliament adopted the Obscene Publications Act, primarily to make enforcement more effective by authorizing judges to issue search warrants upon testimony that an establishment had obscene items for sale. The turn toward broader, more aggressive efforts against obscenity was not limited to Britain; that same year, 1857, the French government brought three separate cases for "offending public morals" against Gustave Flaubert, Charles Baudelaire, and Eugène Sue.[11]

Britain's Obscene Publications Act was not supposed to signal any change in the scope of obscenity prosecutions; in particular, Campbell insisted during parliamentary debate that it would not affect serious literature. Nonetheless, in an obiter dictum in an 1868 case, *Regina v. Hicklin*, Lord Chief Justice Cockburn defined the test of obscenity as whether the "tendency" of a work was "to deprave and corrupt those whose minds are open to such immoral influences, and into whose hands a publication of this sort may fall." In the same ruling, Cockburn declared the intention of an author irrelevant: "Where a man publishes a work manifestly obscene, he must be taken to have had the intention which is implied from that act." Under these principles—which migrated to American courts, even though British law had no force in the United States—the legal regulation of obscenity evolved into a means of enforcing purity and decency in literature generally.[12]

While these developments were taking place in Britain and France, obscenity had not provoked much controversy in the United States, much less the establishment of an organization comparable to the British vice society. The 1842 federal ban on import of indecent pictures (which did not even cover obscene texts) was adopted as part of general tariff legislation and occasioned no recorded congressional debate; states that adopted obscenity statutes usually did so as part of a general codification of their laws.[13] In New York City during the 1850s, prosecutors brought charges against some publishers of pornography, but none went to trial; these cases typically involved works that were European imports or imitations, betraying an American tendency that would become even more pronounced later in the century to associate the obscene with the influence of foreigners and immigrants.[14]

During the antebellum era, the great flash point in free expression was not sex, but slavery. In 1835, postal officials were complicit in local vigilantes' seizure and destruction of abolitionist mailings to the South, but even this episode showed the political barriers to federal censorship at the time. Although President Andrew Jackson proposed legislation authorizing postmasters to destroy incendiary publications, Congress refused to adopt it. Southerners who opposed the abolitionists were even more opposed to any extension of federal power. "Congress has no right in any form or in any matter, to interfere with the freedom of the press," declared John Calhoun, who, far from being a civil libertarian, thought that the federal government should defer to the states' determination of what mail could be circulated.[15] Combined with those who objected on free speech grounds, the states' rights opposition tipped the balance against federal censorship of the mails during the antebellum era.

It was the secession of the South, the absence of its representatives from Congress during the Civil War, and the region's subsequent loss of political power that during and after the 1860s permitted the enlargement of federal power, including new authority for the Post Office. Wartime also brought Lincoln's suspension of habeas corpus, the temporary closing of some opposition newspapers, and federal censorship of telegraph news. The diminished concern for rights of free expression spilled into the Reconstruction era, as was evident in the dragnet searches of telegraph messages ordered during congressional investigations in the 1870s. This was the context—the political conjuncture—for new federal legislation regarding obscenity. In 1865, after reporting that soldiers were receiving "great numbers" of "obscene books and pictures," the postmaster general obtained new authority from Congress to seize obscene materials and prosecute those who mailed them, with penalties of up to a year in prison.[16] Although Reconstruction also saw the adoption of the Fourteenth Amendment (ultimately the basis for applying the First Amendment to the states), the immediate effect of the expanded power of the national government was to breach a long-standing constitutional barrier against federal censorship of the mails and thus of the press. The Civil War and its aftermath thus opened a second era in the history of the First Amendment.[17]

The initial 1865 legislation proved to be only a preliminary step, as Congress failed to provide means of enforcing the statute, but it was not long before a group of Americans persuaded both the federal government and the states to adopt the same solution as in Britain: privately sponsored law enforcement. In the American case, however, the same people who took on the enforcement function also played a critical role as a lobbying group during the formative period of moral censorship. In 1866, the New York chapter of the Young Men's Christian Association (YMCA)—originally founded in 1852, eight years after its counterpart in London—decried the spread of obscenity as an immoral influence on single young men living in boarding houses, and, in 1868, obtained New York State's first antiobscenity legislation. Three years later, a twenty-seven-year-old dry-goods clerk named Anthony Comstock sought on his own initiative to enforce the YMCA-sponsored law against a stationer who sold dirty books, only to find that a local policeman tipped off the vendor ahead of time. Undeterred, Comstock obtained better cooperation from the police in March 1872, when he organized a raid of a Manhattan street where a number of dealers in obscene books and contraceptives were located. Hoping to attack not just the dealers but the publishers, Comstock then appealed for help to the YMCA and there found the patronage that would enable him to convert a personal crusade into a public one. The association's new president, the banker and industrialist Morris K. Jesup, convened a group of influential and wealthy men, who became the YMCA's Committee for the Suppression of Vice and immediately began underwriting Comstock's enforcement work.[18]

The role of these wealthy men in sponsoring moral regulation was part of a more general development in America during the period. Beginning in 1866 with the American Society for the Prevention of Cruelty to Animals—also modeled after a similarly named British society—a series of moral-reform organizations followed the same pattern. In each case, the founders and directors were exclusively men, often of considerable social prominence and wealth, who sought to impose moral regulation through private means they controlled in the belief that public enforcement was unreliable—a genteel, urban, upper-class counterpart to the vigilantes of the western frontier.[19] One interpretation of the elite campaign to suppress obscenity highlights the small-town origins of many of its sponsors and suggests they were reacting against the breakdown of traditional moral norms in the metropolis. Another interpretation points to their recently acquired wealth and suggests that the focus on protecting children from corrupting influences betrayed the sponsors' concern about reproducing their own family status. Still a third account emphasizes their patriarchal ideology and argues they were trying to maintain traditional relationships between the sexes.[20] These concerns may all have been factors in their motivation, but as subsequent events would show, moral censorship enjoyed support not merely from elite men but from others as well, including women—indeed, for a long time it hardly met any opposition. As in Britain, elite-sponsored efforts had a critical early role in the shift toward more stringent moral regulation, though elite concerns were not the sole forces in enlarging and sustaining moral reform over the long term.

A series of sensational developments from the fall of 1872 through the winter of 1873 led to a tighter institutionalization of censorship at the federal level. At first, the YMCA committee preferred to keep a relatively low profile, and Comstock pursued his quarry without much publicity, but in late 1872 a case erupted that became a national scandal. Victoria Claflin Woodhull and her sister Tennessee Claflin operated a brokerage on Wall Street and used its profits to publish a weekly advocating women's suffrage, spiritualism, and free love. Woodhull, who also published the first English translation of the *Communist Manifesto,* was the candidate for president in 1872 of the tiny Equal Rights Party, which she had helped to create. On November 2, the weekly claimed that the eminent preacher Henry Ward Beecher was having an affair with a woman in his congregation—the wife, no less, of Beecher's close friend and neighbor—and Comstock had the sisters arrested for mailing an obscene publication. The basis of the case against them later shifted from the allegations about Beecher to a story they had published accusing a prominent broker of seducing two young girls, and still later to advertisements for contraceptives. All legal charges, however, were eventually dismissed. While this case was proceeding, Comstock had a publisher of popular magazines, Frank Leslie, indicted, also for carrying advertisements for contraceptives, but Leslie said he would stop running the notices and the district attorney let the case drop.[21]

The Woodhull-Claflin prosecution made Comstock into a public figure and raised the salience of moral reform on the public agenda, while the difficulties in obtaining convictions confirmed the view of Comstock and his influential backers that both the federal government and the state needed to adopt stronger legislation. Beginning in December 1872, the YMCA vice committee paid for Comstock and two others to travel to Washington for high-level meetings with Republicans on Capitol Hill. It would have been hard to pick a better moment to invite politicians to make a public display of their moral rectitude. Congress was in the midst of one of the great scandals of American history, the Crédit Mobilier affair, in which prominent Republicans stood accused of profiting unethically from the construction of the transcontinental railroad. In the closing days of its session in March 1873, a besieged Congress struck a blow for righteousness by adopting the measure that Comstock was promoting: "An Act for the Suppression of Trade in and Circulation of obscene Literature and Articles of immoral Use."[22]

The Comstock Act, as it came to be known, was a more wide-ranging, harsher version of the legislation originally enacted in 1865. It provided for one to ten years' imprisonment at hard labor for transporting through the mail any obscene "book, pamphlet, picture, paper, print or other publication of an indecent character, or any article or thing designed or intended for the prevention of contraception or procuring or abortion," or "any article or thing intended or adapted for any indecent or immoral use," or any information about obtaining such things. It also imposed up to five years of prison for distributing the forbidden items in the District of Columbia and federal territories and made the customs ban on importing obscene items more inclusive.[23] Compared to Britain, the United States was a latecomer to moral regulation, but it had come on with a vengeance, imposing stiffer penalties for a wide array of vaguely defined offenses. And unlike Britain's legislation on obscene publications, the Comstock Act specifically targeted contraception and abortion.

Just as remarkable as the sweep of regulation was the system of enforcement the government adopted. Two days after President Grant signed the act on March 3, 1873, the Post Office named Comstock as special agent to take the lead role in carrying it out, but at the request of the Committee for the Suppression of Vice, he received no government salary. That spring, the committee was reorganized as an organization independent of the YMCA, receiving a charter from the state as the New York Society for the Suppression of Vice. The original legislation authorized police assistance to the group in suppressing obscene materials and awarded it half the fines collected under the law, but a month later, at the society's behest, the legislature eliminated the monetary rewards. By rejecting a federal salary for

Comstock as well as bounties from the state, the organization's directors not only tried to avoid any suggestion of self-interested motives but also ensured that Comstock remained dependent on their largess. As secretary and chief agent, he received a full-time salary from the vice society and reported to its board, while holding a federal commission that gave him authority to obtain warrants for arrests and seize and destroy publications and other materials. (He also made arrests without warrants when he caught people in the act of violating the law as he understood it.) Under this extraordinary arrangement, the federal government as well as the state of New York, the leading center of the publishing industry, turned over primary responsibility for the enforcement of moral censorship to a man employed by an elite private society composed exclusively of Christian men.[24] This delegation of federal authority proved remarkably long-lasting: Comstock held his two positions under the Post Office and New York vice society for forty-two years until his death in 1915, a career in law enforcement that rivals J. Edgar Hoover's later forty-eight-year tenure as director of the Federal Bureau of Investigation.

The original adoption of this system occurred with little opposition. While some newspapers raised states' rights objections or criticized the powers concentrated in Comstock, the only sustained protests against the law came from the libertarian fringe of American opinion. In 1876, a group of freethinkers devoted to strict separation of church and state founded the National Liberal League, which denounced the appointment of "a single individual" to inspect the mails as "a delegation of authority dangerous to public and personal liberty" and demanded "that all laws against obscenity and indecency shall be so clear and explicit that none but actual offenders against the recognized principles of purity" be punished. Another group of libertarians, radical advocates of free love, opposed sexual reticence and censorship altogether. But the freethought and free-love movements had little influence, and in 1878, after the National Liberal League obtained more than 50,000 signatures in a call for repeal of the Comstock Act, a congressional committee unanimously rejected the petition. Thereafter, except for a small group called the National Defense Association, which aided defendants in some obscenity and birth-control prosecutions, organized opposition to Comstock was negligible until after the turn of the century.[25]

The courts also did not block the imposition of postal censorship. While the Supreme Court did not take up a direct test, it upheld the constitutionality of the Comstock Act in a related 1877 case, *Ex Parte Jackson,* in which it defined the limits of federal powers over the mails.[26] The case involved a New York lottery promoter who had been convicted of violating a recently amended federal statute barring all lotteries from the postal system. The Court ruled that since Congress had the authority to determine what the Post Office could carry, it "necessarily" had "the right to determine what shall be excluded." Sealed letters and packages, the Court declared for the first time, enjoyed the protection of the Fourth Amendment and could be opened only under warrant, but publications and other material open to inspection enjoyed no such guarantee. Nor did the First Amendment provide any protection. "Liberty of circulating," the Court granted, "is as essential to that freedom [of the press] as liberty of publishing." But because Congress did not bar alternative means of conveyance (and, according to the Court, had no authority to do so), it could constitutionally deny publications access to the mails. Then, citing the Comstock Act, the Court added: "All that Congress meant by this act was, that the mail should not be used to transport such corrupting publications and articles, and that any one who attempted to use it for that purpose should be punished." And this, the Court said, was perfectly constitutional. The decision set no limits on federal authority to exclude publications from the mail, even though the Post Office's monopoly meant that no comparable private substitute existed. And so the Court brought to an end the long abstention of the federal government from using its control of the Post Office to censor communication.

During the late 1870s, the campaign for moral censorship spread throughout the country. Following the leadership of the New York group, clergymen and reformers in other cities set up vice societies and received similar policing powers. The most active groups were the Western Society for the Suppression of Vice, which included branches in Chicago and St. Louis, and the Boston-based New England Society for the Suppression of Vice, later renamed the Watch and Ward Society. Although the founders and directors of these groups were exclusively male, middle-class women's organizations also became active supporters of censorship. The largest of these, the Woman's Christian Temperance Union (WCTU), established a Department for the Suppression of Impure Literature in 1883 and remained a major backer of censorship campaigns for decades. The National Congress of Mothers was also an active supporter of censorship. While the pro-censorship movement was not limited to men, it was organized by gender. Unlike the male vice societies, the female reform organizations did not obtain policing powers from the state, though they aided enforcement by conducting local surveillance to identify sources of smut and also contributed to campaigns for more stringent state legislation.[27] During these years, many states passed "little Comstock laws," drawing on the language of the federal legislation and specifically outlawing information and materials for contraception as well as abortion. By the mid-1880s, state and federal legislation, backed up by private enforcement groups, had effectively created a new regime of moral regulation in America.

Though nativism was not a factor in the passage of the Comstock Act, the pro-censorship groups that originated in the 1870s and 1880s, such as the vice societies and WCTU, were overwhelmingly composed of native-born Protestants, who had long associated obscenity, drunkenness, and other forms of immorality with immigrants. Like the temperance movement, moral censorship offered an older Protestant America a means of resisting an alien new urban culture developing in its midst. As early as its first annual report in 1875, the New York vice society classified arrests by ethnicity and pointedly observed that "a large proportion of those engaged in the nefarious traffic are not native American citizens." Vice campaigns frequently suggested that dirty books and pictures came from foreign sources, particularly France. Writing in 1883 about the dangers of indecent literary classics, Comstock singled out "a well-known book, written by Bocaccio, . . . which I do not purpose to advertise by naming," and denounced many novels from France and Italy as "little better than histories of brothels and prostitutes, in these lust-cursed nations." The rise of European modernist fiction only strengthened this association of foreigners and licentiousness.[28]

Moral censorship in the age of American Victorianism extended far beyond the boundaries of "pornography," as that term later became defined in the mid–twentieth century. Comstock and other supporters of censorship conceived of obscenity as encompassing a vast range of sexual representations, whether found in literary classics, contemporary fiction, or even manuals of medical advice; in their view, no matter the literary or scientific context, the mere reference to sexuality could arouse lust in young people that would destroy their bodies and damn their souls. In addition, Comstock and his allies sought to censor both fiction and journalism that, in their eyes, glorified crime and irresponsibility and encouraged disobedience to law and authority. They also lumped information about birth control in the same category as obscene publications in the belief that both invited sex without procreation and were therefore immoral. And, finally, they sought to suppress certain doctrines such as free love, which they viewed as obscene even if not expressed in titillating language.[29]

The last of these targets, the ideological advocacy of free love, gave rise to a critical test of censorship early in the Comstock era. In 1877, Comstock prosecuted and succeeded in convicting the radical individualist and free-love advocate Ezra Heywood for writing a pamphlet called "Cupid's Yokes" that criticized the institution of marriage. Denouncing the belief "that our Sexual Relations can be better governed by state, than by Personal Choice," Heywood argued that relationships should be based on "mutual discretion—a free compact, dissolvable at will," and he excoriated Comstock for trying to suppress inquiry into "Sexual Science." President Rutherford B. Hayes, however, pardoned Heywood on the grounds that the pamphlet was not prurient, but when Comstock obtained the conviction of a second libertarian, the free-thought activist D.M. Bennett, for mailing a copy of "Cupid's Yokes," President Hayes declined to intervene, and Bennett went to prison for thirteen months.[30]

The great significance of these cases lay in the way they were framed and in the precedent they set. No reformers or radicals at the time challenged the Comstock Act by offering a principled defense of contraception, much less abortion. None anticipated later constitutional challenges by suggesting the act was an unconstitutional infringement of the right to privacy—indeed, no one had yet conceptualized such a right.[31] The challenge to the Comstock Act came instead from libertarians who framed the issue as freedom of speech—an unusual claim for anyone to make at that time in any legal case. When labor organizers in this period met repression during strikes, for example, their lawyers did not even cite the First Amendment or analogous provisions in state constitutions as part of their defense.[32] One reason was judges' unreceptiveness to free-speech claims, amply demonstrated by precedent-setting rulings in the Heywood and Bennett trials. In their jury instructions, the judges used the test for obscenity enunciated ten years earlier by the British court in *Hicklin*: whether the effect of a publication was "to deprave and corrupt those whose minds are open to such immoral influences, and into whose hands a publication of this sort may fall." The American judges also instructed juries only to consider the excerpts singled out by the prosecutor, not the work as a whole, and specified that a work fell within the definition of obscenity if the excerpted passages would evoke impure desires in children.[33] Like Congress, which had enacted more restrictive legislation in

1873 than Parliament had passed in 1857, American judges were now outdoing their British counterparts in the antiobscenity crusade. After a British court acquitted two activists for family limitation in 1877, the American posture toward discussion of birth control stood out as particularly restrictive.[34]

These legal developments in the United States during the 1870s provided the foundation for an era of zealous moral censorship that complemented—and no doubt encouraged—the self-censorship of writers and informal control exercised through publishing houses and other institutions. Comstock's standard method was to pose as a customer or send a decoy, inducing a publisher or dealer to mail a publication or sell forbidden items in person. A large, stocky figure, he would sometimes seize offenders and haul them off to the police for summary trials. Every year he would report a detailed inventory of materials confiscated—by 1900, for example, exactly 877,412 obscene pictures and photographs. Shortly before his death, he told a newspaper that he had destroyed 160 tons of obscene literature and convicted enough people to fill a passenger train with more than "sixty coaches containing sixty passengers each," and he pointed with pride to publishers and abortionists who had died at their own hands while he was hunting them down.[35]

The effectiveness of censorship is impossible to verify, since there are no data on the circulation of forbidden items, and even if there were, it would be difficult to distinguish the impact of law from that of informal controls. But at least some evidence suggests that Comstock's claims of effectiveness were not merely self-serving. Although the Comstock Act did not block all access to contraceptives, advertisements in the press for contraceptives and abortion disappeared, as did manuals of medical advice with birth-control information. The risks of prosecution and imprisonment for publishing or distributing sexually titillating publications almost certainly obstructed dissemination. Radical views of sexuality, marginal to begin with, were driven entirely out of the public sphere.[36]

The antiobscenity crusade probably reached its peak around the turn of the century, when it was part of a larger social-purity movement. In the United States, unprecedented waves of immigrants, coupled with reports of a sharp decline in the birthrate of the native-born, raised the specter of "race suicide" among old-stock Americans. Comstock's prosecutions reached their highest levels in this period, and in line with the preoccupations of the time, he directed his birth-control cases against native-born American women, while bringing obscenity charges primarily against immigrants.[37] Antiobscenity measures also intensified in France and Germany as well as in Britain during the late nineteenth century, though not exactly in the same years. The "breath-taking changes dominating the age," along with new literary experimentation, argues Peter Gay, "generated defensive responses that went far beyond earlier campaigns to contain obnoxious publications."[38]

Purity, moreover, came to be viewed through a distinct ideological prism: "Throughout the western world," E.J. Bristow writes, "the equation of purity and national power led to popular movements and to new legislation against vice." Amid rising imperial tensions, political leaders in various countries, such as Theodore Roosevelt in America, warned that any weakening of moral fiber would undermine a country's military strength. In supporting moral censorship, the American Victorians were not simply responding from an anxious defensive posture; like their British counterparts, they were nothing if not earnestly self-confident about their moral values, saw those values as a basis of power, and had no hesitancy about imposing their principles on others. Convinced that theirs was an age of progress, they viewed the efforts to clean up culture as akin to the efforts to clean up cities and eliminate other poisons and contagions (frequent metaphors in campaigns against obscenity).[39] "Dirt offends against order," Mary Douglas argues in her book *Purity and Danger*. "Eliminating it is not a negative movement, but a positive effort to organise the environment."[40] So, too, the effort to eliminate dirty books and pictures reflected a positive effort to organize the moral environment.

That aim was particularly evident in the efforts of some of the procensorship forces to publicize and disseminate what they regarded as more wholesome literature. The movement to build public libraries drew much of its support from people who were uneasy about popular morality; Andrew Carnegie was the single biggest donor to the New York Society for the Suppression of Vice as well as to library construction throughout the country. The establishment of public libraries, like censorship laws, expressed a widely felt determination to impose moral direction on a cultural marketplace thought to be undermining cherished values. Donors sought to make books available for free in a controlled environment under the authority of a librarian with sober and refined taste. In the 1870s, when the American Library Association was established, its members saw censorship as their professional responsibility. The purpose of libraries, in their view, was not entertainment but education and self-improvement, and they selected books accordingly, banning works that they and their governing boards deemed immoral or sensational. Libraries excluded or put under restricted access many popular stories and novels by such authors as Robert Louis Stevenson, Arthur Conan Doyle, and even Horatio Alger because such books were thought to encourage a "dreamy" and "unrealistic" state of mind in the young.[41]

Even in its heyday, however, moral censorship had its limits. As early as 1887, Comstock met ridicule when he raided New York's Knoedler Gallery for selling photographs of museum works that included nude figures, and the crusade to keep popular fiction out of the libraries eventually fell victim to the libraries' interest in attracting the public. Comstock enjoyed considerable success when he brought down the force of the law on his standard target: a small-time dealer in commercial obscenity or birth control. But popular newspapers were a more formidable foe, and he rarely tangled with them. During the 1880s and 1890s, the WCTU and other pro-censorship groups campaigned against "blood and thunder" papers such as the *National Police Gazette,* which since the 1830s had published sensational reports about crime. By 1880, the *Police Gazette* was so widely available in barbershops, saloons, and other places where men congregated that its estimated circulation of 150,000 vastly understated its audience. In several states, reformers were able to use "little Comstock laws" to ban the story papers; for example, New York in 1884 prohibited newspapers "devoted to . . . criminal news, police reports, or accounts of criminal deeds, or pictures, or stories of deeds of bloodshed, lust or crime"—a striking example of moral concerns trumping freedom of the press in legislation. But though the New York law was not overturned until 1948, it went largely unenforced, and the WCTU's national campaign was unable to hold back the tide of sensational crime reporting. When the *Police Gazette*'s circulation began to fall in the 1890s, the primary cause was not censorship. Rather, its brand of news was now more widely available than ever through the mass-circulation newspapers that William Randolph Hearst and others were publishing.[42] The forces in society that Comstock championed would ultimately be unable to keep in check the forces epitomized by Hearst.

Diversity and Daily Journalism

A widely held view of the mass media conceives of them as a form of mass production and suggests that, like other innovations of the industrial age, they brought about a more homogenized and standardized culture. But from the mid-nineteenth through the early twentieth centuries—that is, before broadcasting and extensive corporate consolidation—this was not the case; the early mass media in America added more to cultural diversity than they subtracted from it.

The equation of the mass media with mass production in manufacturing is misleading. Information and entertainment produced for a large audience are not necessarily less diverse than media produced on a smaller scale. The very drive to reach a broader public may require a diversification of content and style, and the resources available to larger, better-financed organizations may permit innovations and risk-taking impossible in small-scale production. A newspaper is not a single item, but a collection of things; a publisher typically issues many books, not one—and so it is in other media: The greater scale and capacity to bear risk of a few large producers may promote a wider overall range of content, unless the number of firms in an industry is so reduced as to create monopoly power. Much also depends on the public's composition and the political context. A public that is itself becoming more diverse may elicit greater diversity in the media, as long as the state does not view minority or dissident expression as a threat and take steps to repress it.

These considerations help explain why the American media from 1870 until the beginning of World War I came to reflect a greater diversity of expression despite moral censorship and the rise of a mass public. As in the antebellum era, deliberate public choices (reflected in postal subsidies), as well as more efficient means of production and dissemination, cut the costs of print, while sources of revenue increased, making possible a growing profusion of publications. Amid this profusion, mass-circulation newspapers and magazines acquired unprecedented resources that allowed them to address a wider variety of human interests. In addition, the Anglo-Protestant domination of cultural life began to recede as the United States absorbed successive waves of immigrants, who not only created their own newspapers, churches, and other forms of communal expression but also played a central role in the development of the mass press and later the movies. Journalism, literature, and the arts in America had long been distinguished by a more willing embrace of the popular market than was the case in Europe; the rising influence of immigrants in that popular market differentiated America in a new way.[43]

If any single institution or organ dominated the public sphere in this era, it was the daily newspaper. The foundations laid in the early republic and antebellum period for an independent, geographically distributed press now provided the basis for staggering growth. Between 1870 and 1900, the number of dailies nearly quadrupled, from 574 to 2,226, and their average circulation increased by an even larger factor, up from 2,600 to more than 15,000, with the largest newspapers exceeding half a million readers by the century's end. Though some of the growth came in new towns and cities springing up in the West, the ratio of dailies to urban places was also still increasing, from 2.5 in 1870 to 4.1 in 1900. As it had before, growth and competition in the industry spurred cost-cutting technological innovation. Newsprint (paper manufactured from wood pulp rather than rags) was first produced in the late 1860s, spread in the early 1870s, and became standard in the next decade, while Linotype machines and improved rotary presses made production cheaper and faster. Between 1870 and 1900, according to data from one New York paper, the cost of newsprint fell by about 80 percent. During the same period, advertising revenues sharply increased, doubling during the 1870s and growing by another 80 percent the next decade; in 1879, advertisements provided newspapers and periodicals 44 percent of their income, a proportion that rose to 55 percent in 1899 and 60 percent in 1909.[44]

Falling paper and production costs and the growth in advertising, along with improved transportation, enabled newspapers to cut their prices and extend their markets. In 1870, total daily circulation stood at 34 papers per 100 households; by 1900, it reached 94, and ten years later, it hit 121—in other words, an average of more than one daily paper per household. Evening papers, often purchased on a newsstand and read on a streetcar on the way home from work, were responsible for much of the growth and by 1890 outstripped the morning sheets in circulation. As newspapers prospered commercially, they increasingly identified themselves as "independent" or "unaffiliated" rather than as Democratic or Republican. The Associated Press dominated the distribution of national news, but newspapers were in other respects relatively autonomous in their operations; nearly all were independently owned, and larger cities were rife with competition—New York City had fifty-five daily papers in 1889.[45]

The growing numbers of publications and advertisers created opportunities for an intermediary who could facilitate business between the two. Although there had been advertising agents as early as the 1840s, they increased greatly in number and scope of activity toward the end of the nineteenth century. By that time, roughly 4,000 businesses in the United

States sought to promote their products outside of their own local areas and needed skilled help in selecting media and arranging transactions with the thousands of newspapers and magazines in circulation. Advertising agencies originally bought blocks of space in publications and resold it to individual companies, but by the turn of the century they were also preparing copy and designing advertisements. In 1903, the Supreme Court ruled that advertising could receive copyright protection, a change that encouraged investment in advertising content.[46]

Foreign-language dailies also increased during the same period in response to the arrival of new groups of immigrants and the publishing opportunities that American conditions offered. Until World War I, the foreign-language press developed without restriction; the United States, unlike many other countries, did not attempt to prevent linguistic minorities from publishing in their own tongues. Hostility and prejudice in the mainstream press also led some ethnic minorities to create their own independent means of communication; exclusion had been a factor in the origins of African American weeklies in the antebellum era, and it remained an influence, particularly on blacks, Asians, and Jews, in the late nineteenth century. The first foreign daily newspapers had been in French (1828) and German (1834); then came the first dailies in Italian (1859), Polish (1863), Bohemian (1871), and Norwegian/Danish (1871). A torrent arrived after 1885: the first dailies in Yiddish, Slovak, Armenian, Hungarian, Lithuanian, Slovenian, Japanese, Greek, Chinese, Croatian, and Arabic; and between 1900 and 1919, Finnish, Rumanian, Serbian, Bulgarian, Albanian, Russian, Spanish, and Ukrainian. By 1914, as they approached their peak, the German papers had a total daily circulation of 823,000 and the Yiddish papers 763,000, while the Italian and Polish daily press each ran more than 200,000 copies.[47]

Many of the immigrants who read these papers had never read any publications in their own language before coming to America. The reason was not just that more of them became literate after coming to America; in their native countries, the language of the press frequently did not match the spoken vernacular. Through much of Europe, particularly in areas under Russian, German, or Austro-Hungarian control, the educated classes despised the vernacular and preferred another language identified with a higher culture, and the authorities often banned publications in minority tongues in a concerted effort to stifle nationalist movements. As a result, some of the immigrant groups established popular newspapers in America before a press in their own language developed in their countries of origin. "Slovak peasants," the sociologist Robert E. Park wrote in a study of the immigrant press, "learned in America what they were not permitted to do in Hungary—to read their mother tongue." Anarchist and socialist papers in immigrant communities added to the political as well as the ethnic diversity of the press.[48]

The intensely competitive environment of the mainstream, English-language urban press was a continual prod to diversification of content and innovation in journalistic practices. Journalism in America had already undergone several phases of popularization: the mobilization of the popular press in the Revolutionary era, the spread of small-circulation papers through villages and towns of the early republic, and the advent of the penny press in larger cities in the 1830s. Each of these had broadened the public and the scope of interests that newspapers addressed. By 1870, journalism in America had already become more blatant and brash than anywhere else in seeking out news and trumpeting it in dramatic headlines. In the late nineteenth century, yet another phase of innovation further extended this pattern with practices that were sensational for the day, though tame by the standard of later tabloids. Among the conspicuous changes in the "new journalism," as it came to be known, were more prominent use of illustrations, larger type, bolder and blacker headlines, and melodramatic coverage of crime, as a newspaper's first page became a "front page" designed to catch the attention of people passing by a newsstand or a newsboy. Rather than simply reporting news, papers created it through high-profile crusades and stunts, and they made increasing use of that other recent news-generating innovation, the interview, part of a more general trend toward a focus on personalities. Helping readers to economize their scarce time in scanning a paper, news articles increasingly started off with a lead paragraph that condensed the key facts instead of presenting events in chronological order.[49]

With more circulation and advertising, the dailies were also able to add more pages and new features—for example, sports pages and women's sections in the 1880s, personal advice columns and comic strips in the following decade. Increasingly, newspapers became general-interest publications, vehicles of entertainment as much as of information. "The people of today," a trade magazine explained in 1892, "want something more than the mere news in their daily paper. The women and children are newspaper-readers, and there must be stories, and poems, and fashion articles, and correspondence, and illustrations, sermons, and biographies, and holiday specialties, and serials." Compared to newspapers in the Old World, wrote the British journalist William T. Stead in 1902, an American daily simply had more—"more news, more advertisements, more paper, more print"—and "no reader is expected to do more than assimilate just such portion of the mammoth sheet as meets his taste." On Sundays, Stead wrote with some astonishment, Americans "would consider themselves defrauded if they did not have a bale of printed matter delivered at their doors almost equal in bulk to a family Bible."[50]

Tradition-bound British journalists were initially appalled by American journalistic innovations. "Our common idea of the American newspaper," the *British Quarterly Review* commented in 1871, "is that of a print published by a literary Barnum, whose type, paper, talents, morality and taste are all equally wretched and inferior; who is certain to give us flippancy for wit, personality for principle, bombast for eloquence, malignity without satire and news without truth or reliability; whose paper is prolific of all kinds of sensational headings." And this was at a point when the American innovations that made up the new journalism were just beginning. Journalism in Britain was supposed to be impersonal. Reporting of parliamentary speeches, the editor T.P. O'Connor later recalled, gave "no information as to how the speech was delivered or how received . . . nothing of the personality of the persons who made the speech." When change finally came in the late 1880s, it arrived through evening papers under editors such as Stead, O'Connor, and Henry W. Massingham who explicitly said they were imitating the methods that gave the American press its great popularity. O'Connor identified the "main point of difference" as "the more personal tone" of the new style and insisted that the interest of the public in the personalities of its leaders was "healthy" and "rational" and ought to be satisfied. But this was nonsense to defenders of journalistic orthodoxy, such as the critic Matthew Arnold, who in 1887 denounced the "new journalism" (a phrase he coined) as "feather-brained" and consigned it to the bottom of a cultural ranking in which the highest position belonged to art.[51]

In the 1880s, the paradigmatic figure of the new journalism was an American publisher—an immigrant as it happened. Joseph Pulitzer, raised in Budapest, had arrived alone in the United States at age seventeen to serve in the Union army in the final months of the Civil War. Settling in St. Louis, he became a reporter, originally for a German-language paper, made his fortune by buying and building up the *Post-Dispatch*, and in 1883 paid Jay Gould the exorbitant price of $346,000 for the money-losing *New York World*. Pulitzer then succeeded in doing to his higher-priced rivals, including the *Sun*, the *Herald*, and the *Tribune*, what they had done to their entrenched predecessors nearly half a century earlier: He cut the *World*'s price to a penny, adapted the practice of journalism to a new and wider market, and transformed the industry.

In just two years, the *World*'s circulation jumped by a factor of ten to 153,000, making it the biggest in the city, as Pulitzer pioneered or extended a variety of attention-grabbing practices such as detailed and dramatic coverage of murders, prominent use of line-cut illustrations, and teasing headlines about sex (without actually trespassing the boundaries of Victorian convention). In 1887, when an ambitious young journalist calling herself Nelly Bly showed up in desperate need of work, the *World* paid her to feign insanity and go undercover to report on conditions inside a mental asylum for the poor, an assignment that produced one of journalism's great exposés. Two years later, after the publication of *Around the World in Eighty Days*, Pulitzer sent Bly on a race against Jules Verne's fictional record—her telegraphed reports building circulation all along the way—until she arrived back in New York in seventy-two days and the *World* trumpeted her arrival with the headline "Father Time Outdone." As Michael Schudson has argued, while the sober and conservative *New York Times* imparted information, the *World* told stories. That is not to say Pulitzer was indifferent to facts, or that he was interested in stories only for their emotional impact. The young Theodore Dreiser, looking for a job as a reporter, noticed that the only decorations in the *World*'s city room were cards on the wall that read: "Accuracy, Accuracy, Accuracy! Who? What? Where? When? How? The Facts—The Color—The Facts!" But in contrast to the older, less personal style of journalism, Pulitzer wanted his reporters to infuse their articles with color without sacrificing information; when writing up interviews, for example, they were to give "a striking, vivid pen sketch of the subject."[52]

Moreover, Pulitzer's *World* combined sensationalism and storytelling with a crusading liberal reformism and built circulation not just with stunts but with investigations of tenement housing, adulterated food, official misconduct (including police brutality), and corporate malfeasance. He supported the taxation of inheritances, large incomes, monopolies, and "privileged corporations" but remained a nineteenth-century liberal in his reluctance to advocate state regulation, arguing that crime, swindles, and vice "live by secrecy" and that the solution was to expose and ridicule them and "sooner or later public opinion will sweep them away." A lively, popular journalism—"sensationalism" to critics—was therefore the means to a high purpose: "If a newspaper is to be of real service to the public," he said late in life, "it must have a big circulation, first because its news and its comments must reach the largest possible number of people, second because circulation means advertising, and advertising means money, and money means independence." He wanted, as he said on another occasion, "to talk to a nation, not to a select committee."[53]

Pulitzer's initial imperative, however, was to talk to a city where the population of immigrants was surging, and it was his particular genius to develop a journalism that fit this new demographic reality. The use of pictures and emphasis on telling uncomplicated stories may have helped to attract readers with limited English literacy, but Pulitzer appealed to immigrants substantively as well, championing their causes and defending them as a source of America's greatness. In an early editorial, the *World* defined its credo as "justice and equal rights and privileges for all, of whatever color, class, race or condition," and the paper underlined its sympathies with its articles about tenements and sweatshops, positive coverage of Irish nationalism, and a crusade to raise small donations from its readers to complete the installation of the Statue of Liberty when fundraising among the wealthy stalled.[54]

Because Pulitzer himself was an immigrant and the subject of anti-Semitic attacks, the basis of his sympathies scarcely seems mysterious. But even a native-born publisher intent on dominating the daily market in America's great cities could follow the same logic. Supported by the vast fortune his father had made in mining, William Randolph Hearst built one of the earliest and most powerful newspaper chains at the turn of the century, beginning with his father's *San Francisco Examiner.* After the younger Hearst bought New York's floundering *Morning Journal* in 1895, he raided Pulitzer's staff, adopted his formula for mixing sensationalism and reform, followed the same low-price strategy, and set out to do what the *World* had done, except at a higher temperature.

The rivalry between Pulitzer and Hearst is best remembered for the jingoism that characterized both of their New York newspapers before and during the Spanish-American War. But the two publishers were also rivals for immigrant readers, and Hearst no less than Pulitzer sought to become their champion by exposing municipal abuses and devoting attention to international issues they cared about. Hearst, too, attracted immigrant readers by using pictures and simple stories, and he was the first to introduce a color Sunday humor section with comic strips. It was no accident that the Hearst comics were typically populated by mischievous but affectionately portrayed immigrant children going by names such as "Happy Hooligan" and the "Katzenjammer Kids." A comic strip published first by Pulitzer, then by Hearst, and for a while in different versions by both publishers, created the prototype for such characters: a street urchin in a yellow shirt known as the "Yellow Kid." Whence the term "yellow journalism," coined by a hostile critic as a damning label for the kind of high-voltage paper published by the two masters of the urban press.[55]

Detached from party organization, dreaded and abhorred in the upper strata of society, Pulitzer and Hearst represented a new form—or at least a new level—of power available through the medium of journalism. There had been powerful independent publishers before, such as James Gordon Bennett (like Pulitzer, an immigrant), whose *Herald* in the decades before the Civil War drew the same kind of elite condemnation. But Pulitzer and Hearst were more formidable figures in the nation's affairs as a result of metropolitan growth and their papers' vast circulation; they stood at the peak of the press when the press itself was at its peak, in the decades before radio and television. The loathing for them stemmed not just from the standard of journalism they practiced, but from the status of their readers, their own social position, and the political interests they sought to advance. Both men were wealthy upstarts at odds with respectable society, so successful commercially that no political leader or economic interest could control them. In the 1890s, when the elite and most of the press were solidly Republican, the two supported the Democrats (though Hearst belonged to the more populist wing of the party identified with William Jennings Bryan, while Pulitzer did not). Both advocated policies that were radical for their day, attacked corporate and governmental abuses, and gained a following among working-class readers, including immigrants, whom the old-stock elite particularly feared. Muckraking journalism, though it later moved to magazines, had its beginning in the pages of their newspapers; in 1906, when Theodore Roosevelt coined the term "muck-rake," it was a Hearst magazine article that triggered his attack.[56]

So intense was the hatred of Hearst in the 1890s and later that it magnified both his power and his irresponsibility. The idea that he caused the

Spanish-American War does not stand up to scrutiny, and recent studies have also acquitted him of some of the most flagrant journalistic malfeasance of that period. In one legendary story, Hearst supposedly telegrammed the artist Frederick Remington, whom he had sent to Cuba: "Please remain. You furnish the pictures, and I'll furnish the war." A detailed examination of the evidence, however, casts doubt on whether such a telegram was ever sent.[57] No doubt Hearst was demagogic and inflammatory, and everything about him was oversized: his rhetoric and his headlines (he ran the first banners across an entire front page), the big money he spent on his newspapers, and not least of all, his lavish homes and private life. "American journalism, as compared with that of Great Britain, is more enterprising, more energetic, more extravagant, and more unscrupulous," observed the British editor Stead in 1902, and Hearst—just at the beginning of a long career—already embodied those tensions.[58]

Like the mass-circulation dailies, the immigrant press at the turn of the century had its own "new journalism." Immigrant editors, the sociologist Robert Park noted in a 1922 study, "brought to this country the European conception of a press addressed exclusively to the highly educated, deliberately formal and abstruse," but found themselves pressed by their business managers and readers to write more accessibly. The result was a trend toward simpler language, a more personal tone, and more reporting and storytelling.[59]

No editor better exemplifies the shift than Abraham Cahan, who immigrated from Russia in 1882, became a successful writer in both English and Yiddish, and did for the Yiddish press of New York what Pulitzer had done for the big metropolitan papers. In 1897, after New York's Jewish socialists had tried and failed more than once to create a popular, readable newspaper, Cahan and others started up a new daily called the *Forward.* Soon after its launch, however, he fell out with his colleagues, who were more interested in publishing socialist polemics, and left to write for the mainstream press, where he worked for a while under one of the great editors of the day, Lincoln Steffens, and mastered the trade of popular journalism. Despite his success in the general media and the growing acclaim for his short stories and novels in English, Cahan returned permanently in 1903 to edit the *Forward,* then languishing with a circulation of 6,000. He immediately substituted a colloquial, Americanized Yiddish for the Germanic form of the language preferred by intellectuals and told his staff to write about the daily life of their community in terms that made sense to their readers. Eight weeks after he took over, the *Forward*'s circulation tripled, and it continued rising, eventually reaching, at its height in the 1920s, sales of a quarter million, with local editions in eleven cities. The paper did not just inform its readers about the news; it offered them practical advice and moral instruction about everyday problems they encountered. Immigrant papers were preeminently the expression of a particular ethnic group. But rather than keeping immigrants apart, according to Park, they brought "them into contact with the current thought and the current events of their community" and taught them how to get on in America. The *Forward*, which Cahan edited for nearly a half century (he died in 1951), probably did more than any other institution to shape and sustain Yiddish culture in America, but it also—and this was entirely Cahan's intention—helped its readers become Americans. As much as it exemplified cultural pluralism, it also promoted assimilation.[60]

Politics, Markets, and Magazines

Toward the end of the nineteenth century, in yet another phase of the revolution of cheap print, magazines underwent a transformation similar to the one that had already taken place in newspapers. Although there had been some cheap magazines in the early 1800s, they had been short-lived failures. As of the early 1880s, the major national magazines were relatively expensive at 35 cents a copy and had a limited readership concentrated in the more comfortable and conservative classes, in contrast to the newspapers' lower prices and more popular audience. Then, beginning around 1885, several leading magazines cut their prices to 20 or 25 cents, and during the 1890s, prices fell to a dime or even a nickel. But what magazine publishers lost in subscription rates they more than made up in circulation and advertising. A variety of developments had created more positive conditions for publishing inexpensive magazines. The new publications were a superior product compared to their cheap forerunners because new methods of photoengraving and other advances in printing technology made it possible to produce attractively illustrated magazines at a low cost. The growth of the middle classes had also expanded the potential audience for national magazines. But perhaps most important were related changes in postal policy and the volume of advertising.[61]

The usual explanation for the growth of magazine advertising in the late nineteenth century is economic: With the rise of high-volume production, manufacturers of consumer goods began to invest in national brand-name marketing to create and maintain demand for their products and to differentiate them from those of their competitors. This line of argument, however, misses a political aspect of the process that explains why increased expenditures on marketing flowed into magazines in particular.

Between 1874 and 1885, the federal government adopted a series of changes in postal policy that gave companies an incentive to turn to magazines as an advertising medium. During the early nineteenth century, Congress had treated magazines far less favorably than newspapers. Even in 1863, when it invented the new status of "second-class mail" for all regular publications as part of a general revamping of postal classifications, Congress continued to set rates for magazines that were more than twice those for newspapers (though much postage for both went unpaid, since publishers did not need to prepay and postmasters often could not collect from subscribers). Reforms adopted in 1874 followed the earlier model adopted for letter correspondence by requiring prepayment but slashing rates; at this point, the Post Office began charging publications by the pound rather than by the piece, with newspapers paying 2 cents a pound and magazines 3 cents. Meanwhile, manufacturers and retailers made increasing use of the postal system to distribute advertising circulars, some of which evolved into mail-order catalogs; many such mailers mimicked the appearance of magazines in the hope of qualifying for second-class rather than much more expensive third-class mailing rates. But Congress and the Post Office insisted on distinguishing "legitimate" publications from their imitators, and under legislation passed in 1879, all publications eligible for second-class postage had to disseminate "information of a public character, or be devoted to literature, the sciences, arts, or some special industry, and have a legitimate list of subscribers." The increasingly favorable treatment given to magazines stemmed in part from lobbying by publishers and the sensitivity of Congress to an interest group with influence on public opinion. But the congressional decision not to give the same low rates to purely commercial mailers also reflected the traditional understanding that the Post Office had a distinctive mission in supporting public discussion.[62]

The culmination of the shift in policy toward magazines came in 1885, when Congress cut second-class rates to 1 cent a pound, a two-thirds reduction for magazines, making them far cheaper than advertising circulars as a vehicle for marketing. Magazine advertising and publishing boomed in the years that followed, except for a temporary setback during the panic of 1893. Just as rising advertising revenue enabled newspapers to cut prices to readers, so it enabled magazine publishers to follow a low-price, high-volume strategy. The number of periodicals with 100,000 circulation quadrupled from 21 to 85 between 1885 and 1900 and then nearly doubled again to 159 by 1905; the first magazine to hit a circulation of 1 million was the *Ladies' Home Journal* in 1903.[63]

Not only did magazines follow newspapers into the mass market; the very distinction between the two types of publications also began to blur. While newspapers, particularly with their Sunday editions, provided more leisure-time entertainment, magazines increasingly presented reports and interpretations of recent events. The broadened audience for magazines, which encouraged this shift in content, also created the preconditions for the turn toward muckraking in the first decade of the new century. For just as Pulitzer and Hearst used sensational stories to build circulation, so it made sense at least for some magazine publishers to use muckraking as a sensation-creating, circulation-building strategy. In late 1902, when it began publishing Ida Tarbell's series on John D. Rockefeller's takeover of the oil industry, *McClure's* opened a new era in political journalism. No doubt the strong popular response to muckraking exposés testified to the anxieties of the period, but Pulitzer and other newspaper publishers had been exposing graft and abuses for a long time. "What was new in muckraking in the Progressive era," Richard Hofstadter writes, "was neither its ideas nor its existence, but its reach—its nationwide character and its capacity to draw nationwide attention, the presence of mass muckraking media with national circulations, and huge resources for the research that went into exposure." S.S. McClure put his investigative writers on long-term salaries, paying them for their research rather than merely for the copy they produced; Tarbell's fifteen Standard Oil articles, produced over five years, cost McClure, he recalled in his autobiography, $4,000 each. No publisher could have afforded that investment without the mass circulations then achievable under the conditions created by cheap second-class mail rates, lower production costs, and a growing middle-class audience. Muckraking was, therefore, as much a product of the rise of the early mass media as it was a result of the distinct political outlook of the Progressive era.[64]

The Local and Oppositional Press

It may seem logical to assume that the rise of national magazines and the metropolitan press brought about, or reflected, a corresponding eclipse of local and rural publications. But in fact, as national-brand advertising increased, advertising agencies placed a considerable amount of it in small-town papers, strengthening them financially. In addition, as in the early republic, postal policy supported and subsidized a decentralized press. In the mid-1890s, Congress approved the introduction of rural free delivery (RFD)—home delivery along rural postal routes—which meant, under existing rules, that small-town papers could be sent postage-free to rural subscribers within their county. The Post Office had introduced free home delivery of mail in cities in 1863 and by the late 1880s extended the service to towns with at least 10,000 population; the National Grange and other farm organizations then petitioned for extension of the service to rural America, and the Republicans supported the proposal in its effort to win support from farmers in the face of the Populist challenge. The introduction of RFD starting in 1896 produced a boom in rural newspaper circulation and for many farmers meant the beginning of daily rather than weekly newspaper reading. The service not only expanded the potential subscription base of small-town papers but also encouraged local retailers to advertise, since RFD threatened them with greater competition from mail-order houses. As local editors were only too eager to point out, retailers on Main Street now needed to advertise in the local paper to reach farmers who would no longer routinely come into town to get their mail.[65]

No one better illustrates the continuing importance and growing prosperity of independent, small-town editors at the turn of the century than William Allen White, who was to his hometown of Emporia, Kansas, what Cahan was to New York's Lower East Side. In 1895, at age twenty-seven, after working for other papers in Kansas, White returned home and bought the *Emporia Gazette.* During the next decade, he turned it into a thriving enterprise while also acquiring a national reputation for his widely reprinted editorials and articles in national magazines. Though he had begun his career as a loyal supporter of the Kansas Republican organization, White became a major figure in Progressive journalism. According to Sally Foreman Griffith's study of White, the prosperity created by increased advertising and rural free delivery "gave him greater independence from his political patrons" and enabled him to support Progressive reform.[66] The usual view of advertising is that it chained journalism to business interests, and to some degree it did. In an egregious example, patent medicine makers used advertising contracts as a means of pressuring newspapers to oppose drug regulation—a practice that White was responsible for exposing. But just as abundant advertising gave Pulitzer the independence to criticize corporate as well as governmental abuses, so it also gave White the material basis for his editorial independence.

Like Cahan, White had the option of a career in the national media but stuck to his community, and just as Cahan became the archetypal editor of an immigrant paper, so White became the archetypal small-town editor. Each came to symbolize a loyalty to particular communities amid the emerging mass media of the twentieth century. Cahan and White may seem the polar opposites of Pulitzer and Hearst, who were both empire builders. But all four illustrate how the increasingly strong commercial foundation of journalism became a basis of independent power and influence, locally as well as nationally. They exemplified an era when control of the press remained more personal than corporate and the daily newspaper was the paramount medium of the public sphere.

While newspapers were central to the dominant culture in America, they were also crucial for oppositional political movements. Late-nineteenth-century America saw a multitude of anarchist, socialist, and populist publications; no movement, however small, was complete without a journal to establish its identity, propound its ideals, and communicate with its members. Such publications typically had a high mortality rate because they typically carried little, if any, commercial advertising and radical organizations themselves often had only a transitory existence. Some publications were incendiary (*Truth*, an anarchist paper, ran as its motto, "*Truth* is five cents a copy and dynamite is forty cents a pound"), and a few met harassment, or worse, by public officials. But the vicissitudes of oppositional publications generally had little to do with government repression, as the rise and fall of the populist press illustrates. When the agrarian revolt developed in the West and the South during the late 1880s and early 1890s, editors supporting the cause founded hundreds of small papers, almost all of them weeklies, and at the National Farmers' Alliance convention in 1890 created the National Reform Press Association. This network of editors, according to Lawrence Goodwyn, "served as one of the primary organizational bases of Populism throughout the era of the People's Party," disintegrating, however, in 1896, when the party's leadership decided on fusion with the Democrats and nominated Bryan for president. "Ostracized by the business community," Goodwyn writes, "the reform press was kept alive by the faith of its editors and their willingness to work at a level of bare subsistence. When that faith was crushed by fusion, they simply closed their papers."[67]

Socialist papers soon emerged as the major oppositional press but also faced the same material difficulties. Two publications with the largest national circulations—the *Appeal to Reason,* founded by J.A. Wayland in 1895 in Girard, Kansas, and *Wilshire's Magazine* (originally *Challenge*), founded in 1900 by Gaylord Wilshire in Los Angeles—broke with the earlier anticommercialism of socialist publications and accepted advertising. Wayland and Wilshire (after whom Wilshire Boulevard is named) had both made their money investing in real estate and, like good capitalists, adopted aggressive promotion strategies for their publications. The *Appeal* is best remembered for a novel it commissioned in 1904 hoping to create support for workers in Chicago's stockyards. Serialized the next year and republished in 1906 as a book, Upton Sinclair's *The Jungle* instead created outrage about the meatpacking industry's standards. "I aimed at the public's heart," Sinclair said, "and by accident I hit it in the stomach." Boosted by its "army" of subscription salesmen, the *Appeal* was reaching half a million readers by the time it peaked in 1912; that same year, the Socialist Party presidential candidate Eugene Debs—the *Appeal*'s best-known writer—received a million votes, the party's highest total in a national election. But as the party lost support, the *Appeal* lost subscribers; Wilshire's *Challenge* died after the publisher tried to get subscribers to invest in a gold mine that he hoped would finance the socialist revolution.[68] Left-wing magazines have been looking for that gold mine ever since.

From the late nineteenth century to World War I, the oppositional press suffered for lack of advertising revenue—this was the price of its convictions—but it enjoyed the same access to cheap second-class mailing privileges that other publications had. Although the federal government had begun to use its postal powers for purposes of moral censorship, it did not adopt similar measures to control political opinion in print (except insofar as censorship of radical views of sexuality had political implications, or radical publications could be represented as "obscene"). Prevailing judicial doctrine failed to protect dissent, but there was little state repression, and the publishing market remained open. The economic barriers to starting a publication and distributing it were low, and concentrated control of the media had yet to develop. A paper like the *Appeal to Reason* could afford the same printing technology as the largest commercial publications of its time; so could the immigrant newspapers.

Many of these conditions would be inverted later in the twentieth century. Judicial doctrine would become more protective of dissent, but the economic structure of the media would become more of an obstacle to its dissemination. After broadcasting developed, oppositional movements would be unable to match the communications technology of the dominant media. In a real rather than formal sense, then, the public sphere in the decades before World War I was exceptionally open. The forces tending toward the consolidation of "mass culture" were still weaker than the forces favoring diversity in print.[69]

CHAPTER EIGHT

The Rediscovery of the First Amendment

THE RISE of the modern liberal state is often described as a shift from the relatively limited government of the nineteenth century to the more extensive state regulation and spending of the twentieth. This conception, however, neglects a compensating tendency, the repudiation of much of the regulation of moral behavior and free expression built up during the 1800s in both Europe and America. The defining features of the twentieth-century liberal state were not only its greater power and scale but also new and stricter limits on its power so as to protect what came to be called "civil liberties." Though often thought of chiefly as safeguards of individual rights, these guarantees were also intended to shield public discussion, literature, and the arts from state control, and no institutions were more affected by them than the communications media.

By the end of the nineteenth century, two distinct problems for free expression had emerged from developments in American law. As a result of the agitation of Comstock and his allies, moral censorship imposed significant limits on imaginative literature, theater, the visual arts, and public discussion and information related to sex. Indeed, these limits were more severe, in certain respects, than those imposed in Great Britain, the home of Victorianism. And while journalism and political debate in America continued to be exceptionally uninhibited and free of government control, the courts interpreted free-speech rights in a highly restrictive fashion. The tradition of a free press was sustained by other powerful forces: the popular culture of partisan politics and journalism (the customary practice of vehement, even vitriolic criticism of public officials); long-established government policy (postal subsidies to newspapers and magazines irrespective of their political viewpoint); and the structure of media markets (the relative ease, for example, of starting new publications). But when free expression came under attack, the judiciary generally failed to protect it; radicals and labor organizers, for example, could not turn to the courts for vindication of their free-speech rights against hostile public authorities. During the nineteenth century and well into the twentieth, no federal court struck down a law on the basis of the free-speech protections of the First Amendment, and even though state constitutions also included similar guarantees, judges did not give much weight to those provisions. From 1865 to 1917, however, governmental policies toward dissident publications were relatively benign, no federal sedition law was in force, and no crisis tested the limits of political tolerance. It was only after America entered World War I, and the courts provided full backing for the government's crackdown on the war's opponents, that the legal insecurity of dissent became a salient public issue.

The war and the red scare that followed it provoked the generative crisis of modern First Amendment law. The repression of dissenters and the foreign-born led not just the advocates of those groups, but leading figures in philosophy and law, including members of the Supreme Court, to rethink the meaning of freedom of speech. The turn toward a broader defense of free expression, however, began earlier and owed as much to a cultural upheaval as a political one. As a legal matter, the suppression of "immoral" literature had a distinct history from limits on political dissent, but cultural and political radicalism were often socially intertwined. During the 1920s, when radical politics was at low ebb, the liberalizing tendencies in the culture were a powerful factor in the movement for wider freedom of expression. In rediscovering the First Amendment after World War I, the law was registering the end of Victorian moral certainties, removing some of the restraints that had accumulated since the end of the Civil War, and returning to the more open model of the public sphere that had prevailed earlier—but now on the basis of principles compatible with an activist federal government.

Free Speech Becomes a Cause

It was during the Progressive era, particularly between 1910 and 1917, that a free-speech movement began to stir as writers and artists in rebellion against genteel culture discovered a common cause with radical dissenters on the left in the battle against censorship. A new generation of young intellectuals, convinced that America's old "Puritan" hypocrisy stood in the way of an honest understanding and full enjoyment of life, sought to open up discussion of sex, birth control, and other forbidden subjects. European cultural movements were important influences on them. Modernist in their cultural outlook, they looked to such developments as Freudian psychology and literary realism to illuminate areas of consciousness and experience long barred from polite letters and public debate.

Many of the young intellectuals, particularly those who frequented Greenwich Village salons and wrote for such small-circulation left-wing magazines as *The Masses,* favored a broader role for women outside the home, welcomed the diversity brought by the new immigrants, and supported the struggles of workers and the poor for a decent livelihood. The crusade for legalized contraceptives and "voluntary motherhood" led by Margaret Sanger was a characteristic cause of the era, combining concerns about sex, class, and censorship. A public health nurse and socialist, Sanger wrote a series of articles for a socialist publication about birth control (a term she put into circulation), later opened a birth-control clinic in a poor Brooklyn neighborhood, and even turned the story of her struggle into a movie. But because the federal and state Comstock laws treated information about contraceptives as a form of obscenity, she faced an indictment even for writing about the subject, the movie about her work was suppressed, and her campaign became part of the embryonic movement for free speech. Some local authorities also barred public speeches by such radicals as Emma Goldman because of their advocacy of anarchist and revolutionary ideas. In response, "free speech" became a rallying cry for left-wing movements, a way of connecting radical protest to a cause of wider appeal. Members of the International Workers of the World (IWW), who attempted to organize unskilled workers and hoped to replace capitalism altogether, staged "free-speech fights" in cities around the country, giving open-air speeches in defiance of local ordinances and state laws and drawing public officials into battles in which the labor activists could wrap themselves in the Bill of Rights.[1]

But while making free speech into a cause, these struggles had little success in changing laws or institutions and, indeed, hardly affected the main currents of Progressive-era reform. The Comstock laws remained in force, some states enacted new legislation against advocacy of anarchism ("criminal syndicalism," the statutes called it), and many localities shut down theatrical productions or censored motion pictures judged offensive to public morals. Though affirming the principle of free speech, the courts rarely questioned governmental measures punishing what officials viewed as abuses of that right. On the few occasions when the Supreme Court addressed free-speech claims, it was generally hostile to them. In *Patterson v. Colorado* (1907), for example, the Court upheld a finding of criminal contempt against Thomas Patterson, a senator from Colorado, who owned newspapers in his home state in which he had criticized a state court decision upsetting election results in Denver. In his appeal, Patterson claimed that he had not been allowed to prove the truth of his accusations, but the senator did not fare as well as John Peter Zenger had in colonial New York. Writing for the majority and citing Blackstone's *Commentaries,* Justice Oliver Wendell Holmes held that the First Amendment barred only prior restraint of publication and did not limit punishment afterward. "The preliminary freedom," Holmes wrote, "extends as well to the false as to the true; the subsequent punishment may extend as well to the true as to the false."[2] In another case involving a newspaper, *Fox v. Washington* (1915), the Supreme Court upheld the conviction of a writer who had supported the right of members of a group called the Home Colony to bathe in the nude. The article, "The Nudes and the Prudes," was not salacious, but it endorsed a boycott of opponents of skinny-dipping. Justice Holmes, again writing for the Court, found that "by indirection but unmistakably the article encourages and incites a persistence in what we must assume would be a breach of the state laws against indecent exposure."[3]

The central idea in these decisions was that government could properly use its "police power" to restrict any speech that tended to produce a result that government had authority to prevent. The "bad-tendency" doctrine served as a justification for punishing speech even where the connection with the purported effect was remote in time and indirect in route of causation. In the same period, the Supreme Court prohibited the use of the government's police powers to limit the length of the workday or to impose other economic regulations on the grounds that such laws interfered with property rights and employers' and employees' liberty of contract. But the justices did not extend the same constitutional protection to personal or civil liberties. In later years, with the evolution from laissez-faire to modern liberalism, the Supreme Court would reduce the priority of property rights and elevate that of civil liberties, giving government more power to regulate the economy and less power to regulate public discussion and personal behavior. The leading reformers and intellectuals of the Progressive era, however, had not arrived at this position. Determined to overthrow laissez-faire economics, they were wary of allowing individual rights of any kind to trump collective and governmental interests. They tended to see social problems as originating in the environment, and if immoral books or other means of expression contributed to a noxious moral environment, many Progressives had no hesitation in calling for censorship.[4]

Support for free speech at the beginning of the twentieth century came primarily from three sources: newspapers defending the tradition of a free press; conservative libertarian legal scholars (notably Thomas M. Cooley, the author of *Constitutional Limitations*), who put free speech and property rights on the same constitutional plane and favored strong First Amendment protections; and a small contingent of lawyers, journalists, and other liberal activists who in 1902 founded the first of the modern civil libertarian organizations, the Free Speech League. (The difference between the older conservative libertarians and the new group was that the latter were less devoted—indeed, some were downright hostile—to property rights.) In its early years, the Free Speech League devoted most of its work to defending sex reformers indicted under the Comstock laws and anarchists targeted for censorship after the assassination of President William McKinley. Unlike other organizations that made free-speech claims, however, the league was not limited to upholding a particular substantive viewpoint and played the leading role as free-speech advocate in controversies of all kinds between its founding and World War I. Perhaps most noteworthy, it opposed the censorship of allegedly immoral literature just as forcefully as it opposed the censorship of political dissent. The league's central figure, the lawyer Theodore Schroeder, was the single most prolific scholar of First Amendment issues during the prewar years when none of the major Progressive intellectuals gave sustained attention to the problem of free speech.[5]

At least initially, Comstock, the vice societies, and the censorship brigades of the Woman's Christian Temperance Union and other "maternalist" moral-reform groups made the transition into the Progressive era without much difficulty. Indeed, rather than killing off Victorian ideas, Progressivism at first gave them a more up-to-date scientific rationale. The vice crusaders had all along framed their efforts as a means of protecting children, an idea that was also central to Progressive reform; now they presented their work as rooted in social science, which supposedly proved the ill effects of obscenity on adolescents and others susceptible to suggestion. Moral censorship, in this view, was analogous to legislation for pure food and drugs. When concerns about prostitution and venereal disease intensified, the leaders of the new movement for "social hygiene" endorsed censorship as a public health measure. Yet there were discrepant developments at the time. Respectable people and publications began to argue that sex education ought to be part of the instruction of the young, and even before Margaret Sanger took up the issue, some were suggesting that contraceptive devices ought to be legally available.[6]

But perhaps the most serious early sign of trouble for the vice crusaders was the growing ridicule of their efforts among intellectuals, artists, and the more cosmopolitan urban public. In 1905, upon learning from an American reporter that the New York Public Library had removed one of his plays from general circulation, George Bernard Shaw erroneously inferred that Comstock was responsible. "Comstockery," he remarked, adding a new word to the English language, "is the world's standing joke at the expense of the United States. Europe likes to hear of such things. It confirms the deep-seated conviction of the old world that America is a provincial place, a second-rate, country-town civilization after all." Comstock himself only made things worse when, in response, he told the press that he had never heard of Shaw: "Never saw one of his books, so he can't be much." When Shaw's 1893 play *Mrs. Warren's Profession* opened in New York later in 1905, the city's police commissioner had the producer, manager, and two actresses arrested for obscenity. But, on this occasion, America did not turn out to be as "provincial" as Shaw's jab had suggested. While Britain's Lord Chamberlain had denied a license for public performances of *Mrs. Warren's Profession,* a New York court in 1906 threw out the obscenity charges and allowed it to be performed.[7] That same year, in one of the vice crusader's greatest public relations fiascos, Comstock seized the catalogs of the Art Students League because they included drawings of nude figures, and he arrested the league's receptionist for handing out a copy. In the ensuing uproar, the director of the Metropolitan Museum of Art castigated Comstock, newspapers labeled him the "Purifier," and the National Congress of Mothers canceled a speech Comstock had been scheduled to make to the group. The Victorian code, long understood as a means of cultivating higher values, now appeared to be a source of American cultural inferiority and embarrassment. At a vice society meeting in 1906, a speaker indirectly confirmed the shift in sentiment when he implored the group, "We need moral quarantine, and we need men who have got the stuff to enforce it, in spite of public ridicule."[8]

For many years, ridicule did not prevent the vice crusaders from continuing to suppress literature they regarded as obscene. Comstock was reappointed to his position as postal inspector through Roosevelt's and Taft's presidencies and into the Wilson years, and upon Comstock's death in 1915 the Society for the Suppression of Vice appointed a successor who took up the cause with the same zealotry. Moral regulation also became more a matter for bureaucratic enforcement as the Post Office and police departments increasingly internalized and routinized the functions of censorship instead of relying on the vice societies. The Post Office's solicitor excluded books from the mails without any hearing or obligation to obtain evidence, and although publishers could appeal a decision to the courts, judges generally deferred to the agency, even when it banned literary classics from the mails, as it did with some regularity.[9]

When the vice societies sought court approval to suppress books entirely, they were still able to obtain it. In 1908, Boston's Watch and Ward Society demanded that bookstores withdraw Elinor Glin's novel *Three Weeks* because it included suggestive passages about adultery. The case is notable in part because the book had already become a best-seller in both Britain and America, and it only went so far as to describe kissing. A publisher's representative who tested the ban was convicted of obscenity charges in a decision upheld by the Massachusetts Supreme Court, which declared that the book's descriptions "of seductive actions and of highly wrought sexual passion" would be seen in a "light tending towards the obscene and impure" and that Glin "disclosed so much of the details of the way to the adulterous bed" that a jury could reasonably conclude a "general reader" would have "animal" rather than "spiritual" thoughts. In a notorious case in 1915, the mere threat of a vice society prosecution led the publisher of Theodore Dreiser's *The "Genius"* to withdraw the novel from circulation. The publisher's decision was indicative of a deeper pattern during the prewar years, when literary censorship litigation nearly always involved European rather than American fiction. American novels and other writing that would have incurred the wrath of the vice crusaders never made it into print in the first place because of publishers' and bookstore owners' acceptance of the rules of reticence of the genteel tradition.[10]

A small breach in literary censorship resulted, however, from a split between the vice crusaders, who opposed any open discussion of sexuality, and the social hygienists, who favored frank portrayals of prostitution and venereal disease as a way of raising public alarm. In 1913, Comstock secured an indictment of the publisher of *Hagar Revelly*, a novel written by an American physician to highlight the problems of social hygiene, but the defense attorney won an acquittal by emphasizing the book's reformist intent.[11] The idea that the courts should allow publication of a book because it had a redeeming purpose—social, literary, or scientific—would later become crucial in the battle over censorship. But, as of 1917, the courts almost uniformly ignored such considerations in supporting the agencies, governmental and private, concerned with enforcing literary censorship as well as limits on radical dissent. Going into World War I, therefore, although the United States had no federal sedition law in force, legal precedent and current judicial opinion were entirely favorable to governmental measures to suppress speech that officials viewed as having the tendency to undermine law and morality.

War as a Generative Crisis

World War I brought to the surface the repressive potential latent within the inherited legal framework and the dominant currents of Progressive-era thought. An aroused nationalism redirected the moral impulses behind domestic reform into an international crusade, and many Progressives viewed the opponents of this new mission as just as reprehensible as the forces of municipal and business corruption they had fought earlier. At the same time, an aroused nativism redirected its energies against German Americans, sought to eradicate any signs of German language and culture, and demanded that all "hyphenated" ethnic groups shed their older national loyalties and become "100 percent Americans." In short, the war gave new passion and purpose to the old impulses of reform and nativism and merged them into a comprehensive attack on anyone who refused to conform.

Although these impulses were partly expressed through extralegal social pressures, they also took the form of new governmental policies and programs to mobilize national loyalty and suppress dissent, including the first sedition legislation since 1798. By itself, the mere fact of war does not explain these repressive measures, which far exceeded the restrictions on civil liberties during previous wars in American history. Rather, the World War I era crystallized developments that had been in the making during the previous years of peace: the legal doctrines and ideological dispositions that had grown up during the preceding decades and effectively removed constitutional inhibitions, as well as the social tensions from immigration and growing ethnic and racial diversity. All this came to a head under the international and domestic political conditions at the time of America's entry into the conflict in April 1917.

Foreign governments provided models for the wartime restructuring of the public sphere. All of the major belligerents in Europe, despite their varying political traditions, had responded to what appeared to be the imperative demands of "total war" to expand state control of civil society and public opinion as well as of economic life. Already disposed to believe in the superior efficiency of the state, American Progressives generally looked to European wartime state-building as a confirmation of their understanding of political necessity. Besides nationalization of industry, the European powers provided models of intensive government propaganda and censorship (as well as the seizure and surveillance of communications circuits, as we saw in Chapter 6).

The principal belligerents differed in the balance of military and civilian roles. Germany put censorship in the hands of deputy commanding generals, while Britain lodged authority in a civilian-dominated Press Bureau and gave newspaper editors considerable latitude in enforcing censorship guidelines. During the previous century, the British government had not directly operated a propaganda apparatus; its leaders had regarded foreign relations to be an exclusively elite concern and accordingly made little use of mass persuasion to mold opinion about world affairs at home or abroad. In 1914, expecting the war to be quick as well as popular, the government did not immediately change policy, but as the conflict dragged on and war weariness set in, the British government built up propaganda as well as censorship capacities. In January 1917—three months before America's entry into the war—the government created Britain's first central propaganda bureau, the Department (later the Ministry) of Information.[12]

Like Britain in August 1914, the United States in April 1917 had no governmental machinery for mass propaganda or press censorship, but the felt imperatives driving policy were initially more acute than they had been in Britain. Wilson had plausible reasons to worry about domestic opposition. Elected to a second term only the year before on the slogan, "He Kept Us Out of War," the president faced the challenge of converting much of the public from a belief in neutrality that he had encouraged. Eight million Americans looked to Germany as their nation of origin, and much of the German-language press had been sympathetic to the Central Powers, while elements on the left, including the Socialist Party, called on workers to oppose the war effort. Nonetheless, many supporters of the war, including members of the administration, said they wanted to avoid the extremes of European censorship and to emphasize "publicity, *not* suppression," as the Progressive journalist George Creel urged the administration in a memo in March. A few weeks later, after war was declared, Wilson named Creel to direct the Committee on Public Information, the federal office that the president established by executive order to manage public opinion. In the huge propaganda effort that followed, Creel enlisted academics and journalists to compose pamphlets, articles, speeches, and other material vilifying Germany and justifying the war as the great crusade for democracy that Wilson held it to be. Creel's office—the American equivalent of Britain's information ministry—employed every channel of communication, including public speeches, motion pictures, posters, civic organizations, and the press. Among other innovations, it published the first official daily government newspaper in the nation's history. But publicity was not all; despite some dissembling about its intentions, the Wilson administration also turned to censorship.[13]

The gap between pretense and policy at the beginning of America's involvement in the war was evident in the history of the Espionage Act of June 15, 1917, the legislation that became the chief basis of repression. Though the administration denied any intention of restricting criticism, it originally supported a bill that would have given the president authority to censor the press. The House of Representatives, however, rejected this provision in a vote that was widely interpreted to mean that censorship had been defeated. Assuming thereafter that the Espionage Act was directed at spies and saboteurs, public debate and news coverage paid scant attention to two sleeper provisions of the final bill that were later used to suppress dissent. One barred interference with the military through the making of false reports, willful efforts to cause insubordination or mutiny in the armed forces, or willful obstruction of military recruitment or enlistment "to the injury of the service or of the United States." Penalties could include up to twenty years' imprisonment. A second provision authorized the postmaster general to exclude from the mails any matter "advocating or urging treason, insurrection, or forcible resistance to any law of the United States" or that violated the law in other respects; those found guilty faced a possible prison sentence of up to five years.

Although a few members of Congress raised concerns about the potential impact of the law on free speech, the Espionage Act did not appear on its face to prohibit criticism of the government, except insofar as it interfered with the military or called for treason or violent resistance to the law. The postal provisions may have seemed to members of Congress less of a radical step than presidential powers of censorship because the Post Office had long exercised similar authority under the Comstock Act. Moreover, while denying the president the power to censor the press in advance, Congress granted the Post Office a power ostensibly subsequent to publication, which posed fewer constitutional problems, if one believed (as the Supreme Court had held in *Patterson v. Colorado*) that the First Amendment shielded the press only from prior restriction, not subsequent punishment. The Court had also long ruled that a denial of postal service did not violate the First Amendment because other means of distribution were supposedly available.[14]

It did not take long, however, for the implications of the Espionage Act to become apparent. The Post Office soon suppressed issues of *The Masses*, the *Appeal to Reason*, and other socialist and left-wing publications critical of the war, and the agency dealt a devastating financial blow to several of these publications by ruling that they no longer qualified for second-class mail privileges. Pressed to explain the standards he was using, Postmaster General Albert S. Burleson said that, according to his interpretation of the law, no publication could "say that this Government got in the war wrong, that it is in it for the wrong purposes, or anything that will impugn the motives of the Government for going into the war. They can not say that this Government is the tool of Wall Street or the munitions-makers. That kind of thing makes for insubordination in the Army and Navy and breeds a spirit of disloyalty through the country." By the same logic, Rose Pastor Stokes, a socialist, received a ten-year prison sentence for writing a letter to the editor of a Kansas City newspaper in which she said, "No government that is for the profiteers can also be for the people, and I am for the people and the government is for the profiteers." Such statements, the judge said, damaged civilian morale and thereby interfered with the war effort. Under this interpretation, the Espionage Act criminalized any criticism of the government that might be interpreted as discouraging to the military, even indirectly.[15]

As the frenzy of nationalism grew during the war, however, members of patriotic societies and other zealots for conformity began to view the Espionage Act as insufficient. In Montana, a judge acquitted a rancher who had denounced the war and the government in social encounters (for example, at a saloon) because his words could not have affected the war effort, as there were no soldiers or sailors within miles. "The espionage act does not create the crime of attempting to obstruct, only the crime of actual obstruction, and when causing injury to the service," the judge ruled. So immense was the consternation greeting this decision that within a month Montana made it a crime to denigrate key American institutions and symbols. Following Montana's example (and adopting much of its statutory language), Congress eliminated the requirement to show any effect of speech on the military in May 1918, when it adopted an amendment, known as the Sedition Act, which, among other things, barred anyone from uttering "disloyal, profane, scurrilous or abusive language" about the form of government of the United States, the Constitution, the armed forces and their uniforms, or the flag, on penalty of up to $10,000 in fines and twenty years in prison. Like the original Sedition Act of 1798, these additional provisions made words alone a crime, apart from any effect they might have. Altogether, the federal government used the Espionage and Sedition acts to prosecute about 2,200 dissenters, of whom 1,055 were convicted.[16]

Federal officials used these laws almost entirely against socialists and radicals; criticism of the government from other sources, such as the Hearst papers, went unpunished. But the government's supervision of the press during the war was more extensive than the focus on radicals may suggest. Soon after his appointment, Creel asked editors to censor their own papers and clear doubtful articles with his office; particularly after passage of the Espionage Act, editors had reason to err on the side of caution. Although Creel himself had no formal censorship authority, he could turn to the Post Office or the Justice Department for enforcement (as well as to the War Trade Board, which could cut off the supply of newsprint). The Trading With the Enemy Act, passed in October 1917, authorized the president to control all international communications and the Post Office to censor America's foreign-language newspapers, which were required to provide the agency with advance English translations of any article bearing on the war or the government. Under the act's authority, President Wilson established a Censorship Board, which included Creel, Burleson, and Attorney General Thomas W. Gregory. In May 1918, the Censorship Board authorized Creel to require all magazines to clear articles prior to publication.[17]

The silencing of dissent was also carried out by semiofficial national organizations and at lower levels of government. Among the semiofficial groups was a volunteer auxiliary of the Justice Department, the American Protective League (APL), made up of a quarter of a million civilians, mostly businessmen and professionals. Ostensibly acting under federal authority but without court warrants, members of the APL spied on neighbors, wiretapped phones, rifled through private correspondence, and raided the offices of German American papers and other organizations thought to be of doubtful loyalty. Groups demanding "one-hundred-percent" Americanism succeeded in many areas in banning German-language newspapers as well as the teaching of German; after the Soviet Revolution of October 1917, these groups turned their suspicions on Russian-born radicals and groups with communist sympathies. State governments established "councils of defense" to search out disloyalty; by the end of the war, 184,000 councils extended from the local to the national level. These and other loyalty-enforcing efforts were not limited to official purposes. In some states, the councils of defense used their power for partisan gains to destroy left-wing political opposition. "Few people know of the state of terror that prevailed during these years, few would believe the extent to which private hates and prejudices were permitted to usurp government powers," Frederic C. Howe, Wilson's commissioner of immigration, later wrote. In addition, without fear of legal consequences, mobs of vigilantes attacked, beat, and in a few cases murdered people whom they suspected of disloyalty.[18]

President Wilson and his administration bore considerable responsibility for the spiral of repression, though it did not inure to their political advantage. From the beginning of the war and even before it, their repeated denunciations of dissenters and warnings about disloyal subversives and spies stirred up antiradical and nativist anxieties that became impossible to control. "May God have mercy on them [dissenters] for they need expect none from an outraged people and an avenging Government," Attorney General Gregory declared in November 1917—a statement that, following the bad-tendency test, might well be considered an incitement to vigilantism. When mob violence broke out, the administration failed to take any serious steps to stop it. Except for two instances involving personal connections, Wilson refused to intercede with Postmaster General Burleson in cases involving the suppression of left-wing publications. After enacting much of the Progressive agenda during his first term, Wilson had narrowly won reelection in 1916 with an estimated half-million votes from socialists. Wartime repression, however, unleashed forces hostile to the president, split the coalition that elected him, and thereby contributed—as one factor among many—to the Democrats' loss of both houses of Congress in the 1918 elections.[19]

The armistice in November 1918, far from bringing an end to repression, ushered in a new phase of crisis and reaction. In the year after the war's end, industrial conflict and political tensions soared, two communist parties emerged, strikes spread, and some fifty radical papers were started. As alarm grew about the potential spread of revolutionary communism to the United States, foreign-born radicals became the focal point of repression. The war had already transformed public attitudes and public policy toward immigrants. In 1917, Congress had adopted the first major restrictions on European immigration, imposing a literacy requirement and authorizing the Department of Labor to deport aliens involved in radical politics even if they had lived in America for many years. The Alien Act passed by Congress in October 1918 eased the criteria for deporting radicals and, as a result, deportation for the first time became a significant means of controlling dissent. On November 7, 1919, the new attorney general, A. Mitchell Palmer, sent federal agents in eleven cities to seize hundreds of members of the Union of Russian Workers, who were deported the next month, and beginning with raids on January 2, 1920, the Justice Department rounded up 6,000 of the foreign-born members of the two communist parties. Descending on their targets, federal agents in both November and January beat suspects, wrecked offices, tore up books and papers, and made arrests without warrants. Although it would take several months for the full story of official misconduct to come out, the Palmer raids would prove to be the peak of the repressive wave—and the beginning of a civil-liberties backlash.[20]

During the war, neither private organizations nor the courts provided any significant restraint on governmental measures to control speech and the press. Progressive groups overwhelmingly accepted the premise that the war required a temporary suspension of rights in the greater interest of protecting the nation and making the world, as Wilson said, "safe for democracy." The one organization that emerged to defend free-speech rights during the war was the comparatively weak National Civil Liberties Bureau, an offshoot of the pacifist American Union Against Militarism. Although the bureau had some success in working with the War Department to protect conscientious objectors to military service, it was able to do little in free-speech cases given the prevailing views in the executive branch, particularly the Post Office, and the judiciary.[21]

A critical early legal test of free-press rights came in July 1917 when *The Masses* challenged the exclusion of its latest issue from the mails. In defense of suppression, postal officials cited cartoons and passages of articles in the magazine suggesting that the war served the interests only of business and praising draft resisters for their courage. The first court to hear the case affirmed the rights of dissent. District Judge Learned Hand ruled in favor of the magazine on the grounds that none of the material singled out by the Post Office directly incited resistance to the law but rather fell "within the range of opinion and of criticism." Hand's "direct incitement" test would have allowed wartime criticism of the government, unless it expressly called for interference with the military or other violations of the law. Overruling Hand, however, an appellate court reasserted the bad-tendency test, finding that the "natural and reasonable effect" of the objectionable material in *The Masses* was to obstruct military recruiting. Moreover, the judges said they had to abide by the principle that in a "doubtful case" no court should overrule the head of a government department in matters involving "judgment and discretion."[22]

The courts continued throughout the war to defer to the postmaster general in suppressing publications and more generally to support the government in limiting dissent. The Supreme Court did not address these issues until the war was over, and when it first did so, in March 1919, it ruled in favor of the government in four Espionage Act cases. In the most famous of these, the Court upheld the conviction and ten-year sentence of socialist leader Eugene Debs for interfering with recruitment. During a public speech in Canton, Ohio, Debs had, in passing, praised socialists serving prison terms for refusing to register for the draft and told his audience of workers that they were "fit for something better than slavery and cannon fodder." In a unanimous opinion written by Holmes, the Supreme Court found that these words tended to obstruct recruiting and that other statements by Debs in opposition to the war confirmed that he intended that effect.[23]

The Court explained its reasoning about the limits of free speech more fully in another case decided the same day, *Schenck v. United States,* which grew out of a leaflet that Socialist Party members in Philadelphia had mailed to men who had passed the physical examination for the draft. Contrary to many secondary accounts, the leaflet did not expressly call on the draftees to refuse to serve; rather, it denounced conscription as a violation of constitutional rights and urged the men to write their congressmen, sign a petition, and join the Socialist Party. Speaking for a unanimous court in upholding the defendants' convictions for interfering with enlistment, Holmes acknowledged that during peacetime they would have had the right to circulate their appeal. "But the character of every act depends upon the circumstances in which it is done. The most stringent protection of free speech would not protect a man in falsely shouting fire in a theatre and causing a panic. . . . The question in every case is whether the words used are used in such circumstances and are of such a nature as to create a *clear and present danger* that they will bring about the substantive evils that Congress has a right to prevent. It is a question of proximity and degree."[24]

Schenck is often described as the beginning of modern First Amendment law, the case in which the Court established that the federal government could limit speech only when it constitutes a "clear and present danger." But Holmes, according to his own private correspondence three years later, was not intending to articulate a new doctrine with the phrase "clear and present danger." He was merely using what he thought were equivalent words to restate the traditional bad-tendency test. That the Court was not making any innovation was clear from its simultaneously released opinion in *Debs.* Soon, however, civil libertarians, led by the young Harvard law professor Zechariah Chafee, Jr., claimed that "clear and present danger" implied a broader protection of speech because some words that might have a "bad tendency" would not amount to a danger that was "clear and present." Within eight months, Holmes himself would come around to this view and use his own phrase, creatively reinterpreted by Chafee, as a precedent for giving speech greater constitutional protection.[25]

Holmes's defection from the Court's conservative majority came in a case that involved opponents of President Wilson's decision to send

American troops to Russia. The troops landed in August 1918 ostensibly to protect Allied soldiers, Czech in origin, stranded there when Russia withdrew from the war against Germany, though the Czechs were by that time fighting against the Bolsheviks. In New York that month, Jacob Abrams and three other Russian Jewish immigrants distributed leaflets in both English and Yiddish that accused the United States and Wilson of "hypocrisy" in attacking the Russian Revolution and that called on workers to rise up against capitalism in a "general strike." Under the expanded authority in the Sedition Act, which specifically forbade interference with war production, the four were arrested, tried, and convicted. In November 1919, the Supreme Court upheld the convictions, citing the earlier Espionage Act cases.[26]

This time, however, in a dissenting opinion joined by Louis D. Brandeis, Holmes argued that a "silly leaflet" by obscure protesters posed an insufficient danger to meet the clear-and-present-danger test the Court had endorsed and that the defendants evinced no intention of interfering in the struggle against Germany, only of aiding Russia, with which the United States was not at war. Even though Holmes's opinion did not speak for the Court, it marks a break in constitutional interpretation that would transform the free-speech provisions of the First Amendment from what had been, at least to judges, an almost inert text into what Holmes now called a "sweeping command." The peroration of Holmes's dissent came to acquire an almost hallowed status:

> Persecution for the expression of opinions seems to me perfectly logical. If you have no doubt of your premises or your power and want a certain result with all your heart you naturally express your wishes in law and sweep away all opposition. To allow opposition by speech seems to indicate that you think the speech impotent. . . . But when men have realized that time has upset many fighting faiths, they may come to believe even more than they believe the very foundations of their own conduct that the ultimate good desired is better reached by free trade in ideas—that the best test of truth is the power of the thought to get itself accepted in the competition of the market, and that truth is the only ground upon which their wishes safely can be carried out. That at any rate is the theory of our Constitution. It is an experiment, as all life is an experiment. Every year if not every day we have to wager our salvation upon some prophecy based upon imperfect knowledge. While that experiment is part of our system I think we should

> be eternally vigilant against attempts to check the expression of opinions that we loathe and believe to be fraught with death, unless they so imminently threaten immediate interference with the lawful and pressing purposes of the law that an immediate check is required to save the country. . . . Only the emergency that makes it immediately dangerous to leave the correction of evil counsels to time warrants making any exception to the sweeping command, "Congress shall make no law . . . abridging the freedom of speech."[27]

Remarkable though this was as a reversal of his earlier position, Holmes's dissent was not an isolated development. His conversion to a more protective view of free speech during 1919—influenced, it appears, by direct personal communication with Chafee and Learned Hand; by criticism of his Espionage Act opinions from normally friendly sources; by his own reading as he was forced to reconsider his fundamental ideas about freedom; and by the political crisis raging about him—was in line with a shift taking place at the same time among a wider community of Progressive intellectuals. By that fall the Progressives who had supported the war as a liberal crusade to remake the world were bitterly disappointed with the results of the Paris Peace Conference and appalled by the rising intolerance and hysteria at home. They now saw the government's harsh treatment of its critics during the war as having eroded democracy rather than protecting it. And as the red scare spread, the Progressive intellectuals themselves were under suspicion because of their "socialistic" ideas. They had hoped that the war would yield a permanently expanded federal role in setting minimum labor standards and planning the economy. But wartime programs were quickly rolled back, and any broader economic role for government was being denounced as communism. "At this moment," wrote Walter Lippmann in *The New Republic* during the same month that Holmes wrote his dissenting opinion in *Abrams,* "the man who in domestic policy stands about where Theodore Roosevelt stood in 1912 and in foreign affairs where Woodrow Wilson stood when he first landed in Paris, and in his doctrine of toleration where John Milton stood two and a half centuries ago, is certain, absolutely certain to be called pacifist, pro-German and Bolshevist."[28] What was chiefly left of the wartime expansion of state power was the official attack on dissent.

"If the war didn't happen to kill you," George Orwell later wrote, "it was bound to start you thinking." In the United States, the disillusionment with the war and repression of dissent started Progressives thinking more seriously about the value of protections against the abuse of state power. "The war had changed an abiding faith in the state into questionings of it," wrote Howe, who resigned under attack in 1919. "I hated the new state that had arisen, hated its brutalities, its ignorance, its unpatriotic patriotism." While this disillusionment with state power led some reformers to retreat into private concerns, it led others to a deeper appreciation of civil liberties. Journalists and philosophers, from William Allen White to John Dewey, who previously had paid little attention to the problem of free speech, made it a central concern in their postwar writing. Seeing the potential to broaden its appeal beyond its original pacifist supporters, the National Civil Liberties Bureau reorganized in December 1919 and January 1920 under a new name—the American Civil Liberties Union (ACLU)—adding to its board representatives of labor unions and the National Association for the Advancement of Colored People (NAACP) as well as such influential figures as Felix Frankfurter of Harvard Law School.[29]

By this time, many of those who had called themselves "progressives" during the early years of the century were referring to themselves as "liberals." The change had begun in the pages of *The New Republic* during the 1916 campaign, when the editors needed a term to distinguish their viewpoint from that of the collapsing Progressive Party. "Liberal" also had an international cachet because of its wider use in Europe, particularly in Britain, where the social-reformist "new liberalism" called for a more activist state. But by the postwar years, "liberal" also came to have a philosophical basis for onetime progressives that made it a more apt label. Chastened by the experience of the war but still committed to using the state for social reform, they were now also persuaded of the need for vigilant protection of public discussion and personal liberties against the state and collective mob violence. In this sense, they were returning to the classical political liberalism of the eighteenth century, though not to the economic, laissez-faire liberalism of the nineteenth.[30]

Although it would have long aftereffects, the fever of repression began to break during 1920 as fear of an impending revolutionary upheaval eased. Strikes and unrest declined, the weakness of the radicals became clear, and communism remained confined to Russia. But repression didn't just stop by itself; the opponents of Palmerism helped to bring it to a halt. Liberals at the Labor Department held up and ultimately rejected the deportation of most of the aliens arrested by Palmer's agents, and when some in Congress sought to impeach Assistant Secretary Louis F. Post, who had insisted on proof of individual guilt before deporting anyone, he stood his ground and put Palmer on the defensive for violating the law. In June, a group of eminent legal authorities issued a pamphlet detailing the abuses of constitutional rights by the Department of Justice. Although the Senate had passed a peacetime sedition bill in January 1920, the legislation died after groups that had been silent during wartime repression, such as the American Newspaper Publishers Association, spoke up in favor of free speech. In the fall elections, the Republican presidential nominee, Warren G. Harding, swept to victory promising not to continue wartime crusades but to return to "normalcy." Once in office, Harding ordered Debs released from prison, and his postmaster general, Will Hays, ended the controls on left-wing publications that the Wilson administration had continued even after the war was over. "I am not, and will not allow myself to be made, a censor of the press," Hays said.[31]

The Liberal Turn in the Twenties

In accounts of the rise of the modern liberal state in America, the 1920s generally appear only as a historical parenthesis between the Progressive era and the New Deal. No question the decade saw relatively little extension of government social programs and economic regulation. But if we take civil liberties and the rules governing the public sphere to be integral features of the liberal state, the twenties were a crucial decade, for it was then that the courts, and to some extent Congress, began to develop a more protective legal framework for free speech. The twenties also saw the breakdown of Victorian conventions in manners, morals, and the arts and the growing dominance of modern, liberal ideas in intellectual life and urban culture generally.

These trends created an irrepressible cultural conflict with the conservative forces that controlled national politics. Supported primarily by conservative small-town and rural Protestants, moral reformers had succeeded in getting Prohibition enacted during the fervent wartime period—Congress passed the Eighteenth Amendment in late 1917, and the requisite number of states ratified it within a few months of the armistice. The same forces were behind the adoption in 1921 of sharply restrictive immigration quotas, at first temporary, but made permanent three years later when Congress pegged the quotas to the national origins of the 1890 population. The postwar years also saw rising white hostility to African Americans, race riots, and explosive growth in the membership of the Ku Klux Klan. These policies and movements—literally backward-looking in the case of immigration quotas—sought to check the changes in society being carried along by such tidal forces as the rise of the big cities, the growing influence of the new immigrants, black migration to the North, the expansion of consumer culture, and the increasing penetration of the national media into every sphere of American life. In the culture wars of the era, including the battles over free expression, these were the framing polarities—old-stock Protestants against new ethnic immigrants and African Americans, Victorian against modern, an insular conservatism with political power against a cosmopolitan liberalism with rising cultural influence.

Despite liberalizing cultural tendencies, the twenties were hardly a time of earnest public spirit. The war had exhausted the nation's crusading energies and left in its wake widespread disillusionment that undercut social and economic reform. But the same disillusionment also undercut moral reform and in that sense had a liberalizing impact. Like the old Progressivism, Comstockery seemed foolish and discredited, and as Prohibition failed to prevent Americans from drinking alcohol and gave rise instead to bootleggers, speakeasies, and organized crime, it only reinforced doubts about other forms of moral regulation. When Prohibition was first introduced, vice crusaders saw a positive analogy with moral censorship; according to the *Christian Century,* Prohibition was "the censorship of beverages," while censorship was merely "the prohibition of harmful literature and spectacle." If the government could legitimately dictate what Americans could drink, surely it could dictate what they could read. But the analogy turned out to work even more powerfully in reverse: If the government couldn't, after all, dictate what Americans could drink and the effort to do so proved a fiasco, censorship might not make sense either.[32]

Postwar cultural changes at three levels—popular manners and morals, literature and the arts, and institutional control of resources and rewards—radically altered the context of political and legal battles over censorship. The entire tradition of sexual reticence came under siege during the 1920s. Throwing aside Victorian inhibitions, women shed layers of clothing, wore short skirts and short hair, and began using cosmetics and patronizing beauty salons. To the consternation of moral traditionalists, popular music and dance grew more overtly sensual, and sex became a legitimate topic of conversation. With the popularization of Freudian ideas many people came to believe that the healthy attitude toward sex was to bring it into the open rather than repress it. "'Victorian' and 'Puritan' were becoming terms of opprobrium," Frederick Lewis Allen wrote in his 1931 history of the twenties, *Only Yesterday*. "It was better to be modern—everybody wanted to be modern—and sophisticated, and smart, to smash the conventions and to be devastatingly frank. And with a cocktail glass in one's hand, it was easy at least to be frank."[33]

The postwar generation of writers and intellectuals similarly disdained convention and despised what they viewed as the dishonest sentimentality of their Victorian predecessors. The war had disabused them of optimism and faith in fine words, and rather than obscure ugly facts with euphemisms and hide from the difficult truths of life, they "prided themselves," Ann Douglas writes, "on facing facts, the harder the better."[34] This was the attitude that underlay the unashamed, matter-of-fact writing about sex in novels of the period, such as Ernest Hemingway's *The Sun Also Rises*. Although Victorian conventions had come under intellectual attack in the prewar era, they had still enjoyed the preponderant support of the literary elite, but during the 1920s, the balance of intellectual firepower shifted to the new generation, with its disillusioned, hard-boiled sensibility. The postwar writers were modernists in the sense that they believed the truth lay beneath the surface of life and needed to be ferreted out with an unrelenting honesty, even if it offended popular beliefs and tastes. True art, like science, defied both piety and public opinion. It was a staple among major writers of the period—Sinclair Lewis and H.L. Mencken, for example—that the stifling conventions of everyday life kept Americans from a deeper knowledge of themselves and the world, and it was testimony to the mood of the time that mockery of Main Street and scorn for the "booboisie" did not prevent their books from finding a large popular audience.

Changing cultural institutions reflected these new tendencies and enabled them to develop and reach a wider public. Along with the new writers of the period came new publishers, drawn in many cases from first- or second-generation immigrant backgrounds. New publishing houses—and some old houses in the hands of a younger generation—championed the new literary sensibility and sponsored and defended books that vice crusaders abhorred as immoral. The change in publishing was representative of a larger phenomenon, the emergence of what the historian Stanley Coben calls "a structure to support intellectual dissent." The decade also saw tremendous growth in universities and private foundations, some of them now led by men with liberal sympathies who provided sources of financing and professional advancement for research and scholarship critical of the society. These institutions and their leaders played a key role in supporting new lines of investigation in the social sciences—for example, the work of Franz Boas and his student Margaret Mead in anthropology challenging the scientific racism and repressive sexual practices of Victorian America.[35] Just as changes in popular manners and morals were undercutting Victorianism from below, the emerging literary and intellectual elite was assaulting it from the redoubts of high culture.

The old literary censorship was not able to withstand this onslaught. After the armistice, Comstock's successor, John Sumner, sought to renew the battle against indecent literature. In cases involving books from established publishers, however, judges in New York not only found for the defendants but also awarded them damages against the vice society for malicious prosecution. In 1922, refusing to determine obscenity any longer on the basis of isolated passages, the state's Court of Appeals adopted the "whole-book" test and effectively thwarted attempts to block serious literary works from publication. In response, conservative civic and religious groups formed a coalition called the Clean Books League, which in 1923 pressed for new legislation authorizing juries to base judgments of obscenity on any part of a book, defining obscenity more broadly to include anything that was "filthy" or "disgusting," and forbidding expert testimony. At this point, the vice crusaders still enjoyed considerable prestige, and none of the major organizations representing publishers, authors, or librarians was willing to testify against the proposed toughening of censorship. Even the ACLU, conceiving its mission as the defense of political dissent, refused to become involved in obscenity cases in the early 1920s. It was left to one of the upstart book publishers, Horace Liveright, to lead the meager opposition to the Clean Books bill, which nearly passed but for the Democratic majority leader in the state senate, Jimmy Walker. A songwriter and veteran of the popular entertainment world—soon to be elected New York City's mayor—Walker embodied the popular repudiation of Victorian morals. "No woman was ever ruined by a book," he said during the censorship debate, stalling and eventually killing the legislation.[36]

When the Clean Books League tried to get the obscenity bill passed again the next year, not only was the measure decisively defeated but, for the first time, the National Association of Book Publishers, the Authors' League, and the American Library Association openly opposed censorship. Massachusetts went through a surge of censorship activity in the same period—Boston banned more than sixty novels in 1927 alone, with the Irish police now assuming leadership in the fight against indecency—but book censorship became a local embarrassment, and the crusade there ended in 1930 when the legislature liberalized the state's censorship law. In New York by this time, instead of suppressing books, vice society attacks actually helped to increase their sales, and some publishers virtually invited prosecutions as a publicity strategy. There is no surer sign that a crusade has had it than when its targets decide that being attacked is good for business.[37]

The battle over literary censorship reached the federal government only at the end of the 1920s and then played out as the conflict already had in New York. Officials of the U.S. Customs Bureau and Post Office made decisions to suppress books on a largely ad hoc basis until representatives of the two agencies in 1928 drew up a list of about 700 forbidden books by authors running from Boccaccio and Rabelais to contemporary writers such as D.H. Lawrence and James Joyce. That same year, seeking to make the customs law consistent with rules in effect since the war under the Post Office, the House of Representatives added a provision to a tariff bill forbidding imports of treasonable books. These steps toward bureaucratic rationalization had the unintended effect, however, of exciting the attention of anticensorship forces. One of the Senate's more literate members, Bronson Cutting of New Mexico, moved to eliminate customs censorship of books altogether, and though Congress did not accept this proposal, it devoted four days of debate to the subject and eventually agreed to an amendment requiring a court trial for the suppression of any work, specifying whole books as the basis of judgment, and authorizing the secretary of the treasury to exempt works of literary and scientific merit.[38]

The culmination of the liberalization trend came in December 1933, when a federal judge exonerated Joyce's novel *Ulysses*, one of the few serious literary works that the courts and Customs Office had continued to suppress. The "obscene," according to Judge John Woolsey, legally meant tending "to stir the sex impulses or to lead to sexually impure and lustful thoughts," but he insisted that the law's concern was the effect on the "average" or "normal" person, not on a child (as courts had earlier ruled in applying the Hicklin test), and that Joyce's novel was not an "aphrodisiac." Pornography, Woolsey held, was material "written for the purpose of exploiting obscenity," but he said he found no evidence that *Ulysses* was written with that intent—no "dirt for dirt's sake." Woolsey's criteria for evaluating a book's effect and an author's intent were far more protective of free expression than the legal rules that had prevailed for the previous half-century. Three years earlier, a speaker had told the American Booksellers' Association, "Censorship is to the book business what the flea is to the dog," and though this had been an exaggeration, it was increasingly apt.[39]

While legislators as well as judges were lifting censorship from serious literature in the years after World War I, the Supreme Court remained the focal point in battles over the limits of political advocacy. In a series of dissenting opinions after *Abrams,* Holmes and Brandeis continued to develop their more expansive view of free speech, until the Court began slowly to move in the direction they had been charting. A key step came in the 1925 case *Gitlow v. New York,* involving a radical, Benjamin Gitlow, who had been convicted of violating New York State's ban on advocacy of "criminal anarchy" for helping to publish a manifesto that called for a "revolutionary dictatorship of the proletariat." Though, as usual, it upheld the suppression of radical speech, the Court's majority declared for the first time that free speech and other rights protected under the First Amendment were fundamental liberties guaranteed against state infringement by the Fourteenth Amendment. This decision not only expanded free-speech rights by requiring state governments to abide by federal constitutional guarantees (as Madison had originally wanted to do in a separate amendment in 1791); it also increased the volume of free-speech cases reaching the Supreme Court, a change that made the Court far more important than it previously had been in determining the legal framework of communications. In 1927, the Court overturned a Kansas conviction of an IWW organizer for violating the state's "criminal syndicalism" statute, the first time in its history that the Court ruled in favor of a radical in a free-speech case. And, in 1931, it set another landmark when in two cases it overturned state laws as violations of the First Amendment.[40]

The Court's decision in one of these 1931 cases, *Near v. Minnesota,* represented a dramatic reversal from prewar rulings on the rights of the press. In 1927, an anti-Semitic, anti-Catholic Minneapolis journalist named Jay

M. Near had established a weekly paper called the *Saturday Press* in which he accused the chief of police and other public officials of protecting "Jew gangsters" who "practically" controlled the city. One of the accused public officials, the county prosecutor, then invoked Minnesota's Public Nuisance Law, which declared that a "malicious, scandalous, and defamatory newspaper" was a nuisance and authorized judges to shut such a publication down permanently. Under the law, the state did not have to prove that the charges in Near's paper were false; the burden lay on Near, instead, not only to prove that he had published the truth, but also to show that he had acted "with good motives and for justifiable ends." Unable to satisfy a court that he had done so, Near saw his paper closed after nine issues, a decision upheld by the Minnesota Supreme Court.

With the backing of the ACLU and Robert Rutherford McCormick, the conservative publisher of the *Chicago Tribune,* Near then appealed to the U.S. Supreme Court. In a landmark 5–4 ruling, the Court declared the Minnesota law to be an unconstitutional form of prior restraint of the press, in that the state required publishers, before they issued any further numbers of a publication, to demonstrate the truth of charges against public officials as well as the goodness of their own motives and ends. (The issue in the case was not libel; any of those defamed by Near, the Court recognized, still had the right to sue him.) Besides Holmes and Brandeis, the Court's majority consisted of three recently appointed justices, including Chief Justice Charles Evans Hughes, who wrote the opinion. The decision has since been interpreted as nearly always barring prior restraint of the press.[41]

Stronger legal protections for political dissent as well as imaginative literature were thus already emerging before the New Deal. An ideological watershed divided the Progressivism of 1900–1918 from the liberalism in place by 1932. Both earlier Progressives and later liberals favored the use of state authority in regulating the economy, but the two movements had different approaches to free expression. In their struggle against laissez-faire, the Progressives had conceived a general skepticism about claims of individual rights; continuing to uphold Victorian ideals, they were as much moral as economic reformers, worried about impure influences on the young and the poor, and therefore endorsed moral censorship for what they saw as benign and scientifically justified purposes. When America entered World War I, they were intellectually disarmed on the subject of individual liberty.

Two processes arising independently then turned onetime progressives and their successors in a liberal direction. On the one hand, the war and the red scare chastened them about the uses of state power; on the other, the Victorian certainties that underlay moral reform were undergoing a long-term erosion, generating at first, before the war, the revolt of the young intellectuals, and then, during the twenties, a far more pervasive questioning of Victorian conventions of sexual reticence. The failure of Prohibition reinforced these tendencies. By the early 1930s, these currents of political and cultural change had come together in a new set of liberal principles for the public sphere, upheld by a civil liberties movement and increasingly sympathetic judges, who gave the text of the First Amendment an institutionalized force and "sweeping" scope that it had previously lacked. The New Deal incorporated these ideas, and the judges Roosevelt appointed consolidated the transformation.

As liberals gave free expression more importance, so many of them also came to emphasize the virtues of "cultural pluralism" rather than the Americanization stressed by the earlier Progressives.[42] But with the enactment of restrictive quotas in the early 1920s, the United States had turned away from the openness at least to white Europeans that had previously characterized American immigration policy. The combined effect of strengthened civil liberties and restricted immigration was to invert the pattern of cultural change. From the 1870s to the early 1900s, the dominant tendencies had been tighter moral regulation and growing ethno-religious diversity, but now America moved in the opposite directions—toward greater cultural relaxation and ethno-religious closure and conformity. Not until the 1960s was America able to accept simultaneous moves toward wider diversity among immigrants and greater freedom of expression.

The liberal cultural and legal turn of the 1920s needs to be qualified in other ways. Even though courts were rejecting obscenity cases against established publishers brought by the vice societies, they did not overturn the Hicklin test or enunciate a new definition of the obscene. Similarly, as of the early 1930s, the Supreme Court had not yet adopted a clear alternative to the bad-tendency test in free-speech cases; indeed, it was just at the beginning of a long line of cases in this area. Perhaps most important, the trend toward stronger protection of free speech did not apply to all media. Just as the British had maintained theater licensing for centuries after the licensing of the press was abolished, so, too, the United States maintained censorship of other media even as it relaxed censorship of books. The Post Office continued to regulate the sexual content of magazines, and the 1920s saw the advent of broadcast licensing. One reason that public and judicial opinion about books may have relaxed is that the focus of concern was now shifting to other media believed to be more powerful than print. To many Americans, the most worrisome of these influences was the flickering silver screen that millions of young people watched every week, unchaperoned in the dark.

CHAPTER NINE

The Framing of the Movies

THE EARLY development of the motion pictures in the 1890s and their rapid growth after 1900 were subject to the same dynamic tensions as the rise of the other popular media between the Civil War and World War I. America's transformation into a more diverse, urbanized, industrial society energized and propelled both the burgeoning market for the movies and the anxious reaction that developed against them. During their first two decades, the motion pictures in America had a primarily urban, working-class audience drawn heavily from new immigrant groups, and the movie industry itself, after an initial phase in the hands of men of Anglo-Protestant descent, soon came under the control of immigrant entrepreneurs, most of them Jewish. The United States did not originally dominate international film production; before World War I, the leading role belonged to the French. But as immigrants generally lent a new vitality to American culture, so they imparted it to motion pictures, by the end of the war turning the production center they built in Hollywood into the world's movie capital.

A variety of religious, social-reform, and other groups, however, saw the movies as a seductive and all-too-popular source of moral subversion and, beginning in 1907, persuaded some municipalities and states to censor the new medium. As the Supreme Court generally took a narrow view of free-speech rights at this time, so it upheld governmental censorship of motion pictures, ruling in 1915 that the movies lay outside the sphere of constitutionally protected free expression. As a result, not only did officials, primarily at the state and local level, gain authority to screen and censor movies; the motion-picture industry also subjected itself to privately organized censorship in the hope of preventing more comprehensive and stringent federal legislation.

The political framework of the movies therefore developed differently from that of the press. From the beginning of the republic, the government aided the press and influenced its development through subsidies in postal rates, government printing contracts, and other means. But actual governmental control of publishers was relatively circumscribed, even after the rise of moral censorship after the Civil War. The motion pictures, in contrast, depended neither on a state-run distribution system nor on public subsidy, and for that reason the state may seem to have had little to do with them. But because of the absence of constitutional protection, political influence on the content of the movies was greater than on that of the press. Movie censorship laws upheld by the Supreme Court called for government approval before exhibitors showed any individual work in a state or locality, a form of control ("prior restraint") that the courts had never generally approved in relation to periodicals or books. The federal government also shaped the movie industry through patent decisions, antitrust law, and international trade policy. In contrast to most other governments, the United States did not carry out censorship at the national level, but the constitutional insecurity of film producers, distributors, and exhibitors exposed them to control by state and local authorities and made them highly susceptible to pressure from private interest groups threatening political retribution. Faced with such threats at a moment of vulnerability in the early 1930s, the leaders of the motion-picture industry capitulated and accepted a censorship regime more rigid than imposed in peacetime on any other medium. Politics mattered for the movies as it did for the press, but in a different way.

The Path to the Nickelodeon

The social origins of motion pictures were a critical early influence on their path of development. Whereas newspapers and magazines had begun among the elite and evolved in a more popular direction, movies acquired a lowbrow image at an early point in their history and faced a challenge in achieving respectability. (Even the name "movies" was thought demeaning; in 1915, industry boosters tried to get Americans to call them "photoplays.") The movies did not start out with low-status patronage everywhere. In Europe, they originally attracted a more middle-class audience, and early exhibitions of "high-class" motion pictures were common in America as well. But while the higher-status markets on both sides of the Atlantic expanded slowly, the popular movie audience in America grew to enormous dimensions in a relatively short time. The rapid pace of diffusion in the United States recalls similar patterns in the adoption of the telephone and other new technologies and products in the nineteenth century; as a general rule, American society tended to provide more fertile ground for commercial innovations aimed at broad popular markets. The movies were unusual, however, in that working-class immigrant communities played so critical a role early in the process of popularization.

The movies' low-status beginnings were of particular importance because of the deepening divide between high culture and popular entertainment at the turn of the century. During the late 1800s, many Americans of higher status began to draw sharper distinctions between forms of culture they revered and diversions that they believed were scarcely worthy of being considered "culture" at all. Previously, museums, theaters, and musical presentations had promiscuously mixed different genres and adapted older works to current popular tastes. Because the promoters of exhibitions and performances depended on paying customers, they had clear incentives to respond to what their often boisterous audiences demanded to see and hear. But in the 1880s and 1890s, wealthy patrons began organizing symphony orchestras, art museums, and other cultural institutions as nonprofit organizations under their own control. Relieved of the need to make a profit, and often led by artistic directors trained in Europe, these new organizations distinguished the true culture they represented from mere entertainment and relegated the audience to a secondary, passive role. Cultural distinctions acquired strong racial overtones; the very terms "highbrow" and "lowbrow," derived from nineteenth-century phrenology, associated aesthetic refinement with racial types.[1] In this hierarchy, the movies belonged to a lower order of cultural activity stigmatized by their crass commercial, low-status, and immigrant associations.

At the same time as wealthy patrons were removing high culture from the marketplace, cheap commercial amusements were proliferating in an "entertainment discount revolution"—another intensive phase of the long-term fall in prices for various kinds of cultural commodities. Like the penny papers and dime novels before them, some new forms of cheap entertainment were named for their low price: dime museums (which presented various novelties, freaks, and live entertainment), penny arcades, and "ten-twenty-thirties" (popular theaters where prices ranged from 10 to 30 cents depending on the seat).

After the Civil War, theater prices had risen until, by the mid-1880s, the average price for a ticket was $1, which put commercial performances out of reach for the majority of the public. For women and children, going out after dark had been widely thought not only unsafe, but also indecent; in the evening, their proper place was at home. Toward the end of the nineteenth century, however, rising real wages increased workers' discretionary income, while a shorter workweek increased their discretionary time. Street lighting and improved transportation connecting residential neighborhoods to downtown areas encouraged a diverse population, including women, to go out for entertainment even after dark. Under these conditions, David Nasaw argues, showmen could make money on the basis of a "new calculus of public entertainment" (lower prices, larger audiences), but they "had to provide forms and places of entertainment that were public in the sense that they belonged to no particular social groups, exciting enough to appeal to the millions, and respectable enough to offend no one." The storefront dime or family museums, ten-twenty-thirties, amusement parks, vaudeville theaters at "popular prices," and eventually the motion pictures were among the new urban amusements to fit this pattern. Vaudeville, the most popular live-entertainment medium of the late nineteenth century, evolved out of "variety"—informal performances in saloons and music halls—when impresarios made the entertainment the primary attraction and cleaned up the acts to appeal to respectable audiences. By the 1890s, the regional vaudeville circuits built by the major entrepreneurs in the business represented the most extensive exhibition networks in America.[2]

Several public amusements began as a novelty entertainment or craze that enjoyed a brief popularity before eventually evolving into a more stable cultural form. Two streams of development converged here: rapid innovation in electrical technology and the growth of commercialized forms of leisure. In 1877, the year after Alexander Graham Bell's first exhibition of the telephone, Thomas Edison invented a relatively crude phonograph, imagining that it would serve a variety of purposes, including entertainment as well as practical applications in business. But a market failed to develop, and after a brief flurry of interest the phonograph fell into disuse for some years until Bell's associates in the early 1880s came out with an improved sound-recording system. (Reversing the name Edison had given the device, they called it a "graphophone," making it seem more like a sibling to the telephone.) Spurred by the competition, Edison in 1888 improved his own design, expecting businesses to adopt the phonograph for dictation and other uses. Almost by accident, however, the phonograph's distributors discovered that it had more of a market as an entertainment medium than as a business apparatus. By 1890, the phonograph was enjoying a wave of popularity as a coin-in-the-slot music machine (an early version of the jukebox) located in storefront phonograph parlors as well as in such venues as hotel lobbies and train stations. The parlors would later evolve into penny arcades where a penny or nickel could buy a variety of amusements.[3]

The motion pictures were also a product of the convergence of innovation in entertainment and electrical technology and entered the marketplace by the same path as the phonograph. Edison approached motion pictures with the phonograph as a paradigm, seeing the two as companions. "I am experimenting upon an instrument that does for the Eye what the phonograph does for the Ear, which is the recording and reproduction of things in motion," he wrote in 1888. Edison now was an independent entrepreneur, with his own laboratory and manufacturing facilities. Although his personal contributions to the invention of motion pictures were more limited than the public later took them to be, the Edison organization became pivotal to the industry's early history, largely because of the patents Edison acquired and the characteristically aggressive litigation he undertook in defense of them. Encounters during 1888 and 1889 with two pioneers in the field—the photographer Eadweard Muybridge, who had devised a primitive motion-picture system, and French scientist Etienne-Jules Marey, who had invented the first motion-picture camera—shaped Edison's early efforts. And in his own laboratory, much of the work on motion pictures fell to one of his assistants, William Laurie Dickson, later an important figure in his own right. A simultaneous development greatly facilitated the development of a workable system for both taking and exhibiting motion pictures: In 1889, George Eastman introduced transparent, celluloid film produced in a continuous roll for the Kodak camera he had introduced the year before. But however diverse the sources of invention may have been, it was Edison's laboratory that produced the first commercial application of motion pictures, a system consisting of two devices: a motion-picture camera, which Edison called a "kinetograph," and a peephole viewing machine, or "kinetoscope." In 1891, even before this work was finished, Edison filed broad patent claims that, after some legal vicissitudes, would be sustained by the courts in 1907 and provide him, for a brief time, with the leverage to control the motion-picture business.[4]

The kinetoscope itself had a short career. Exhibited in 1893 and introduced commercially in storefront parlors the following year, the device enabled one person at a time to look through an eyepiece to watch a filmstrip that ran at most a minute and a half. The films, which Edison's technicians produced in a studio built at their laboratory in West Orange, New Jersey, showed such scenes as vaudeville acts, a cockfight, and a boxing match. By 1895, the novelty was already wearing off and the kinetoscope business was fading. But it was just at this point that cinema was about to get its real start as inventors in France, Britain, Germany, and the United States independently devised machines to project motion pictures onto screens. In France, Auguste and Louis Lumière began using the projector they invented, the *cinématographe,* to show films to audiences during 1895. That same year, two Americans, Charles Francis Jenkins and Thomas Armat, demonstrated a large-screen projector in Atlanta, but the public event that launched the movie industry in the United States came in April 1896, when essentially the same projector—rechristened "Edison's Vitascope," though Edison was only its manufacturer—made its New York debut before a paying audience at Koster and Bial's Music Hall. Within three months, motion-picture shows had taken place in cities across the country, mostly at vaudeville theaters.

In America, movies had a rapid takeoff partly because the prior development of vaudeville circuits had created a system of exhibition with a modular program that readily accommodated novelty performances. The movies also spread rapidly because a variety of improved projectors came on the market: Edison's competitors first imported the Lumière cinématographe; then, having left Edison for a new company, Dickson introduced his projector, the Biograph; and by the following year, new models came from other sources, including Edison himself, who dumped the Vitascope in favor of a model of his own. The economic advantages of movie projection were clear. Far more people could watch a screened motion picture than could use a kinetoscope, and once the investment was made in a first copy, movies had lower labor costs than live theater. As a result, motion-picture shows fit the new high-volume, low-price entertainment calculus perfectly.[5]

The earliest motion pictures were not movies in the sense they later acquired. A show typically consisted of a series of short subjects, including filmed vaudeville turns, short scenes from the theater, and views of everyday life ("actualities"), such as people walking in a park or waves crashing on a beach. Some of these subjects soon showed newsworthy people or events, such as a campaign appearance of William McKinley (McKinley's inauguration in 1897 was the first to be recorded on film). Initially, the sheer novelty of cinema was sufficient to draw people to the screen; pictures of oncoming locomotives, an onrushing cavalry charge, or distant places and exotic people were thrilling to audiences that had either never seen anything like them or never seen them from the perspective that the motion pictures offered.

The month the Vitascope made its debut in 1896, a one-minute Edison film of a middle-aged couple kissing at the climax of a scene from a Broadway show caused a sensation. "For the first time in the history of the world," declared an article in the New York *World*, "it is possible to see what a kiss looks like. . . . Scientists say kisses are dangerous, but here everything is shown in startling directness. What the camera did not see did not exist. The real kiss is a revelation. The idea has unlimited possibilities." But in a culture that fought so hard to keep many things hidden, not everyone welcomed the possibilities of "startling directness." A Chicago critic pronounced the kiss "absolutely disgusting . . . no more than a lyric of the Stock Yards." Like sex, violence on the screen was also controversial from the start. Prize fights, illegal in nearly all states, were a major early film attraction and a particular source of outrage to moral reformers, who sought to have fight films banned. One early historian of the movies dates their lowbrow image from the public furor over the filming of the "vicious and bloody" Corbett-Fitzsimmons fight in 1897.[6]

Yet, through the 1890s, the audience of the motion pictures seems to have been drawn from all classes, though people from different backgrounds did not necessarily see the same films in the same places. Higher-status audiences saw motion pictures not only at vaudeville theaters in big cities but also at traveling exhibitions in small towns or even under the sponsorship of churches—venues that often had films of a more uplifting or educational nature, such as views of foreign countries. In contrast, working-class audiences were more likely to seek out entertainment in the form of slapstick farces or fight films and to see them at cheaper vaudeville theaters or penny arcades. The exhibitors who brought motion pictures to these diverse locations were not mere distributors; they assembled the shows and sometimes narrated as the films were shown. And to provide the attractions, there emerged a new industry of film production, including Edison Manufacturing, Biograph, and the major French producers, Georges Méliès and Pathé Frères. While exhibition was organized regionally, film production was international from the start as a result of both legal sales and piracy ("duping").[7]

Movie production rose steadily from 1896 to about 1900, but a number of problems impeded the industry's growth as the new century began. Like many other technologies in their early stages, the motion pictures lacked uniform standards; the Edison and Biograph projection systems worked on incompatible formats, limiting the supply of films any individual exhibitor could use. Copyright protection was not yet secure. Edison's suits against other firms in the movie industry for patent infringement also threatened their ability to do business and discouraged investment in new production capacities. And production companies were still struggling to come up with material that would sustain audience interest. Before 1903, the overwhelming majority of American films—more than 80 percent, according to one estimate based on copyright data—were of a topical nature, including news, travel, documentary, and sports subjects. This early pattern might have indicated that the movies would develop primarily into a visual newspaper. After the turn of the century, however, filmmakers turned increasingly to comedies; then, around 1903, they began developing techniques for narrating more complicated stories, and these "story films"—such as Edwin S. Porter's landmark *The Great Train Robbery*, a 1903 Edison release—were huge commercial successes.[8] According to a study of Edison's records for 1904–1905, staged films sold three and a half times better than actualities.[9] Pathé Frères, the world's largest film production company at the time, opened a New York sales office in 1904, gaining a major share of the American market with its story films, and soon the major American film producers were focusing their resources on fiction films aimed at popular audiences. The two segments of the film exhibition industry were growing at sharply different rates: While the market for genteel, uplifting, high-class motion pictures was stagnating, the popular, lowbrow, working-class market for movie entertainment was booming.[10]

Up to this point, motion-picture exhibitors had relied on vaudeville theaters and other existing venues, but the surging popular demand for movies created the basis for a new down-market exhibition space. In June 1905, an entrepreneur in Pittsburgh set up a cheap storefront theater for showing films and called it the "Nickelodeon" (5 cents being the price of admission and "odeon" the Greek word for theater). Within a year, hundreds of nickelodeons had sprouted across the country, and by the beginning of 1907, there were 2,500, according to the new entertainment paper *Variety*. In November of that year, an article in *The Saturday Evening Post* put the number of nickelodeons at between 4,000 and 5,000 and calculated that just to meet expenses, they had to have a weekly attendance of at least 16 million—a conservative estimate, as the nickelodeons were highly profitable. The new storefront movie houses, charging 5 or sometimes 10 cents, were not only cheaper than traditional theaters but also more accessible to working-class neighborhoods. With continuous shows lasting a half hour or so, customers could squeeze in a visit at any time—housewives while shopping, workers after a day on the job. Entire families came in the evening and on Sundays. Children, often on their own, made up a large part of the audience, perhaps as much as a third. A typical nickelodeon had fewer than 300 seats, changed its program three times or more a week (obtaining new films through rental exchanges), and provided some kind of musical accompaniment, perhaps a piano player or a small orchestra. Individual films were short, typically lasting five or six minutes, sometimes ten, and derived their subject matter, as Lewis Jacobs writes, "from American life—from the exploits of the policeman and burglar, cowboy and factory worker, farmer and country girl, clerk and politician, drunkard and servant girl, storekeeper and mechanic." Between movies, there were "illustrated songs" by local performers, with audience sing-alongs on the chorus. Writing about the nickelodeons of his childhood, the writer James Agee later recalled "the barefaced honky-tonk and the waltzes by Waldteufel, slammed out in a mechanical piano, . . . the laughter of unrespectable people having a hell of a fine time, laughter as violent and steady and deafening as standing under a waterfall." Nickelodeon audiences shouted, cheered, and stamped their feet. The films may have been silent, but the theaters shook.[11]

Although more middle-class people would soon be going to the movies, the audience in the nickelodeon era was predominantly working-class. A New York survey sponsored by the Russell Sage Foundation in 1910 found that although people from working-class backgrounds made up just 2 percent of the audience for legitimate, high-priced theater, they accounted for 72 percent of all moviegoers. The survey also identified 25 percent of the movie audience as "clerical" and just 3 percent as "leisured." Unlike traditional theaters, which segregated members of the audience according to the price they paid, nickelodeons followed the democratic practice of letting people take any open seat—except that many smaller theaters excluded African Americans, and some larger ones admitted them only to the balcony.[12]

Much of nickelodeon audience consisted of first- and second-generation immigrants, though no data are available on ethnic variation in attendance. An obvious advantage of the movies for immigrants was that they could understand the pantomime of the silent films even without knowing English; indeed, filmmakers in the early 1900s may have been uninterested in adding sound to pictures partly because their audience spoke not one language, but several. In poor immigrant neighborhoods, the nickelodeons also served as centers of social life for the young. A study mapping Manhattan's nickelodeons in 1908 shows the theaters were overwhelmingly clustered in neighborhoods such as the Lower East Side that shared two features: high population densities and large numbers of working-class immigrants, mostly Jews and Italians. Many contemporary sources report the particular affinity of Jews for the movies. Of Manhattan's nickelodeon owners, about 60 percent were Jewish, with Italians next at 18 percent. Since opening a theater cost as little as $400 and the business was too new for native-born elites to have entrenched themselves in it, immigrants were able to get a start in the movie business without facing either the financial barriers or the prejudice they encountered in other businesses and professions. And having gotten a foothold, some of the Jewish exhibitors would later rise to the top of the industry: William Fox, Adolph Zukor, and Marcus Loew, who each owned about a half-dozen New York movie houses in 1908, would later build, respectively, Fox, Paramount, and Metro-Goldwyn-Mayer.[13]

The immediate effect of the nickelodeon boom was to create a spurt in demand for motion pictures that American producers were unable to meet. As demand rose, the film historian Charles Musser argues, storefront theaters could be opened faster than new movie production facilities could be built. The skills involved in distributing and exhibiting films were also easier to acquire than the skills needed to produce motion pictures. In addition, the lawsuits brought by Edison Manufacturing were discouraging other production companies from making the investments needed for expansion, while Edison itself used its facilities to make more prints of its movies rather than to increase the number of new movies it made. The failure of the American movie industry to respond to rising demand fast enough created an opening for foreign filmmakers to seize a larger share of the American market. In 1907, two-thirds of the films released in the United States were imported from Europe; Pathé Frères alone supplied one-third of all movies shown in America, more than any domestic firm.[14] During the previous two years, its films had contributed to the nickelodeon boom, so in a sense Pathé Frères was merely harvesting the fruits of a market it had helped to build.[15] The same period also saw a decisive shift from topical to narrative forms of cinema; the share represented by comedy and drama, according to copyright data, reached two-thirds in 1907 and more than 90 percent in 1908.[16] These changes signaled not only the birth of the modern cinema but also the onset of a political crisis over the control of a medium that to many stunned onlookers appeared to be a new form of "urban vice."

Censorship and Diversity on the Screen

By 1907, a new domain of communication and cultural expression had grown up outside the supervision of customary authority. Many films of this period told stories or showed scenes that guardians of the moral order regarded as overly suggestive, excessively violent, or likely to encourage lawlessness. Comedies made fun of Victorian morality, and melodramas often depicted the rich and powerful as dissolute and corrupt while portraying workers as victims of injustice. At the time, many Americans of older stock were already in a panic over the effects of the new immigration, the changing role of women, fears of "race suicide," and industrial strife. In that context, the movies were suspect, not just because of their content but also because so much of the movie audience was foreign-born and so many of the films were foreign-made. Before 1907, however, the rise of the motion pictures took place outside the field of vision of the press, the professional classes, and the arbiters of culture and morality. Then, as if suddenly awakening to a threat that had stolen upon them, moral reformers began to raise concerns about the motion-picture "problem." They especially feared that the illusory world portrayed on the screen was leading children into careers of crime and delinquency.

Not all the reactions were hostile. Some Progressive reformers approved of the cinema, seeing it as an opportunity for uplift, and thought that with proper guidance movies could become a positive moral influence. As had long been the pattern in the moral regulation of print, reformers tended to divide into two camps, though there was much overlap between them: the advocates of repression, who called for government censorship, and the advocates of amelioration and uplift, who emphasized the need for wholesome and appealing alternatives to the cheap temptations of the marketplace. Some of the concern about the motion pictures, unlike print, also focused on a physical space, the storefront movie theater, which often did present serious risks of overcrowding, inadequate fire safety, and poor ventilation. But this was not all; a darkened theater where youth went unchaperoned created worrisome opportunities for sexual experimentation. "There should be a police woman at the entrance of every moving picture show and another inside," declared one feminist reformer. "These places are the recruiting stations of vice."[17] As an unregulated space for unregulated messages, the movies were, in a sense, doubly dangerous.

The two regulatory responses to the movies, the repressive and ameliorative, became evident in one of the earliest battles over motion-picture censorship. In New York the day before Christmas 1908, Mayor George B. McClellan, Jr., closed the city's more than 600 nickelodeons, requiring them to reapply for licenses under new rules that would bar them from opening on Sundays and from showing movies that tended to "degrade or to injure the morals of the community." A court injunction obtained by the nickelodeon owners, led by William Fox, thwarted the mayor's edict, allowing the theaters to reopen. But another option emerged during the controversy when representatives of the People's Institute, a Progressive-reform organization in the city, called for a voluntary mechanism to clean up the movies. Opposed to government censorship and generally approving of the cinema, the institute's leaders invited various educational and Protestant reform associations to join together to create a private board that would review films submitted by the industry and recommend cuts or complete suppression. With an advisory committee that included such notables as Andrew Carnegie and Samuel Gompers, the board was directly descended from older mechanisms of privatized elite censorship such as the Society for the Suppression of Vice, except that it had no delegated legal authority. Nothing would compel the movie industry's participation or acquiescence, but film companies would be able to publicize the board's seal of approval. The board would also help to promote films that embodied higher moral qualities. Established in March 1909, originally as the New York Board of Censorship of Motion Pictures, it quickly changed "New York" to "National" in its name after obtaining the cooperation of the movie industry. Within six months, the board was scrutinizing three-quarters of all movies released in the country.[18]

The National Board of Censorship was able to work out this relationship with the movie industry for two reasons—first, because the industry was under siege and needed a means of legitimation; and second, because just at that moment, an economically motivated effort to monopolize the industry produced a willing partner for the Progressive moral reformers. The fractious patent litigation among the leading film companies came to an end in 1908 in the wake of a court decision the previous year that appeared to favor Edison over its rivals, except for Biograph, which had strong patent claims of its own. But even Biograph decided that further litigation would be too costly and struck a bargain with Edison to share in the profits of a new Motion Picture Patents Company that would also license eight other firms: the other major American production companies, one foreign producer (Pathé Frères), and two importers.

Finalized in December 1908—the same month as the closure of the New York nickelodeons—the Edison trust (as it became known) pooled sixteen patents on motion-picture projectors, cameras, and film and brought together companies accounting for virtually all domestically made films and the majority of foreign imports. The trust aimed to enrich its members, above all Edison, by controlling competition and shifting profits from the distributors and exhibitors back (in the supply chain) to the producers and patent holders. The Patents Company established a uniform set of prices per foot of film that the distributors (rental exchanges) would pay film producers, and it exacted royalties from three different groups: manufacturers of cameras and projectors ($5 per machine), motion-picture exhibitors ($2 a week), and movie producers (one-half cent per foot of film). Exhibitors and rental exchanges that wanted any films from licensed companies would also have to agree not to show or distribute films from unlicensed firms. In addition, Eastman Kodak, the preeminent manufacturer of movie film worldwide, would supply raw film stock only to licensed companies in return for becoming their exclusive supplier. At the time the trust was created, the domestic entrepreneurs who were excluded or refused to cooperate—so-called "independents," many of them small-time Jewish theater and exchange owners—seemed to be of no consequence. The trust held a commanding position over the industry, and as one of its early actions, hoping to improve public regard for motion pictures, it offered the cooperation of its member companies to the National Board of Censorship.[19]

Both the moral and economic drives to control the industry drew upon nationalist sentiment. Although many of the offending films had been domestically produced, public criticism of the movies focused on foreign imports and played upon the image of European—particularly French—decadence and licentiousness. Explaining its cooperation with the National Board, the Patents Company said it hoped to bar "cheap and inferior foreign films" and attract "the better class of the community" to movie theaters, but the trust itself excluded the lesser European producers entirely, without regard to the moral character of their films. Even Pathé Frères, despite its membership in the trust, found itself under continued attack, shifted investment back to Europe, and after 1910 played a smaller role in the United States than it had before.[20] In part, domestic producers were catching up with the rise in demand for story films that they had been unable to meet a few years earlier. Hostility toward foreign films and growing production at home together cut imports to less than 20 percent of the titles released in the United States by the end of 1912.[21]

This shift toward domestically produced movies did not, however, reflect the triumph of the Edison trust, which soon after its formation began to lose control of the industry. The independents—led by such figures as Fox in New York and Carl Laemmle in Chicago, both owners of rental exchanges—proved to be a formidable source of opposition both in the marketplace and in court. They imported films from foreign producers excluded by the trust and soon began producing their own movies by obtaining raw film stock from abroad, pretending to use motion-picture cameras not covered by the trust's patents, and otherwise foiling the trust's continual harassment. Laemmle's Independent Moving Picture Company (IMP), which later evolved into Universal, released its first film in October 1909. By June 1910, independent companies were distributing two-thirds as many reels of film as the licensed companies and serving 30 percent of the nation's approximately 10,000 movie theaters. Meanwhile, hoping to defeat resistance from distributors, the members of the trust created their own distribution company, General Film, which bought out existing exchanges and by 1912 virtually monopolized the distribution of films from licensed sources. The federal government finally stepped in when President Taft's attorney general charged the Patents Company and General Film with violating the Sherman Antitrust Act in August 1912—a time when Taft was under fire from his two principal opponents in the fall election, Woodrow Wilson and Theodore Roosevelt, for being too soft on the trusts. That same month, a court decision overturned one of the key patents controlled by the Edison trust and eliminated the barriers to the independents' use of standard movie cameras. By this point, the independents were producing nearly as many films as the licensed companies.[22]

The shifting tides of the law were only one factor favoring the independents. In October 1915, a federal court found the Patents Company and General Film guilty of antitrust violations and several months later ordered them to dissolve, but by then the independents already had the trust beaten. During this same period, a growing middle-class market for the movies emerged, and new and more luxurious theaters were built as the nickelodeon era came to an end. The independents, despite their origins in the world of nickelodeons and small-time vaudeville, anticipated this shift earlier and responded to it more effectively than members of the trust did. On the face of things, the independents were improbable victors. The trust consisted almost entirely of Anglo-Protestant businessmen, and their central figure, Thomas Edison, was an American legend, while the independents were nearly all socially marginal Jewish immigrants, originally without significant financial backing or political connections. The explanation for the Jewish independents' conquest of the industry cannot solely be that they had an early start. The companies in the Edison trust had an earlier start, and they created a rationalized organization of the kind that controlled many other sectors of the economy. For a while, they were sufficiently disciplined to maintain a profitable order in an expanding industry. But their "first-mover" advantages, control of patents, and initial market power were ultimately unavailing.

The trust's failure arose not only from legal and political intervention but also from intertwined aspects of its own economic practices and cultural assumptions. The very rules the Patents Company used to suppress competition contributed to its ultimate demise. By setting a uniform price per foot for films, it eliminated any incentive for the licensed companies to invest in more costly and elaborate productions. For a long time, the trust also stubbornly insisted on limiting its members to short films, one- or two-reelers. The independents, in contrast, invested in more expensively produced, multi-reel "feature" films that they correctly judged would appeal to upscale audiences in better theaters. The independents were not responsible, as is often argued, for introducing the "star system" into the movies, but some independent producers, such as Laemmle, were especially aggressive in paying actors and actresses unprecedented sums of money and using publicity to build up audience identification with them. In general, the trust followed a conservative, risk-averse strategy, attempting to maintain not only its monopoly power but also the motion-picture business as it had evolved up to 1908, while the independents were more willing to make high-risk investments in pursuit of an enlarged audience that only a more ambitious conception of motion pictures could create.

Even after the trust's error in opposing feature films became clear, the companies in the trust were unable to match the independents' grasp of the market. This disparity may be traceable to differences in the origins of the two sets of firms. The trust's members, as Neal Gabler argues, typically entered the industry "by inventing, bankrolling, or tinkering with movie hardware," while the independents entered the business by running theaters. Several of the independents, such as Zukor, who started out as a furrier, had also come from fashion-conscious industries where success depended on alertness to changing tastes. Reflecting on the refusal of the Patents Company to grant him a license when he was first planning to produce feature films, Zukor later said of the trust: "What they were making belonged entirely to technicians. What I was talking about—that was show business." Astonishingly, not one firm in the Edison trust survived to become part of the modern movie industry; indeed, only one company, Vitagraph, lasted beyond 1920, and it disappeared in 1925. All the great film companies were built by the independents.[23]

Like the Edison trust, the National Board of Censorship failed to achieve its original aims. Lacking the authority to compel producers to submit their films or to accept its guidance, the board was unable to extend its supervision over the entire industry. Nor did it succeed in speaking for all those who thought the movies were in need of restraint; moral judgments about films turned out to be far more contentious even among reformers than they had initially imagined. Led from 1910 to 1915 by the reformer Frederic Howe, the National Board attempted to make the movies into a progressive moral force. In reviewing films, it was especially concerned about anything that might lead youth into the ways of crime; for example, it censored one film for making a burglary look too easy. It also rejected films concerned with such themes as infidelity and suicide and sought to remove sexually suggestive material. The board's leadership was relatively tolerant, however, by the standards of the day, and unlike European government censors, it was not preoccupied with suppressing oppositional political ideas. Conservative critics believed the board was insufficiently vigilant and instead supported comprehensive state censorship.

The federal government adopted a few censorship measures in this period. In 1909, Congress authorized the Treasury Department to censor imported films, and a few years later it banned prize-fight films from interstate commerce after a widely distributed fight film showed an African American boxer defeating a white man. The principal steps in controlling the movies, however, came at lower levels of the federal system. In 1911, Pennsylvania became the first state to create a motion-picture censorship board; Ohio and Kansas followed in 1913, then Maryland and Virginia. Many cities across the country also adopted procedures for local censorship, often lodging authority with the police. The National Board strenuously fought official censorship; Howe warned about the danger of having the state pass upon "the portrayal of labor questions, of Socialism, the Industrial Workers of the World, and other insistent issues." In 1915, hoping to clarify its philosophy, the National Board dropped the word "censorship" from its name, recast itself as the "National Board of Review of Motion Pictures," and focused its efforts on the promotion of better films rather than the suppression of bad ones. Some public officials also opposed official censorship. In 1912, a new mayor of New York, William Gaynor, vetoed an ordinance that included movie censorship provisions, insisting that the constitutional guarantee of freedom of the press covered "all methods of expression by writing or pictures."[24]

But this view did not prevail. In 1915, the constitutionality of motion-picture censorship came before the U.S. Supreme Court in a landmark case, *Mutual Film Corporation v. Industrial Commission of Ohio,* testing the Ohio censorship law, which authorized a state board to approve only those films that it judged to be "of a moral, educational or amusing and harmless character." Because the Court had not yet held the First Amendment to apply to the states, the free-press guarantees of the Ohio state constitution were the chief basis of Mutual Film's appeal (though even if the Court had found the First Amendment applicable, its reasoning indicates it would not have decided the case any differently). In a unanimous decision, the Court upheld the Ohio law and movie censorship, declaring, "The exhibition of moving pictures is a business pure and simple, originated and conducted for profit, like other spectacles, not to be regarded, nor intended to be regarded by the Ohio Constitution, we think, as part of the press of the country or as organs of public opinion. They are mere representations of events, of ideas and sentiments published and known, vivid, useful and entertaining no doubt, but . . . capable of evil, having power for it, the greater because of their attractiveness and manner of exhibition."[25]

Three distinct arguments appear in this opinion. First, by identifying the movies as "a business pure and simple," the Court implied that their commercial status made them unworthy of constitutional protection, even though publishers of newspapers, books, and magazines had never lost their free-speech rights because they ran their businesses for profit. Second, the Court distinguished between two classes of expression, the press and "spectacles," and put the movies in the latter category along with theatrical presentations and circuses. While acknowledging that such spectacles and performances are also "mediums of thought," the Court denied that "guaranties [*sic*] of free opinion and speech" extended "to the multitudinous shows which are advertised on the bill-boards of our cities and towns. . . . The judicial sense supporting the common sense of the country is against the contention." Here the Court invoked an implicit distinction between ideas and entertainment, but this was not ultimate grounds of the decision, for the Court readily conceded that the movies often did convey ideas. In the third and decisive step in its reasoning, it declared that movie censorship lay within government's police powers because the movies were "capable of evil," or, as a particularly evocative passage put it: "Their power of amusement and, it may be, education, the audiences they assemble, not of women alone nor of men alone, but together, not of adults only, but of children, make them [motion pictures] the more insidious in corruption."[26]

The Supreme Court's opinion in *Mutual Film,* which set no constitutional limitation whatsoever on movie censorship, guided state as well as federal law for the next thirty-seven years. At an analytical level, the Court was dealing with a problem of translation—that is, it was translating legal principles from old contexts (the press, live spectacles) into a new one (cinema). But the justices' language, far from being strictly analytical, was laden with the anxieties and prejudices of their time when they described the audience ("not of women alone nor of men alone, but together, not of adults only, but of children") and the movies themselves ("a business pure and simple," advertised on billboards, similar to circuses, unworthy of being accorded the rights of the press as a matter of "common sense"). The difference between the press and the movies was not simply that the press enjoyed a long tradition of constitutional protection, whereas the movies were a novelty. The people who produced and exhibited the movies were also parvenus, easily dismissed in crass terms as interested in nothing but money. Unlike the press, with its powerful newspaper and magazine publishers, the movie industry consisted at this point of small enterprises run by social outsiders. Support for censorship was an expression of distrust of their motivations. The same kinds of concerns surrounded moviegoers. During the New York censorship controversy, Mayor Gaynor suggested that censorship measures reflected a prejudice against the low-income people who made up the movie audience. "Why are we singling out these people as subjects necessary to be protected by a censorship?" he asked. "Are they any more in need of protection by censorship than the rest of the community?"[27] Although moral reformers and judges may not have wanted to put it so baldly, their implicit assumption was that the movie audience did require their benevolent supervision.

Yet movie censorship in the period before World War I should not be overstated. Like publishing, the early movie industry was remarkably open to diverse points of view because the costs of production were low and access to the marketplace was relatively easy, given the thousands of locally run movie houses. As a result, films were produced by many different types of organizations, including reform groups, labor and business organizations, and women's rights advocates and their opponents. On public issues, the movies were anything but silent. Many film melodramas attacking corrupt businessmen were counterparts to muckraking journalism, and some even took their plots from the news and magazine stories of the day. (Upton Sinclair produced *The Jungle* for the screen in 1914 and cast himself in the role of a heroic socialist leader.)

The early movies, with their predominantly working-class audience, often explored the lives and struggles of workers with great sympathy. In a study of the numerous worker films from the early twentieth century, Steven J. Ross distinguishes three general types: comedies and dramas that used workers and immigrants as their protagonists, when they could just as easily have had middle-class characters; films that dramatized workers' daily hardships, often focusing on women in sweatshops, mills, and offices or on child labor; and "labor-capital" films that depicted often violent conflicts involving male workers, business, and the police. In an analysis of 244 labor-capital films made between 1905 and 1917, Ross classifies 46 percent as liberal, 34 percent as conservative, and 20 percent as antiauthoritarian, populist, or radical. In the same period, women film writers, directors, and producers were responsible for movies that dealt with issues of sexual equality, birth control, and women's suffrage, while other films were harshly critical of these ideas. As Ross writes, "Movies were far more political and varied in their ideological perspectives during the silent era than at any subsequent time." And, partly because movies theaters reflected the ethnic makeup of the neighborhoods in which they were located, many films were produced for particular groups—Irish films for Irish audiences, Yiddish films for Jews, and after 1913 all-black movies (so-called "race films") for the roughly 200 theaters in African American neighborhoods.[28]

When the Supreme Court denied movies the constitutional status of the press, therefore, it was not simply reflecting what some may suppose to have been the irrelevance of silent film to public debate. In March 1915, only months before the Court issued its decision, the opening of D.W. Griffith's *The Birth of a Nation*, with its racist portrayal of blacks and glorification of the Ku Klux Klan, set off a major national controversy that, if nothing else, demonstrated the growing power of the movies as an organ of opinion. After 1911, movie theaters also regularly presented newsreels, a direct counterpart to newspapers, though in subsequent years the courts ruled that newsreels were just as much subject to government censorship as fiction films.[29]

The rise of the mass media in the United States, I have been arguing, came just at the moment when America was becoming a more diverse, urbanized, industrial society, and that conjuncture had twin effects: It brought new vitality to the emerging media, while setting off an alarmed reaction against them. The new urban working-class and immigrant neighborhoods provided the movies with their most enthusiastic audience and many of their most inventive producers and entrepreneurs. And the predominance of these groups in the industry intensified the anxious response of an older America worried about the direction the society was taking.

That the motion pictures were produced outside local communities, bypassing local means of control, contributed to the anxiety about the movies' influence. The result was an uneasy division of control: The immigrant entrepreneurs rose to dominate the motion pictures, while anxious elites instituted a second level of scrutiny over them. In the long term, the political framework that emerged in this period would have great consequence for the movies: By approving censorship, the Supreme Court stripped the industry of any constitutional recourse and encouraged it, in later years, to adopt increasingly stringent means of self-censorship. In the short term, however, censorship had only a limited impact. Film production, distribution, and exhibition were so fragmented that control over the industry was difficult without direct federal regulation. And even where local and state censorship existed, compliance was often only superficial. Censorship as actually practiced was too uneven and crude to block all the subtle ways in which the movies disrupted older beliefs and traditions. As a result, despite the limitations that censorship created, the silent pictures before World War I were a powerfully disturbing—and liberating—aspect of American culture and the public sphere.

The Consolidation of Control

At the time of the Supreme Court's decision in *Mutual Film* in 1915, the limited reach of state and local municipal censors, as well as the competitiveness and diversity of the movie industry, prevented any single public or private organization from controlling the content of the movies. But transformations in both the political context and economic structure of the movie industry between the late 1910s and the early 1930s supplied the impetus and conditions for centralized control missing earlier. The result was the establishment of a censorship code more systematic than ever previously imposed during peacetime on any medium in the United States.

World War I and its immediate aftermath had a profound impact on both the role of the American film industry and the political pressures it faced. The war elevated the movies to new importance and subordinated them to new constraints. By the time the United States entered the war, the movies were attracting 10 to 13 million people daily. And with European film production decimated, American motion-picture companies also gained a dominant share of international markets; by 1918, the United States produced an estimated 80 percent of films worldwide. The vast audiences, both at home and abroad, made American movies an ideal instrument of war propaganda. The federal government's Committee on Public Information organized a separate motion-picture division, which exercised tight control over all film footage of the war, financed three feature films of its own, and sent thousands of volunteers, known as "four-minute men," to give short, patriotic speeches in movie theaters. Movie censorship, previously focused on moral concerns, took on a thoroughly political character. Under the authority in the Espionage Act of 1917 barring any speech that interfered with recruitment or encouraged insubordination in the armed forces, the government even suppressed a film about the American Revolution, *Spirit of '76*. Atrocities by British redcoats portrayed in the movie might "make us a little bit slack in our loyalty to Great Britain," said the judge, who gave producer Robert Goldstein a prison sentence of ten years (later reduced to three). The film industry as a whole was scarcely in need of censorship to bring it into line with government policy. The war gave the immigrant entrepreneurs who now dominated moviemaking an opportunity to demonstrate their Americanism, and they responded with patriotic films demonizing Germany and glorifying the Allied cause, while movie stars played a new public role in boosting such efforts as the sale of Liberty Bonds. The wartime role of the industry testified to the distance it had traveled in public esteem since its early days of dubious respectability.[30]

Many Americans remained deeply ambivalent, however, about the moral character of the movies and the people who made them. By the war's end, southern California had become the center of filmmaking, and "Hollywood" soon came to symbolize both the glamour and irresponsibility of a dream-like, alien world. Filmmakers—members of the Edison trust as well as independents—had been using southern California as a production site since about 1910. Unlike New York and Chicago, which had been the trade's early centers, the Los Angeles area allowed year-round filmmaking, but the industry didn't migrate there just for the climate. Low production costs and a cooperative, antiunion municipal government helped to attract movie production. Still early in its development and largely without any industrial base, Los Angeles also enabled the new movie moguls, producers, and stars to build a new community around the ideals of leisure and consumption that they were projecting on the screen. The area held particular appeal to the Jewish movie producers. Far removed from the East's social hierarchies, it enabled them to escape the snubs of eastern Anglo-Protestant elites, shed their pasts, and create a new society of their own. But the very distinctiveness of Hollywood as a community added to the uneasy relationship of many Americans to the "Hollywood" of the imagination.[31]

This uneasy relationship erupted into a new crisis of control over the movies during the early postwar years. America at the time was rent by a broader conflict between the new, urban, "flapper" jazz-age culture with its frank acceptance of sex and the still-powerful, small-town, Anglo-Protestant elements that had secured the adoption of Prohibition and continued to oppose the discussion and representation of sex in literature and the arts. In the more relaxed moral climate just after the war, a flurry of risqué movies from such Hollywood producers as Cecil B. DeMille openly defied Victorian sensibilities, even as these films sought to reconcile modernity with tradition by promoting an ideal of sexual passion within marriage. Several Hollywood sex scandals—the suspicious death of a young woman at a party held by movie star Fatty Arbuckle; the murder of a prominent film director; the divorce of "America's sweetheart" Mary Pickford and her remarriage to Douglas Fairbanks—added to the image of a decadent Hollywood debauching American morals. Thoroughly fed up with what they saw as the laxity and ineffectiveness of the National Board of Review, Protestant moral reformers once again turned to proposals for state censorship. Nearly 100 bills to regulate the movies were introduced into state legislatures in 1921; when New York State enacted a movie censorship law that year, it was a major blow to the industry because of the pivotal importance of the New York market.[32]

The defeat in New York led to a strategic shift and organizational upheaval in the movie industry. During the previous decade, the industry had relied on its voluntary relationship with the National Board of Review to deflect demands for government censorship. In 1916, after the Supreme Court's decision in *Mutual Film,* firms in the various sectors of the trade had also established the National Association of the Motion Picture Industry (NAMPI) to forge a unified front against government control; among its actions, the organization had unsuccessfully sponsored a constitutional amendment for freedom of the screen. But internal tensions, particularly between the exhibitors and the producers, had weakened the association. After NAMPI's failure to stop the New York legislation, the leading movie companies decided to leave out the exhibitors in creating a new group, the Motion Picture Producers and Distributors of America (MPPDA), which would restore public confidence by promising to clean up Hollywood and exercise effective self-censorship. To take charge of this organization, the industry's leaders called on the former national chairman of the Republican Party, Will Hays, who as President Harding's postmaster general had just ended the political censorship of the mails still in effect under the Espionage Act. Generally opposed to a wider role for government, Hays could be counted on to fight state censorship of the movies. And as an elder in the Presbyterian Church, he was perfectly cast to serve as chief of public relations for the largely Jewish producers and to represent them to the conservative Protestant groups that as of 1922 represented the major source of agitation for moral reform of motion pictures.[33]

The Hays Office, as the new trade association's headquarters became known, initially proved far more successful than its predecessor in resisting external control of the movies. Taking charge of the industry's fight against a Massachusetts referendum to institute movie censorship, Hays succeeded in getting the measure defeated by a more than two-to-one margin. A master of co-optation, he invited representatives from a variety of civic organizations to join in providing advice to the industry, often paying them for their services. Though his main early accomplishments were in public relations, Hays did attempt to reform Hollywood by bringing about several changes in industry practices, such as the addition of morals clauses to actors' contracts. From 1924 to 1930, through a voluntary review that enabled producers to submit synopses of stories or books they were considering for screen development, the Hays Office killed 125 movie projects that it judged offensive. A department was also established to work with the studios to clean up films before censorship, and in 1927 one member of Hays's staff drew up a list of "Don'ts and Be Carefuls" that attempted to summarize the requirements of state censorship boards. The "don'ts" included profanity and nudity, while the "be carefuls" urged discretion in connection with sex, crime, and violence. Based in New York, Hays had no authority over the studios and no staff in Hollywood to exercise close supervision of movie production. Nonetheless, his efforts prevented any extension of government censorship for the remainder of the 1920s: No additional states adopted a censorship board after New York.[34]

The twenties were boom years of massive growth and capital investment for the movies, initially strengthening the major motion-picture companies but ultimately leaving them deeply in debt and vulnerable to external control. The decade saw the construction of the great picture palaces across the country, and audiences soared—by 1927, weekly attendance reached 100 million. The controversial issues that the movies had addressed before the war now nearly vanished from the screen. According to an analysis by the historian Lary May of the 6,600 films produced during the decade, only fifteen dealt with labor and fifty-one with modern politics—a total of just 1 percent. The disappearance of social-problem films probably had less to do with the Hays Office than with the general decline of political dissent, the shift to a predominantly middle-class movie audience, and the changing economics of the motion-picture industry. In 1912, at the height of the Progressive era, there had been about sixty production companies and hundreds of independent exhibitors; about 2,000 films were produced annually at a cost typically ranging between $1,000 and $10,000 per film. These conditions were congenial to a wide spectrum of subject matter and viewpoints. By 1920, as a result of the shift to longer feature films and the rise of the star system, costs had increased to between $40,000 and $80,000 per movie, the total number of movies produced had fallen (it would average around 800 annually during the decade), and the industry was consolidating into a smaller number of firms.[35]

The first of the motion-picture giants emerged in 1916 when Zukor engineered a takeover of the leading distributor of features, Paramount, and combined it with his own Famous Players production company and the operations of producer Jesse Lasky. Two years later, Paramount distributed 220 features, far more than any other company. One combination led to others. After some of the biggest first-run movie theaters formed First National Exhibitors Circuit to gain bargaining leverage against the film producers, First National went into production; Zukor then bought hundreds of theaters across the country to assure his company access to screens and tap the profits in exhibition. Other leading movie producers followed suit, until the movie industry consisted of a few large, vertically integrated giants with production studios, distribution networks, and theater chains. These companies also dictated terms to independent exhibitors, imposing a system known as "block booking," which required them to accept a series of films, including a company's lesser output, if they wanted to obtain its hit movies with big-name stars. Vertical integration and block booking left little room for smaller rivals. The shift to talking pictures between 1926 and 1930 delivered the final blow to small firms, which could not afford the necessary investments. By 1930, production costs averaged $375,000 per film, and the industry was almost entirely concentrated in eight firms: the five "majors" (Paramount, Fox, Warner Brothers, Radio-Keith-Orpheum [RKO], and Loews—the parent company of MGM) and the "little three" (Universal, Columbia, and United Artists). These firms operated as an oligopoly, effectively locking up access to first- and second-run movie houses. Several of the film companies, however, had become seriously overextended; the massive investments in theaters and talking pictures had made the giants dependent on their bankers and vulnerable to external pressure, particularly after the Great Depression hit.[36]

Political trouble began mounting for the movie industry at the end of the twenties. Several Protestant leaders, convinced that Hays was merely pacifying them, refused to continue to work with his office and renewed their calls for government action. In addition to censorship, they sought a federal ban on block booking on the grounds that the practice forced local theaters to show morally questionable films. Not only was legislation against block booking pending in Congress; the new president in 1929, Herbert Hoover, was considering antitrust action against the movie industry. At the state and local level, censorship boards requested an unprecedented number of cuts; in 1928, New York State alone required deletions in 4,000 scenes in 600 movies. Silent films were relatively cheap to edit, but cuts in talking pictures were more complicated and expensive. And if censors entirely banned a movie, the studios faced a larger loss than in earlier years given their larger average investment in films. According to an internal memo to Hays in 1929, the states and municipalities with censorship boards accounted for more than half the American market measured by movie attendance and more than 60 percent measured by revenue.[37] Even before the Depression struck, therefore, the industry was already facing increased pressure to censor movies prior to distribution.

As these problems mounted, an additional source of pressure—and a new solution to the industry's woes—presented itself. Catholic organizations had thus far played no role in what had been a Protestant-led movement to censor the movies. In 1929, however, a group of Catholics, both lay and clerical, began meeting at the initiative of Martin Quigley, publisher of the trade magazine *Exhibitors Herald-World*, to discuss the formulation of a censorship code for the movies, to be enforced through the movie industry at the point of production. That this Catholic effort began at a time when the movie industry was in dire shape was no coincidence. Thoroughly familiar with the industry's financial problems, Quigley saw an opportunity for Catholics to reform the movies by seizing the moment and offering an alternative to government censorship. The movement had its deeper origins in long-standing Catholic objections to moral currents in the broader society and an increasing sense of urgency as Catholic immigrants in America assimilated. A new generation of Catholic intellectuals saw themselves as taking up the standard of natural law and fixed moral values that many liberal Protestants were abandoning. One of the Catholic intellectuals opposed to modern liberal tendencies was a Jesuit professor and prolific writer in Catholic publications, Daniel Lord, who devoted his columns and books to attacks on modern literature and drama, the theory of evolution, birth control, and secular education. Working with Quigley, Father Lord assumed the principal role in writing what became the Motion Picture Production Code.[38]

The code Lord and Quigley drafted was concerned with far more than prohibiting obscenity and upholding sexual modesty. Motion pictures, they stipulated, should chiefly be regarded as entertainment, but they drew a sharp distinction between "correct" and "wrong" entertainment according to its effect on moral standards and insisted that the movies had a special moral obligation because of their broad audience and emotional impact. The code set forth three general principles: First, motion pictures should never lower the viewers' moral standards and thus should never throw "the sympathy of the audience . . . to the side of crime, wrong-doing, evil or sin"; second, movies should always present "correct standards of life, subject only to the requirements of drama and entertainment"; and third, movies should never ridicule the law, "natural or human." One of the themes of the Lord-Quigley code was support for authority. The court system, for example, "should not be presented as unjust," and motion pictures must never use "ministers of religion" as "comic characters or villains" or otherwise undermine religious faith. Evil might be presented in a film only if "throughout, the audience feels sure that *evil is wrong* and *good is right*." The particular applications of the code to the treatment of crime, sex, and other matters all followed from these general premises about "correct entertainment."[39]

Rather than oppose the Catholic code, Hays welcomed it. "This was the very thing I had been looking for," he later wrote. The code—and subsequent Catholic pressure—offered Hays the opportunity to achieve the control of the movies that much of the public believed he already had. The Presbyterian elder now became the Catholics' chief ally in reining in the Jewish filmmakers. In January 1930, after some initial resistance, the studio heads bowed to the demands for self-regulation and voted for a version of the code incorporating the principles Lord and Quigley had formulated and spelling out a variety of specific rules. For example, in its provisions related to sex, the code pledged to uphold the sanctity of marriage, prohibited adultery from being "explicitly treated, or justified, or presented attractively," ruled out "scenes of passion" that would "stimulate the lower and baser element," and forbade any portrayal of "sex perversion" (homosexuality was never explicitly mentioned) or any sex relationships between blacks and whites.[40] The producers agreed to obtain Hays Office approval of scripts prior to production and of films prior to release but insisted on retaining ultimate authority: A producer who disagreed about a particular decision could call for a jury of fellow producers to resolve the dispute. Sure enough, although the Hays Office began to obtain cuts and revisions in movies based on the code, it quickly ran into resistance. As the Depression deepened and box-office receipts fell, some of the studios desperate for hits simply flouted the code or used producers' juries to overrule the Hays Office. Known in the history of the movies as "pre-code" Hollywood (actually, it was pre-enforcement), the era saw such films as Mae West's risqué hit *She Done Him Wrong* (1933), the early gangster movies beginning with *Little Caesar* (1930) and *Public Enemy* (1931), and a series of highly political films that reflected the despair of the early Depression years. Mae West's double entendres provided the era's signature lines: "I like restraint if it doesn't go too far," she said at the time.[41]

The battle over formally endorsing the Production Code, however, was a mere warm-up to the more decisive struggle over enforcing it. From 1930 to 1933, movie attendance fell from an estimated 80 million to 50 million per week, leaving nearly all movie companies in the red and plunging three of them into receivership. During the spring of 1933, several independent developments created new political risks for the filmmakers. The New Deal's National Industrial Recovery Act called for the creation of industry-wide management codes, which some moral reformers saw as an opening for federal censorship of the movies—a mistaken expectation, but nonetheless a new front in the continuing battle over government control. Coincidentally, a conservative, pro-censorship organization threw the motion-picture companies on the defensive by publishing nine volumes of social science research on the effect of the movies on children. The research reports—known as the Payne Fund studies because of the foundation that sponsored them—were qualified in their conclusions, but a summary volume written for a popular audience, *Our Movie Made Children*, claimed definitive evidence that the movies damaged children's health, aroused dangerous sexual fantasies, and led to higher crime rates.[42] The apparently scientific basis for moral attacks on the movies compounded the industry's problems in the wake of its failure to uphold the Production Code.

Outraged by the apparent spinelessness of the Hays Office, the Catholic activists who had formulated the code called on the Catholic hierarchy to apply pressure on the studios, and a collaborative relationship with the industry now turned into a confrontational one. During the summer of 1933, Bishop John Cantwell of Los Angeles sent the president of the Bank of America, A.H. Giannini, and attorney Joseph Scott to meet with the top studio heads in Hollywood. Giannini, a major lender to the companies, delivered the bishop's message that unless they enforced the code, the Catholic Church would launch a public attack on them in the fall. Scott was rougher, warning that the "dirty motion pictures" produced by Jews and the predominance of Jews among "communistic radicals" were "build[ing] up an enormous case against the Jews in the eyes of the American people." There were Americans, he observed, who sympathized with the Nazis (Hitler had seized power six months earlier) and were "even now organizing further to attack the Jew in America." The Jewish producers had better stop this "damnable business" if they wanted to avoid the public's wrath.[43] All but one of the producers at the meeting said they would do so, but their words weren't enough. In November, a conclave of American bishops voted in favor of organizing a mass movement against immoral pictures, to be called the Legion of Decency. The next month, even before the movement got under way, Hays made a further concession, putting one of the lay Catholics involved in the movement, Joseph I. Breen, in charge of censorship in Hollywood. But Breen still lacked final authority, and the Catholic clerics went ahead with their campaign, denouncing the movies from the pulpit, condemning specific films, and asking millions of churchgoers to take a Legion of Decency oath to shun movies that the Church declared indecent.

By July 1934, although Catholic boycotts continued, the battle was effectively over. The studio heads gave Breen the authority over both scripts and finished films that he had previously lacked, eliminated the producers' juries, and set stiff fines for any company that released a picture without a seal of approval from the new Production Code Administration. Thus began decades of stringent moral censorship of motion pictures. During the next several years, controversies continued even among Catholics as to what constituted indecency in the movies, and a dual structure evolved. After a movie received a seal of approval from the Production Code Administration, it went to the National Legion of Decency, which could obtain further cuts and revisions.[44] By the mid-1930s, with movie attendance recovering, the movie companies discovered that although censorship ruled out certain kinds of films (Mae West's, for example), it did not prevent the industry from being a highly profitable business. And so the moviemakers learned to work in harness.

The sequence of events may suggest that the Church's boycott of films finally brought the industry to its knees because it threatened box-office receipts. During the summer of 1934, however, an employee sent by Hays to twenty cities to report on the impact of the Legion's boycotts found that they were ineffective. Indeed, when the Church declared a movie indecent, the result was sometimes record-breaking attendance. The Catholic hierarchy was unable to control audiences even in the major Catholic population centers in the Midwest, much less in the South, where anti-Catholicism undercut the Legion's efforts.[45] Thus, the Catholic campaign did not achieve its effect through demonstrations of raw power at the box office. While the movie companies may have feared the Legion's long-run impact on movie attendance, they faced an immediate threat in 1934 to their financial credit—and their lenders did not want any trouble with the Church. The moviemakers also faced political risks at a moment of national political upheaval; if rebuffed, the Catholics might join the Protestants in supporting government censorship. The timing of the Legion of Decency campaign was crucial. In a more secure and prosperous period, the industry might have refused to concede any of its autonomy and merely sought to pacify Catholic activists as it had Protestant critics in the past. But for the Jewish movie company owners and executives, the collective risks in the early 1930s were simply too great—not least of all, the risk that anti-Semitism would spiral into a mass movement in America as it had in Europe. A prolonged confrontation with the Catholic Church could tilt the balance in any one of the struggles they faced.[46]

Although the conjuncture of economic crisis and political upheaval in the early 1930s precipitated the advent of the Production Code, the longer-term sources of the new censorship regime lay in the legal and economic conditions created during the previous two decades. Denied constitutional protection by the Supreme Court, the movie industry had faced a continual struggle to minimize state censorship that led it to make one concession after another until its abject surrender in 1934. But a non-governmental system of censorship was enforceable only because the consolidation of the movie industry had reduced it to a tight oligopoly; if the industry had still consisted of dozens of production companies and distributors and hundreds of independent exhibitors, a trade association that adopted a censorship code would almost certainly have found it difficult, if not impossible, to assure compliance. The system that operated under the Hays Office was exceptional not just as a limit on freedom of expression but as a means of industrial control. It represented a kind of "neocorporatist," industry-based alternative to government regulation much discussed in the 1920s but otherwise decisively rejected during the New Deal (after the Supreme Court declared the National Industrial Recovery Act unconstitutional). The federal government's tolerance of the movie oligopoly was crucial. Had it taken strong antitrust measures against the movie industry during the 1920s or 1930s (as it later did in the 1940s), there would not have been the unified control of production, distribution, and exhibition that made a neocorporatist system of movie regulation effective.[47]

The censorship of the movies imposed in the early 1930s resembled that other great experiment in moral regulation—Prohibition—which came to an end in the same period. But if Prohibition had shown the futility of enforced morality, the lesson was lost on the authors of the Motion Picture Production Code. Although the forces of modernity had weakened Victorianism during the 1920s, the moral conflict over contemporary culture was far from over. The movies, ironically, had been far less subject to ideological and moral restraint before World War I and came under moral censorship just when they should have been freed of control if the general trends in American culture neatly translated to the screen. But the advent of movie censorship did not stem from the culture at large. It reflected the strategic calculations of an oligopoly faced with a powerful institution representative of only a segment of the society. That the Jewish moviemakers came under the censorship of the Catholic Church in a predominantly Protestant society was, on its face, a highly improbable development, explainable only by the peculiar sequence of developments that had unfolded since the turn of the century.

The same Catholic intellectuals who agitated for movie censorship also called for censorship of modern literature, but while they succeeded in limiting the cinema, they failed to impose comparable restrictions on print. Indeed, censorship descended on the movies just at the moment that the courts began to lift censorship from serious literature and to undo the long legacy of Comstockery; by coincidence, Breen took over as censor of the screen the same month, December 1933, that Judge Woolsey handed down his decision in the *Ulysses* case. The differences in outcomes between print and screen reflected the different legal and economic conditions of the two media. Not only did the Constitution and the courts afford stronger protection to the press; the far more fragmented publishing industry had no central organization comparable to the Hays Office that could have carried out a neocorporatist form of censorship. The movies became the target of Catholic pressure in the 1930s because key figures in the movement understood that the industry was vulnerable to pressure and because moral reformers, both Catholic and Protestant, had come to believe that the movies were singularly important as a destructive influence. In their original rationale for the Production Code, Quigley and Father Lord argued that films could not be given the same "latitude" as books. "A book describes; a film vividly presents," they wrote. "One presents on a cold page; the other by apparently living people." Such arguments echoed the Supreme Court's opinion in 1915 that the motion pictures had a special "power" for evil and recapitulated earlier attacks on the theater going back to the Puritans.[48]

The disparity between the *Ulysses* decision and the advent of the Motion Picture Production Code did not necessarily signify an inconsistency or rupture with earlier understanding. Nineteenth-century censorship was chiefly concerned with cultural forms that reached a popular, not an elite, audience. If the focus of censorship had moved from literature to the movies by the 1930s, that was entirely in line with concerns that had animated movements for cultural regulation for a long time. Such movements logically direct their efforts at regulating media that are both popularly influential and institutionally vulnerable. By the 1930s, the focal point of regulatory pressure had moved from print to the movies—and to another new medium, broadcasting.

CHAPTER TEN

The Constitution of the Air (1)

The Origins of Broadcasting

RADIO was reinvented in the 1920s. At the close of World War I, the corporations and government agencies involved in radio around the world still thought of the medium chiefly as a wireless telegraph, even though experiments in broadcasting dated back to the early 1900s and manufacturers were now turning out reliable equipment to send and receive sound. During the war, the military had begun to use radio telephones (as in air-to-ground communication), and the telephone industry was planning to use radio links where wires couldn't reach. There was clearly a business in conveying conversation from point to point, but there didn't seem to be any profit or justifiable purpose in sending voices out to the world—who but a few radio enthusiasts would be listening? And how could broadcasting make money?

Nonetheless, some tentative efforts to broadcast music and talk, at first without any definite plan, began at about the same time on both sides of the Atlantic. In Great Britain, the Marconi Company started making brief experimental transmissions in early 1920, culminating in June in a widely publicized broadcast of a celebrated opera singer, but in August the Post Office banned further use of radio for entertainment because of complaints of interference with military and other "important" communications. In the

United States, once wartime restrictions on radio use were lifted in 1919, a few pioneers in several cities set up transmitters on the roofs of garages and offices and carried on broadcasting as a hobby. One of these pioneers was an employee of the radio-manufacturer Westinghouse in Pittsburgh. A conceptual breakthrough came in September the next year, when a Westinghouse vice president noticed a department store advertisement for radio sets and suddenly had visions of a consumer market for receivers if broadcasting could be made into a regular service. Historians generally date the popular radio boom from the evening of November 2, 1920, when Westinghouse's newly licensed Pittsburgh station, KDKA, went on the air to broadcast the results of the presidential election.[1]

There couldn't have been a more fitting occasion for the debut of American broadcasting than an election night. In the following years, political decisions about the basic structural arrangements and rules of broadcasting would determine what kind of medium radio was going to become. With the advent of broadcasting, moreover, the age of the print-dominated public sphere would begin to wane: Within two decades, according to public opinion surveys, radio would overtake newspapers as Americans' primary source of news, and national political leaders would use radio to communicate directly with the public, bypassing newspapers, parties, and other locally based organizations. In short, the institutional framework adopted for radio would become a significant part of the framework of politics itself. And because the structure adopted for radio would later be carried over to television in the United States and other countries, the political decisions made during the 1920s were to have especially significant and long-lasting effects.

Like any new medium, broadcasting posed a series of constitutive choices. Now that radio was no longer conceived only as a means of point-to-point communication, governments had to reexamine earlier decisions about carving up the spectrum into different regions and regulating the use of the airwaves. These decisions, however technical in appearance, were often deeply political in their significance, as they determined, for example, the number of broadcasting stations, the range and quality of their reception, and the extent of their autonomy. A variety of options were available for disposing of the spectrum, ranging from purely governmental to purely private ownership and control. While the Europeans opted by the 1930s primarily for tax-financed, government-run broadcasting systems, the United States might have taken the diametrically opposite course, auctioning frequencies to the highest bidder or allowing private radio stations to claim ownership of the wavelengths they were already using. But rather than privatizing the spectrum, the United States decided to retain the airwaves in public ownership and create a licensing system for their use by private broadcasters. At least in a formal sense, this decision represented a middle ground; in practice, the system created was overwhelmingly commercial, dependent on advertising revenue and driven by competition for listeners, in keeping with the commercial incentives dominating newspapers, magazines, and movies. The licensing of broadcasters, however, departed radically from earlier practices in communications, as the federal government had never licensed the press, moviemakers, or other creators of culture (though state and local governments did license theaters).

Many of the choices about radio involved translating basic principles about rights and powers in communication into a new context. Would Congress and the courts, despite the licensing system, conceive of radio broadcasters as part of the press and extend to them the same protections enjoyed by the print media under the First Amendment? Or would they treat broadcasting, like the movies, as mere entertainment, outside the scope of constitutionally protected expression and therefore subject to state censorship? Or in still another possibility, would the government view broadcasters as common carriers like telephone and telegraph companies and therefore require stations to provide access to potential speakers on an equal basis? Each paradigm—press, entertainment, common carrier—brought with it a different body of legal understandings. A particularly important question about rights concerned the rights of political candidates and others concerned with matters of public controversy: What access would they have to the air? Broadcasting also raised questions about property rights—for example, whether broadcasters had to obtain permission and pay for the right to broadcast performances of copyrighted music or play-by-play reports of professional sports games.

The most important of these questions about rights involved the right to broadcast at all. With the technology available at the time, the radio spectrum was a scarce resource, which made it impossible (as soon became evident) to accommodate all who wanted entry into broadcasting. But how were authorities to choose among would-be broadcasters? As a result of legislation adopted in 1927, the United States vested licensing authority in an independent regulatory commission, which then adopted criteria for assigning frequencies that, in practice, favored commercial over nonprofit organizations. In countries where broadcasting developed as a tax-financed, public function, the analogous question of organizational selection involved the locus of broadcasting within the state. One option was to locate radio in a bureaucracy under direct political control—a system of official state broadcasting that was adopted not only by authoritarian governments but also by some democracies. Another option for radio was a quasi-independent, professionally run public corporation—an approach, pioneered by Great Britain, that came to be known as public-service broadcasting. There might also be hybrid systems mixing private and governmental broadcasters—the path taken in Canada. Americans were not keenly aware of the varying systems as they emerged elsewhere in the world; by the 1930s, insofar as the issue was debated at all, both the critics and the defenders of American commercial radio contrasted it with the British public-service model. These two institutional paradigms were widely seen as the fundamental alternatives for broadcasting in the English-speaking world.

The different constitutive choices in radio, particularly the contrasting roles of the state and private business in Europe and the United States, may seem simply to correspond to general ideological patterns, but before 1927 it was far from obvious what the outcome would be. Britain and several other European countries started out with private broadcasting monopolies, while there was widespread opposition in America to advertising on radio and no consensus among the leaders of the industry or public officials about how broadcasting would be financed and organized. After being established on different bases in the late 1920s, however, European and American broadcasting diverged further in the following decade. Even as America turned toward a fully commercial model, some influential groups opposed the path of development that radio was taking and waged a rearguard struggle to change it. The airwaves, by their nature, might appear to be the most adaptable and alterable of media. Nonetheless, the choices that different countries made at an early stage in broadcasting proved remarkably tenacious.

Clashes in the Ether

Technological advances in Europe and America during World War I made radio ripe for reinvention, but wartime political decisions gave a particularly sharp jolt to radio's development in the United States. The prewar American radio industry, paralyzed by legal battles over patents and dominated by British-owned Marconi, had been an unlikely candidate to take on a leading role in the world. The war, however, led the federal government to intervene in uncharacteristic ways, suspending patent rights for the war's duration, seizing control of foreign assets, standardizing radio components for war production, and training servicemen in skills they carried into civilian life. The suspension of patent conflicts facilitated innovation and enabled companies such as Westinghouse to get into the market for radio equipment. Although Americans would later view radio broadcasting entirely as a triumph of private business, the government played a key role in the industry's birth, including the creation of the dominant company, the Radio Corporation of America (RCA), established at the prompting of Navy officials to maintain American control of radio after the war.[2] The reinvention of radio didn't happen overnight; after KDKA's debut in November 1920, it took another year before broadcasting took off. During the first eleven months of 1921, the Department of Commerce licensed only 5 radio stations; then it licensed 23 in December. The explosion came in 1922, when more than 500 stations received licenses and a radio craze swept the country, exciting wide-eyed predictions that broadcasting would perfect democracy, create world peace, and solve innumerable other problems. In March 1922, the *New York Times* noted that "radio phoning" had become "the most popular amusement in America."[3]

Radio technology before the war was of interest primarily to the military, to corporations involved in the chiefly maritime and transoceanic wireless-telegraph business, and to amateur radiotelegraphers. The relative weight of these three interests was evident in the prewar allocation of spectrum. Choice wavelengths from 187.4 to 499.7 kHz were reserved for the government (mainly the Navy), while private companies could operate below and above the government band. Amateurs, the least powerful interest, got the short end of the spectrum—the shortwaves (above 1,500 kHz), which were mistakenly thought to have no practical value. The 1912 Radio Act, the primary legislation governing use of the ether, gave the Department of Commerce no authority to restrict the number of radio licenses or to deny one to a qualified applicant. Assuming that the spectrum was an unlimited resource, the law regarded its use for radio communication as a right, not a privilege.[4]

The advent of broadcasting upset the technical assumptions and political balance underlying the earlier constitutive choices about radio.

Broadcasting required more bandwidth than radiotelegraphy, lured new parties into the ether, and turned it into a medium for reaching the public. The new interests in radio consequently questioned the earlier allocation of spectrum, dominated by military priorities that no longer seemed compelling. As radio stations multiplied and the airwaves grew congested, it also became apparent that the government could no longer treat use of the spectrum as a right and would need to develop criteria for denying licenses to some applicants in favor of others. Existing legislation, however, did not allow any executive agency to reallocate spectrum from government to private use, nor did it authorize any selection among license applicants. Empowering the federal government to determine who could (and could not) broadcast also raised difficult ideological and constitutional problems, especially as radio developed into a means of expressing ideas and opinions.

Broadcasting gave rise to problems in private law as well. The postwar patent-pooling agreement among the major corporations in the radio industry, drawn up before they appreciated the potential of broadcasting, left unclear which firms were entitled to profit from the new field—for example, who could sell radio receivers to "amateurs" (that is, the public at large) and who was entitled to operate a broadcast station. Once broadcasting emerged, RCA, GE, and Westinghouse (the "Radio Group") insisted that their rights in radio receivers and radiotelegraphy embraced the new business, while AT&T and its Western Electric subsidiary (the "Telephone Group") saw broadcasting as a logical extension of their rights in radio transmitters and radiotelephony. The emergence of broadcasting affected the two groups unequally. Both faced rampant patent infringement by other firms, but the Radio Group nonetheless profited enormously from the sale of radio receivers, while the Telephone Group found itself confined to the far less profitable business of making transmitters and by 1923 had sold only 35 of the roughly 600 broadcast transmitters in use. Dissatisfied with its position, AT&T fell out with its former partners, sold its shares in RCA, and began preparing its own plans to dominate radio. As the rise of broadcasting set corporate interests against the military in the struggle over spectrum, so it also set corporate interests against each other in the contest for new markets.[5]

The resolution of these conflicts during the 1920s proceeded on both a public-law (Washington) track and a private-law (New York) track. In postwar Washington, three federal agencies vied for dominance in radio policy: the Navy, which had played the leading role in radio since 1904; the Post Office, which in 1919 received an appropriation from Congress to develop radio stations in connection with air mail and envisioned itself as the government's principal communications agency; and the Department of Commerce, which under the 1912 Radio Act held the chief administrative responsibilities related to private use of radio, including the distribution of licenses and inspection of apparatus. This was not merely a bureaucratic struggle; each of the agencies represented a different type of relationship of the state to radio: safeguarding the technology for military defense, supervising it as a governmental medium, and promoting its development by private business. The Navy, despite its role in creating RCA, soon antagonized the radio industry by continuing to put military interests ahead of commercial development (for example, in international negotiations over use of the spectrum). Business did not take long to gravitate to its natural ally, the Department of Commerce. By mid-1921, representatives of the major radio companies were turning for help to the department's new secretary, who proved ready to act as their protector and champion.[6]

Herbert Hoover, secretary of commerce in both the Harding and Coolidge administrations before being elected president in 1928, would become the key figure in framing American policy toward broadcasting during the medium's constitutive phase. A successful businessman trained as an engineer, Hoover was singularly well prepared to promote a technology-based industry that few other public officials understood. Radio fit his agenda perfectly in the early twenties, when he saw his role at Commerce as fostering economic growth, including the promotion of new industries. Hoover's general approach to business, known as "associationalism," involved the facilitation of what he thought of as industrial self-government: By serving as an honest broker, often bringing together groups of businessmen to advise him, he aimed to help them resolve their disputes and coordinate their relations free from state control. In line with this strategy, beginning in 1922 Hoover organized a series of four annual national radio conferences, inviting representatives of business and engineering groups to deliberate on the industry's problems, and then framed his decisions as issuing from their recommendations. In the business-minded 1920s, perhaps it was inevitable that Commerce would emerge triumphant in its interdepartmental struggle with the Navy and the Post Office. But Hoover did not merely depend on the ideological climate; he cultivated business support, consulted his fellow engineers in the corporate world, and invoked both business and technical authority in legitimizing his policies. Supported by his private-sector allies, he defeated his bureaucratic rivals and set the public agenda for broadcasting.[7]

During the early 1920s, Hoover did not succeed, however, in gaining new statutory authority over radio. In June 1921, his allies in Congress introduced the first of a series of bills that would have centralized regulation of radio in the Department of Commerce. Radio, Hoover said, was "one of the few instances on record in which the people of the United States were united in their desire for more regulation." While awaiting congressional action, Hoover took a series of tentative steps on his own—setting aside one frequency for private-sector broadcasting and another for government broadcasts in September 1921; instructing all amateurs at the beginning of 1922 to stop broadcasting and limit themselves to short-wave radiotelegraphy and telephony; and a few months later, opening a second channel for private-sector broadcasts. The perils of his legal position, however, were underlined by an appellate court decision in November 1921 in a case involving a radio station that had caused interference with government transmissions, according to the Department of Commerce. The court ruled that the department had no authority to deny a license, but the case became moot when the company went out of business before the Supreme Court could rule on the government's appeal. In February 1922, hoping to build support for legislation giving him clear authority, Hoover convened the First National Radio Conference, but radio legislation stalled amid conflicting proposals, the absence of any sense of urgency in Congress, and unease in some quarters about permanently vesting power over radio in a single federal official. Content to work with Hoover on an ad hoc basis, some business leaders preferred to defer legislation until broadcasting stabilized and they had a better understanding of their long-term interests.[8]

A year later, in March 1923 when the Second National Radio Conference convened, prospects for action by Congress had faded, and Hoover determined to move ahead even without new legal authority to deal with the mounting problem of signal interference among the nation's proliferating broadcast stations. That spring, rooting his actions in the second conference's proposals, Hoover carried out a comprehensive reorganization of the spectrum, dedicating the band from 550 to 1365 kHz to broadcasting and creating three classes of broadcast stations at varying power levels: high-powered stations (at that time from 500 to 1,000 watts) serving wide areas without any interference; moderate-powered stations (not more than 500 watts) serving smaller regions; and low-powered stations, crammed together on a single frequency, serving only local areas, and often authorized to broadcast only during the daytime. To make room for the broadcast band, Hoover moved ship-to-shore, air-to-ground, and other commercial radio services to frequencies formerly reserved to the government. These actions would later be held illegal; shifting commercial services into the government band, for example, was clearly barred by both U.S. and international law.[9] But broadcasting was a growing industry and immensely popular, and Hoover had built up support so effectively that his assumption of extralegal powers would stand unchallenged for three years. And because radio became so well established during that time, much of what Hoover ordered illegally became entrenched and eventually gained the force of law.

In these years, radio was gradually passing from a novelty to a familiar, though far from universal, feature of American life. From 1922 to 1925, the number of receivers in use climbed to an estimated 2.75 million, the proportion of homes in the United States with radios grew from 0.2 to 10.1 percent, and the quality of reception improved as cheap crystal sets with limited capacities gave way to better models with vacuum tubes. Headphones became unnecessary when Western Electric put loudspeakers on the market in 1922–1923, and in 1925 GE produced an electrodynamic loudspeaker with improved fidelity. (All radio at this point, however, was AM—that is, based on "amplitude modulation"—with its characteristically high static and limited sound range.) Improved reception and speakers encouraged a change in the mode of listening from the early preoccupation with "DXing" (tuning in the farthest stations) to more relaxed listening to music. By this time, radio sets were moving out of attics and garages into parlors and living rooms, evolving from equipment into furniture, and holding the attention not merely of male hobbyists but of entire families. Many people, especially in working-class communities, continued to assemble their own radio sets out of parts they purchased. Fully assembled receivers were relatively expensive, and even though radios were available in many different models at a wide range of prices, they were more common among middle- and upper-class families than among the poor.[10]

Initially, broadcasting was entirely local, stations were on the air only a few hours a week, and programming was ad hoc and amateurish. But the idea of putting radio broadcasts on a national and more professional basis did not take long to emerge. In June 1922, David Sarnoff, at the time vice president of RCA, proposed to GE (RCA's parent company) the establishment of a high-quality, nationwide broadcasting organization to be called the "Public Service Broadcasting Company or National Radio Broadcasting Company or American Radio Broadcasting Company, or some similar name." Sarnoff urged that RCA, GE, Westinghouse, and their licensees agree to pay over 2 percent of gross radio sales to finance the service.[11] This was the germ of the idea for a national radio network, and in fact, a public-service broadcasting company with financing along the lines Sarnoff proposed would be established—but in Great Britain, not in the United States, and on the basis not of a private license fee but of a governmental one. American radio networks would have a different economic foundation.

Although early radio attracted a great variety of enthusiasts and enterprises, four principal types of broadcasting—each with a different rationale—went on the air in America during the early twenties. Seeing profit in the hardware, not in broadcasting per se, RCA, Westinghouse, and other radio manufacturers operated stations to promote sales of receivers. A second group of businesses, such as department stores and newspapers, launched broadcasting stations to publicize themselves; they did not yet sell on-the-air advertising—the entire station was an advertisement. And, third, many colleges and churches as well as other nonprofit organizations ran stations as an extension of their general mission.[12] All three of these types of broadcasters were hoping for benefits that were indirect and hard to evaluate. (Here and elsewhere I use the term "broadcasters" to refer to the station and network organizations, not to the individuals on the air.) Only the fourth, AT&T, envisioned broadcasting as profitable in itself.

During 1922, AT&T established a station in New York City—WEAF would be its name—to sell time to customers who wanted to get on the air without establishing a station of their own. Drawing its model from the long-distance ("toll") telephone business, the company conceived of the customers of WEAF as placing a call to the listening public, and hence AT&T labeled the system "toll broadcasting." The business started off slowly; after weeks without any revenue, a real-estate development corporation paid $50 to present a ten-minute talk about its new residential project. WEAF would subsequently be seen as the first station to carry commercials, but unlike later sponsor-supported broadcasting, AT&T's initial model envisioned the radio station as merely a common carrier for anyone willing to pay to broadcast a message or performance. The common-carrier conception, however, not only overestimated the demand at that time for such a service; it also ignored the interest of a broadcaster in building up its audience by airing programs of dependable quality. WEAF would turn profitable only after AT&T began to arrange for high-quality programming to be produced for sponsors, who were content at first merely to be identified with a show in order to promote goodwill and brand recognition. No sales pitches interrupted these programs. Other broadcasters nonetheless considered the practice of selling airtime inappropriate, even scandalous, but WEAF broke the taboo against commercial sponsorship, and the industry watched its progress closely.[13]

In another key innovation, AT&T used its long-distance lines during 1922 to link together distant stations. Within two years it had created a network of sixteen stations called the National Broadcasting System that reached 65 percent of America's radio homes, primarily in the Northeast and Midwest. And by late 1924, the company was able to set up a coast-to-coast network of twenty-six stations to broadcast a speech by President Calvin Coolidge. In addition, the Bell System controlled the lines used for remote pickups enabling radio stations to broadcast from sports arenas, churches, dance halls, and other locations. To strengthen its position further, the telephone company's equipment division, Western Electric, developed a radio receiver that could be used to threaten the core business of the Radio Group. Jealously guarding its chief competitive advantage, AT&T denied RCA and its allies access to its long-distance network ("Transmission by wire is ours," AT&T allegedly told Sarnoff).[14]

Seeking alternative means of interconnection, RCA and its allies tested the use of telegraph lines, tried to develop "superpower" stations that could broadcast over the entire country, and used shortwave radio to relay broadcasts from one station to another. None of these technological options, however, proved to be reliable. AT&T, as the only company capable of achieving the economies of scale afforded by a network, might have been able to dominate radio—that is, if the government would have allowed the Bell System to extend its monopoly from long-distance telephone services to broadcasting. But given widespread public hostility to the Bell "octopus" and the stake that other influential business interests already had in radio, AT&T could scarcely have counted on political acquiescence in a dual monopoly, and by early 1924 it had secretly agreed with the Radio Group to submit their conflict to binding private arbitration. No sooner had they reached this understanding than the Federal Trade Commission (FTC) issued an antitrust complaint against all the patent allies for monopolizing the receiver business. But it would be seven years before the Justice Department began an antitrust prosecution, and in the interim the radio industry would settle its internal conflicts through private negotiations conducted in the shadow of federal authority.[15]

Beyond the dispute within and about the "radio trust," there were other disagreements and uncertainties about the institutional destiny of broadcasting. Because listeners could not be charged for programs, many in the industry as well as among the general public believed that broadcasting would have to be financed by a tax on radio receivers, other public revenues, a private license fee, or philanthropy. One analogy compared radio stations to libraries and suggested that there might someday be an Andrew Carnegie with the vision to endow community broadcast stations. Radio advertising, it was universally agreed, was highly undesirable. At the first radio conference in 1922, Hoover had said it was "inconceivable that we should allow so great a possibility for service, for news, for entertainment, for education, and for vital commercial purposes, to be drowned in advertising chatter." Listing priorities for radio, the business and engineering representatives at that conference had put "toll broadcasting" in last place and recommended prohibiting "direct" advertising and allowing only "a statement of the call letters of the station and of the name of the concern responsible for the matter broadcasted." In other words, the first radio conference conceived commercial radio along the lines of what later became noncommercial radio. So general was the belief in radio's special mission to raise the tone of American culture that even the advertising trade papers originally disapproved of advertising on the air. Rejecting radio as an "objectionable advertising medium," *Printer's Ink* declared that "the family circle is not a public place, and advertising has no business intruding there unless it is invited."[16]

Americans, in other words, do not appear to have been any more culturally predisposed toward commercialism in radio than Europeans were, but the political response in the United States, unlike Europe, was to let private industry set its own course. While Hoover initially echoed the widespread anticommercial sentiment, he made no effort to carry out the first radio conference's recommended restrictions on advertising, insisting that the matter be left to industry to resolve. Artfully appealing to different groups, he also made public statements critical of any radio monopoly while giving out valuable licenses for high-powered stations to the patent allies that were the subject of the FTC's antitrust complaint.[17]

During these early years, radio was also the scene of an emerging conflict over intellectual property rights. The initial reaction of most broadcasters was outrage in 1922 when the American Society of Composers, Authors and Publishers (ASCAP) demanded royalties for music played on the air. A 1909 copyright revision passed by Congress had given copyright holders rights to public performances of their work for profit, and in 1914 composers and music publishers had created ASCAP to demand royalties for music played in public places. In a key test case brought by ASCAP, the Supreme Court ruled in 1917 that even without a specific entertainment charge, a restaurant with an orchestra owed royalties because it wasn't providing music for charitable purposes. In 1923, a court similarly upheld ASCAP's position that radio broadcasts were not charitable and that stations therefore had to pay royalties even if they were not making a profit. Beginning with AT&T's WEAF, some broadcasters settled with ASCAP for a flat annual license fee, but the diehards in the industry met in Chicago to found a new organization, the National Association of Broadcasters (NAB), to carry on the fight. It was the beginning of a long struggle over the spoils of radio.[18]

As the broadcasters saw it, the copyright holders were being greedy—wouldn't exposure on the air boost sales of sheet music and records? In fact, radio in the 1920s, like the Internet three-quarters of a century later, plunged record (as well as sheet-music) sales into a deep downturn; rather than pay for disks, many people preferred to listen to broadcast music for free. Desperate for sales, the major recording companies turned to a market that small labels had only recently begun to exploit successfully: "race records" of black musicians, who weren't being invited to perform on the air. During the 1920s, jazz recordings exploded in popularity, transforming American popular music. Even through its side effects, the impact of radio was rippling through the culture.[19]

Divergent Paths

While radio stations were proliferating in the United States during the early 1920s, broadcasting in Europe evolved more slowly and in a different direction. Not only were the Europeans still recovering from the devastation of the war; European governments also continued to leave less latitude for private initiative and decentralized innovation. The radio craze took off in America without any effective legal restraint. In Great Britain, in contrast, the 1904 Wireless Telegraphy Act required all receivers and transmitters to be licensed by the Post Office; this was the statutory basis on which the government shut down the Marconi Company's initial foray into broadcasting in 1920. By early 1922, the excitement about radio in Britain stimulated by American developments forced the government to allow broadcasting to resume on a limited basis. Pressed by the radio manufacturers to allow a more substantial broadcasting service, the Post Office invited them to meet together and come up with a proposal. The ensuing negotiations resulted in the formation of a unified private broadcasting organization, the British Broadcasting Company (BBC), wholly owned by Britain's radio manufacturers, licensed by the Post Office, and financed primarily by a license fee of ten shillings on radio receivers (of which the Post Office kept half as general revenue).[20]

From the start, even though it was a private company created by manufacturers to boost their sales of radio receivers, the BBC had three features sharply distinguishing it from its American counterparts: a monopoly structure, tax financing, and subordination to the Post Office. These features outlasted the BBC's private career. Within a few years, the government accepted the recommendation of an official committee—strongly supported by the BBC's own general manager, John Reith—to convert the organization into a public corporation to be run as a public service. Nationalized in 1927 and renamed the British Broadcasting Corporation, it received a royal charter to emphasize its (relative) autonomy from political control. Under the new arrangement, however, the postmaster general retained authority not only over the wavelengths, power levels, and hours of broadcasting but over the content as well; he directed the BBC not to take editorial positions of its own on public policy and to avoid all matters of political and religious controversy. This evolution from private to national control followed more or less the same pattern as the telegraph industry (originally private but nationalized in 1870) and the telephone industry (also private at first, but nationalized in 1911).

The key figure in the formative phase of the BBC was Reith, who served as director-general until 1938. His conception of the organization as a force for integrating the nation and elevating its cultural standards left a deep and lasting imprint on the public-service broadcasting tradition. Rather than creating a plurality of local stations, Reith built a centralized service based on high-power stations across the country. The chief focus of the BBC was its national program produced in London, though in each of several provincial centers it broadcast a regional program as well. The schedule mixed light entertainment with educational programs, opening up previously exclusive forms of musical and theatrical performance, lectures, and national events to the wider nation. The result, as two British historians have noted, was the creation of "a radically new kind of public—one commensurate with the whole of society." But while extending access to culture more widely, the BBC also carried an unmistakable class accent. Influenced by Matthew Arnold's conception of culture and deeply religious, Reith saw the BBC as an opportunity to raise the knowledge, morals, and taste of the British public. He aimed to rescue the lower ranks from vulgarity, not to allow them to satisfy or express it. The BBC's responsibility, he wrote, was "to carry into the greatest possible number of homes everything that is best in every department of human knowledge, endeavor, or achievement."[21] In the mid-1920s, much of American radio had a similar cultural tone—the predominant form of music on the air at the time was known as "potted palm" music, the kind "played at tea time by hotel orchestras"[22]—but as a monopoly the BBC had less incentive to go down-market in search of a wider audience. Differently structured, the two systems set off on paths of development that in time would take them further apart as American radio turned to advertising and British public-service broadcasting remained more or less insulated from market pressures and kept to its mission of cultural uplift.

Developments in France illustrated another path in broadcasting policy. In 1923, following its earlier pattern in telecommunications, the state placed radio broadcasting under the same authority as the post office. But it also awarded ten-year franchises to about a dozen private stations (as it had originally allowed limited private development of the telephone). A separate state radio administration established under the Ministry of Posts, Telegraph and Telephone in 1927 controlled all broadcasts concerning political and economic questions, whether on state or private stations. Six years later, the state purchased the privately owned Radio-Paris and began building a regional radio network. Although private stations survived until 1939, broadcasting came under increasingly stringent political control during the 1930s. German radio moved even more dramatically in that direction. Before 1932, ten private corporations with government representatives on their boards held regional broadcasting monopolies; then the Nazis centralized control under their Ministry of Propaganda. Throughout continental Europe, governmental supervision of broadcasting became the rule, even where the stations were nominally in the hands of private corporations.[23]

In the United States, the system of extralegal regulation that Hoover and the industry had contrived to govern the airwaves collapsed in 1926. The Fourth National Radio Conference had resolved in November 1925 that because of rampant signal interference among the nation's more than 500 broadcasters, the Department of Commerce should announce a moratorium on any further radio licenses, and Hoover had agreed. The next month, a station run by the radio manufacturer Zenith—whose president opposed Hoover's "one-man" rule of radio—deliberately challenged the department by switching to an unused frequency reserved for Canada. But after the federal government sued Zenith, a court ruled that the Department of Commerce had no authority to assign frequencies, deny licenses, or impose many of the other regulations it had established for radio. Hoover himself asked for guidance from the attorney general about what to do. In July 1926, after privately informing the commerce secretary that it agreed with the judge's decision, the Justice Department released an opinion forcing the government to abandon its regulation of broadcasting. A free-for-all then broke out as more than 200 new stations appeared, while others jumped to new frequencies, changed their hours, or increased their power.[24]

The resulting cacophony produced the impetus for change that Hoover had been unable to provide on his own. This was the second generative crisis of radio regulation. As the sinking of the *Titanic* had precipitated the Radio Act of 1912, so the anarchic deregulation of 1926 finally jolted Congress into action. But the legislation it passed the next year did not confer authority on the Department of Commerce. By this time, Hoover was expected to run for the Republican nomination for president, putting himself in competition with prospective rivals in the Senate, including the majority leader, who believed that Hoover would enjoy an unfair advantage if he controlled the award of radio licenses during the campaign. The compromise that emerged from House and Senate bills created an independent Federal Radio Commission (FRC) on a temporary basis for a year, with authority reverting to the Department of Commerce thereafter. In the following years, however, Commerce would never regain power over broadcasting; an independent commission proved to be so durable a political compromise that, just seven years later, Congress would use it to refashion the radio commission into a more general regulatory authority over communications.

The Radio Act of 1927 gave the FRC the powers that Hoover had long sought. The act authorized the five-member commission to divide up the spectrum among different classes of stations and to select which applicants would receive licenses to run stations at specific wavelengths, power levels, geographic locations, and hours. (Control over military and other governmental radio channels, however, was reserved to the president.) The law unambiguously reaffirmed public ownership of the airwaves; it terminated all existing licenses and required applicants to waive any claim of ownership of spectrum in seeking a new license. Unlike the 1912 law, which implied that applicants had a right to use the spectrum, the new statute treated it as a privilege, authorizing the FRC to grant a license "if public convenience, interest or necessity will be served thereby." The law did not spell out the meaning of this language, but it included some specific restrictions, denying radio licenses to foreign owners and to any company convicted of monopolizing or attempting to monopolize radio communication. To balance geographic interests, Congress required each of the commission's members to be drawn from one of five regions of the nation. To provide a check on partisan control, it said no more than three of the five commissioners could be members of the same political party. In other key provisions, the law denied the FRC authority to censor radio communication and required any station providing time to a political candidate to "afford equal opportunities to all other such candidates for that office."[25]

The same year that Congress passed the Radio Act, the United States hosted representatives of other governments at a conference in Washington that resulted in a new, two-part international agreement about radio. The first half, signed by the United States, established general rules that American negotiators saw as appropriately governmental; these included a division of the spectrum along lines close to those adopted at Hoover's second radio conference. Broadcasting received the band from 550 to 1,500 kHz. The agreement's second half, which the United States did not sign, dealt with operational issues that in the American view were best left to the marketplace. This approach satisfied the private-sector interests that had objected to earlier international accords shaped primarily by statist assumptions and military priorities.[26]

While the regulatory framework of broadcasting was taking shape through legislation and international agreements, the organizational framework of the American broadcasting industry began to emerge through a private settlement of the dispute between the Radio Group and AT&T. In late 1924, in secret proceedings, the arbitrator agreed upon by all parties issued a ruling that represented a triumph for the Radio Group. But AT&T refused to abide by the outcome and presented a private memorandum by an eminent lawyer holding that if the arbitrator's understanding of the original patent agreements was correct, those agreements violated the antitrust laws and the telephone company could not be required to comply. The memorandum's author, John W. Davis, the Democratic candidate for president that year, had been involved in drafting the Clayton Antitrust Act when he was Wilson's solicitor general. Already facing the threat of an antitrust prosecution, RCA and its allies could not take AT&T to court and risk disclosure of Davis's legal memorandum. Instead, they proposed a compromise: the creation of a separate broadcasting network, to be formed out of the stations owned by all the various parties and the network that AT&T had already developed. The terms of a deal were reached during 1925 and carried out the following year. RCA, GE, and Westinghouse would own the new National Broadcasting Company (NBC), which would guarantee AT&T at least $1 million in revenue annually in a ten-year contract for interconnection of NBC stations over long-distance telephone lines. In addition, RCA would buy AT&T's station, WEAF, for $1 million. AT&T also obtained the right to market radio receivers, though it later decided not to do so.[27]

In backing out of broadcasting, AT&T repeated what Western Union had done nearly half a century earlier when it backed out of telephone service. Both firms controlled the primary backbone of national communications at the time a new medium emerged. Like Western Union in 1879, AT&T in 1926 had gained a strong position in the new industry and possessed the raw economic power to dominate it, but legal and economic complications led to second thoughts. During the late nineteenth century, Western Union generally held back from extending its monopoly power into new areas because of the likely hostile political reaction. Now the telephone company had to forego an extension of its monopoly because of the risk of generating so much political opposition as to jeopardize the firm's immensely profitable core business. After running WEAF for three years, AT&T was also wary that broadcasting might entangle the company in controversial issues and damage the goodwill it enjoyed in high political circles. As a result, by the time RCA proposed a compromise, some influential figures within AT&T had doubts about the wisdom of pursuing a business in broadcasting. The deal gave AT&T a new stream of revenue from interconnecting stations—indeed, radio networks would become the telephone company's single biggest customer group—without the political risks of direct involvement in broadcasting. The deal also implicitly settled another question. RCA and its allies had been highly critical of advertising on radio. When they took over WEAF, they accepted the premise that broadcasting would be sponsor-supported. As NBC expanded, its station affiliates not only began broadcasting national programs with national advertisers; one by one, they also started finding sponsors for locally originated programs.

The different outcomes in European and American radio broadcasting confirmed three earlier patterns. First, European governments had a long tradition of taxing communications, whereas Americans had consistently rejected any special tax on communications ever since the founding of the republic—indeed, going back to the Stamp Act crisis of 1765. In a sense, the tax on radio receivers in Britain and elsewhere was a twentieth-century reincarnation of the stamp tax on newspapers. To be sure, the motivations of the new tax were different, but the license fee supporting the BBC also had the effect of giving a more elite character to a medium that developed in a more popular direction in the United States.

Second, American policies toward communications had characteristically favored a rapid rollout of new technologies; this was the case with AM radio. To the British, American radio was chaotic and vulgar; to its defenders, American broadcasting demonstrated its virtue by its pluralism and sheer scale. "With only 6 percent of the world's population," one senator bragged in 1926, "we have more than 80 percent of all the receiving sets on earth and five times as many broadcast stations as all the rest of the world combined."[28] As commerce secretary, Hoover had set out to build a flourishing industry, and by that standard his policies had succeeded.

Third, the Europeans were more willing to concentrate control of communications media not just in the state, but in a single bureaucracy. After the telegraph and telephone emerged, European governments had typically given responsibility for the new networks to their post offices;

now some European governments also gave the same organizations authority over broadcasting. America was not exactly devoted to free-market competition in communications; the Post Office, Western Union, and the Bell System were all monopolies or nearly so, and a network oligopoly came to dominate radio. But "legacy" institutions in America were not allowed to control new media. The Post Office lost its bid to control the telegraph in 1846, Western Union abandoned the telephone in 1879, and AT&T withdrew from broadcasting in 1926. In 1913, the federal government had used an antitrust prosecution to separate control of the telegraph and telephone networks; the year after AT&T sold its broadcast interests, the 1927 Radio Act barred telegraph and telephone companies from holding radio licenses if the purpose or effect would be to "substantially lessen competition or to restrain commerce." In short, the United States had a checks-and-balances paradigm for communications just as it did for government itself. But the paradigm would have its limitations in assuring diversity and free expression on the air.

CHAPTER ELEVEN

The Constitution of the Air (2)

Creating the New Public Sphere

THE AIRWAVES in the 1920s were like newly discovered virgin land that attracts colonists eager for adventure, wealth, or the opportunity to build a glorious new civilization. Like many a frontier territory, radio quickly became a battleground of legal claims and political deals, of new industry, dashed hopes, and great business empires. That had always been the course of American settlement whether on the prairie or on the spectrum. Broadcasting, however, was not simply a field of enterprise or an extension of society into a new domain. It promised to change society. The promise of broadcasting, even more than earlier media, was to make culture accessible to all, to enable the electorate to become better informed, to put people instantaneously in touch with the news of the world. Here was a new, buzzing and booming public sphere, an updated means of forming public opinion and public taste appropriately scaled to the age of mass democracy.

Yet, by comparison with the traditional medium of the public sphere—the press—radio suffered from several disabilities. Its entire basis of operation, the radio spectrum, was a scarce resource allocated by the state. As radio developed during the late 1920s and 1930s, control devolved on only a few hands, and the new medium provided less latitude for cultural diversity and political dissent than did print. While the press was increasingly independent of politics, there developed an interdependence between those who held political power (and needed radio) and those who controlled radio (and needed political goodwill). Instead of extending democracy, therefore, radio threatened to distort it. Such was the promise—such were the dangers—as the political framework of broadcasting was established in the period from 1927 to World War II.

New Networks, New Powers

Although the 1927 Radio Act resolved that broadcasting in America would be privately operated under federal licenses, the legislation left much to be determined, including the allocation of spectrum and the selection of who would own and control radio. The law did not set any priorities among the commercial, educational, religious, and other groups interested in retaining or acquiring licenses to the air. And it did not address networks directly, saying only that the radio commission might adopt "special regulations" of "stations engaged in chain broadcasting." It was not so much the law as its interpretation by the new regulators—backed up by the courts—that would determine how radio would be run. One factor guaranteed philosophical continuity: The Republicans retained control of all three branches of the federal government, and the same political leader who had dominated radio regulation from 1921 to 1927 remained the decisive influence for five additional critical years. Despite the Senate's desire to limit his power over radio, Hoover chose the initial nominees to the Federal Radio Commission at Coolidge's invitation and then made his own nominations after being inaugurated as president in 1929. These commissioners maintained the close, supportive relationship with commercial radio interests that Hoover had earlier fostered.

By 1927, radio was emerging as a primary medium of popular entertainment and had found a place in about one-quarter of American households.[1] Receivers were now available that ran on house current rather than cumbersome batteries, and new models reduced static and produced sound with greater range and fidelity (though still within the limits of AM radio). Broadcast transmitters were also increasing in power, up to 10,000 watts (later to 50,000), further improving reception for a widening range of listeners. At the same time, a new structure of the broadcasting industry was taking shape to give local stations and their audiences access to national programs, particularly from America's entertainment capital in New York. By the end of 1927, the first full year of operations, NBC had forty-eight affiliated stations, and the following year it divided its affiliates into two "basic" networks: NBC-Red, originating primarily from WEAF (later renamed WNBC), and NBC-Blue, originating from WJZ, also in New York. Though the two networks overlapped, NBC-Red was the more popularly oriented and profitable, while NBC-Blue distributed more refined offerings. Another network, established by a shaky start-up called United Independent Broadcasters, briefly received financing from a record company and went on the air as the Columbia Phonograph Broadcasting System, with sixteen station affiliates, in September 1927. Soon it simplified its name to the Columbia Broadcasting System (CBS). Most of the affiliates of both NBC and CBS were independently owned and managed, except for a small number of key stations in large metropolitan areas owned by the networks themselves.[2]

The great constitutive choice facing the FRC at its inception was the design of the spectrum, particularly how to divide the bandwidth allotted to radio broadcasting among different kinds of channels. Radio engineers at the time believed that to avoid interference, broadcast signals needed to be 10 kHz apart, which meant that ninety-six channels could fit on the broadcasting band. Six of these were set aside for Canada. The number of stations that the remaining ninety channels could carry in the United States depended on decisions the FRC would make about the location and power levels of broadcast transmitters. The more powerful a station's transmitter, the more distant the interference it created. The interference caused by a particular station, in fact, could extend even beyond its own listening range, particularly at night, when signals traveled farther. At the highest power levels, only one station could occupy a frequency (labeled a "clear channel" when a single broadcaster was assigned to it). In contrast, at moderate power levels there could be several regional stations at the same frequency spread around the country, and at the lowest power many dispersed local stations could use the same wavelength. By a straightforward logic, then, the greater the number of clear channels, the less space remained on the spectrum for regional and local stations to stay on the air, especially in the key evening hours. Because high-powered stations required more expensive equipment, the interest in clear channels was greatest among well-financed commercial broadcasters, who could most readily take advantage of such licenses to reach the widest possible listening audience. Convincing the FRC to set aside clear channels was a high priority for the emerging national radio networks. Nonprofit broadcasters, in contrast, generally preferred an allocation creating a greater number of more affordable local stations.[3]

The spectrum-allocation choice facing the FRC, therefore, pitted commercial broadcasters against nonprofits, and national against local interests. Other considerations, however, complicated the issue. The stronger signals of clear-channel stations would reach rural listeners who might otherwise have no access to radio at all, and those stronger signals also meant better reception for people with cheaper radios. The ideal of universal service, therefore, provided a justification for allocating a large share of the broadcast spectrum to clear-channel stations. But there was an implicit trade-off: More equal access to listening meant more concentrated control of broadcasting. If there had been a well-financed public radio network, it, too, would have been interested in obtaining clear channels. The gap in resources between commercial and nonprofit broadcasters shaped their views on the spectrum and enabled the commercial interests to champion an approach that promised better radio reception for rural and low-income Americans.

During the FRC's troubled first year—the Senate initially failed to confirm two of the five original nominees, and two who were confirmed died shortly after assuming office—the commission put off any comprehensive redesign of the broadcasting spectrum. Instead, it made ad hoc assignments, forcing many stations to share frequencies and setting aside about two dozen clear channels, nearly all of which it awarded to commercial broadcasters that became affiliates of NBC. These early decisions, however, provoked criticism in Congress, particularly from southern and western representatives who saw the rise of "chain broadcasting" as a new form of northeastern cultural domination. When the lawmakers renewed the tenure of the FRC in 1928, they adopted a provision known as the Davis Amendment that required the commission to make a comprehensive reallocation of spectrum assuring equal allotments of stations to the five regions identified in the 1927 Radio Act.[4]

For expert guidance in spectrum reallocation, the FRC turned to a committee drawn from a professional association, the Institute of Radio Engineers, whose most influential members worked for RCA or other corporations. The key recommendation of the engineers was to increase the number of clear-channel stations to 50, with the remaining channels divided up so as to allow 90 regional stations and 100 local ones. Such a drastic reduction from the 733 stations on the air in 1927 drew opposition, however, from the National Association of Broadcasters. Issuing its order in August 1928, the FRC set the number of clear-channel stations at 40, making room for more regional and local stations than the engineers had recommended, though still forcing many broadcasters to time-share frequencies. The reallocation immediately changed the position on the radio dial of more than nine out of ten stations. While time-sharing allowed the number of stations to stabilize for the next several years at around 600, the new design of the broadcast band was highly congenial to the big commercial networks. Even though the clear and regional channels were equally divided among the five regions, nearly all of the licenses for those stations went to commercial broadcasters that either already were or soon would become affiliates of NBC and CBS.[5]

As the law required, the FRC defended its decisions about clear-channel and other licenses on the grounds of the "public convenience, interest, or necessity." Some members of Congress believed that the public interest justified allocating a share of stations to broadcasters with an educational, religious, or civic mission, but this was not how the FRC viewed the matter. The commission held that the public interest meant the interest of the listeners, and it offered two justifications for interpreting that interest to favor commercial broadcasters. The first emphasized technical criteria. Because listeners had an interest in the best possible reception and the most extensive radio service, stations were most deserving of licenses if they had superior technical equipment, trained personnel, and the capacity to operate full-time rather than merely a few hours a week. The commission deemed it vital, for example, that stations prevent their signals from drifting from their assigned frequencies and interfering with those of other stations. Broadcasters with strong financial resources were better able to maintain high engineering standards. Such criteria gave an edge to commercial stations over many low-budget college and other nonprofit stations that had limited facilities and broadcast schedules.

According to a second justification, presented in the FRC's annual report in 1929, the public interest dictated a preference for stations serving the general public rather than stations serving "private or selfish interests." To be sure, the FRC acknowledged, commercial stations carried advertising, but this was merely a practical necessity to support a "well-rounded" program. Commercial stations actually served the general public because they were interested in obtaining the largest possible audience, while nonprofit stations served only particular groups such as students or members of a church. A commercial station would present alternative views on a subject, while a nonprofit would naturally tend only to present its own perspective. Indeed, the commission characterized stations supported by advertising as "general public service" stations, while it described noncommercial broadcasters as "propaganda" stations and declared that when contending for the same frequency, a public-service station had "a claim of preference over a propaganda station."[6]

While the FRC gave commercial broadcasters licenses for the high-power clear-channel and regional stations, it gave colleges, religious groups, and other nonprofit broadcasters licenses only for low-power local stations, often authorizing them to broadcast just a few hours a week on shared frequencies. Stations receiving limited hours then often found it difficult to survive. At that time, the FRC licensed stations for only three months, and anyone could challenge a station for its frequency or hours when the license came up for renewal. Such challenges forced nonprofit stations to mount continual legal defenses, which they could ill afford. Often they were forced to change frequencies. In 1927, for example, the Connecticut State College station at Storrs was ordered to move around the radio dial eight times before the college finally gave up and turned off the microphone. The director of the dying University of Arkansas station declared that while the commission might say it had not closed down any educational station, "It merely cuts off our head, our arms, and our legs, and then allows us to die a natural death." Between 1927 and 1930, nonprofit stations fell by more than two-thirds, down from more than 200 to 65. During the entire period from 1921 to 1936, 204 educational stations were established, and 80 percent of these lost or sold their licenses.[7] In another key decision (or rather "nondecision"), the FRC allowed stations to be bought and sold without any review of purchasers' records in serving the public interest. Although Congress had rejected private ownership of the airwaves, the commission's practices resulted in a de facto market in spectrum.

The FRC's reallocation of frequencies, the consolidation of the networks, and the conversion of radio to advertising all came about in the same years and were closely interrelated. Economic forces shaped by political decisions helped to drive the transformation. Before 1927, stations were able to operate on minimal budgets. As of 1925, the average station was on the air only five hours *per week.*[8] Most broadcasters operated at relatively low power, and programming was inexpensive, in part because performers appeared for free and many stations paid no royalties to composers. By the late 1920s, however, regulatory and competitive pressures were both contributing to sharply increased costs. Under the FRC's guidance, stations moved to higher power levels, stricter engineering standards, and seventeen-hour daily broadcast schedules. Programming costs increased as listening audiences demanded higher-quality shows and composers and musicians demanded payment. Many businesses and nonprofit organizations that originally launched stations hoping for indirect benefits could no longer justify the mounting costs that radio entailed, unless they could make broadcasting pay on its own. Here the absence of any public finance for broadcasting in the United States was critical. Without a license fee or tax support to bear its mounting cost—or a great benefactor to provide an endowment—American radio was certain to be dominated by commercial broadcasters, and those broadcasters were bound to turn to the only two sources capable of controlling their costs and producing the revenue needed to make a profit: networks and advertising.

The networks served in part as intermediaries between national advertisers and individual stations. They gave advertisers of brand-name consumer products efficient access to a large national audience, and out of their advertising revenue they provided stations with a stream of dependable income to run the programs that advertisers sponsored. They also gave their affiliates a competitive advantage by supplying popular and high-quality programs at low or zero cost that unaffiliated stations in their local markets found it difficult to match. Even in countries with noncommercial broadcasting systems, networks have an economic logic, based ultimately on the relatively high cost of producing content (programming) relative to the costs of transmission or reproduction. The additional role of American networks in connecting national advertisers and national audiences gave them an unbreakable hold on broadcasting. NBC was the first titan of the industry, building its Red and Blue networks on the stations originally created by AT&T and Radio Group companies and then capturing most of the early clear-channel licenses. As an upstart, CBS was at a decided disadvantage and faced considerable financial instability during its early years. But in 1928, William S. Paley and his father, a cigar manufacturer, bought CBS, and under the young man's leadership the network took several steps that turned it into a thriving enterprise.

One of Paley's key innovations involved the network-affiliate relationship. Networks supplied their station affiliates with programming of two types: "sponsored" programs paid for by advertisers and "sustaining" programs paid for by the networks themselves. Under its original arrangement, NBC allowed affiliates to choose among its offerings, paying them to carry sponsored programs and charging them for use of sustaining programs. Under Paley's system, CBS offered sustaining programs at no direct charge—during the Depression years, a huge benefit for stations, giving them about fifteen hours of programming at no cost. In return, Paley got an option on any part of the affiliates' schedules for the network's sponsored programs as well as the right to transmit a certain number of hours of sponsored programs without payment to the local station. The option gave CBS a marketing edge by enabling it to guarantee advertisers time on as many of its stations as they wanted without worrying about local clearance. By the mid-1930s, CBS catapulted ahead of NBC in profitability, though not in the total power of station affiliates.[9]

These were years of tremendous expansion in the radio audience. While the Depression led many families to drop telephone service, the proportion with radios climbed sharply. The share of American households with receivers went from 23.6 percent in 1927 to 45.8 percent in 1930 and 65.2 percent in 1934—in absolute terms, from 6.8 to 20.4 million homes. Radio was now approaching total coverage in large cities, where 93 percent of households in 1935 had radios, compared to 77 percent in towns with under 1,000 population and 34 percent in rural areas. Listening was not a solitary pursuit. Most families gathered together to tune into favorite shows, often friends came over to listen, and during the day radios blared in shops and workplaces. While radio ownership was predictably higher in higher-income families, that relationship did not apply to listening. Studies repeatedly found that listening was highest among middle- and lower-income people, least among the affluent. According to several studies, by the mid-1930s Americans were averaging about four hours of radio listening a day.[10]

With so vast an audience at hand, the reluctance of advertisers to use radio in the early 1920s gave way to a growing enthusiasm for the new medium by the end of the decade. Hesitant at first about invading the sanctity of the home and offending listeners, sponsors and stations had delicately refrained from explicit commercials or sales talks and allowed only "indirect" advertisements, such as giving the sponsor's name to the show (as in WEAF's first regular series, the *Eveready Hour*) or to the performers (as in the Vicks Vaporub Quartette). Palmolive Soap used both devices, identifying the soloists on the *Palmolive Hour* as Olive Palmer and Paul Oliver. Brand names were also interwoven into dialogue among performers and announcers. Even as sales pitches gained acceptance during the late 1920s, networks and stations continued to ban any mention of prices or special offers and to exclude such products as deodorants and laxatives. But by the early 1930s, these genteel restraints had collapsed; radio gave itself wholly over to commercialism as some sponsors adopted the theory that in a publicity-saturated world sponsors had to be direct, insistent, and intrusive to get their message across. Increasingly, advertisers viewed radio as an especially effective medium precisely because it reached listeners in their homes and could impress a message distinctively and repeatedly on a listener's awareness and memory.[11]

Not only did advertising become the economic basis of radio in America; in addition, sponsors and advertising agencies became far more powerful in radio than they had been in the press. Newspapers and most magazines depended on advertisers for only part of their income, and some publications survived entirely by selling subscriptions and individual copies to readers. Commercial broadcasters, however, derived all of their revenue from advertising. Rather than selling shows to listeners, they only sold listeners' attention to sponsors. Advertising revenue in the print media also typically came from many different sources, while the sponsorship of radio programs was far more concentrated. Although spot advertising began on local and independent stations in the mid-1920s, network programs typically had single sponsors, who frequently intervened in shaping and censoring the shows' content. Perhaps the most distinctive feature of radio as an advertising medium lay in the critical role and power of advertising agencies. Although the agencies started out by preparing copy for radio advertisements and negotiating with stations on behalf of sponsors, they quickly assumed the central role in program production. Increasingly, the agencies came up with the ideas for programs, wrote the scripts, hired the performers, found sponsors, and presented shows to the networks as a complete package. By 1929, advertising agencies were producing 33 percent of programs; individual sponsors, another 20 percent; the networks, 28 percent; and special program builders, 19 percent. Within a few years, the agencies took over virtually all but the sustaining programs the networks produced for use during unsold airtime. The magnitude of the shift in radio was stunning: It had taken only a few years for radio to undergo a total reversal from utterly rejecting advertising, to allowing it, and then to ceding to advertising agencies the dominant role in the creation of radio entertainment.[12]

By the late 1920s, the development of radio took place in the awareness that there was another broadcasting technology on its way, already referred to as "television." In fact, television had a false start during the 1920s, when inventors in both Europe and America developed prototypes based on the 1884 work of a German inventor, Paul Nipkow. The concept involved a mechanical apparatus, a spinning disk with perforated holes, used for both transmitting and receiving moving images. By 1925, the Scottish inventor John Logie Baird was demonstrating a primitive working model, and during the mid-1920s, using a related system, the independent inventor Charles Francis Jenkins gave the first public demonstrations of television in America. In 1927, Hoover appeared on an AT&T television demonstration transmitted from Washington to a receiver in New York. With backing from Wall Street and an experimental license from the FRC, Jenkins went into production of television sets and began regular broadcasts from a television station in Washington; by the end of 1928, the FRC had granted twenty-eight experimental licenses.

Perhaps as many as 100,000 Americans saw a Jenkins television during this period. Television caught the tail end of the 1920s speculative fever on Wall Street—but when the stock market crashed, so did television in its first incarnation. Because television licenses were only experimental, the FRC allowed no advertising; Jenkins's company depended on sales of receivers, and when those faltered, the company failed. But the British and German state broadcasting systems, not dependent on commercial success, continued telecasts during the early 1930s when there were none in America. In the United States, the initial failure of television stood as a cautionary lesson about the dangers of premature deployment of a new technology. The fundamental problem, as some understood it at the time, lay in the attempt to base television on a mechanical device that severely limited the size and clarity of images; when television development revived during the 1930s, the technology would be fully electronic. But while television's initial failure signaled caution, it also convinced key figures in the business world that whoever gained a dominant position in radio would be well-positioned to do the same as broadcasting moved on to television and became an even bigger industry. And in that respect, they were right.[13]

The turn toward a network-dominated, commercial radio system did not occur without criticism or protest. Cultural conservatives as well as socialists condemned what they viewed as the degradation of a promising new medium. Although some of these critics favored nationalization of radio on a BBC model, the major political challenge came from advocates of educational broadcasting, who in 1930 organized the National Committee on Education by Radio (NCER) and proposed that 15 percent of broadcast channels be reserved for government or government-chartered educational stations. Backed by the Payne Fund, the committee included representatives from the National Educational Association and eight other organizations representing such interests as college broadcasters, land-grant colleges, and Catholic educators. But 1930 also saw the establishment of an opposing group, the National Advisory Council on Radio in Education, which included several illustrious university presidents and drew support from one of the Carnegie philanthropies. The council called for collaboration with commercial broadcasters and claimed that the networks were willing to make adequate provision for educational programs. To these educators, it made sense to compromise with the networks because they could provide access to a far larger audience than the low-power educational stations could reach. NBC and CBS, for their part, seemed to show reciprocal interest and did provide some educational programming in unsold slots on their schedule. As of the early 1930s, moreover, the networks were still anxious about their respectability and had an interest in winning over part of the education lobby and demonstrating that there was no compelling need to set aside channels for noncommercial use.

Educational reformers were not the only group in the broadcast reform movement vulnerable to a divide-and-conquer strategy. In 1930, organized labor proposed a measure that would have obtained three clear channels—one each for groups concerned with labor, agriculture, and education. A bill granting a clear channel to labor actually passed the Senate, though it failed to win the approval of the House. In 1932, however, the unions abandoned the attempt to build a coalition among nonprofit broadcasters after the Chicago Federation of Labor's WCFL—the country's one labor-controlled station—struck a deal with NBC and gained the right to broadcast full-time at 5,000 watts. That year, instead of granting 15 percent of channels to the nonprofits, the Senate asked only for a report on the subject from the FRC. The agency concluded that "educational programs can be safely left to the voluntary gift of the use of facilities by commercial stations."[14]

The political weakness of the broadcast reformers had deeper roots than their own internal divisions. Although they claimed wide support in public opinion, the reformers were never able to build a popular membership organization; a brief effort by the NCER to create an American Listeners Society in support of nonprofit radio came to nothing, and a campaign to inspire newspaper opposition to the commercialization of radio also flopped. The educators' conception of radio as a means of edification may simply not have enjoyed the popular approval they imagined. A study of listeners' correspondence with Wisconsin's state university station suggests a good deal of public ambivalence toward the station's uplifting mission. In 1925, in response to a farmer who requested some old fiddle music ("I said fiddle don't mean a VIOLIN"), the broadcast director replied, "The air is overcrowded every night with jazz and other worthless material, and it would be quite beneath the dignity of the University to add to it." Survey data indicate that educational programs on the networks tended to draw relatively small audiences, which, moreover, were disproportionately composed of more highly educated listeners, not the less-educated ones they were ideally supposed to instruct.[15]

Nor does the available evidence suggest that radio was actually an effective medium for teaching. During the early twentieth century, technological enthusiasts in education saw the new media of the time—the movies and radio—as the basis for a revolution in the classroom, yet new technologies proved a disappointment in practice. Teachers found them far more difficult to integrate into classroom practice than the older and cheaper technologies of chalk and blackboard, pencil and paper.[16] This is not to suggest that the outcome of the battle over the allocation of spectrum depended on a rational evaluation of the competing uses of radio. Once the networks were established, they represented not merely a powerful economic interest but also the gateway to the national public. And, as the experience after the inauguration of Franklin Roosevelt in 1933 showed, the control of the airwaves gave the broadcasters sufficient political leverage in Washington to overwhelm the scattered advocates of noncommercial radio.

While broadcast reformers saw Roosevelt's election as reason for renewed hope for a reallocation of spectrum, another idea for radio reform was gaining support. This was a proposal to create a unified communications commission that would assume the FRC's functions as well as the responsibilities of the Interstate Commerce Commission for regulating the telephone industry. (The ICC was primarily concerned with transportation and widely believed to have neglected its responsibilities for telecommunications.) Hoover had supported the reorganization plan, and Congress had already been considering it for several years; now a shift in the international system gave the proposal added momentum. At a conference in Madrid in 1932, the nations represented in the International Telegraph Union combined the international agreements regulating the telegraph (dating to 1865), the telephone (dating to 1885), and radio (dating to 1906) into a single International Telecommunications Convention and changed the organization's own name to the International Telecommunications Union. Key leaders in American industry and government concluded from this development that to represent American interests effectively in the international arena, the United States needed a single agency to make consistent regulatory policy for communications. This is a common basis of the international diffusion of governmental structures; once "international regimes" emerge, individual countries often have an incentive to adjust their own policy-making process to match. Another development at the time helped to ease the way for enactment of a new regulatory structure in the United States. In early 1933, two years after the Department of Justice had finally brought suit against the "radio trust" for restraint of trade, GE and Westinghouse agreed to give up control of RCA, which became an independent company and the sole owner of NBC. The antitrust settlement removed an issue that might have been a stumbling block for new legislation. Furthermore, the Democratic victory in the 1932 elections put the key committees in both the House and Senate in the hands of strong advocates of a new communications commission. Everything was set for a reorganization, unless Roosevelt had a different agenda.[17]

Although Roosevelt had taken no position on communications reform during the 1932 campaign, the new administration and its supporters included some advocates of radical change. Josephus Daniels, who as secretary of the Navy in World War I had been Roosevelt's superior and remained one of his close political allies, privately urged the president during the summer of 1933 to consider nationalizing radio. Roosevelt had already made Secretary of Commerce Daniel C. Roper responsible for an internal review of communications policy, and in a confidential report to the president Roper rejected nationalization as politically and economically impractical. Instead, the administration convened a committee under Roper that included key congressional leaders, and this group endorsed a unified regulatory commission in a report that became the administration's official policy. During the ensuing congressional debate on legislation to create the new commission, supporters of radio reform in the Senate introduced an amendment to reserve 25 percent of channels to nonprofit broadcasters, only to see the proposal go down to defeat by a nearly two-to-one margin as the administration stood by. The legislation itself passed the House and Senate with no real opposition and included nothing to disturb commercial broadcasting interests. "When we read it," an NBC vice president later said of the final bill, "we found that every major point we had asked for was there."[18]

Signed by the president on June 18, the Communications Act of 1934 created a single seven-member body, the Federal Communications Commission (FCC), to regulate radio as well as interstate and international telegraph, cable, and telephone services. Although it formally repealed the Radio Act of 1927, the new measure reenacted nearly all the provisions of the earlier legislation, much of it verbatim. The FCC is often described as a New Deal agency, but this is primarily the result of a coincidence of timing. Though the legislation had Roosevelt's signature, the actual substance had Hoover's name written all over it. It was Hoover who had presided over the key constitutive choices in broadcasting and broadcast regulation; the 1934 legislation ratified and consolidated these earlier decisions.

Roosevelt's motivations for accepting this system do not appear to be deeply mysterious. On assuming office in the midst of a national economic crisis, he had other battles to fight besides taking on commercial radio interests. In the 1932 election, six out of ten newspapers had opposed him, and Roosevelt believed that he was the victim of a deep hatred among newspaper publishers who slanted press coverage against his programs. The radio networks, in contrast, gave the president their full cooperation, opening the airwaves to him whenever he wanted, and Roosevelt used radio to reach the public directly and explain his policies. He never showed any inclination to jeopardize this vital political asset for what might be a hopeless and even unpopular crusade to change the structure of broadcasting. Roosevelt's early appointments to the FRC and then the FCC also showed more of a concern for defending political interests than for reform of radio.[19] Unlike other areas of policy, broadcasting would have no new deal—at least not in the early years of Roosevelt's presidency.

A reversal of broadcasting policies in Canada during this period provides a sharp counterpoint to the outcome in the United States. Before 1932, Canadian radio developed along American lines as a private industry, except that stations in Canada were typically smaller and weaker enterprises than their American counterparts. Radio ownership in Canada ran at about half the rate in the United States, partly because broadcasters outside of Toronto had only low-power transmitters, putting many Canadians, especially in sparsely populated areas, beyond the range of any of the country's stations. In the more densely populated areas, generally close to the United States, listeners tended to tune in American stations because of Canadian broadcasters' weak signals, limited schedules, and relatively unexciting programs. As a result, a consensus emerged across the political spectrum in favor of governmental intervention to strengthen Canadian radio. Under a Conservative government in 1932, Canada created a federal commission to regulate and carry on broadcasting and established a license fee on receivers to pay for the new service. While existing stations remained in private hands, the commission produced and distributed national programming. Four years later, a Liberal government established the Canadian Broadcasting Corporation (CBC), modeled after the BBC in that it received greater autonomy and more ample funding than the earlier commission. The CBC still did not take over Canadian radio entirely, but it built a national network of high-power public stations and generally limited private broadcasters to a low-power, local role. In the resulting hybrid system, the CBC served as both national network and national regulator of private radio stations, a majority of which became CBC affiliates. Canadian public broadcasting was itself a hybrid; though modeled after the BBC, the CBC relied partly on advertising to supplement tax revenue, and its offerings included popular American radio shows.[20]

One of the central figures in Canada's radio reforms later described the 1932 legislation as stemming from two "driving motives": first and most important, the "national motive," and second, "the free use of broadcasting by all sections of opinion." The appeal to national sentiment gave Canada's broadcast reformers the kind of wide popular support that the American advocates of nonprofit radio were unable to achieve. To Canadians, a stronger role for government seemed the only feasible way to resist domination by American broadcasting, maintain a distinct national identity, extend coverage to distant and dispersed citizens, and make possible a national public sphere for discussion of Canadian problems. In addition, Canada's leaders, like those in other British Commonwealth countries, continued to look to Britain for models of a well-ordered state; the CBC's first director was a Canadian who had served in a leading role at the BBC. By the 1930s, Australia also developed a hybrid system, consisting of a governmental radio network, the Australian Broadcasting Corporation, financed by a license fee on receivers, and a commercial radio sector dependent on advertising, which captured about 80 percent of the national audience.[21]

In the United States, a hybrid system like Canada's or Australia's was a far more plausible alternative than a BBC-style broadcasting monopoly. Centralized governmental control of communications was deeply suspect in America, and after the federal censorship of dissenting publications during World War I, many liberals as well as conservatives shared a heightened suspicion of centralized power. Recognizing the breadth of opposition, broadcast reformers made no serious effort to nationalize the industry, nor did they try to pass a license fee on radio receivers. They focused instead on the modest aim of making radio more pluralistic and diverse by reserving some channels for nonprofit use. This measure, attractive partly because it imposed no cost on taxpayers, also would not have fundamentally changed American radio; commercial broadcasters would still have remained the dominant force on the air. Mild reforms of this sort did not threaten capitalism as such; they only threatened particular commercial interests—but they failed nonetheless because they emerged when those interests were so strong that they had no need to make concessions.

Broadcasting, in other words, is another case that illustrates the importance of the constitutive moment. The key decisions came in the 1920s, when conservative Republicans were in power and business enjoyed sway over policy; by the time Roosevelt was elected, the networks commanded the electronic portals to the public. If radio broadcasting had developed earlier or later—if the constitutive choices about broadcasting had been made at the height of Progressivism in 1912, or if they had arisen for the first time in 1935 at the height of the New Deal—the Progressives or New Dealers might have made different choices, and a public broadcasting network might have developed as part of a hybrid system at radio's beginnings instead of waiting for decades. Even if Americans had faced a clear-cut choice about radio in 1922, they might well have decided against a purely commercial system; at that time, after all, on-the-air advertising met condemnation from every direction. But broadcasting evolved step by step during the twenties without any single definitive moment of public decision. Advertising developed slowly at first, only becoming explicit and intrusive as the public grew accustomed to it. Americans may not have wanted on-the-air advertising in the first place, but they came to accept it, and they certainly weren't willing to pay taxes to avoid it. In a 1938 survey conducted by the American Institute of Public Opinion, 47 percent of respondents said they thought the time devoted to advertisements was just "about right," while only 36 percent said it was "too much." Perhaps even more telling was a survey question that asked people how much they were willing to pay to eliminate commercials: 79 percent said they wouldn't pay anything.[22] Commercial radio did not merely become entrenched as an interest group; it became embedded in culture and consciousness, and it gathered legitimacy until it seemed impossible that it could be any other way.

Censorship and Diversity on the Dial

The framework of American broadcasting that emerged during the late 1920s and 1930s—federal licensing and regulation, network domination, and control by advertisers and advertising agencies—stood in uneasy tension with the traditions of a free press. To be sure, unlike European countries, the United States had hundreds of private, independently owned radio stations, and there was no direct governmental censorship. But federal regulators and commercial interests more severely constrained freedom and diversity of expression on the air than in print.

Licensing represented only the most obvious form of control. No newspaper or magazine in America had to satisfy a government agency's definition of the "public convenience, interest, or necessity" to stay in business. In 1927 and 1934, even as it declared that no regulation "shall interfere with the right of free speech by means of radio communication," Congress gave radio's regulators broad and flexible authority to develop the medium as it evolved. The law left it to the regulatory commission to define the public interest and, rather than locking in control of stations, required broadcasters to reapply for licenses at least every three years (more frequently if the commission so decided). The free-speech problem in radio was not merely that broadcasters, unlike publishers, needed to keep a government license; the licensing criteria were also vague, and the cost of failing to satisfy them was the commercial equivalent of a hanging, well known for its powers of concentrating the mind. Even though, as it turned out, regulators rarely imposed that penalty, the mere possibility was sufficient to make broadcasters highly attentive to signals of displeasure in high places. Regulation by "raised eyebrow," it came to be called. Moreover, whereas the founding of one publication did not automatically extinguish another, the scarcity of channels meant that a license for one broadcaster came at another's expense. The broadcast spectrum could not support the range of expression available in print. To some extent, this limit on diversity reflected the limits of available technology, but federal regulatory and licensing decisions had accentuated the problem.

Scarcity of spectrum wasn't the only basis for differences in the treatment of radio and the printed word. Many believed that restrictions on broadcasting were legitimate because radio invaded the sanctity of the home. When the medium evolved from a pastime of male hobbyists into a form of family entertainment during the 1920s, radio entered a sphere that served as a compelling rationale for moral censorship. In a sense, this was the inverse situation from the movies, where the fear was that the young were viewing films in a dimly lit, unchaperoned space. Radio weakened parental control by the opposite means, entering the home unchecked. The sanctity of home life was one of the grounds for the early opposition to radio advertising—conveniently forgotten as commercialism became established. But it remained a basis for regulation of song lyrics, plays, and even political invective. Immediately after guaranteeing free speech on radio, the Radio Act of 1927 banned "any obscene, indecent, or profane language" on the air. This provision reflected a moral consensus that broadcasters themselves attempted to enforce.

The FRC (and later the FCC) saw no contradiction between affirming rights of free speech and basing licensing decisions on the content of a broadcaster's programming. While recognizing that it had no authority to censor radio, the commission interpreted the bar against censorship to preclude only prior restraint of a broadcast, not the use of past programs as a basis for a decision about whether a station served the public interest. Of course, by signaling that it viewed some kinds of broadcasts as inconsistent with the public interest, the commission had the effect of restraining them. For example, after the commission held that lotteries and fortune-telling did not serve the public interest, stations dropped them from their schedules.

In 1928, the commission signaled its disapproval of stations that "consume much of the valuable time allotted to them" for "distinctly private" purposes. This was a central issue in a case involving one of the best-known radio personalities in the Midwest, John R. Brinkley, a doctor of dubious credentials who promised to cure male impotence by implanting goat glands in the scrotum. Based in Milford, Kansas, Brinkley ran a pharmaceutical business, a hospital where he performed his operations, and station KFKB. At 5,000 watts, KFKB could be heard from the Rocky Mountains to the Mississippi and in 1929 won a listeners' poll as America's most popular radio station. On the air for an hour and a half a day, Brinkley would explain his treatments and read letters from patients he had never seen, generally prescribing his own secret-formula drugs. Although some objections to his broadcasts involved indecency ("Tell your husband to sleep in the barn," he advised a woman who complained about her spouse's excessive virility), the FRC denied KFKB's bid to renew its license in 1930 on the grounds that Brinkley conducted the station only in his "personal interest" and that his practice of prescribing drugs to unseen patients, solely on the basis of their letters, was "inimical" to public health. (That same year, Kansas rescinded his medical license.) Rejecting Brinkley's claim that revocation of his station's license represented censorship, the District of Columbia Court of Appeals declared that "because the number of available broadcasting frequencies is limited, the commission is necessarily called upon to consider the character and quality" of a broadcast service, taking into account past conduct: "By their fruits ye shall know them." The burden, the court said, was on Brinkley to show that a license renewal was in the public interest, and in rendering its judgment, the commission had "merely exercised its undoubted right" to consider his previous broadcasts, "which is not censorship."[23]

A second case from 1930 brought out even more clearly the limited application of the First Amendment to broadcasting. Like Brinkley, the

Reverend Bob Shuler of KGEF, Los Angeles, had a large listening audience, but Shuler's interests were religious, moral, and political—the kind of speech generally regarded as deserving the highest constitutional protection. Shuler used his station to crusade against drinking and prostitution and to make charges of criminal and immoral conduct against the mayor, chief of police, and other local leaders, some of whom left office as a result of his attacks and exposures. Shuler's attacks on judges, however, had twice led to contempt-of-court judgments against him. He was also anti-Semitic and anti-Catholic. In 1928, when the Catholic Al Smith was the Democratic candidate for president, Shuler declared that "Rome and liquor" were trying "to take over" and "wring the life out of this country."

In 1930, local opponents of Shuler challenged his license when it was up for renewal. Before the FRC heard the case, Shuler said on the air that the "Catholic commissioner" might be against him—an instance cited by the opposing side as evidence of Shuler's recklessness because, as it happened, the commission had no Catholic members at all. In its decision against Shuler, the FRC found that his attacks on religious minorities as well as his unsubstantiated charges against civic leaders were "certainly not in the interests of the public." Shuler's broadcasts were "sensational rather than instructive," the commission later declared to the court of appeals. Affirming the regulators' decision in 1932, the court emphasized that Shuler had offended religious sensitivities, stirred up civic discord, and defamed public officials without being able to produce evidence to support his accusations.[24] The Supreme Court declined to review the decision.

Only the year before, in *Near v. Minnesota,* the Supreme Court had held that Minnesota could not shut down a publication that the state judged to be "malicious, scandalous, and defamatory." The Shuler and Near cases led to different results despite striking similarities. Jay Near was also anti-Catholic and anti-Semitic and leveled charges of corruption against public officials, who instead of suing for libel attempted to deny him his means of public expression. But in that case, the Supreme Court held that Minnesota had wrongly placed the burden on Near to prove the truth and good motives of his accusations and that the state's action in barring him from continuing to publish represented an unconstitutional prior restraint on the press.[25] In contrast, the final decision in Shuler's case affirmed the government's termination of his broadcast license, in part because he failed to show that his charges were not reckless. As the courts saw it, limited spectrum necessarily meant a lower level of protection for free speech. Not only was the public-interest standard for broadcasting held constitutional; in this and other cases, the FCC received a sweeping mandate to interpret that standard and determine the limits of programming on the air.

While federal law constrained the diversity of broadcasting in one way, the ascendancy of the networks curtailed it in another. Before the late 1920s, there was a profusion of stations with a local orientation. As Lizabeth Cohen shows in a study of Chicago, early radio listeners found "familiar distractions" on the air: "talk, ethnic nationality hours, labor news, church services, and vaudeville-type musical entertainment by hometown, often ethnic talent." Rather than being melded into a mass culture, Americans listening to radio in the 1920s were able to sustain their varied cultural and class identities. The rise of the networks brought a shift to entertainment created for a national audience: comedy and variety shows with national celebrities, soap operas, westerns and detective shows, and sports programs.[26] Network radio during the 1930s followed a pattern that was later duplicated in television. When the number of broadcast networks is small, each one will rationally produce lowest-common-denominator programming aimed at the broad consumer market sought by advertisers. Specialization in niche markets (narrowcasting) only makes sense with an increase in the number of channels. Like television in the 1950s, AM network radio in the 1930s (and after) avoided programming that appealed only to particular cultural groups. In a city as large as Chicago, the rise of the networks did not entirely drive out ethnic, religious, and labor programming, which remained on some local stations, but the balance shifted toward more standardized mass entertainment.

During the 1930s, the networks extended their reach through the country. The NBC-Red, NBC-Blue, and CBS networks grew from 21 percent to 38 percent of all stations, but these numbers understate the true picture. NBC and CBS had nearly all of the high-powered stations, accounting for more than 85 percent of the nation's nighttime wattage. In 1934, independent broadcasters created a fourth national network, the Mutual Broadcasting System, which grew to include a large number of mostly low-power stations, lagging far behind the leaders in total wattage and audience share. Partly in response to Mutual, NBC and CBS tightened their control of affiliated stations, requiring them to sign five-year (instead of one-year) affiliation contracts that excluded the use of programming from any other network. The basic problem facing Mutual was the difficulty of gaining access to key cities in the country where all the existing stations were controlled by NBC and CBS. Less than fifty of the ninety-two cities with more than 100,000 people had three or more full-time stations, even including low-power local outlets.[27] The shortage of stations in major metropolitan areas was the key factor preventing additional networks from forming—and the underlying reason for the emphasis on lowest-common-denominator mass entertainment rather than more diverse programming for particular cultural groups.

Competing for the broad consumer market and the largest number of listeners, the networks tried to keep off the air anything controversial or potentially offensive to conventional values and tastes. Combined with the FCC's regulation by raised eyebrow, the moral regulation by networks and sponsors sharply restricted the range of subjects and ideas on the air. By the 1930s, for example, advocates of birth control were able to publish their views, but they couldn't get on radio. In 1936, surveying censorship by radio stations, the ACLU found, "Radicals, liberals and even the Republican Party have suffered. Minority political parties, doctors seeking to warn the public of syphilis, trade unions and opponents of lynching have all felt the censor's hand." As in the movies, censorship extended even to the slightly suggestive or profane. Cole Porter's "Let's Put Out the Lights and Go to Bed" became "Let's Put Out the Lights and Go to Sleep." A Philadelphia station cut a general off the air for using the word "hell" when describing an episode of combat for which he had received the Congressional Medal of Honor.[28]

For black Americans, the restrictive regime of the radio networks had especially serious consequences. The networks did not employ blacks during the 1930s in any capacity—not as announcers or commentators, not as executives, not even as technicians. Black performers, particularly musicians, had some limited success in the mid-1920s when local stations, particularly in New York and Chicago, began to broadcast jazz. But as the networks gained sway, blacks lost ground, though not for lack of listener interest in the music and culture of black America. By the late 1920s, jazz found a receptive mass audience on the air, but the vocalists and bands that the networks featured were typically white. The first weekly series on national radio to become a huge popular hit was *Amos 'n' Andy*, a broadcast version of the old blackface minstrel show, in which two white entertainers, using exaggerated Negro dialect, portrayed a pair of hapless southern blacks who had moved to Chicago. During the 1930s, as radio moved to more emphasis on narrative forms, such as soap operas, mysteries, and westerns, blacks found it difficult to get any regular parts; even the few black roles usually went to white actors. (Amazingly, when Quaker Oats put "Aunt Jemima" on the air in a morning series, a white actress played the part.) Some network programs had black performers as guests, but except for a show that Louis Armstrong had on CBS for thirteen weeks in 1937 and a Sunday morning program of gospel music on NBC, the networks avoided featuring African Americans as hosts or stars. Breakthroughs for blacks came at the local level. Beginning in the late 1920s, Jack Cooper—a black journalist who covered entertainment for the *Chicago Defender*—rented time on a low-power Chicago station for a variety show called *The All-Negro Hour.* The networks during the 1930s didn't showcase black talent for fear of alienating southern station affiliates, and advertisers did not want to sponsor such shows, much less pay African American performers for product endorsements, for fear of having their brands associated with blacks.[29]

Given their economic position, blacks had little leverage with the networks. In 1930, when 45.8 percent of American homes had radios, the proportion of black households with radios stood at 14.4 percent in cities and just .03 percent in rural areas. By 1940, the rate of radio ownership in black households was up to 43.4 percent—almost exactly half the white rate—but the pervasive poverty in the black community still limited its appeal to business as a consumer market. Blacks literally had no ownership of radio; not a single radio station, network-affiliated or independent, was black-owned during the 1930s. To make matters worse, the American Federation of Musicians had segregated locals, and the white locals controlled the jobs in network radio. The problem had a political as well as an economic dimension. The black community mounted a protest against *Amos 'n' Andy* as a demeaning portrayal of African American life, but the campaign was unable to gain any wider public or political support. The networks studiously avoided addressing race itself; network news and public affairs programs during the 1930s regarded the subject of racial discrimination as taboo. Just as the Democratic Party sought to maintain support from southern white voters by ignoring the problems of race, so the national radio networks steered clear of racial issues to keep the support of southern stations and listeners. Advocates of racial integration had a few symbolic victories on radio in the late 1930s, but the emergence of radio as a force breaking down racial barriers and as a means of communication in the black community itself would wait until after World War II.[30]

Politics and the New Public Sphere

The limitations of broadcasting as a means of free expression had potentially ominous implications for democratic politics. The traditional theory of republican government hadn't only guaranteed freedom of the press—it had assumed the centrality of the press as a medium of political communication. There were two distinct sources of difficulty in translating that theory from print to broadcasting. First, the scarcity of spectrum provided a rationale for subjecting the airwaves to far greater government control than the print media; in none of the liberal democracies did broadcasters enjoy the same autonomy that the press did. And second, whether ownership of stations and networks was private, as in America, or governmental, as elsewhere, control of radio was far more heavily concentrated than was control of the press. Together, these two features posed a risk that even in countries with free elections, people in power would use their sway over the command centers of broadcasting to deny the opposition an equal opportunity to disseminate its views and compete for votes.

Radio, however, also fit certain tendencies that were already under way in election campaigning, at least in the United States. As Michael McGerr has shown, the late nineteenth century saw a decline of political spectacle—torchlight processions and other forms of participatory political display—in favor of two alternatives: campaigns of education and campaigns based on the techniques of modern advertising. Political advertising was already central in the McKinley-Bryan election of 1896, and it dominated Wilson's reelection campaign in 1916 and his propaganda effort during World War I. Another key aspect of the new political style that emerged in this period was a more active role for individual candidates. Instead of running "front-porch" campaigns, for example, presidential candidates were increasingly expected to tour the country to give speeches and generate local news coverage. Often they traveled by rail, speaking at stops to local crowds. Franklin Roosevelt, who was the vice presidential candidate on the Democratic ticket in 1920 (before he was stricken with polio), said that the Democrats needed to run a "strenuous" campaign around the country to reach the voters because the newspapers were overwhelmingly Republican. Not just candidates, but presidents themselves, beginning with Theodore Roosevelt, devoted far more time to public speeches than their predecessors had during the nineteenth century. In short, even before broadcasting emerged, political advertising and the personal focus on candidates were already well established, and national leaders were increasingly using the spoken, not just the written, word to communicate with the public. Broadcasting did not inaugurate these changes, but it helped to bring them to full development.[31]

These tendencies added to the challenge to democracy posed by broadcasting. Radio advertising was expensive. What rules would govern political advertising on the air and the financial relationships that would emerge between parties and radio networks? And what might prevent a politician—an extremist on the left or right or even a member of one of the traditional parties—from using radio to manipulate public opinion and suppress opposition? The American response to these questions came through the development of special legal requirements and informal rules for regulating political access to radio that did not apply to the press or any other medium.

The legal requirements concerned candidates for public office. American law did not generally treat broadcasters as common carriers—that is, broadcasters were not obliged, as were telephone companies, to carry the messages of anyone willing and able to pay. Only during political campaigns did the law make radio a common carrier, and even then the broadcasters' obligations were limited. In the campaign-related provisions of the 1927 Radio Act and the 1934 Communications Act, Congress carefully required stations to "afford equal opportunities" to opposing candidates, not to provide them with free airtime. Indeed, the law did not require stations to provide any time at all to campaigns; it merely said that if they aired one candidate's message, they had to afford equal opportunities to other legally qualified candidates for the same office. Although some stations decided against running any campaign messages, most offered time to candidates at the same rates they charged commercial advertisers. During the early 1930s, some members of Congress sought to expand this provision by requiring stations to afford equal opportunities to opposing sides in public controversies (an anticipation of what later came to be called the "fairness doctrine"). But before the 1940s, neither the Congress nor the regulatory officials imposed any formal requirements for fairness beyond the "equal opportunities" that the law guaranteed candidates.[32]

Federal law also barred broadcasters from censoring what candidates said on the air, but this requirement put radio stations in a difficult position. In 1930, the owner of station KVEP in Oregon lost his license after broadcasting a speech by a political candidate who charged that his opponent was a "sodomite." According to the FRC, the mere "imputation of immorality" was obscene and a threat to the "sanctity of home life," and the station owner was responsible because he had failed to prevent it. That same year, a Nebraska court held a station liable for a candidate's slander of another politician during a campaign speech on the radio. Broadcasters argued that if Congress was going to bar them from censoring candidates, it ought to give them immunity from prosecution for the words the politicians used. But although the stations were unable to get immunity, they did not close the airwaves to campaign debate. Some politicians, however, were abruptly cut off the air when they made statements that station managers thought potentially libelous.[33] Thus, broadcasters' liability may have indirectly inhibited harshly personal campaigning on the radio.

Informally, even before the Radio Act of 1927, American broadcasters began to work out a set of rules for political access to the airwaves that virtually amounted to a system of private regulation of politics. The key element was a distinction between speech that was news (to be covered at the expense of the broadcaster) and speech that was advertising (to be paid for by the candidate or party). Broadcasters themselves decided what fell into each category, though parties sometimes contested the decisions. Beginning with the 1924 presidential election, the major national broadcasters offered free coverage of national party conventions and certain other events that they deemed newsworthy, while charging for other political broadcasts. They also adopted the practice of giving equal treatment to the two major parties, while devoting much less attention to third parties and other groups. Broadcasters opposed any legal requirement of free airtime for candidates, partly out of concern that it would force them to open the airwaves to radicals and fringe candidates. Political advertising didn't only generate revenue for broadcasters; it also enabled the two major parties to dominate the air because they were best able to pay for it. Federal law did make it possible for radical parties to purchase some network time; in 1936, for example, the Communist Party bought 4 percent of the political advertising on NBC. By requiring payment for most political messages, however, broadcasters could comply with the legal requirement to treat all candidates for the same office equally, while effectively marginalizing radicals whom they did not want to put on the air.[34]

By the late 1920s, Republicans and Democrats were spending as much as a fifth of their campaign budgets on radio and, in the process, becoming heavily dependent on the networks for credit. After the 1928 election, when they spent a combined total of more than $1 million on radio advertising, both parties ended up with debts they were unable to pay off for several years. The same thing happened in 1932; in fact, going into the 1936 election, the Democrats had still not paid off their debts to NBC and CBS from four years earlier. Ordinarily, the networks insisted on immediate payment by advertisers, but they extended long-term credit to the two major parties without charging interest, a favor not generally extended to others. The parties' indebtedness may actually have been to the broadcasters' advantage. Although the Republicans and Democrats may not have paid their bills promptly in 1932, they more than paid back the broadcasters in the Communications Act they passed two years later. The parties and networks needed each others' good will. In internal NBC correspondence in 1940, the executive who had been in charge of political broadcasting for fourteen years cautioned against "putting the screws on" the parties: "We must not lose sight of the fact that we have been very fortunate in radio in getting away with the selling of time for presidential candidates. We might awaken some morning and find that we are going to have to *give* time to national campaigns, instead of selling it."[35]

While legally bound to give candidates "equal opportunities" during campaigns, broadcasters tended to favor incumbents at other times. As newsmakers, often with authoritative information, public officials legitimately command attention even from an independent press with constitutional protections. The dependence of radio on government regulation reinforced this tendency to give those in power a preponderant role in public discussion. The incumbent bias in radio particularly benefited the party in control of the White House—Republicans until 1933, Democrats for the twenty years afterward. When presidents and other high administration officials wanted airtime, they were usually able to get it without charge. The advantage that presidents enjoyed from radio also depended, however, on their own skill with the new medium and their grasp of its possibilities. Coolidge, who came across more effectively on radio than in person, was the first president to use it to political advantage. Hoover went on air twice as much as his predecessor, but his radio appearances, like Coolidge's, consisted of speeches to public gatherings, not talks addressed specifically to radio listeners. Paley of CBS actually advised Hoover to give "exclusive radio talks to the whole Nation . . . from your study in the White House," but the suggestion fell on deaf ears.[36] Ironically, Hoover had little gift for the medium he had done so much to shape, whereas Roosevelt, who did little to shape radio, knew instinctively how to use it.

Roosevelt's presidency saw "a revolution in the pattern of communication between Americans and their Chief Executive," Lawrence and Cornelia Levine observe in a recent study. In his "fireside chats," Roosevelt used a conversational style, straightforward language, and a personal form of address that encouraged listeners to feel that he was speaking directly to them. The talks averaged only twenty-six minutes, and the president gave relatively few of them—just thirty-one during his nearly twelve years in office. Radio perfectly fit Roosevelt's needs, helping him to conceal his paralysis and present himself as a powerful leader while conserving his energy. But during his first term, he was actually on the radio for less time than Hoover had been during his four years in office. By avoiding overexposure, Roosevelt made the chats national events, drawing not only immense audiences but also an avalanche of correspondence. "You are the first President to come into our homes; to make us feel you are working for us; to let us know what you are doing," a woman from Illinois wrote to him after the first of the fireside chats. "Until last night, to me, the President of the United States was merely a legend. . . . But you are real. I know your voice; what you are trying to do."[37]

The usual criticism of broadcasting is that it is a one-way medium that puts the listener in an isolated and passive position, but the fireside chats were not just a leader's monologue. Roosevelt's conversational style—and his actual words—invited response. While Hoover was president, the White House mailroom had been handling about 800 letters a day; under Roosevelt, it began receiving 8,000 daily, with peaks of 150,000. Even compared to other national crises, the volume was large; one study calculates that Lincoln received 44 letters per year per 10,000 literate adults during the Civil War; Wilson 47 during World War I; and Roosevelt, 160. Roosevelt's mail came predominantly from Americans of modest backgrounds—46 percent from laborers, according to an analysis of letters received over five days in March 1934. The president used the mail to gauge public opinion, and he instructed his staff to answer all of it. The letters afford a rare picture of radio from the listeners' perspective. The Levines note that "the majority of listeners heard the Fireside Chats not in isolation but as part of groups, large and small, . . . with families and friends at home; in churches and synagogues; in offices, hotel lobbies, and movie theaters, in barracks and camps; in the streets and in parks." And rather than inculcating passivity, radio tended "to stimulate audiences to thought and action, and to give a sense of participation and inclusion—often for the first time in their political lives."[38]

Radio served as a great equalizer for a Democratic president. The Republicans' political ascendancy during the preceding decades had been matched by their ascendancy in the press, although Roosevelt's estimates that Republicans controlled 85 percent of newspapers exaggerated the picture. (In 1936, the Republican Alf Landon received 57 percent of newspaper endorsements, Roosevelt 36 percent.) A study of the 1940 presidential campaign found each party's members favoring one medium: "In exposure, in congeniality of ideas, in trust, and in influence—in all of these characteristics the Republicans inclined in favor of the newspaper and the Democrats in favor of the radio."[39] The networks provided airtime not just to Roosevelt but to his administration more generally. By the end of the decade, forty-two New Deal agencies were producing radio programs, often broadcast over the networks during their sustaining time. Many of these programs were informational, such as "Help Yourself to Health" from the Public Health Service, but others were aimed at shaping political sentiment. A twenty-six-part series broadcast on CBS, "Americans All—Immigrants All," underwritten by the U.S. Office of Education in the Department of Interior, sought to increase tolerance by highlighting the positive contributions to American history by the nation's ethnic groups, including African Americans and Jews.[40]

But although Roosevelt benefited tremendously from radio as a medium and from the cooperation of the networks, the president and his administration were not in a position to monopolize the air. The networks gave free time to congressional Republicans and conservative groups, such as America First, that opposed Roosevelt. The Ford Motor Company and other corporations sponsored programs that included attacks on the New Deal, and the news commentators on the air included conservatives as well as liberals. The Republicans outspent Democrats in radio advertising during the campaigns of the 1930s. And Senator Huey P. Long and Father Charles E. Coughlin—the "radio priest"—were able to use the airwaves to build political movements that seriously threatened Roosevelt during his first term. In April 1931, CBS had refused to renew a contract with Father Coughlin, but he had created his own ad hoc network, including more than thirty stations covering most of the country—though radio stations finally closed off the airwaves to Coughlin in 1940 after he turned openly anti-Semitic and sympathetic to the Nazis.[41]

Constrained though American radio was, it offered a far greater diversity of political opinion than was available in Europe at the time. The BBC during the interwar period severely restricted political debate. Before elections, it meted out equal time for speeches to the major parties, but only the official representatives of parties with seats in Parliament were able to get on the air. Under those rules, the BBC not only banned the Scottish and Welsh nationalists but also kept Winston Churchill off the radio when he was out of power in his own party. French radio offered even less to the political opposition. Before an election in 1932, for example, the opposition leader was allowed just one broadcast speech amid a torrent of radio addresses by the governing party. And in Germany, even before the Nazi takeover radio was entirely the creature of the government. Hitler did not use radio to gain support because the state didn't allow him on the air; then, after he seized power, radio became wholly an instrument of Nazi propaganda. The use of radio by the state as a means of controlling public opinion was so widespread that a survey in 1932 concluded, "American private broadcasting gives a more hospitable welcome to contending and contradictory schools of political and economic thought than any other broadcasting known at present to the world." Ironically, European governmental broadcasting was doing more for "man as home student," while American radio was doing more for "man as active citizen."[42]

Networks and News

In fact, American radio in the early 1930s wasn't doing all that much for active citizenship. The networks at that time emphasized entertainment above all else and devoted little investment or airtime to news and public affairs. By 1932, however, radio was showing signs of its potential as a news medium. In March that year, the kidnapping of the baby of Charles and Anne Morrow Lindbergh set off a frenzy of radio coverage, and on election night in November the networks beat the newspapers in reporting Roosevelt's victory. As CBS began building a news department, alarm spread in the newspaper industry. Already hit by declining circulation and revenue with the deepening of the Depression, many publishers worried that radio would siphon off more of their readers and advertisers, and early in 1933 the American Newspaper Publishers Association and major wire services, including the Associated Press, resolved to stop selling news bulletins to broadcasters. So began what came to be called the press-radio war. As debate over the Communications Act developed, the last thing the networks wanted was to have the press line up with the advocates of non-profit broadcasting in support of restrictions on radio advertising. Knuckling under, NBC and CBS disavowed any intention of building up news divisions and accepted a set of rules known as the Biltmore agreement, dictated by the publishers in December 1933. The networks agreed to provide only two five-minute newscasts a day, one late enough in the morning and the other late enough in the evening so as not to undercut the sales of either morning or evening papers. All radio news would have to be at least twenty-four hours old, no single item could be longer than thirty words, a single combined wire service bureau would supply all items, and every broadcast would end with the words, "For further details, consult your local newspaper." The agreement symbolized network radio's early indifference to journalism.[43]

Needless to say, the newspaper industry's attempt to strangle broadcast news in its cradle didn't succeed. Although the networks were powerful, they did not control radio in its entirety, and independent stations continued newscasts. The publishers were powerful, but not powerful enough to prevent the startup of new wire services specifically for radio stations or to keep the two smaller rivals of the Associated Press from breaking ranks and selling bulletins to broadcasters. Once Congress passed the Communications Act in 1934, broadcasters also did not have to worry about the political clout of the press. Soon the networks were ignoring any limitations on the news they could break. During the mid-1930s, however, the networks primarily featured news commentators rather than original news reporting. It was only toward the end of the decade that broadcast journalism came into its own—and when it did, it set off a new round of conflict about the power of the networks.

The emergence of broadcast journalism in the late 1930s reflected a more general coming-of-age of the medium. As the critics of American radio saw it, the networks were "shackled" to advertisers, but there was one area where the networks did not face the usual incentives: the sustaining programs provided to affiliates to fill unsold time. While the networks made their money off sponsored programs, they also competed for cultural distinction and social cachet; CBS enjoyed great success in these efforts, perhaps more than it deserved. During the late 1930s, the network began to use its sustaining time to experiment with new ideas and to offer programs of real substance and quality—original drama such as the Mercury Theater of the Air, directed by Orson Welles and John Houseman, and more extensive news coverage, including reports from Europe from a group of journalists hired by its European director, Edward R. Murrow.

CBS originally sent Murrow to London primarily to book European entertainment acts and to arrange for broadcasts of notable events. Shortwave transmission, though unreliable, now made it possible to broadcast live from European capitals. At first resistant to devoting airtime to news reports, the CBS hierarchy gave way in the face of two developments in 1938—Hitler's annexation of Austria in March and the Munich crisis in September—which led to a surge of American interest in European news. On March 13, immediately after the Germans marched into Vienna, CBS provided its first *World News Roundup,* taking its listeners on a tour of key cities where reporters, soon to be household names, recounted the latest developments. An even bigger turning point came with the Munich crisis in September, when the networks issued frequent flash reports from Europe and radio commentators played a leading role in making sense of breaking developments as Britain and France capitulated to Hitler's demands in Czechoslavakia. On CBS, H.V. Kaltenborn made eighty-five broadcasts in eighteen days; later, he described radio itself as "one of the most significant events of the crisis." A poll in October 1938 found that by a margin of three to one, Americans said they were "more interested" in radio news than in newspaper reports of the crisis.[44] The sudden preoccupation with urgent news on the air invited dramatic invention. Only weeks after the Munich crisis, on the eve of Halloween, Welles created a sensation with a production of *The War of the Worlds* in which listeners heard a supposed news bulletin reporting that Martians had landed in New Jersey. The vast majority of listeners knew it was theater, but even so, according to a study of the response, the broadcast frightened roughly a million people—the panic indirectly testifying to the increased importance of broadcast news and the edginess so many felt in the midst of international crisis.[45]

Broadcast news became more important partly because radio itself was becoming pervasive. The proportion of households with radios rose from 65 percent in 1934 to 81 percent in 1940, and a rising proportion of new cars had radios. The radio was a fixture in bars, clubs, and other public venues. Six out of ten people reported listening regularly to radio newscasts, according to an April 1939 survey that excluded the South (and therefore probably overstated the proportion for the nation as a whole). The lower the education and socioeconomic status of respondents, the greater was the preference for radio over newspapers as a source of news. Other surveys show that, by September 1939, Americans were about equally likely to identify radio or newspapers as the source of most of their news—but that by December 1941 far more people relied on radio. The great advantage of radio was its immediacy, and in dire times that advantage propelled broadcast news ahead of the press.[46]

Popular attention to broadcast journalism, however, intensified a long-simmering conflict over its role. The news commentators on the air frequently received warnings from both their sponsors and the networks to tone down their views and present themselves as objective analysts. When war broke out in Europe in September 1939, CBS insisted that its reporters' voices be as neutral as the network's policy toward the belligerents. But even though the "Murrow boys" adopted a sober, factual tone, their sympathy for the Allies was unmistakable. During the Blitz, despite the misgivings of CBS brass, Murrow took his microphone to rooftops and streets to let Americans hear the sounds of war and stories of ordinary Britons' quiet endurance. "You burned the city of London in our houses and we felt the flames that burned it," the poet Archibald MacLeish later said at a dinner honoring Murrow. "You laid the dead of London at our doors and we knew the dead were ours—were all men's dead." But what to many Americans seemed a journalism of heroic proportions seemed to others to be propaganda aimed at getting the United States to enter the fighting. And it wasn't only the isolationists who demanded neutrality from broadcast news. The broadcast industry shared the premise that radio journalists should not take sides. "Since the number of broadcasting channels is limited, news broadcasts shall not be editorial," the NAB declared in its code of ethics in 1939.[47]

The FCC had long looked askance at "propaganda" stations, and in a licensing decision in May 1941, the commission declared that "the broadcaster cannot be an advocate." The case involved a challenge by a company called Mayflower Broadcasting to the renewal of a license for Boston station WAAB, whose management had aired editorials that, according to some testimony, attacked local politicians unfairly. The FCC did not take away WAAB's license—by the time the FCC heard the case, the station had abandoned editorials altogether. In its ruling, however, the regulatory agency went beyond its earlier policies by declaring that radio stations could not broadcast their own editorials at all. The ruling did not bar the expression of opinion by individuals on the air, such as radio commentators who spoke for themselves. The idea was that, unlike the press, which had a categorical right to advocate a particular viewpoint, broadcasting stations could best serve democracy by remaining open to competing views: "Freedom of speech on the radio must be broad enough to provide full and equal opportunity for the presentation to the public of all sides of public issues." The FCC would renounce its ban on station editorials in 1949 when it adopted the Fairness Doctrine (which would require stations both to broadcast controversial news and public-affairs programs and to offer reply-time to people who disagreed with management's views). The Mayflower decision proved the FCC's first, unsteady step as it attempted to work out an alternative model of free speech for broadcasting.[48] In a key case in 1939, the Supreme Court defined certain kinds of public property (parks, streets, and so on) as a public forum where government authorities had to accommodate the widest possible freedom of expression.[49] Although the Court did not extend the public-forum model to the airwaves, the FCC effectively did so by calling on broadcasters to make their stations available to a diversity of voices rather than simply using them as a platform for their own. James Lawrence Fly, the New Dealer whom Roosevelt appointed as chairman of the FCC in 1939, wrote that "if printing presses were few and their output severely limited, a democratic society could not allow small groups of owners unlimited discretion as to what is and what is not printed." Scarcity of channels, in other words, required a model of free expression and public discussion based not on the rights of the channel owner, but on the rights of the listeners (or later viewers) to hear different points of view.[50]

The effort by federal regulators to assure a diversity of voices on the air was also evident in an unprecedented series of FCC measures aimed at opening network radio to greater competition. During Roosevelt's second term, the New Deal had entered a new phase with a revival of antitrust enforcement, and the FCC reflected this turn. In 1941, culminating a three-year investigation into "chain broadcasting," the FCC concluded that the control exerted by the networks was not only anticompetitive but also inimical to a "free radio system." America, the commission said, had rejected government ownership of radio because "the power inherent in control over broadcasting is too great and too dangerous to the maintenance of free institutions to permit its exercise by one body, even though elected by or responsible to the whole people." But in avoiding one danger, the commission continued, "we must not fall into an even more dangerous pitfall: the concentration of power in the hands of self-perpetuating management groups."[51]

Taking aim particularly at RCA—which owned both the Red and Blue NBC networks as well as more than one station in each of several major metropolitan areas—the FCC ruled that it was against the public interest for any organization to own more than one network and for any network to own more than one station in an area. Although the commission did not set a numerical cap on the number of stations a network could own in the nation as a whole, it also ruled that no license be given to a network for a station in any area where the stations were so few or unequal that the network's acquisition of an outlet would "substantially" restrict competition. These rulings effectively barred the networks from assuming direct ownership of all but a few radio stations. The commission also sought to loosen the hold of the networks over their affiliates. Under the FCC's new rules, networks could not require stations to enter into affiliation contracts longer than a year or prevent them from taking programs offered by other networks. The FCC's concern was that networks enjoyed so much power over stations that they were not only blocking new networks from developing but also preventing stations from serving the interests of their local communities. In 1943, the Supreme Court would uphold the FCC's orders, and NBC would be forced to sell off its less profitable Blue network to the new American Broadcasting Company (ABC).[52]

Some critics and historians belittle the significance of the chain broadcasting rules, noting, for example, that the proportion of radio stations with network affiliations rose to 95 percent by 1945. But the FCC's purpose was not to discourage the growth of networks; the commission recognized that network affiliation was essential to profitable operation of stations. The rules aimed to increase competition among networks and to give local stations some independence—in short, to deny NBC and CBS the nearly complete dominion over radio they had previously enjoyed. This was an extension of the long-standing American checks-and-balances model of democratic communications, and it was not entirely unavailing.

In 1941, the sociologist Paul Lazarsfeld took note of the division of power between the broadcasting industry and a New Deal agency "with its well-known progressive tendencies." Radio, he wrote, "is probably at this moment the most neutral and fairest institution in the country. The businessmen who own it and the civil servants who watch over it balance each other very well." Lazarsfeld was attempting to explain why radio had "so far been a conservative force in American life" in the sense that it had not greatly altered public opinion, at least according to his own research.[53] From the outset, broadcasting had the effect of concentrating media power in America far more than it had ever been before. The belated New Deal in broadcasting attempted only to restrain that tendency. There was no possibility of reversing it.

Was American radio the censored and homogeneous medium its critics portrayed, or did it exemplify American free enterprise and liberty as its defenders claimed? As the United States stood on the verge of entering World War II, the picture looked different depending on the point of comparison. Relative to the press in the United States, American broadcasting was more centralized, more subject to government control, less diverse, and less open to ideological contention. But the opposite was true if the comparison was to broadcasting in Europe; from that perspective, American radio seemed decentralized, free of government censorship, and more diverse, competitive, and contentious. But if national policy had been different during radio's constitutive phase in the 1920s, American broadcasting might have been more pluralistic from the outset—or for that matter, more monopolistic. As two new media technologies took shape in the 1930s and 1940s, these issues arose anew.

In 1933, the radio inventor Edwin Howard Armstrong patented a new system for radio called "frequency modulation" (FM). Armstrong initially had the support of RCA in his field tests, which showed FM to be dramatically superior to AM. FM virtually eliminated static and provided a wider range of sound. As a result, the new system could have provided the technological basis not only for improved service but also for an expanded number of stations—in other words, for greater competition and diversity in radio. Armstrong himself expected that because of its superiority, FM would replace AM. But in April 1935, RCA suddenly abandoned support for Armstrong's work while announcing a major investment in another technology—television. The following years proved difficult for Armstrong, who became convinced that RCA was attempting to "sabotage" his invention by disparaging it and lobbying the FCC against it. There was probably some truth in his accusations; Sarnoff, RCA's president, saw television as the future and regarded FM as a rival for available spectrum as well as investment capital. Far from promising to improve RCA's profits, FM threatened to make many of its patents obsolete and to undermine the position of its NBC subsidiary as the dominant radio network.[54]

Nonetheless, in 1936 Armstrong was able to get the FCC to allocate sufficient bandwidth for four experimental FM channels, and four years later—with the strong backing of its antimonopolist New Deal chairman—the commission authorized commercial development of FM in a band wide enough for forty channels, including five reserved for educational stations (as the nonprofit broadcasters had long demanded for AM). The commission authorized sixty-seven FM stations by the time the United States entered the war and suspended development; later, in 1945, the FCC would kick FM "upstairs" to a new band, making the early FM equipment obsolete but providing room for many more FM channels. The usual story about the long-delayed development of FM radio—it floundered for decades, until finally taking off in the late 1960s—is Armstrong's tale of a conspiracy between big business and bureaucracy, but the case for collusion doesn't withstand close analysis.[55] The chief reasons for FM's delayed success were the twin difficulties of introducing an alternative radio technology when AM was already well-entrenched and of obtaining spectrum and investment capital at the same time as television. To be sure, if policy makers had given high enough priority to greater diversity in radio, FM offered the technological basis for achieving it. FM was radio's "second chance," but for decades it was a missed opportunity.

Television also stalled during the late 1930s, but for a different reason: the specter of monopoly. The FCC and much of the radio industry feared that a single company was positioning itself to dominate the new industry. With its healthy profits from radio and other businesses, RCA was able to make an investment in television research that gave it an overwhelming technological edge. In a key move, Sarnoff had hired the Russian refugee Vladimir Zworykin, who built on the invention of electrical scanning by his mentor in St. Petersburg, Boris Rosing. Zworykin's work, along with Philo T. Farnsworth's image dissector (which RCA had to license), provided the basis for a fully electronic television system. But when RCA was ready to roll out television commercially, it met sharp resistance from its competitors and the FCC over the architecture for the medium. Television wouldn't work unless both transmitters and receivers were synchronized for the same number of lines and picture frames per second. While RCA's system called for 441 scanning lines and 30 frames per second, its rivals were using other standards, and repeated attempts to achieve a technical consensus were unsuccessful.

Averse to giving a monopoly to RCA, the FCC repeatedly deferred a final decision about commercialization, allowing RCA to operate television only on an experimental basis. In countries where monopoly power wasn't an issue—as in Germany and Britain—television was able to proceed more easily during the 1930s. The Nazi government began the first regular public television service in Berlin in March 1935, and by the late 1930s, the BBC had regular telecasts. In this case, the Europeans were running ahead, while the attempt to provide for competition—and to avoid a repeat of the earlier commercial debacle with television in the 1920s—held back American development.[56]

After World War II, of course, television would take off in the United States, but there was a remarkable continuity in institutional structure with radio. Early regulatory decisions had led to domination of radio by NBC and CBS. Now, too, early decisions about the spectrum available to television would create a shortage of channels in major urban areas and again lead to domination by NBC and CBS, with ABC emerging more slowly as the third network. Once more, a network oligopoly would usher in a long era of lowest-common-denominator mass entertainment. Different decisions about the spectrum at the outset (and later about community-antenna television, now known as cable) could have produced additional television networks, but policy makers long failed to exploit the possibilities.[57]

As so often had been the case in communications, the path of development was not easily diverted from familiar channels. In both Europe and America, the predominant pattern in broadcasting was the persistence of early constitutive choices—whether those choices concerned the role of the state and private enterprise, freedom of expression, or the extent of diversity. Change would come, but it would come slowly. Even today much of the system of power established by early decisions remains with us—and the media world those decisions helped to create is now ubiquitous and inescapable.

CHAPTER TWELVE

Coda

The Advent of the Media

BY THE late 1920s, the media in America and other advanced societies formed a new constellation of power. At its center was an array of large organizations dominating communication in print, on the screen, and in the air, while the constellation's most brilliant lights—movie stars, radio personalities, influential columnists and commentators, and other luminaries—were visible to a vast public, national in scope. The press had long been a force to be reckoned with; now the motion pictures, broadcasting, and allied entertainment and advertising industries represented additional channels of influence.

What was new, however, was not simply the plurality of media, nor even their mass character. The media were increasingly a source of wealth, and power relations had accordingly changed in the United States and to some extent in other liberal democracies. In the eighteenth and early nineteenth centuries, the press depended on governments and political parties for subsidy; it was only with the growth of advertising and circulation in the mid- to late 1800s that newspapers were able to become formidable institutions in their own right apart from politics. Radio and the motion pictures had also emerged as sources of wealth and fame. Now, moreover, the modes of political communication had changed, and parties and politicians increasingly depended on independently financed media for access to the public's eyes and ears. Indeed, in the United

States, where the private broadcast networks in the 1930s extended interest-free, long-term credit to the two major parties to buy political advertising, the subsidy relationship had even been reversed.

The ability of the media to exert a force of their own depended on both their autonomy from state control and their commercial independence. In both these respects, America had provided especially fertile ground for their development, and as a phenomenon of power the media were more fully advanced in the United States than anywhere else: a potent but still decentralized press, practicing a brand of aggressive, often sensational journalism; a movie business concentrated in a handful of companies that dominated screens abroad as well as at home; and the world's only significant commercial broadcast industry, with hundreds of local stations and two national network organizations. These institutions were the harbingers of a new era when the media were an independent factor in politics—no less important, for example, than the political parties that had once held sway over many of them. Reporting a president's State of the Union address, for example, journalists by the early 1900s were far more likely than their nineteenth-century predecessors to assume the role of independent interpreters of politics and provide their own analyses of the speech's significance.[1] Syndicated political columnists began to appear in the 1920s, and some of the most influential newspaper columnists doubled as radio commentators, commanding a larger audience on a regular basis than any political figure, except possibly the president.

The media had also become a phenomenon of power in another sense. Their reach through space and time was far greater than ever before. In a sense, they had fulfilled the democratic hope of universal access so well that they were developing into a nearly ubiquitous aspect of daily experience. Cultural forms that had once been hard to acquire were becoming hard to escape. The change had begun, if not with printing itself, then with the revolution of cheap print and the growth of penny newspapers, dime novels, and other throwaway reading matter available for quick scanning on the go. The printed word also became part of the built environment as signs, electric lights, and advertising billboards went up in nineteenth-century cities. A similar process then happened with the environment of sound. The phonograph, radio, and the talkies reshaped aural experience. Broadcasting invaded the routines of daily life at home, at work, in private automobiles, and in public places as a growing majority of people listened to the radio for hours every day—an average of more than four hours daily in the United States, according to several studies during the 1930s. Particularly after the rise of the networks, radio brought professional entertainment, advertising jingles, news from abroad, and the voices of political leaders directly into the home. Playing at all hours of day and night, Susan Douglas writes, radio "made music a more integral, structuring part of everyday life and individual identity."[2] As in other areas, easy access bred a continual taste for novelty; melodies became familiar so much more quickly than before that the average lifetime of a popular song was now measured in months instead of years.

The plenitude of popular media ratcheted up the competition for eyes and ears. Banner headlines in American papers had begun to scream in the 1890s, and now tabloid newspapers—in Britain beginning with the *Daily Mirror* in 1903 and in the United States with New York's *Daily News* in 1919—exemplified the media's frenzied quest for attention.[3] By the early 1930s, advertising men were already saying that the public had become saturated with messages and that effective advertising consequently needed to be more emphatic and intrusive.

At the same time, communications continued to be a factor in economic growth and military power. Broader access to telecommunications, more advanced long-distance networks, more rapid diffusion of innovation in communication technologies and products—these were sources of economic and strategic advantage. Both wired and wireless networks connected buyers and sellers, facilitating their transactions and enabling them to operate more efficiently. In the military, advances in radio were critical at first for naval operations and then more generally enhanced command-and-control of mobile units. World War I highlighted the vital importance of both communications infrastructure and mass media. The belligerents struggled over control of submarine cables and radiotelegraphy, invested in new radio technology, and conscripted the mass media into propaganda campaigns to mobilize patriotism at home and demoralize the enemy abroad. The manipulation of the press, the creation of false newsreel footage, and the intensive use of advertising during the war left a sense of disgust afterward, but the war experience also sharpened critical awareness of the media's role in what Walter Lippmann in 1920 called "the manufacture of consent."[4] The explosion of radio during the following decade reinforced this growing awareness of media power.

The reach and pervasiveness of the mass media, as well as the economic and military value of communications networks and technologies, made constitutive choices about them all the more important. In the 1930s, the world was witness to a stark contrast in political models of communications between the totalitarian and liberal worlds. The fascists in Germany and communists in Russia viewed the communications media as essential means for extending the power of their regimes more comprehensively than was conceivable ever before. Totalitarian states differed from merely authoritarian ones in their capacity to reach into civil society, private life, and even (so they hoped) the interior of consciousness—and the modern media were a key aspect of this all-embracing form of rule.

The liberal democracies denied the state such complete control of communications, culture, and civil society, but the modern media nonetheless posed a dilemma for them as well. The traditional conceptions of liberal democracy had assumed and exalted a press that was not only free from state control but also at the service of public discussion, readily accessible to contending parties and interests. The technology and economics of the print media were compatible with the easy entry of diverse viewpoints into the public sphere. The new mass media, however, did not fit this model as well as the press did. They did not receive the same degree of protection from state supervision; control was more highly centralized; and advertising and mass marketing drove their content, particularly in the case of commercial radio in the United States. The origins of modern communications had been, in critical respects, liberal and democratic. How, then, had the media developed along lines that were so deeply in tension with those ideals? Could the mass media do the job that democracy classically assigned to the press—or did the commercially driven media and new techniques of mass persuasion so distort public knowledge and degrade public discussion as to make popular self-government impossible?

The Sources of Media Power

The structure of the media, I have been arguing, resulted from constitutive choices at key junctures that affected the long-run path of development of communications. From the seventeenth to the mid–twentieth century, these decisions were made in the context of three overarching realities: the primacy of the nation-state, the emergence of liberal constitutionalism, and the expansion of the reading public and other cultural markets. The power of the modern media is a byproduct of decisions made in the context of these developments as they played out in different societies.

National interests, as political leaders variously understood them, guided critical choices about communications, and differences among states—their structure, situation, and ideology—figured at key points in the constitutive process. Centralizing absolutist regimes in seventeenth-century Europe used communications to consolidate their power. They sought to control the press not only by censoring it but also by limiting it exclusively to printing guilds concentrated in the national capital. The earliest newspapers were typically court gazettes. While opening up postal systems to public use, state officials used postal monopolies to generate tax revenue, to regulate news reported in manuscript or print, and to conduct surveillance and espionage. In the nineteenth century, the continental European states also developed the electric telegraph as a state monopoly, conceiving it at first as a military technology and then treating it as an extension of postal functions. Britain's concern about coordinating its far-flung imperial interests led to a focused effort to build up international submarine cable networks under favored private companies. In the nineteenth century, as before, multilingual states in Europe required the use of an official language and suppressed the culture of national minorities, and many of those groups, in turn, sought to achieve national independence, partly through the cultivation of their own literature and establishment of their own media. The creation of national broadcast monopolies in the twentieth century reflected the same interest in configuring the public in the image of the nation. In short, interests in state- and nation-building were driving forces in development of the media, often leading to state monopolies or other direct state involvement.

The greater role of private enterprise in communications in the United States is partly attributable to the distinctive conditions of American political development. Military and other security-related concerns figured far less prominently in the constitutive decisions about communications in America from the founding of the republic to World War I. The geographical position of the United States offered protection from threatening foreign powers; immigrants came in great numbers, but they were so fragmented among themselves and had such strong incentives for assimilation that they posed no challenge to the primacy of English or prevailing patterns of cultural and political authority. When new communications technologies appeared, the government did not reserve them first for military use, and when foreign-language papers proliferated in the late nineteenth century, the government made no effort to control them.

Nonetheless, American decisions about communications did reflect an interest in nation-building of a particular kind. The early design of the Post Office as a comprehensive network for circulating political news as well as private correspondence reflected a deliberate effort to use communication to hold the new nation together. Law and policy in nineteenth-century America generally fostered an open, continent-wide, national market—and American postal and telecommunications development formed part of that project. America was not immune to security concerns. During the Civil War and World War I, the federal government restricted freedom of expression, and the World War I period also saw a demand for "100 percent" Americanism that departed from the earlier tolerance for immigrant cultures. In general, however, security interests were not the governing criteria in constitutive choices about communications. Postal confidentiality, the privatization of the telegraph, and the Navy's loss of control over policy toward radio after World War I all reflected this general tendency to give priority to private and commercial interests.

In both Europe and America, weak or divided state authority in the eighteenth century helped to incubate the earliest form of media power—an independent press. The absence of any strong central authority in the Netherlands created the basis in its commercial centers for a flourishing, export-oriented press and a de facto public sphere that extended into France through illicit circulation that royal authorities were unable to suppress. In England beginning in the 1690s, and in colonial America beginning in the 1720s and 1730s, divisions among political elites and the advent of competition in printing were both factors in the stirring of open public controversy and the beginnings of a free press. In the first instance, then, a public sphere and relatively autonomous press emerged from the breakdown of monopolies in both politics and markets—even before the press enjoyed any affirmative guarantee of its rights.

The emergence of liberal constitutionalism, however, institutionalized the autonomy of the press from the state and provided for important correlative protections. Liberal state-building involved the building-in of limitations on the state, not just the expansion of its functions, and these limitations gave a greater role to the press as an agent of public accountability. For example, the demand that not only trials, but also legislative sessions, be open to the public gave the press a right of access to certain kinds of political news. Even during the colonial period, these rights advanced further in America than in England itself. While the English press, after the end of licensing in 1695, enjoyed a limited freedom, the government used a combination of policies—high stamp taxes, prosecutions for seditious libel, and bribery and intimidation—to keep dissent in line and to prevent the emergence of a popularly based opposition press.

In contrast, the Revolutionary period in America, beginning with the resistance to the Stamp Act, created an alliance between patriots and printers that elevated freedom of the press to high symbolic importance and gave it a force in political tradition beyond its codification in the Bill of Rights and prevailing judicial interpretation. The Stamp Act resistance became the precedent for resisting and rejecting any special taxes on the press. Although newspapers routinely put their liberty into practice by vilifying public officials, postal policies were nonetheless designed to subsidize newspapers of all kinds without limit. In addition to these general subsidies, printers also received more selective benefits from their political sponsors in the form of government contracts. But the fragmented structure of the state—the division among the executive, legislative, and judicial branches, as well as federal, state, and local authority—prevented any single party from monopolizing subsidies and consolidating press power. Before 1860, when political subsidies were most important, frequent changes in party control of the presidency and houses of Congress led to high turnover in the newspapers enjoying special privileges. Unlike their counterparts in Paris and London, newspapers based in Washington were never able to gain a dominant position over newspapers outside the capital (for example, through local editions of national papers). The suspicion of centralized power that Americans embodied in governmental checks and balances carried over to the press and helped to keep it highly decentralized during its formative period in America.

Liberty of the press became the paradigm for claims of free expression through all means of communication, but governments did not necessarily extend the same protection to other media. Indeed, laws and norms regarding free expression have tended to be media-specific. Despite the end of licensing of the press, England long maintained prior censorship of the theater. Similarly, on both sides of the Atlantic, the new popular media of the early twentieth century—the motion pictures and broadcasting—did not receive the same autonomy as the press.

The history of freedom of expression looks different once this varied pattern is taken into account. According to the usual American narrative, the rights of free speech guaranteed in the Constitution went into a long legal twilight until the emergence of modern First Amendment jurisprudence on the Supreme Court in the 1920s. The twenties did represent a watershed in both the judicial and broader cultural understanding of free speech. But the nineteenth century was neither so grim nor the period after the 1920s so bright as this picture suggests. With certain well-known exceptions—the Sedition Act crisis in 1798, southern suppression of abolitionist literature, and Lincoln's control of war news and brief suspension of papers during the Civil War—the press in America enjoyed an exceptional degree of political autonomy throughout the period before World War I. Populist and socialist newspapers, for example, circulated freely. An important break occurred, however, with the growing use of the federal government's postal powers for purposes of moral censorship after 1865; the postal powers were also the basis for much of the political censorship during World War I. While court decisions began overturning censorship of both literature and political dissent during the 1920s and 1930s, they upheld censorship of the movies and radio. By this period, the pro-censorship groups previously concerned about indecent literature increasingly turned their attention to the movies and broadcasting; to some extent, the press enjoyed greater liberty after the 1920s because the focus of moral regulation turned toward media that seemed to many people, including judges, to be more dangerous.

The power of the media, however, has its roots not only in legal rights but also in commercial success, and the movies and broadcasting, like the press, became highly profitable industries in America. Commercial independence itself had a political basis; newspaper, magazine, and book publishing flourished in nineteenth-century America because the press was not only free but favored. The policies benefiting the press included postal subsidies, which enabled first newspapers and then magazines to reach more subscribers and thereby attract more advertising; intellectual property rights, which provided an incentive for investment in publishing (and later other media); and the absence of taxes on publications. The press also benefited indirectly from the early state support for roads, canals, and railroads, which promoted the development of a national market for print media, and federal as well as local support of education, which expanded the reading public. Innovations in printing and paper-making worked in the same direction—that is, making it profitable for entrepreneurs to adopt high-volume, low-price, mass-market publishing strategies, beginning with the penny press. Advertising was the key here as it enabled newspapers, magazines, and other media to be sold at a price below cost—in the case of radio programs, to be given to listeners at no price, in exchange for their attention.

Under these conditions, the American press and other media became more oriented than their European counterparts to a popular audience. Comparisons between American and European newspapers were already highlighting this contrast in the nineteenth century. American innovations in journalism and graphic design made American papers easier to read. The great urban newspapers of the late 1800s made more use of illustration, comic strips, and easily grasped narratives as they competed for a mass audience that included large numbers of immigrants.

The same orientation to a polyglot urban market later affected the motion pictures. The ethnic diversity of the movie audience in America's cities at the turn of the century required moviemakers to create films that could appeal across cultural boundaries. One of the reasons that American movie companies proved so successful in exporting films to Europe is that they had already figured out how to appeal to Europeans who had come to America. Entrepreneurial talent from immigrant communities also wrested control of the movie industry from the largely native-born Edison movie trust and proved more adept in responding to new tastes and business opportunities. In short, the American popular market and the diversity of the society helped to generate cultural enterprises enjoying competitive advantages over their international rivals.

Another aspect of American development contributed to comparative advantage in telecommunications and later broadcasting. American policy did not block single organizations from dominating the postal, telegraph, and telephone networks. But the United States consistently barred organizations controlling a dominant network from extending their power to a newly emerging one. Congress declined to give the Post Office permanent control of the telegraph in 1846. Western Union lost control of the telephone in 1879, and a federal antitrust suit forced AT&T to separate itself from Western Union in 1913. None of the foregoing was able to control broadcasting in America, although AT&T had the raw economic power to monopolize network radio in the 1920s. In other words, while allowing a high level of concentrated ownership within any mode of communications, American policy consistently favored "intermodal" competition. This was the checks-and-balances framework applied to restraining private power in communications.

The American bar against the expansion of legacy organizations contrasts sharply with the European policy of consolidating telegraph, telephone, and often broadcasting under the unified control of postal authorities. The significance of the European practice is not only that it put the government in control of all the major networks and sacrificed competition; it also put postal (and later telegraph) officials with little orientation to new technology in charge of more technically complex and dynamic networks. America's twentieth-century lead in telecommunications technology, especially long-distance land lines, stemmed largely from this difference. Similarly, despite the rise of network oligopolies in American broadcasting, talent in radio and later television had a variety of local as well as national outlets, whereas European states concentrated decision-making power in a single national broadcast authority and thereby discouraged competition and private investment in program production. As a result, when broadcast programming began to be exported, the ratings-driven, market-oriented, popular-minded American industry was far better positioned to seize opportunities for international expansion.[5]

Here, then, were the political origins of the power and wealth of the media as well as of the competitive edge of the communications industries in the United States: From the founding of the republic, the federal government had given the press constitutional guarantees, postal subsidies, and other benefits that enabled newspaper, book, and magazine publishing to become economically as well as formally independent of the state and political parties. Unlike the major European states, the United States privatized telecommunications, promoted communications development on a continental scale, and resisted any special tax on the media, from the eighteenth-century stamp taxes on the press to the twentieth-century radio (and later television) license fees that other countries imposed to support broadcasting. Under these conditions, the press, and later other media in America, became more popularly oriented than their counterparts in Europe, were driven to find ways of appealing to audiences that cut across cultural boundaries, and were positioned to become successful cultural exporters. The rise of a private, advertising-supported, and competitively driven broadcasting system was the culmination of the distinctive path of development that American communications had taken.

This was the American achievement—and the American dilemma—in communications. At its origins, liberal democracy cherished the press as a public guardian, little anticipating its metamorphosis into a powerful industry with its own imperatives. In the twentieth century, particularly in the aftermath of World War I and other developments that raised concerns about manipulation of public opinion, some critics began to ask how to reconcile democratic ideals with the media's power and limitations. The problem has never been entirely resolved—it never will be—but some productive efforts to address it emerged in the decades between the two world wars.

The Media and Democracy

The relationship between the commercial media and democracy has always had two sides. Commerce both distorts and enlarges the public sphere; the incentive to attract more readers, listeners, or viewers sometimes produces reckless sensationalism and sometimes engages new groups in public debate. In the nineteenth century, as newspapers became increasingly dependent on advertising, editors and publishers began to see their readers less as members of the polity and more as consumers; yet advertising revenue also enabled papers to field far more reporters and provide a wider range of news independent of political subsidy. Pulitzer's equation—"circulation means advertising, and advertising means money, and money means independence"—captured the potential relationship between commercial success and editorial autonomy. It was on this basis that journalism produced both the greatest muckraking and the worst jingoism.

As the press and other media grew in scale and influence during the early twentieth century, however, a variety of countervailing efforts emerged to mold public opinion. Business leaders turned to a new kind of expert—the public relations specialist—for advice about how to present themselves to the media and the world. Advertising became concerned not just with selling products but also with enhancing corporate images, and publicity agents proliferated, peddling ready-to-use material to reporters and editors who routinely printed it in their papers. Government departments created press bureaus, and presidents, beginning with Wilson, instituted regular press conferences. The vast apparatus that Wilson established to manage public opinion during World War I epitomized these developments. That effort involved not just government propaganda and censorship but also self-censorship and misrepresentation by the press, and when the war was over, critics attacked the complicity of journalists in public deception. The concerns about the press went beyond the familiar objections to the sensationalism of Hearst and struck at the elite papers as well. In 1920, with Charles Merz, Lippmann reviewed three years' coverage of the Russian Revolution in the *New York Times* and found the paper's reporting riddled with bias and inaccuracies; on ninety-one occasions, the *Times* had said the Bolshevik regime was near collapse or reported it had already fallen. "The news about Russia," Lippmann and Merz wrote, "is a case of seeing not what was, but what men wished to see."[6]

Part of the remedy, it seemed to Lippmann, lay in a reform of journalism and the creation of new means of disciplined, scientific investigation of the public world. In *Liberty and the News*—the first and most prescriptive of three books on public opinion and democracy that he wrote during the 1920s—Lippmann argued that "in an exact sense the present crisis of western democracy is a crisis in journalism." The original essay in *Liberty and the News* was about the idea, as he explained in a letter, "that freedom of thought and speech present themselves in a new light and raise new problems because of the discovery that opinion can be manufactured." No liberty, he wrote in the book itself, exists "for a community which lacks the information by which to detect lies." If democracy was to work, the press owed the public, above all else, a "steady supply of trustworthy and relevant news": "There can be no higher law in journalism than to tell the truth and shame the devil." Certainly the truth was "slippery," but precisely for that reason, "good reporting requires the exercise of the highest of the scientific virtues," such as the habit "of ascribing no more credibility to a statement than it warrants."

Lippmann was urging reporters to be more "objective," a term that was just coming into use in writing about journalism. Critics now often dismiss objectivity as a professional ideology, but it is important to understand the practices that Lippmann was urging reporters to adopt. He wanted journalists to emulate science by developing a "sense of evidence" and forthrightly acknowledging the limits of available information; he urged them to dissect slogans and abstractions and to refuse to withhold news or put moral uplift or any other cause ahead of veracity. What Lippmann was demanding of journalists was, above all, accountability. He called on newspapers to identify the sources of articles, whether from a press bureau or by an individual reporter; to publish the names of individual staff members; and to be held responsible for errors and falsehoods. The entire field of journalism, he said, needed to be upgraded to a profession to attract first-class educated talent. But journalists could not do the necessary work alone; they needed experts to organize information for them, and Lippmann called for the creation of "political observatories"—research institutes both inside and outside of government—to provide systematic evidence that could be used, for example, to evaluate the performance of government agencies.[7]

A few years later, in his larger work *Public Opinion,* Lippmann shifted his emphasis to a greater role for expertise; by this time, he was more despairing about both the press and the public on the grounds that neither reporters nor citizens were likely to overcome the stereotyped "pictures in our heads" that most people have of the public world.[8] *Public Opinion* had the greater academic influence—James W. Carey calls it the "founding book in American media studies."[9] But it was the earlier program of journalistic professionalism and expanded data-gathering and research in organizations insulated from political control that actually became central to the response of liberal democracies to the problem of manipulated opinion that World War I had exposed.

But the problem itself might not be as dire as Lippmann thought. Social science research during the 1930s raised doubts about whether, in fact, the media could "manufacture" opinion. Instead of conceiving of society as consisting of isolated individuals, American sociologists in the early twentieth century saw instead a honeycomb of social organization. And, partly because they took civil society and social structure into account, the sociologists who first studied the media empirically found the effects of advertising and political campaigns to be more limited than was widely believed. The single most influential work was a study by Paul Lazarsfeld, Bernard Berelson, and Hazel Gaudet of how voters in one Ohio county made their decisions during the 1940 presidential campaign. Relatively few voters seemed to change their minds because of anything they read in the press or heard on the radio; social relationships and personal influence were more important. Much of the impact of the media, insofar as there was any, came in what the study called a "two-step flow" via "opinion leaders" who paid close attention to public affairs and then talked with others in the community. Lazarsfeld and his coauthors drew an optimistic inference from their findings: "In the last analysis," they wrote, "more than anything else people can move other people. From an ethical point of view, this is a hopeful aspect in the serious social problem of propaganda. The side which has the more enthusiastic supporters and which can mobilize grass-roots support in an expert way has great chances of success."[10]

As this analysis became codified as the "dominant paradigm" in the sociology of communications, two explanatory factors stood out. First, the media had limited effects in changing opinions—Lazarsfeld recognized the media had a strong reinforcing effect—because of self-selection: People tended to read or listen to things they agreed with; they interpreted material according to their preconceptions; and their memory was selective. And, second, social ties and patterns of personal communication tended to "anchor" people's opinions and render them less susceptible to media influence. Lazarsfeld's "effects" paradigm is sometimes said to have assumed readers and listeners to be passive, but it is almost the opposite: People's choices about what to read or listen to and how to interpret it, as well as their own relationships and communications with each other, were the principal reasons Lazarsfeld cited for the media's limited capacity to move opinion.

This research corrected the earlier, exaggerated view of the public as easily susceptible to mass suggestion, but it suffered from its own limitations. As subsequent work on the "agenda-setting" function of the media has shown, the media could not tell people what to think but strongly affected what they thought about. Moreover, the kind of political and consumer choices Lazarsfeld and his colleagues studied often minimized media effects; at the time of the 1940 presidential election, partisan identities were strong, and most people already had opinions one way or the other about Roosevelt after he had been in office for two terms. In a situation where people had much less prior information—for example, in understanding the Russian Revolution in 1917—the media would likely have a much larger effect on public opinion.

Perhaps most important, the limited-effects model drew its conclusions from research on short-term changes in opinions and tastes and did not address other kinds of shifts, particularly those that develop over the long term.[11] Lazarsfeld's research, for example, did not address change from one generation to the next—between an older generation that had grown up with more traditional cultural practices and a younger generation that became more attuned from an early age to the new popular media. During the 1920s and 1930s, as older cultural traditions broke down, many parents were convinced that the media were, in a sense, alienating their children's affections, and as Lizabeth Cohen writes in her study of Chicago, "Ethnic, working-class parents were right to observe that their children craved stylish fashions, the latest motion pictures, popular tunes on the radio, and evenings at commercial dance halls." Adolescents were using the media then, as they have in other contexts, to escape "the confining ethnic worlds of their families." Yet, as Cohen points out, this was not a simple repudiation: "Rather, more like their parents than was at first apparent, young people looked to their ethnic peer groups to mediate mass culture."[12] Once again, the media were filtered through the honeycomb of social relations.

One long-term change in the media with uncertain effects was a narrowing of ideological diversity. The system of print communication that prevailed up to World War I accommodated political viewpoints across a broad spectrum. Radical newspapers such as the *Appeal to Reason* were at no technological advantage; they had the same printing presses as other publications, and the Post Office distributed them nationally on the same subsidized terms. Populist and socialist papers, though they suffered for lack of advertising revenue, rose and fell according to the vicissitudes of the movements they spoke to and for.

It was not technological change per se that narrowed the ideological spectrum. Before World War I, movies varied widely in viewpoint. With rising costs in the 1920s, however, the movies came under the control of a small number of large firms that dominated the entire industry from production to exhibition, and the next decade the industry succumbed to pressure to censor itself according to the Production Code. By the 1930s, broadcasting had followed the same course as the movies in going from an early pluralism to corporate consolidation and a narrowing of ideological boundaries.

The contrast in the operating principles of the dominant communication networks could hardly be clearer. During the nineteenth century, political views circulated via a network (the Post Office) to which even radical papers enjoyed a right of access. Advocates of the corresponding viewpoints in the twentieth century had no comparable right to get on the radio. And while the Supreme Court provided stronger protections of political dissent beginning in the 1930s, radio and the movies were deemed outside the scope of the First Amendment. Nonetheless, in comparative terms, American radio in the 1930s was still more ideologically diverse than systems in Europe; even the BBC was less open to political controversy than commercial radio in the United States.

Some critics, particularly on the left, reacted to the popular media of the period by overgeneralizing about the homogeneity of the "culture industry," a term introduced by Max Horkheimer and Theodor Adorno, who came to America from the Institute of Social Research in Frankfurt, Germany, in the late 1930s (Adorno at first worked on Lazarsfeld's radio research in an ill-fated partnership). To the "critical theorists" of the Frankfurt School, the culture industry was a system of "mass deception" that lulled people into accepting oppression and converted art and culture into standardized commodities. What was new about the culture industry, in fact, was the "exclusion of the new." The radio, they wrote, "turns all participants into listeners and authoritatively subjects them to broadcast programs which are all exactly the same." Indeed, Horkheimer and Adorno equated American radio with fascism: "In America [radio] collects no fees from the public, and so has acquired the illusory forms of disinterested, unbiased authority which suits Fascism admirably. The radio becomes the universal mouthpiece of the Führer. . . . The inherent tendency of radio is to make the speaker's word, the false commandment, absolute." The public, in this view, was entirely passive; according to Horkheimer and Adorno, cartoons "hammer into every brain" the lesson that all individual resistance is useless. "Donald Duck in the cartoons and the unfortunate in real life get their thrashing so that the audience can learn to take their own punishment."[13]

Critical theory itself, however, was a cartoon of culture. Like many European immigrants, Horkheimer and Adorno were so hostile to popular sensibilities—Adorno abhorred jazz, for example—that they could not imagine that the new forms of culture they encountered in America were capable of yielding work of value and originality comparable to the high culture that they thought the public should be taught to appreciate.

Although radio and the movies in the 1930s had homogenizing tendencies, these weren't inherent in capitalism; the mass audience would break up in future decades. Even during the late 1930s, New Deal policies were attempting to limit monopoly power and promote diversity and localism in the media. The FCC's Chain Broadcasting rules in 1941 not only forced NBC to disgorge its second network (which became ABC) but also limited network control of affiliated stations. In 1938, the Department of Justice initiated an antitrust suit against the big movie studios that would eventually force the companies to give up control of local theaters. Another federal antitrust suit of this period would compel the Associated Press to serve all papers. These measures were consistent with a long tradition of policy (embodied in postal rates, for example) that gave a decentralized local press more of a role in the United States than in Europe.

The Frankfurt School critics, of course, were not interested in restoring competition or checks and balances—they objected to the conversion of the public into "mere media markets,"[14] as if printers had not been producing for the marketplace ever since Gutenberg. But markets, however much reviled, make vital contributions to a democratic public sphere that are unlikely to be made any other way. The production of original books, movies, music, and television is inherently risky: No one knows for sure whether an audience for any new work exists beforehand. Public tastes are fickle; precisely what distinguishes a hit from a dud may be unpredictable. These uncertainties give strategic importance to those who put capital at risk. As publishers and other producers of cultural goods search for new works on which to place their bets, they are continually testing the popular appeal of new genres, styles, and subjects. This entrepreneurial activity expands the scale and scope of the public sphere, extending its known frontiers.

Sometimes even a single influential work—a book, a movie, a song—can give a latent public its voice and bring it into full awareness of itself. The discovery of a new market may thereby trigger public (and private) self-discovery and alter what politics is about. While most writers and publishers and others involved in making such choices mostly stick to familiar terrain, the industry's hunger for new products is a spur to cultural as well as economic risk-taking. More amply capitalized organizations are better able to assume that kind of risk—and are far more likely to do so in a legal environment that protects free expression. Moreover, the growth of markets does not extinguish noncommercial interests in culture and public life. The market, even when its products are distasteful, is a continual stimulus to innovation outside the market and in reaction to it. In a dynamic sense, markets in liberal societies enrich the public sphere far more than they impoverish it. If, however, all were left to the market—if government had not promoted communications networks, the press, education, and innovation while attempting to check tendencies toward excessive concentrations of power—the public sphere would be poor indeed. Our public life is a hybrid of capitalism and democracy, and we are better off for it, as long as the democratic side is able to keep the balance.

Our story stops at a point—the entry of the United States into World War II in December 1941—when some changes in the media paused and a new political framework of communications emerged. While commercial development of television and FM radio was suspended for the war's duration, the war set in motion two political changes with long-term implications: Military investment began to drive innovation in electronics, telecommunications, and computers. And the United States moved irreversibly into a central role in international political economy. Whereas the primacy of the nation-state had earlier been the overarching reality, many of the crucial decisions about communications and the media would now be made in an international context. In the coming decades—at first slowly and then with greater force—the American model of privately owned, competitively driven communications would also become far more influential in other parts of the world. The United States would export not only its culture, but also its institutions. And the global media—not all of them American by any means, but structured along the commercial lines pioneered in the United States—would become a factor of power everywhere.

All this is another story—but in many ways it is still the story this book tells. Political choices have continued to be pivotal in the constitution of the media, and the great constellation of power emerging from those choices now extends far beyond any individual country's horizon.

More than 2,000 years ago, Archimedes is supposed to have said, "Give me a lever long enough and a place to stand, and I will move the world." Many people hoping to move the modern world have thought that the media offered them a lever long enough and a place to stand—the place being in front of a microphone, camera, or computer screen. Mostly this is a delusion, as so many people are pushing in different directions. But the media certainly are mighty levers, and where our world moves in the future will depend on critical choices about them we have yet to make.

Notes

INTRODUCTION

1. A communications revolution, in other words, involves radical, discontinuous change in communication itself. But rather than defining equally abrupt social consequences as essential to the concept, this approach leaves the second-order effects on society as an open question, to be resolved entirely through empirical and historical inquiry.

2. The theoretical approach outlined here borrows from several different bodies of work concerning law and constitutions, the social construction of technology, network externalities, and path dependence. The quoted words regarding path dependence come from Paul A. David, "Historical Economics in the Long Run: Some Implications of Path Dependence," in Graeme Donald Snooks, ed., *Historical Analysis in Economics* (London: Routledge, 1993), 29–40 (quotation, 29). A trivial but evocative example of path dependence is the keyboard design with the letters QWERTY on the upper left, adopted originally to slow down typists to prevent keys from jamming but still in use for computers despite alternatives that are demonstrably more efficient. See Paul A. David, "Clio and the Economics of QWERTY," *American Economic Review, Papers and Proceedings* 75 (1985), 332–337.

3. For further discussion of the concept of the public sphere, see Chapter 1.

4. On the significance of technological architectures, see Lawrence Lessig, *Code and Other Laws of Cyberspace* (New York: Basic Books, 1999). The argument that "architecture is politics" does not apply only to modern technologies. For example, Jack Goody and Ian Watt, following David Diringer, argue that the alphabet, unlike earlier writing systems, was a "democratic script" because of its relative simplicity. See Jack Goody and Ian P. Watt, "The Consequences

of Literacy," *Comparative Studies in History and Society* 5 (1963), 304–345. By economizing on cognitive effort, and therefore on the time and resources that individuals and societies needed to invest in order to become literate, a simplified writing code opened up possibilities for more widespread literacy. Analogous arguments also apply to the advent of printing, which involved a variety of architectural choices, such as the use of Latin versus the vernacular, with varying consequences for textual accessibility.

5. For a classic discussion of transitions in legal frameworks, see Ithiel de Sola Pool, *Technologies of Freedom* (Cambridge: Harvard University Press, 1983).

6. S. Frederick Starr, "New Communications Technologies and Civil Society," in Loren Graham, ed., *Science and the Soviet Social Order* (Cambridge: Harvard University Press, 1990), 19–50. See also Steven L. Solnick, "Revolution, Reform and the Soviet Telephone System, 1917–1927," *Soviet Studies* 43 (1991), 157–176, and Bradley Jay Buchner, "Social Control and the Diffusion of Modern Telecommunications Technologies: A Cross-National Study," *American Sociological Review* 53 (June 1988), 446–453. My discussion of Russian telecommunications reflects discussions with telecommunications consultants and executives who have worked in former Soviet-bloc countries.

7. Stephen Holmes and Cass R. Sunstein, *The Cost of Rights* (New York: W.W. Norton, 1999).

8. See, for example, Charles Tilly, ed., *The Formation of National States in Western Europe* (Princeton, NJ: Princeton University Press, 1975), and other works by Tilly in which the state is equated with executive capacities.

9. On the relationship of intellectual property law to economic growth, see Douglass C. North, *Institutions, Institutional Change, and Economic Performance* (Cambridge: Cambridge University Press, 1990), and David C. Mowery and Nathan Rosenberg, *Paths of Innovation: Technological Change in 20th Century America* (New York: Cambridge University Press, 1998).

10. The quoted words are Byron Shafer's definition of "American exceptionalism"; see Byron E. Shafer, ed., *Is America Different? A New Look at American Exceptionalism* (Oxford: Clarendon Press, 1991), v. The difficulty with the term "American exceptionalism" is that some analysts identify it with a normative belief in America's unique values or with a theory of American development emphasizing values or political ideas exclusively. Social scientists have used the concept in a neutral sense to refer to the deviation of American institutions from prevailing patterns, particularly in Europe, but it is probably impossible to eliminate the phrase's normative overtones, and historians have repudiated it. See, for a defense of the concept, Seymour Martin Lipset, *American Exceptionalism: A Double-Edged Sword* (New York: W.W. Norton, 1996), and, for a critique, Ian Tyrell, "American Exceptionalism in an Age of International History," *American Historical Review* 96 (October 1991), 1031-1055.

My approach differs from exceptionalist theories such as Lipset's that attempt to explain American patterns on the basis of distinctive cultural and ideological orientations with continuing causal impact. The constitutive approach taken here views the influence of values in a more institutional and historical way. Once values are applied and entrenched in stable institutional structures (as they were, for example, through the Constitution), the institutions channel development along particular paths and "carry" the values to some extent independently of public belief. Value orientations are not irrelevant. In any conflict, the opposing sides are likely to try to mobilize widely shared values in support of their position, but the outcome may depend on institutional structures and the resources and strategies each side employs as well as the resonance of its appeal in public sentiment. Values are always at the mercy of politics; their influence is not direct but mediated by the forces at work in a given historical time.

Moreover, rather than explain American institutions solely on the basis of internal factors, the analysis here follows other recent work in viewing America within a larger world context. For example, much recent colonial and early American history has located American developments in a wider Atlantic economy, a framework that has influenced my account (see Chapter 2). But an Atlantic perspective does not seem to me to preclude an emphasis on the causal significance of political and other developments specific to the United States.

The degree to which America has been an exception has also varied through history. The United States started out as a republic at a time when none of the major European countries had a republican system of government. America was, in that respect, more exceptional at the time it established its founding institutions than it is today. In the case of communications, the United States stood alone among major nations in placing the telegraph, telephone, and broadcasting entirely in private ownership. American exceptionalism in communications has as its point of reference clear differences in law and social organization, and the problem of explaining that deviation from European patterns remains even if one rejects American exceptionalism (particularly in its celebratory "city-on-a-hill" version) as a general interpretive framework.

11. Stephen Skowronek, *Building a New American State: The Expansion of National Administrative Capacities, 1877–1920* (New York: Cambridge University Press, 1982). On the Constitution as a "European" state-building project under distinctively American political conditions, see Max M. Edling, *A Revolution in Favor of Government: Origins of the U.S. Constitution and the Making of the American State* (New York: Oxford University Press, 2003), especially 55-58.

12. On the distinction between knowledge and information, see Daniel Bell, "The Social Framework of the Information Society," in Michael L. Dertouzos and Joel Moses, eds., *The Computer Age: A Twenty-Year View* (Cambridge: MIT Press, 1979), 167–168.

13. Alexis de Tocqueville, *Democracy in America,* ed. J.P. Mayer, trans. George Lawrence (Garden City, NY: Doubleday, 1969 [1835]), 459–460.

14. Jean K. Chalaby, "Journalism as an Anglo-American Invention: A Comparison of the Development of French and Anglo-American Journalism, 1830s–1920s," *European Journal of Communications* 11 (1996), 303–326.

15. Michael Schudson, *Discovering the News* (New York: Basic Books, 1978).

CHAPTER ONE

1. James Moran, *Printing Presses: History and Development from the Fifteenth Century to Modern Times* (Berkeley and Los Angeles: University of California Press, 1973), 30–31.

2. Here I borrow some language from my discussion in "The Meaning of Privatization," *Yale Law & Policy Review* 6 (1988), 6–41.

3. The term "public sphere" comes from Jürgen Habermas (who in turn draws on earlier writers), but the definition and analysis here depart from his work. In *The Structural Transformation of the Public Sphere,* Habermas presents a class-specific formation: the "bourgeois" public sphere, "the sphere of private people come together as a public," where they confront the authorities with the "public use of their reason." See Jürgen Habermas, *The Structural Transformation of the Public Sphere* (Cambridge: MIT Press, 1989), esp. 1–5, 27–31. The discussion here, in line with much subsequent work, rejects Habermas's assumptions about the class character of the early modern public sphere (see n. 7 below). I also make no assumptions about the rationality of the public sphere, nor do I accept Habermas's explanation of its emergence or his narrative of its decline. There are particular problems with his treatment of the English case (see n. 42 below). In accounting for the creation of the public sphere, I put greater emphasis on politics (the unintended effects of political conflict, changes in the structure of politics, and political choices about communications). That a public sphere did emerge in the early modern world at the level of the nation-state and serve for a time as a relatively unified field for the formation of public opinion seems to me, however, an indispensable idea. Among the voluminous literature on the subject, see Craig Calhoun, ed., *Habermas and the Public Sphere* (Cambridge: MIT Press, 1992), and Hannah Barker and Simon Burrows, eds., *Press, Politics, and the Public Sphere in Europe and North America* (New York: Cambridge University Press, 2002).

4. For a classic formulation, see Robert E. Park, "News as a Form of Knowledge," *American Journal of Sociology* 45 (1940), 675–677.

5. See David Zaret, *Origins of Democratic Culture: Printing, Petitions, and the Public Sphere in Early-Modern England* (Princeton, NJ: Princeton University Press, 2000), especially Chapter 3 (quotation from Bacon, 56); on parliamentary decision-making before the English Revolution, see Mark Kishlansky, "The

Emergence of Adversary Politics in the Long Parliament," *Journal of Modern History* 49 (December 1977), 617–640.

6. Lucien Febvre and Henri-Jean Martin, *The Coming of the Book: The Impact of Printing, 1450–1800,* ed. Geoffrey Nowell-Smith and David Wootton, trans. David Gerrard (London: NLB, 1976 [1958]), 249; Rudolf Hirsch, *Printing, Selling and Reading, 1450–1550,* 2d ed. (Wiesbaden: Otto Harrasowitz, 1974), 22–24.

7. Habermas emphasizes these themes in his account; see *The Structural Transformation of the Public Sphere,* 14–31. But, under the lingering influence of a Marxian theory of history, he also argues that the bourgeoisie played the leading role in the transformation (and that England was the "model case" because the "capitalist mode of production" had advanced to the highest stage there). "The 'capitalists,' the merchants, bankers, entrepreneurs, and manufacturers," he writes, were "the real carrier of the public, which from the outset was a reading public" (23). Research on the social composition of the reading public and other aspects of the public sphere has not sustained this view; for a review of the evidence, see Robert Wuthnow, *Communities of Discourse: Ideology and Social Structure in the Reformation, the Enlightenment, and European Socialism* (Cambridge: Harvard University Press, 1989), 204–206, 209–211.

8. On the transition to a commercial system emphasizing the role of the stationers, or *cartolai,* see Anthony Grafton, "The Humanist as Reader," in Guglielmo Cavallo and Roger Chartier, eds., *A History of Reading in the West,* trans. Lydia G. Cochrane (Amherst: University of Massachusetts Press, 1999), 179–212 (*cartolai,* 189–196). For the standard account of the impact of printing, see Elizabeth L. Eisenstein's one-volume work, *The Printing Revolution in Early Modern Europe* (New York: Cambridge University Press, 1983); for a skeptical perspective, see Adrian Johns, *The Nature of the Book: Print and Knowledge in the Making* (Chicago: University of Chicago Press, 1998); and for Eisenstein's defense as well as Johns's rebuttal, see *American Historical Review* (February 2002).

9. Febvre and Martin, *The Coming of the Book,* 89.

10. Hirsch, *Printing, Selling and Reading, 1450–1550,* 69.

11. Jean François Gilmont, "Protestant Reformations and Reading," in Cavallo and Chartier, *A History of Reading in the West,* 213–237; Dominique Julia, "Reading and the Counter-Reformation," ibid., 238–268; and Roger Chartier, "The Practical Impact of Writing," in Roger Chartier, ed., *A History of Private Life,* vol. 3, *Passions of the Renaissance* (Cambridge: Harvard University Press, 1989), 119–120, 130–133. Much of the statistical association between Protestantism and literacy disappears once economic status is taken into account; see Rab A. Houston, *Literacy in Early Modern Europe: Culture and Education, 1500–1800* (New York: Longman, 1988), 147–150.

12. The association between Protestantism and economic development arose in the first place because the areas that converted to Protestantism were already

developing more rapidly; see Wuthnow, *Communities of Discourse,* Chapter 2, for an interpretation emphasizing the effects of commercial expansion on the relative autonomy of the states converting to Protestantism.

13. John Feather, *A History of British Publishing* (New York: Croom Helm, 1988), 12–13.

14. Elizabeth L. Eisenstein, *Grub Street Abroad: Aspects of the French Cosmopolitan Press from the Age of Louis XIV to the French Revolution* (Oxford: Clarendon Press, 1992). See also David W. Davies, *The World of the Elseviers, 1580–1712* (The Hague: Martinus Nijhoff, 1954), 122–131.

15. Febvre and Martin, *The Coming of the Book,* 310–311. For England, see Frederick S. Siebert, *Freedom of the Press in England, 1476–1776* (Urbana: University of Illinois Press, 1952), 30–51; Philip Hamburger, "The Development of the Law of Seditious Libel and the Control of the Press," *Stanford Law Review* 37 (February 1985), 666–673; and Cyndia S. Clegg, *Press Censorship in Elizabethan England* (Cambridge: Cambridge University Press, 1997).

16. Feather, *A History of British Publishing,* 31–34.

17. Ibid., 38. New patents, however, continued to be issued to individual printers by the Stuarts after 1603; see Siebert, *Freedom of the Press in England,* 127–133.

18. Joseph Klaits, *Printed Propaganda Under Louis XIV* (Princeton, NJ: Princeton University Press, 1976), 36–37; Robert Darnton, *The Literary Underground of the Old Regime* (Cambridge: Harvard University Press, 1982); Carla Hesse, "Economic Upheavals in Publishing," in Robert Darnton and Daniel Roche, eds., *Revolution in Print: The Press in France, 1775–1800* (Berkeley: University of California Press, 1989), 69–97.

19. Annabel Patterson, *Censorship and Interpretation: The Conditions of Writing and Reading in Early Modern England* (Madison: University of Wisconsin Press, 1984).

20. J. W. Saunders, "The Stigma of Print: A Note on the Social Bases of Tudor Poetry," *Essays in Criticism* 1 (1951), 139–164.

21. Jan Albert van Houtte, "La Poste des Tour et Tassis, 1489–1794," in Luc Janssens and Marc Meurrens, eds., *La Poste des Tour et Tassis, 1489–1794: dossier accompagnant l'exposition du même nom aux Archives générales du Royaume, Bruxelles 2 octobre–19 décembre 1992* (Brussels: Archives générales du Royaume, 1992), 11–20; Howard Robinson, *The British Post Office: A History* (Princeton, NJ: Princeton University Press, 1948), 24–28; Anthony Smith, *The Newspaper: An International History* (London: Thames and Hudson, 1979), 19–20.

22. John J. McCusker and Cora Gravesteijn, *The Beginnings of Commercial and Financial Journalism: The Commodity Price Currents, Exchange Rate Currents, and Money Currents of Early Modern Europe* (Amsterdam: Neha, 1991), 22–24.

23. Michael Stephens, *A History of News* (New York: Viking, 1988), 151–156.

24. Harold Love, *Scribal Publication in Seventeenth-Century England* (Oxford: Clarendon Press, 1993), 9–12; Lawrence Stone, *The Crisis of the Aristocracy* (Oxford: Clarendon Press, 1965), 388.

25. C. John Sommerville, *The News Revolution in England: Cultural Dynamics of Daily Information* (New York: Oxford University Press, 1996), 19–20.

26. Stephens, *A History of News,* 149–150.

27. Joseph Frank, *The Beginnings of the English Newspaper, 1620–1660* (Cambridge: Harvard University Press, 1961), 5–12.

28. Howard M. Solomon, *Public Welfare, Science and Propaganda in Seventeenth-Century France* (Princeton, NJ: Princeton University Press, 1972), 100–161.

29. Smith, *The Newspaper,* 15.

30. Zaret, *Origins of Democratic Culture,* 11–12.

31. Sheila Lambert, "The Beginning of Printing for the House of Commons, 1640–32," *The Library,* 6 ser., 3 (1981), 43–61; Joad Raymond, *The Invention of the Newspaper: English Newsbooks, 1641–1649* (Oxford: Clarendon Press, 1996), esp. 80–126; Siebert, *Freedom of the Press in England,* 147–233; Zaret, *Origins of Democratic Culture,* 174, 177; Nigel Smith, *Literature and Revolution in England, 1640–1660* (New Haven, CT: Yale University Press, 1994), 54–70; Kishlansky, "The Emergence of Adversary Politics in the Long Parliament," 640; Mark A. Kishlansky, *Parliamentary Selection: Social and Political Choice in Early Modern England* (New York: Cambridge University Press, 1986), 108–109.

32. Quoted in Charles E. Clark, *The Public Prints: The Newspaper in Anglo-American Culture, 1665–1740* (New York: Oxford University Press, 1994), 24.

33. Hamburger, "The Development of the Law of Seditious Libel and the Control of the Press," 714–725.

34. Peter D.G. Thomas, "The Beginnings of Parliamentary Reporting in Newspapers, 1768–1774," *English Historical Review* 74 (1959), 623–636.

35. On newspapers after 1695, see Jeremy Black, *The English Press in the Eighteenth Century* (Philadelphia: University of Pennsylvania Press, 1987); Hannah Barker, *Newspapers, Politics, and English Society, 1695–1855* (Harlow, England: Longman, 2000); Clark, *The Public Prints*; Geoffrey A. Cranfield, *The Development of the Provincial Newspaper, 1700–1760* (Oxford: Clarendon Press, 1962).

36. See Chapter 4.

37. Kishlansky, *Parliamentary Selection,* 12–21, 105–135, 225–230; J.A. Downie, *Robert Harley and the Press: Propaganda and Public Opinion in the Age of Swift and Defoe* (New York: Cambridge University Press, 1979).

38. Hamburger, "The Development of the Law of Seditious Libel and the Control of the Press," 734–758 (Holt quoted, 735).

39. Downie, *Robert Harley and the Press,* 160, 176–177.

40. On the origins of the stamp tax, see Downie, *Robert Harley and the Press,* 149–161.

41. Black, *The English Press in the Eighteenth Century,* 106–108; Bob Harris, *Politics and the Rise of the Press: Britain and France, 1620–1800* (London: Routledge, 1996), 15.

42. On the press and politics in this period, see Michael Harris, *London Newspapers in the Age of Walpole: A Study of the Origins of the Modern English Press* (Rutherford, NJ: Fairleigh Dickinson University Press, 1987), Chapters 7 and 8. One reason for Habermas's mischaracterization of the public sphere in early eighteenth-century Britain may be the sources on which he relied, such as Lawrence Hanson, *Government and the Press, 1695–1763* (Oxford: Clarendon Press, 1936). According to Harris, Hanson generally underestimates the damage to the press from the government's prosecutions: "Arrest, seizure of property, confinement, payment of bail, and delay before trial hit all those concerned in newspaper production and distribution and even in the case of an eventual acquittal there was no prospect of recouping the often considerable costs involved. The journalists of this period were as vulnerable to arbitrary harassment as other newspaper employees, and Hanson in his account considerably overemphasized the security of the author" (136, 140). Partly because of Hanson, Habermas portrays the English press in the early 1700s as being an effective instrument of public opinion and minimizes the various ways in which the government controlled it. Habermas, for example, refers to the original stamp tax as a "temporary setback" (59), failing to mention later increases and stricter enforcement. See Habermas, *The Structural Transformation of the Public Sphere,* 57–64.

43. Vincent J. Liesenfeld, *The Licensing Act of 1737* (Madison: University of Wisconsin Press, 1984).

44. Kenneth Ellis, *The Post Office in the Eighteenth Century* (London: Oxford University Press, 1958), viii.

45. Ian K. Steele, *The English Atlantic, 1675–1740: An Exploration of Communication and Community* (New York: Oxford University Press, 1986), 137.

46. On the growth of literacy in England, see Lawrence Stone, "Literacy and Education in England, 1640–1900," *Past and Present* 42 (1969), 61–139; David Cressy, *Literacy and the Social Order: Reading and Writing in Tudor and Stuart England* (Cambridge: Cambridge University Press, 1980); Michael Sanderson, *Education, Economic Change and Society in England, 1780–1870* (London: Macmillan, 1983); and W.B. Stephens, "Literacy in England, Scotland, and Wales, 1500–1900," *History of Education Quarterly* 30 (Winter 1990), 545–571.

47. For general discussions of circulation and readership, see Black, *The English Press in the Eighteenth Century,* 104–106; John Brewer, *Party Ideology and Popular Politics at the Accession of George III* (Cambridge: Cambridge University Press, 1976), 139–148. For the number of copies published weekly in 1704,

see James R. Sutherland, "The Circulation of Newspapers and Literary Periodicals, 1700–30," *The Library,* 4th ser. 15 (June 1934), 110–124; for 1750, the stamp tax data are reported in Black, *The English Press in the Eighteenth Century,* 105; for population estimates, see B.R. Mitchell, ed., *British Historical Statistics* (Cambridge: Cambridge University Press, 1988), 8.

48. Brewer, *Party Ideology and Popular Politics at the Accession of George III,* 142.

49. Daniel Roche, "Censorship and the Publishing Industry," in Darnton and Roche, *Revolution in Print,* 3–26 (data on the Bastille, 23).

50. Stephen Botein, Jack R. Censer, and Harriet Ritvo, "The Periodical Press in Eighteenth-Century English and French Society: A Cross-Cultural Approach," *Comparative Studies in Society and History* 23 (1981), 464–490; see also Harris, *Politics and the Rise of the Press: Britain and France, 1620–1800.*

51. J.C.D. Clark, *English Society, 1688–1832: Ideology, Social Structure and Political Practice during the Ancien Regime* (Cambridge: Cambridge University Press, 1985).

52. Roche, "Censorship and the Publishing Industry."

53. Darnton, *The Literary Underground of the Old Regime.*

54. Jeremy D. Popkin, *News and Politics in the Age of Revolution: Jean Luzac's Gazette de Leyde* (Ithaca, NY: Cornell University Press, 1989), 34–45; Simon Burrows, "The Cosmopolitan Press, 1760–1815," in Barker and Burrows, *Press, Politics, and the Public Sphere in Europe and North America,* 23–47.

55. Simon Schama, "The Enlightenment in the Netherlands," in Roy Porter and Mikulas Teich, eds., *The Enlightenment in National Context* (Cambridge: Cambridge University Press, 1981), 54–71 (books banned, 60–61).

56. Popkin, *News and Politics in the Age of Revolution,* x, 68–98.

57. Ibid., 37.

58. Zaret, *Origins of Democratic Culture,* 266–275.

59. James Scott, *Seeing Like a State* (New Haven, CT: Yale University Press, 1998), 64–71, 79–82.

60. Scott gives no sense that legibility could work in the reverse way: "Legibility implies a viewer whose place is central and whose vision is synoptic" (ibid., 79).

61. See Wuthnow, *Communities of Discourse,* for an interpretation emphasizing the causal importance of state-building projects in the development of the public sphere. Although I am indebted to Wuthnow's analysis, particularly his emphasis on divisions within the state, I disagree with his characterization of the public sphere as "an adjunct of the growth of bureaucracy and patronage" in both Britain and France (219) and his disparagement of the role of the market.

CHAPTER TWO

1. Ian K. Steele, *The English Atlantic, 1675–1740: An Exploration of Communication and Community* (New York: Oxford University Press, 1986). According

to Steele, the average age of London-datelined news reported in Boston dropped from 162 days in 1705 to 128 days by 1717, and then to 83 days by 1739 (figure, 159). See also T.H. Breen, "An Empire of Goods: The Anglicization of Colonial America, 1690–1776," *Journal of British Studies* 25 (October 1986), 467–499.

2. Alexis de Tocqueville, *Journey to America,* ed. J.P. Mayer, trans. George Lawrence (London: Faber and Faber, 1959), 283, 356–357; Alexis de Tocqueville, *Democracy in America,* ed. J.P. Mayer, trans. George Lawrence (Garden City, NY: Doubleday, 1969 [1835]), 303.

3. For a general argument that the differences between Canada and the United States are traceable to the American Revolution, see Seymour Martin Lipset, *Continental Divide: The Values and Institutions of the United States and Canada* (New York: Routledge, 1990).

4. Hugh Amory and David D. Hall, "Introduction," in Amory and Hall, eds., *A History of the Book in America,* vol. 1, *The Colonial Book in the Atlantic World* (New York: Cambridge University Press, 2000), 8.

5. Roger Magnuson, *Education in New France* (Montreal: McGill-Queen's University Press, 1992), 86, 90–91, 107–108.

6. The following discussion of colonial development relies extensively on Jack Greene, *Pursuits of Happiness: The Social Development of Early Modern British Colonies and the Formation of American Culture* (Chapel Hill: University of North Carolina Press, 1988); but see also John M. Murrin, "The Irrelevance and Relevance of Colonial New England," *Reviews in American History* 18 (1990), 177–184.

7. B. Katherine Brown, "The Controversy over the Franchise in Puritan Massachusetts, 1954 to 1974," *William and Mary Quarterly,* 3rd ser., 33 (1976), 212–241.

8. This text is from a 1653 book by Cotton Mather, but "the 1634 version of the oath . . . remained in force with minor changes until 1665," according to Marcus A. McCorison, "Found at Last? The 'Oath of a Freeman,' the End of Innocence, and the American Antiquarian Society," in James Gilreath, ed., *The Judgment of Experts: Essays and Documents about the Investigation of the Forging of the Oath of a Freeman* (Worcester: American Antiquarian Society, 1991), 66. For the 1653 text of the oath, see ibid., 172.

9. McCorison, "Found at Last?" 66; on the meaning of freemanship, see B. Katherine Brown, "Freemanship in Puritan Massachusetts," *American Historical Review* 59 (1954), 865–883.

10. Darren Staloff, *The Making of an American Thinking Class: Intellectuals and Intelligentsia in Puritan Massachusetts* (New York: Oxford University Press, 1998). For a more benign view of political stability under the Puritans, see Timothy H. Breen and Stephen Foster, "The Puritans' Greatest Achievement: A Study of Social Cohesion in Seventeenth-Century Massachusetts," *Journal of American History* 60 (1973), 5–22.

11. Larry D. Eldridge, *A Distant Heritage: The Growth of Free Speech in Early America* (New York: New York University Press, 1994), 97, 103, 107.

12. Michael Warner, *The Letters of the Republic: Publication and the Public Sphere in Eighteenth-Century America* (Cambridge: Harvard University Press, 1990), 19.

13. Jane Kamensky, *Governing the Tongue: The Politics of Speech in Early New England* (New York: Oxford University Press, 1997), 7.

14. Hugh Amory, "Printing and Bookselling in New England, 1638–1713," in Amory and Hall, *The Colonial Book in the Atlantic World,* 83–116; David. D. Hall, "The Atlantic Economy in the Eighteenth Century," ibid., 155.

15. On literacy and education in the colonies, see Kenneth A. Lockridge, *Literacy in Colonial New England: An Enquiry into the Social Context of Literacy in the Early Modern West* (New York: W.W. Norton, 1974); Lawrence A. Cremin, *American Education: The Colonial Experience, 1607–1786* (New York: Harper and Row, 1970); and (regarding compliance with school laws) Robert Middlekauf, *Ancients and Axioms: Secondary Education in Eighteenth-Century New England* (New Haven, CT: Yale University Press, 1963), 31–40, as well as the sources cited below on female literacy.

16. Lockridge, *Literacy in Colonial New England,* 15–23. Lockridge's reliance on wills as a source of signature data has been subject to much criticism. See Ross W. Beales, Jr., "Studying Literacy at the Community Level: A Research Note," *Journal of Interdisciplinary History* 9 (1978), 93–102, and the sources cited below on female literacy. For a review of the literature, see Carl F. Kaestle, "Studying the History of Literacy" and "The History of Readers," in Carl F. Kaestle et al., *Literacy in the United States* (New Haven, CT: Yale University Press, 1991), 3–72.

17. For the estimates of female literacy, which are higher than Lockridge's, see Joel Perlmann and Dennis Shirley, "When Did New England Women Acquire Literacy?" *William and Mary Quarterly,* 3rd. ser., 48 (January 1991), 50–67, and Joel Perlmann, Silvana R. Siddali, and Keith Whitescarver, "Literacy, Schooling, and Teaching Among New England Women, 1730–1820," *History of Education Quarterly* 37 (Summer 1997), 117–139. See also E. Jennifer Monaghan, "Literacy Instruction and Gender in Colonial New England," in Cathy N. Davidson, ed., *Reading in America: Literature and Social History* (Baltimore: Johns Hopkins University Press, 1989), 53–80.

18. Rhys Isaac, *The Transformation of Virginia, 1740–1790* (Chapel Hill: University of North Carolina Press, 1982), 122–123.

19. David D. Hall, "The Chesapeake in the Seventeenth Century," in Amory and Hall, *The Colonial Book in the Atlantic World,* 56.

20. Ibid., 55–82 (scribal legal publication, 61–65); Amory, "Printing and Bookselling in New England, 1638–1713," in Amory and Hall, *The Colonial Book in the Atlantic World,* 115–116; Warner, *Letters of the Republic,* 26–27; for later

developments, see Cynthia Z. Stiverson and Gregory A. Stiverson, "The Colonial Retail Book Trade: Availability and Affordability of Reading Material in Mid-Eighteenth-Century Virginia," in William L. Joyce et al., eds., *Printing and Society in Early America* (Worcester: American Antiquarian Society, 1983), 132–173.

21. James N. Green, "The Book Trade in the Middle Colonies, 1680–1720," in Amory and Hall, *The Colonial Book in the Atlantic World,* 201.

22. Ibid., 218.

23. Charles E. Clark, *The Public Prints: The Newspaper in Anglo-American Culture, 1665–1740* (New York: Oxford University Press, 1994), 71–73; Wm. David Sloan and Julie Hedgepeth Williams, *The Early American Press, 1690–1783* (Westport, CT: Greenwood Press, 1994), 1–10.

24. Clark, *The Public Prints,* 77–102; Sloan and Williams, *The Early American Press,* 17–23.

25. John J. McCusker and Russell R. Menard, *The Economy of British America, 1607–1789* (Chapel Hill: University of North Carolina Press, 1985), 55; Greene, *Pursuits of Happiness,* 182.

26. Harold Nelson, "Seditious Libel in Colonial America," *American Journal of Legal History* 3 (1959), 162.

27. Eldridge, *A Distant Heritage,* 3, 97, 103.

28. Ibid., 137.

29. Norman L. Rosenberg, *Protecting the Best Men: An Interpretive History of the Law of Libel* (Chapel Hill: University of North Carolina Press, 1986), 12–28.

30. Clark, *The Public Prints,* 123–140.

31. James N. Green, "English Books and Printing in the Age of Franklin," in Amory and Hall, *The Colonial Book in the Atlantic World,* 255.

32. Sloan and Williams, *The Early American Press,* 62–63.

33. On the background of the case, see Stanley N. Katz, "Introduction," in Katz, ed., *A Brief Narrative of the Case and Trial of John Peter Zenger* (Cambridge: Harvard University Press, 1963), 1–35, and Leonard W. Levy, *Emergence of a Free Press* (New York: Oxford University Press, 1985), 37–45. The Zenger case, despite its legendary status, has undergone considerable deflation. "The Morrisites were slightly ahead of contemporary American thinking on the subject of libel, but hardly the radical exponents of free speech which history has held them to be," writes Katz (16).

34. Nelson, "Seditious Libel in Colonial America," 160–172.

35. Carol Sue Humphrey, *"This Popular Engine": New England Newspapers During the American Revolution, 1775–1789* (Newark: University of Delaware Press, 1992), 58–61; Stephen Botein, "'Meer Mechanics' and an Open Press: The Business and Political Strategies of Colonial American Printers," *Perspectives in American History* 9 (1975), 127–225.

36. Sloan and Williams, *The Early American Press,* 63; Humphrey, *"This Popular Engine,"* 78–80.

37. See Levy, *Emergence of a Free Press,* 16–61.

38. Stephen Botein, "Printers and the American Revolution," in Bernard Bailyn and John B. Hench, eds., *The Press and the American Revolution* (Worcester: American Antiquarian Society, 1980), 11–57.

39. Botein, "Printers and the American Revolution," 19–23; Sloan and Williams, *The Early American Press* (Franklin quoted, 65).

40. Clark, *The Public Prints,* 216, 221–222, 228.

41. Gordon S. Wood, *The Radicalism of the American Revolution* (New York: Knopf, 1992), 29–30.

42. Bernard Mandeville, *The Fable of the Bees,* cited in Lawrence Stone, "Literacy and Education in England, 1640–1900," *Past and Present* 42 (1969), 68–139 (quotation, 85).

43. Bernard Bailyn, *The Ideological Origins of the American Revolution* (Cambridge: Belknap Press, 1967), 34–36; John Trenchard and Thomas Gordon, *Cato's Letters, or, Essays on Liberty, Civil and Religious, and Other Important Subjects,* ed. Ronald Hamowy (Indianapolis: Liberty Fund, 1995).

44. *The Papers of Benjamin Franklin,* ed. Leonard Labaree (New Haven, CT: Yale University Press, 1959), 1: 27.

45. Quoted in Wood, *Radicalism of the American Revolution,* 110.

46. Jack A. Goldstone, *Revolution and Rebellion in the Early Modern World* (Berkeley: University of California Press, 1991), 483n. Randall Collins calls Goldstone's book "the state of the art . . . surely the best work on revolutions yet produced." Collins, *Macrohistory: Essays in Sociology of the Long Run* (Stanford, CA: Stanford University Press, 1999), 21.

47. My view of this debate is indebted to Wood, *Radicalism of the American Revolution,* and R.R. Palmer, *The Age of the Democratic Revolution: A Political History of Europe and America, 1760–1800* (Princeton, NJ: Princeton University Press, 1959), 9–10, 185–188. For a recent skeptical analysis, see Jack P. Greene, "The American Revolution," *American Historical Review,* February 2000, http://www.historycooperative.org/journals/ahr/105.1/ah000093.html (December 24, 2000).

48. Wood, *Radicalism of the American Revolution,* 57–92, 169–189.

49. Raymond Williams, *Culture and Society, 1780–1950* (New York: Columbia University Press, 1958), xiv; Palmer, *The Age of the Democratic Revolution,* 14–20.

50. "Thus when the King instructed the governor to obtain a law, and the governor communicated the royal command," writes Main, "the legislature listened not to an individual figurehead but to the spokesman for a power elite extending from Whitehall to the county seats, and including many of the most important

colonials." Jackson Turner Main, *The Sovereign States* (New York: New Viewpoints, 1973), 99–101. Historians who minimize the revolutionary character of the Revolution tend to minimize the importance of sovereignty. For example, in his essay "The American Revolution," Greene refers to the colonial societies as "settler republics" even though their governments were not republics by any acceptable definition.

51. According to R.R. Palmer's estimate, there were 24 émigrés per 1,000 people from the American colonies, compared to only 5 per 1,000 from France. Palmer, *The Age of the Democratic Revolution,* 188. Wood notes that the numbers were less important than who the loyalists were: "A disproportionate number of them were well-to-do gentry operating at the pinnacles of power and patronage. . . . Because they commanded important chains of influence, their removal disrupted colonial society to a degree far in excess of their numbers." Wood, *Radicalism of the American Revolution,* 176.

52. Gordon S. Wood, *The Creation of the American Republic, 1776–1787* (Chapel Hill: University of North Carolina Press, 1969); Palmer, *The Age of the Democratic Revolution,* 213–235; Bailyn, *Ideological Origins of the American Revolution* (Madison quoted, 55).

53. Richard D. Brown, "Afterword," in William L. Joyce et al., eds., *Printing and Society in Early America* (Worcester: American Antiquarian Society, 1983), 304–305.

54. Levy, *Emergence of a Free Press,* 188.

55. Arthur M. Schlesinger, *Prelude to Independence: The Newspaper War on Britain, 1764–1776* (New York: Knopf, 1958), 68–69 (Franklin quoted, 69).

56. Pauline Maier, *From Resistance to Revolution: Colonial Radicals and the Development of American Opposition to Britain, 1765–1776* (New York: Knopf, 1972), 53–63.

57. Maier, *From Resistance to Revolution,* 91.

58. Richard L. Merritt, *Symbols of American Community, 1735–1775* (New Haven, CT: Yale University Press, 1966), 143.

59. Ruth L. Butler, *Doctor Franklin, Postmaster General* (Garden City, NY: Doubleday, Doran, 1928). Hunter died in 1761 and was replaced by John Foxcroft; Franklin continued to run the colonial post office until 1774.

60. John Adams, "A Dissertation on the Canon and the Feudal Law," in *Papers of John Adams,* ed. Robert J. Taylor et al. (Cambridge: Harvard University Press, 1977), 1: 113, 120–121, 128.

61. Levy, *Emergence of a Free Press,* 66.

62. See Botein, "Printers and the American Revolution."

63. Eric Foner, *Tom Paine and Revolutionary America* (New York: Oxford University Press, 1976), 79–86 (Paine quoted, 79, 83). On the later debate over

Paine's style, see Olivia Smith, *The Politics of Language, 1791–1819* (Oxford: Clarendon Press, 1984).

64. Sidney Kobre, *The Development of the Colonial Newspaper* (Pittsburgh: Colonial Press, 1944), tables 6 and 7, 147–148. Counting only those listed by Kobre that were published during 1775, twenty-six sided with the Revolution, ten with the British. Botein notes that exact numbers are meaningless because some printers changed sides and others fudged their views. Botein, "Printers and the American Revolution," 32n.

65. Humphrey, *"This Popular Engine,"* 72–73.

66. The low figure refers to copies printed per capita; the high figure refers to subscriptions per capita. For the American data on copies per capita, I use the circulation estimates by William A. Dill, *Growth of Newspapers in the United States* (Lawrence: Department of Journalism, University of Kansas, 1928), and the population estimate in U.S. Department of Commerce, Bureau of the Census, *Historical Statistics of the United States: Colonial Times to 1970* (Washington, DC: Government Printing Office, 1975), Part 1, 8. The English figure for copies printed in 1775 is based on stamp tax data reported in Jeremy Black, *The English Press in the Eighteenth Century* (Philadelphia: University of Pennsylvania Press, 1987), 105. The relative subscription estimates are based on Cremin, *American Education: The Colonial Experience, 1607–1786,* 547. Cremin estimates 35,000 subscribers in the American colonies as of 1775; Dill estimates only 23,000. Using Dill's numbers, the relative density of newspaper subscriptions in the colonies would be about 60 percent, not 91 percent, of the English level.

67. Jeremy D. Popkin, *Revolutionary News: The Press in France, 1789–1799* (Durham, NC: Duke University Press, 1990), 26–33.

68. Carla Hesse, "Economic Upheavals in Publishing," in Robert Darnton and Daniel Roche, eds., *Revolution in Print: The Press in France, 1775–1800* (Berkeley: University of California Press, 1989), 97.

69. Popkin, *Revolutionary News,* 53, 84–85.

70. Schlesinger, *Prelude to Independence,* 189–190, 223–227; Janice Potter and Robert M. Calhoon, "The Character and Coherence of the Loyalist Press," in Bailyn and Hench, *The Press and the American Revolution,* 229–265.

71. See Dwight L. Teeter, "Press Freedom and Public Printing: Pennsylvania, 1775–83," *Journalism Quarterly* 45 (1968), 445–451 (quotation, 450); Rosenberg, *Protecting the Best Men,* 52–53.

72. Cushing to Adams, Feb. 18, 1789, quoted in Levy, *Emergence of a Free Press,* 199.

73. Samuel Miller, *A Brief Retrospect of the Eighteenth Century. Part First; In Two Volumes: Containing a Sketch of the Revolutions and Improvements in Science, Arts, and Literature During That Period* (New York: T. and J. Swords, 1803), 2: 251.

74. Wood, *Creation of the American Republic,* 259–343 (Paine quoted, 259); Warner, *Letters of the Republic,* 97–117.

75. Max M. Edling, *A Revolution in Favor of Government: Origins of the U.S. Constitution and the Making of the American State* (New York: Oxford University Press, 2003), 15-30; Robert Allen Rutland, "The First Great Newspaper Debate: The Constitutional Crisis of 1787–88," *Proceedings of the American Antiquarian Society* 97 (1987), 43–58; John K. Alexander, *The Selling of the Constitutional Convention: A History of News Coverage* (Madison, WI: Madison House, 1990); Elaine F. Crane, "Publius in the Provinces: Where Was *The Federalist* Reprinted Outside New York City?" *William and Mary Quarterly,* 3rd ser. 21 (1964), 589–592; Charles E. Clark, *Printers, the People and Politics: The New Hampshire Press and Ratification* (Portsmouth: New Hampshire Humanities Council, 1989).

76. Saul Cornell, *The Other Founders: Anti-Federalism and the Dissenting Tradition in America, 1788–1828* (Chapel Hill: University of North Carolina Press, 1999), 19–50, 121–124 (Madison quoted, 27); Lance Banning, "Republican Ideology and the Triumph of the Constitution, 1789–1793," *William and Mary Quarterly,* 3rd ser. 31 (1974), 167–188; Gordon S. Wood, "The Democratization of Mind in the American Revolution," in Robert H. Horwitz, ed., *The Moral Foundations of the American Republic* (Charlottesville: University Press of Virginia, 1977), 108–135.

77. On the origins of the First Amendment, see Levy, *Emergence of a Free Press*; David A. Anderson, "The Origins of the Press Clause," *U.C.L.A. Law Review* 30 (February 1983), 455–541; David P. Currie, *The Constitution in Congress: The Federalist Period, 1789–1801* (Chicago: University of Chicago Press, 1997), 110–115; and, regarding Madison's role, Ralph Ketcham, *James Madison: A Biography* (New York: Macmillan, 1971), 175–303.

78. Cornell, *The Other Founders,* 158–160 (William Grayson quoted, 159); Anderson, "Origins of the Press Clause," 477–480 (Madison's draft, 478); Lance Banning, *The Sacred Fire of Liberty: James Madison and the Founding of the Federal Republic* (Ithaca, NY: Cornell University Press, 1995), 265–290.

79. Anderson, "Origins of the Press Clause," 480–481; for a different view of the Senate amendment, suggesting it would have been open to contrary interpretations, see Rosenberg, *Protecting the Best Men,* 70.

80. Helen E. Veit et al., eds., *Creating the Bill of Rights: The Documentary Record from the First Federal Congress* (Baltimore: Johns Hopkins University Press, 1991), 188–189; Anderson, "Origins of the Press Clause," 48–84. By a strange coincidence, the article barring the states from infringing essential rights was the fourteenth amendment in the original House resolution of August 24, 1789. Veit et al., *Creating the Bill of Rights,* 41. The Fourteenth Amendment, adopted in 1868, later became the basis for applying the First Amendment to the states.

81. "Address to the Inhabitants of Quebec (1774)," in Bernard Schwartz, ed., *The Bill of Rights: A Documentary History* (New York: Chelsea House Publishers, 1971), 223.

82. Anderson, "Origins of the Press Clause."

83. In a 1960 book, *Legacy of Suppression,* Leonard Levy claimed that the framers did not intend to overturn the law of seditious libel and that the suppression of the loyalists and other infringements of free speech showed that, at the time of the Bill of Rights, "the American experience with freedom of political expression was as slight as the conceptual and legal understanding was narrow." Leonard W. Levy, *Legacy of Suppression: Freedom of Speech and Press in Early American History* (Cambridge: Harvard University Press, 1960). Twenty-five years later, in a revised edition of his book pointedly retitled *Emergence of a Free Press,* Levy retracted his claims about the practice of free expression. Regardless of legal doctrine, American newspapers at the time of the Bill of Rights were filled with unrestrained attacks on public officials. But Levy continued to maintain that before the crisis over the Sedition Act in 1798, no Americans questioned seditious libel. Among the weaknesses in Levy's revised position were that he made categorical opposition to seditious libel the supreme test of free speech and ignored changes in political and legal thought that drastically curtailed seditious libel prosecutions in practice. He also missed examples of sharp criticism of seditious libel law during the 1780s. For the full critique, see David M. Rabban, "The Ahistorical Historian: Leonard Levy on Freedom of Expression in Early American History," *Stanford Law Review* 37 (February 1985), 795–856; Anderson, "Origins of the Press Clause"; Lucas A. Powe, Jr., *The Fourth Estate and the Constitution: Freedom of the Press in America* (Berkeley: University of California Press, 1991), 22–50; and Cornell, *The Other Founders,* 128–135.

84. Rosenberg, *Protecting the Best Men,* 54.

85. Levy, *Emergence of a Free Press,* 251.

86. David Yassky, "Eras of the First Amendment," *Columbia Law Review* 91 (1991), 1699–1755.

87. Michael J. Sandel, *Democracy's Discontent* (Cambridge: Harvard University Press, 1996), 38, citing Louis Henkin, "Constitutional Fathers, Constitutional Sons," *Minnesota Law Review* 60 (1976), 1113–1147. The original words in Henkin's article appear on p. 1118. Henkin's point, however, is not to minimize the early historical basis of constitutionally guaranteed rights but to emphasize, contrary to Sandel, that state constitutions embodied these principles even more than the federal Constitution did: "It is in the early state constitutions that we find full expression of a theory of republican government based on popular sovereignty, a social compact expressed in a written constitution, natural unalienable rights. . . . Early declarations of rights suggest principles not even implied in the United States Constitution, even as amended by the Bill of Rights—the right to be protected in life, liberty, and property (not merely that government shall

not deprive us of them); the right to justice and to a judicial remedy; the principle and the aspiration of equality" (1117–1118).

88. Jeffrey L. Pasley, *"The Tyranny of Printers": Newspaper Politics in the Early American Republic* (Charlottesville: University Press of Virginia, 2001), 60–104; Richard N. Rosenfeld, *American Aurora: A Democratic-Republican Returns* (New York: St. Martin's Press, 1997). For background on the Sedition Act crisis, see John C. Miller, *Crisis in Freedom: The Alien and Sedition Acts* (Boston: Little, Brown, 1951); James Morton Smith, *Freedom's Fetters: The Alien and Sedition Laws and American Civil Liberties* (Ithaca, NY: Cornell University Press, 1956); Rosenberg, *Protecting the Best Men,* 79–100; and Currie, *The Constitution in Congress,* 253–273.

89. Miller, *Crisis in Freedom,* 59.

90. For the text, see Smith, *Freedom's Fetters,* 435–442.

91. Pasley, *"The Tyranny of Printers,"* 109–111, 125–126; Anderson, "Origins of the Press Clause," 515–516.

92. Popkin, *Revolutionary News,* 171–174.

93. Pasley, *"The Tyranny of Printers,"* 117, 124–131, 200–203.

94. David Hackett Fischer, *The Revolution of American Conservatism: The Federalist Party in the Era of Jeffersonian Democracy* (New York: Harper and Row, 1965), 129–149 (Ames quoted, 135).

95. Ketcham, *James Madison,* 396, 401–403; Levy, *Emergence of a Free Press,* 293–294.

96. Leonard W. Levy, *Jefferson and Civil Liberties: The Darker Side* (Cambridge: Harvard University Press, 1963), 42–69.

97. Levy, *Emergence of a Free Press,* 338–339. On the background of the Croswell case, see Milton W. Hamilton, *The Country Printer: New York State, 1785–1830* (New York: Columbia University Press, 1936), 176–177, 197–198.

98. See Chapter 8. It was not until 1964 that the Supreme Court declared the Sedition Act unconstitutional. *New York Times Co. v. Sullivan,* 376 U.S. 967 (1964).

99. On freedom of the press during the Mexican War, see Paul H. Bergeron, *The Presidency of James K. Polk* (Lawrence: University Press of Kansas, 1987), 182.

100. Russel B. Nye, *Fettered Freedom: Civil Liberties and the Slavery Controversy, 1830–1860* (n.p.: Michigan State University Press, 1963).

101. François Furet, *Interpreting the French Revolution* (New York: Cambridge University Press, 1981); Philippe Raynaud, "American Revolution," in François Furet and Mona Ozouf, eds., *A Critical Dictionary of the French Revolution* (Cambridge: Harvard University Press, 1989), 593–603.

CHAPTER THREE

1. Washington Irving, "Rip Van Winkle," in Irving, *The Sketchbook of Geoffrey Crayon, Gentn.* (New York: George P. Putnam, 1852), 56.

2. Joanne B. Freeman, *Affairs of Honor: National Politics in the New Republic* (New Haven, CT: Yale University Press, 2001), xxii, 131–132 (Jefferson quoted, 131).

3. Frank Luther Mott, *American Journalism: A History, 1690–1960,* 3d ed. (New York: Macmillan, 1962), 169.

4. Isaiah Thomas, *The History of Printing in America,* 2 vols. (Worcester, MA: 1810), 18.

5. Gerald J. Baldasty, *The Commercialization of News in the Nineteenth Century* (Madison: University of Wisconsin Press, 1992), 11–35; John C. Nerone, "The Mythology of the Penny Press," *Critical Studies in Mass Communications* 4 (December 1987), 389–390; Richard P. McCormick, *Party Formation in the Jacksonian Era* (Chapel Hill: University of North Carolina Press, 1966), 30–31; Robert Remini, *The Election of Andrew Jackson* (Philadelphia: Lippincott, 1963), 77; Jeffrey L. Pasley, *"The Tyranny of Printers": Newspaper Politics in the Early American Republic* (Charlottesville: University Press of Virginia, 2001), 10–17, 348–356, 389–397.

6. Mott, *American Journalism,* 201–202; Alfred McClung Lee, *The Daily Newspaper in America* (New York: Macmillan, 1937), 59, 314.

7. William A. Dill, *Growth of Newspapers in the United States* (Lawrence: Department of Journalism, University of Kansas, 1928), 11.

8. William Gilmore, *Reading Becomes a Necessity of Life: Material and Cultural Life in Rural New England, 1780–1835* (Knoxville: University of Tennessee Press, 1989), 18, 25 (national estimates, 194). Historians disagree about how widespread newspapers were. Jack Larkin writes that "even in the countryside of Massachusetts, no more than one household in ten or twelve received a newspaper." Unfortunately, the date Larkin has in mind is unclear; though he cites no data, he may be right about 1800, but Gilmore's study indicates that newspapers were far more widespread in rural New England by the 1830s. Jack Larkin, *The Reshaping of Everyday Life, 1790–1840* (New York: Harper and Row, 1988), 36.

9. Richard Cobden, *England, Ireland, and America,* in *Political Writings of Richard Cobden,* 2 vols. (New York: D. Appleton, 1867), 1: 124. Cobden's estimate for 1834 of 90 million copies a year in the United States is almost identical to the 90.3 million copies for 1835 in Dill.

10. American circulation works out to 6.02 copies per person per year; British, 1.8. The British numbers, however, do not include the illegal, unstamped press. For U.S. circulation figures, see Dill, *Growth of Newspapers in the United States,* 11, and for population estimates, see U.S. Department of Commerce, Bureau of the Census, *Historical Statistics of the United States: Colonial Times to 1970* (Washington, DC: Government Printing Office, 1975), Part 1, 8. For Britain, the estimate is based on the number of newspaper stamps sold in 1835, as reported in F. W. Bateson, ed., *Cambridge Bibliography of English Literature*

(New York: Macmillan, 1941), iii, 789–790, 795–797; population estimates come from B.R. Mitchell, ed., *British Historical Statistics* (Cambridge: Cambridge University Press, 1988), 9.

11. Michael G. Mulhall, *The Progress of the World* (London: Edward Staford, 1880), 90. As of 1830, when the United States had 1,300 newspapers, there were 23 in German-speaking Europe (excluding Austria and the north of Schleswig), though the German population at this time was estimated to be about twice as large as America's. See Hans-Friedrich Meyer, *Zeitungspreise in Deutschland im 19. Jahrhundert und ihre gesellschaftliche Bedeutung* (Hamburg: Stiftung Wissenschaft und Presse, 1969), 529 *ff.*

12. Tocqueville explicitly rejected the view that taxes explained the lower circulation of newspapers in Britain and France. See *Democracy in America,* ed. J.P. Mayer, trans. George Lawrence (Garden City, NY: Doubleday, 1969 [1835]), 519. But elsewhere he identified the absence of any regulatory burdens on newspapers as a primary reason for their dispersed development throughout the United States. Ibid., 184.

13. Milton W. Hamilton, *The Country Printer: New York State, 1785–1830* (New York: Columbia University Press, 1936), 139–141; Baldasty, *The Commercialization of News in the Nineteenth Century,* 49.

14. Richard R. John, *Spreading the News: The American Postal System from Franklin to Morse* (Cambridge: Harvard University Press, 1996). The analysis of the Post Office that follows is heavily indebted to John and to two earlier books: Wayne E. Fuller, *The American Mail: Enlarger of the Common Life* (Chicago: University of Chicago Press, 1972), and Richard B. Kielbowicz, *News in the Mail: The Press, Post Office, and Public Information, 1700–1860s* (Westport, CT: Greenwood Press, 1989).

15. Mail volume per capita seems actually to have been lower in the United States than in France in 1830 but higher in 1840. For the French postal and population data, see B.R. Mitchell, *European Historical Statistics, 1750–1975,* 2d rev. ed. (New York: Facts on File, 1980), 30, 678. For the U.S. postal data, see John, *Spreading the News,* 4; for the U.S. population data, see Bureau of the Census, *Historical Statistics of the United States,* Part 1, 8.

16. John, *Spreading the News,* 52.

17. Rush, quoted in John, *Spreading the News,* 30.

18. Fuller, *The American Mail,* 79–86; John, *Spreading the News,* 49.

19. Richard D. Brown, "The Emergence of Urban Society in Rural Massachusetts, 1760–1820," *Journal of American History* 61 (June 1974), 29–51.

20. William Smith, *The History of the Post Office of British North America, 1670–1870* (Cambridge: Cambridge University Press, 1920, 157, 161, 165–166, 242.

21. John, *Spreading the News,* 31–37.

22. Lee Soltow and Edward Stevens, *The Rise of Literacy and the Common School in the United States: A Socioeconomic Analysis to 1870* (Chicago: University of Chicago Press, 1981), 77.

23. I base this estimate on the following calculations: Kielbowicz, *News in the Mail,* 71, reports the Post Office carried 16 million newspapers in 1830 and that the number grew at 2.3 million copies a year until 1845. Dill, *Growth of Newspapers in the United States,* 11, estimates total circulation (copies printed) at 90.3 million for 1835 and 195.8 million for 1840. Thus, the average proportion sent by mail over the 1835–1840 period was roughly one-fourth, but by 1840 it was down to 20 percent, perhaps because of the relatively faster growth of urban newspapers.

24. John, *Spreading the News,* 37.

25. Kielbowicz, *News in the Mail,* 71; John, *Spreading the News,* 38.

26. Smith, *The History of the Post Office in British North America, 1670–1870,* 165–166, 197, 200.

27. George L. Parker, *The Beginnings of the Book Trade in Canada* (Toronto: University of Toronto Press, 1985), 57, 158. See also Paul Rutherford, *A Victorian Authority: The Daily Press in Late Nineteenth-Century Canada* (Toronto: University of Toronto Press, 1982), 36–37.

28. Joel H. Wiener, *The War of the Unstamped: The Movement to Repeal the British Newspaper Tax, 1830–36* (Ithaca, NY: Cornell University Press, 1969), 1–9. On religious and moral tracts, see Maurice J. Quinlan, *Victorian Prelude: A History of English Manners, 1700–1830* (Hamden, CT: Archon Books, 1965), 180–192. On differences in advertising between Britain and the United States, see Wiener, *The War of the Unstamped,* 12 (citing *The Scotsman,* October 1, 1828); T.R. Nevett, *Advertising in Britain: A History* (London: Heinemann, 1982), 49; *Niles' Weekly Register* 28, no. 11 (May 14, 1825), 176. On taxes and newspaper circulation, see A. Aspinall, *Politics and the Press:* c. *1789-1850* (London: Home and Van Thal, 1949), 6-32, 57-59.

29. Culver H. Smith, *The Press, Politics, and Patronage: The American Government's Use of Newspapers, 1789–1875* (Athens: University of Georgia Press, 1977), 12–42; William E. Ames, *A History of the* National Intelligencer (Chapel Hill: University of North Carolina Press, 1972), 111.

30. Smith, *The Press, Politics, and Patronage,* 56–99. On the decline of patronage, see Chapter 4 below.

31. Smith, *The Press, Politics, and Patronage,* Appendix 1, 249.

32. Jacob W. Landynski, *Search and Seizure and the Supreme Court: A Study in Constitutional Interpretation* (Baltimore: Johns Hopkins University Press, 1966).

33. Kenneth Ellis, *The Post Office in the Eighteenth Century* (London: Oxford University Press, 1958), 60–67.

34. David H. Flaherty, *Privacy in Colonial New England* (Charlottesville: University Press of Virginia, 1972), 114–127.

35. Ibid., 122.

36. Freeman, *Affairs of Honor,* 70.

37. *Ex Parte Jackson* 96 U.S. 727 (1877).

38. The following discussion of the census draws on my article "The Sociology of Official Statistics" in William Alonso and Paul Starr, eds., *The Politics of Numbers* (New York: Russell Sage Foundation, 1987), 7–57.

39. Walter F. Willcox, "Census," in *Encyclopaedia of the Social Sciences* (New York: Macmillan, 1930), 2: 295–300.

40. Jean Bodin, *The Six Bookes of a Commonweale,* ed. Kenneth Douglas McRae (Cambridge: Harvard University Press, 1962 [English translation, 1606]), 637, 641.

41. William Petty, *Political Arithmetick* (London: 1690).

42. Gregory King, "Natural and Political Observations and Conclusions upon the State and Condition of England" (1696), in George E. Barnett, ed., *Two Tracts by Gregory King* (Baltimore: Johns Hopkins University Press, 1936), 12–56.

43. Peter Buck, "People Who Counted: Political Arithmetic in the Eighteenth Century," *Isis* 73 (1982), 28–45.

44. James Madison, "Federalist No. 54," in Alexander Hamilton, John Jay, and James Madison, *The Federalist* (New York: Modern Library, n.d. [1787–1788], 359.

45. Patricia Cline Cohen, *A Calculating People: The Spread of Numeracy in Early America* (Chicago: University of Chicago Press, 1982).

46. Steven Kelman, "The Political Foundations of American Statistical Policy," in Alonso and Starr, *The Politics of Numbers,* 275–302.

47. David J. Siepp, "The Right to Privacy in American History" (Cambridge, MA: Program on Information Resources Policy, 1978).

48. Gerald L. Grotta, "Philip Freneau's Crusade for Open Sessions of the U.S. Senate," *Journalism Quarterly* 48 (1971), 667–671.

49. Freeman, *Affairs of Honor,* 15–16; see also 31–38, 48–53.

50. Lawrence A. Cremin, *American Education: The National Experience, 1783–1876* (New York: Harper and Row, 1970), 124–125. On theories of child-raising, see Jacqueline S. Reinier, "Rearing the Republican Child: Attitudes and Practices in Post-Revolutionary Philadelphia," *William and Mary Quarterly,* 3rd ser. 39 (January 1982), 150–163.

51. Bernard Bailyn, *Education in the Forming of American Society* (Chapel Hill: University of North Carolina Press, 1960), 45–46.

52. Carl F. Kaestle, *Pillars of the Republic: Common Schools and American Society, 1780–1860* (New York: Hill and Wang, 1983), 8–9.

53. For the enrollment growth in New York and elsewhere, see Kaestle, *Pillars of the Republic,* 24; for the national estimates, see Albert Fishlow, "The American Common School Revival: Fact or Fancy?" in Henry Rosovsky, ed., *Industrialization in Two Systems: Essays in Honor of Alexander Gerschenkron* (New York: Wiley, 1966), 40–67. For European countries in 1830, Fishlow cites the "conjectural" figures in Mulhall's *The Progress of the World.*

54. David Tyack, Thomas James, and Aaron Benavot, *Law and the Shaping of Public Education, 1785–1954* (Madison: University of Wisconsin Press, 1987), 34.

55. See Gloria L. Main, "An Inquiry into When and Why Women Learned to Write in Colonial New England," *Journal of Social History* 24 (Spring 1991), 579–589; Joel Perlmann and Dennis Shirley, "When Did New England Women Acquire Literacy?" *William and Mary Quarterly,* 3rd ser. 48 (January 1991), 50–67.

56. Linda Kerber, *Women of the Republic: Intellect and Ideology in Revolutionary America* (Chapel Hill, NC: University of North Carolina Press, 1980), 199–202. See also Gilmore, *Reading Becomes a Necessity of Life,* 44–45.

57. Benjamin Rush, "Thoughts upon Female Education, Accommodated to the Present State of Society, Manners, and Government in the United States of America" (1787), in Frederick Rudolph, ed., *Essays on Education in the Early Republic* (Cambridge: Harvard University Press, 1965), 27–40.

58. Nancy F. Cott, *The Bonds of Womanhood: "Woman's Sphere" in New England, 1780–1835* (New Haven, CT: Yale University Press, 1977).

59. On this and related points about education within the family, see Maris A. Vinovskis, *Education, Society, and Economic Opportunity: A Historical Perspective on Persistent Issues* (New Haven, CT: Yale University Press, 1995), 3–16.

60. Noah Webster, *Dissertations on the English Language* (Boston: Isaiah Thomas, 1789), 405–406, quoted in Thomas Gustafson, *Representative Words: Politics, Literature, and the American Language, 1776–1865* (Cambridge: Cambridge University Press, 1992), 312.

61. Gustafson, *Representative Words*; E. Jennifer Monaghan, *A Common Heritage: Noah Webster's Blue-Back Speller* (Hamden, CT: Archon Books, 1983). Among the many biographies, see John S. Morgan, *Noah Webster* (New York: Mason/Charter, 1975), and Richard M. Rollins, *The Long Journey of Noah Webster* (Philadelphia: University of Pennsylvania Press, 1980).

62. Cohen, *A Calculating People.*

63. Kaestle, *Pillars of the Republic,* 22–23, 62.

64. Tyack, James, and Benavot, *Law and the Shaping of Public Education,* 28–29.

65. Bureau of the Census, *Historical Statistics of the United States,* Part 1, 370.

66. U.S. Department of Commerce, Bureau of the Census, *Education of the American Population,* by John K. Folger and Charles B. Nam, a 1960 Census Monograph (Washington, DC: U.S. Government Printing Office, 1967), 113.

67. Carlo Cipolla, *Literacy and Development in the West* (Harmondsworth, England: Penguin Books, 1969), 71.

68. Allan Greer, "The Pattern of Literacy in Quebec, 1745–1899," *Histoire Sociale/Social History* 11 (November 1978), 295–335 (quotation, 331); Bruce Curtis, "Some Recent Work on the History of Literacy in Canada," *History of Education Quarterly* 4 (Winter 1990), 613–624.

69. Soltow and Stevens, *The Rise of Literacy and the Common School in the United States,* Chapter 4.

70. Harvey Graff, *The Literacy Myth: Literacy and Social Structure in the Nineteenth-Century City* (New York: Academic Press, 1979).

71. William J. Baumol, Sue Anne Batey Blackman, and Edward N. Wolff, *Productivity and American Leadership: The Long View* (Cambridge: MIT Press, 1989).

72. Samuel Bowles and Herbert Gintis, *Schooling in Capitalist America* (New York: Basic Books, 1976), 151–179.

73. Lewis J. Perelman, *School's Out: Hyperlearning, the New Technology, and the End of Education* (New York: William Morrow, 1992).

74. John Meyer et al., "Public Education as Nation-Building in America," *American Journal of Sociology* 85 (1979), 978–986. For a more general account along similar lines, see John Boli, Francisco O. Ramirez, and John W. Meyer, "Explaining the Origins and Expansion of Mass Education," *Comparative Education Review* 29 (May 1985), 145–170.

75. Kaestle, *Pillars of the Republic,* 67–70; Diane Ravitch, *The Revisionists Revised* (New York: Basic Books, 1978), 28–31, 36–72. For a Marxist analysis that tries to rescue a Marxist explanation from the empirical wreckage, see Richard Rubinson, "Class Formation, Politics, and Institutions: Schooling in the United States," *American Journal of Sociology* 92 (November 1986), 519–548.

76. Kaestle, *Pillars of the Republic,* 206–210.

77. U.S. Bureau of the Census, *Compendium of the Seventh Census,* by J.D.B. De Bow (Washington, DC: 1854), 153.

78. Dill, *Growth of Newspapers in the United States,* 63.

79. John, *Spreading the News,* 257–280.

80. Clement Eaton, *Freedom of Thought in the Old South* (Durham, NC: Duke University Press, 1940); Russel B. Nye, *Fettered Freedom: Civil Liberties and the Slavery Controversy, 1830–1860* (East Lansing: Michigan State University Press, 1963); George Fitzhugh, "Uniform Postage, Railroads, Telegraphs, Fashions, etc.," *Debow's Review* 26 (June 1859), 657–664 (quotation, 661); see also Eugene D. Genovese, *The World the Slaveholders Made: Two Essays in Interpretation* (New York: Pantheon Books, 1969), 151–164.

81. Alvin Toffler, *The Third Wave* (New York: Bantam, 1981), 33.

82. Meyer et al., "Public Education as Nation-Building in America."

83. Edward W. Stevens, Jr., *Literacy, Law, and Social Order* (Dekalb: Northern Illinois University Press, 1988).

84. Gordon S. Wood, *The Radicalism of the American Revolution* (New York: Knopf, 1992), 6–7.

85. Alice Hanson Jones, *The Wealth of a Nation to Be: The American Colonies on the Eve of the Revolution* (New York: Columbia University Press, 1980), 310; Mark Egnal, *Divergent Paths: How Culture and Institutions Have Shaped North American Growth* (New York: Oxford University Press, 1996), 4–7, 18; Richard Easterlin, "Interregional Differences in Per Capita Income, Population, and Total Income, 1840–1850," in National Bureau for Economic Research, *Trends in the American Economy in the 19th Century,* Studies in Income and Wealth, vol. 24 (Princeton, NJ: Princeton University Press, 1960), 97–98.

CHAPTER FOUR

1. [Sydney Smith], "[Review of] Statistical Annals of the United States of America, by Adam Seybert," *Edinburgh Review* 33 (January 1820), 79; Harriet Martineau, *Society in America* (London: Saunders and Otley, 1837), 3: 205; Van Wyck Brooks, *The World of Washington Irving* (New York: E.P. Dutton, 1944), 331–332, 416–417, 468; Ralph Waldo Emerson, "The American Scholar" (August 31, 1837), in Alfred R. Ferguson, ed., *The Collected Works of Ralph Waldo Emerson* (Cambridge: Belknap Press, 1971), 1: 52.

2. Rosalind Remer, *Printers and Men of Capital: Philadelphia Book Publishers in the New Republic* (Philadelphia: University of Pennsylvania Press, 1996), 16–19.

3. James N. Green, "English Books and Printing in the Age of Franklin," in Hugh Amory and David Hall, eds., *A History of the Book in America,* vol. 1, *The Colonial Book in the Atlantic World* (New York: Cambridge University Press, 2000), 276, 283.

4. Hugh Amory, "Reinventing the Colonial Book," in Amory and Hall, *The Colonial Book in the Atlantic World,* 33–34.

5. John Feather, *A History of British Publishing* (New York: Croom Helm, 1988), 67–68.

6. Daniel Defoe, *An Essay on the Regulation of the Press* (Oxford: Basil Blackwell, 1958 [1704]), 25–29 (quotation, 28); Mark Rose, *Authors and Owners: The Invention of Copyright* (Cambridge: Harvard University Press, 1993), 34–41.

7. Lyman Ray Patterson, *Copyright in Historical Perspective* (Nashville: Vanderbilt University Press, 1968), 143–150.

8. Feather, *History of British Publishing,* 80–83; Rose, *Authors and Owners,* 92–103; Patterson, *Copyright in Historical Perspective,* 151–161.

9. See Rose, *Authors and Owners,* 5–6, and Martha Woodmansee, "The Genius and the Copyright: Economic and Legal Conditions for the Emergence of the Author," *Eighteenth-Century Studies* 17 (1984), 425–448. Patterson emphatically rejects the view that the Statute of Anne was enacted to benefit the author or that it had that effect: "It was a trade-regulation statute enacted to bring order to the chaos created in the book trade by the final lapse in 1694 of its predecessor, the Licensing Act of 1662, and to prevent a continuation of the booksellers' monopoly." Patterson, *Copyright in Historical Perspective,* 143. And the subsequent legal interpretations to the 1770s precluded the development of "a satisfactory law to protect the interests of the author as author" (ibid., 151). See also David Saunders, *Authorship and Copyright* (New York: Routledge, 1992), Chapter 2.

10. Locke's memorandum on the Licensing Act is reprinted, without any heading, in Peter King, *The Life and Letters of John Locke* (London: 1884), 202–209 (quotations, 205, 208). There is a striking similarity between Locke's arguments and the reasons cited by the House of Commons for failing to renew the Licensing Act. See Patterson, *Copyright in Historical Perspective,* 139–140.

11. On the French developments, see Carla Hesse, "Enlightenment Epistemology and the Law of Authorship in Revolutionary France, 1777–1793," *Representations* 30 (1990), 109–137. With the law of July 19, 1793, limiting copyright to the life of the author plus ten years, "the cultural capital of the Old Regime was definitively remanded from the private heirs and publishers into the public domain. . . . Progress in human understanding depended not on private knowledge claims but rather on free and equal access to enlightenment. . . . The intention and the result of this redefinition of the author's claims to his text as property was not to enhance the author's power to control or determine the uses and meanings of the text. In fact, it was quite the opposite" (128, 129, 130).

12. Feather, *History of British Publishing,* 116–125 (quotation, 124).

13. Bruce W. Bugbee, *Genesis of American Patent and Copyright Law* (Washington: Public Affairs, 1967), 2, 65–67.

14. Ibid., 108; Harry R. Warfel, ed., *Letters of Noah Webster* (New York: Library Publishers, 1953), 1–4.

15. Bugbee, *Genesis of American Patent and Copyright Law,* 107–110.

16. Ibid., 111–112.

17. *The Federalist,* no. 43; Bugbee, *Genesis of American Patent and Copyright Law,* 125–131; Patterson, *Copyright in Historical Perspective,* 192–193.

18. Bugbee, *Genesis of American Patent and Copyright Law,* 111–112.

19. A congressional report in 1906 put the point in unambiguous language: "[Copyright] is not based upon any natural right that the author has in his writings . . . but upon the ground that the welfare of the public will be served." H.R. Rep. No. 2222, 60th Cong. 2d sess. (1909), quoted in Jane C. Ginsburg, "A Tale of Two Copyrights: Literary Property in Revolutionary France and America," in

Carol Armbruster, ed., *Publishing and Readership in Revolutionary France and America* (Westport, CT: Greenwood Press, 1993), 95. The natural-rights conception is a pure expression of Locke's labor theory of value, while the incentive model is fundamentally utilitarian. The shifting emphases in thinking about copyright in the era of the framers may reflect the larger intellectual transition from natural-rights to utilitarian political thought in progress at the time. The intention of the framers has been subject to dispute. For the case against the natural-rights theory, see Howard B. Abrams, "The Historic Foundation of American Copyright Law: Exploding the Myth of Common Law Copyright," *Wayne Law Review* 29 (1983), 1119–1191.

20. *Clayton et al. v. Stone et al.*, 5 F. Cas. 999 (1829).

21. *Wheaton v. Peters,* 33 U.S. 591 (1834).

22. *Stowe v. Thomas,* 22 F. Cas. 201 (1853).

23. Benjamin Kaplan, *An Unhurried View of Copyright* (New York: Columbia University Press, 1967); Saunders, *Authorship and Copyright,* 150–161; Meredith L. McGill, "The Matter of the Text: Commerce, Print Culture, and the Authority of the State in American Copyright Law," *American Literary History* 9 (Spring 1997), 21–59.

24. John Tebbel, *A History of Book Publishing in the United States,* vol. 1, *The Creation of an Industry, 1630–1865* (New York: R.R. Bowker, 1972), 141–142.

25. Ibid., 223.

26. On the various modes of control of publishing risk, see Remer, *Printers and Men of Capital,* Chapter 4; for a general sociological analysis of the relationship between risk and the structure of cultural production, applied to twentieth-century industries, including publishing, see Paul M. Hirsch, "Processing Fads and Fashions: An Organization-Set Analysis of Cultural Industry Systems," *American Journal of Sociology* 77 (1972), 639–659.

27. Tebbel, *A History of Book Publishing in the United States,* 1: 208–210; Eugene Exman, *The Brothers Harper: A Unique Publishing Partnership and Its Impact upon the Cultural Life of America from 1817 to 1853* (New York: Harper and Row, 1965), especially Chapter 5.

28. Clarence Gohdes, *American Literature in Nineteenth-Century England* (New York: Columbia University Press, 1944), 19; Saunders, *Authorship and Copyright,* 156.

29. The term "price revolution" commonly refers to substantial, long-lasting movements in the general level of prices; I use the term for such movements in one sector. On price revolutions, see David Hackett Fischer, *Price Revolutions: Rhythms of Change in World History* (New York: Oxford University Press, 1996).

30. Roger Chartier, *The Cultural Uses of Print in Early Modern France,* trans. Lydia G. Cochrane (Princeton, NJ: Princeton University Press, 1987); Margaret

Spufford, *Small Books and Pleasant Readers* (Athens: University of Georgia Press, 1982).

31. For a recent review, see Reinhard Wittmann, "Was There a Reading Revolution at the End of the Eighteenth Century?" in Guglielmo Cavallo and Roger Chartier, eds., *A History of Reading in the West,* trans. Lydia G. Cochrane (Amherst: University of Massachusetts Press, 1999), 284–312.

32. David M. Henkin, *City Reading: Written Words and Public Spaces in Antebellum New York* (New York: Columbia University Press, 1998), 69–100.

33. Quoted by David Hall, *Cultures of Print: Essays in the History of the Book* (Amherst: University of Massachusetts Press, 1996), 54; S. G. Goodrich, *Recollections of a Lifetime* (New York: Arundel, 1856), 1: 86.

34. *Grosjean, Supervisor of Public Accounts of Louisiana, v. American Press Co., Inc., et al.*, 297 U.S. 233 (1936). On the Massachusetts taxes, see Carol Sue Humphrey, *"This Popular Engine": New England Newspapers During the American Revolution, 1775–1789* (Newark: University of Delaware Press, 1992), 93–97. During the Civil War, the federalist government imposed a 3 percent tax on advertising, and some states and cities in the nineteenth century enacted mostly minor, short-lived taxes on publications. See Randall P. Bezanson, *Taxes on Knowledge in America* (Philadelphia: University of Pennsylvania Press, 1994), 105–132.

35. Joel H. Wiener, *The War of the Unstamped: The Movement to Repeal the British Newspaper Tax, 1830–1836* (Ithaca, NY: Cornell University Press, 1969), 1.

36. Aubert J. Clark, *The Movement for International Copyright in Nineteenth Century America* (Washington, DC: Catholic University of America Press, 1960), 43–44, 81–83.

37. Nathan Rosenberg, *Technology and American Economic Growth* (New York: Harper and Row, 1972), 43–45, 50.

38. William Charvat, *Literary Publishing in America, 1790–1850* (Philadelphia: University of Pennsylvania Press, 1959), 61–84.

39. Feather, *History of British Publishing,* 131–132; Judith A. McGaw, *Most Wonderful Machine: Mechanization and Social Change in Berkshire Paper Making, 1801–1885* (Princeton, NJ: Princeton University Press, 1987), 93–116, 185; Alfred McClung Lee, *The Daily Newspaper in America* (New York: Macmillan, 1937), 98–103.

40. Sean Wilentz, *Chants Democratic: New York City and the Rise of the American Working Class, 1788–1850* (New York: Oxford University Press, 1984), 129–132; Ronald Zboray, *A Fictive People: Antebellum Economic Development and the American Reading Public* (New York: Oxford University Press, 1993), 8.

41. Rollo G. Silver, *The American Printer: 1787–1825* (Charlottesville: University Press of Virginia, 1967), 47–56; Exman, *The Brothers Harper,* 36; James

Moran, *Printing Presses: History and Development from the Fifteenth Century to Modern Times* (Berkeley and Los Angeles: University of California Press, 1973), 115, 186.

42. Rollo G. Silver, *The American Printer: 1787–1825*, 59–61; Remer, *Printers and Men of Capital*, 96–98; Michael Winship, "Printing with Plates in the Nineteenth-Century," *Printing History* 5 (1983), 15–27.

43. David Paul Nord, "The Evangelical Origins of Mass Media in America, 1815–1835," *Journalism Monographs*, no. 88 (1984) (quotation, 2).

44. According to the online reference World Financial Data, the exchange rate as of December 31, 1829, was $4.79 to the pound.

45. Exman, *The Brothers Harper*, Chapters 2 and 3.

46. Alexander Keyssar, *The Right to Vote: The Contested History of Democracy in the United States* (New York: Basic Books, 2000), 29, 51–52.

47. Ibid., 40. On the political background, including the use of newspapers in party building, see Richard P. McCormick, *The Second American Party System: Party Formation in the Jacksonian Era* (Chapel Hill: University of North Carolina Press, 1966); Ronald P. Formisano, *The Transformation of Political Culture: Massachusetts Parties, 1790s–1840s* (New York: Oxford University Press, 1983); and Wilentz, *Chants Democratic*.

48. Jeffrey L. Pasley, *"The Tyranny of Printers": Newspaper Politics in the Early American Republic* (Charlottesville: University Press of Virginia, 2001), 10–17.

49. Alexis de Tocqueville, *Democracy in America*, ed. J.P. Mayer, trans. George Lawrence (Garden City, NY: Doubleday, 1969 [1835]), 517–518.

50. On the development of the penny press, see, generally, Oliver Carlson, *The Man Who Made News: James Gordon Bennett* (New York: Duell, Sloan and Pearce, 1942); Michael Schudson, *Discovering the News* (New York: Basic Books, 1978); Dan Schiller, *Objectivity and the News: The Public and the Rise of Commercial Journalism* (Philadelphia: University of Pennsylvania Press, 1981); John D. Stevens, *Sensationalism and the New York Press* (New York: Columbia University Press, 1991); Andie Tucher, *Froth and Scum: Truth, Beauty, and the Ax Murder in America's First Mass Medium* (Chapel Hill: University of North Carolina Press, 1994); and William E. Huntzicker, *The Popular Press, 1833–1865* (Westport, CT: Greenwood Press, 1999) (Day quoted, 2). For a critical review, see John C. Nerone, "The Mythology of the Penny Press," *Critical Studies in Mass Communications* 4 (December 1987), 376–404, which includes a historiographical discussion. In his rejection of the idea that the penny press was the revolutionary birthplace of modern journalism, Nerone writes: "The expansion of the press in the United States was a result of ideas and expectations popularized in the period of the American Revolution. The change, beginning in the eighteenth century, was deeply affected by two grand developments in the nineteenth century: the

rise of popular partisan politics and the appearance of a market economy." This is the view I take, but Nerone goes too far in minimizing the significance of the penny press and suggesting that those who emphasize its importance are legitimizing the current practices of journalism. See the response by Michael Schudson, "A Revolution in Historiography?" ibid., 405–408.

51. Some historians seem to suggest a sudden shift to street sales, but Nerone argues there are no data to support that contention; the one breakdown of sales available suggests the continued predominance of subscriptions. Of the more than 19,000 copies of the *Sun* sold in 1835, only 2,000 were sold on the street. Nerone, "Mythology of the Penny Press," 384.

52. Schudson, *Discovering the News,* emphasizes Bennett's middle-class readers; Schiller, *Objectivity and the News,* sees the penny press audience as predominantly artisanal; Tucher, *Froth and Scum,* 211–212, questions an emphasis on either.

53. Huntzicker, *The Popular Press, 1833–1865,* 74.

54. Gerald J. Baldasty, *The Commercialization of News in the Nineteenth Century* (Madison: University of Wisconsin Press, 1992), 123.

55. See Frank Luther Mott, "Facetious News Writing, 1833–1883," *Mississippi Valley Historical Review* 29 (June 1942), 35–54.

56. Patricia Cline Cohen, *The Murder of Helen Jewett: The Life and Death of a Prostitute in Nineteenth-Century New York* (New York: Knopf, 1998), 25, 26.

57. *New York Herald,* April 12, 1836 (under "Visit to the Scene").

58. Tucher, *Froth and Scum,* 35–36, 38.

59. Alfred McClung Lee, *The Daily Newspaper in America: The Evolution of a Social Instrument* (New York: Macmillan, 1937), 314–317; Frank Luther Mott, *American Journalism: A History, 1690–1960,* 3d ed. (New York: Macmillan, 1962), 201–202.

60. U.S. Department of Commerce, Bureau of the Census, *Historical Statistics of the United States: Colonial Times to 1970* (Washington, DC: Government Printing Office, 1975), Part 1, 12.

61. Baldasty, *The Commercialization of News in the Nineteenth Century,* 6–7, 11–35.

62. Horace Greeley, *Recollections of a Busy Life* (New York: J.B. Ford, 1868), 136.

63. Lee, *The Daily Newspaper in America,* 167.

64. J. Cutler Andrews, *The North Reports the Civil War* (Pittsburgh: University of Pittsburgh Press, 1955), 20–21.

65. Donald Lewis Shaw, "At the Crossroads: Change and Continuity in American Press News, 1820–1860," *Journalism History* 8 (1981), 38–53, 76.

66. David J. Russo, "The Origins of Local News in the U.S. Country Press, 1840s–1870s," *Journalism Monographs,* no. 65 (1980).

67. Shaw, "At the Crossroads."

68. David S. Reynolds, *Beneath the American Renaissance: The Subversive Imagination in the Age of Emerson and Melville* (New York: Knopf, 1988), 54–91 (quotations, 58, 59, 63).

69. Reynolds, *Beneath the American Renaissance,* 177; see also Schiller, *Objectivity and the News,* 96–178.

70. In an analysis of fiction titles published by American authors, Reynolds finds that conventional sentimental-domestic narratives, which accounted for 80 percent of titles before 1800 and represented about half before 1830, dropped to just 20 percent between 1831 and 1860. In the latter period, the explosion of "cheap sensational literature (particularly yellow-covered pamphlet novels)" lifted two other types of narrative, "romantic adventure" and "subversive" fiction, to almost 60 percent of the total. While tales of romantic adventure were "action-packed and sometimes dark but usually stylistically restrained," the writers of subversive fiction went to hyperbolic extremes of violence and irrationality, often in radical exposés of the betrayal of democratic ideals. See Reynolds, *Beneath the American Renaissance,* 8, 183.

71. Ibid., 3–10.

72. Michael Denning, *Mechanic Accents: Dime Novels and Working-Class Culture in America* (London: Verso, 1987).

73. Frank Luther Mott, *Golden Multitudes: The Story of Best Sellers in the United States* (New York: Macmillan, 1947), 79; Madeleine B. Stern, ed., *Publishers for Mass Entertainment in Nineteenth Century America* (Boston: G.K. Hall, 1980).

74. Charvat, *Literary Publishing in America, 1790–1850,* 61–84.

75. Anne C. Rose, *Voices of the Marketplace: American Thought and Culture, 1830–1860* (New York: Twayne, 1995), 130–161.

76. Schudson, *Discovering the News,* 57–59.

77. Larzer Ziff, *Literary Democracy: The Declaration of Cultural Independence in America* (New York: Viking Press, 1981), xiv.

78. Brooks, *The World of Washington Irving,* 268; Thomas Nelson Page, *The Old South* (New York: C. Scribner's Sons, 1892), 74.

79. Alexis de Tocqueville, *The Old Regime and the French Revolution,* trans. Stuart Gilbert (Garden City, NY: Doubleday Anchor Books, 1955), 74; for Tocqueville's contrast between the United States and France in this regard, see *Democracy in America,* 184. On the persistence of earlier patterns in French book publishing during the Napoleonic era, Jeremy Popkin writes: "The dominant trend . . . remained what it had been throughout the eighteenth century: Paris sucked the life out of the provincial printing centers. . . . In this, as in so many other respects, the Revolution worked to increase Paris's domination over the rest of the country." "The Book Trades in Western Europe during the Revolutionary Era," *Papers of the Bibliographical Society of America* 78 (1984), 420.

80. David Madsen, *The National University: Enduring Dream of the USA* (Detroit: Wayne State University Press, 1966), 25–56 (quotations, 38, 49).

81. Ibid., 58–63.

82. See Culver H. Smith, *The Press, Politics, and Patronage: The American Government's Use of Newspapers, 1789–1875* (Athens: University of Georgia Press, 1977); Timothy E. Cook, *Governing with the News: The News Media as a Political Institution* (Chicago: University of Chicago Press, 1998), Chapters 2–3.

83. Wayne E. Fuller, *The American Mail: Enlarger of the Common Life* (Chicago: University of Chicago Press, 1972), 113.

84. Chapter 5 discusses the 1840 reform of the British Post Office in connection with the later nationalization of the telegraph on the same model.

85. Richard R. John, *Spreading the News: The American Postal System from Franklin to Morse* (Cambridge: Harvard University Press, 1996), 159–160; Fuller, *The American Mail,* 123–125.

86. Humphrey, *"This Popular Engine,"* 24; Richard D. Brown, "The Emergence of Urban Society in Rural Massachusetts, 1760–1820," *Journal of American History* 61 (June 1974), 43. In 1820, Massachusetts still included Maine.

87. David Jaffee, "The Village Enlightenment," *William and Mary Quarterly,* 3d ser., 47 (July 1990), 327–346.

88. Charvat, *Literary Publishing in America, 1790–1850,* 18–26.

89. Ibid., 20–22.

90. Seymour Martin Lipset, *Continental Divide: The Values and Institutions of the United States and Canada* (New York: Routledge, 1990), Chapter 11.

91. These calculations are based on data in S.N.D. North, *The Newspapers and Periodical Press* (Washington, DC: Government Printing Office, 1884), 186–187 (Table XI); the population data come from Bureau of the Census, *Historical Statistics of the United States,* 1: 24–37. States classified as belonging to the North for all years were the free states as of 1860, plus Maryland and the District of Columbia. California, Oregon, and western territories without statehood were excluded from the analysis.

92. Mark E. Neely, *The Fate of Liberty: Abraham Lincoln and Civil Liberties* (New York: Oxford University Press, 1991).

93. Smith, *The Press, Politics, and Patronage,* 242.

94. Richard Burket Kielbowicz, "Origins of the Second-Class Mail Category and the Business of Policymaking, 1863–1879," *Journalism Monographs,* no. 96 (1986), 17.

95. Baldasty, *The Commercialization of News in the Nineteenth Century,* 66–71, 83, 140.

96. A. Aspinall, *Politics and the Press, c. 1780–1850* (London: Home and Van Thal, 1949), 66–106; Allen Hutt, *The Changing Newspaper: Typographic Trends in Britain and America, 1622–1972* (London: Gordon Fraser, 1973), 47–50; Jean K. Chalaby, "Journalism as an Anglo-American Invention: A Comparison of the Development of French and Anglo-American Journalism, 1830s–1920s," *European Journal of Communications* 11 (1996), 303–326.

97. Michael Schudson, "Question Authority: A History of the News Interview," in *The Power of News* (Cambridge: Harvard University Press, 1995), 72–93; Chalaby, "Journalism as an Anglo-American Invention," 312.

98. Denning, *Mechanic Accents*, Chapters 2–3; Raymond Howard Shove, *Cheap Book Production in the United States, 1870 to 1891* (Urbana: University of Illinois Library, 1937), 1–4, 32.

99. Clark, *The Movement for International Copyright in Nineteenth Century America*; Saunders, *Authorship and Copyright*, 167–185; Wendy Griswold, "American Character and the American Novel: An Expansion of Reflection Theory in the Sociology of Literature," *American Journal of Sociology* 86 (1981), 740–765.

CHAPTER FIVE

1. Tom Standage, *The Victorian Internet* (New York: Walker, 1998).

2. On the contemporary response to the telegraph, see Daniel Czitrom, *Media and the American Mind: From Morse to McLuhan* (Chapel Hill: University of North Carolina Press, 1982), 3–14.

3. Allan R. Pred, *Urban Growth and the Circulation of Information: The United States System of Cities, 1790–1840* (Cambridge: Harvard University Press, 1973), 38, 54, 55.

4. See, particularly, Richard R. John, "Recasting the Information Infrastructure for the Industrial Age," in Alfred D. Chandler, Jr., and James W. Cortada, eds., *A Nation Transformed by Information: How Information Has Shaped the United States from Colonial Times to the Present* (New York: Oxford University Press, 2000), 55–105. David Hochfelder argues that the telegraph was revolutionary as a technology, but not in its early impact on society. See David Paul Hochfelder, "Taming the Lightning: American Telegraphy as a Revolutionary Technology, 1832–1860" (Case Western Reserve University, Ph.D. dissertation, 1999). For cautionary conclusions on the telephone, see Claude S. Fischer, *America Calling: A Social History of the Telephone to 1940* (Berkeley: University of California Press, 1992).

5. Carter Goodrich, *Government Promotion of American Canals and Railroads, 1800–1890* (New York: Columbia University Press, 1960), 5–11, 270–271; John Lauritz Larson, *Internal Improvement: National Public Works and the Promise of Popular Government in the United States* (Chapel Hill: University of North Carolina Press, 2001), 73–80, 230–232; Colleen A. Dunlavy, *Politics and Industrialization: Early Railroads in the United States and Prussia* (Princeton, NJ: Princeton University Press, 1994).

6. Carter Goodrich, "The Revulsion Against Internal Improvements," *Journal of Economic History* 10 (November 1950), 161.

7. My emphasis on conjunctural factors goes along with the general argument here that the development of communications was path-dependent: Early

choices biased later ones, sending American communications down a distinctive path of development. Although private control of telecommunications did crystallize into a dominant paradigm further down that path, several types of institutions offered widely understood alternative models at the inception. These included the federally run Post Office and mixed public-private state transportation enterprises. As a result, it is hard to see how a cultural account emphasizing paradigm persistence can be a satisfactory explanation of the telegraph's privatization. On policy paradigms, see Frank Dobbin, *Forging Industrial Policy: The United States, Britain, and France in the Railway Age* (New York: Cambridge University Press, 1994).

8. Gerard Holzmann and Bjorn Pehrson, *Early History of Data Networks* (Los Alamitos, CA: IEEE Computer Society Press, 1995), 47–96; Jeffrey Kieve, *The Electric Telegraph in the UK* (Newton Abbott, England: David and Charles, 1973), 15–16 (quotation, 17); A.N. Holcombe, *Public Ownership of Telephones on the Continent of Europe* (Cambridge: Harvard University Press, 1911), 4–6.

9. Levi Woodbury, "Circular to certain Collectors of the Customs, Commanders of Revenue Cutters, and other persons," March 10, 1837, reprinted in Thomas C. Cochran, ed., *The New American State Papers, 1789–1860, Science and Technology*, vol. 8, *Telegraphs, Military Technology* (Wilmington, DE: Scholarly Resources, 1973), 16; Lewis Coe, *The Telegraph: A History of Morse's Invention and Its Predecessors in the United States* (Jefferson, NC: McForland, 1993), 7–9; Robert L. Thompson, *Wiring a Continent: The History of the Telegraph Industry in the United States, 1832–1866* (Princeton, NJ: Princeton University Press, 1947), 11–12; John, "Recasting the Information Infrastructure for the Industrial Age," 74–75.

10. Hochfelder, "Taming the Lightning," 104–116; Carleton Mabee, *The American Leonardo: A Life of Samuel F.B. Morse* (New York: Knopf, 1943), 149–154, 189–225.

11. Kieve, *The Electric Telegraph in the UK*, 29–72.

12. Holcombe, *Public Ownership of Telephones on the Continent of Europe*, 9–12.

13. Ibid., 8–9.

14. Daniel R. Headrick, *The Invisible Weapon: Telecommunications and International Politics, 1851–1945* (New York: Oxford University Press, 1991), 12–13, 44–45; James Foreman-Peck and Robert Millward, *Public and Private Ownership of British Industry, 1820–1990* (Oxford: Clarendon Press, 1994), 58.

15. Hochfelder, "Taming the Lightning," 52–71; Albert E. Moyer, *Joseph Henry: The Rise of an American Scientist* (Washington, DC: Smithsonian Institution Press, 1997), 72–77, 142–144.

16. "Electro-Magnetic Telegraphs," U.S. House of Representatives, 25th Cong., 2d sess., report no. 753, April 6, 1838, reprinted in Cochran, *New Ameri-*

can State Papers, 1789–1860, Science and Technology, vol. 8, 52–61; Mabee, *The American Leonardo*, 210–211.

17. Samuel F.B. Morse to F.O.J. Smith, February 15, 1838, in Cochran, *New American State Papers, 1789–1860, Science and Technology*, vol. 8, 59–60.

18. Quoted in Hochfelder, "Taming the Lightning," 117.

19. Mabee, *The American Leonardo*, 258–259; *Congressional Globe*, 27th Cong., 3d sess. (February 23, 1843), 339.

20. There is some uncertainty as to whether May 24 or May 25 was the actual date of Morse's original transmission. Mabee, *The American Leonardo*, 262–280; Menahem Blondheim, *News over the Wires: The Telegraph and the Flow of Public Information in America, 1844–1896* (Cambridge: Harvard University Press, 1994), 31–34. On the Democratic platform, see Charles Sellers, "Election of 1844," in Arthur M. Schlesinger, Jr., ed., *History of American Presidential Elections, 1789–1968* (New York: Chelsea House, 1971), 1:799.

21. Thompson, *Wiring a Continent*, 29–33 (quotations: Bennett, 31; Johnson, 33); Richard R. John, *Spreading the News: The American Postal System from Franklin to Morse* (Cambridge: Harvard University Press, 1996), 86–88 (Clay quoted, 87).

22. Paul H. Bergeron, *The Presidency of James K. Polk* (Lawrence: University Press of Kansas, 1987), 261.

23. Richard Bensel, *Yankee Leviathan: The Origins of Central State Authority in America, 1859–1877* (New York: Cambridge University Press, 1990), 64–78.

24. Goodrich, "The Revulsion Against Internal Improvements," 145–169.

25. Ibid., 152.

26. Larson, *Internal Improvement*, 233–240.

27. Tilly writes: "War made the state, and the state made war." Charles Tilly, "Reflections on the History of European State-Making," in Charles Tilly, ed., *The Formation of National States in Western Europe* (Princeton, NJ: Princeton University Press, 1975), 42.

28. It is not clear, according to recent definitions of the concept, whether all of these industries were "natural monopolies"—that is, whether in a given market, "a single firm [could] produce the desired output at lower cost than any combination of two or more firms." William Sharkey, *The Theory of Natural Monopoly* (New York: Cambridge University Press, 1982), 54. The emergence during the late nineteenth century of the theory of natural monopoly, however, was a political factor in its own right, even when it may have been mistaken. On network industries and their development, see Foreman-Peck and Millward, *Public and Private Ownership of British Industry, 1820–1990*, 1–3, 340–347.

29. Kieve, *The Electric Telegraph in the UK*, 51–52; Foreman-Peck and Millward, *Public and Private Ownership of British Industry, 1820–1990*, 56, 59. The

development of Britain's global submarine cable network is dealt with at length in the next chapter.

30. For the Edinburgh Chamber report and Association petition, see *British Parliamentary Papers, Transport and Communications, Posts and Telegraphs*, 5 (Shannon, Ireland: Irish University Press, 1971), 59–66.

31. "Memorandum, in Support of the Expediency of the Telegraphic Communication of the Kingdom being Placed in the Hands of Her Majesty's Government," June 1861, reprinted in *BPP, Posts and Telegraphs*, 5, 56–59. On Ricardo's background, see Kieve, *The Electric Telegraph in the UK*, 42–43, 120–121.

32. Kieve, *The Electric Telegraph in the UK*, 125–126.

33. On Hill, see M.J. Daunton, *Royal Mail: The Post Office since 1840* (Dover, NH: Athlone, 1985), 3–54.

34. Ibid., 22–25; Foreman-Peck and Millward, *Public and Private Ownership of British Industry, 1820–1990*, 66–69.

35. C.R. Perry, *The Victorian Post Office: The Growth of a Bureaucracy* (Rochester, NY: The Boydell Press, 1992), 91–97 (Jevons quoted, 93); Frank Ives Scudamore, "A Report to the Postmaster General upon Certain Proposals Which Have Been Made for Transferring to the Post Office the Control and Management of the Electric Telegraphs Throughout the United Kingdom," July 1866, reprinted in *BPP, Posts and Telegraphs*, 5, 13–47 (quotation, 28 [20 in orig.]).

36. Kieve, *The Electric Telegraph in the UK* (*The Economist*, April 4 1868, quoted, 145), 138–153; Perry, *The Victorian Post Office*, 100–116.

37. U.S. Bureau of the Census, *Compendium of the Seventh Census* (1854), 189; Kieve, *The Electric Telegraph in the UK*, 51; Foreman-Peck and Millward, *Public and Private Ownership of British Industry, 1820–1990*, 54.

38. Blondheim, *News over the Wires*, 39–43. Some of the telegraph entrepreneurs also came from the stagecoach and private express businesses; the Post Office Act of 1845 had ended subsidies for stagecoaches and banned private expresses competing with the Post Office. (Richard R. John, personal communication).

39. Blondheim, *News Over the Wires,* 41.

40. Thompson, *Wiring a Continent*, 97–165. On the difference between British and American railroad construction, see H.J. Habakkuk, *American and British Technology in the Nineteenth Century* (New York: Cambridge University Press, 1962), 86–88.

41. On subsidies, see Richard B. Du Boff, "The Rise of Communications Regulation: The Telegraph Industry, 1844–1880," *Journal of Communication* 34 (Summer 1984), 52–66; Thompson, *Wiring a Continent*, 348–355; Tomas Nonnmacher, "State Promotion and Regulation of the Telegraph Industry, 1845-1860," *Journal of Economic History* 61 (March 2001), 19-36; Charles S. Morgan, "Problems in the Appraisal of the Railroad Land Grants," *Mississippi Valley Historical Review* 33 (1946), 443–454.

42. Alexander James Field, "The Magnetic Telegraph, Price and Quantity Data, and the New Management of Capital," *Journal of Economic History* 52 (June 1992), 401–413.

43. *Western Union Telegraph Co. v. Carew*, 15 Michigan 525 (1867); *Primrose v. Western Union Telegraph Co.*, 154 U.S. 1 (1893).

44. Morton Horwitz, *The Transformation of American Law, 1780–1860* (Cambridge: Harvard University Press, 1977), 63–108.

45. Kenneth L. Sokoloff and B. Zorina Khan, "The Democratization of Invention During Early Industrialization: Evidence from the United States, 1790–1846," *Journal of Economic History* 50 (June 1990), 363–378; B. Zorina Khan, "Property Rights and Patent Litigation in Early Nineteenth-Century America," *Journal of Economic History* 55 (March 1995), 58–97.

46. *O'Rielly v. Morse*, 56 U.S. 62 (1854). On the patent history, see Hochfelder, "Taming the Lightning," 167–243.

47. Thompson, *Wiring a Continent*, 194–202, 259–330.

48. Quoted in Hochfelder, "Taming the Lightning," 270.

49. Richard D. Du Boff, "The Telegraph in Nineteenth-Century America: Technology and Monopoly," *Comparative Studies in Society and History* (July 1984), 580–581. On commodity exchanges, futures trading, and intercity price variations, see Richard B. Du Boff, "The Telegraph and the Structure of Markets in the United States, 1845–1850," *Research in Economic History* 8 (1983), 253–277. Markets would have become more integrated without the telegraph. If information had moved at the speed of railroads instead of the telegraph, there would still have been a narrowing of price differences. The unification of disparate markets in the continental United States should be associated not with the telegraph alone but with the rise of both rail and wire networks, which were in any event closely related.

50. Dating the origins of the NYAP is complicated by the informal nature of the association in its early years. Citing a memorandum in the papers of Moses S. Beach, Blondheim fixes the origin as the spring of 1846 and argues that relays of news from the Mexican War prompted the papers' agreement to share costs. See Blondheim, *News over the Wires*, 48–55. But Richard Schwarzlose finds no evidence of Mexican War news actually being shared and dates the AP from the spring of 1848, when the member papers chartered a steamer to expedite delivery of European news from Halifax, entered into a joint agreement with F.O.J. Smith for telegraph dispatches from Boston, and purchased a steamer to collect New York harbor news. See Richard A. Schwarzlose, *The Nation's Newsbrokers*, vol. 1, *The Formative Years, from Pretelegraph to 1865* (Evanston, IL: Northwestern University Press, 1990), 89–107.

51. Blondheim, *News over the Wires*, 71–117, 143–168; Du Boff, "The Telegraph in Nineteenth-Century America: Technology and Monopoly," 579.

52. Thompson, *Wiring a Continent*, 426.

53. "An Act to aid in the Construction of Telegraph Lines, and to secure to the Government the Use of the same for postal, military, and other Purposes," in George P. Sanger, ed., *Statutes at Large, Treaties and Proclamations of the United States of America, from December 1865 to March 1867* (Boston: Little, Brown, 1868), 221–222. In an error repeated by some other scholars, Ithiel de Sola Pool suggests that the 1866 Telegraph Act imposed common-carrier obligations on telegraph companies, but there was nothing in the act to that effect. Ithiel de Sola Pool, *Technologies of Freedom* (Cambridge: Belknap Press, 1983), 95. On the politics of the legislation, see Richard R. John, "The Significance of Postal Telegraphy: Toward an Alternative Genealogy of the Information Age," Economic History Workshop, Harvard University, March 2001. John points out that Western Union preferred a government buyout to the entry of the Post Office into the telegraph business, which would have been likely to cut into the company's earnings and share values.

54. David Hochfelder, "A Comparison of the Postal Telegraph Movements in Great Britain and the United States, 1866–1900," *Enterprise and Society* 1 (December 2000), 739–761.

55. John, "The Significance of Postal Telegraphy." Press criticism of Western Union increased in the 1880s, however, after Jay Gould's takeover of the company.

56. David Homer Bates, *Lincoln in the Telegraph Office: Recollections of the United States Military Telegraph Corps During the Civil War* (Lincoln: University of Nebraska Press, 1995 [1907]).

57. Perry, *The Victorian Post Office*, 138–142; Foreman-Peck and Millward, *Public and Private Ownership of British Industry, 1820–1990*, 73–78.

58. Kieve, *The Electric Telegraph in the UK*, 71–72, 216–218. See also testimony in "Report from the Select Committee on Post Office (Telegraph Department); Together with the Proceedings of the Committee, . . . July 13, 1876," reprinted in *BPP*, *Posts and Telegraphs*, 5, 560–574.

59. Alan J. Lee, *The Origins of the Popular Press in England, 1855–1914* (Totowa, NJ: Rowman and Littlefield, 1976), 60–63, 91; Kieve, *The Electric Telegraph in the UK*, 220–222.

60. Fritz Stern, *Gold and Iron: Bismarck, Bleichröder, and the Building of the German Empire* (New York: Knopf, 1977), 264–268; Graham Storey, *Reuters: The Story of a Century of News-Gathering* (New York: Crown, 1951), 48; Donald Read, *The Power of News: The History of Reuters* (New York: Oxford University Press, 1999), 12–29, 65–68; Anthony Smith, *The Geopolitics of Information: How Western Culture Dominates the World* (New York: Oxford University Press, 1980), 75–77.

61. Smith, *The Geopolitics of Information*, 77–81; Read, *The Power of News*, 55–61.

62. John and Hochfelder both argue that postal telegraph agitation influenced Western Union's business strategy and created, in Hochfelder's phrase, "a quasi-

regulatory environment." See John, "The Significance of Postal Telegraphy," and Hochfelder, "A Comparison of the Postal Telegraph Movements in Great Britain and the United States, 1866–1900," 756–757.

63. Blondheim, *News over the Wires*, 149–150, 164–166; Richard A Schwarzlose, *The Nation's Newsbrokers*, vol. 2, *The Rush to Institution, from 1865 to 1920* (Evanston, IL: Northwestern University Press, 1990), 2: 91–104; Paul Israel, *Edison: A Life of Invention* (New York: John Wiley and Sons, 1998), 49–63.

64. William J. Baumol, "Contestable Markets: An Uprising in the Theory of Industry Structure," *American Economic Review* 72 (March 1982), 1–15.

65. Maury Klein, *The Life and Legend of Jay Gould* (Baltimore: Johns Hopkins University Press, 1986), 197–205, 277–282.

66. Ibid., 394.

67. Western Union Telegraph Co., "Remarks of Norvin Green, President, to the Board of Directors, September 13, 1882," 5.

68. *Pensacola Telegraph Company v. Western Union Telegraph Company* 96 U.S. 1 (1877); Richard Franklin Bensel, *The Political Economy of American Industrialization, 1877–1900* (New York: Cambridge University Press, 2000), 289–354.

69. For the 1868 data, see Foreman-Peck and Millward, *Public and Private Ownership of British Industry, 1820–1990*, 71. For the United States, Foreman-Peck and Millward used data on Western Union messages; if we assume total telegraph use was 10 percent greater, the ratio of telegraph use to income per capita was almost identical in the two countries. For 1880 British data, see B.R. Mitchell, ed., *British Historical Statistics* (Cambridge: Cambridge University Press, 1988), 12, 566; for the U.S. data, see U.S. Department of Commerce, Bureau of the Census, *Historical Statistics of the United States: Colonial Times to 1970* (Washington, DC: Government Printing Office, 1975), Part 1, 9; Part 2, 788. The telegraph use for 1880 comes from Census, not Western Union, data. For France and Germany, see Foreman-Peck and Millward, *Public and Private Ownership of British Industry, 1820–1990*, 140.

70. John, "Recasting the Information Infrastructure for the Industrial Age," 81–82; Gardiner G. Hubbard, "Government Control of the Telegraph," *North American Review* 325 (December 1883), 522.

71. On productivity differences, see Foreman-Peck and Millward, *Public and Private Ownership of British Industry, 1820–1990*, 142–143. While concluding that state telegraph subsidies did not increase output, Foreman-Peck and Millward also write that "differences in performance between Victorian state and private enterprise were small enough to be statistically insignificant. Each had their distinctive inefficiencies but the net effects were not so dissimilar." Foreman-Peck and Millward, *Public and Private Ownership of British Industry, 1820–1990*, 80; see also 148.

72. Blondheim, *News over the Wires*, 151; Schwarzlose, *The Nation's Newsbrokers*, 2: 21–28.

73. S.N.D. North, *History and Present Condition of the Newspaper and Periodical Press of the United States with a Catalogue of the Publications of the Census Year* (Washington, DC: Government Printing Office, 1884), 109.

74. W.A. Swanberg, *Pulitzer* (New York: Charles Scribner's Sons, 1967), 29–30, 44, 68; Charles A. Barker, *Henry George* (New York: Oxford University Press, 1955), 112–120; Schwarzlose, *The Nation's Newsbrokers*, 2: 25, 28.

75. Blondheim, *News over the Wires*, 170; Schwarzlose, *The Nation's Newsbrokers*, 2: 111–115, 145–146.

76. North, *History and Present Condition of the Newspaper and Periodical Press*, 107; Schwarzlose, *The Nation's Newsbrokers*, 2: 133.

77. *International News Service v. Associated Press*, 248 U.S. 215 (1918).

78. Schwarzlose, *The Nation's Newsbrokers*, 2: 139–212; *Associated Press v. United States,* 326 U.S. 1 (1945).

79. Blondheim, *News over the Wires*, 130–140; L.A. Gobright, *Recollection of Men and Things at Washington* (Philadelphia: Claxton, Remsen and Haffelfinger; Washington, DC: W.H. and O.H. Morrison, 1869), 318.

80. Marl Wahlgreen Summers, *The Press Gang: Newspapers and Politics, 1865-1878* (Chapel Hill: University of North Carolina Press, 1994), 303; Blondheim, *News over the Wires*, 177–184.

81. David J. Seipp, *The Right to Privacy in American History* (Cambridge: Harvard University Program on Information Resources Policy, 1978), 30–37.

82. *Ex Parte Jackson* 96 U.S. 727 (1877). The constitutional authority was Judge Thomas Cooley, who in the fourth edition of his treatise *Constitutional Limitations* wrote that "the reasons of a public nature for maintaining the secrecy of telegraphic communication are the same with those which protect correspondence by mail." Seipp, *The Right to Privacy in American History*, 38.

83. *Primrose v. Western Union Telegraph Company,* 154 US 1 (1894) (quotation, 14); W. M. Williams, "Applicability of the Interstate Commerce Act to Telegraph Companies," *Central Law Journal* 90 (January–June 1920), 370–378.

CHAPTER SIX

1. Paul Israel, *From Machine Shop to Industrial Laboratory: Telegraphy and the Changing Context of American Invention, 1830-1920* (Baltimore: Johns Hopkins University Press, 1992), 100-122.

2. Ibid., 135–139; Paul Israel, *Edison: A Life of Invention* (New York: John Wiley and Sons, 1998), 49–81; Robert V. Bruce, *Bell: Alexander Graham Bell and the Conquest of Solitude* (Boston: Little, Brown, 1973) (Orton quoted, 127).

3. Stephen B. Adams and Orville R. Butler, *Manufacturing the Future: A History of Western Electric* (New York: Cambridge University Press, 1999), 29–38; Bruce, *Bell,* 113–116, 130–131, 197–198.

4. Sidney H. Aronson, "Bell's Electrical Toy: What's the Use? The Sociology of Early Telephone Usage," in Ithiel de Sola Pool, ed., *The Social Impact of the*

Telephone (Cambridge: MIT Press, 1977), 15–39; Asa Briggs, "The Pleasure Telephone: A Chapter in the Prehistory of the Media," ibid., 40–65.

5. Bruce, *Bell,* 83–87, 125–127; Gardiner G. Hubbard, "Government Control of the Telegraph," *North American Review* 325 (December 1883), 521–535 (quotation, 522); Robert W. Garnet, *The Telephone Enterprise: The Evolution of the Bell System's Horizontal Structure,1876–1909* (Baltimore: Johns Hopkins University Press, 1985), 11–19, 25–28. By 1878, Hubbard's responsibilities were limited to legal affairs, and two years later William H. Forbes became president of the new National Bell Telephone. I make no effort here to follow the Bell System through all its corporate reorganizations and simply refer to it as "Bell."

6. W. Bernard Carlson, "Entrepreneurship in the Early Development of the Telephone: How Did William Orton and Gardiner Hubbard Conceptualize the New Technology? *Business and Economic History* 23 (Winter 1994), 161–192; Rosario Joseph Tosiello, *The Birth and Early Years of the Bell Telephone System, 1876–1880* (Boston University, Ph.D. dissertation, 1971), 223. The story that Hubbard asked $100,000 of Orton was first published half a century after the alleged event by Bell's assistant, Thomas A. Watson, in his reminiscences: *Exploring Life: The Autobiography of Thomas A. Watson* (New York: D. Appleton, 1926), 107. But there is no contemporary corroboration of the amount of money or record of the conversation. See Richard R. John, "Recasting the Information Infrastructure for the Industrial Age," in Alfred D. Chandler, Jr., and James W. Cortada, eds., *A Nation Transformed by Information: How Information Has Shaped the United States from Colonial Times to the Present* (New York: Oxford University Press, 2000), 88.

7. Tosiello, *The Birth and Early Years of the Bell Telephone System, 1876–1880,* 452–491. Hochfelder emphasizes that Western Union failed to protect its long-term interests in the contract with Bell. See David Hochfelder, "Constructing an Industrial Divide: Western Union, AT&T, and the Federal Government, 1876-1971," *Business History Review* 76 (Winter 2002), 705-732.

8. Garnet, *The Telephone Enterprise,* 20–24; Claude S. Fischer, *America Calling: A Social History of the Telephone to 1940* (Berkeley: University of California Press, 1992), 49.

9. Milton Mueller, *Universal Service: Interconnection, Competition and Monopoly in the Making of the American Telephone System* (Cambridge: MIT Press, 1996), 15–17.

10. On the returns to investors, see J. Warren Stehman, *The Financial History of the American Telegraph and Telephone Company* (Boston: Houghton Mifflin, 1925), 72–73; Richard Gabel, "The Early Competitive Era in Telephone Communication, 1893–1920," *Law and Contemporary Problems* 34 (1969), 343.

11. John V. Langdale, "The Growth of Long-Distance Telephony in the Bell System: 1875–1907," *Journal of Historical Geography* 4 (1978), 145–159; Garnet, *The Telephone Enterprise,* 74–89; Robert Bornholz and David S. Evans,

"The Early History of Competition in the Telephone Industry," in David S. Evans, ed., *Breaking Up Bell* (New York: North-Holland, 1983), 9–10; Mueller, *Universal Service,* 40.

12. Bell was told that the Post Office would not be "bound to secrecy" and "that in the event of your method of telegraphy appearing to be both original and useful, all questions of remuneration shall rest entirely with the postmaster-general." He decided to pursue his opportunities in America. Bruce, *Bell,* 110.

13. James Foreman-Peck and Robert Millward, *Public and Private Ownership of British Industry, 1820–1990* (Oxford: Clarendon Press, 1994), 102.

14. Ibid., 97–112; C.R. Perry, *The Victorian Post Office: The Growth of a Bureaucracy* (Rochester, NY: The Boydell Press, 1992), 145–200; Charles R. Perry, "The British Experience, 1876–1912: The Impact of the Telephone During the Years of Delay," in Pool, *The Social Impact of the Telephone,* 69–96; quotation from the *Times,* January 14, 1902, in Perry, *The Victorian Post Office,* 200.

15. Raymond M. Duch, *Privatizing the Economy: Telecommunications Policy in Comparative Perspective* (Ann Arbor: University of Michigan Press, 1991), 169.

16. A.N. Holcombe, *Public Ownership of Telephones on the Continent of Europe* (Cambridge: Harvard University Press, 1911), 267–309, 433; Duch, *Privatizing the Economy,* 165–171.

17. Data for 1895 come from U.S. Department of Commerce, Bureau of the Census, *Historical Statistics of the United States: Colonial Times to 1970* (Washington, DC: Government Printing Office, 1975), Part 2, 784; Holcombe, *Public Ownership of Telephones on the Continent of Europe,* 421; and Perry, *The Victorian Post Office,* 198. The British population data come from B.R. Mitchell, ed., *British Historical Statistics* (Cambridge: Cambridge University Press, 1988), 12. On Germany, see Duch, *Privatizing the Economy,* 123–132.

18. Mueller, *Universal Service,* 55–60.

19. Fischer, *America Calling,* 92–101; Claude S. Fischer, "The Revolution in Rural Telephony, 1900–1920," *Journal of Social History* 21 (Fall 1987), 5–26; Ronald R. Kline, *Consumers in the Country: Technology and Social Change in Rural America* (Baltimore: Johns Hopkins University Press, 2000), 23–54; Steven J. Keillor, *Cooperative Commonwealth: Co-ops in Rural Minnesota, 1859–1939* (St. Paul: Minnesota Historical Society Press, 2000), 236–255; Mueller, *Universal Service,* 68–69.

20. Mueller, *Universal Service,* 60–67.

21. For the data on revenue per phone, see *1910 Annual Report of the Directors of American Telephone & Telegraph Company to the Stockholders, Year Ending Dec. 31, 1910* (New York, 1911), 26; Bornholz and Evans, "The Early History of Competition in the Telephone Industry," 20–25.

22. Kline, *Consumers in the Country,* 38–39; Fischer, *America Calling,* 48–49.

23. Bureau of the Census, *Historical Statistics of the United States: Colonial Times to 1970,* Part 2, 783–784; American Telephone and Telegraph Company,

"Telephone Statistics of the World" (New York: Office of the Statistician, May 1912), 15. Fischer estimates the growth rate at roughly 30 percent. *America Calling,* 49.

24. As of January 1911, cities with population of more than 100,000 accounted for 14 percent of Europe's population, but 55 percent of its telephones, while such cities represented 26 percent of the U.S. population and 33 percent of its telephones. See AT&T, "Telephone Statistics of the World," 18.

25. Perry, "The British Experience, 1876–1912: The Impact of the Telephone During the Years of Delay," 76.

26. Fischer, "The Revolution in Rural Telephony, 1900–1920," 7–8.

27. Ibid., 14; U.S. Department of Agriculture, *Yearbook of Agriculture, 1904* (Washington, DC: Government Printing Office, 1905), 16, quoted in Kline, *Consumers in the Country,* 43.

28. Fischer, "The Revolution in Rural Telephony, 1900–1920," 16.

29. James J. Storrow to John E. Hudson, Nov. 17, 1891, quoted in Leonard S. Reich, *The Making of American Industrial Research: Science and Business at GE and Bell, 1876–1926* (New York: Cambridge University Press, 1985), 137.

30. Reich, *The Making of American Industrial Research,* 138.

31. Kenneth Lipartito, "When Women Were Switches: Technology, Work, and Gender in the Telephone Industry, 1890–1920," *American Historical Review* 99 (October 1994), 1075–1111; Venus Green, "Goodbye Central: Automation and the Decline of 'Personal Service' in the Bell System, 1878–1921," *Technology and Culture* 36 (October 1995), 912–949.

32. On the limitations of the telephone cooperatives, see the sympathetic but devastating analysis in Keillor, *Cooperative Commonwealth: Co-ops in Rural Minnesota, 1859–1939,* 245–250.

33. Bornholz and Evans, "The Early History of Competition in the Telephone Industry"; Mueller, *Universal Service,* 69–79.

34. For studies exploring the Bell System's economic behavior during this period, see Kenneth Lipartito, "System Building at the Margin: The Problem of Public Choice in the Telephone Industry," *Journal of Economic History* 49 (June 1989), 323–336; David Gabel, "Competition in a Network Industry: The Telephone Industry, 1894–1910," *Journal of Economic History* 54 (September 1994), 543–572; and David Weiman and Richard C. Levin, "Preying for Monopoly? The Case of Southern Bell Telephone Company, 1894–1912," *Journal of Political Economy* 102 (February 1994), 103–126.

35. On business regulation during the Progressive era, see Morton Keller, *Regulating a New Economy: Public Policy and Economic Change in America, 1900–1933* (Cambridge: Harvard University Press, 1990); Morton Keller, "Regulation of Large Enterprise: The United States Experience in Comparative Perspective," in Alfred D. Chandler, Jr., and Herman Daems, eds., *Managerial Hierarchies: Comparative Perspectives on the Rise of the Modern Industrial Enterprise*

(Cambridge: Harvard University Press, 1980), 161–179; Louis Galambos and Joseph Pratt, *The Rise of the Corporate Commonwealth* (New York: Basic Books, 1988), 44–56; and the classic indictment of Progressive regulation, Gabriel Kolko, *The Triumph of Conservatism: A Re-interpretation of American History, 1900–1916* (New York: Free Press of Glencoe, 1963). For a critical survey of theories of regulation, including its origins, see Robert Britt Horwitz, *The Irony of Regulatory Reform: The Deregulation of American Telecommunications* (New York: Oxford University Press, 1989), 22–45.

36. Bornholz and Evans, "The Early History of Competition in the Telephone Industry," 25.

37. *1910 Annual Report of the Directors of American Telephone & Telegraph Company to the Stockholders, Year Ending Dec. 31, 1910* (New York: 1911), 22–23. The following year's report endorsed cross-subsidies to achieve a qualified universalism: "Rates must be so adjusted as to make it possible for everyone to be connected who will add to the value of the system to others." *1911 Annual Report . . .* (New York: 1912), 34. Such statements do not bear out Mueller's assertion, "Universal service did not mean rate subsidies to make telephone service more affordable. It meant the elimination of fragmentation and the unification of telephone service under regulated local exchange monopolies." Mueller, *Universal Service,* 92. While Vail put the emphasis on the latter, he repeatedly said universal service held the promise of extending to "every man's door." For an interpretation emphasizing the postal ancestry of Vail's outlook, see Richard R. John, "Theodore N. Vail and the Civic Origins of Universal Service," *Business and Economic History* 28 (Winter 1999), 71–81. For details on Vail's background, see the hagiographic treatment in Albert Bigelow Paine, *In One Man's Life; Being Chapters from the Personal and Business Career of Theodore N. Vail* (New York: Harper and Brothers, 1921).

38. Mueller, *Universal Service,* 108–112; Bornholz and Evans, "The Early History of Competition in the Telephone Industry," 13.

39. Jeffrey E. Cohen, "The Telephone Problem and the Road to Telephone Regulation in the United States, 1876–1917," *Journal of Policy History* 3 (1991), 42–69; Mueller, *Universal Service,* 121–127.

40. "Annual Report of Postmaster General Albert Sidney Burleson, 1913," reprinted in Katherine B. Judson, *Selected Articles on Government Ownership of the Telegraph and Telephone* (White Plains, NY: H.W. Wilson, 1914), 117–118.

41. Cohen, "The Telephone Problem and the Road to Telephone Regulation in the United States, 1876–1917," 63–64; Mueller, *Universal Service,* 129–135. On the press response to the settlement, see "The Telephone-Telegraph Divorce," *Literary Digest* 48 (January 3, 1914), 3–4, reprinted in Judson, *Selected Articles on Government Ownership of the Telegraph and Telephone,* 24–27. Ironically, AT&T revitalized Western Union during the brief period it had control over the

telegraph company. See Hochfelder, "Constructing an Industrial Divide: Western Union, AT&T, and the Federal Government, 1876-1971," 720-724.

42. John Brooks, *Telephone: The First 100 Years* (New York: Harper and Row, 1976), 157–159.

43. On early telephone regulation, see Lipartito, "System Building at the Margin," 331–336; Horwitz, *The Irony of Regulatory Reform,* 100–104; Cohen, "The Telephone Problem and the Road to Telephone Regulation in the United States, 1876–1917"; and Alan Stone, *Public Service Liberalism: Telecommunications and Transitions in Public Policy* (Princeton, NJ: Princeton University Press, 1991).

44. Bureau of the Census, *Historical Statistics of the United States: Colonial Times to 1970,* Part 2, 783; Norton Long, "Public Relations Policies of the Bell System," *Public Opinion Quarterly* 1 (October 1937), 5–22.

45. Fischer, *America Calling,* 49.

46. American Telephone and Telegraph Company, "Telephone and Telegraph Statistics of the World, January 1, 1929" (n.p.: Chief Statistician's Division, April 1, 1930).

47. Fischer, "The Revolution in Rural Telephony, 1900–1920"; Claude S. Fischer, "Technology's Retreat: The Decline of Rural Telephony in the United States, 1920–1940," *Social Science History* 11 (Fall 1987), 295–327.

48. Peter J. Hugill, *Global Communications Since 1844: Geopolitics and Technology* (Baltimore: Johns Hopkins University Press, 1999), 79.

49. Ibid., 56–57.

50. Ibid., 76.

51. Daniel R. Headrick, *The Invisible Weapon: Telecommunications and International Politics, 1851–1945* (New York: Oxford University Press, 1991), 28–49; Hugill, *Global Communications Since 1844.*

52. Jeffrey Kieve, *The Electric Telegraph in the UK* (Newton Abbott, England: David and Charles, 1973), 118; Headrick, *The Invisible Weapon,* 17–24.

53. Daniel R. Headrick, *The Tools of Empire: Technology and European Imperialism in the Nineteenth Century* (New York: Oxford University Press, 1981).

54. Headrick, *The Invisible Weapon,* 28–49 (for data on global cable ownership, see charts, 38–39); Hugill, *Global Communications Since 1844,* 39–41.

55. Headrick, *The Invisible Weapon,* 93–111.

56. Susan J. Douglas, *Inventing American Broadcasting, 1899–1922* (Baltimore: Johns Hopkins University Press, 1987), 3–28; W.J. Baker, *A History of the Marconi Company* (London: Methuen, 1970), 15–84.

57. Headrick, *The Invisible Weapon,* 117–120; Douglas, *Inventing American Broadcasting,* 64–80.

58. Baker, *A History of the Marconi Company,* 129–135; Headrick, *The Invisible Weapon,* 116–124; Douglas, *Inventing American Broadcasting,* 106, 120–123,

137–142; Hugh G.J. Aitken, *The Continuous Wave: Technology and American Radio, 1900–1932* (Princeton, NJ: Princeton University Press, 1985), 251–252.

59. Douglas, *Inventing American Broadcasting,* 102–131; Aitken, *The Continuous Wave,* 252–255; Bureau of the Census, *Historical Statistics of the United States: Colonial Times to 1970,* Part 2, 1114.

60. Douglas, *Inventing American Broadcasting,* 124–126; Aitken, *The Continuous Wave,* 193–194.

61. Douglas, *Inventing American Broadcasting,* 216–239.

62. Aitken, *The Continuous Wave,* 28–161, 250–251.

63. George Leverett to Frederick Fish, Oct. 17, 1901, quoted in Langdale, "The Growth of Long-Distance Telephony in the Bell System: 1875–1907," 148.

64. Neil Wasserman, *From Invention to Innovation: Long Distance Telephone Transmission at the Turn of the Century* (Baltimore: Johns Hopkins University Press, 1986).

65. Reich, *The Making of American Industrial Research,* 153–160.

66. David C. Mowery and Nathan Rosenberg, *Paths of Innovation: Technological Change in 20th Century America* (New York: Cambridge University Press, 1998), 13–18; Reich, *The Making of American Industrial Research,* 39–40.

67. Reich, *The Making of American Industrial Research,* 5, 180. On AT&T's public relations, see Roland Marchand, *Creating the Corporate Soul: The Rise of Public Relations and Corporate Imagery in American Big Business* (Berkeley: University of California Press, 1998), 48–87, and Long, "Public Relations Policies of the Bell System."

68. Douglas, *Inventing American Broadcasting,* 240–252.

69. Hugill, *Global Communications Since 1844,* 139–151; Headrick, *The Invisible Weapon,* 138–150.

70. Headrick, *The Invisible Weapon,* 140–143.

71. Ibid., 167–179. The data on *New York Times* coverage come from Harry S. Foster, Jr., "Studies in America's News of the European War (University of Chicago, Ph.D. dissertation, 1932), cited in Headrick, *The Invisible Weapon,* 148. On the limited impact of Allied naval power early in the war, see Paul Kennedy, *The Rise and Fall of the Great Powers* (New York: Random House, 1987), 256–260.

72. Aitken, *The Continuous Wave,* 282–287; Douglas, *Inventing American Broadcasting,* 258–266.

73. Douglas, *Inventing American Broadcasting,* 28–82.

74. Aitken, *The Continuous Wave,* 302–424.

75. Reich, *The Making of American Industrial Research*, 219-220.

76. Ibid., 220–224; Aitken, *The Continuous Wave,* 432–479.

77. Alfred D. Chandler, Jr., *The Visible Hand: The Managerial Revolution in American Business* (Cambridge: Belknap Press, 1977); Alfred D. Chandler, Jr.,

Scale and Scope: The Dynamics of Industrial Capitalism (Cambridge: Belknap Press, 1990); Chandler and Daems, *Managerial Hierarchies.* On Chandler's neglect of "the political construction of the national market," see Richard Franklin Bensel, *The Political Economy of American Industrialization, 1877–1900* (New York: Cambridge University Press, 2000), 6–8, 289–354. Chandler's argument about the effect of family-run firms on productivity in Britain and France cannot apply to the network industries, where state ownership prevailed; see Foreman-Peck and Millward, *Public and Private Ownership of British Industry,* 343. For a balanced assessment, also noting Chandler's tendency to downplay government organization as a source of large-scale administrative methods, see Richard R. John, "Elaborations, Revisions, Dissents: Alfred D. Chandler, Jr.'s *The Visible Hand,* after Twenty Years," *Business History Review* 71 (Summer 1997), 151–200.

78. Richard R. Nelson and Gavin Wright, "The Rise and Fall of American Technological Leadership," *Journal of Economic Literature* 30 (December 1992), 1942.

79. Reich, *The Making of American Industrial Research,* 180–184; Brooks, *Telephone,* 14; Adams and Butler, *Manufacturing the Future,* 107, 138–142.

80. Bradley Jay Buchner, "Social Control and the Diffusion of Modern Telecommunications Technologies: A Cross-National Study," *American Sociological Review* 53 (June 1988), 446–453; S. Frederick Starr, "New Communications Technologies and Civil Society," in Loren Graham, ed., *Science and the Soviet Social Order* (Cambridge: Harvard University Press, 1990), 19–50.

CHAPTER SEVEN

1. Karl Polanyi, *The Great Transformation* (Boston: Beacon Press, 1957), 130.

2. As a conceptual abstraction, "mass media" only begins to make sense when there is more than one means of reaching a mass public—that is, some means besides the press. In discussing historical developments until now, therefore, I have generally avoided using the term "mass media," which in any event only came into use at a later date. With the advent of motion pictures, the multiplication of alternative channels to the mass public began.

3. Pornography originally meant "writing about prostitutes"; see Walter Kendrick, *The Secret Museum: Pornography in Modern Culture* (Berkeley: University of California Press, 1996), 1. Since much of what Americans described as "obscenity" in the nineteenth century would not be classified as pornography today, I prefer the former term in this historical discussion. In general, wherever I use such terms as "obscenity," "vice," and "indecency," they should be understood in the dominant sense of the period—not as we might use them today.

4. For this distinction, see Joseph R. Gusfield, *Symbolic Crusade: Status Politics and the American Temperance Movement* (Urbana: University of Illinois Press, 1963), 6–7.

5. Elizabeth Bainum Hovey, "Stamping Out Smut: The Enforcement of Obscenity Laws, 1872–1915" (Columbia University, Ph.D. dissertation, 1998), 35–37.

6. Edward J. Bristow, *Vice and Vigilance: Purity Movements in Britain Since 1700* (Totowa, NJ: Rowman and Littlefield, 1977); Maurice J. Quinlan, *Victorian Prelude: A History of English Manners, 1700–1830* (New York: Columbia University Press, 1941); M.J.D. Roberts, "The Society for the Suppression of Vice and Its Early Critics, 1802–1812," *The Historical Journal* 26 (March 1983), 159–176; Donald Thomas, *A Long Time Burning: The History of Literary Censorship in England* (New York: Routledge and Kegan Paul, 1969); Peter Gay, *The Bourgeois Experience: Victoria to Freud,* vol. 1, *Education of the Senses* (New York: Oxford University Press, 1984).

7. Kendrick, *The Secret Museum,* 50–53; Quinlan, *Victorian Prelude*, 240–250.

8. On the early legal history of obscenity, see Thomas, *A Long Time Burning,* 74–85. The 1728 case involved the prosecution of Edmund Curll for republishing *Venus in the Cloister* (1683). On the vice society as a downward-bearing pressure group and other points, see Brian Harrison, "State Intervention and Moral Reform in Nineteenth-Century England," in Patricia Hollis, ed., *Pressure from Without in Early Victorian England* (London: Edward Arnold, 1974), 289–321; Roberts, "The Society for the Suppression of Vice and Its Early Critics, 1802–1812," 174–175; M.J.D. Roberts, "Making Victorian Morals? The Society for the Suppression of Vice and Its Critics, 1802–1886," *Historical Studies* 21 (October 1984), 157–173 (quotation from the *Christian Observer* [1811], 162–163); Bristow, *Vice and Vigilance,* 43.

9. James Q. Wilson and George L. Kelling, "The Police and Neighborhood Safety," *The Atlantic* (March 1982), 29–38; George L. Kelling and Catherine M. Coles, *Fixing Broken Windows: Restoring Order and Reducing Crime in Our Communities* (New York: The Free Press, 1996).

10. Roberts, "Making Victorian Morals?" 168–169.

11. Gay, *Education of the Senses,* 309, 358–360.

12. Kendrick, *The Secret Museum,* 116–123 (Cockburn quoted, 121, 122).

13. James C.N. Paul and Murray L. Schwartz, *Federal Censorship: Obscenity in the Mails* (New York: Free Press of Glencoe, 1961), 12.

14. Donna I. Dennis, "Sexual Speech and the Regulation of Obscenity in the 1850s," paper presented to the Center for Arts and Cultural Policy Studies, Princeton University, March 5, 2001.

15. Paul and Schwartz, *Federal Censorship,* 7–8 (Calhoun quoted, 8). Southerners, Gaines Foster argues, were "united behind a central tenet of the antebellum moral polity, that any legislation of morality should be left to the states" because of their fear of creating a precedent for antislavery measures by the federal government. See Gaines M. Foster, *Moral Reconstruction: Christian Lobbyists and the Federal Legislation of Morality, 1865–1920* (Chapel Hill: University of

North Carolina Press, 2002), 19. Once slavery was abolished, southern representatives gradually shifted to support for federal moral regulation. See ibid., 119, 227–228.

16. Paul and Schwartz, *Federal Censorship,* 17–18.

17. David Yassky, "Eras of the First Amendment," *Columbia Law Review* 91 (1991), 1699–1755.

18. Heywood Broun and Margaret Leech, *Anthony Comstock, Roundsman of the Lord* (New York: A. & C. Boni, 1927), 76–85; Hovey, "Stamping Out Smut," 41–45.

19. Timothy J. Gilfoyle, "The Moral Origins of Political Surveillance: The Preventive Society in New York City, 1867–1918," *American Quarterly* 38 (1986), 637–652.

20. For these interpretations, see, respectively, Paul S. Boyer, *Purity in Print: The Vice-Society Movement and Book Censorship in America* (New York: Scribner, 1968); Nicola Kay Beisel, *Imperiled Innocents: Anthony Comstock and Family Reproduction in Victorian America* (Princeton, NJ: Princeton University Press, 1997); and Janet Farrell Brodie, *Contraception and Abortion in Nineteenth-Century America* (Ithaca, NY: Cornell University Press, 1994).

21. Helen Lefkowitz Horowitz, "Victoria Woodhull, Anthony Comstock, and Conflict over Sex in the United States in the 1870s," *Journal of American History* 87 (September 2000), 403-444; Hovey, "Stamping Out Smut," 47-54.

22. Horowitz, "Victoria Woodhull, Anthony Comstock, and Conflict over Sex in the United States in the 1870s"; Hovey, "Stamping Out Smut," 54–57; Broun and Leech, *Anthony Comstock,* 129–132.

23. 17 *Statutes at Large* 598.

24. Hovey, "Stamping Out Smut," 58–64. According to another study, the Post Office's own inspectors devoted little of their time to enforcement of the Comstock Act. See Andrea Tone, *Devices and Desires: A History of Contraceptives in America* (New York: Hill and Wang, 2001), 26–27.

25. Broun and Leech, *Anthony Comstock,* 176–179; Carol Flora Brooks, "The Early History of the Anti-Contraceptive Laws in Massachusetts and Connecticut," *American Quarterly* 18 (Spring 1966), 3–23 (National Liberal League resolution reprinted, 17); Hal D. Sears, *The Sex Radicals: Free Love in High Victorian America* (Lawrence: Regents Press of Kansas, 1977), 170, 199–200.

26. *Ex Parte Jackson* 96 U.S. 727 (1877).

27. On the role of the WCTU and the maternalist wing of the censorship movement, see Alison M. Parker, *Purifying America: Women, Cultural Reform, and Pro-Censorship Activism, 1873–1933* (Urbana: University of Illinois Press, 1997).

28. New York Society for the Suppression of Vice, *First Annual Report* (New York, 1875), 6; Anthony Comstock, *Traps for the Young* (Cambridge: Belknap

Press, 1967 [1883]), 173, 179. On the Protestant base of support for temperance, see Gusfield, *Symbolic Crusade.*

29. Hovey, "Stamping Out Smut," 73–119.

30. Martin Henry Blatt, *Free Love and Anarchism: The Biography of Ezra Heywood* (Urbana: University of Illinois Press, 1989), 100–141 (Heywood quoted, 103–104); Hal D. Sears, *The Sex Radicals: Free Love in High Victorian America* (Lawrence: Regents Press of Kansas, 1977), 153–182.

31. Linda Gordon, *Women's Body, Women's Right: A History of Birth Control in America* (New York: Grossman, 1976), 97–115; Samuel D. Warren and Louis D. Brandeis, "The Right of Privacy," *Harvard Law Review* 4 (1890), 191–220.

32. Mark Graber, *Transforming Free Speech: The Ambiguous Legacy of Civil Libertarianism* (Berkeley: University of California Press, 1991), 25 (citing Clarence Darrow's defense in *In re Debs* 158 U.S. 564 [1895]).

33. *U.S. v. Bennett,* 24 F. Cas. 1093 (Cir. Ct. S.D.N.Y. 1879).

34. Kendrick, *The Secret Museum,* 159–160; Tone, *Devices and Desires,* 23.

35. Robert Bremner, "Editor's Introduction," in Comstock, *Traps for the Young,* vii–xxxi; New York Society for the Suppression of Vice, *Twenty-Sixth Annual Report* (New York, 1900), 8; Broun and Leech, *Anthony Comstock,* 15–16.

36. Horowitz, "Victoria Woodhull, Anthony Comstock, and Conflict over Sex in the United States in the 1870s"; Hovey, "Stamping Out Smut," 137. On Comstock's limited impact on access to contraceptives, see Tone, *Devices and Desires,* 25–45.

37. Hovey finds that for the first six years after 1873, about a third of Comstock's cases involved birth control, while most of the rest targeted obscene publications, but around 1879 both kinds of cases diminished greatly. Comstock claimed considerable success in suppressing these offenses and increasingly turned his attention as postal inspector to gambling and mail fraud. By the mid–1890s, however, he had resumed prosecuting birth control and obscenity cases in larger numbers than ever, a pattern that continued until about 1907. See Hovey, "Stamping Out Smut," 121, 184, 202–203.

38. Gay, *Education of the Senses,* 360.

39. Bristow, *Vice and Vigilance,* 6; Daniel Walker Howe, "American Victorianism as a Culture," *American Quarterly* 27 (December 1975), 507–532.

40. Mary Douglas, *Purity and Danger: An Analysis of Concepts of Pollution and Taboo* (New York: Frederick A. Praeger, 1966), 2.

41. Dee Garrison, *Apostles of Culture: The Public Librarian and American Society, 1876–1920* (London: Free Press, 1979); Rosemary Ruhig Du Mont, *Reform and Reaction: The Big City Public Library in American Life* (Westwood, CT: Greenwood Press, 1977); Evelyn Geller, *Forbidden Books in American Public Libraries, 1876–1939: A Study in Cultural Change* (Westport, CT: Greenwood Press, 1984); Parker, *Purifying America,* Chapter 3.

42. On the story papers and the campaign against them, see Hovey, "Stamping Out Smut," 189–190; Parker, *Purifying America,* 56–63; and Elliot J. Gorn, "The Wicked World: The National Police Gazette and Gilded-Age America," *Media Studies Journal* 6 (Winter 1992). The Supreme Court overturned the New York statute in *Winters v. New York,* 333 U.S. 507 (1948).

43. On the role of immigrants in American culture in this period, see Nathan Glazer, "The Immigrant Groups and American Culture," *The Yale Review* 48 (Spring 1959), 382–397, and John Higham, "Immigration," in C. Vann Woodward, ed., *The Comparative Approach to American History* (New York: Oxford University Press, 1997 [1968]), 102–103.

44. U.S. Department of Commerce, Bureau of the Census, *Historical Statistics of the United States: Colonial Times to 1970* (Washington, DC: Government Printing Office, 1975), Part 2, 810; Alfred McClung Lee, *The Daily Newspaper in America* (New York: Macmillan, 1937), 64-67, 103, 748-749; Frank Luther Mott, *American Journalism: A History, 1690-1960,* 3d ed. (New York: Macmillan, 1962), 503.

45. Bureau of the Census, *Historical Statistics of the United States: Colonial Times to 1970* Part 2, 810; Lee, *The Daily Newspaper in America,* 82, 731; Jeffrey B. Rutenbeck, "Newspaper Trends in the 1870s: Proliferation, Popularization, and Political Independence," *Journalism and Mass Communications Quarterly* 72 (Summer 1995), 361–375; Bruce M. Owen, *Economics and Freedom of Expression: Media Structure and the First Amendment* (Cambridge, MA: Ballinger, 1985), 69 (Table 2A–5).

46. Daniel Pope, *The Making of Modern Advertising* (New York: Basic Books, 1983), 113–139; *Bleistein v. Donaldson Lithographic Co.,* 188 U.S. 239 (1903). The opinion was by Justice Holmes, who defended paid-for speech even before he became a defender of free speech; for an analysis, see Benjamin Kaplan, *An Unhurried View of Copyright* (New York: Columbia University Press, 1967), 34–35.

47. Robert E. Park, *The Immigrant Press and Its Control* (New York and London: Harper and Brothers, 1922), 252; Lee, *The Daily Newspaper in America,* 88-94; 738 (Table XXIII).

48. Park, *The Immigrant Press and Its Control,* 14–48, 50–55, 67 (quotation, 50). See also Sally M. Miller, *The Ethnic Press in the United States: A Historical Analysis and Handbook* (Westport, CT: Greenwood Press, 1987); Stephen Harold Riggins, "The Media Imperative: Ethnic Minority Survival in the Age of Mass Communications," in Riggins, ed., *Ethnic Minority Media: An International Perspective* (Newbury Park, CA: Sage, 1992), 1–20.

49. Allen Hutt, *The Changing Newspaper: Typographic Trends in Britain and America, 1622–1972* (London: Gordon Fraser, 1973), 54–67; George Juergens, *Joseph Pulitzer and the New York World* (Princeton, NJ: Princeton University

Press, 1966); Helen MacGill Hughes, *News and the Human Interest Story* (New York: Greenwood Press, 1968 [1940]), 31–33.

50. Lee, *The Daily Newspaper in America,* 323 (quoting the trade journal *Newspaperdom*); William T. Stead, *The Americanization of the World; or, The Trend of the Twentieth Century* (New York: H. Markley [1902]), 291.

51. *British Quarterly Review* 53 (January 1871), 4, quoted in Piers Brendon, *The Life and Death of the Press Barons* (London: Secker and Warburg, 1982), 69; T.P. O'Connor, "The New Journalism," *The New Review* 1 (1889), 423–434 (quotations, 423, 428); Hutt, *The Changing Newspaper,* 67; Laurel Brake, "The Old Journalism and the New: Forms of Cultural Production in London in the 1880s," in Joel Wiener, ed., *Papers for the Millions: The New Journalism in Britain, 1850s to 1914* (New York: Greenwood Press, 1988), 1–24 (quoting Arnold, 1, 15).

52. W.A. Swanberg, *Pulitzer* (New York: Scribner's, 1967), 67–70, 157; Juergens, *Joseph Pulitzer and the New York World,* 35 (Dreiser quoted, 31); Brooke Kroeger, *Nellie Bly: Daredevil, Reporter, Feminist* (New York: Times Books, 1994), 79–103, 161–173; Michael Schudson, *Discovering the News* (New York: Basic Books, 1978), 88–120.

53. Swanberg, *Pulitzer,* 75–76; Alleyne Ireland, *An Adventure with a Genius: Recollections of Joseph Pulitzer* (New York: E.P. Dutton, 1920), 115; Juergens, *Joseph Pulitzer and the New York World,* 16, 267–269.

54. Juergens, *Joseph Pulitzer and the New York World,* 46–47, 234–262 (quotation, 236).

55. David Nasaw, *The Chief: The Life of William Randolph Hearst* (Boston: Houghton Mifflin, 2000), 108–109, 163; Lisa Yaszek, "'Them Damn Pictures': Americanization and the Comic Strip in the Progressive Era," *Journal of American Studies* 28 (1994), 23–38; on the origins of the term "yellow journalism," see W. Joseph Campbell, *Yellow Journalism: Puncturing the Myths, Defining the Legacies* (Westport, CT: Praeger, 2001), 25–33.

56. On Pulitzer as the "original" muckraker, see Juergens, *Joseph Pulitzer and the New York World,* 234–286; John Tebbel and Mary Ellen Zuckerman, *The Magazine in America, 1741–1990* (New York: Oxford University Press, 1991), 117.

57. Campbell, *Yellow Journalism,* 71–95. Nasaw suggests that even if Hearst did send the telegram to Remington, it was referring only to the war then in progress between Cuban revolutionaries and the Spanish army. Nasaw, *The Chief,* 127–128. On the origins of the Spanish-American War, see John Offner, *An Unwanted War: The Diplomacy of the United States and Spain over Cuba, 1895–1898* (Chapel Hill: University of North Carolina Press, 1992).

58. Stead, *The Americanization of the World,* 292.

59. Park, *The Immigrant Press and Its Control,* 68, 77.

60. Sanford E. Marovitz, *Abraham Cahan* (New York: Twayne, 1996), 39–59; Park, *The Immigrant Press and Its Control,* 87, 99–109.

61. Frank Luther Mott, *A History of American Magazines,* vol. 4, *1885–1905* (Cambridge: Harvard University Press, 1957), 2–8; Tebbel and Zuckerman, *The Magazine in America,* 66–67, 108–109; David Reed, *The Popular Magazine in Britain and the United States, 1880–1960* (London: The British Library, 1997), 19–22, 27–49.

62. Richard Burket Kielbowicz, "Origins of the Second-Class Mail Category and the Business of Policymaking, 1863-1879," *Journalism Monographs,* no. 96 (1986).

63. Kielbowicz, "Origins of the Second-Class Mail Category and the Business of Policymaking, 1863–1879"; Mott, *A History of American Magazines,* vol. 4, 17, 20.

64. Richard Hofstadter, *The Age of Reform: From Bryan to F.D.R.* (New York: Vintage Books, 1955), 186–188; S.S. McClure, *My Autobiography* (New York: Frederick A. Stokes, 1914), 244–245.

65. Wayne E. Fuller, *R.F.D.: The Changing Face of Rural America* (Bloomington: Indiana University Press, 1964), 13–14, 30–58, 293–297; Sally Foreman Griffith, *Home Town News: William Allen White and the Emporia Gazette* (New York: Oxford University Press, 1989), 67–91.

66. Griffith, *Home Town News,* 91.

67. Lawrence Goodwyn, *Democratic Promise: The Populist Moment in America* (New York: Oxford University Press, 1976), 230–231, 492–494 (quotations, 231, 494); Elliott Shore, *Talkin' Socialism: J.A. Wayland and the Role of the Press in American Radicalism, 1890–1912* (Lawrence: University Press of Kansas, 1988), 99–100; Laureen Kessler, *The Dissident Press: Alternative Journalism in American History* (Beverly Hills, CA: Sage, 1984), 111–136.

68. Shore, *Talkin' Socialism,* 103–110, 167–171, 197–200.

69. For another treatment of these issues, see Carl F. Kaestle, "Standardization and Diversity in American Print Culture, 1880 to the Present," in Kaestle et al., *Literacy in the United States* (New Haven, CT: Yale University Press, 1991), 272–293.

CHAPTER EIGHT

1. Henry May, *The End of American Innocence: A Study of the First Years of Our Own Time, 1912–1917* (New York: Knopf, 1959), ix–xiv, 340–347; Christine Stansell, *American Moderns: Bohemian New York and the Creation of a New Century* (New York: Metropolitan Books, 2000), 75–119, 234–241.

2. *Patterson v. Colorado,* 205 U.S. 454 (1907) (quotation, 462).

3. *Fox v. Washington,* 236 U.S. 273 (1915) (quotation, 277). On this case and others involving free speech during this period, see David M. Rabban, *Free*

Speech in Its Forgotten Years, 1870–1920 (New York: Cambridge University Press, 1997), 129–176, esp. 132–147. For further discussion of state courts, see Margaret A. Blanchard, "Filling in the Void: Speech and Press in State Courts Prior to *Gitlow*," in Bill F. Chamberlin and Charlene J. Brown, eds., *The First Amendment Reconsidered* (New York: Longman, 1982), 14–59.

4. Rabban, *Free Speech in Its Forgotten Years*, 211–247; Paul S. Boyer, *Purity in Print: The Vice-Society Movement and Book Censorship in America* (New York: Scribner, 1968), 24–29; on differences among Progressive journalists, see John A. Thompson, *Reformers and War: American Progressive Publicists and the First World War* (New York: Cambridge University Press, 1987), 71–74.

5. Mark Graber, *Transforming Free Speech: The Ambiguous Legacy of Civil Libertarianism* (Berkeley: University of California Press, 1991), 17–49; Thomas M. Cooley, *A Treatise on the Constitutional Limitations Which Rest upon the Legislative Power of the States of the American Union*, 4th ed. (Boston: Little, Brown, 1878), 518–579; Hal D. Sears, *The Sex Radicals: Free Love in High Victorian America* (Lawrence: Regents Press of Kansas, 1977), 200–201; Rabban, *Free Speech in Its Forgotten Years*, 25–26, 44–55.

6. Boyer, *Purity in Print*, 24–29; John C. Burnham, "The Progressive Era Revolution in American Attitudes Toward Sex," *Journal of American History* 59 (March 1973), 885–908.

7. "Bernard Shaw Resents Action of Librarian; Calls 'American Comstockery' World's Standing Joke," *New York Times*, Sept. 26, 1905; "Who's Bernard Shaw? Asks Mr. Comstock," *New York Times*, Sept. 28, 1905; Felice Flanery Lewis, *Literature, Obscenity, and Law* (Carbondale: Southern Illinois University Press, 1976), 54–59.

8. Elizabeth Bainum Hovey, "Stamping Out Smut: The Enforcement of Obscenity Laws, 1872–1915" (Columbia University, Ph.D. dissertation, 1998), 287–296; Boyer, *Purity in Print*, 43 (vice society speaker quoted).

9. James C.N. Paul and Murray L. Schwartz, *Federal Censorship: Obscenity in the Mails* (New York: Free Press of Glencoe, 1961), 34, 38–41.

10. *Commonwealth v. Joseph Buckley*, 200 Mass. 346 (1909); Lewis, *Literature, Obscenity, and Law*, 59–63; Boyer, *Purity in Print*, 32–39.

11. Boyer, *Purity in Print*, 44–48.

12. M.L. Sanders and Philip M. Taylor, *British Propaganda During the First World War, 1914–1918* (London: Macmillan, 1982), 1–12, 18–32, 55–65; Gary S. Messinger, *British Propaganda and the State in the First World War* (Manchester, England: Manchester University Press, 1992); Deian Hopkin, "Domestic Censorship in the First World War," *Journal of Contemporary History* 5 (1970), 151–169; Stephen Vaughn, *Holding Fast the Inner Lines: Democracy, Nationalism, and the Committee on Public Information* (Chapel Hill: University of North Carolina Press, 1980), 214–215.

13. Vaughn, *Holding Fast the Inner Lines,* 3–38 (Creel quoted, 17); George Creel, *How We Advertised America* (New York: Harper and Brothers, 1920); James R. Mock and Cedric Larson, *Words That Won the War: The Story of the Committee on Public Information, 1917–1919* (Princeton, NJ: Princeton University Press, 1939). For broader discussions, see David M. Kennedy, *Over Here: The First World War and American Society* (New York: Oxford University Press, 1980), 45–92, and Ronald Schaffer, *America in the Great War* (New York: Oxford University Press, 1991), 3–30.

14. H.C. Peterson and Gilbert C. Fite, *Opponents of War, 1917–1918* (Madison: University of Wisconsin Press, 1957), 14–17; Paul I. Murphy, *World War I and the Origin of Civil Liberties in the United States* (New York: Norton, 1979), 41–80; Rabban, *Free Speech in Its Forgotten Years,* 249–255; *Ex Parte Jackson* 96 U.S. 727 (1877).

15. Murphy, *World War I and the Origin of Civil Liberties in the United States,* 96–103 (Burleson quoted, 100); Peterson and Fite, *Opponents of War,* 185–186 (Stokes quoted, 185).

16. Richard Polenberg, *Fighting Faiths: The Abrams Case, the Supreme Court, and Free Speech* (New York: Viking, 1987), 27–36 (judge quoted, 28); Peterson and Fite, *Opponents of War,* 208–221; Schaffer, *America in the Great War,* 15.

17. Vaughn, *Holding Fast the Inner Lines,* 217–225; Murphy, *World War I and the Origin of Civil Liberties in the United States,* 80–81.

18. Murphy, *World War I and the Origin of Civil Liberties in the United States,* 87–91; Peterson and Fite, *Opponents of War,* 17–20, 194–205; Frederic C. Howe, *The Confessions of a Reformer* (New York: C. Scribner's Sons, 1925), 278.

19. Peterson and Fite, *Opponents of War,* 149 (Gregory quoted), 205–207; Murphy, *World War I and the Origin of Civil Liberties in the United States,* 61–62, 100–103; Kennedy, *Over Here,* 236–244.

20. John Higham, *Strangers in the Land: Patterns of American Nativism, 1860–1925* (New York: Atheneum, 1985), 222–231; Donald Johnson, *The Challenge to American Freedom: World War I and the Rise of the American Civil Liberties Union* ([Lexington]: For the Mississippi Valley Historical Association, University of Kentucky Press, 1963), 119–145.

21. Murphy, *World War I and the Origin of Civil Liberties in the United States,* 153–164.

22. *Masses Publishing Co. v. Patten,* 244 F. 535 (S.D. N.Y. 1917) (quotation, 539); *Masses Publishing Co. v. Patten,* 246 F. 24, 38 (2d Cir. 1917) (quotation, 39); John Sayer, "Art and Politics, Dissent and Repression: The Masses Magazine Versus the Government, 1917–1918," *American Journal of Legal History* 32 (January 1988), 42–78.

23. *Debs v. United States*, 249 U.S. 211 (1919). For background, see Peterson and Fite, *Opponents of War*, 248–255.

24. *Schenck v. United States*, 249 U.S. 47 (1919) (quotation, 52); on the leaflet, see Polenberg, *Fighting Faiths*, 213–215.

25. Fred D. Ragan, "Justice Oliver Wendell Holmes, Jr., Zechariah Chafee, Jr., and the Clear and Present Danger Test for Free Speech: The First Year, 1919," *Journal of American History* 58 (June 1971), 24–45; Polenberg, *Fighting Faiths*, 218–228; Rabban, *Free Speech in Its Forgotten Years*, 285–286.

26. *Abrams et al. v. United States*, 250 U.S. 616 (1919); Polenberg, *Fighting Faiths*, 36–55, 228–235.

27. *Abrams et al. v. United States*, 250 U.S. 630–631 (1919).

28. Polenberg, *Fighting Faiths*, 218–228; Rabban, *Free Speech in Its Forgotten Years*, 350–355; Thompson, *Reformers and War*, 236–237, 258–260, 267–272 (Lippmann quoted, 260).

29. George Orwell, *Coming Up for Air* (New York: Harcourt Brace, 1950), 144, quoted in Kennedy, *Over Here*, 45; Howe, *The Confessions of a Reformer*, 279; Thompson, *Reformers and War*, 271–272; Johnson, *The Challenge to American Freedom*, 145–148; Rabban, *Free Speech in Its Forgotten Years*, 299–316.

30. Richard Crockatt, "American Liberalism and the Atlantic World, 1916–1917," *Journal of American Studies* 11 (April 1977), 123–143; Thompson, *Reformers and War*, 272–273.

31. Higham, *Strangers in the Land*, 231–233; Johnson, *The Challenge to American Freedom*, 83–84 (Hays quoted, 84).

32. Boyer, *Purity in Print*, 152–153 (*Christian Century* quoted, 152).

33. Frederick Lewis Allen, *Only Yesterday: An Informal History of the Nineteen-Twenties* (New York and London: Harper and Brothers, 1931), 89–112 (quotation, 112).

34. Ann Douglas, *Terrible Honesty: Mongrel Manhattan in the 1920s* (New York: Farrar, Straus, and Giroux, 1995), 33.

35. Stanley Coben, *Rebellion Against Victorianism: The Impetus for Cultural Change in 1920s America* (New York: Oxford University Press, 1991), 48–68.

36. Boyer, *Purity in Print*, 99–118 (Walker quoted, 118); Walter Kendrick, *The Secret Museum: Pornography in Modern Culture* (Berkeley: University of California Press, 1996), 178–180.

37. Boyer, *Purity in Print*, 119–127, 134–135, 167–206.

38. Boyer, *Purity in Print*, 209–238.

39. Lewis, *Literature, Obscenity, and Law*, 126–127; *United States v. One Book Called "Ulysses,"* 5 F. Supp. 182 (S.D.N.Y. 1933); Boyer, *Purity in Print*, 135 (speaker to booksellers quoted).

40. *Gitlow v. New York*, 268 U.S. 652 (1925); *Stromberg v. California*, 283 U.S. 359 (1931); *Near v. Minnesota*, 283 U.S. 697 (1931).

41. *Near v. Minnesota,* 283 U.S. 697 (1931); Fred W. Friendly, *Minnesota Rag* (New York: Vintage Books, 1982).

42. Horace Kallen, *Culture and Democracy in the United States* (New York: Boni and Liveright, 1924).

CHAPTER NINE

1. Lawrence W. Levine, *Highbrow/Lowbrow: The Emergence of Cultural Hierarchy in America* (Cambridge: Harvard University Press, 1988).

2. David Nasaw, *Going Out: The Rise and Fall of Public Amusement* (New York: Basic Books, 1993), 1–18 (quotation, 5); Kathy Peiss, *Cheap Amusements: Working Women and Leisure in Turn-of-the-Century New York* (Philadelphia: Temple University Press, 1986); Michael Kammen, *American Culture, American Tastes: Social Change and the 20th Century* (New York: Knopf, 1999), 31–32; Roy Rosenzweig, *Eight Hours for What We Will: Workers and Leisure in an Industrial City, 1870–1920* (New York: Cambridge University Press, 1983), 171–182; Robert Allen, *Vaudeville and Film, 1895–1915: A Study of Media Interaction* (New York: Arno Press, 1980), 23–25.

3. Paul Israel, *Edison: A Life of Invention* (New York: John Wiley and Sons, 1998), 277–292; Nasaw, *Going Out,* 120–133.

4. Charles Musser, *The Emergence of Cinema: The American Screen to 1907* (New York: Scribner, 1990), 62–72 (Edison quoted, 64); Elizabeth Brayer, *George Eastman: A Biography* (Baltimore: Johns Hopkins University Press, 1996), 68–70, 109–112.

5. Musser, *The Emergence of Cinema,* 81–105; Allen, *Vaudeville and Film,* 75–115.

6. Raymond Fielding, *The American Newsreel, 1911–1967* (Norman: University of Oklahoma Press, 1973), 3–25; "The Anatomy of a Kiss," *World,* April 26, 1896, quoted in Lary May, *Screening Out the Past: The Birth of Mass Culture and the Motion Picture Industry* (New York: Oxford University Press, 1980), 39; Terry Ramsaye, *A Million and One Nights; A History of the Motion Picture* (New York: Simon and Schuster, 1926), 1: 259, 286–289; Musser, *The Emergence of Cinema,* 115–122.

7. Musser, *The Emergence of Cinema,* 183–189, 284.

8. Ibid., 298–336; Allen, *Vaudeville and Film,* 127–128, 151–159, citing data from Richard Arlo Sanderson, "A Historical Study of the Development of American Motion Picture Content and Techniques Prior to 1904" (University of Southern California, Ph.D. dissertation, 1961).

9. Musser, *The Emergence of Cinema,* 375.

10. Ibid., 368–369.

11. Eileen Bowser, *The Transformation of Cinema, 1907–1915* (Berkeley: University of California Press, 1994), 1–11; Musser, *The Emergence of Cinema,*

417–447; Lewis Jacobs, *The Rise of the American Film: A Critical History* (New York: Harcourt Brace, 1939), 67; Russell Merritt, "Nickelodeon Theaters, 1905–1914: Building an Audience for the Movies," in Tino Balio, ed., *The American Film Industry*, rev. ed. (Madison: University of Wisconsin Press, 1985), 83–102 (Agee quoted, 83–84).

12. Michael M. Davis, Jr., *The Exploitation of Pleasure: A Study of Commercial Recreations in New York City* (New York: Russell Sage Foundation, 1911), 30. To determine class, Davis relied on subjective observations by a small group of researchers but claimed there was "remarkably little" disparity in their judgments: "The classification was more difficult in appearance than in reality" (31). See also Rosenzweig, *Eight Hours for What We Will*, 191–195. On discrimination against African Americans, see Douglas Gomery, *Shared Pleasures: A History of Movie Presentation in the United States* (Madison: University of Wisconsin Press, 1992), 155–159, and Gregory Waller, *Main Street Amusements: Movies and Commercial Entertainment in Lexington, Kentucky, 1896–1930* (Washington, DC: Smithsonian Institution Press, 1995), 161–179.

13. Ben Singer, "Manhattan Nickelodeons: New Data on Audiences and Exhibitors," *Cinema Journal* 34 (Spring 1995), 5–35; Richard Abel, *The Red Rooster Scare: Making Cinema American, 1900–1910* (Berkeley: University of California Press, 1999), 70–73; Neal Gabler, *An Empire of Their Own: How the Jews Invented Hollywood* (New York: Crown, 1988), 3–5; Robert Sklar, *Movie-Made America: A Social History of American Movies* (New York: Random House, 1975), 40–42.

14. Musser, *The Emergence of Cinema*, 449–489.

15. Abel, *The Red Rooster Scare*, 20–37, 48–49.

16. Allen, *Vaudeville and Film*, 212.

17. Dr. Alice Shaw, quoted in Bowser, *The Transformation of Cinema*, 37–38; Kathleen D. McCarthy, "Nickel Vice and Virtue: Movie Censorship in Chicago, 1907–1915," *Journal of Popular Film* 5 (1976), 37–55.

18. Nancy J. Rosenbloom, "Between Reform and Regulation: The Struggle over Film Censorship in Progressive America, 1909–1922," *Film History* 1 (1987), 307–325; Daniel Czitrom, "The Politics of Performance: From Theater Licensing to Movie Censorship in Turn-of-the-Century New York," *American Quarterly* 44 (December 1992), 525–553; Garth Jowett, *Film: The Democratic Art* (Boston: Little, Brown, 1976), 111–116, 126–130.

19. Bowser, *The Transformation of Cinema*, 21–36; Janet Staiger, "Combination and Litigation: Structures of U.S. Film Distribution, 1891–1917," *Cinema Journal* 23 (Winter 1983), 41–72; Robert Anderson, "The Motion Picture Patents Company: A Reevaluation," in Balio, *The American Film Industry*, 133–152.

20. Abel, *The Red Rooster Scare*, 94–101, 136–139; Rosenbloom, "Between Reform and Regulation," 310.

21. Bowser, *The Transformation of Cinema*, 85.

22. Ibid., 73–85; Staiger, "Combination and Litigation: Structures of U.S. Film Distribution, 1891–1917," 50–55.

23. Gabler, *An Empire of Their Own*, 30, 59–61 (quotations, 30, 59); Bowser, *The Transformation of Cinema*, 33–36, 83–85.

24. Ruth A. Inglis, *Freedom of the Movies* (New York: Da Capo Press, 1974 [1947]), 68–76; Rosenbloom, "Between Reform and Regulation," 314–316 (quotations, 314, 316); on the development of film censorship abroad, see Neville March Hunnings, *Film Censors and the Law* (London: George Allen and Unwin, 1967).

25. *Mutual Film Corp. v. Industrial Com. of Ohio*, 236 U.S. 230 (1915) [at 244].

26. Ibid., at 242–244.

27. Rosenbloom, "Between Reform and Regulation," 314.

28. Steven J. Ross, *Working-Class Hollywood: Silent Film and the Shaping of Class in America* (Princeton, NJ: Princeton University Press, 1998), 6–10, 34–35, 45–48, 57–71 (quotation, 35). See also Kay Sloan, *The Loud Silents: Origins of the Social Problem Film* (Urbana: University of Illinois Press, 1988), and Kevin Brownlow, *Behind the Mask of Innocence* (New York: Knopf, 1990).

29. Jowett, *Film: The Democratic Art*, 101–103; Michael Rogin, "'The Sword Became a Flashing Vision': D.W. Griffith's *The Birth of a Nation*," in Rogin, *"Ronald Reagan," the Movie: and Other Episodes in Political Demonology* (Berkeley: University of California Press, 1987), 190–235; Fielding, *The American Newsreel*, 70–71, 284–285; *Pathé Exchange, Inc. v. Cobb*, 195 N.Y.S. 661 (1922).

30. Alfred E. Cornebise, *War as Advertised: The Four Minute Men and America's Crusade, 1917–1918* (Philadelphia: American Philosophical Society, 1984), 2–12; Stephen Vaughn, *Holding Fast the Inner Lines: Democracy, Nationalism, and the Committee on Public Information* (Chapel Hill: University of North Carolina Press, 1980); *United States v. Motion Picture Film "The Spirit of '76,"* 252 F. 949, 947–948 (S.D. Cal. 1917), aff'd sub nom, *Goldstein v. United States*, 258 F. 908 (9th Cir. 1919).

31. May, *Screening Out the Past*, 167–199; Gabler, *An Empire of Their Own*, 5–6; Bowser, *The Transformation of Cinema*, 149–165.

32. Inglis, *Freedom of the Movies*, 62–70.

33. Francis G. Couvares, "Hollywood, Main Street, and the Church: Trying to Censor the Movies Before the Production Code," *American Quarterly* 44 (December 1992), 584–616; Donald Johnson, *The Challenge to American Freedom: World War I and the Rise of the American Civil Liberties Union* ([Lexington]: University of Kentucky Press, 1963), 83 (Hays quotation).

34. Gregory D. Black, *Hollywood Censored: Morality Codes, Catholics, and the Movies* (New York: Cambridge University Press, 1994), 31–34; Stephen Vaughn, "Morality and Entertainment: The Origins of the Motion Picture Production Code," *Journal of American History* 77 (June 1990), 39–65.

35. May, *Screening Out the Past,* 177, 214.

36. Tino Balio, "Struggles for Control, 1908–1930," in Balio, *The American Film Industry,* 116–131; Halsey, Stuart and Co., "The Motion Picture Industry as a Basis for Bond Financing," ibid., 195–217; Richard Koszarski, *An Evening's Entertainment: The Age of the Silent Feature Picture, 1915–1928* (New York: Scribner, 1990), 63–94; Douglas Gomery, *The Hollywood Studio System, 1930–1949* (New York: St. Martin's Press, 1986), 1–25.

37. Couvares, "Hollywood, Main Street, and the Church," 596–598; Black, *Hollywood Censored,* 34; Leonard J. Leff and Jerold L. Simmons, *The Dame in the Kimono: Hollywood, Censorship, and the Production Code,* 2d ed. (Lexington: University Press of Kentucky, 2001), 8.

38. Vaughn, "Morality and Entertainment," 50–52; Black, *Hollywood Censored,* 34–39; Couvares, "Hollywood, Main Street, and the Church," 500–609.

39. See "Working Draft of the Lord-Quigley Code Proposal," in Black, *Hollywood Censored,* Appendix A, 302–308.

40. Black, *Hollywood Censored,* 40–43 (Hays quoted, 40); Appendix, "The Motion Picture Production Code," in Leff and Simmons, *The Dame in the Kimono,* 286–288.

41. Thomas Doherty, *Pre-code Hollywood: Sex, Immorality, and Insurrection in American Cinema, 1930–1934* (New York: Columbia University Press, 1999); Leff and Simmons, *The Dame in the Kimono,* 11–33 (West quoted, 24).

42. Douglas Gomery, "U.S. Film Exhibition: The Formation of a Big Business," in Balio, *The American Film Industry*, 226; Black, *Hollywood Censored,* 149–156; Henry James Forman, *Our Movie Made Children* (New York: Macmillan, 1933); see also Garth S. Jowett, Ian C. Jarvie, and Kathryn H. Fuller, eds., *Children and the Movies: Media Influences and the Payne Fund Controversy* (New York: Cambridge University Press, 1996).

43. Black, *Hollywood Censored,* 157–160 (Scott quoted, 159, from letter from Breen to Quigley, Aug. 4, 1933).

44. Black, *Hollywood Censored,* 182–187; Gregory D. Black, *The Catholic Crusade Against the Movies, 1940–1975* (New York: Cambridge University Press, 1997), 1–3.

45. Black, *Hollywood Censored,* 187–190.

46. On the economic vulnerabilities, see Vaughn, "Morality and Entertainment."

47. Ellis Hawley, "Three Faces of Hooverian Associationalism: Lumber, Aviation, and Movies, 1921–1930," in Thomas K. McCraw, ed., *Regulation in Perspective: Historical Essays* (Cambridge: Harvard University Graduate School of Business Administration, 1981), 95–123.

48. "Working Draft of the Lord-Quigley Code Proposal," 304; Jonas Barish, *The Antitheatrical Prejudice* (Berkeley: University of California Press, 1981).

CHAPTER TEN

1. Asa Briggs, *The BBC: The First Fifty Years* (New York: Oxford University Press, 1985), 14–15; Susan J. Douglas, *Inventing American Broadcasting, 1899–1922* (Baltimore: Johns Hopkins University Press, 1987), 298–300.

2. See Chapter 6.

3. Erik Barnouw, *A Tower in Babel* (New York: Oxford University Press, 1966), 91; Douglas, *Inventing American Broadcasting*, 303.

4. Hugh R. Slotten, *Radio and Television Regulation: Broadcast Technology in the United States, 1920–1960* (Baltimore: Johns Hopkins University Press, 2000), 6–8.

5. Kenneth Bilby, *The General: David Sarnoff and the Rise of the Communications Industry* (New York: Harper and Row, 1986), 70–73; Barnouw, *A Tower in Babel*, 81–82, 105–118.

6. Philip T. Rosen, *The Modern Stentors: Radio Broadcasters and the Federal Government, 1920–1934* (Westport, CT: Greenwood Press, 1980), 21–33.

7. Rosen, *The Modern Stentors*, 35–46; Douglas B. Craig, *Fireside Politics: Radio and Political Culture in the United States, 1920–1940* (Baltimore: Johns Hopkins University Press, 2000), 45–48.

8. Rosen, *The Modern Stentors*, 35–40, 49–50 (Hoover quoted, 49); Slotten, *Radio and Television Regulation*, 15–21.

9. Rosen, *The Modern Stentors*, 50–59; Barnouw, *A Tower in Babel*, 121–122.

10. Christopher H. Sterling, *Electronic Media: A Guide to Trends in Broadcasting and Newer Technologies, 1920–1983* (New York: Praeger, 1984), 216, 222; Leslie J. Page, Jr., "The Nature of the Broadcast Receiver and Its Market in the United States from 1922 to 1927," *Journal of Broadcasting* 4 (Spring 1960), 174–182; Craig, *Fireside Politics*, 10–11; Susan J. Douglas, *Listening In* (New York: Times Books, 1999), 55–82.

11. David Sarnoff, "Letter to E.W. Rice, Jr., Honorary Chairman of the Board, General Electric Co., June 17, 1922," in Lawrence W. Lichty and Malachi C. Topping, eds., *American Broadcasting: A Source Book on the History of Radio and Television* (New York: Hastings House, 1975), 163–164.

12. Available data do not break out the distribution of stations according to the categories used here; but see Malcolm M. Willey and Stuart A. Rice, *Communication Agencies and Social Life* (New York and London: McGraw-Hill, 1933), 196 (Table 54), using Commerce Department data showing, for 1925, "commercial broadcasting companies," 21; educational institutions, 110; churches, 50; newspapers and publishers, 33; electric and radio stories and service companies, 91; miscellaneous, 266. Unfortunately, the final entry undermines the usefulness of the earlier ones.

13. Barnouw, *A Tower in Babel*, 105–114, 158–159; William Peck Banning, *Commercial Broadcasting Pioneer: The WEAF Experiment, 1922–1926* (Cambridge: Harvard University Press, 1946).

14. Craig, *Fireside Politics*, 27-28; Bilby, *The General*, 76-79; Barnouw, *A Tower in Babel*, 143-145,160-161.

15. Bilby, *The General*, 76–79; Barnouw, *A Tower in Babel*, 161–162; Susan Smulyan, *Selling Radio: The Commercialization of Radio Broadcasting, 1920–1934* (Washington, DC: Smithsonian Institution Press, 1994), 42–58.

16. Barnouw, *A Tower in Babel*, 154–157; Hoover quoted in Slotten, *Radio and Television Regulation*, 17; Roland Marchand, *Advertising the American Dream: Making Way for Modernity, 1920–1940* (Berkeley: University of California Press, 1985), 89–94 (*Printers' Ink* quoted, 89).

17. Barnouw, *A Tower in Babel*, 177–178.

18. John Ryan, *The Production of Culture in the Music Industry: The ASCAP-BMI Controversy* (Lanham, MD: University Press of America, 1985), 16–17, 19–20, 31–52.

19. William Barlow, *Voice Over: The Making of Black Radio* (Philadelphia: Temple University Press, 1999), 18–19; Barnouw, *A Tower in Babel*, 128–129.

20. Briggs, *The BBC: The First Fifty Years*, 17–37.

21. Paddy Scannell and David Cardiff, *A Social History of British Broadcasting* (Oxford: Blackwell, 1991), 1: 7–17 (quotation, 14); Briggs, *The BBC: The First Fifty Years*, 53–55 (Reith quoted, 55).

22. Barnouw, *A Tower in Babel*, 126.

23. Ruth Thomas, *Broadcasting and Democracy in France* (London: Crosby Lockwood Staples, 1976), 1–3; Jerome G. Kerwin, *The Control of Radio* (Chicago: University of Chicago Press, 1934), 9–10.

24. Rosen, *The Modern Stentors*, 93–94; Slotten, *Radio and Television Regulation*, 37–40.

25. Radio Act of 1927, 44 Stat. 1162–1174.

26. Rosen, *The Modern Stentors*, 121–123.

27. Bilby, *The General*, 82–87; Rosen, *The Modern Stentors*, 87–92.

28. Louise M. Benjamin, *Freedom of the Air and the Public Interest: First Amendment Rights in Broadcasting to 1935* (Carbondale and Edwardsville: University of Illinois Press, 2001), 73–74 (quoting Sen. Clarence Dill).

CHAPTER ELEVEN

1. Christopher H. Sterling, *Electronic Media: A Guide to Trends in Broadcasting and Newer Technologies, 1920-1983* (New York: Praeger, 1984), 222. This commonly used measure—the proportion of households with radio—understates access to radio in its early years, when many people listened to broadcasts at a neighbor's home or in a public place. There is an analogous difficulty in using the proportion of households with telephones as a measure of access to the phone system. Especially in urban areas, many people relied on public (pay) telephones. The subsequent near-total shift of radios and telephones to house-

hold or individual ownership tends to bias the understanding of media use in the past.

2. Philip T. Rosen, *The Modern Stentors: Radio Broadcasters and the Federal Government, 1920–1934* (Westport, CT: Greenwood Press, 1980), 116–121; Federal Communications Commission, *Report on Chain Broadcasting* ([Washington: Government Printing Office], 1941), 14–16.

3. Hugh R. Slotten, *Radio and Television Regulation: Broadcast Technology in the United States, 1920–1960* (Baltimore: Johns Hopkins University Press, 2000), 44–45; Robert McChesney, *Telecommunications, Mass Media and Democracy: The Battle for Control of U.S. Broadcasting, 1928–1935* (New York: Oxford University Press, 1993), 22–23.

4. McChesney, *Telecommunications, Mass Media and Democracy,* 19–22.

5. Slotten, *Radio and Television Regulation,* 52–66; Rosen, *The Modern Stentors,* 135–136.

6. Slotten, *Radio and Television Regulation,* 49–51; McChesney, *Telecommunications, Mass Media and Democracy,* 26–28 (FRC Annual Report quoted, 27, 28).

7. Erik Barnouw, *A Tower in Babel* (New York: Oxford University Press, 1966), 259–261; Rosen, *The Modern Stentors,* 140; McChesney, *Telecommunications, Mass Media and Democracy,* 30–31 (Arkansas station director quoted, 31); Slotten, *Radio and Television Regulation,* 58–59.

8. Louise M. Benjamin, *Freedom of the Air and the Public Interest: First Amendment Rights in Broadcasting to 1935* (Carbondale and Edwardsville: University of Illinois Press, 2001), 65 (citing Hiram Jome, *Economics of the Radio Industry* [Chicago: A.W. Shaw, 1925], and internal AT&T study).

9. Sally Bedell Smith, *In All His Glory: The Life and Times of William S. Paley* (New York: Simon and Schuster, 1990), 62–67, 116; Barnouw, *A Tower in Babel,* 251.

10. Sterling, *Electronic Media,* 222; Hadley Cantril and Gordon W. Allport, *The Psychology of Radio* (New York and London: Harper and Brothers, 1935), 86–88; F.H. Lumley, *Measurement in Radio* (Columbus: Ohio State University Press, 1934), 196.

11. Roland Marchand, *Advertising the American Dream: Making Way for Modernity, 1920–1940* (Berkeley: University of California Press, 1985), 94–108.

12. J. Fred MacDonald, *Don't Touch That Dial! Radio Programming in American Life, 1920–1960* (Chicago: Nelson-Hall, 1979), 30–32.

13. Kenneth Bilby, *The General: David Sarnoff and the Rise of the Communications Industry* (New York: Harper and Row, 1986), 117–120; Christopher H. Sterling and John M. Kittross, *Stay Tuned: A Concise History of American Broadcasting* (Belmont, CA: Wadsworth, 1978), 99–102; Asa Briggs, *The BBC: The First Fifty Years* (New York: Oxford University Press, 1985), 155–161.

14. McChesney, *Telecommunications, Mass Media and Democracy,* 38–62, 146–150 (FRC quoted, 148).

15. Ibid., 158–177; Derek Vaillant, "'Your Voice Came in Last Night . . . But I Thought . . . It Sounded a Little Scared': Rural Radio Listening and 'Talking Back' During the Progressive Era in Wisconsin, 1920–1932," in Michele Hilmes and Jason Loviglio, eds., *The Radio Reader* (New York: Routledge, 2001), 63–88 (quotation, 63–64); Paul F. Lazarsfeld, *Radio and the Printed Page* (New York: Duell, Sloan and Pearce, 1940), 21–47.

16. Larry Cuban, *Teachers and Machines: The Classroom Use of Technology Since 1920* (New York: Teachers College Press, 1986), 19–26.

17. McChesney, *Telecommunications, Mass Media and Democracy,* 177–179.

18. Rosen, *The Modern Stentors,* 170–178; McChesney, *Telecommunications, Mass Media and Democracy,* 179–209 (NBC vice president quoted, 209).

19. Rosen, *The Modern Stentors,* 178; Lawrence W. Lichty, "The Impact of FRC and FCC Commissioners' Backgrounds on the Regulation of Broadcasting," *Journal of Broadcasting* 6 (Spring 1962), 97–110; Douglas B. Craig, *Fireside Politics: Radio and Political Culture in the United States, 1920–1940* (Baltimore: Johns Hopkins University Press, 2000), 93; McChesney, *Telecommunications, Mass Media and Democracy,* 182–183.

20. Frank W. Peers, *The Politics of Canadian Broadcasting, 1920–1951* (Toronto: University of Toronto Press, 1969), 17–20, 48–51, 75–79, 101–105, 166–188, 210–211, 244, 346–365.

21. Peers, *The Politics of Canadian Broadcasting,* 440–443 (quotation, 441); Craig, *Fireside Politics,* 42–43.

22. Craig, *Fireside Politics,* 27.

23. Benjamin, *Freedom of the Air and the Public Interest,* 89–94 (Brinkley quoted, 92); Lucas A. Powe, Jr., *American Broadcasting and the First Amendment* (Berkeley: University of California Press, 1987), 22–30; *KFKB Broadcasting Association, Inc., v. FRC,* 47 F.2d 670 (D.C. Cir. 1930) (quotation: 672).

24. *Trinity Methodist Church v. FRC,* 62 F. 2d 850 (D.C. Cir., 1932); Benjamin, *Freedom of the Air and the Public Interest,* 97–106 (Shuler quoted, 99, 104); Powe, *American Broadcasting and the First Amendment,* 11–18 (FRC quoted, 16).

25. Powe, *American Broadcasting and the First Amendment,* 18–21. On the Near case, see above, Chapter 8.

26. Lizabeth Cohen, *Making a New Deal: Industrial Workers in Chicago, 1918–1939* (Cambridge: Cambridge University Press, 1990), 129–143, 327–328 (quotation, 135).

27. FCC, *Report on Chain Broadcasting,* 31–32, 35, 51.

28. ACLU study quoted in Craig, *Fireside Politics,* 101; Benjamin, *Freedom of the Air and the Public Interest,* 142–146. See also Matthew Murray, "'The Ten-

dency to Deprave and Corrupt Morals': Regulation and Irregular Sexuality in Golden Age Radio Comedy," in Hilmes and Loviglio, *The Radio Reader,* 135–156.

29. William Barlow, *Voice Over: The Making of Black Radio* (Philadelphia: Temple University Press, 1999), 16–30, 50–58; Douglas, *Listening In,* 83–99. Douglas writes that while "radio reined in black jazz," it also "took the music of African Americans into the heart of white America and made it our first genuine national music" (95).

30. U.S. Department of Commerce, Bureau of the Census, *Sixteenth Census of the United States, 1940: Housing,* vol. 2, *General Characteristics* (Washington, DC: Government Printing Office, 1943), table 10, 38; Barlow, *Voice Over,* 28, 31–34; Barbara Dianne Savage, *Broadcasting Freedom: Radio, War, and the Politics of Race, 1938–1948* (Chapel Hill: University of North Carolina Press, 1999), 10–12.

31. Michael McGerr, *The Decline of Popular Politics: The American North, 1865–1928* (New York: Oxford University Press, 1986), 138–183 (Franklin Roosevelt quoted, 173); Jeffrey K. Tulis, *The Rhetorical Presidency* (Princeton, NJ: Princeton University Press, 1987), 139–140.

32. Craig, *Fireside Politics,* 114–116.

33. Benjamin, *Freedom of the Air and the Public Interest,* 117–127.

34. Craig, *Fireside Politics,* 117–118, 132; Benjamin, *Freedom of the Air and the Public Interest,* 36–47.

35. Louise Overacker, *Money in Elections* (New York: Macmillan, 1932), 28–29; Craig, *Fireside Politics,* 133–137 (quotation, 137: John Royal to Niles Trammel, NBC Interdepartment Correspondence, Feb. 13, 1940).

36. Craig, *Fireside Politics,* 124–127, 142, 150–151 (Paley quoted, 151).

37. Lawrence W. Levine and Cornelia R. Levine, eds., *The People and the President: America's Extraordinary Conversation with FDR* (Boston: Beacon Press, 2002), x–xi, 12–20 (quotation, x; Illinois woman quoted, 27); Craig, *Fireside Politics,* 156–157.

38. Levine and Levine, *The People and the President,* 5–11, 20–23 (quotations, 20, 22–23).

39. Paul F. Lazarsfeld, Bernard Berelson, and Hazel Gaudet, *The People's Choice: How the Voter Makes Up His Mind in a Presidential Campaign* (New York: Duell, Sloan, and Pearce, 1944), 129-133 (quotation, 129). On newspaper endorsements and coverage, see Graham J. White, *FDR and the Press* (Chicago: University of Chicago Press, 1979), 51-91.

40. Levine and Levine, *The People and the President,* 12; Savage, *Broadcasting Freedom,* 21–62.

41. Erik Barnouw, *The Golden Web: A History of Broadcasting in the United States,* vol. 2, *1933 to 1953* (New York: Oxford University Press, 1968), 14–16, 34; David Holbrook Culbert, *News for Everyman: Radio and Foreign Affairs in*

Thirties America (Westport, CT: Greenwood Press,1976), 47–53; Alan Brinkley, *Voices of Protest: Huey Long, Father Coughlin, and the Great Depression* (New York: Knopf, 1982), 99–101, 265–267.

42. William Hard, "Europe's Air and Ours," *Atlantic Monthly* 150 (October 1932), 499–509 (quotations, 499, 509). The later Canadian policy toward controversial broadcasting, formulated in 1939, may have been more open than the American system; see Peers, *The Politics of Canadian Broadcasting,* 279.

43. Giraud Chester, "The Press-Radio War: 1933–1935," *Public Opinion Quarterly* 13 (Summer, 1949), 252–264; Barnouw, *The Golden Web,* 18–22; McChesney, *Telecommunications, Mass Media and Democracy,* 171; Douglas, *Listening In,* 166–168.

44. Barnouw, *The Golden Web,* 55, 66–83; Culbert, *News for Everyman,* 73–76; Stanley Cloud and Lynne Olson, *The Murrow Boys: Pioneers on the Front Lines of Broadcast Journalism* (Boston: Houghton-Mifflin, 1996), 31–41; H.V. Kaltenborn, *I Broadcast the Crisis* (New York: Random House, 1938), 3, 9; Douglas, *Listening In,* 176–180; Hadley Cantril and Mildred Strunk, *Public Opinion, 1935–1946* (Princeton, NJ, Princeton University Press, 1951), 524.

45. Hadley Cantril, *The Invasion from Mars: A Study in the Psychology of Panic* (Princeton, NJ: Princeton University Press, 1940).

46. Lazarsfeld, *Radio and the Printed Page,* 204, 218–219; Cantril and Strunk, *Public Opinion, 1935–1946,* 524.

47. Cloud and Olson, *The Murrow Boys,* 57–60; Douglas, *Listening In,* 180–188; Barnouw, *The Golden Web,* 135–137 (NAB code quoted, 137).

48. Hugh Carter Donahue, *The Battle to Control Broadcast News: Who Owns the First Amendment?* (Cambridge: MIT Press, 1989), 33–36.

49. *Hague v. Committee for Industrial Organization,* 307 U.S. 496 (1939).

50. James Lawrence Fly, "Regulation of Radio in the Public Interest," *Annals of the American Academy of Political and Social Science* 213 (January 1941), 106–107. The high-water mark of this alternative model came nearly thirty years later in *Red Lion Broadcasting v. FCC,* 395 U.S. 367 (1969).

51. FCC, *Report on Chain Broadcasting,* 72.

52. Ibid., 91–92; *NBC v. United States,* 319 U.S. 192 (1943).

53. Paul F. Lazarsfeld, "The Effects of Radio on Public Opinion," in Douglas Waples, ed., *Print, Radio, and Film in a Democracy* (Chicago: University of Chicago Press, 1942), 66–78 (quotations, 66, 69, 70).

54. Barnouw, *The Golden Web,* 41–42; Slotten, *Radio and Television Regulation,* 113–117.

55. Slotten, *Radio and Television Regulation,* 118–144.

56. Bilby, *The General,* 120–134; Briggs, *The BBC: The First Fifty Years,* 161–171.

57. Robert Britt Horwitz, *The Irony of Regulatory Reform: The Deregulation of American Telecommunications* (New York: Oxford University Press, 1989), 174–195.

CHAPTER TWELVE

1. Michael Schudson, "The Politics of Narrative Form," in *The Power of News* (Cambridge: Harvard University Press, 1995), 53–71; on the growth of "interpretive" journalism, see also Schudson, *Discovering the News* (New York: Basic Books, 1978),145–148. (Note: Sources already referenced for facts or arguments earlier in this book are not cited again in this chapter.)

2. Susan J. Douglas, *Listening In* (New York: Times Books, 1999), 84.

3. Piers Brendon, *The Life and Death of the Press Barons* (New York: Atheneum, 1983), 108–115; Simon Michael Bessie, *Jazz Journalism: The Story of the Tabloid Newspapers* (New York: E.P. Dutton, 1938), 79–95.

4. Walter Lippmann, *Liberty and the News* (New York: Harcourt, Brace and Howe, 1920), 5.

5. On American comparative advantage in television, see Eli Noam, *Television in Europe* (New York: Oxford University Press, 1991), 11–27.

6. "A Test of the News," *The New Republic,* Aug. 4, 1920; see Phillip Knightley, *The First Casualty* (New York: Harcourt, 1975), 138–170.

7. Lippmann, *Liberty and the News,* 5, 9, 11, 13, 64, 72–73, 87, 94–95; Ronald Steel, *Walter Lippmann and the American Century* (New York: Vintage Books, 1980), 171; Marion Tuttle Marzolf, *Civilizing Voices: American Press Criticism, 1880–1950* (New York: Longman, 1991), 81.

8. Walter Lippmann, *Public Opinion* (New York: Harcourt, Brace, 1922). The third of Lippmann's books on the subject was *The Phantom Public* (New York: Harcourt, Brace, 1925).

9. James W. Carey, *Communication as Culture: Essays on Media and Society* (Winchester, MA: Unwin Hyman, 1989), 75.

10. Paul F. Lazarsfeld, Bernard Berelson, and Hazel Gaudet, *The People's Choice: How the Voter Makes Up His Mind in a Presidential Campaign* (New York: Duell, Sloan, and Pearce, 1944), 150–158 (quotation, 158).

11. For the full elaboration of the limited-effects model, see Elihu Katz and Paul F. Lazarsfeld, *Personal Influence* (Glencoe, IL: Free Press, 1955), and Joseph Klapper, *The Effects of Mass Communication* (Glencoe, IL: Free Press, 1960); for criticism, see Todd Gitlin, "Media Sociology: The Dominant Paradigm," *Theory and Society* 6 (1978), 205–253. On agenda-setting, the original discussion was in Bernard Cohen, *The Press and Foreign Policy* (Princeton, NJ: Princeton University Press, 1963); the key empirical study was Maxwell E. McCombs and Donald L. Shaw, "The Agenda-Setting Function of Mass Media," *Public Opinion Quarterly* 36 (1972), 176–187. See Everett M. Rogers, *A History of Communication Study: A Biographical Approach* (New York: The Free Press, 1994), 237–315.

12. Lizabeth Cohen, *Making a New Deal: Industrial Workers in Chicago, 1918–1939* (Cambridge: Cambridge University Press, 1990), 143–145 (quotations, 144). On later intergenerational differences in civic engagement possibly

related to the advent of a new medium (television), see Robert Putnam, *Bowling Alone: The Collapse and Revival of American Community* (New York: Simon and Schuster, 2000), 216–276.

13. Max Horkheimer and Theodor W. Adorno, *Dialectic of Enlightenment,* trans. John Cumming (New York: Herder and Herder, 1972 [orig. ed. in German, 1944]), 120–167 (quotations, 120, 122, 134, 138, 159). For background and a sympathetic exposition, see Martin Jay, *The Dialectical Imagination: A History of the Frankfurt School and the Institute of Social Research, 1923–1950* (Boston: Little, Brown, 1973), 173–218.

14. Jürgen Habermas, *The Structural Transformation of the Public Sphere* (Cambridge: MIT Press, 1989), 160.

Index